INTRODUCING

COMPUTERS

CONCEPTS, SYSTEMS, AND APPLICATIONS

ROBERT H. BLISSMER

INTRODUCING

COMPUTERS

CONCEPTS, SYSTEMS, AND APPLICATIONS

**1991–92
EDITION**

John Wiley & Sons, Inc.

New York • Chichester • Brisbane • Toronto • Singapore

Cover photos (clockwise from top left)
courtesy of: IBM; Apple Computer,
Inc.; Compaq Computer Corp.; IBM;
Apple Computer, Inc.; IBM; IBM

Acquisitions Editor	Joe Dougherty
Production Manager	Katharine Rubin
Production Supervisor	Micheline Fredericl
Digital Production Supervisor	Jennifer Dowling
Copy Editor	Marjorie Shustak
Photo Researcher	Elyse Rieder
Photo Research Manager	Stella Kupferberg
Manufacturing Manager	Lorraine Fumoso
Marketing Manager	Carolyn Henderson

Recognizing the importance of preserving what has been
written, it is a policy of John Wiley & Sons, Inc. to have books
of enduring value published in the United States printed on
acid-free paper, and we exert our best efforts to that end.

Library of Congress Cataloging in Publication Data:
Blissmer, Robert H.
Introducing Computers: Concepts, Systems, and
Applications

    Robert H. Blissmer. –1991–1992 ed.
        p.   cm.
      Includes index.

ISBN 0471-53443-9

1. Computers.   I. Title.
QA76.B564 1991   88-79217
004--dc19   CIP

Printed in the United States of America
10 9 8 7 6 5 4 3 2 1

This book is dedicated to
Dean, Staci, and Jennifer.

CONTENTS IN BRIEF

SECTION ONE   **OVERVIEW**

1   Getting Started
2   Personal Computer Applications
3   Computers, Society, and Ethics
4   Computers at Work

SECTION TWO   **HARDWARE**

5   Input
6   Output
7   Processors and Memories
8   Mass Storage
9   Communications

SECTION THREE   **INFORMATION SYSTEMS**

10   Management Information Systems
11   Database Management Systems
12   Artificial Intelligence and Expert Systems

SECTION FOUR   **DEVELOPING APPLICATIONS**

13   Systems Analysis and Design
14   Programming
15   End-User Development

SECTION FIVE   **APPENDIXES**

A   The History of Computers
B   Shopping Guide
C   Number Systems, Data Representation, and Codes
D   Glossary

PREFACE

OVERVIEW

Introducing Computers is a textbook for students with little or no computer background who want to make the most out of their first course in computers. This comprehensive, up-to-date resource outlines the skills necessary to achieve computer literacy and teaches the key concepts, systems, and applications that are essential to making the computer a useful and productive tool.

Benefits of *Introducing Computers* include

• An annual update to keep pace with the dizzying speed of technological innovation and change.

• An easy-to-understand writing style that demystifies computer concepts, applications, and technology.

• An application focus with practical examples that clearly explains what can and cannot be done with computers.

• Coverage of the broader issues of how computers are used and their role in business, government, and education.

• Modular chapters that can be taught in any order.

• A built-in study guide with answers at the end of each chapter.

• A remarkably affordable price.

The book can be used for a one-semester or one-quarter introductory computer course, or as the text for a general computer literacy course. In addition, it can be used as supplementary reading in a variety of computer-related classes, from freshman-level microcomputer application courses to graduate-level business courses.

ORGANIZATION

Introducing Computers is organized into five sections. Take a look at the Contents in Brief at the beginning of the preface. The chapters are modular, so you can teach them in any order you choose. But the rationale behind this particular order is as follows.

• **Section One—Overview** gives students the big picture and lays the ground rules for further learning. If you want to begin your course with history, start with Appendix A, The History of Computers. This visual timeline presentation can make history come alive.

If you would rather save the "Computers, Society, and Ethics" chapter for the end of the course, just cover history and Chapters 1, 2, and 4.

• **Section Two—Hardware** contains detailed coverage of how basic computer hardware subsystems are applied to information processing. To help put these concepts in perspective, I provide examples of their tangible manifestations: products that accomplish these tasks and applications for each of the devices mentioned.

Chapter 7 also includes a discussion of the evolution from mainframe computers to personal computers and a useful comparative analysis of the different types of computer systems. Chapter 9 contains a brief history of communication.

• **Section Three—Information Systems** discusses the role, uses, and implications of computer-based technology in organizations. Take a look around nearly any organization today and you'll see that the computing environment has changed markedly from that of only a few years ago. Powerful desktop computers linked to minis and mainframes in networks have created fundamental changes in the workplace.

• **Section Four-Developing Applications** is a nontechnical overview of systems analysis and programming methods used to develop computer applications. Chapter 15 features end-user development and highlights the many nonprogramming tools now available.

If you'd rather cover systems analysis, programming, and end-user development before applications, simply teach Section Four before Section Three.

• **Section Five—Appendixes** covers important and useful resource information. These appendixes can be used alone or to augment specific chapters in the text.

Appendix A is a visual timeline. Appendix B dovetails nicely with Chapters 2 or 13. Appendix C works well with Chapter 7. Appendix D, the glossary, goes well beyond the key terms in the book.

WHAT'S NEW?

The most exciting and noticeable change this year is the addition of two completely new chapters—"Computers at Work" and "End-User Development." (See the Contents for more description.) With the help of reviewers and readers, I've also fine-tuned each chapter, adding new information and deleting old and unnecessary details. I can't list the many new photographs and illustrations, but here's a listing of the major changes in the new edition.

• **Chapter 1** has a revised section on information and codes.

• **Chapter 2** updates and revises the Operating System section and the User Interface section. The chapter does not cover all personal computer applications. It leaves the more complex applications such as expert systems, advanced database management, and interface builders to later chapters in which they can better be explained in the appropriate context.

• **Chapter 3** has been revised to accommodate the new Chapter 4. I've changed the Information Society section and also enhanced the Information as a Strategic Resource section and the Computer Crime section.

• **Chapter 4** is a brand new chapter. It surveys the many uses for computers in various professions and incorporates the former Appendix B, "Computers and Careers," into the chapter. You can use this chapter to familiarize your students with the diverse and interesting computer applications and technologies related to the career they choose.

• **Chapter 5** adds new information about digitizing audio and video. This has become more important with the emphasis on multimedia applications covered in Chapters 4 and 15.

• **Chapter 6** has added information on laser printers and graphics.

• **Chapter 7** adds a new section on specialized processors to cover coprocessors and ASICs. The minihistory Trends in the Evolution of Computer Systems section has been revised, as has the section on supercomputers.

• **Chapter 8** contains all new information on PC Cards, a new solid-state technology that may eventually replace rotating memory, and all new information on disk arrays.

• **Chapter 9** updates the Facsimile section and the Networking section.

• **Chapter 10** has changes in the Personal Computing section.

• **Chapter 11** has minor changes to enhance the presentation of material.

• **Chapter 12** has a new organization with a section on Neural Networks. I've also revised the Expert System section and added new information about chess-playing computers.

• **Chapter 13** has a new section on Computer-Aided Software Engineering (CASE).

• **Chapter 14** has a new name, Programming. It also has new information about CASE, and I've enhanced and clarified the Object-Oriented Programming section.

- **Chapter 15** is a brand-new chapter. With today's emphasis on decentralized computing, end users are playing a more important role in developing applications. This chapter surveys the tools and trends in this emerging area and points out examples of how and where they are used.
- **Appendix A** adds recent developments at the end of the timeline.
- **Appendix B** contains a reorganized Hardware section that focuses on notebook computers and adds a workstation category.

In all, I think you'll find that the changes make *Introducing Computers* the most complete up-to-date textbook on the market; the easiest book from which to teach, and the easiest book for your students to read without insulting their intelligence. Thanks again for your help.

CHAPTER STRUCTURE

This book has been organized to aid the learner. Each chapter contains the following information to reinforce learning:

- **Preview**. This is a succinct overview of each chapter that states the major concepts clearly and concisely, so that the body of the chapter can hone in on the details. It includes a bulleted-list summary of the learning objectives presented in the chapter.
- **Highlights**. When a new or key term, idea, or important concept is introduced, it is highlighted in *boldface italic* type, then defined. Important terms are highlighted in *italic only*. This keeps the number of key terms in each chapter to a manageable level.
- **Applications**. Each concept or system is accompanied by an explanation in the form of an application (i.e., how the idea or device is used).
- **Photographs and Illustrations**. Each major concept and idea is accompanied by a visual illustration or photograph to enhance and reinforce the narrative material.
- **Spotlight On**. Several chapters feature boxed sidebars. They contain a discussion of applications for the technology included in the chapter and provide additional material for stimulating class discussion.
- **Review**. Chapter summaries provide a review of key points and ideas.
- **References and Resources**. An annotated bibliography is provided to direct the student to additional in-depth reading on the subject.
- **Study Guide**. A built-in workbook at the end of each chapter includes matching key terms with definitions, true/false, multiple choice, thought questions, and projects. Answers to matching, true/false, and multiple choice are printed in the book to reinforce learning.
- **Software Exercises**. A set of generic exercises serves two purposes: (1) to provide additional projects for classes that don't have a hands-on application software component and (2) for hands-on exercises to complement your own use of word processing, spreadsheet, and database application software.

SUPPLEMENTS

- **Instructor's Manual.** The Instructor's Manual contains suggested syllabi, classroom teaching suggestions, chapter-by-chapter outlines, transparency masters, and additional background information.
- **Test Bank.** There are 2600 questions available on disk, as well as in printed and bound form.
- **Data Disk.** An MS-DOS disk contains files for the software exercises at the end of each chapter. Developed in Microsoft Works, these files can be used as is or modified to better suit your needs.
- **Computer Applications Using Lotus 1-2-3, dBase IV, and WordPerfect 5.0.** This hands-on tutorial guide to Lotus, dBase, and WordPerfect emphasizes how to use these packages as productivity tools. Narrative discussions are, as such, minimized in favor of concise, step-by-step instructions (accompanied by a student data disk).

- **A Short Course in Structured BASIC Programming.** The BASIC supplement teaches problem-solving skills and the fundamentals of computer programming in structured BASIC.

In addition to these important ancillaries, *Introducing Computers* is available with some of the most powerful and functional educational software on the market today.

- **Getting Started with VP-Planner, Getting Started with dBase III Plus, Getting Started with WordPerfect 4.2.** These brief, tutorial-style introductions to VP-Planner, dBase, and WordPerfect include educational versions of the software and are the perfect compliment to *Introducing Computers*.

- **Discovering Microsoft Works for the IBM Personal Computer.** This best selling integrated software features word processing, spreadsheet with charting, database with reporting, and communications capabilities as well as an extremely easy-to-use interface (accompanied by an Instructor's Manual and a Student Projects Workbook).

- **Enable: Educational Version.** This powerful integrated software package includes word processing, spreadsheet, database, graphics, and telecommunications as well as an 80,000-word spelling checker and two extensive student manuals (accompanied by an Instructor's Manual, Test Bank, Educational and Full-Version software, and a Student Applications Workbook).

For more information about any of these supplements, please contact your local Wiley representative.

whose foresight continues to allow the book to grow and evolve. My sincere thanks for the help and assistance that was provided during the design and production phases of the book by the following people at Wiley: Katharine Rubin, Gilda Stahl, Marjorie Shustak, Micheline Frederick, Jennifer Dowling, and Maddy Lesure.

I thank the following reviewers whose comments, ideas, and feedback greatly influenced the contents, scope, and form of the 1991-92 edition of *Introducing Computers*:

Janet M. Urlaub, *Sinclair Community College*

Daniel M. Everett, *University of Georgia*

Terence Ryan, *Southern Illinois University at Edwardsville*

Chung Lee, *California State Polytechnic University, Pomona*

Mr. David Preston, *Eastfield College*

Mr. Noah Barnette, *Virginia Tech University*

Prof. Brian MacGuire, *Univeristy of Regina*

The text for *Introducing Computers* was written with the MS-DOS version of Microsoft Word. These files, along with style sheets, were transferred to the Macintosh version of Microsoft Word. Page layouts were produced with Aldus PageMaker and camera-ready pages were produced on a high resolution, plain paper, PostScript laser printer.

Robert H. Blissmer

ACKNOWLEDGMENTS

Books are only possible through the combined efforts of many people. My special thanks go to Roland Alden who criticized the text and supplied the Pascal, C, and Ada examples for Chapter 14. My thanks go also to Gwenn Bell and Oliver Strimpel of the Boston Computer Museum who provided insight into material for Appendix A.

This book would not have been possible without its editor, Joe Dougherty,

ABOUT THE AUTHOR

Robert H. Blissmer is professor of computer applications at the Community College of Micronesia, Kolonia, Pohnpei, Federated States of Micronesia.

When he graduated from college, Mr. Blissmer had no idea that he would wind up in a career focused on computers, but his first job was as a COBOL computer programmer. He then became a systems analyst.

As a college professor in the 1970s at Orange Coast College and Cypress College in California, he taught computer, business, and general design courses. In addition, he designed, implemented, and directed a collegewide interdisciplinary studies program. While on sabbatical he worked with R. Buckminster Fuller, directing a World Game international design conference and designing an exhibit for the United Nations Habitat conference in Canada.

It wasn't long before his interest in computers led him into a position as a journalist. His work as an editor gave him exposure to a variety of companies, people, and state-of-the art computer systems, and his articles have appeared in several computer industry publications. But the lure of teaching proved too much. He now enjoys the challenge of teaching computer literacy in a developing island nation.

CONTENTS

SECTION ONE

OVERVIEW   1

CHAPTER 1

GETTING STARTED   3

What Is a Computer? **4**
The Three Rs of Computer Literacy **6**
Overview Part I: Computer Concepts **9**
Overview Part II: Personal Computer Systems **15**

CHAPTER 2

PERSONAL COMPUTER APPLICATIONS   27

Personal Computer Software **28**
Operating Systems **30**
Application Software **34**
Software for Writing **35**
Desktop Publishing **39**
Spreadsheet Software **40**
Database Software **42**
Graphic Software **45**
Communications Software **47**
Integrated Software **48**

CHAPTER 3

COMPUTERS, SOCIETY, AND ETHICS   55

The Computerization of Society **56**
The Information Society **56**
The Economics of Information **58**
How Technology Fuels Change **62**
Responses for a Changing World **66**
Computers and Ethics **70**
Software Piracy **74**

CHAPTER 4

COMPUTERS AT WORK   81

The Changing Nature of Work **82**
Computers in Manufacturing **82**
Computers in Retailing **87**
Computers in Health Care and Medicine **88**
Computers in the Arts and Design **89**
Computers in Government, Military, and Law **92**
Computers in Education **95**
Computers and Careers **97**
Jobs, Training, and the Future **99**

SECTION TWO

HARDWARE   107

CHAPTER 5

INPUT   109

Computer System Input **110**
Keyboards **111**
Pointing Devices **113**
Scanners **117**
Sensors **122**
Voice Input **123**

CHAPTER 6

OUTPUT   131

Computer System Output **132**
Printers **133**
Video-Display Technology **139**
Graphics: Another View **143**
Specialized Output Systems **144**
Voice Output **145**

CHAPTER 7

PROCESSORS AND
MEMORIES   153

The Central Electronic Complex 154
The Evolving Central Electronic Complex
    161
Trends in the Evolution of Computer
    Systems 163
Supercomputers 170
Parallel Processing 171

CHAPTER 8

MASS STORAGE   179

Files and Mass Storage 180
Sequential, Random, and Index
    Sequential Files 181
Magnetic Tape Devices 182
Magnetic Disk Devices 184
Improving the Disk's Capacity 189
Other Magnetic Storage Media 190
Optical Disks 191

CHAPTER 9

COMMUNICATIONS   199

Computers and Communications
    Converge 200
Communication Channels 202
Communication Technology 205
Computer Networking 210
Communications Industry Issues 213
Optional Communication Concepts 215

SECTION THREE

INFORMATION SYSTEMS   223

CHAPTER 10

MANAGEMENT INFORMATION
SYSTEMS   225

What Is a Management Information
    System? 226
The Structure of MIS 227
Organizational Perspectives 228
Personal Computing 231
Workgroup Computing 233
Network Computing 236
The Effects on People 238

CHAPTER 11

DATABASE MANAGEMENT
SYSTEMS   245

Data Basics 246
Database Models 248
Data Manipulation 251
Distributing Databases 256
Optional Database Management Concepts
    257

CHAPTER 12

ARTIFICIAL INTELLIGENCE AND
EXPERT SYSTEMS   267

Can Machines Really Think? 268
From Thinking to Intelligent Behavior 269
Natural Language Processing 270
Expert Systems 272
Neural Networks 275

SECTION FOUR

DEVELOPING
APPLICATIONS   281

CHAPTER 13

SYSTEMS ANALYSIS
AND DESIGN   283

The MIS Department 284
Phase I: Definition 285
Phase II: Design and Development 290
Phase III: Implementation 292
Case Study: Selecting A Personal
    Computer System 293

CHAPTER 14

PROGRAMMING   303

The Evolution of Programming 304
Structured Program Design 306
The Phases of Software Development 309
Object-Oriented Programming 315
Comparing Programming Languages 316

CHAPTER 15

END-USER DEVELOPMENT   327

The Need for End-User Development 328

Alternatives to Traditional Programming
 328
Macro Languages **329**
Program Generators **330**
Database Programming Languages **331**
Interface Builders **332**
Hybrid Approaches **334**
Authoring Systems **335**
Object Environments **336**
End-User Development Trade-offs **337**

SECTION FIVE

APPENDIXES 343

APPENDIX A
THE HISTORY
OF COMPUTERS 345

APPENDIX B
SHOPPING GUIDE 375

APPENDIX C
NUMBER SYSTEMS,
DATA REPRESENTATION,
AND CODES 419

APPENDIX D
GLOSSARY 431

PHOTO CREDITS 449

INDEX 453

OVERVIEW

PREVIEW

Everyone is telling you that you must become computer literate. That simply means using computers as problem-solving tools—a goal that is accomplished when using a computer becomes fluent, productive, and enjoyable. How do you become computer literate? First, you must become fluent in the language and vocabulary of computers. Chapter 1 will get you started, by explaining the major concepts, ideas, and terms and by putting them in the context of the big picture of computers.

As with any problem-solving tool, you must understand for what computers can and cannot be used. What is the value of computers to you as an individual? Chapter 2 presents the computer as a personal tool, discusses the applications for personal computers, and sets the stage for hands-on exploration with computers.

Computer literacy, however, could be shallow without an understanding of how the computer's influence goes far beyond personal uses. In Chapter 3, you will see that there is indeed a big picture, but it is not always a rosy one. Computers are changing our work, education, and everyday lives. Chapter 3 discusses the causes, implications, and problems of the computerization of society. Finally, to round out the big picture, Chapter 4 presents a survey of the technology and issues surrounding the use of computers at work.

The major topics introduced in this section include

- What is a computer?
- The three Rs of computer literacy.
- An overview of computer concepts.
- An overview of personal computer systems.
- Operating system software.
- Application software.
- Software for writing and desktop publishing.
- Spreadsheet software.
- Database software.
- Graphic software.
- Communications software.
- Integrated software.
- The computerization of society.
- The information society.
- The economics of information.
- Crime, security, and privacy.
- Software piracy.
- Computers in manufacturing.
- Computers in retailing.
- Computers in medicine and health care.
- Computers in the arts and design.
- Computers in education.
- Computers and careers.

ALEXEY PAJITNOV

Profession: Soviet software game author and scientific assistant, Computing Center of the U.S.S.R. Academy of Sciences.

Profile: As a scientific assistant, Pajitnov works on artificial intelligence, voice recognition, and CAD/CAM software. He is best known in the United States for developing *Tetris* and *Welltris*, two games published by Spectrum HoloByte. Both games have won the Software Publishers Association's Excellence in Software Award in the action/arcade program category.

Quote: "*The main thing is to construct…always adding, improving, developing. This is my motto.*"

CHAPTER 1

GETTING STARTED

PREVIEW

Learning about computers is like taking a journey to an interesting country. It is an adventure—filled with creative, interesting, and challenging excursions. On any journey, you will find shortcuts, alternative routes, and interesting places to stop for a while. You may also get lost as you come across the use of unfamiliar language and customs; therefore, it is wise to consult a guide before starting out. This chapter serves as such a guide—a description of the territory you are going to encounter in the rest of the book.

To do this, it will provide you with an up-to-date map of the territory. First, it will define the term *computer* and show you some different types of computers and different uses for them. Second, it will give you some tips and guidelines that you can use for learning about computers and their uses. Third, it will translate the terminology that you will find along the way into an easy-to-learn and easy-to-use set of concepts for everyday use. Finally, it will give you an overview of personal computer systems so that you can apply the concepts and understand what computers are and how they can be used.

In this chapter, you'll learn

- What a computer is and what it can do for you.
- The types, sizes, and categories of computer systems.
- The three Rs of computer literacy.
- The basic concepts of systems, information, communication, hardware, software, and applications.
- The role of personal computing in larger systems.
- The function of a keyboard, display, system unit, disk drive, and printer.

WHAT IS A COMPUTER?

Have you ever been asked the question, "What is a computer?" If not, try to answer the question now. If you have some difficulty, do not be surprised. The term computer has been used in a wide variety of ways and tends to mean different things to different people.

A *computer* can be thought of as an electronic device that is capable of performing the following tasks:

• Responding in a predictable way to input.

• Processing that input according to a set of instructions.

• Storing the instructions and the results of processing.

• Providing output in the form of information.

This general definition may be applied to a wide variety of devices. It also emphasizes function: it tells what the computer does rather than what it is. The only mention of equipment appears in the words "electronic device." To help put this definition in perspective, let us look at some examples of what a computer can do for you.

WHAT COMPUTERS DO FOR YOU

People's perceptions of computers are often determined by the reasons they use them. Not long ago, computers were used only for rather routine tasks, such as keeping records for government agencies, tracking paychecks for accountants, and "crunching numbers" for scientists and engineers. Today, computers are used in more imaginative ways. Artists, writers, and historians have discovered that computers can help them, too. Computers are being used to choreograph dances, compose music, and inspire reading through gamelike simulations. Painters and illustrators augment their list of conventional tools, such as pen and paintbrush, with computers.

More people are using computers in one way or another, whether playing a game, learning a history lesson, or ob-taining information. Why is this so? Dazzling technology aside, sociologists and psychologists point to a basic human need. In this age of big business, big government, television viewing, and spectator sports, people sometimes feel detached and uninvolved. In contrast, the computer offers involvement, participation, and immediate feedback.

• The computer is active, not passive.

• The computer can question you and respond to questions in a two-way conversation.

• The power to take control of a computer and make it respond to your bidding is literally at your fingertips.

TYPES OF COMPUTERS

Computers come in a wide variety of types and sizes, so it is useful to sort them out by their categories. The broadest categories are special purpose and general purpose.

Special-purpose computers are dedicated to only one function: controlling the machines in which they are embedded. They have been given a permanent set of instructions. In effect, they have been preprogrammed to perform their specific purpose.

For example, tiny, hidden special-purpose computers tell you what time it is on your digital watch, control traffic signals, and inject fuel into your car's engine as you drive. Some even speak to you, telling you that your car door is open or that your car is low on gas. They help you scramble eggs in your microwave oven or unscramble programs on your cable TV decoder box. In your telephone, they remember numbers and dial them for you at the press of a button.

Not all special-purpose computers are small. The navigational computers aboard the space shuttle, the computers found in sophisticated military aircraft, and those found in medical diagnostic equipment are typical examples of medium- to large-scale special-purpose computers.

Other computers that you might be aware of have such brand names as IBM, Apple, Atari, or Commodore.

Types of computer. Some of the many uses for special-purpose and general purpose computers.

Special Purpose	General Purpose
Watches	Data Processing
Traffic signals	Writing
Automobiles	Calculating
Appliances	Record keeping
Telephones	Education
Airplanes	Accounting
Spaceships	Graphics
Instruments	Entertainment

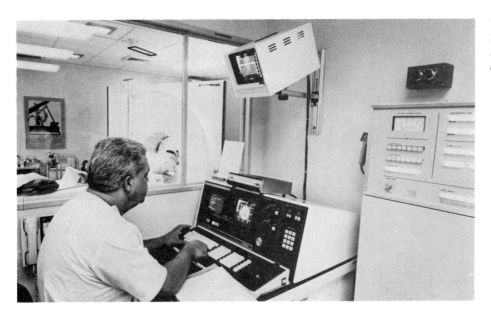

Types of computers. *Computer-aided tomography scanner (CAT scanner) uses a special-purpose computer to collect, analyze, and display medical information.*

These computers differ from their special-purpose cousins by being programmable; that is, their operation can be changed by altering the instructions or programs they are given. Being programmable, they become *general-purpose computers*. They can be adapted to many situations if given appropriate programs. For example, there are programs that can help store and organize data, sort data alphabetically (or any other way you choose), write letters and reports, and generate charts and graphics. Like special-purpose computers, general-purpose computers also come in a wide range of sizes and capabilities.

Some smaller general-purpose computers, often known as *personal computers,* are designed for use by individuals, such as executives, office workers, and engineers. A close cousin of the personal computer is called a *workstation.* Although it resembles a personal computer in appearance, it is used in complex scientific and technical applications that require more computational power. Larger and far more expensive computers, called *mainframes,* are designed to process large amounts of data and to be shared by many different people in businesses, government agencies, and scientific and educational institutions. In the midrange of size and price are the *minicomputers,* which are suitable for use in departments, branch offices, factories, and scientific laboratories. In Chapter 7, you will learn more about

these traditional categories of computers and their uses.

Of course, we have barely begun to scratch the surface. Later in this chapter, the term *system* will be used to describe a computer; after that, you will learn about what is inside the computer. Be aware that technical people have a tendency to describe computer concepts in complex specialized terms. This is the major reason the computer is understood so poorly by the general public. Therefore, you must acquire some fundamental knowledge and skills before you can fully appreciate what a computer is or what it can do for you. The following set of guidelines will help you become computer literate.

Types of computers. *With the right program, a general-pupose personal computer can be used for many tasks.*

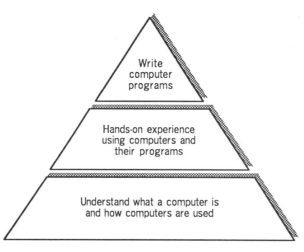

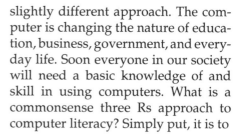

slightly different approach. The computer is changing the nature of education, business, government, and everyday life. Soon everyone in our society will need a basic knowledge of and skill in using computers. What is a commonsense three Rs approach to computer literacy? Simply put, it is to

- Read about computers.
- Obtain real experience with computers.
- Write computer programs.

Levels of computer literacy. Not everyone needs to be computer literate to the same degree. Few people need to write programs. Many people need to use programs as problem-solving tools. Almost everyone needs to know what computers are and how they are used.

THE THREE Rs OF COMPUTER LITERACY

Computer literacy is the knowledge and skills required to use a computer as a problem-solving tool. As an analogy, think of the little red schoolhouse of yesteryear. There, reading, writing, and arithmetic were considered to contain the fundamental knowledge and skills required for people to solve problems in the world in which they lived and worked. Those three Rs were always associated with the commonsense rules for preparing oneself for life; even though they seem quite simple, they took years to learn and master.

Today, common sense may dictate a

Keep in mind that not everyone needs to be computer literate to the same degree. A travel agent needs to know how to operate a computer to book airline, hotel, and car reservations. This usually requires less computer literacy than a manager needs, who must know how to use a computer to write, calculate, analyze, and communicate. Note that neither needs to know how to program a computer to do their jobs effectively.

READ ABOUT COMPUTERS

The day will come when computers will be just like other consumer products. You will buy them, take them out of their box, read a few simple directions on a single sheet of paper, and begin using them immediately. Because this is not the case today, reading is an excellent way to acquire basic knowledge about computers and their uses. There are two approaches for reading about computers.

As a novice, the first approach is to gather general knowledge. This book will help you to translate a highly specialized and computer-related language into an easy-to-learn language for everyday use. Discovering a new language for communicating knowledge about something means discovering a new tool for solving problems. To aid you in this pursuit, appropriate references and resources are listed at the end of each chapter. They will point you to more detailed knowledge about the subjects discussed. Reading these selections will help you gain the knowledge needed to make intelligent choices about computers and their uses. These selections will also help you discover uses for computers that

Computer literacy. Cal Tech students designed this interactive program for use at the National Air and Space Museum gallery.

you could not have imagined in advance. Whether you are a novice or a professional, you should read these selections.

You should also start to read computer magazines. The field of computers changes rapidly. Because magazines are more current than books, they are sometimes better indicators of new trends. For example, go to your library and browse through several issues of one magazine. This will show you the differences between this year's products and topics and those of last year. A subscription to one of the many weekly or monthly computer magazines will keep you abreast of current changes.

You should also consider purchasing one of the many low-priced paperback computer dictionaries available in your local bookstore. Although you will find all the key terms used in this book in the glossary, a dictionary of computer terms is a more comprehensive reference guide to the language of computers. Several of these dictionaries are listed in the resource section of this chapter.

After you have gained general knowledge, your second reading approach may be to learn about a specific computer or program. The books and manuals that accompany a computer-related product are called *documentation.* All computer-related products should at least have a quick reference guide or card that summarizes the important instructions, a training manual, and a reference manual. Ignoring the documentation can lead to problems in operating the computer or program. You will want to start using the documentation right away to answer your basic questions. When you advance to higher levels of computer literacy, such as using or writing computer programs, you will start using the documentation to help you answer more detailed or complex questions.

REAL EXPERIENCE WITH COMPUTERS

Although reading about computers may raise your knowledge level and understanding of computers, there is no substitute for sitting down in front of a computer and experiencing what it

can do. In the beginning, it does not matter where you start. In fact, many low-cost commercial software packages are designed to help you get started with computers. For example, use one of the game packages to play an adventure game. Try an educational package for drill and practice in spelling or arithmetic. Use a word processor to write a letter to a friend. These experiments will show you that the computer is not intimidating. If you make a mistake, the computer will not get mad at you; it will simply provide you with a way to correct your mistake. That fact alone might free you to experiment with novel uses of the computer, which you might otherwise be afraid of trying.

Doing this will give you some of the basic skills necessary to operate computers and computer programs, and it is also a commonsense approach to computer literacy. Remember that many computers are general-purpose tools, and the fact that you can operate one type of computer or computer program usually means that you can generalize that skill and learn more easily how to operate other types of computers and computer programs.

After a little experimenting, you will soon begin to discover for yourself the areas of interest you want to pur-

Documentation. Shown here are a user's manual, tutorial disks, keyboard diagram and key labels, and a quick-reference guide for a word processing program.

Real experience with a computer. Hands-on instruction is a commonsense method for achieving computer literacy.

sue. If you still doubt your computer ability after your trial run, a tutorial might help you to learn about computers. In this context, a *tutorial* is a computer program that contains step-by-step directions for learning how to use a computer or a computer program. Sitting at the computer and practicing while following the directions that appear on the computer's display screen is an effective method of introduction. With a good tutorial, you can teach yourself the fundamentals of a computer or computer program in a few hours through real hands-on experience.

You do not have to learn to program a computer to be able to use it for problem solving and learning. The vast majority of today's computer users simply buy ready-made programs. One such program, a *spreadsheet*, enables you to organize numbers and formulas into rows and columns of cells, similar to the paper spreadsheets that have been used in businesses for years. For example, if you are having a problem balancing your household budget, you can use a spreadsheet to type in the numbers and formulas for a monthly budget. Then, you can change the numbers or formulas to see how different budgets might affect your personal finances. All the calculating is accomplished by the spreadsheet. You can concentrate on exploring solutions to the problem. You will learn more about spreadsheets in Chapter 2.

WRITE COMPUTER PROGRAMS

After you read about computers and become more familiar with them by experimenting with them, your interest in computers may rise to new levels. If so, you are probably ready for the next level of computer literacy—writing a program.

Writing a program means creating a set of instructions that the computer can follow. For the computer to understand you, the instructions must be written in a programming language, such as BASIC or Pascal. A *programming language* is a formally constructed artificial language in which the syntax and grammar rules are stated so precisely that a computer can analyze, interpret, and understand the meaning of that language.

Tutorials. *Shown here is the Learning Works tutorial opening screen that provides a tour of Works and its capabilities.*

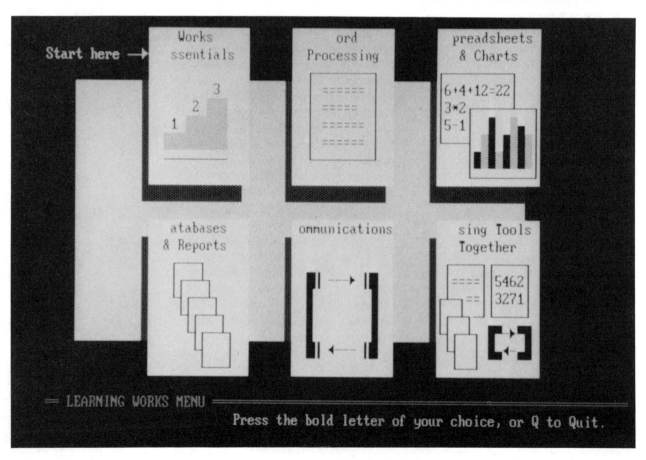

All programming languages include a *vocabulary*—the set of words used to make instructions—and a grammar or *syntax*—a precise set of rules that determines the set of possible instructions in the language. Writing a program can be an intellectually demanding task. You must first map out exactly what you want the program to do, apply some commonsense rules of logic, and be willing to follow a problem from its conception to completion at a very high level of detail.

You do not have to learn how to program a computer to use one. Just as the person who learns something about cars would probably leave fixing a car to a mechanic, so the average computer user would leave programming to a programmer. But learning about the concepts of programming will take you behind the scenes where you will discover firsthand many of the principles and concepts of how computers work.

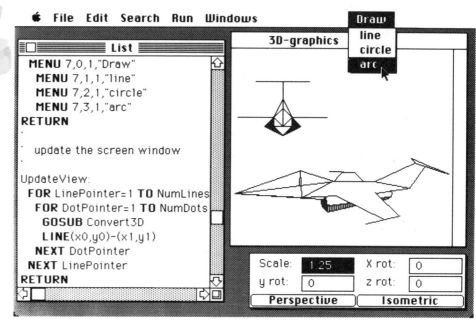

Write computer programs. Microsoft BASIC, a programming language for the Macintosh, is a specially adapted version of BASIC that can also provide graphics and animation.

OVERVIEW PART I: COMPUTER CONCEPTS

You may have noticed that experienced computer users often speak a different language. In a field of study such as computers, it is easy to become overwhelmed with new words that represent new concepts and ideas.

This set of specialized words, called *jargon,* is used to speed up communication between people. For example, on a trip to your local computer store, you may encounter a salesperson who says, "The Model 50 comes with 2 megabytes of RAM, a $3\frac{1}{2}$-inch floppy, a 40-megabyte hard disk, an 80286 processor, and OS/2." If you are not persistent or motivated enough to learn the jargon, this "technobabble" is guaranteed to widen the gap between you and computer users.

Jargon is used by all professional people. It is a shortcut they use to communicate effectively with their colleagues. Because it assumes prior knowledge, the beginner cannot be expected to know what it means. For

example, our salesperson's monolog is actually a very condensed description of a popular IBM Personal System/2. By the time you finish Chapter 2, you will understand what most of the jargon in that monolog means.

There is no point in accumulating more and more words without some method for organizing or categorizing them. A real stumbling block for most people is recognizing where words fit into the overall picture. You need a frame of reference for coping with new concepts and ideas.

You will come across computer concepts on the following pages again and again. They are overall guidelines for better understanding the subject of computers. Use them as you would use a set of maps: to keep from getting lost and to cover a lot of territory quickly.

SYSTEMS

A *system* is a set or arrangement of parts that act together to perform a function. The term *system* is used to describe organization, and it helps you to put other concepts in order. As you become more familiar with systems and computers, you will see the advantages of using this term to help organize your thinking.

Sometimes the parts of a system can also be systems. For example, suppose an office wants to install a computer to

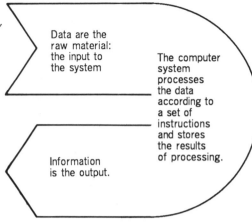

Systems. *Diagram showing the major functional components of a computer: input, processing, storage, and output.*

Data are the raw material: the input to the system

The computer system processes the data according to a set of instructions and stores the results of processing.

Information is the output.

automate its paperwork. There is a system to be computerized (the paperwork), and there is a system that surrounds that system (the office itself). There may be other systems involved. The office, for example, may be one department in a large company.

When using the term system as a concept, a good method for thinking about how things are organized is to start with the whole and work toward the parts.

The field of medicine provides us with a good example of how this method is applied. Doctors think of the human body in terms of an arrangement of parts: a respiratory system, a circulatory system, a nervous system, a digestive system, and so on. These subsystems interact with each other to perform a function: keeping the human body alive, healthy, and growing. When you are sick, doctors will examine your symptoms and ask you lots of seemingly unrelated questions. The doctors are simply starting with the whole and are working toward the parts because they know that all the parts are acting together. They are using systems as a concept to aid their diagnosis.

Auto mechanics use the same method when diagnosing a problem with a car. First, they listen and look at the whole system; then they try to work down to the specific subsystem (e.g., fuel system, ignition system, electrical system) before they begin to examine a specific detail, such as a gas filter, a spark plug, or a fuse.

A computer is also a system. It is a set of parts or subsystems. The main subsystems are input, output, processor, and storage. Each subsystem per-

forms a specific subfunction, and the subsystems work together to perform *information processing*—responding to input, processing that input according to instructions, and communicating the output. You will learn about these subsystems in detail in Section Two. They provide the basic frame of reference when organizing and categorizing many aspects of computers.

INFORMATION

In the broadest sense, *information* is data that has a context. This concept is useful because the context helps us to make decisions and solve problems using data and information. Because we have defined information in terms of data, let us examine in more detail the relationship between the two.

Data

Data are simply facts, numbers, letters, or symbols, whereas information always has a context. A simple example will illustrate this. If I were to hand you a piece of paper with the letter *A* written on it, what have I given you? A piece of data—and rather raw data at that. If I hand you the same piece of paper and tell you that it is your grade for this course, that is information.

Take another example, a name and address. If you found it scribbled on a scrap of paper lying in the street, it would probably mean nothing. But suppose you ran a mail-order business and I told you that the name and address was that of a person who buys products via mail order. Now you have some information because the name and address have a context: they become the pathway to a potential customer.

Suppose I gave you a list of names and addresses. Now you have even more valuable information—a mailing list. What if the list consisted of subscribers to *Business Week* magazine? You could make some assumptions about what these people might buy (e.g., most are probably executives,) by consulting *Business Week*'s reader profile. You can begin to see how the context transforms data into information, and why information is more valuable than data. In an upcoming section, we will talk about how mailing lists can be put to use in information systems.

Codes

As a practical matter, the speed, reliability, and usefulness of computers partially stem from the fact that data and information can easily be represented as electrical signals. This was first demonstrated by the early telegraph. At the transmitter end, a telegrapher would transform a series of letters in the alphabet into pulses of electric current by a pattern of long and short switch closings. At the receiving end, the pulses of electric current were converted into a series of clicks that a human receiver could translate back into letters of the alphabet.

One of the key concepts in this process is the idea of a code. Samuel F. B. Morse, the inventor of the telegraph, had to invent a code to make his technology workable and practical. A *code* is a set of symbols, such as the dots and dashes of the Morse code, that represents another set of symbols, such as the letters of the alphabet. After the telegraph, the idea of using electricity for transmitting coded information quickly caught on.

A circuit is required for electricity to work as a carrier of information. The common lamp is a circuit with which you are familiar. It consists of a power source, wire, a light bulb, and a switch; its function is to provide illumination. How could you use this simplest of circuits to convey information? You could use your porch light as a signal to indicate to a friend whether or not you were home.

To a computer engineer, a *circuit* is an interconnected set of electronic components that performs a function. A circuit can be as simple as a switch, a light bulb, and some wire, but computers need far more complex circuits. The circuits used in computers are called *integrated circuits*—combinations of thousands or more circuits built on tiny pieces of silicon that are called *chips*.

The porch light as a signal also demonstrates the idea of a binary signal. Either there is current flowing and the

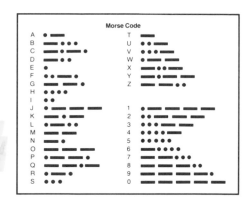

Information. *The International Morse Code was one of the first codes that could be represented by electrical pulses to transmit information.*

light is on, or there is no current flowing and the light is off. In a computer circuit, the on-and-off combinations are represented by two different levels of voltage. The first (usually the higher) level of voltage is said to be on, whereas the second level of voltage is said to be off.

This on-and-off pattern is the basic building block for the coding of all patterns of information used in computer and communication systems. The pattern is often referred to as the binary system (binary simply means two). By combining binary and digit (for the digits 0 and 1 used in the binary system), we derive the term bit. A *bit* is the smallest possible unit of information because one bit is enough to tell the difference between two alternatives, such as on or off. Bits are the means by which the data that flow through the circuits of a computer are represented. Groups of bits can be arranged to represent numbers, letters, and special symbols in the form of a code. A bit has an interesting feature that expands the potential of computer capability: a bit is capable of storing the same amount of information regardless of its physical size. To get a feel for this, try to remember your high school geometry. Do you remember that an angle is also completely independent of size? If you draw a triangle as small as your pencil will allow or draw the same triangle big enough to cover the floor of a room, the angles will remain the same.

In computer hardware, the bit's counterpart—the switch—has the same distinguishing feature. You can make a switch as big as the one Dr. Frankenstein used to "turn on the juice" to give life to his monster, or you

One coin			One bit can describe 2 alternatives
Two coins			Two bits can describe 4 alternatives
Three coins			Three bits can describe 8 alternatives
Four coins			Four bits can describe 16 alternatives
Eight coins			Eight bits can describe 256 alternatives

Information. *A bit is the smallest possible unit of information because one bit is enough to describe the difference between two alternatives. Groups of bits can be arranged to represent numbers, letters, and special symbols in the form of a code.*

uct of decades of development and represents a stretching of technological limits from the time when computers existed only in the laboratory.

INFORMATION SYSTEMS

An *information system* is a system that takes data, processes it, and provides information as output. The previously mentioned names and addresses, for example, combined with a computer to do the processing and a printer for output, can provide a mail-order business with a simple but useful information system. The business could sort the names by ZIP code, for example, and print mailing labels. (Presorting mail by ZIP code allows the company to send mail at a cheaper rate.) An information system does not necessarily include a computer. However, if the mailing list becomes very large, say, several thousand names, it becomes exceedingly difficult to do the tasks of sorting and preparing the mailing labels by hand.

By adding some more data, such as age, sex, income, and marital status, to the mailing list, the information processing possibilities begin to multiply rapidly. Mail-order businesses rely heavily on their information systems to help them develop special lists of people that may buy specific merchandise. By using information systems in innovative ways, a mailing list can be created for almost any conceivable use. For example, a mailing list consisting of first-time home buyers might be the ideal audience for a furniture catalog. A list of people whose ZIP codes fall in coastal regions and who are under age 30 might be the ideal audience for a surf wear and accessories catalog. Also, if sending a catalog results in a purchase, then even more information about what a customer is willing to buy becomes available, and the information becomes even more valuable.

can make it so small that it would literally be dwarfed by the head of a pin. They both represent the same amount of information—a binary digit. Computer builders make faster, cheaper, and more reliable computer circuits simply by packing more and more switches and other circuit elements onto a tiny piece of silicon called a chip. Today's chips contain so many transistors and circuits that one chip can now do all the tasks that used to require a roomful of electronic components. That tiny silicon chip is the artful prod-

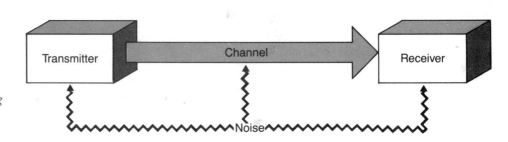

Communications. *Block diagram showing the basic components of a communication system.*

Networks. *Digital's All-In-1 allows multiple personal computers to be networked together and provides services such as file sharing and electronic messaging.*

Even the mailing list itself becomes a marketable commodity. Many businesses will rent their customer mailing lists for prices of $50 per thousand to several hundred dollars per thousand names. (Most companies that do this will remove names on request.)

Information systems are not, of course, confined to mail-order businesses. They are found in banks, insurance companies, government agencies, space probes, and automated factory machines, to name a few. We will explore information systems in greater detail in Section Three.

COMMUNICATION SYSTEMS

No study of computers would be complete without including communication systems. Information systems and communication systems are closely related. ***Communication*** is the transfer of meaningful information. If no information is present, the communication becomes noise. And, if information can't be communicated, it can't be used.

In its simplest technical form, a communication system consists of a sender (the technical term for sender is transmitter), a physical channel over which to send the information, and a receiver.

Communication is most important in the study of computers because information (like people) is widely distributed in the world. It would be impractical as well as highly undesirable to collect all the information in the world and store it in one place. Unscrupulous leaders and decision makers might use it to consolidate and centralize their own power. What would happen, for example, if the United States had only one national newspaper or one government-controlled television station? A better solution is to communicate the information between decentralized locations.

Network is the term that is used to describe at least two but usually more communication devices connected to each other. There are two common categories of networks with which everyone is familiar. The first category is a network that broadcasts information from a single source. Radio and television networks are an example: a group of stations are linked together so that the same programs can be carried to a wider audience. An airline reservation system is a computer example of this type of network. Thousands of per-

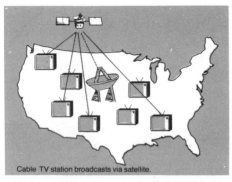
Cable TV station broadcasts via satellite.

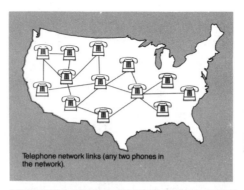
Telephone network links (any two phones in the network).

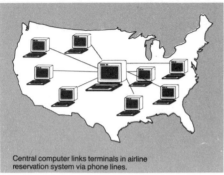
Central computer links terminals in airline reservation system via phone lines.

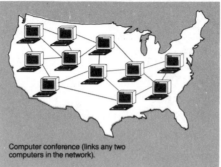
Computer conference (links any two computers in the network).

Networks. The two broad categories of communications networks (A, B) are shown here.

Hardware and software. Although software does have a form, it is different from hardware because it is information recorded on a medium such as a disk.

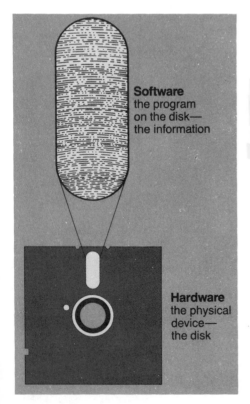
Software
the program on the disk— the information

Hardware
the physical device— the disk

sonal computers located in travel agencies are connected to a central computer that stores information on the flight schedule and availability of seats on each flight. Another example is the central computer that electronically stores volumes of information, such as the *Academic American Encyclopedia, The Wall Street Journal,* or *The New York Times.* This information is available for a subscription fee to customers who have a terminal or a computer that can connect to the central computer.

The second category is a network that transfers information among many sources. A telephone system is the prime example: the focus is input oriented, that is, switching messages from one location to another. In a computer example, the manager of a department is preparing a pay raise report using the personal computer on her desk. The manager needs to know the start date and current salary of all employees in the department. Using a decentralized network, she communicates to a mainframe computer in which payroll records are kept and incorporates that data into the report. Then, she sends electronic messages to each employee in the department, asking for updated job descriptions to incorporate into the report. By using a network of computers, the manager is

able to produce a more effective and accurate report, and do it much faster than if it had been done manually.

HARDWARE AND SOFTWARE

Hardware is the physical equipment in a computer system. The first people who sold computer hardware had a unique phrase that related to their line of work. If sales were down, a conversation between sales manager and salesperson was likely to include the following phrase: "You've got to push more iron" (translation: "sell more hardware"). The substitution of the word iron for hardware probably occurred in some legendary sales meeting when early computers were housed in fairly large metal cabinets and were sometimes known as hunks of iron.

Many of today's smaller computers are housed in plastic or fiberglass, but the phrase still exists because, without software, the computer would just sit there like a hunk of iron. Software tells the hardware what to do. *Software* is the term used to describe the programs that control the operation of the computer system. The words "software" and "program" are used interchangeably.

A lot of confusion arises in using computers because people do not always make the distinction between hardware and software. For example, many people confuse a program, which is software, with the disk on which it resides, which is hardware. This is because hardware and software are necessarily complementary. You usually don't find one without the other. The reason that hardware is still better accepted and understood than software is that hardware has a tangible form you can see and touch. Software does have a form, but it is intangible in the sense that it is really just information or a program that is loaded into the memory of a computer system.

APPLICATIONS

Applications are the things computers can be used to do. The previously mentioned mailing list examples are applications. The computer was originally designed to solve mathematical problems; therefore, the first applied use of computers involved number processing. It soon became apparent that the computer was capable of manipulating and processing any kind of symbol, not just numbers, so the applied uses of computers branched into information processing.

Computer applications are moving far beyond their early round of uses, such as payroll processing, inventory, and record keeping. The following list of applications shows the rapid evolution of computer use today.

• Dispatchers for shipping firms pinpoint trucks on electronic maps and determine exactly where each truck is located.

• Robot assemblers count parts, detect shortages, and inform humans when and how to make replacements.

• Graphic designers design; lay out; and produce advertising, magazines, brochures, and books.

• Political candidates analyze voting patterns and trends.

• Sports teams score events, collect information for scouting, organize ticket sales, and control the environment of domed stadiums.

• Consumer product brand managers analyze shopping data by individual product and package size, store location, and time of day when the product was purchased.

In the past only a relatively small percentage of people had hands-on contact with computers. Today, computer applications leave virtually no aspect of life or work untouched. With the personal computer, you have the potential to organize your work and life in ways that are not only better for you as a person, but are dramatically more effective and efficient.

What you do with computers depends to a large extent on your application for computers. Thinking about applications will help you to sort out the wide variety of computers and computer programs available for specific purposes. You will discover more detail about applications for personal computers in Chapter 2.

OVERVIEW PART II: PERSONAL COMPUTER SYSTEMS

Combining the words personal and computer may give you the impression that personal computers are less sophisticated than their larger mainframe and minicomputer relatives. This is a misconception. Advances in technology have almost eliminated the gap that once existed between personal computers and larger machines.

Because of this evolution, most organizations are on the threshold of a new style of computing in which increasing amounts of computer resources are allocated to individual users in the form of personal computer systems. This new style of computing relies on the communication concepts already discussed to link groups of computers of different sizes and types so their users can communicate and share information. You will learn more details about computers and communications in Chapters 9 and 10.

In fact, all the computer concepts already discussed apply to personal computer systems. A good way to understand these abstract concepts is to apply them to the hardware and software components of a personal computer system. It is highly unlikely at this stage of your learning that you

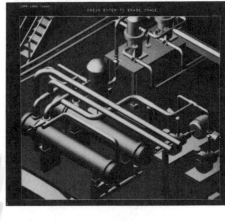

Applications. *An industrial process plant modeled with computer-aided design using three-dimensional design capabilities.*

Applications. *At the Olympic Games, a network of computers scores events and links officials and reporters through an electronic message system.*

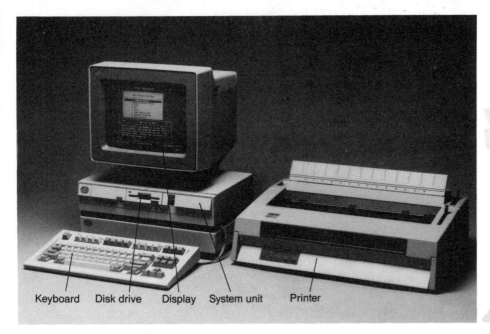

Keyboard   Disk drive   Display   System unit   Printer

Personal computer systems. *The IBM Personal System/2 Model 30.*

computer. It allows you to enter commands or data into the computer. The keyboard may contain from 70 to 105 keys. A personal computer keyboard includes a typewriter layout and a set of keys marked with arrows that control the movement of a visual aid—a *cursor*—on the display screen. Some keyboards include a numeric keypad for number-intensive data entry and calculations as well as a set of function keys. These are general-purpose keys that, depending on the application, perform special functions.

Keyboards are not the only way to communicate with a computer. A variety of input devices are available, including pens, touch screens, and mice. A *mouse* is a device used to position the cursor on a display screen in lieu of cursor control keys. A mouse also has a button for selecting options. We will discuss each of these devices in Chapter 5, but for the moment, the primary advantage to these alternative input devices is the ease with which you can move a cursor around on the screen and execute commands.

would be able to gain the same kind of hands-on experience with a minicomputer or mainframe computer that is possible with a personal computer. The basic hardware components of a personal computer system consist of the

- Keyboard.
- Display.
- System unit.
- Disks and disk drives.
- Printer.

These components perform similar functions in computers of all types and sizes. Familiarizing yourself with what they are and what they do will help you make the connection between computer concepts and tangible hardware components. In Chapter 2, the software components of a personal computer system will be discussed.

KEYBOARDS

A *keyboard* is a device that converts keystrokes into special codes that can be electronically manipulated by the

DISPLAYS

A display, often called a monitor, is one of the output parts of the system. A *display* is a device that is used (1) to give you feedback while you operate the computer and (2) to view the computer's output. For example, when you type on the keyboard, the letters are immediately displayed along with the cursor that indicates where the next letter you type will appear.

The display is typically a CRT (cathode ray tube), the same type of tube that is found in a television set. CRTs can be found with green-phosphor, amber-phosphor, black-on-white (the background is white and the text and images are black), or color displays. Color monitors are common, but are more expensive than single-color

Keyboards. *Shown is an IBM Personal Computer keyboard with a mouse to the right.*

(monochrome) monitors. Also, flat screens, such as LCDs (liquid crystal displays), are commonly used in portable computers. LCDs are larger versions of the displays found in digital watches and calculators.

THE SYSTEM UNIT

A system unit houses the processor and memory of a personal computer system. If you were to remove the cover of the system unit and look inside, you would see the parts that make up a system unit. Note, however, that some computers do not come apart easily and that others have a warranty that is invalidated if you take the computer apart. Although it is not necessary to know how each of these parts works, it is useful, from a systems point of view, to know something about how each part contributes to making up the whole system.

If you ignore for the moment all the wires and connections that link the various parts together, you will see the fundamental building blocks of all computer systems and subsystems— the integrated circuit chips. All the functional hardware parts of the computer—input, processor, storage, and output—can be made from integrated circuits.

You cannot actually see the integrated circuit chips. They are housed in sealed rectangular blocks of black plastic to protect them. One of the most important of these chips is called the *central processing unit (CPU)* or simply the processor. In a personal computer, the CPU is the *microprocessor* chip. It carries out the processing tasks by interpreting and executing the instructions in a program.

Working in close conjunction with the microprocessor is a form of storage called the computer's *memory.* This is where the programs, along with the data to be input and the results to be output, are stored. A computer's memory is actually a collection of chips that are functionally divided into two types—ROM (read-only memory) and RAM (random-access memory).

ROM (read-only memory) is permanent memory that the microprocessor can read information from, but whose contents can be neither erased nor written over—thus the name, read-only memory. ROM stores the instructions that start up the computer when the power is turned on as well as some additional programs that need never be changed.

RAM (random-access memory) is

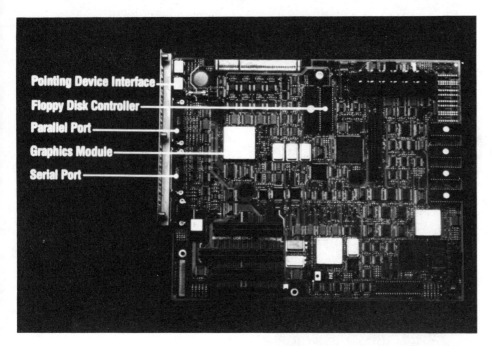

Pointing Device Interface
Floppy Disk Controller
Parallel Port
Graphics Module
Serial Port

The system unit. *The mother board of an IBM Personal System/2 Model 30 computer.*

grated circuit chips require so little electricity to operate, a power supply is also housed in the system unit. This converts ordinary household current into the low-voltage direct current that the integrated circuits require.

Many personal computers also contain a series of sockets, called *expansion slots,* into which additional circuit boards can be plugged. These additional circuit boards expand the capabilities of the computer. Some can contain additional memory chips, whereas others can provide the ability to connect additional external devices: for example, a modem, a printer, extra disk drives, or other input/output devices, such as a color display screen.

DISKS AND DISK DRIVES

Disks have become the most widely used medium for the storage part of the system. A *disk* is a circular platter on which a recording surface has been applied. The most common type of disk is *magnetic.* It is coated with the same material found on audio tape, and it can be erased and used over and over. Another type, the *optical disk,* uses laser beams of light instead of the magnetic method to record and retrieve information.

There are two types of magnetic disks: floppy disks and hard disks. Floppy disks are made from thin sheets of flexible plastic; hard disks are made from rigid platters of aluminum. The device that plays the disk is called a disk drive. It contains the mechanical equipment needed to spin or rotate the disk and the read/write head needed to record and retrieve information to and from the disk.

The most common hard disk drives are called Winchester drives, after the code name for the IBM project that developed them. In a Winchester drive, one or more disks along with the read/write head and the spinning mechanism are housed in a sealed container. A common size for Winchester drives is $5\frac{1}{4}$ inches. For several technical reasons, which will be discussed in Chapter 8, hard disks are capable of storing much more information than floppy disks. For example, a $5\frac{1}{4}$-inch Winchester disk might store 20 to 40 million characters of information,

temporary memory that is empty until the microprocessor needs to use it, that is, until it loads programs and data into it. RAM is often called read/write memory, meaning that the microprocessor can read its contents and write programs or data into it. Most RAM is temporary because it loses its contents when the computer's power is turned off. For long-term storage of information or programs, disk drives (which we will discuss soon) are connected to the system.

Memories for personal computers are rated according to their capacity, which is measured in thousands of bytes. A *byte* consists of eight consecutive bits and is the equivalent of one character, such as a letter, a number, or a punctuation mark. A standard abbreviation for thousands of bytes is K, which represents the number 1024 (i.e., 2^{10}), so the capacity of a memory that is expressed as 640K means 640 x 1024, or 655,360 bytes. Most personal computers come with 640K or 1024K memories, and their memories are expandable beyond that number.

By themselves, the chips cannot do much—they have to be connected and fed with electricity. The chips are usually mounted on a *mother board*—a fiberglass circuit board that contains sockets into which the chips are plugged and a set of tracks (printed on the circuit board) that connects the various chips. Because these tiny inte-

whereas a $5\frac{1}{4}$-inch floppy disk might only store 360,000 characters of information.

Today, many personal computers come with one floppy disk drive that uses $3\frac{1}{2}$-inch disks, and one hard disk drive. The hard disk is used for storing large quantities of information and provides fast access to that information. The floppy disk drive is convenient for making backup copies of the data on the hard disk, making copies of files that can be mailed to friends or coworkers, and, of course, to input new information into the system.

PRINTERS

A **printer** is a device that produces paper-copy output from a computer system. Printers come in a wide variety of shapes, styles, and prices. Most print in one color (black), but technological breakthroughs are making color printing a feasible alternative for graphics applications. The typical printer for a personal computer is connected to the computer by a cable. It usually accepts continuous-form paper, but some printers will accept single sheets, such as letterhead.

Your applications for a personal computer will determine the type of printer to use. One way to classify printers is by the method used to form the printed images. *Dot-matrix printers* form characters with a pattern of dots. This method can include striking a ribbon with a hammer, spraying ink with a nozzle, or transferring the pattern with heat or a laser. The quality of the output from such printers ranges from a very rough and highly visible grainy pattern of dots to an extremely fine high-resolution pattern. The former is quite adequate for printing drafts of documents; the latter is more desirable for printing graphic images.

Fully formed character printers for personal computers are commonly called *letter-quality printers* because their printing looks as if it were produced by an electric typewriter. These printers use a cylinder, a typeball, a thimble, or a daisy wheel—a plastic wheel with spokes that contain letters on the tips—to strike a ribbon and transfer a fully formed character to the paper. Letter-quality printers produce typewriter-quality documents and are desirable for correspondence. However, these printers are limited to printing characters and are not capable of printing graphic images.

All printers are connected to the computer through a **port**—the location through which the computer exchanges information with an external device. A port has a physical connector and an address, so that programs know where to send information. The two basic types of ports are serial and parallel, but you need not be concerned with the technical differences here. Some computers come with ports built into the mother board. Others use circuit boards that plug into the computer's expansion slots.

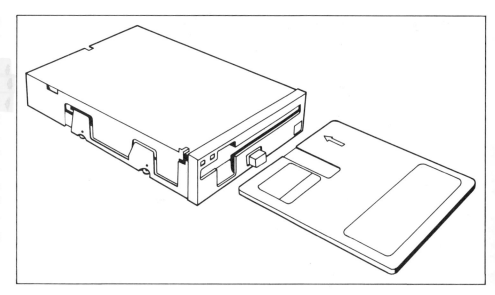

Disks and disk drives.

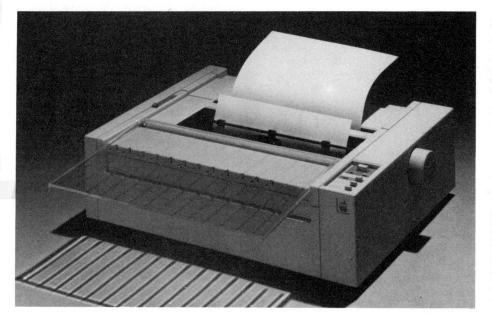

Printers. *The Apple Imagewriter is a low-cost dot-matrix printer.*

REVIEW

A computer is an electronic device that is capable of responding to input, processing that input, storing instructions and the results of processing, and providing output in the form of information. The broadest categories of computers are special and general purpose. Computer literacy encompasses some commonsense guidelines that include reading about computers, obtaining real experience with computers, and writing computer programs.

However, you do not have to learn to program to use a computer. Computers are systems: they have gone far beyond number processing to become information processing systems. Information systems are found in banks, insurance companies, government agencies, space probes, and automated factory machines, to name a few. Communication plays an important role in the study of computers because computers are often connected together in networks and because information must be communicated to be useful.

Personal computer systems are highly evolved descendants of earlier larger systems and are having a major impact on organizations. Hardware is the physical equipment in a computer system; software is the programs that control the operation of the system. Applications are what you do with computers, and they can be found everywhere. The fundamental components of any computer system include a keyboard for input, a display screen for output, a system unit for processing and memory, disk drives for storage, and a printer for output.

RESOURCES

BOOKS

Bolter, J. David. *Turing's Man: Western Culture in the Computer Age.* Chapel Hill: University of North Carolina Press, 1984. An interesting book that contrasts the impact that earlier technology had on culture with the impact computers have on our culture.

Crichton, Michael. *Electronic Life.* New York: Ballantine, 1984. The author of *The Andromeda Strain* and *Congo* presents a short, nontechnical introduction to computers. It is well worth the few hours that it takes to read.

Eames, Charles, and Ray Eames. *A Computer Perspective.* Cambridge, Mass.: Harvard University Press, 1973. Originally an exhibit for IBM, this graphic history of the origin and development of the computer from 1890 to 1950 was made into an interesting history book.

Evans, Christopher. *The Micro Millennium.* New York: Washington Square Press, 1981. An excellent overview of the past, present, and future of computers. Easy and fast reading that focuses on the people who made it happen.

Freiberger, Paul, and Michael Swaine. *Fire in the Valley: The Making of the Personal Computer.* Berkeley, Calif.: Osborne/ McGraw-Hill, 1984. Easy, fun, and informative reading about the history of personal computers and the people who were involved in it.

Kidder, Tracy. *The Soul of a New Machine.* Boston: Little, Brown, 1981. An interesting story, understandable by anyone even moderately interested in technology. It deals with the trials and tribulations of the group of engineers and programmers who built a new minicomputer for Data General Corporation.

Macaulay, David. *The Way Things Work.* Boston: Houghton Mifflin, 1988. Part 4, *Electricity and Automation*, is of special interest, but don't neglect the rest of this highly illustrated, informative book.

Nelson, Theodor. *Computer Lib/Dream Machines.* Redmond, Wash.: Microsoft Press, 1987. As the author puts it, "a wildly utopian introduction to computers," this is a reprint of a book that first appeared in the 1960s and is reminiscent of the *Whole Earth Catalog*. Still, it's worth reading. Original ideas never go out of style, only out of print.

COMPUTER DICTIONARIES

Downing, Douglas, and Michael Covington. *Dictionary of Computer Terms.* New York: Barron's, 1989. An excellent pocket-sized technical dictionary with personal computer software products and companies.

Porter, Kent. *The New American Computer Dictionary.* New York: New American Library, 1985. A good pocket-sized dictionary with a few illustrations added.

Rosenberg, Jerry M. *Dictionary of Computers, Data Processing, & Telecommunications.* New York: John Wiley, 1984. A very large reference with over 10,000 terms, complete and comprehensive.

Webster's New World Dictionary of Computer Terms. New York: Simon & Schuster, 1983. A good pocket-sized dictionary with clear explanations.

MAGAZINES

Computer Shopper. New York: Ziff-Davis. A monthly tabloid complete with classifieds and product reviews. A good place to look for new and used computers.

InfoWorld. Menlo Park, Calif.: CW Communications. A weekly newspaper that covers the microcomputer end of the industry. Good for first sources of information and gossip about computer people. Excellent coverage and reviews of software products for small business and personal computers.

PC Computing. New York: Ziff-Davis. A monthly magazine targeted to the novice computer user. It contains an interesting mix of stories and factual reviews.

STUDY GUIDE

Match the following key terms to the appropriate definition:

A.

1. __C__ Computer
2. __e__ Special-purpose computer
3. __b__ General-purpose computer
4. __f__ Computer literacy
5. __a__ Documentation
6. __h__ Tutorial
7. __g__ Spreadsheet
8. __d__ Programming language

a. The books and manuals that accompany a computer-related product.

b. A computer whose operation can be changed by altering its programs.

c. An electronic device that responds to input, processes that input according to instructions, stores the instructions and the results of processing, and provides output.

d. A formally constructed artificial language in which the syntax and grammar are stated so precisely that a computer can analyze, interpret, and understand the meaning of that language.

e. A computer that is dedicated to a single purpose.

f. The knowledge and skills required to use a computer as a problem-solving tool.

g. A ready-made program that enables you to organize numbers and formulas into a rectangular array of cells.

h. A computer program that contains step-by-step directions for learning how to use a computer or a computer program.

B.

9. __e__ Jargon
10. __g__ System
11. __k__ Information
12. __m__ Code
13. __a__ Circuit
14. __h__ Integrated circuit
15. __b__ Bit
16. __n__ Data
17. __i__ Information system
18. __d__ Communication system
19. __j__ Network
20. __f__ Hardware
21. __l__ Software
22. __c__ Applications

a. An interconnected set of electronic components that performs a function.

b. The smallest unit of information used in computer and communication systems.

c. The things computers can be used to do.

d. Two or more communicating devices that are connected to each other.

e. The vocabulary of specialized words that is used to speed up communication between people.

f. The physical components of a computer or other system.

g. A set or arrangement of parts acting together to perform a function.

h. A system that consists of a sender, a physical channel, and a receiver.

i. A system that takes input, processes it, and produces information as output.

j. Combinations of thousands of circuits built on tiny pieces of silicon, which are called chips.

k. Any data that have a context.

l. Programs that control the operation of a computer system.

m. A set of symbols that represents another set of symbols.

n. The facts, letters, numbers, or symbols used to produce information.

C.

23. ____ Keyboard
24. ____ Display
25. ____ Microprocessor
26. ____ Memory
27. ____ ROM (read-only memory)
28. ____ RAM (random-access memory)
29. ____ Byte
30. ____ Mother board
31. ____ Expansion slot
32. ____ Disk
33. ____ Printer
34. ____ Port

a. A form of storage where programs, data to be input, and results to be output are stored.

b. A device that converts keystrokes into special codes that can be electronically manipulated by the computer.

c. A device that produces hard copy output from a computer system by transferring an image onto paper.

d. Eight consecutive bits that are the equivalent of one character.

e. A device that is used to give you feedback and to view the computer's output.

f. A circular platter on which a recording surface has been applied.

g. The central processing unit of a microcomputer.

h. Temporary memory that is empty until the microprocessor needs to use it, that is, until it loads programs and data into it.

i. A fiberglass circuit board that contains sockets into which chips are plugged and tracks that connect the various chips.

j. Permanent memory that the microprocessor can read information from, but whose contents can be neither erased nor written over.

k. A socket into which additional circuit boards can be plugged.

l. The location through which the computer exchanges information with an external device.

True/False:

35. _____ A primary task of a computer is to provide output in the form of information.

36. _____ The broadest categories of computers are microcomputers, minicomputers, and mainframes.

37. _____ Special-purpose computers can be adapted to many situations by giving them an appropriate program.

38. _____ A minicomputer is the smallest and least expensive type of computer.

39. _____ Learning how to program is a requirement for using a computer as a problem-solving tool.

40. _____ A programming language is a formally constructed artificial language.

41. _____ Writing a program is an intellectually simple task.

42. _____ The main subsystems of a computer are input, processor, storage, and output.

43. _____ One of the problems with computers is that information cannot be represented as electrical signals.

44. _____ A binary signal combines the three possibilities of yes, no, and maybe.

45. _____ When no information is present, communication becomes noise.

46. _____ A telephone system is an example of a network that processes centralized output.

47. _____ The first step in getting started with computers involves finding a computer or hardware.

48. _____ The two types of disks are magnetic and optical.

49. _____ Random access means that it takes the same amount of time to access any one piece of information from memory as it does another.

50. _____ A microprocessor can read and write information to and from RAM.

Multiple Choice:

51. Which of the following is not considered to be one of the basic tasks that a computer is capable of performing?

   a. Responding to output in a predictable way.
   b. Processing input according to instructions.
   c. Storing instructions and the results of processing.
   d. Providing output in the form of information.

52. Large-scale general-purpose computers are called

   a. Microcomputers.
   b. Mainframes.
   c. Minicomputers.
   d. Personal computers.

53. Advances in computer technology have led to

   a. The creation of less sophisticated computers.
   b. The elimination of the gap that was inherent in computer sizes.
   c. The widening of the gap that was inherent in computer sizes.
   d. The elimination of the need for mainframe computers.

54. Ready-made programs such as spreadsheets

   a. Help you to learn programming.
   b. Help your reading about computers.
   c. Are tutorials that help you to learn about computers.
   d. Help you to concentrate on solving problems.

55. Which of the following is the way in which computer people use the word system?

   a. Authority.
   b. Organization.
   c. Logic.
   d. Ideas.

56. When using the term system as a concept, a good method for thinking about organization is to

   a. Take things apart, decide what they are, and put them back together.

   b. Use system as a frame of reference to translate and categorize more specialized words.

   c. Start with the whole and work toward the parts.

   d. Translate a highly specialized and complex computer terminology into an easy-to-learn language.

57. A bit is the smallest possible unit of information because a bit

   a. Can be represented by two different levels of voltage in a computer circuit.

   b. Is enough to tell the difference between two opposites, such as on and off.

   c. Can be grouped with other bits to represent numbers, letters, or special symbols.

   d. Is any pattern that has a commonly understood meaning.

58. The difference between data and information is that

   a. Data always contain information.

   b. Data have a context; information may not.

SOFTWARE EXERCISES

Your instructor wants to find out how comp to use a word proc you will be exp tions involve ment. For t you di

     ...processor.

   d. Mother board.

Thought Questions:

61. In this chapter, we covered the basic concepts of systems, information, information systems, communication, hardware, software, and applications. Which concept did you find the easiest to understand? Why? Which concept was the most difficult or obscure? Why?

62. To understand how a computer system works, you should understand how each of the parts contributes to the functioning of the whole system. Which parts (keyboard, display, system unit, disk and disk drive, printer) are easiest to understand? Why? Which parts are the most incomprehensible? Why?

Projects:

63. Obtain a current issue of a computer magazine from your school library or local bookstore. Examine the magazine in terms of questions such as "Who is the magazine written for?" and "Is it suitable for novices?" Then make a presentation to your class about the magazine. Include whether or not you would recommend the magazine. Defend your position.

64. Visit an office in your area that uses computers. Make a list of where all the computers are in the office and what they are used for. Prepare a report for your class.

survey your college or university ...uters are being used. You are going ...essor to create a report. In the process, ...osed to the basic word processing opera-... in creating, composing, and saving a docu-...

...his exercise, your instructor has obtained a copy of ...school's catalog, which lists all the departments or ...visions in the school. The class will be divided into teams, one team per department or division. In addition, one team will be assigned to the library, and another will be assigned to administration.

Each team is responsible for contacting the chairperson or the appropriate person in charge. The team will find out

- What types of computers are used.
- How many computers are used.
- For what applications are the computers used.
- What future plans each department has for computers.

Each team will then use a word processor to prepare a two-page report on their findings. By the time you have completed this assignment, you will have learned the basic skills of using a word processor.

ANSWERS

1. c, **2.** e, **3.** b, **4.** f, **5.** a, **6.** h, **7.** g, **8.** d, **9.** e, **10.** g, **11.** k, **12.** m, **13.** a, **14.** j, **15.** b, **16.** n, **17.** i, **18.** h, **19.** d, **20.** f, **21.** l, **22.** c, **23.** b, **24.** e, **25.** g, **26.** a, **27.** j, **28.** h, **29.** d, **30.** i, **31.** k, **32.** f, **33.** c, **34.** l, **35.** T, **36.** F, **37.** F, **38.** F, **39.** F, **40.** T, **41.** F, **42.** T, **43.** F, **44.** F, **45.** T, **46.** F, **47.** F, **48.** T, **49.** T, **50.** T, **51.** a, **52.** b, **53.** b, **54.** d, **55.** b, **56.** c, **57.** b, **58.** c, **59.** c, **60.** c.

ALAN C. KAY

Profession: Kay is associated with Apple Computer, Inc., in Cupertino, California, as an Apple Fellow.

Profile: After obtaining a Ph.D from the University of Utah, Kay joined the artificial intelligence project at Stanford University going on to then become a founding principal at Xerox Palo Alto Research Center (PARC). In his position as an Apple Fellow, he has an independent charter to pursue unconventional ideas for Apple's future. He has often been called the father of personal computing.

Quote: "The best way to predict the future is to invent it."

CHAPTER 2

PERSONAL COMPUTER APPLICATIONS

PREVIEW

Ten years ago, there wasn't much application software for personal computers. But as the demand for personal computing escalated, vendors have developed application software that can be sold at reasonable prices. Today, personal computer applications are commonplace in the business world. Secretaries are agile with word processing, accountants with spreadsheets, and managers with databases. They, like others, have learned that using personal computers is a strategic job skill.

The personal computer is now accepted as a vital part of the overall information system strategy of large and small organizations. Personal computers can handle many of the tasks that were once relegated to their larger ancestors.

This chapter will highlight the advantages and benefits of personal computers by giving you a broad overview of personal computer software, including operating systems and application software.

In this chapter, you'll learn

- The major categories of personal computer software.
- The role of a user interface.
- The functions of an operating system.
- Characteristics of popular operating systems.
- The functions of word processing software.
- Characteristics of desktop-publishing software.
- The functions of a spreadsheet program.
- The functions of a database program.
- Characteristics of graphics, communications, and integrated software.

PERSONAL COMPUTER SOFTWARE

When you think about using a personal computer, the first question you should ask yourself is, "What do I want to do with it?" Even if you have a specific application in mind, such as writing your next term paper, the answer to the question lies in finding the right software for your application. Once you do that, you can start using a personal computer right away.

Personal computer software comes in many different varieties, and the applications number in the thousands, so it is useful to know how individual programs are categorized. The broadest classifications of software are system software and application software.

System software includes

- Operating systems.
- Programming languages.

Programming languages will not be discussed in this chapter. More information about them will be provided in Chapter 14.

Application software includes

- Special-purpose programs.
- General-purpose programs.

Using a personal computer involves getting used to the conventions of the user interface and the operating system, then developing an understanding of what a computer can do by becoming familiar with some of the application software for personal computers.

USER INTERFACES

When using personal computer software, you will interact with the **user** *interface*—the software that is responsible for passing information to and from the person using a program. As an analogy, think of a car as a system for providing personal transportation. Some components of the car—the engine, the transmission, the wheels, and so on—provide the basic means of transportation. Other components of the car, including the steering wheel, the brake and gas pedals, and the instrument panel, provide the means for controlling the operation of the car. Those components can be thought of as the car's user interface.

A software user interface provides a running *dialog* between the computer system and the user. Its purpose is to allow the user to communicate with and control the computer. It takes requests from a user and distributes them to other parts of the program that perform the actual processing tasks. It also provides feedback to the user while the software is running and provides output from the results of the processing tasks.

Although communication and control are the two fundamental concepts on which user interfaces are based, different computer systems use them in different ways. As a consequence, you will find a wide variety of user interfaces as you begin to use personal computers. For example, the user interface of an Apple Macintosh is entirely different from that of an IBM Personal Computer. On the Macintosh, the user interface is presented as a series of pictures called *icons* to indicate functions. A mouse is used to select them. On earlier IBM Personal Computers, the user interface is presented as a prompt with a blinking cursor. You enter commands or data by typing on the keyboard.

User interfaces also differ in the way you give them commands. Interacting with software can be accomplished with a command-driven, menu-driven, graphical, natural language interface, or a combination of two or more types of interfaces.

Command-driven interfaces request or prompt the user to type in a single letter, word, or line that is then translated into an instruction for the program to follow. The typical command begins with a verb, such as

Personal computer software. *Categories of software for personal computers.*

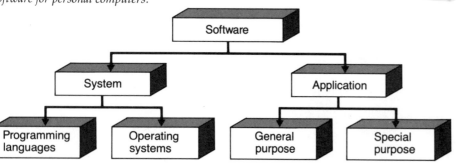

COPY. The verb is followed by one or more words called *arguments* that specify in more detail what the command is to accomplish. For example, in the operating system command COPY OLDDATA NEWDATA, COPY is the verb, and the arguments are two filenames separated by a space. When the command is executed, the resulting action is to copy the data in the file named OLDDATA to the file named NEWDATA.

Some application programs have command-driven interfaces too. For example, spreadsheet programs often have a command-driven interface to perform such functions as save, clear, print, or load a spreadsheet. An advantage is that once you master the commands, using the program becomes fast and easy. A disadvantage is that command-driven interfaces are difficult for nontechnical users to learn and apply.

Menu-driven interfaces offer the user a list of choices or options, called a menu, as a way of letting a user choose from several different commands or functions. For example, a word processing program might offer a menu of numbered choices. You type the number that corresponds to your choice.

A popular form of menu-driven interfaces uses two levels to provide more choices. At the first level, a menu bar provides a list of all the available menus. When you select a choice from the menu bar, a list of choices will drop down from the menu bar. This type of menu is called a pull-down menu.

Menu-driven interfaces are generally easier to learn than are command-driven interfaces. However, if the menu-oriented system is not flexible (i.e., if it requires you to continue working your way through menus long after you have mastered the use of the system), it can become annoying to use.

Graphical user interfaces, often abbreviated GUIs, use pictures and graphic symbols to represent commands, choices, or actions. They often present the user with a graphic representation of a desktop, complete with pictures or icons of disks, a trash can,

Command-driven interface. *User's of Microrim's R:Base program type in commands in response to the program's R> prompt. The program interprets the commands and provides the users with the requested information.*

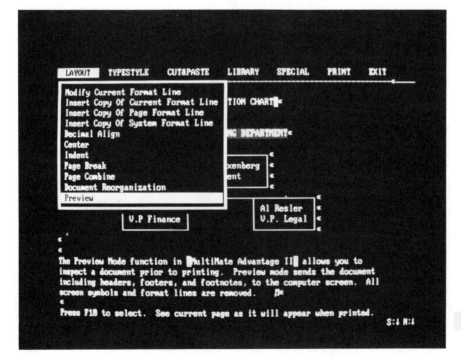

Menu-driven interface. *The MultiMate word processor uses a menu to indicate choices among program functions.*

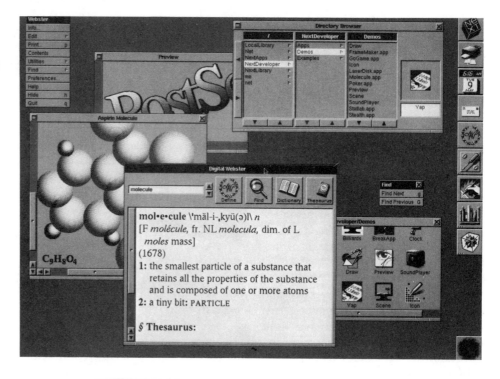

Graphical user interface. The Next Computer System's NextStep user interface and development environment makes extensive use of graphics and icons to present information. (Copyright (c) 1989, Next, Inc. Reprinted by permission.)

file folders, and programs. In addition, they provide *windows*—a method for dividing the display screen into variable-sized rectangles for viewing two or more applications or parts of an application at the same time. The two most widely known examples of graphical user interfaces are the Macintosh user interface and the Microsoft Windows user interface for MS-DOS–based computers.

Natural language interfaces allow the user to input simple English phrases that are translated into commands or actions by the application program. They are most commonly found in applications where it is not practical to train people in a more formal command language or interface before they begin to use a computer.

For example, to give the sales force of a large company the means of accessing information stored in computer files, the company might choose to implement a natural language system whereby the salespeople could query the contents of the files by asking free-form questions in English.

The term *user friendly* has come to be associated with how easy software is to learn and use. Although this is naturally somewhat subjective, command-driven interfaces are considered to be the most difficult to learn and use, whereas graphical user interfaces are considered the easiest to learn and use. However, trade-offs still exist between making a program easy to learn and use and making a program perform a wide variety of complex tasks.

Natural language interface. Microrim's Clout provides a method for entering an English phrase instead of a command in order to access information.

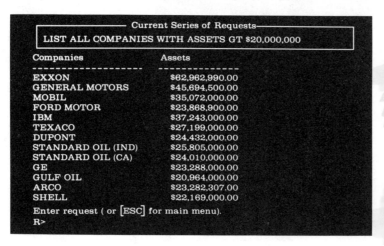

Current Series of Requests—	
LIST ALL COMPANIES WITH ASSETS GT $20,000,000	

Companies	Assets
EXXON	$62,962,990.00
GENERAL MOTORS	$45,694,500.00
MOBIL	$35,072,000.00
FORD MOTOR	$23,868,900.00
IBM	$37,243,000.00
TEXACO	$27,199,000.00
DUPONT	$24,432,000.00
STANDARD OIL (IND)	$25,805,000.00
STANDARD OIL (CA)	$24,010,000.00
GE	$23,288,000.00
GULF OIL	$20,964,000.00
ARCO	$23,282,307.00
SHELL	$22,169,000.00

Enter request (or [ESC] for main menu).
R>

OPERATING SYSTEMS

An *operating system* is software that manages the overall operation of the computer system. Its primary purpose is to support application programs. The parts of an operating system can be grouped into four broad functional categories. One set of parts forms the shell or user interface; another set of parts is responsible for coordinating multiple computers in a network; a third set coordinates multiple tasks, or basic units of work within a single computer; and, finally, the *kernel* of the operating system is software that ties the hardware to the software and performs such tasks as keeping track of everything in memory and managing the flow of information to and from disks, the keyboard, and the display screen.

An analogy can be drawn between a computer user and someone who attends a live performance, such as a play or concert. When you attend a performance, you are seeing the end result of a carefully coordinated production. What you don't see in a good performance are the technical details, the behind-the-scenes activities that are making the performance run smoothly. Technicians manage light and sound, stagehands manage props and change scenes, and actors change costumes and wait for their cues. Similarly, an operating system manages the details needed to support a smoothly running application program.

All application programs share some tasks in common. They include accepting characters typed at the keyboard, displaying information on the screen, managing information on a disk, and managing information in memory. The operating system takes care of the details of these tasks. A most important example of how operating systems support application programs is the task of managing files. To a computer program, a *file* is simply a named collection of information. Whether your application is general or special purpose, your program will need to store information in files.

By itself, a disk is an empty container waiting to be filled. The operating system takes care of

• Formatting the disk, which involves electronically preparing the disk to be able to store files.

• Managing the location of information on the disk.

• Checking to make sure that errors do not occur when reading to and writing from the disk.

• Performing the input and output necessary to retrieve and store information on the disk.

Personal Computer Operating Systems		
Parts	Functions	Trends
Shell	Interface with user	Windowing Graphics-oriented interface
Network Management	Communicate with other computers	Internetworking Standard protocols
Task Management	Coordinate multiple applications	Multitasking Advanced memory management
Kernel	Interface with hardware	Virtual environments Richer variety of files

More details of how information is organized, stored, and retrieved on a disk will be covered in Chapter 8.

Operating systems also manage the other components of a computer system. They support programs, called *device drivers*, that control the various hardware devices, such as the keyboard, display screen, and printer. The device driver is responsible for translating instructions from the application into commands the hardware understands. For example, if an application program wants to print something, it simply sends the information and the appropriate instructions to the operating system, which, in turn, calls upon the printer device driver to manipulate the printer to perform the desired task.

More complicated computer sys-

Operating systems. An operating system is a set of software that manages the overall operation of a computer system.

Multitasking. Deskview can manage several programs at once and allow the user to easily switch among several programs.

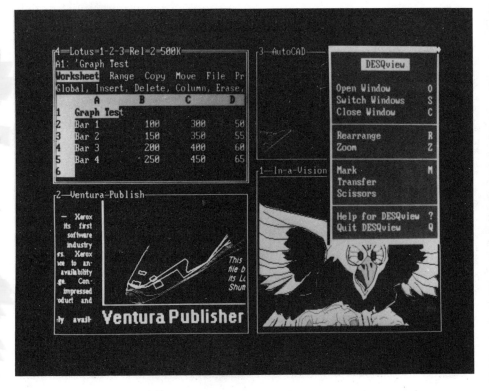

tems support more sophisticated operations. For example, it is possible for a computer system to be operating on two or more *tasks*, or pieces of work, at the same time. This type of operating system is called a ***multitasking system***. It takes care of the details that are required to manage several tasks at once and allows the user to switch between tasks.

Some computer systems are designed to serve several users at once. These systems, called ***multiuser systems***, usually have several terminals connected to a single central processor. A multiuser operating system has to keep track of what each user is doing, know where the user's programs and data are in memory, manage shared data on disks so that users do not destroy each other's data, and allocate a fair share of computing services to each user.

Some operating systems allow large-sized programs to run in small-sized computers. To accomplish this, the operating system uses virtual memory techniques. ***Virtual memory*** creates the illusion of a computer with more memory by moving some data to disk. When a program needs to be larger than the size of available memory, the program is divided into a number of pieces. To run such a program, the first piece is brought into memory and executes until another section of the program is needed. Then, the second piece is brought in, and so on. An operating system using

virtual memory techniques automatically takes care of managing the pieces and bringing them in and out of memory as needed.

GETTING TO KNOW YOUR OPERATING SYSTEM

Although in theory all operating systems perform very similar functions, in practice there are many different operating systems. One reason is that different personal computers are built around different CPUs (central processing units), or microprocessors, each with its own unique characteristics. Another reason is the subjective nature of user-interface design.

MS-DOS

The ancestor of MS-DOS was developed in the early 1970s by Tim Patterson of Seattle Computer Products, Inc. Later, Microsoft Corporation, under the leadership of William H. Gates, acquired the rights and began licensing it as MS-DOS (Microsoft disk operating system).

When IBM decided to enter the personal computer market in 1981, it licensed MS-DOS from Microsoft and renamed it PC DOS (Personal Computer disk operating system). The IBM Personal Computer quickly became very popular and because of IBM's reputation, the race was on to make computers compatible with the IBM Personal Computer. Manufacturing a computer that was IBM compatible generally meant using MS-DOS as the operating system of choice.

MS-DOS has a command-driven user interface. It prompts the user, who responds by typing a command and pressing the Enter key. Its commands can be used to format disks; copy, rename, delete, and backup files; and organize and manage files on the disk.

As high-capacity hard disks increased in popularity, it became necessary to devise a method to keep track of large numbers of files. Microsoft added variations of MS-DOS (versions 2.0 and up) that incorporated a tree-structured hierarchical file management scheme in which files can be organized into groups called *directories*.

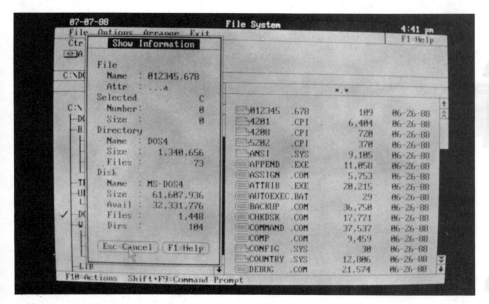

MS-DOS. *Microsoft's MS-DOS Version 4.0 allows commands to be accessed through pull-down menus.*

A disk contains one master or root directory, which may contain both files and subdirectories. Each subdirectory may contain files and lower-level subdirectories. Using this method, subdirectories can be given names that indicate what type of files may be found in them. Later variations of MS-DOS (versions 3.0 and up) added additional enhanced commands and support for networks. Version 4.0 added a user interface called the DOS Shell with pull-down menus.

MS-DOS users who want a graphical user interface can obtain Microsoft Windows, which provides a window- and icon-based user interface for DOS's file management functions and allows applications to share data among themselves.

Macintosh Operating System

Apple's Macintosh operating system is a descendant of research done at Xerox PARC (Palo Alto Research Center) and Apple's Lisa computer, the user interface of which was designed by a team headed by Larry Tesler.

The Macintosh operating system uses a graphical user interface. Icons indicate functions, and a mouse is used to select them. Major parts of the operating system include QuickDraw for drawing text and graphics on the screen and a hierarchical file system called the Finder that allows the user to group files in a number of different ways and to rearrange the groupings. Newer versions of the operating system include MultiFinder for managing and switching among programs.

Unix

Unix was developed by Ken Thompson and Dennis Ritchie in 1969 at Bell Laboratories, the research and development arm of AT&T. Unix was designed as a programmer's tool and was used primarily by programmers who were developing new software. After that, it became popular in universities, and then it evolved into a general-purpose operating system.

Unix is a multiuser, multitasking operating system designed to work on a variety of computers from personal computers to mainframes. There are

Unix. *Sun Microsystem's Open Look is a graphical user interface for Unix.*

two standard versions of Unix. System V.4 is offered by Unix International, an organization led by AT&T and Sun Microsystems. OSF 1 is offered by the Open Software Foundation, an organization led by IBM, Digital, and Hewlett-Packard. Both versions offer similar graphical user interfaces: System V.4's is called Open Look, and that of OSF 1 is called Motif. In addition, proprietary versions of Unix are available from individual companies, such as A/IX from IBM, Ultrix from Digital, A/UX from Apple, and Mach from Next.

Unix's major advantage is that it is a very modular operating system that can be assembled like building blocks to perform various functions. Unix's major drawback is that there is no single cohesive operating system. Programs that run under one version often do not run under another version.

Operating System/2

When IBM decided to introduce a second generation of personal computers in 1987, they named them Personal Systems/2. The operating system, called Operating System/2

(OS/2), is a single-user multitasking operating system for this generation of personal computers. It was developed under a joint agreement between IBM and Microsoft.

OS/2 provides a standard graphical user interface called the Presentation Manager. It provides a window-based user interface for the operating system's file management functions and allows applications to share data among themselves. The OS/2 kernel supports multitasking so that applications can be written as closely cooperating sets of tasks.

OS/2 also incorporates an extension called local-area network (LAN) manager, which permits groups of computers to interact with one another and share resources, such as disks and printers.

A *distributed filing* capability, such as that offered by OS/2 and Unix, gives a computer access to files that reside on another computer's disk on a network and manages the details of many linked computers sharing the same communication link, hardware devices, and programs. More detail on the operating system and what it implies for hardware can be found in Chapters 7 and 8.

Operating System/2. OS/2 provides Presentation Manager, a built-in graphical user interface.

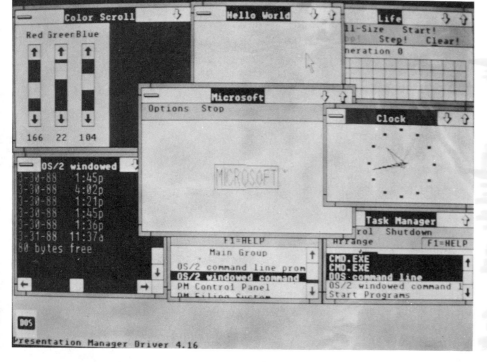

Presentation Manager Driver 4.16

APPLICATION SOFTWARE

In contrast to operating systems, *application software* performs work not related to the computer system itself. Almost any kind of application that you would need is already written and tested and may be purchased off the shelf in retail computer stores or through mail-order outlets. This application software falls into two categories: special purpose and general purpose.

• *Special-purpose programs*. Dedicated to performing tasks such as payroll, accounting, bookkeeping, education, entertainment, or statistical analysis, the programs contain built-in problem-solving features specially designed for those particular tasks.

• *General-purpose programs*. Adaptable to a wide variety of tasks, such as word processing, spreadsheet calculating, record keeping, graphics, or communications, the user defines the problem and the procedure and uses the software to assist in preparing a solution.

Special-purpose programs have been developed in response to the specific needs of individuals, professionals, and small businesses. Because there are so many different programs, each one quite application specific, it is beyond the scope of this chapter to discuss special-purpose application software. Some categories of special-purpose application software are the following:

• *Managing*. Includes project management, decision modeling, and statistical analysis programs.

• *Accounting and bookkeeping*. Ranges from simple personal finance systems and income tax programs to complex accounts payable, accounts receivable, and general ledger systems.

• *Vertical market applications*. Customized programs dedicated to the specific needs of such professions as lawyers, dentists, doctors, real estate agents, contractors, and distributors.

• *Entertainment*. Consists primarily of computer games.

• *Education.* Can easily overlap with the entertainment category in the form of simulations and games, but the education category also includes tutorials, computer-aided instruction, and computer-based training.

• *Scientific and engineering.* A wide variety of statistical, data-gathering, analytical, design, and testing programs.

• *Utilities.* This category includes disk and file management; data protection and recovery; and desktop utilities such as calendars, calculators, and notepads.

General-purpose programs have been developed in response to the general problem-solving needs of people whose work involves such common tasks as planning, writing, record keeping, calculating, and communicating. Part of general-purpose software's usefulness derives from the fact that it is not dedicated to any specific use but can be adapted to a wide variety of tasks. The categories of general-purpose application software include the following:

• *Writing.* One of the most common general applications for computers, this category includes *word processors,* which allow you to write anything from a simple note to a book about computers; *outline processors,* which allow you to enter ideas and reorganize them in outline form; *desktop publishing,* which allows you to prepare and print typeset- or near-typeset-quality documents; and spelling checker, mail merge, and indexing programs that work in conjunction with word processors.

• *Spreadsheets.* Another common general application, the spreadsheet allows you to build and analyze financial models, balance sheets, budgets, and other types of numerical models.

• *Databases.* Database programs let you create, index, and access files, such as personal notes, customer lists, or inventories. You can also create and print reports based on those files.

• *Graphics.* This category includes drawing, computer-aided design, analytical graphics, and presentation graphics programs.

• *Communications.* Communications software allows you to link your personal computer to information-providing networks such as The Source or CompuServe, or it gives you the option of communicating directly with other personal computer owners.

• *Integrated.* These multifunction general-purpose programs combine at least two functions with the ability to share data among the functions. For example, integrated accounting programs might combine accounts receivable, accounts payable, and general ledger into one program. Other integrated programs might combine word processing, spreadsheet, database, and communications functions.

These categories of general-purpose software may not meet all your application needs, but learning about them, understanding how they work, and learning about some of the problems that can be solved by using them may give you several immediate reasons for using a personal computer.

SOFTWARE FOR WRITING

Writing with a word processing program is similar in many ways to writing with an ordinary electric typewriter, but a word processor offers significant features above and beyond the typewriter that make writing faster, easier, and perhaps better. Word processing is a common application for personal computers because it seems that everyone at one time or another needs to work with words. The benefits of word processing over manual methods quickly become apparent to even the novice user. You are familiar with the written word. You learn to organize and write documents, such as letters, papers, reports, short stories, and even business correspondence in school. If you have already used a typewriter, word processing will be an easy application to learn.

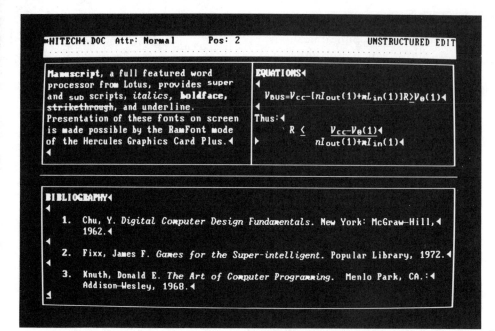

The screen shows:

```
HITECH4.DOC  Attr: Normal        Pos: 2           UNSTRUCTURED EDIT

Manuscript, a full featured word    EQUATIONS◄
processor from Lotus, provides super  ◄
and sub scripts, italics, boldface,   V_BUS=V_cc-[nI_out(1)+mL_in(1)]R>V_0(1)◄
strikethrough, and underline.         Thus:◄
Presentation of these fonts on screen       R <     V_cc-V_0(1)
is made possible by the RamFont mode        ►    nI_out(1)+mI_in(1)◄
of the Hercules Graphics Card Plus.◄
◄

BIBLIOGRAPHY◄
◄
   1. Chu, Y. Digital Computer Design Fundamentals. New York: McGraw-Hill,◄
      1962.◄
◄
   2. Fixx, James F. Games for the Super-intelligent. Popular Library, 1972.◄
◄
   3. Knuth, Donald E. The Art of Computer Programming.  Menlo Park, CA.:◄
      Addison-Wesley, 1968.◄
◄
```

Word processing. *A sample screen of the Lotus Manuscript word processor.*

Word processing. *A sample screen of the Microsoft Word for Windows word processor.*

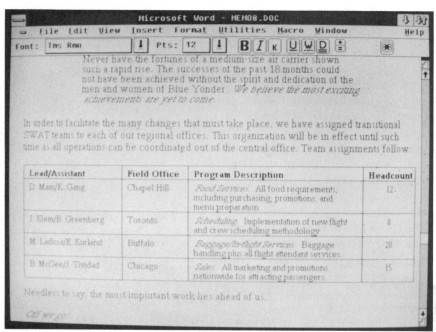

WHAT IS WORD PROCESSING?

Word processing is a term coined by IBM in 1964 to describe electronic ways of handling a standard set of office activities—composing, revising, filing, and printing written documents. For years, computers have been used in the office to accomplish these tasks, but they were usually large, complex, and inaccessible systems. Often, it was easier to write by hand than it was to gain access to use these word processing systems. The development of word processing programs for personal computers made the electronic handling of words practical even for the person who only wanted to write a letter, proposal, or business plan.

USING WORD PROCESSING SOFTWARE

Suppose that on your first job, your boss tells you to analyze a competitor's product line and write a report based on your findings. How might a word processor help you to accomplish this task? Let's see.

Composing

Assume that you have accomplished your preliminary research, organized your notes, and thought about what you are going to write; you are now ready to compose your report.

Composing a document simply means typing the text on your computer keyboard. With most word processors, you select an option that lets you create a new document and begin typing. When you start with a blank screen, a small blinking box or underline, called a *cursor*—a visual aid on the display screen—will be positioned at the beginning of the document. As you type, the cursor will mark where the next character you type will appear.

With most word processors, you will notice that when you reach the end of a line, the cursor will automatically jump down to the next line and any words extending past the right margin will automatically drop with the cursor. This feature is called *word wrap*; it allows you to continue typing without having to use the Enter key. And effects that make your work look professional, such as centered titles, headers and footnotes, indented paragraphs, and boldfaced and underlined words or phrases, are all easily accomplished with special commands.

Revising

If all a word processor could do was compose a document, you could hardly justify the cost of a personal computer system to do it. One of the most powerful features of word processing is its ability to revise a document.

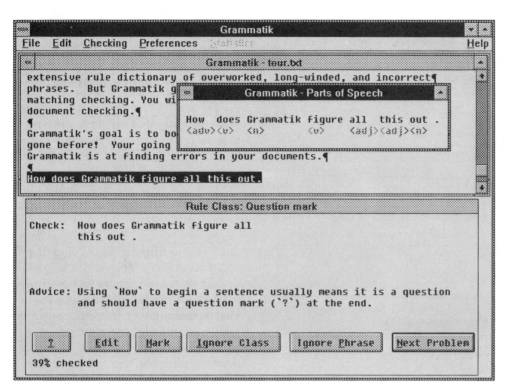

Word processing options. Grammatik is a writing tool that includes sentence analysis, a style and usage guide, spell checking, readability analysis, and proofreading.

Although revisions can be accomplished during the process of composing your document, assume that you have completely typed a first draft of your report on your word processor. You wish to check it for errors and polish it into a final draft. You can move to any location in the document by using the cursor movement arrow keys, or other specially marked keys, such as Page Up, Page Down, Home, or End. Because many documents are larger than can be displayed on the screen, *scrolling*—the process of using the directional keys to move the contents of a screen up, down, left, or right—can be used to view any portion of the document. In our example, you could return to the beginning of your report by pressing the Home key, or you could scroll to the beginning of the document by using the up arrow key. By using the cursor movement keys, you can quickly move through a document and make changes, corrections, additions, and deletions.

For more extensive revisions, you can move, copy, or delete entire paragraphs or other specially marked blocks of text. If, for example, you decide you do not like the order of paragraphs in your report, you can keep moving them around, polishing draft after electronic draft until you are satisfied. If you are revising a previously

written document and want to search for specific words or phrases, you can easily search forward or backward from any point in the document and find letters, words, or phrases to make changes. Revising also includes changing how the document appears, which is called reformatting. This capability includes changing from single to double spacing—or vice versa—as well as changing the width of the printed text by resetting the left and/

Word processing options. Microsoft Bookshelf includes a U.S. ZIP code directory, which is useful for word-processing documents containing addresses.

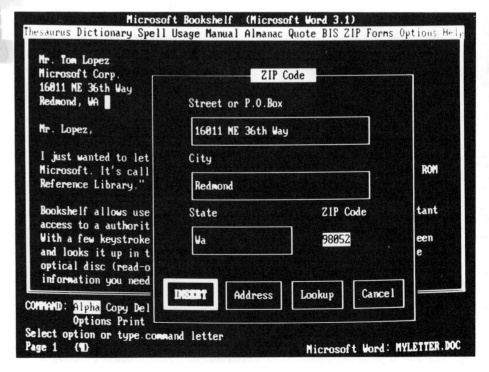

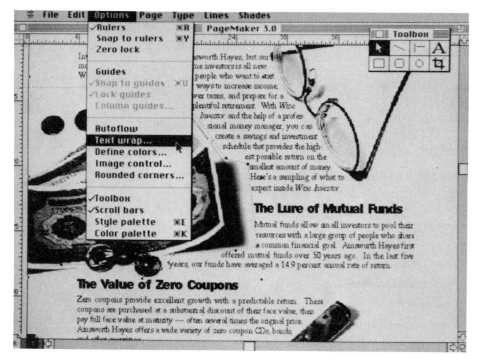

File Edit Options Page Type Lines Shades

Desktop publishing *requires high-resolution displays, such as the screen shown here.*

or right margins. All changes in revising a document are usually accomplished with a few keystrokes.

Word processors come with options that help you to revise documents. They include automatic spelling checkers, punctuation correctors, thesaurus programs, form-letter addressing programs, and programs that can create customized forms, such as purchase orders or bills. For example, a spelling checker program compares the words in your report with a list of words in the program's spelling dictionary. As the spelling checker searches through your document, comparing your spelling to what it has stored in its dictionary, it will stop at any word where it finds a discrepancy and allow you either to change the word or to continue on through the document. A spelling checker might contain 100,000 commonly used words in its dictionary plus the capability to add 20,000 or more of the words you need to custom-tailor the dictionary to your work.

Filing

Whatever you compose or revise in a document stays in the computer's memory until you save or file it on a disk. To a word processing program, a file is a collection of words that is given a name. Most often, it is the equivalent

of a document, but long documents, such as a book, may be made up of separate files, perhaps one file for every chapter. Filing is accomplished by using commands that name and save a fully or partially finished document on a disk. Suppose that you had only finished half of your report and that you decided to take a lunch break. You save your work by filing it on a disk; when you are ready to return to it, you simply use the command that retrieves an existing file.

People who use word processing extensively accumulate many files. It is good to name the files with easy-to-remember names because keeping track of several disks of files can become perplexing when you want to retrieve an old file that you have not used for some time.

Printing

Printing a document involves turning what you have accomplished on the screen into words printed on paper. Some word processors have a feature called page preview that allows you to view a screen representation of how pages will be produced by the printer. Others are designed to reproduce the words on the page in exactly the same format as they appear on the display screen. Of course, you can print any number of draft copies, but one of the benefits of word processing is its ability to revise and edit draft copies without having to print out each version. Only the finished draft need be printed.

TYPES OF WORD PROCESSORS

All word processors can accomplish the basic tasks of composing, revising, filing, and printing. But some users have special needs that require more advanced features such as precise control over word, paragraph, and document formatting, the ability to create custom tables, automatic footnoting, and the ability to incorporate graphics into a document.

Differentiating among different types of word processors is a matter of examining your specific needs, then discovering which word processors have the features that match your needs. Because there are many word processors that offer a wide variety of advanced features, your final choice will be quite subjective.

A good overall rule of thumb in choosing any application software is to use simple tools for simple tasks and complicated tools for complex tasks. The more casual user of word processing will be satisfied by an inexpensive program with a limited number of special features. The more dedicated word processing user, such as a writer or secretary, usually wants a word processor with more functions and capabilities.

DESKTOP PUBLISHING

One application that has grown in popularity recently is desktop publishing, a term that was coined in 1985 by Paul Brainard, founder of Aldus Corporation.

In all organizations, there is the fundamental need to produce written communications that not only deliver a message clearly but have a professional look as well. Desktop publishing can satisfy that need. In its simplest form, *desktop publishing* entails the use of personal computers to prepare and print a wide variety of typeset- or near-typeset-quality documents.

Desktop-publishing software, often called *page composition software*, shares some characteristics with its progenitor word processing software; however, desktop-publishing programs are quite different from word processing programs. A word processor's features are designed to let users control and manipulate a document's content, whereas a desktop-publishing program is more concerned with changes in style, format, placement, and shaping of text and graphics. Anyone who is considering using a desktop-publishing program should be prepared to learn the basics of graphic design and typography. Effective design is the key to publishing clear, professional-looking communications.

The process involves designing or laying out the publication; making up or composing the document by assembling the text and graphics created by other programs; making changes such as repositioning items, editing text, and manipulating graphics; and publishing the finished product on a high-quality printer.

Desktop publishing can be used to create

• Manuals and technical documentation.

• Low-volume specialty publications.

• Proposals, press releases, letters, and newsletters.

• Financial statements.

• Business forms.

• Proof copies for commercial typesetting and printing.

In these applications, desktop publishing can accomplish the following:

• Reduce the time and number of steps required to print pages.

• Print on demand (where and when needed).

Desktop-publishing programs allow users to control style, format, placement, and shaping of text and graphics.

SPOTLIGHT ON...
Desktop-Publishing Applications

Users of desktop-publishing software have discovered that the smallest organization or group within an organization can produce documents on a par with large organizations or outside typesetting houses. No job is too small for near-typeset-quality appearance:

• Marketing people have found myriad uses for desktop publishing: *Yellow Pages* display ads, direct mail pieces, press releases, flyers, brochures, catalogs, and slide presentations.

• Newsletter, magazine, and newspaper publishers have discovered that these programs are viable alternatives to traditional manual processes that involve graphic designers, layout and production artists, typesetters, and printers.

• Documentation—the manuals and references that accompany a product—are also ideal candidates for desktop publishing. Producing documentation is a complex affair. Many people have a hand in its creation, and documentation must go through revision after revision as it evolves from a rough draft to a finished product. Desktop publishing speeds up the process of producing documentation, so that accurate documentation gets out the door at the same time the product does.

As writing tools go, desktop-publishing programs bear little resemblance to word processors; desktop publishing is not simply advanced word processing. You'll have to begin to deal with typestyles of various sizes and shapes, so familiarize yourself with such concepts as fonts, points, picas, and copyfitting. Integrating graphics into a document requires some knowledge of design and layout. You don't need to become a professional graphic designer to use desktop publishing, but a little knowledge of graphic design will go a long way.

To learn more, read Looking Good in Print *by Roger C. Parker. Illustrated, 221 pp. Chapel Hill, N.C.: Ventana Press, 1988.*

	A	B	C	D	E				CASH FLOW (000) FORECAST FY 19?						
		OCT	NOV	DEC	JAN		FEB	MAR	APR	MAY	JUN	JUL	AUG	SEPT	TOTAL
USES OF FUNDS:															
PROF/LOSS		0.00	0.00	0.00	-39.00										
AMORT		0.00	0.00	0.00	0.14										
OP FUNDS		0.00	0.00	0.00	-38.86		-62.10	-81.41	-77.17	-82.43	-90.16	-97.64	-104.13	-127.42	-761.46
							0.14	0.14	0.14	0.14	0.14	0.14	0.14	0.14	1.26
ACT REC		0.00	0.00	0.00	0.00		-61.96	-81.27	-77.03	-82.29	-90.02	-97.50	-103.99	-127.28	-760.20
INV		0.00	0.00	0.00	0.00		0.00	0.00	0.00	0.00	0.00	0.00	0.00	0.00	0.00
OTHER		0.00	0.00	0.00	5.00		0.00	0.00	0.00	0.00	0.00	0.00	0.00	0.00	0.00
FIX ASST		0.00	0.00	0.00	0.00		0.00	0.00	0.00	0.00	0.00	0.00	0.00	0.00	0.00
TOTAL		0.00	0.00	0.00	5.00		0.00	0.00	0.00	0.00	0.00	0.00	0.00	0.00	0.00
							0.00	0.00	0.00	0.00	0.00	0.00	0.00	0.00	0.00
SOURCE OF FUNDS:															
ACY PAY		0.00	0.00	0.00	19.39		11.30	9.30	3.40	2.74	2.94	3.28	2.75	11.07	11.07
LT DEBT		0.00	0.00	0.00	0.00		0.00	0.00	0.00	0.00	0.00	0.00	0.00	0.00	0.00
EQUITY		0.00	0.00	28.00	0.00		0.00	0.00	1200.00	0.00	0.00	0.00	0.00	0.00	0.00
TOTAL		0.00	0.00	28.00	19.39		11.30	9.30	1203.40	2.74	2.94	3.28	2.75	11.07	11.07
CHANGE IN WKG CAP		0.00	0.00	28.00	-24.47		-50.66	-71.98	1126.37	-79.56	-87.08	-94.22	-101.24	-116.20	-749.13
BEGINNING CASH		0.00	0.00	0.00	28.00		3.53	-47.13	-119.10	1007.27	927.71	840.63	746.42	645.18	528.97
ENDING CASH		0.00	0.00	28.00	3.53		-47.13	-119.10	1007.27	927.71	840.63	746.42	645.18	528.97	

Spreadsheets. A spreadsheet is much larger than can be displayed on the screen, so you can scroll up, down, left, or right to view any portion of the entire spreadsheet.

Spreadsheets. A spreadsheet consists of rows and columns. The intersection of a row and column is called a cell. Each cell can contain text, numbers, or formulas.

Status line to indicate position of cursor

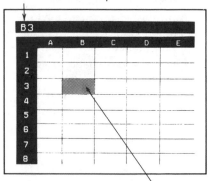

Highlighted cursor at cell B3

- Produce customized documents.
- Produce documents that can be corrected and reprinted in minutes.

In addition to high-quality printers, desktop publishing requires a good deal of graphic display capability on a personal computer. For example, desktop-publishing software first became available on the Macintosh with its built-in graphics user interface. Advanced video-display technology plays a key role in making possible desktop publishing, as well as other graphic applications. We will discuss these output devices in Chapter 6.

SPREADSHEET SOFTWARE

Computers have always been noted for their ability to perform fast and accurate calculations. Even the smallest personal computers can perform arithmetic operations at speeds measured in millions of calculations per second. Also, computers have the capability to model or simulate real-world items or events in detail.

A spreadsheet model consists of rows and columns of interrelated numbers. All spreadsheet programs allow you to build such a model, enter information into the model, and change or modify the model based on your analytical questions about what the model is supposed to represent. For example, it is a common practice in business to create a model of a com-

pany based on historical financial data, and then to manipulate that data to solve problems or answer questions about what will happen to the company under various circumstances.

WHAT IS A SPREADSHEET PROGRAM?

As mentioned in Chapter 1, a *spreadsheet* program, often simply called a spreadsheet, is an interactive program that enables you to organize numbers and formulas into rows and columns. It is a descendant of the paper spreadsheets long used by financial analysts to solve such problems as budgets, estimates, financial projections, income taxes, and financial ratios. But spreadsheets can be used by anyone who needs a general problem-solving tool that organizes information in such a manner. A spreadsheet's workspace is divided into rows and columns. At the intersection of each row and column is a *cell* where text, numbers, or formulas can be entered and stored. The entire workspace is much larger than the screen can display at any one time, so it is possible to scroll up, down, left, or right to view any portion of the workspace on the screen.

Any cell in the workspace can refer to any other cell or combination of cells in the workspace by using the appropriate cell number(s). For example, building a budget model might include columns of values that represent specific expenses in a projected budget, whereas the rows represent months of the year. The sum of the columns can easily be represented by formulas that add all the cells in a column. The sum of the rows can also be represented by formulas that add monthly expenses to obtain yearly totals. Both rows and columns can be labeled to describe what they are.

A spreadsheet program eliminates the need to calculate the sums manually by performing the calculations automatically or on command. For example, if the numbers in the columns are changed, the sums are recalculated by the program, saving the time and effort of manual recomputing. Automatic recalculation improves accuracy and makes it easy to change complex models. Writing a program to accom-

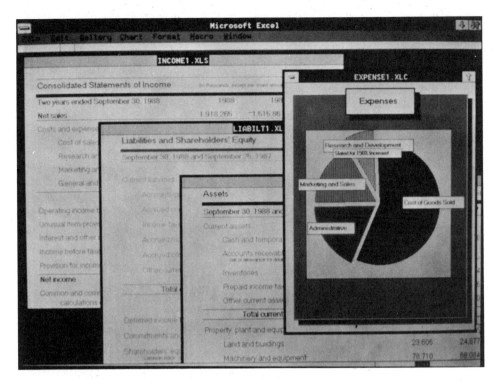

Spreadsheets. *A sample screen of the Microsoft Excel spreadsheet.*

plish the same tasks would take weeks of programming time.

BUILDING A SPREADSHEET MODEL

Recall the previous section in which you were asked to perform an analysis of your company's competition. Suppose that your analysis turns up a new business opportunity. A good example of using a spreadsheet to analyze the opportunity is to create a business plan. No matter how big or small the proposed opportunity might be, if you ask the question, "Where should I start?" the answer will be a unanimous "Start with a business plan." A business plan is a written proposal of how you would go about starting a new business. That business might be a totally new company or a new product for an existing company. One of the most important parts of a business plan is the financial proposal; this contains such estimates as your projected sales, profits, and expenses. For example, if you are trying to interest investors in financing the new business, a sound financial proposal will be one of their requirements. A spreadsheet program can greatly simplify the task of creating the financial proposal of a business plan. It can help you prepare your sales forecasts, expense forecasts,

cash flow, and balance sheets. Perhaps even more important, it allows you to ask *what-if* questions by comparing alternative models.

COMPARING ALTERNATIVE MODELS

As an example of comparing alternatives, imagine that your company produces educational software. You have an idea for a new educational game program. You think that the game is unique and interesting and that it would be a big hit if it were produced and marketed properly. A coworker

Spreadsheets. *A sample screen of the SuperCalc5 spreadsheet.*

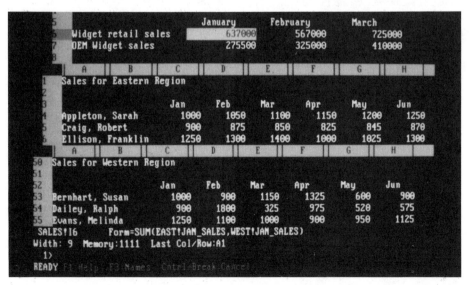

	A	B	C
1	REVENUE:	Mail Order	Royalty
2	Units Sold	1000	1000
3	Unit Revenue	29.95	3.00
4	TOTAL REVENUE	29,950.00	2,995.00
5			
6	FIXED EXPENSES:		
7	Overhead	12,000.00	12,000.00
8	VARIABLE EXPENSES:		
9	Marketing	10,000.00	
10	Production	2,500.00	
11	TOTAL EXPENSES	24,500.00	12,000.00
12	PROFIT OR -LOSS	5,450.00	-9,005.00

(1)

	A	B	C
1	REVENUE:	Mail Order	Royalty
2	Units Sold	500	500
3	Unit Revenue	39.95	4.00
4	TOTAL REVENUE	19,975.00	1,997.50
5			
6	FIXED EXPENSES:		
7	Overhead	12,000.00	12,000.00
8	VARIABLE EXPENSES:		
9	Marketing	10,000.00	
10	Production	2,500.00	
11	TOTAL EXPENSES	24,500.00	12,000.00
12	PROFIT OR -LOSS	-4,525.00	-10,002.50

(3)

	A	B	C
1	REVENUE:	Mail Order	Royalty
2	Units Sold	1000	1000
3	Unit Revenue	39.95	4.00
4	TOTAL REVENUE	39,950.00	3,995.00
5			
6	FIXED EXPENSES:		
7	Overhead	12,000.00	12,000.00
8	VARIABLE EXPENSES:		
9	Marketing	10,000.00	
10	Production	2,500.00	
11	TOTAL EXPENSES	24,500.00	12,000.00
12	PROFIT OR -LOSS	15,450.00	-8,005.00

(2)

	A	B	C
1	REVENUE:	Mail Order	Royalty
2	Units Sold	1000	1000
3	Unit Revenue	29.95	3.00
4	TOTAL REVENUE	29,950.00	2,995.00
5			
6	FIXED EXPENSES:		
7	Overhead	12,000.00	12,000.00
8	VARIABLE EXPENSES:		
9	Marketing	20,000.00	
10	Production	2,500.00	
11	TOTAL EXPENSES	34,500.00	12,000.00
12	PROFIT OR -LOSS	-4,550.00	-9,005.00

(4)

Spreadsheets. *Building a spreadsheet is a process of translating your model into a spreadsheet model. The process is interactive and can be changed or modified at any step in the process.*

1. Build the model by entering text, numbers, and formulas.

2. What if you raise the price to $39.95? Reenter unit revenue numbers in cell B3. Note that all dependent numbers have been recalculated (i.e., cells B4, B12, C3, C4, C12).

3. What if you only sell 500 units instead of 1000 units? Reenter units sold number in cell B2. Note that all dependent numbers have been recalculated.

4. What if you double your marketing expense? Reenter marketing expense number in cell B9. Note that all dependent numbers have been recalculated.

suggests that the game be offered through mail-order sales. Your boss suggests that the firm should sell it through a software distributor. The software distributor sounds like the easiest route, but direct mail-order sales sound more profitable. What should you do?

Once you start to think through the problem, you can see that making a decision such as this would be enhanced if you knew more about the financial aspects of the problem. That's where a spreadsheet can help you. Even this simplified example requires a set of interrelated variables. The variables are your estimates of sales and the costs of doing business.

Estimated profits can be calculated by deducting the costs of doing business from the income from sales. Sales of the game would also be affected by the price you plan to charge. What should the price of the game be? Suppose that you estimate an initial price of $29.95. What is the cost of producing the game? You check with a company who will manufacture the game disk for $4.50 in quantities of 250 or for $2.50 in quantities of 500. There are also such marketing costs as placing direct-mail ads. On the other hand, the software distributor will take care of production, marketing, and distribution and pay your company a 10 percent royalty on each copy sold. And,

you can't forget that in either case there are the overhead costs of designing and writing the game.

You are now ready to begin comparing the alternatives. Keep in mind that the model has been deliberately simplified. Only the concepts will be discussed. In thinking through the model, you must consider such estimates as (1) the number of units that can be sold, (2) the expenses of doing business, and (3) the effects of changing the values of each of these estimates.

The beauty of the spreadsheet program as a forecasting tool is your ability to revise the figures to help answer such questions as: "What if I raise the selling price to $39.95?" "What if I sell only 500 units instead of 1000?" "What if I doubled the marketing expenses?" Once your initial model is built, you can change your entire model by simply changing one number, such as units sold. The recalculating ability of the spreadsheet program makes it easier to explore the alternatives, come up with best case and worst case outcomes, and prepare a more detailed and informed financial proposal.

This is but one example of the many different problems that can be solved with a spreadsheet program. In the example, you could project a five-year sales plan based on a growth rate of 10 percent per year and let the program calculate sales figures based on that formula.

A company considering the decision to lease or buy their cars could use a spreadsheet program to build a model of the costs associated with each alternative. A company considering a real estate investment could calculate monthly payments based on different interest rates. Generally, learning to use a spreadsheet program for less complicated problems can be accomplished with a few hours of hands-on experience.

DATABASE SOFTWARE

Database software for personal computers is general-purpose application software used for computerized record keeping. Keeping records requires two things: a place to store the information and a way to organize it that permits timely and easy retrieval. Simple filing cabinets perform both functions. Computerized record-keeping programs or database programs go beyond the simple filing cabinet because they automate the manual tasks of entering, modifying, cross-referencing or indexing, and retrieving information. They also allow you to display specific items of interest and create reports and summaries of your information.

WHAT IS A DATABASE?

A *database* is a collection of data organized according to a structure that facilitates the manipulation of the data. The database capabilities for personal computers vary widely. Very simple databases are nothing more than computerized filing cabinets. Sophisticated multiple-file systems are suitable for organizing large amounts of information and retrieving that information in many different ways.

Database software for personal computers falls into two categories:

• A *file manager* is a program that manages basic data management tasks, such as entering, modifying, retrieving, and printing information from one file at a time.

• A *database manager* is a more sophisticated program that manages two or more files at the same time. In addition to the functions of a file manager, a database manager has the capability to index, cross-reference, and maintain relationships among information contained in the files.

A database manager allows you to sort data into alphabetical order; perform mathematical calculations on various data items, such as automatically calculating totals; and create several different ways of indexing or cross-referencing your data. In short, it allows you to build a rather complex application. Unfortunately, this power is usually provided at the expense of ease of use: building a sophisticated application requires becoming familiar with technical terms and spending a substantial amount of time becoming

familiar with the application.

Learning the principles and concepts of database software for personal computers gives you a simplified subset of many of the data management concepts that you would encounter if you worked with mainframe computers in a large organization. However, the concepts of database software for large computer systems go far beyond what will be discussed in this chapter. Those concepts will be covered in greater detail in Chapter 11.

A SIMPLE DATABASE

Remember the mailing list applications that were discussed in Chapter 1? Each individual in the mailing list could logically be thought of as a *record*—a collection of related data treated as a unit. In turn, each record contains a number of *fields*—the smallest units of named data that have a meaning in a record. In the basic example, the fields include name, street address, city, state, and ZIP code. The collection of records (the whole mailing list) taken together forms the database.

The usefulness of database application programs generally depends on whether or not the benefits outweigh the cost of establishing, maintaining, updating, and using the software. For example, a checkbook, converted into the form of a database, is capable of

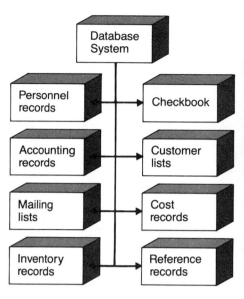

Database. *Some of the many uses for a database system.*

Database. *Reflex shows all of the details of an individual record in a form.*

```
=PROFIT / SALES * 100
  Views    Edit    Print/File    Records    Search    Form
 FORM

    Sales Record

  MONTH: Jan-85

  STORE: Haven

  PRODUCT: VCR

  QUANTITY: 425

  SALES: $297              PROFIT: $86

  COST: $211              % Margin: 29
```

Database. Reflex can also show records in a row and column format.

2/01/85

| Views | Edit | Print/File | Records | Search | List |

LIST

MONTH	STORE	PRODUCT	QUANTITY	SALES	COST	PROFIT	% Margin
Jan-85	Haven	VCR	425	$297	$211	$86	29
Jan-85	NewPark	Camera	193	$172	$101	$71	41
Jan-85	NewPark	TV	168	$64	$50	$14	22
Jan-85	NewPark	VCR	398	$307	$197	$110	36
Jan-85	Pierce	Camera	219	$170	$115	$55	32
Jan-85	Pierce	TV	188	$92	$56	$36	39
Jan-85	Pierce	VCR	537	$319	$266	$53	17
Jan-85	Tremont	Camera	234	$161	$123	$38	24
Jan-85	Tremont	TV	153	$59	$45	$14	24
Jan-85	Tremont	VCR	350	$206	$173	$33	16
Feb-85	Haven	Camera	255	$219	$134	$85	39
Feb-85	Haven	TV	246	$35	$74	($39)	-111
Feb-85	Haven	VCR	458	$361	$227	$134	37

providing you with such information as an alphabetical listing of the people to whom you write, check listings by expense category, total expenses for a given period of time (e.g., a given month or year), and listings by various check amounts. Simply having your checkbook in database form lets the computer do the adding, subtracting, and reconciling of your balance.

If these benefits are attractive, you should then consider the cost of establishing and maintaining your checkbook database. Remember that the data on your checks are not going to appear automatically in your data-

Database. Reflex provides a cross-tab view that can perform arithmetic calculations on numeric fields.

3851.12

| Views | Edit | Print/File | Records | Search | Crosstab |

CROSSTAB

Summary: @SUM   Field: PROFIT

	PRODUCT			
		Camera	TV	VCR	ALL
S	Haven	$512	($105)	$670	$1,077
T	NewPark	$361	$107	$478	$946
O	Pierce	$387	$243	$375	$1,005
R	Tremont	$296	$108	$419	$823
E	ALL	$1,556	$353	$1,942	$3,851

base. Somebody has to enter those data and, what is more important, make sure that they are accurate.

SORTS, SEARCHES, AND REPORTS

A database system derives much of its power through the ability to perform three simple tasks: sorting, searching, and generating reports. To show how a database system allows you to perform these tasks, it is helpful to look at a general example. Almost all businesses keep a set of records known as a customer list. In its simplest form, it might just be a Rolodex file, in which each record is a card that contains a customer's name, address, and phone number. A more complex example might include a record for each customer that contains enough information to generate all the company's billing information.

Suppose that the customer list database is made up of one record for each customer that includes the previously mentioned customer information along with some general information about the customer's purchases. *Sorting*, which involves arranging the records into a preidentified sequence, makes it possible to generate a list sorted by customer number, alphabetically by customer name, by ZIP code for mailing purposes, or even by items purchased. Sorting a database

```
File: C:\AGENDA\FILES\SCRIPT
View: Initial View  When Date: 07/31/88          03/24/88   16:55

Tasks and Ideas                              People      When
  • Bob is working on a draft of the budget for  ·Bob     ·03/12/88
    tomorrow; will present it at the monthly
    management meeting
  ♪ Forward the contract details to Sue tomorrow  ·Sue     ·03/25/88
  ♪ Can we get the cost of goods sold under $12 by  »Ton    ·07/31/88
    the end of July?
  • Jim says the marketing team will be set by the  ·Jim    ·03/01/88
    beginning of next month
  • Ton will have his business plan in by a week  ·Ton     ·03/24/88
    from Thursday; make sure it covers  pricing,
    strategy, and distribution.
  • decision needed on department-wide computer  ·Sue     ·03/11/88
    upgrades -- hold meeting with Jim and Sue on  Jim
    Friday
  • Liz will present ten-point incentives program  ·Liz     ·02/20/88
    to distributors next week

 F1     F2     F3     F4     F5     F6     F7     F8     F9     F10
Help  Edit   Copy   Done   Note   Move   Mark  Vw Mgr Cat Mgr  Menu
```

Personal information managers. Lotus
Agenda makes it easy to enter, edit, organize,
view, and manipulate personal information.

also makes it possible to search and generate reports in various sequences. For example, you can sort a database alphabetically by customer name to print a report and then sort the database by ZIP code to generate and print mailing labels in ZIP code order.

Searching involves the ability to find information in a database. This might include a most general case in which you want to list the entire contents of a database on the computer's display screen or a special case in which you want to search for a specific record or set of records. For example, if you want to know the name of every customer who purchased more than $10,000 worth of goods last year, you could search the customer list database to display only those customers who meet the criterion—more than $10,000 in sales. Or, if the customer list database were being used by a software distributor, you would be able to search for all customers who purchased Lotus 1-2-3.

A report generator allows you to create nicely formatted reports, including headings, subheadings, columns of data from the database, columns of data computed from existing fields in the database, and computed intermediate and final totals. Once the format of the report has been defined, it can be saved as a file on a disk and used over and over again to print copies of the report.

PERSONAL INFORMATION MANAGERS

A class of software similar to database programs is called *personal information managers*. Like databases, these programs help you manage information. Unlike databases, they can manage information without using the record and field structure common to databases. You do not have to think about the structure of your data ahead of time. For example, you can use a personal information manager to type in notes about a project you are working on, then filter through them and reorganize them by categories of your own choosing.

GRAPHIC SOFTWARE

Computer graphics is a broad term that refers to the methods and techniques used to draw pictures or images on display screens or on graphic printers and plotters. You have probably seen computer graphics in arcade and educational games and in special effects on television programs and films. Another use for graphics is in the graphical user interfaces, discussed earlier in the chapter, where pictures are used in conjunction with words to communicate with the user.

Graphic software for personal computers can be used to create charts,

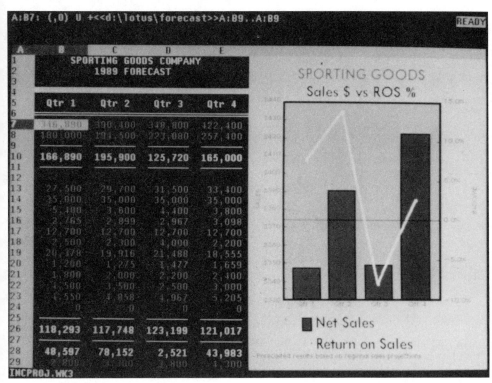

A:B7: (,0) U +<<d:\lotus\forecast>>A:B9..A:B9   READY

SPORTING GOODS
Sales $ vs ROS %

■ Net Sales
Return on Sales

Analytical graphics. Lotus 1-2-3 allows the user to generate analytical graphics directly from spreadsheet data.

or rectangles, can be resized or moved around on the screen without affecting other objects. Draw programs are better suited for diagrams that must often be changed, whereas paint programs are preferred for more artistic illustrations. Computer-aided design (CAD) programs use very sophisticated draw-program features to allow engineers to use their display screens as electronic drafting tables and eliminate the tedium of manually redrawing their designs in much the same way that the users of spreadsheet programs eliminate the tedium of manual recalculation.

The largest application for personal computer graphic software is producing business graphics. Application software for business graphics includes two categories, analytical and presentation graphics.

• *Analytical graphics* are intended to help you analyze data from spreadsheets and databases.

• *Presentation graphics* analyze the same kind of data but are designed to help you communicate data to other people.

maps, drawings, diagrams, and pictures. The simplest graphic software consists of paint and draw programs. A *paint program*, such as MacPaint for the Macintosh or Windows Paintbrush for MS-DOS computers, provides commands to create lines, circles, rectangles, and other shapes, as well as do freehand sketching. A *draw program*, such as MacDraw and Windows Draw, provides similar capabilities, but the objects created, such as circles

For example, virtually all spreadsheet programs offer built-in analytical graphics capabilities. These programs are capable of transforming data that are contained in their

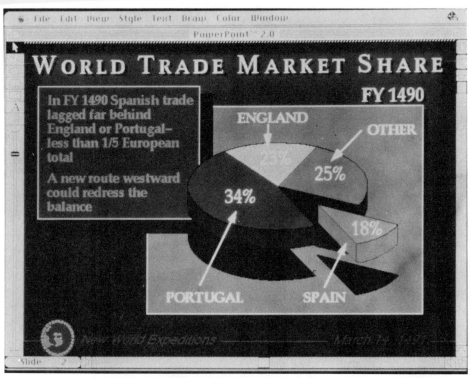

Presentation graphics. Microsoft PowerPoint is a desktop presentation package that can produce overheads and slides.

spreadsheet into analytical graphics, such as bar, line, and pie charts, through a few simple commands.

Although analytical graphics are relatively quick and easy to produce, they are usually not of high enough quality for a formal presentation. Presentation graphics programs, sometimes called *desktop presentation* programs, coupled with a plotter, a laser or inkjet printer, or a slidemaker can produce presentation-quality bar, line, and pie charts from data that are typed at the keyboard or from data contained in database and spreadsheet files. Most of these packages offer you the ability to edit and change graphics while viewing them on the display screen and then make a slide or a transparency. For example, with such a graphics program, you can input some data, make a bar chart, quickly change it to an exploded pie chart, and decide which one to use for your presentation.

After the overhead transparency, the next most widespread medium for presentation graphics is the 35-mm slide. Computerized slidemaking systems that attach to a personal computer can produce color presentation graphics inexpensively and quickly on 35-mm slides. It should be noted that a personal computer system can display graphic images only if it is equipped with special graphics hardware. This is sometimes found in the form of an add-on board, called a *graphics adapter board*, that plugs into one of the expansion slots that were mentioned in Chapter 1. Other computers are equipped with special-purpose graphics processor chips that take care of the details of displaying graphic images on the display screen. In Chapter 6, we will discuss tools that can add animation, audio, and video to presentations.

COMMUNICATIONS SOFTWARE

By itself, a personal computer is a powerful and interesting tool, but when it can communicate with other computers, a whole new world of applications opens up. Groups of computers linked together in networks can share programs and information. For example,

Presentation graphics. *The Polaroid Palette electronically records screen images to create full-color 35-mm slides.*

you can communicate with another personal computer by sending and receiving electronic messages. You can subscribe to an information-providing system, such as The Source or CompuServe. Services include home shopping; bill paying; directory services; weather and sports updates;

Modems. *Shown here is an Apple modem that plugs into a wall outlet, thereby freeing up space on a desktop.*

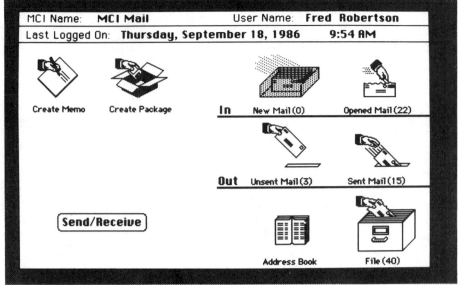

Communications software. Desktop Express gives Macintosh users electronic mail and document-delivery capabilities.

Integrated software. In addition to providing a graphic environment, the Macintosh version of Microsoft Works allows several documents, spreadsheets, charts, or databases to be displayed in windows.

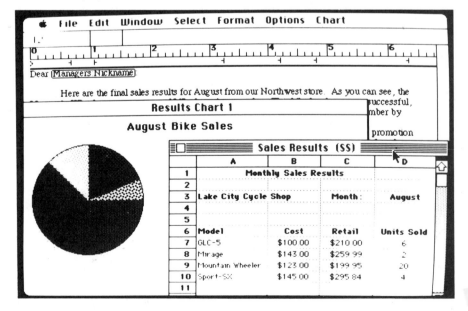

banking; airline, hotel, and car reservations; financial and legal services; electronic news services, magazines, and encyclopedias; and electronic messaging services.

Most computer-to-computer communication occurs over the telephone system, so you need a device called a modem. A *modem*—short for *modu*late and *dem*odulate—is a hardware device that enables two computers to exchange data over standard telephone lines. A modem may be a device that is separate from the computer, or it may be built into the computer. Modems generally include such useful features as automatic dialing, automatic answering, and options for various modes of communication.

In addition to a modem, *communications software* is necessary to provide the interface between one computer with a modem and another computer with a modem. A communications program automates many of the functions involved in getting the computer to communicate. In effect, it provides you with a set of commands so that you can easily perform such operations as dialing the phone, redialing if connection is not established on the first try, putting your computer in automatic answer mode so that it can receive calls from other modem-equipped computers, storing and retrieving a list of frequently called numbers, automatically logging on to the system you are calling, and capturing data or transferring files automatically. You will learn more about communications software in Chapter 9.

INTEGRATED SOFTWARE

All the programs discussed in the categories of general- and special-purpose application software can be combined or *integrated*. Integration provides the benefits of easy switching between functions without having to go back to the operating system and the ability to share data between functions. For example, with integrated software, it might be possible to "cut" a graphic image from a graphics program and "paste" it into a word processing document. Integration can be accomplished in a variety of ways. Families of programs, such as the PFS:Professional Series or an integrated accounting application, can share data between programs. Operating environments, such as Microsoft Windows, can provide a unified environment in which data can be shared among programs. Multiple functions can also be incorporated into a single program, such as in the Enable or Works packages.

On the negative side, however, critics of multifunction integrated programs claim that functionality is sacrificed by having too many components in a single program. The critics say that the power of each component is less than that of an equivalent stand-alone program. For example, the spreadsheet component of an integrated program may be less powerful and, therefore, not as useful as the best stand-alone spreadsheet programs.

REVIEW

Computer software falls into two broad categories: system and application software. System software includes operating systems and programming languages. Application software includes special-purpose programs and general-purpose programs. The user interface is software that passes information to and from the user. Types of user interfaces include command-driven, menu-driven, graphical, and natural language. An operating system manages the overall operation of the computer system. MS-DOS has become the de facto standard for personal computers, but others include Unix, Macintosh, and OS/2. Software for most applications is already written so that you only have to buy it to begin using it.

General-purpose software for writing, record keeping, calculating, graphics, and communicating forms the basis for accomplishing many of the tasks associated with using a personal computer. Word processors can help you write faster and more professionally; desktop-publishing programs combine text and graphics into effective publications; spreadsheet programs are useful tools for estimating and planning; database programs can help you manage your records; graphics software helps you create, summarize, analyze, and present information; communication software allows you to link into larger networks of computers; and integrated software combines several functions into one multifunction program.

RESOURCES

BOOKS

Davis, William S. *Operating Systems: A Systematic View*. Reading, Mass.: Addison-Wesley, 1987. Covers MS-DOS, Unix, and IBM's job control language (JCL). A good technical textbook reference.

Kelly, Kevin, ed. *Signal: Communication Tools for the Information Age*. New York: Harmony, 1988. The Whole Earth gang is back again with another one of their catalogs of tools and resources. Fascinating for casual reading and finding offbeat resources.

Letwin, Gordon. *Inside OS/2*. Redmond, Wash.: Microsoft Press, 1988. Letwin is a programmer who wrote much of OS/2, and he describes the operating system with a combination of developer's insight and incredible technical detail. If you're interested in operating systems, this is a good book to read.

Lichty, Tom. *Design Principles for Desktop Publishers*. Glennview, Ill.: Scott, Foresman, 1989. An easy to read book that is filled with background information for desktop publishers.

Lu, Cary. *The Apple Macintosh Book*. Redmond, Wash.: Microsoft Press, 1988. If you own or plan to buy a Macintosh computer, this is a must-buy book. Lu is an excellent explainer, and his book is full of tips and advice for Macintosh users.

Topham, Douglas. *A DOS User's Guide to Unix*. New York: Simon & Schuster, 1990. A practical guide to Unix that builds on prior knowledge of DOS. This book teaches Unix by comparing the similarities and the differences between Unix and DOS.

Wolverton, Van. *Running MS-DOS*. Redmond, Wash.: Microsoft Press, 1989. A practical hands-on reference guide to using MS-DOS with plenty of examples, tips, and explanations. This book has several editions, so be sure to buy the latest version.

MAGAZINES

Personal Publishing. Wheaton, Ill.: Hitchcock. A monthly desktop-publishing magazine slanted toward the do-it-yourselfer.

Publish! San Francisco, Calif.: PCW Communications. A monthly desktop-publishing magazine slanted toward the professional graphic designer. It does, however, contain good ideas about design and desktop publishing.

STUDY GUIDE

Match the following key terms to the appropriate definition:

A.

1. ____ Special-purpose programs   4. ____ Command-driven interface   7. ____ Windows

2. ____ General-purpose programs   5. ____ Menu-driven interface   8. ____ Natural language interface

3. ____ User interface   6. ____ Graphical user interface

a. An interface that uses pictures and graphic symbols to represent commands, choices, or actions.

b. A method for dividing the display screen into variable-sized rectangles.

c. Programs that are dedicated to performing single-use tasks.

d. An interface that allows the user to input simple English phrases in lieu of complex computer commands.

e. Programs that are adaptable to a wide variety of tasks.

f. An interface that prompts the user to type in a single letter, word, or line that represents an instruction.

g. Software that passes information to and from the person using the program.

h. An interface that offers a list of choices or options as a way of getting the user to make a selection.

B.

9. ____ Operating system   12. ____ Device driver   15. ____ Virtual memory

10. ____ Kernel   13. ____ Multitasking system   16. ____ Distributed filing

11. ____ File   14. ____ Multiuser system

a. A named organized collection of information.

b. Functional units that control the operation of the hardware components of a personal computer system.

c. A capability that gives a computer access to files that reside on another computer's disk on a network.

d. A set of programs that manages the overall operation of a computer system.

e. A set of software that ties the hardware to the software.

f. An operating system that allows two or more tasks to be operating at the same time.

g. An operating system that manages two or more users sharing the same computer system.

h. A technique for storing programs on mass-storage devices and creating the illusion that data are in memory by swapping pieces in and out of memory when needed.

C.

17. ____ Application software   20. ____ Word wrap   22. ____ Desktop publishing

18. ____ Word processing   21. ____ Scrolling   23. ____ Spreadsheet

19. ____ Cursor

a. An interactive program that enables you to organize numbers and formulas into a rectangular array of cells.

b. The process of using the directional keys to move the contents of a display screen up, down, left, or right.

c. A blinking box or underline that marks where the next character you type will appear.

d. Programs that perform work not related to the computer system itself.

e. Electronic ways of handling a standard set of office activities—composing, revising, printing, and filing written documents.

f. A feature that allows you to type beyond one line without having to use the Enter key.

g. The use of personal computers to prepare and print a wide variety of typeset- or near-typeset-quality documents.

D.

24. _____ File manager
25. _____ Database manager
26. _____ Database
27. _____ Record

28. _____ Field
29. _____ Sorting
30. _____ Computer graphics
31. _____ Analytical graphics

32. _____ Presentation graphics
33. _____ Modem
34. _____ Communications software

a. A collection of raw data, the relationships among the data, and the capability to manipulate the data.

b. Graphics that are intended to help a person analyze typed-in data or data from spreadsheets and databases.

c. Software that provides the interface between one computer with a modem and another computer with a modem.

d. A collection of related data treated as a unit.

e. A device that enables two computers to exchange data over standard telephone lines.

f. Arranging records into a preidentified sequence.

g. The smallest unit of named data that has meaning in a record.

h. The methods and techniques used to draw pictures or images on display screens or special graphic printers and plotters.

i. Graphics that are intended to help a person communicate with other people.

j. A program that manages two or more files at the same time.

k. A program that manages entering, modifying, retrieving, and printing information from one file at a time.

True/False:

35. __T__ System software includes operating systems and programming languages.

36. __F__ Using a personal computer primarily involves finding the right hardware that will meet your application needs.

37. __T__ One of the main purposes of an operating system is to support application programs.

38. __F__ One trend in operating systems is to make the user interface command driven.

39. __T__ Even though operating systems perform similar functions, using one computer's operating system is not the same as using another.

40. __T__ One advantage of a word processor is the accuracy with which you can make corrections, additions, and deletions.

41. __T__ Word processors require special commands to type in multiple-line documents.

42. __F__ Whatever you compose or revise in a word processing document is automatically transferred to disk.

43. __T__ Desktop-publishing users need to learn the basics of graphic design and typography.

44. __F__ Only financial people can use spreadsheet programs effectively.

45. __T__ An important aspect of a database is the relationships among the data.

46. __F__ Searching the database involves arranging the records into a preidentified sequence.

47. __F__ The largest application for personal computer graphics software is freehand drawing.

48. __T__ A computer must be equipped with special graphics adapters or chips in order to display graphic images.

49. __F__ Modems are software programs that provide an interface between two or more computers.

Multiple Choice:

50. Which of the following is not considered application software?

    a. Spreadsheet programs.
    b. Operating systems.
    c. Word processors.
    d. Communications programs.

51. Which of the following are not usually stored in a spreadsheet cell?

    a. Values.
    b. Formulas.
    c. Labels.
    d. Models.

52. Which of the following is not a basic function of a spreadsheet program?

    a. Writing.
    b. Forecasting.
    c. Planning.
    d. Modeling.

53. Computerized record-keeping systems allow you to

    a. Check for spelling and punctuation errors.
    b. Communicate with other computers.
    c. Enter, modify, and retrieve

data.

d. Manage files on disks.

54. The job of managing files belongs to the
   a. Word processor.
   b. Communications program.
   c. Database program.
   d. Operating system.

55. Which of the following is a multiuser, multitasking operating system?
   a. Unix.
   b. OS/2.
   c. MS-DOS.
   d. Macintosh.

56. Which of the following types of user interfaces usually requires that you type in abbreviated instructions?
   a. Command-driven interface.
   b. Menu-driven interface.
   c. Graphical user interface.
   d. Natural language interface.

57. Which of the following is not a function of a word processing program?
   a. Document management.
   b. Composing.
   c. Record keeping.
   d. Revising.

58. A primary purpose of computer graphics is to
   a. Change the user interface of computers.
   b. Communicate with other computers.
   c. Create formatted reports.
   d. Draw pictures on display screens.

59. Creating a 35-mm slide for a sales meeting would most likely involve the use of which of the following?
   a. Communications software.
   b. Presentation graphics.
   c. Analytical graphics.
   d. Free-form drawing.

Thought Questions:

60. Among the three general-purpose categories of software—word processing, spreadsheet, and database—which do you find easiest to understand? Why? Which is the most difficult? Why?

61. Using your major as a starting point, which types of application software discussed in this chapter would you find most applicable to your studies? Why?

Projects:

62. Choose one of the categories of special-purpose application software mentioned in this chapter; then visit a computer store and find a program that fits the category you choose. Find out as much as you can about the program (ask for a demonstration if possible), and prepare a report describing the program.

63. You have been asked to design a user interface for a computer-aided instruction program that allows you to practice simple addition, subtraction, multiplication, and division. In a presentation to the class, briefly describe or show what the options for the initial display screen of the user interface might look like.

SOFTWARE EXERCISES

Recall the example of comparing mail-order versus software distributor sales described on page 42. This exercise will show you how to build a spreadsheet model to compare these two alternatives. Begin the exercise by using the worksheet shown on page 42 to lay out the model.

Entering Text

To begin building the model, enter the text entries in column A and the two headings in cells B1 and C1. Note that you will have to expand the width of column A before you begin entering the text.

Entering Formulas

Next enter the appropriate formulas in the proper cells. Total Revenue (cells B4 and C4), for example, is Units Sold multiplied by Unit Revenue; Total Expenses (cells B11 and C11) is the sum of Fixed Expenses plus Variable Expenses. Profit or Loss (cells B12 and C12) can be calculated by subtracting Total Expenses from Total Revenue. Note that while entering formulas, the spreadsheet displays the results of the formula (rather than the formula itself), and because there are not yet numbers to calculate, the values of cells will be 0.

Entering Numbers

Entering a number into a cell is very straightforward. Use the sample data supplied by the spreadsheet on page 42 Note that if the spreadsheet automatically recalculates every time you enter a new number, you will have to be careful to finish entering all the data for the spreadsheet to show the correct results.

What-If Analysis

Revise the model by

- Changing the Selling Price to $39.95 and the Royalty to $3.95.
- Changing Units Sold to 500.
- Changing Marketing Expenses to $20,000.
- Changing the Selling Price to $49.95 and the Royalty to $4.95.
- Changing Units Sold to 750.
- Changing Marketing Expenses to $15,000.

Use the spreadsheet program to add a new row at the top of the spreadsheet. Then type your name and the number of this class in the upper left-hand corner of the spreadsheet. After you finish the assignment, print it to turn in to your instructor.

ALTERNATIVE ASSIGNMENT

If the software you are using can copy data from a spreadsheet and paste it into a word processing document, prepare a financial report by copying the completed assignment to a word processing document, adding the title "Business Plan: Financial Section" and your name and class number.

ANSWERS

1. c, 2. e, 3. g, 4. f, 5. h, 6. a, 7. b, 8. d, 9. d, 10. e, 11. a, 12. b, 13. f, 14. g, 15. h, 16. c, 17. d, 18. e, 19. c, 20. f, 21. b, 22. g, 23. a, 24. k, 25. j, 26. a, 27. d, 28. g, 29. f, 30. h, 31. b, 32. i, 33. e, 34. c, 35. T, 36. F, 37. T, 38. F, 39. T, 40. F, 41. F, 42. F, 43. T, 44. F, 45. T, 46. F, 47. F, 48. T, 49. F, 50. b, 51. d, 52. a, 53. c, 54. d, 55. a, 56. a, 57. c, 58. d, 59. b.

CLIFF STOLL

Profession: Astronomer by training, computer security expert by accident.

Profile: After receiving his Ph.D. in Planetary Science from the University of Arizona in Tuscon, Stoll built image processing software for the space telescope and designed the optical system of the Keck Observatory. For two years, he tracked a computer hacker who was selling military data to the Soviet KGB. As a result, he wrote *The Cuckoo's Egg*, a true story about computer espionage and security. He is now working at the Harvard-Smithsonian Center for Astrophysics, building databases for X-ray astronomy.

Quote: "On computer networks, you can bang on forty doors before someone notices. With this kind of guard our computers are sitting ducks. Almost nobody's watching for intruders trying to break in."

CHAPTER 3

COMPUTERS, SOCIETY, AND ETHICS

PREVIEW

In 1989, the computer as we know it celebrated its 50th birthday. Although the event went largely unnoticed, it is interesting to observe that in this relatively short lifetime, the computer has evolved from a one-of-a-kind laboratory curiosity into a worldwide phenomenon. Compare this rate of change with the 5000 years it took to progress from writing to printing and the 500 years it took to progress from printing to media such as the telephone, radio, and television.

Computers have pervaded every aspect of our society by restructuring work, education, and leisure. What does the computerization of society mean? What are the economic and technological trends that are fueling the phenomenon? What are some of the current problems that are caused by these trends? What are some of the ethical issues that arise because of the use of computers? These questions will be discussed in this chapter.

This chapter will discuss the impacts that computers have on our everyday lives. It expands the discussion to include the social and ethical effects of the computerization of society.

In this chapter, you'll learn

• What the computerization of society means.

• How society has shifted toward information work.

• How information is used as a strategic resource.

• How technology fuels change.

• How to respond to a changing society.

• The impacts of microelectronic technology.

• The effects of technological change.

• The ethics of crime, security, and privacy.

• The ethics of software piracy.

THE COMPUTERIZATION OF SOCIETY

Computerization is a broad term that refers to the restructuring of society caused by the widespread use of computers. The computerization of society is the result of two related trends. The first is economic. As you learned in Chapter 1, information—stored electronically in computers—can be processed and communicated to enhance its own value and add value to products and services. The second trend is technological. The widespread growth of microelectronic technology changes both the nature of the products that are produced and the process by which those products are designed and manufactured.

The effects and implications of computerization are complex issues. The positive social impacts include new products and services, new jobs, and an overall increase in the quality of living. The negative social impacts include the pressures that change brings to individuals, organizations, and the work force.

THE INFORMATION SOCIETY

A term you will often hear mentioned is the ***information society***. As popularized in sociologist Alvin Toffler's book *The Third Wave*, it means a society structured around the principles of information as a commodity and as a strategic resource. The first wave was launched by the Agricultural Revolution and the second by the Industrial Revolution. Toffler calls the third wave the Information Revolution and says it launched the United States and other developed countries into the information society.

One of the most interesting ways to look at how we are changing from an industrial society into an information society is to look at how people work. The United States was at the peak of its industrialization in the 1950s. At that time, a little over 62 percent of the work force was employed in blue-collar ***industrial work***, meaning work that involves the production of goods. At the same time, roughly 17 percent of the work force was employed in white-collar positions. The remaining 21 percent worked on the farm.

White-collar work or ***information work*** involves the delivery of services. Information workers in service industries include professionals and technicians (doctors, dentists, lawyers, teachers, engineers, computer programmers, computer operators, etc.), managers and administrators (who make up a substantial part of our government), and clerical workers. Information workers do not produce anything physically, but they spend their working time receiving, processing, and transmitting information. In other words, they create economic value without creating a tangible product.

By the 1980s the work force figures we just cited had practically reversed. According to John Naisbitt, author of *Megatrends*, 60 percent of the work force is now engaged in service-related work, and the percentage is climbing. Less than 20 percent of the work force is engaged in factory work, and the percentage is declining.

To put it another way, by the mid-1980s the wages of production workers represented only 6.2 percent of the U.S. gross national product (GNP). Manufactured goods will, of course, continue to be produced in great quantities. But goods production will continue to employ fewer people and generate a smaller share of the nation's income.[1]

The transition to information work. *The U.S. work force has been shifting dramatically toward the service category, which includes information workers. (From* Employment Projections for 1995, *U.S. Bureau of Labor Statistics, April 1986.)*

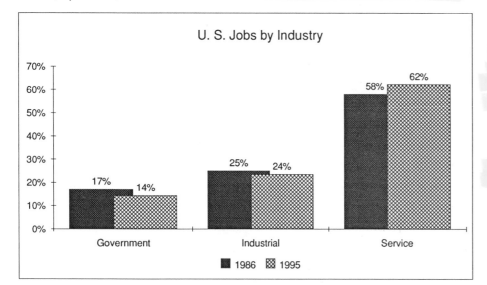

U. S. Jobs by Industry

	1986	1995
Government	17%	14%
Industrial	25%	24%
Service	58%	62%

Another interesting way to look at how society and jobs are changing is to look at the skill levels required for work.

INDUSTRIAL WORK

Industrial work has long been associated with low-skilled manual labor. Often, these jobs did not even require basic literacy as many assembly-line jobs were designed with such simple schemes as assembling color-coded parts or following diagrams that required minimal know-how. To be sure, some of these antiquated jobs can still be found in isolated pockets. But the number of low-skilled jobs is declining.

In *Workforce 2000*, a study performed for the U.S. Department of Labor, researchers ranked jobs by skills rather than by education. They gave jobs numerical ratings according to the math, language, and reasoning skills they require and grouped them into six categories. (On the 0-to-7 scale for example, a laborer is ranked 1.3, a salesperson 3.4, a teacher 4.2, and a scientist 5.7). Their findings showed that only 27 percent of all new jobs fall into the lowest two skill categories, whereas 41 percent of new jobs are in the three highest skill categories.[2]

Why do most industrial jobs require high skill levels? Because the vast majority of these jobs have been augmented by computers, robots, or automated machinery. When that happens, work becomes more demanding, and workers must have higher skill levels to perform their jobs. Today, work requires more responsibility and abstract thinking, as well as more decision making, and problem-solving skills and far less manual labor.

In progressive manufacturing industries, for example, the assembly-line approach, in which each worker works alone performing specific tasks, is being replaced by teams of interchangeable workers who together set goals and make decisions. In addition, mechanical systems are being replaced by computerized automated systems. The people who work with these systems must read complex manuals and be able to conceptualize how the sys-

The information society. Engineers often use personal computers as a routine part of their job.

tems run. They must also be able to monitor the computerized systems' progress, and if need be, make corrective changes based on the abstract information presented on the computer's display screens.

INFORMATION WORK

Like industrial work, service work has often been characterized by low-quality, low-wage jobs. Certainly jobs, such as the legendary "hamburger-flipper," leave nothing to individual skill and initiative. And not all service workers are intensive users of information. But a large percentage of these workers are information workers. They do not work on factory or department store floors, but in offices.

The types of information-based jobs being created demand much higher levels of skills than the jobs that exist today. As offices have become more complex, and as computers and automation take over the routine tasks, jobs have become more broadly defined. Secretaries, office clerks, salesclerks, and nurses, for example, may find themselves with more decision-making and managerial responsibility than in the past. Thus the amount of knowledge and skill needed to make a productive contribution at work becomes greater. Information workers in education, health care, government, and finance rank in the highest U.S. Depart-

Industrial work. *Automated technologies are playing an important role in the way most products are manufactured.*

- Before computers, information was considered to be limited, expensive, and hard to get.
- After computers, information can be plentiful, cheap, and easy to get.

However, this raises some tricky economic questions. Information is not like a commodity such as oil, steel, or food in that (1) it does not go away when you consume it and (2) the traditional economic theories that place limits on how much of any product you can consume do not seem to hold true. Economists will continue to struggle with the concept of information as an economic resource simply because it is often difficult to measure the worth or value of information.

Keep in mind that the concept of information as an economic resource is different from the more familiar concept of information as a political resource, that is, when individuals withhold or consolidate information to gain or establish power and influence in an organization.

Two interesting ways to describe how computers are changing the economics of information are to look at (1) how businesses are beginning to treat information as a commodity and (2) how some are treating that commodity as their primary strategic resource.

ment of Labor skill categories.

How do you prepare for work in such an environment? The college degree has become the major form of job certification. According to the U.S. Department of Labor, corporate America has come to rely on the college degree as the safest guarantee that an applicant has the skills, maturity, and discipline to tackle a job.[3]

In the long term, all the developed nations of the world are evolving from the era of industrialization to the era of information. The United States and Japan provide good examples of countries that look for future economic growth in selling the knowledge of their highly educated people instead of the strength of their people's muscles. The shift from producing goods to producing services will continue to reshape nation's jobs and industries.

THE ECONOMICS OF INFORMATION

The economics of information have been revolutionized by the computer. The cost of storage per unit of information has decreased from dollars to hundredths of a cent. Therefore, the amount of information that companies can afford to bring to bear on a given question is vastly increased.[4]

INFORMATION AS A COMMODITY

The traditional publishing industry has long recognized the strategic value of information and has been able to assign an economic value to it by treating it as a commodity. People all over the world are linked together by radio, telephone, television, telex, cable TV, satellite, and, most recently, computer networks. More than one publishing company has its eye on information as a commodity. The New York Times, Time, Inc., and Warner Communications, traditionally considered newspaper, magazine, film, and television publishers, are all experimenting with *computerized information services*—on-line databases to which subscribers can gain access via telephone lines. Like a gas or electric utility, these companies attach a meter to the flow of information coming into your home

Information work. Shown here is a terminal used to access Mead Data Central's Nexis information service.

through the service, and they charge for the service based on how much time you use it.

A subscriber can already access approximately 3000 different on-line databases from a personal computer or terminal. They are still more expensive than traditional print media, such as newspapers or magazines. The user must pay a one-time initial charge and then an hourly connect charge, which ranges from $6 per hour to over $100 per hour, depending on the service.

A sampling of some of the on-line databases includes

• Dow Jones News/Retrieval. Offers news, including articles from *The Wall Street Journal*, financial information, and stock market quotes.

• Dialog Information Services. Offers access to hundreds of databases, with references to articles in journals.

• Nexis. Offers the major wire services, 10 newspapers, and 48 magazines.

Prodigy Services Company, a partnership of IBM and Sears, enables subscribers with personal computers to choose among a broad range of computer-based services such as news, electronic mail, home shopping, travel reservations, consumer reports, and banking. Unlike the on-line databases that charge by the hour, Prodigy charges a flat monthly fee, supple-

menting subscription revenues with on-line advertising.

INFORMATION AS A STRATEGIC RESOURCE

The computer, with its capability to store, organize, retrieve, and communicate vast amounts of information in many different ways, allows organizations to consider information as a strategic resource that adds value to the other good or service the company offers. Information processing then becomes a new way of organizing economic and social activity.

Computerized information services. A sample screen shows access to historical stock quote information.

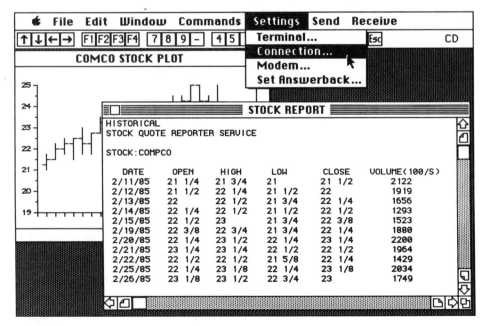

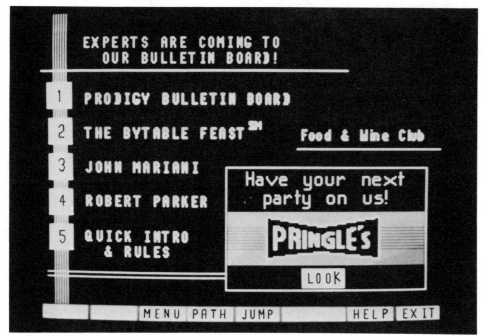

Computerized information services. *Advertisers buy space on the Prodigy personal videotex system, which helps lower the cost of subscribing to the service.*

For example, in financial markets, the commodity traded is not stocks, bonds, and other financial instruments but information, such as prices, volumes, yields, and values. A system that can process information faster and present it to those who are making the trading decisions is essential. On trading floors from Tokyo to New York to London, computers are used to assimilate vast amounts of information and distill it into trading strategies. The linking of financial markets around the world and the emergence of financial instruments that are traded 24 hours a day means that traders must have the technology to give them a strategic advantage over the competition.

You will learn more about strategic information systems in Chapter 10. For now, let's look at some before and after examples of how organizations treat information as a strategic resource to help explain this concept.

Insurance

• *Before.* If an insurance company uses information in its databases to keep track of its clients and send them bills, the company is using its information system as an administrative tool. It may be a more efficient way to keep track of and to bill customers, but it is essentially only part of the overhead or the cost of doing business.

• *After.* The company develops client profiles and sends those profiles to its agents. The agents match the insurance company's services, such as loans and additional insurance, to the client's needs. By using information to better understand its customers, the company generates additional business and improves the overall service the company offers.

Airlines

• *Before.* Passengers make or change reservations by using the telephone to call an airline or travel agent and find out the availability of seats. The system is simply a way of keeping track of passengers and seats.

• *After.* With extensive information on seat availability and travel patterns, the airlines can apply lower fares to selected cities and vary the number of lower fares on a given flight. The airlines improve efficiency and sell more tickets; the passengers may benefit by paying lower fares.

Perhaps the most widely known example of a strategic information system is American Airlines' computerized reservation system called Sabre (semiautomated business research environment). It started as a rudimentary reservation system and has grown to be the world's largest travel agency reservation system. American Airlines uses it to generate new sources of revenue and to outperform its competition. You will learn more about reservation systems and databases in Chapter 11.

Retailing

• *Before.* A nationwide chain of retail stores uses its information system primarily for record keeping to keep track of sales and produce profit and loss statements for each store as well as for the entire corporation.

• *After.* The chain uses its information system to investigate consumer trends and to offer a greater variety of goods and services on a store-by-store basis to meet customer demand. The system is also linked into an order-entry system to trim inventory, an inventory management system to control the product mix, and a delivery system to keep perishable items fresh.

Accounting

• *Before.* Companies exchange paper-based documents, such as purchase orders and invoices. Much time and effort are expended in typing information on those documents into computer systems, which adds greatly to the company's overhead.

• *After.* Companies use *electronic data interchange (EDI)*—the computer-to-computer electronic transmission of documents such as invoices and purchase orders. EDI makes possible the translation of documents into and out of a generic form so they can be electronically transferred among different computers. For example, Company *A* electronically sends a purchase order to Company *B*. The purchase order is entered directly into Company *B*'s database. No physical documents are delivered, and no entries are posted in manual ledgers.

By executing their accounting transactions electronically, companies cut the clerical costs involved in manually processing such documents, improve the accuracy of routine transactions, and speed up the process of doing business.

Banking

• *Before.* Individuals and organizations exchange paper-based checks and cash to pay bills and other debts.

• *After.* Individuals insert a magnetically encoded card with a personal identification number (PIN) into an *automatic teller machine (ATM)*—a special-purpose computer that allows bank customers to perform routine banking transactions themselves, rather than having to wait for a bank employee. People can use an ATM to obtain cash and pay many of their utility, department store, and credit card bills by electronic debiting and crediting of various accounts.

Computerized banking. *Customers waiting to use an automatic teller machine.*

Much time and effort has been invested in technology to replace paper transactions with electronic transactions. The benefits include (1) the movement of transactions is greatly speeded up, (2) the error rates drop dramatically, and (3) the cost per transaction drops.

However, as more and more individuals and organizations swing toward electronic transactions in lieu of conventional paper transactions such as checks, new problems will have to be addressed. One problem is working out the legal implications and issues surrounding the security, control, and authorization of electronic transactions. Originally, paper with a signature or a company seal was the only document considered to be a legal receipt. As of 1978, the Electronic Funds Transfer Act makes your receipt from an automated teller machine a legal receipt. Eventually, society may need some sort of legal paperless receipt.

Types of electronic banking.

Type	Example
Authorization	Pay bills by telephone
	Make direct deposit of paychecks
	and social security checks
	Make automatic electronic payments
Automatic teller machine	Deposit and withdraw funds on a 24 hour basis
Point-of-sale machine	Verify credit cards
	Check guarantee
	Debit card payments
National bank card networks	Transfer funds electronically from account to account
Automatic clearing	Transfer funds electronically between banks
	Substitute for paper check clearing

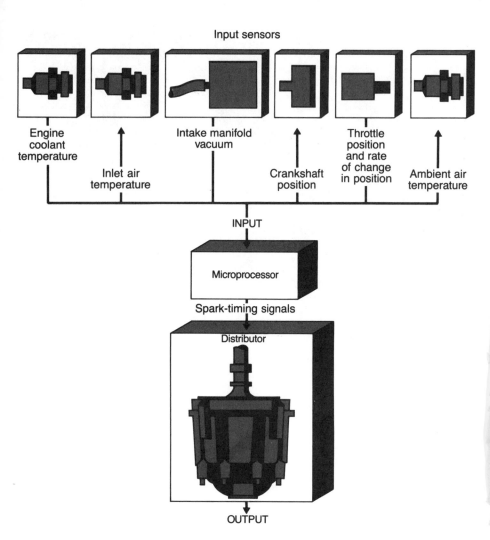

Input sensors

Engine coolant temperature

Inlet air temperature

Intake manifold vacuum

Crankshaft position

Throttle position and rate of change in position

Ambient air temperature

INPUT

Microprocessor

Spark-timing signals

Distributor

OUTPUT

Microelectronic technology. Special-purpose computers are used extensively in today's automobiles.

Once these problems are solved, and people accept the changes, banks and businesses will be well on the way to a cashless society.

This kind of computerization almost guarantees that the trend toward using information as a strategic resource will continue to grow. In all our examples, the computer is not just another machine but a strategic tool that is being used to reorganize economic activity.

HOW TECHNOLOGY FUELS CHANGE

To adapt to change in the next decade, every industry and every person should be thinking about the implications of computerization. How and why has it come about? In the beginning of the chapter, it was mentioned that computerization was stimulated by the technological trend toward the use of microelectronics. Such technological change can produce rapid and sweeping results.

Technological change is a complex process, but, simply put, a need or demand triggers the invention or discovery of new technology by which new products, services, or techniques are created. Applying new technology, such as microelectronics, can completely restructure economic and social activity in our society. The following sections will explain how.

WHAT IS TECHNOLOGY?

Throughout history, technology has played a dominant role in the development of society. *Technology* is most broadly defined as the practical application of knowledge and is considered to be "those activities directed to the satisfaction of human needs, which produce alterations in the material world."[5] The last 50 years have witnessed a flood of new inventions and discoveries that are based on *microelectronics*—the electronic logic represented as microscopic circuits on a chip.

Microelectronic technology exerts an influence on products because (1) it is restructuring the process by which products are designed and manufactured and (2) it is rapidly being incorporated into a wide range of products. The most dramatic application of microelectronic technology is the microprocessor, which has been incorporated into large and small computers, communication systems, industrial products, and consumer products. The trend toward greater and greater use of microelectronic technology will continue to bring important and perhaps radical transformations to the economy. To illustrate the magnitude of such changes, let us take a look at the automobile industry as an example.

Microelectronic technology, in the form of microprocessors and integrated circuits, has been applied to many of the mechanical functions in a car. These functions include everything from spark-timing systems, ignition, fuel injection, turbocharging, monitoring engine conditions with display for the driver, digital instrument panels, and suspension systems to diagnostic detection systems that mechanics can read when the car is in for service.

By equipping a car with a multipurpose display screen linked to ground- and satellite-based navigation and tracking systems, the car becomes a part of a much larger automated transportation system. Such a system might enable a driver to plot a route and have appropriate maps electronically displayed in the car. The system would also monitor traffic, spot congested areas, and warn the driver of a traffic jam along his or her route. While these systems are experimental today, they are expected to play a major role in easing traffic congestion and improving safety.

Drivers of today's computerized automobiles may be impressed by digital displays or the talking computer that nags about the open door, but these changes will eventually be taken for granted. The mechanic who has to service the car is faced with another set of problems. For example, after having spent years perfecting tune-up techniques, the mechanic is suddenly faced with an electronic ignition. Adjusting a carburetor in the past was a skill that could be practiced with a simple set of tools and a fine-tuned ear. Fuel injection requires a different set of skills and tools. Adaptation through retraining becomes the mechanic's way of coping with the

Automobile navigation system. *The screens next to the cellular phone display maps and navigation data recorded on map cassettes.*

changing technology. The alternative is watching his or her skills become obsolete.

HOW CHANGE AFFECTS SOCIETY

Not only do the mechanics who service the cars we just discussed have to be retrained in new technologies, but the entire support industry for the mechanics also has to change. The tool-producing industry that supports the mechanics must develop new tools to work on these new electronic parts. The industries that supply the primary automobile-manufacturing plants

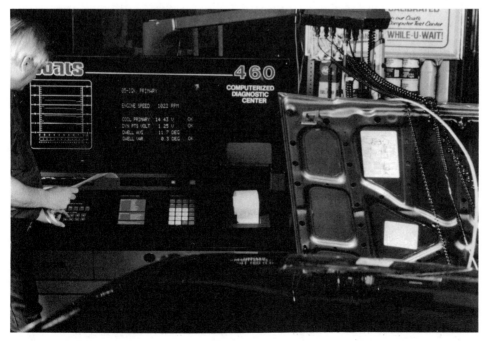

Computerization of the automobile. *An auto mechanic using computerized diagnostic tools.*

must also change the way in which parts are made based on the new technologies. The sales people who sell the automobile must be retrained in the new technologies. And the people who work in the automobile-manufacturing plants must be retrained as factories convert to automated techniques. This is only one example of the chain of events that must occur when even the simplest change upsets the status quo. In all industries and at all levels, technological change forces people to change their patterns of work and play and, ultimately, their life-styles.

The conversion of manual operations and procedures to the use of computer-aided techniques also exerts a great influence on the organization of the work force and brings up new problems and issues that have to be addressed. Every technology must be accompanied by a work force with an associated set of skills that can attend to that technology. In terms of work, microelectronic technology has two important impacts. First, it places a demand for higher levels of skills in the work force and changes the nature of work. Second, microelectronic technology in the form of automation could put much of the work force out of work.

OBSOLESCENCE AND THE COMPUTER

Although change does bring about new products, services, and jobs, obsolescence is also a rather unfortunate by-product. Obsolescence, from a systems point of view, is what happens when a part of the system spurts ahead and another part of the system lags behind. Technology in general and microelectronic technology in particular play a major role in pointing out this contrast. Because technology speeds up change, it can shorten the life cycle of a particular product. As technology clips along at its rapid pace, it begins to make people and their skills appear to be obsolete.

A recent example of how computerization is forcing us to focus on the future is the slowing down of what are called America's smokestack industries—steel and automobiles. Al-

though it is a more complex issue, computerization allowed other industrial countries to leap ahead, making American industries noncompetitive in the world economy. Many of the factories were shut down because they were not technologically up to date, and many of the people who were laid off by factory closings did not foresee changes coming. Many of the unemployed from the steel- and automobile-manufacturing industries, along with the smaller industries that support these giants, will never work at their former occupations again. These people are the victims of rapid technological change.

On the brighter side, however, change always produces new opportunities. According to a report commissioned by the Club of Rome—a worldwide organization composed of scholars, scientists, business people, and government leaders—

The promise of the microprocessor is that through its ubiquitous applications in the automation of industry and the tertiary sector, it is capable of increasing productivity to the extent that it should be able to provide all the resources required by a country, including those of defense, health, education, nourishment, and welfare, to provide a reasonably high material standard of living for everyone, without depleting or degrading the resources of the planet, with only a fraction of the physical work expended today.[6]

Although this utopian view is compelling, it is still difficult to ascertain the long-term consequences of such computerization. In the shorter term, however, the change in the established work force is directly related to obsolescence. The unemployment in the unskilled and semiskilled work force that occupies much of the media's attention is only a small part of the total picture. Skilled work is vulnerable to obsolescence, too, precisely because it is tied to specialized expertise. People who tie their future to a specific skill may be in for a rude awakening as computer technology brings about rapid change.

Two Service-Oriented Jobs

Consider, for example, the difference between the following two service-oriented jobs and the effect that computer technology has on the relative obsolescence of these jobs.

A travel agent is an information worker whose job has been enhanced by computer technology. A customer can contact a travel agent and take care of planning a trip, booking an airline reservation, making car and hotel reservations, and paying for the entire transaction. The travel agent has access to a vast network of computers that allows this to happen.

In contrast, a social worker is an information worker whose job has not yet been enhanced by computer technology. Customers seeking welfare, unemployment, or child care are faced with a complex bureaucracy. They may spend an enormous amount of time determining which plan best suits their needs or just meeting eligibility requirements before receiving any services. Have you ever waited in a line to receive a service, only to be told that the service is in another department, with another line?

Both Face Obsolescence

Which type of information worker just discussed faces obsolescence? The answer is both. The travel agent is likely to become obsolete before the social worker because the travel agent faces competition from the very computer network that allows him or her to perform so efficiently. Eaasy Sabre, a version of American Airlines' reservation system; the electronic version of the *Official Airline Guide;* and Travelshopper, which links to the Northwest Airlines and Trans World Airlines reservation system are offered as a part of the computerized information services that were mentioned earlier. Any individual with a personal computer can connect directly to these services by phone (for a fee, of course). The customer is then provided with up-to-date information about schedules and prices. These services have evolved to the point where the customer can make all reservations—airline, hotel, and car—and charge it to his or her credit card. What happens to the travel agent's job when this be-comes commonplace?

The social worker faces a similar type of obsolescence, although it should enhance service to the recipients. As computerization proceeds in government bureaucracies, computers will eliminate much of the bureaucracy. The social worker's function of gatekeeper, pointing out specific services for specific customers, will be enhanced by a network of computers that can perform the searching, checking, and qualifying tasks much more efficiently. Social workers will be free to concentrate on counseling and other people-oriented tasks.

The examples we have given imply that specific education, usually called vocational education, might not be the best path to pursue in the face of rapid change and obsolescence. What we need to ask is whether schools are training people for skills that are already obsolete. Most of the people now out of work were trained for a specific vocation, and they are often unable to change to new occupations. It can be argued that generalized work skills are more desirable than specialized expertise because the former allow better and more effective adaptation to a changing environment.

THE NEED TO ADAPT

Adaptation means looking to the future, seeing potential changes, and making a positive response to those changes. On a technological time scale, changes are measured in years or less, and microelectronic technology provides the most dramatic example of rapid change. For example, the competitive world of computers has a tremendous appetite for new ideas. It provides opportunities for new jobs and new talent. The potential financial rewards are enormous. Furthermore, it does not appear that this rapid-pace change is going to slow down in the future.

Throughout your life, you will be affected by technology and change. To keep control of your life, you will need to understand technology, learn to adapt, and learn to use it in a positive and productive way.

```
Key Line * for Booking details, or
RF-Return Flights  CP-Change Parameters
[F] Fares  >3

 Leave:01MAR BOS  BOSTON           900A
 Arrive:01MAR SFO  SAN FRANCISCO    125P
 Airline: AMERICAN         Flight: 117
 Equipment: D10    Meal: Breakfast
 Stops: 1
   Class:    Booking Code:  Seats:
 1 First         F          Available
 2 Coach         Y          Waitlist Only
 3 Special       B          Waitlist Only
 4 Special       Q          Waitlist Only
 5 Special       M          Waitlist Only
```

Computerized information services. Travelshopper, a service offered by TWA, allows you to book airline flights through Compuserve on a personal computer.

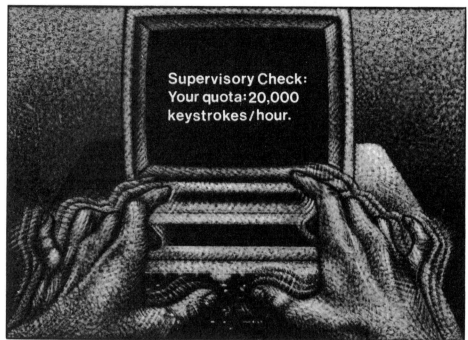

The electronic sweatshop. Many managers feel that computer monitoring motivates employees to meet company standards and makes them more productive workers.

The electronic sweatshop. Many employees, union officials, and government officials worry that computer monitoring causes stress and dehumanizes employees.

RESPONSES FOR A CHANGING WORLD

How should we cope with the effects of computerization? Accepting, reshaping, or rejecting are all options when looking toward your future. Viewing the phenomenon of computerization from several different perspectives helps us comprehend the many different effects it has on society. We have just considered some examples of the difficulties that societies have in coping with the many new ideas and uses for computers and information that cannot be foreseen in advance. There are, however, some basic attitudes about computers that color our perceptions. These attitudes can make us more or less fearful of computers.

THE ALL-COMPUTER TECHNOCRACY

On one hand, some envision a vast all-computer technocracy, in which computers in glass-enclosed rooms are gathering, storing, and processing information about us, our lives, and our society. They are monitoring us as they collect and dispense taxes, welfare payments, Medicare payments, licenses, and hundreds of other services.

An example of a form of automation that is causing some concern is taking place in the American office. There, information systems are helping to increase worker efficiency while lowering labor costs. This is officially referred to as back-office automation, but many people are unofficially referring to it as the electronic sweatshop, as the following example points out.

The Electronic Sweatshop

The people who work here [Plymouth, Mass.] process health-insurance claims for Blue Shield of Massachusetts. The facility is highly automated, and the work is done with video display terminals (VDTs). Six hours a day, except for one 15-minute break, processors sit before their terminals transferring data from claims forms to a company computer system. The computer revolution came to Plymouth a little more than a year ago, and a claims processor here offers a counterrevolutionary criticism: "The girls at work call it a sweatshop. Most of them figure they won't last more than two years."[7]

Several issues are being raised by concerned workers and labor unions about the conditions under which back-office employees must work. For example, the computer systems themselves monitor the workers' performance. The workers are often paid on a piecework basis, that is, by how many keystrokes are processed per hour. Every keystroke at every computer terminal can be tabulated and recorded, and reports can be generated that show the number of keystrokes per hour and how many mistakes were made by each individual worker. Managers claim that computer monitoring has brought about increases in productivity. They also claim that monitoring via computer allows them to rate employee performance objectively and to determine promotions and bonuses without giving employees special treatment.

Such computer monitoring, say the workers, does not enhance productivity but instead encourages a work pattern that tends to be monotonous, leads to stress, and dehumanizes the employee. A growing number of labor unions, government officials, and labor experts have rallied against computer monitoring, and several states have considered legislation to restrict the practice. Twenty unions have adopted official positions against computer monitoring, and one union negotiated a contract that limits computer monitoring of workers.[8]

In response to such problems, many companies are adopting new and innovative solutions. For example, one insurance company, Travelers Corporation, that formerly relied on a back-office claims-processing department is replacing its clerical workers with highly skilled nurses, called patient advocates, who work at personal computers answering inquiries and dispensing information on how customers can reduce costs or obtain second opinions. This is also an example of the transition to information work that was discussed earlier in the chapter.

The Computerless Society

At the opposite end of the spectrum are the people who believe that we would do just as well without computers at all. Although we might find it difficult to imagine such a society, it is worth remembering that the entire Industrial Age, from the invention of the steam engine to the late 1950s, ran its course without the aid of computers.

Computers only emerged at the tail end of the Industrial Age. Jacques Vallee points out the modern case of automation in reverse:

After the fall of Saigon, writes French author Jean Larteguy, who remained in Vietnam after the American withdrawal, the men who took over the economy closed the banks and instructed an army of clerks to take all the computer listings and copy them by hand onto regular ledgers. They went through every account and every aspect of the banks' operations. When the task was completed, the banks opened their doors to the public again, their entire accounting having returned to the days of bean counting.[9]

Although the modern corporation is far removed from the bean-counting accountants of yesteryear, a small number of businesspeople have expressed their disillusionment with computers. Their attitude is that computers have not delivered the efficiency and effectiveness as promised and that running their businesses could be done just as well without them.

SPOTLIGHT ON...
Enabling Applications

Computer and communication technology are enabling tools; they can be used to maintain control over your life. And perhaps nowhere is this more useful than with disabled people. Personal computers equipped with adaptive devices and specially written software enable the disabled to become more productive and independent.

Stephen W. Hawking, the Cambridge University physicist and author of *A Brief History of Time*, has Lou Gehrig's disease (amyotrophic lateral sclerosis) and has lost his voice as a result of pneumonia complications. Confined to a computer-equipped wheelchair, Hawking uses a hand switch to choose the words and commands he needs to speak through a synthesizer, run a word processor, or even play chess. His only complaint: the speech synthesizer has an American, not a British accent.

A variety of input and output devices have been adapted for use by the disabled. Enlarged keyboards, large-screen and magnifying displays, voice synthesizers, and Braille screens and printers have been designed for the blind or visually impaired.

Pressure-sensitive switches and joysticks, touch tablets, light pens, modified keyboards, scanners, and voice-recognition systems can ease the effects of almost any physical disability.

Computers and communications make knowledge and people more accessible and provide the tools to lessen the effects of disability—much to the disabled individual's advantage.

To learn more, read Apple Computer Resources in Special Education and Rehabilitation, *DLM Teaching Resources, P.O. Box 4000, Allen, Texas 75002; or* Curriculum Methods for Mastery: How to Make Education Special for All Learners, *Mindscape Educational Division, 3444 Dundee Road, Northbrook, Ill. 60062.*

High-tech/high-touch in the computer industry. Shown here is the Comdex computer show, an annual gathering of computer buyers and sellers.

Telecommuting. Some workers link their personal computers to the main office by telephone lines and work at home.

HIGH-TECH/HIGH-TOUCH

Somewhere in the middle of this dispute, in thousands of homes and businesses, people are using computers for their own pleasure and challenge. They are exchanging information with each other by personal contact, by swapping software, and by conversations through electronic mail and conferences. They see computers as interesting tools to be used in solving their problems. This points to an interesting resolution to the negative aspects of the computerization of society.

The term high-tech/high-touch, coined by John Naisbitt in *Megatrends*, describes the situation well. The term refers to the fact that whenever high technology is introduced, it is either accompanied by a compensatory human response or it is rejected. One example is the high technology of modern nuclear warfare that led to an interest in human safety. High-tech medical practice, such as cancer treatment, organ transplants, and artificial hearts, led to a high-touch interest in preventive health care and such concerns for the dying as the hospice movement. In the high-tech computer industry, the growing popularity of conventions and conferences increases the high-touch, face-to-face contact among computer industry workers.

Telecommuting

The growing popularity of personal computers coupled with the ease of connecting them to a corporate network of electronic information has led to a new way for many workers to spend their working hours. *Telecommuters*, a term coined in 1973 by researcher Jack Nilles, are people who work at home or at a satellite office and use computers and telephones instead of physical transportation to commute. With the advent of low-cost computer and communication technology, your office may travel with you wherever you go. A growing number of people already work this way.

People who write for a living exemplify this trend. Some journalists have inexpensive portable computers on which they can compose and edit their stories in the field. The information is stored in the computer, and the reporter can go to the nearest phone, dial the newspaper or magazine, and transmit the story to the office computer, where it is prepared for typesetting. For example, the book you are now reading was revised in Pohnpei, a small island in Micronesia between Hawaii and the Philippines. I wrote the manuscript on a word processor, sent disks via conventional mail to my publisher in New York, and transmitted all my changes and revisions via electronic mail and facsimile.

Some insurance companies are giving up the back office for the home office. Workers are processing claims on their personal computers at home; several companies encourage their programming staffs to use personal computers at home. They write and correct their programs at home and transmit the results or mail disks to the main office. Telecommuting is also an attractive option for parents with young children and for disabled persons who might not be able to hold traditional jobs.

Telecommuting, however, is not without its detractors. The Service Employees International Union (SEIU) voted to fight telecommuting. It has asked the Department of Labor to issue a ban against "home work." SEIU's reasoning is that all the benefits to telecommuting are on the company side. Workers themselves have cited several reasons for not wanting to telecommute when given the option.

The reasons, workers say, are that they do not want to be cooped up at home and do not want to miss the social contact of an office. These are similar to the reasons given by students who do not opt to take courses by television.

The Center for Futures Research at the University of Southern California in Los Angeles predicts that as much as 7 percent of the work force may be telecommuting by the turn of the century. A survey by New York-based Electronic Services Unlimited estimated that the number of people who work at home exceeded 20 million in 1987. It should be noted that the figure includes self-employed people and part-time telecommuters.

If the social aspects of work and education can positively benefit by telecommuting, then we will surely witness a growing number of people who will integrate their work, play, and total life-styles through computers.

Education and the Future

How might the computerization of society filter down into the educational environment? Would it simply mean that all students would have their own computers, or would it mean a difference in how courses are taught? Here is one scenario.

Lori, a 21-year-old college senior, lounged on the grass in the center of the campus quadrangle. On her lap was a notebook-sized portable computer. She was putting the finishing touches on her proposed spring schedule.

"Hey Lori, want to go over to the cafeteria and have a cup of coffee?" her boyfriend John called to her.

"Can't now," Lori said. "I've got to go to the media center and see if I can get this schedule approved."

Although Lori was on a traditional college campus in Boston, the schedule she was preparing was far from traditional. She needed 15 units to complete her degree and was contemplating an anthropology course at the University of Chicago, an economics course at Harvard, and a computer science course at the University of California at Berkeley. Her local campus was still the center of her social life, but her academic life consisted of many classes taken through a combination of interactive video and computer networks. Most colleges had long since joined the Electronic Educational Consortium, a nonprofit foundation that jointly produced and marketed live and interactive, video/computer-based courses. Students were issued electronic vouchers, which they could use at any school to complete their degree programs. Computer networks had made classroomless learning a practical everyday matter, and students were free to take courses wherever and from whomever they chose.

After checking her schedule, Lori walked to the media center—a campuswide information system as well as the local node in a nationwide network of electronic educational services. She plugged her portable computer into the media center's network, entered her password, and accessed the ETV interactive course channel to scan the course offerings. She smiled as she watched a brief advertisement for the anthropology course. Her father once told her that in the 1980s, the music industry had tried a similar technique with artists making videos of selected songs and broadcasting them over a channel called MTV.

She found that the only way to take the anthropology course was to use an interactive self-pacing video disk and to communicate her assignments to the professor through electronic mail. Be-

Electronic classroom. *The computer science department at Brown University uses personal computer workstations connected together in a network. The instructor can introduce an animated sequence of images viewed by all students an then let each one of them confront the material directly by working independently on the same "interactive movie."*

cause her portable computer used an inexpensive compact video disk drive similar to the Tandy compact audio disk drive on which she played her favorite music, her portable computer had full color, motion, and sound capabilities.

The computer science course would be no problem. She simply had to tap into a teleconference that linked her into an ongoing interactive computer science program. The economics course was a problem. The economics professor she had heard so much about and wanted to see on live interactive video was on a leave of absence in Washington serving on the President's Economic Advisory Council.

"It figures," muttered Lori. "The only course that originates right here in Boston." She copied the schedule of other economics courses into her portable computer and decided to catch up with John and have that cup of coffee while she pondered her alternatives.

Although this particular scenario may not be exact as to its time or technical description, it does point out some significant possibilities for education, many of which are already under way.

Several universities are installing campuswide networks that will connect dorm rooms to classrooms, libraries, and mainframe computers. Each student is encouraged to purchase his or her own personal computer. In addition to providing students with a personal problem-solving tool for writing papers and performing research tasks, the personal computers are linked into the network to access data in mainframe computers and can communicate with other personal computers. As more and more students start learning how to use computers, these experiments will become more widely known and used. And, as these computer innovations are assimilated into everyday campus life, the computerization of education will change the thinking patterns and work methods of students, faculty, and administrators.

COMPUTERS AND ETHICS

Computerization is having an impact on the information society that goes far beyond the change in economic and technical trends. The smooth functioning of an information society is highly dependent on electronic technology. Such a society is also quite sensitive to disruption through various forms of computer crime, such as unauthorized access to information, embezzlement, and invasions of security and privacy.

CRIME

Computer crime takes many forms, from unintentional disruption to vengeful acts to embezzlement. For example, on November 2, 1988, students at the University of California at Berkeley noticed that something was repeatedly and rapidly trying to gain access to their computer system. That something was a *worm*—a program that reproduces itself by creating copies of itself. By the next day, the worm had replicated uncontrollably and infected 2000 computers all around the country on the Internet series of national research networks. The Internet was overwhelmed. The program's creator Robert T. Morris, Jr., was a computer science graduate student at Cornell University.

Although Cornell suspended Morris and condemned him for more

Education and the future. In many colleges, students are strongly encouraged to purchase their own personal computers.

of a juvenile act rather than one of malicious intent, the federal government was far less tolerant. In January 1990, Morris was found guilty of writing a program that disrupted a nationwide computer network. His sentence: three years' probation, a $10,000 fine, and 400 hours of community service. Morris's prosecution and conviction sent a message from the federal government that tampering with computers, even when not intentionally destructive, was not acceptable.

Although the characteristics of this case were not considered to involve fraud and deceit, it raised several concerns about the security of computer systems, and it prompted the federal government to begin prosecuting individuals under the Federal Computer Fraud and Abuse Act of 1986.

In another incident, an unknown intruder gained illegal access to the Jet Propulsion Laboratory (JPL) computer system, browsed through the system for several hours, and left behind a *Trojan horse*—an unauthorized program hidden inside or attached to a legitimate program. Although no classified material was compromised, JPL was forced to rebuild its computer system and add additional security measures in fear that the intruder's Trojan horse might have permitted easy access to the computer system in the future.

These computer criminals are known as *hackers*—people who gain access to computer systems without authorization. Hackers have become a serious problem because of the widespread use of networks and personal computers. This opens up new possibilities for people to (1) easily obtain access to information that is stored in institutional systems or (2) destroy information, usually by erasing or changing data or programs stored on disks.

Embezzlers, people who unlawfully appropriate money for their own use, have wasted no time in using computers to perpetrate their crimes. Using electronic transactions, embezzlers can transfer funds from one account to another. For example, using what SRI International computer crime expert Donn Parker calls data diddling, a bank employee might use the com-

Computer crime headlines.

puter to transfer funds into his or her personal account and cover up the switch with phony transactions. However, a routine audit will normally uncover such a crime.

In another scheme, often called salami slicing, criminals use computer programs to slice off tiny fractions of dollar amounts in ordinary transactions and add them to a separate account (usually one of their own). Salami slicing is particularly hard to detect because each individual slice is a fraction of a penny and while the slicing is going on, all account totals appear to be in balance.

Another serious and destructive form of computer crime is the spreading of computer viruses. A *virus program* is any program developed specifically to interfere with a computer's normal operation. It is called a virus because, like its biological counterpart, it can clone copies of itself and then infect other programs with those copies. Then the virus program activates, usually triggered by a certain date or after it makes a certain number of copies of itself. Depending on the intent of the programmer, a virus program might simply display an annoying message on the computer's display, or begin to destroy data on the disk or in memory.

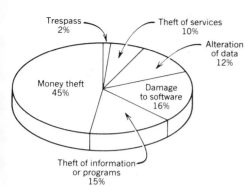

Types of computer crime. (*From* Computer Crime, Computer Security, Computer Ethics, *National Center for Computer Crime Data. Copyright (c) 1986. Reprinted by permission.*)

Virus programs can be transmitted by passing an infected floppy disk from one computer to another, or over telephone lines. For example, a virus program attached to another program on a computerized bulletin board can rapidly infect many computer systems.

A widely documented incident at Lehigh University during the 1987-88 school year shows how potentially damaging a virus program can be. Now known as the Lehigh virus, the program attached itself to the DOS operating system. It would then count the number of new disks it had infected, and when the count reached four, it began to erase program and data files on the infected disk. The virus probably spread through the willingness of students to share data and programs.

Although the infection was largely confined to the computer laboratory at Lehigh University, the virus has not been completely contained and is thought to have spread to other computers outside the university.

Other computer viral infections have been reported at the University of Delaware, Georgetown University, the University of Pittsburgh, IBM, Aldus Corporation of Seattle, and in Israel, where a destructive virus program designed to erase all disk files on May 13, 1988, was apparently intended as a political protest. Although it had begun to spread, the virus was fortunately discovered and destroyed before May 13.

There are some simple precautions that anyone can take against the threat of virus programs. They include using only software that comes in factory-sealed packages, not downloading programs from computerized bulletin boards, and not using copied software.

It is possible that virus programs may be more widespread than reported. Many corporations, fearing adverse publicity, will not disclose information about alleged or real viruses.

SECURITY

As you can see from our examples, the security of information stored in computers is in question. Even though sensitive computer systems, such as those that contain financial data or deal with national security, require elaborate clearances and codes to use them, most computer systems are vulnerable to those who would misuse them for their own personal gain. A large number of computer crimes occur because of lax security. What can an individual or organization do about the problems of security?

There are several solutions for dealing with various aspects of the problem. The simplest solution is to lock up disks and computers when they are not in use. A locking file drawer or cabinet is sufficient to protect floppy disks. Putting a physical lock on a hard disk or a computer will prevent unauthorized tampering with the device.

In addition, a backup copy of any disk that contains sensitive or important data should always be made and stored in a different location than the original. Backing up disks should become a routine procedure for the user, not only to prevent theft and contamination by viruses, but also to prevent accidental loss of data owing to human or computer error or natural disaster.

Large organizations, for example, not only back up their data, but also have remote disaster recovery sites where the duplicate data are stored. The consequences of a major theft, fire, or other natural disaster would be too severe for these organizations to ignore.

In multiuser computer systems, where many users share a computer or group of computers, more security is needed. ***Password protection***—a software form of security that relies on the use of a code the user must enter to gain access to a computer system—may help to solve the problem. To use the system, the user must enter his or her password on the computer's keyboard. More complicated password-protection schemes are designed to facilitate different levels of access to computer systems. For example, the president of a company may have a password that allows access to any information, whereas a salesperson's password may only offer restricted access to certain sales and marketing information. Sophisticated password-protection software is capable of tracing who signed on, what computer or terminal was used, and what information was requested.

In situations where communication between two or more computers is involved, such as a network of computers, a common security method involves *encryption*, the scrambling of data to render it unintelligible to an unauthorized recipient, and *decryption*, the reversal of a previous scrambling of data to make it intelligible. For example, a simple method for coding and decoding messages might be to take the alphabet and assign each letter to a number so that A = 1, B = 2, C = 3, and so on. To create a coding scheme used in encrypting and decrypting electronic transmissions requires an elaborate computer program, the details of which are beyond the scope of this book. Encryption/decryption systems are used extensively by banks in their automatic teller machine networks, and are required for all defense-related federal government computer systems. The controversial aspect of encryption is that no code has yet proved to be completely unbreakable.

However, many solutions are not technological. There are five major strategies that any security-conscious organization should implement.[10] They are

• *Authenticate.* Always check who is accessing which information.

• *Authorize.* Make sure that the person who owns the information has given permission to use it.

• *Audit.* Keep records of who accesses what.

• *Supervise.* Most computer criminals are insiders. Make sure that the staff who use the computer are properly supervised when accessing critical systems.

• *Establish strict computer crime policies* and stick to them.

PRIVACY

In a society where increasing amounts of personal data are being stored in computer systems and where computers are capable of easily communicating with one another, the concern for privacy is a legitimate issue. Take, for example, the simple sharing of information by organizations that have a common set of interests, such as businesses that subscribe to credit-record services. Subscribers use such systems to screen applicants for various forms of credit, and the system was set up with good intentions.

The problem with such systems is that the information is gathered without the subject's participation; thus, it may be difficult for an individual to gain access to his or her records and correct any errors. The Fair Credit Reporting Act of 1971 gives consumers who have credit reports on file certain basic rights, such as the right to dispute inaccurate or incomplete information and have it reinvestigated and the right to disclosure of the nature and substance of all information about them. But it does not stop the information from being gathered in the first place.

Another example involves attempts by the Federal Bureau of Investigation (FBI) to expand its National Crime Information Center files into a nationwide system that would enable law enforcement agencies to exchange information on people who are suspected of committing a crime but have not been charged. The system already contains information on stolen property, missing people, and people for whom arrest warrants have been issued.[11] The problem with the system involves the questionable nature of the information stored in the FBI files. Studies have shown that arrest records are notoriously inaccurate. Furthermore, it has been estimated that one out of five Americans has been arrested for nontraffic offenses, which means that quite a few people could end up in the FBI files. The effects of inaccuracies could be quite unsettling to the individuals involved. For example, what would happen if an advisor to the president seriously proposed that all children of a certain age be examined to see if they had any criminal tendencies, and he or she had access to computer records from the FBI?

The Privacy Act of 1974 was enacted to provide safeguards against invasions of personal privacy by federal agencies. The rights include limits on the types of personal information an organization may collect and the right to see, copy, and correct information maintained by a record-keeping organization. Legislation such as the Fair Credit Reporting Act and the Privacy Act provide guidelines for the development of new laws to help individuals safeguard their personal information.

SOFTWARE PIRACY

Software piracy is the illegal or unauthorized copying of software. Software, like a book or an audio or video recording, is protected by copyright law. An important point about software is that it is licensed, not purchased. The software publisher retains the ownership; since the users do not own the software, they are not free to do what they want with it. Software is usually accompanied by a license agreement that contains a fair use clause that restricts copying the software and the documentation. For example, the clause usually states that the user can make a copy of the software to use as a backup copy but cannot make multiple backup copies, cannot make copies for friends or colleagues, and, of course, cannot make copies for resale.

Copy Protection

In an effort to combat software piracy, individual software companies have devised several protection schemes. The most common method of *copy protection* takes the form of codes that are recorded on the disk and are designed to prevent people from copying disks. Copy protection was widespread in the 1980s, but consumer reaction to it was negative. As a result, most software publishers have abandoned copy protection schemes for software sold in the United States. Copy protection is, however, still widely used outside the United States.

Site Licensing

One alternative to copy protection is a plan known as *site licensing*—a contract in which the customer is allowed to make copies of a software package for use at one site (e.g., the software would only be used by the accounting department). The plan is favored by customers, such as large companies, that might purchase hundreds or thousands of copies of a particular software package for use within their organizations.

Shareware

An innovative, but far less widely used scheme, is called shareware. The software publisher distributes copies of a software package for free, often encouraging potential users to give copies to their friends. A potential user tries out the software, and, if satisfied, pays the software publisher. There are several incentives to buy the software. First, only those people who have bought the software are eligible to receive updated copies of the program and the documentation. Second, if person *A* gives a copy of the software to person *B* and that person buys the software, person *A* gets a rebate. Supporters of shareware claim that it is an ideal way for entrepreneurial programmers to make money without incurring large overhead and marketing costs. Larger software publishers, however, consider the idea impractical for high-volume, high-priced, or complex software.

So far, software publishers have been unable to stop software piracy. It is difficult to police the violators, except in isolated instances. Software publishers have had moderate success with publicity campaigns that inform and educate consumers about the ethical and legal issues involved in copying software. This has been effective in large corporations where the adverse publicity and the possibility of paying for expensive litigation might be a factor. But the fact remains that software is legally protected by copyright law, so anyone who makes a copy of software to avoid paying for it is breaking that law.

REVIEW

Computerization is the result of two trends: the increasing use of information as a strategic resource and the growth of microelectronics. An information society is one in which most of the population spends its time gathering, processing, and communicating information rather than physically producing goods.

The economics of information have been revolutionized by the computer. Today, information can be plentiful, cheap, and easy to get. Computerized information services allow subscribers to access information directly through personal computers or terminals. When information is treated as a strategic resource, it adds value to the good or service that an organization produces. Insurance companies, airlines, and banks are examples of organizations that use information strategically.

Technology is responsible for much of the change in our society. In all industries and at all levels, technology forces people to change their lifestyles. Adaptation to such change means looking to the future, seeing those changes, and making a positive response. People's attitudes color their perceptions of computers. Some view computerization as an all-computer technocracy; others would just as soon have no computers at all. In the middle, people are adapting to computers by using them as creative problem-solving tools.

The smooth functioning of an information society creates a dependence on electronic technology. Institutions become vulnerable to disruption through various forms of computer crime and invasions of security and privacy. Software piracy is the unauthorized or illegal copying of software; making a copy of software to avoid paying for it is a crime.

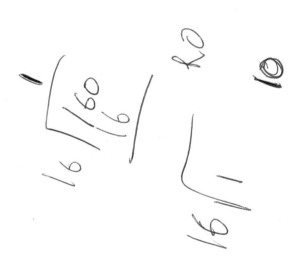

REFERENCES

1. *Workforce 2000: Work and Workers for the Twenty-first Century* Indianapolis, Ind.: Hudson Institute, 1987. pp 26–27.

2. Ibid, p. xxi.

3. Uchitelle, Louis. "Surplus of College Graduates Dims Job Outlook for Others." *New York Times,* June 18, 1990, p. 1.

4. Nolan, Richard L., and Alex J. Pollock. "Organization and Architecture, or Architecture and Organization." In *Stage by Stage.* Lexington, Mass.: Nolan, Norton & Company, September-October 1986, p. 2.

5. Rae, John B. "The Know-How Tradition: Technology in American History." In *Technology and Culture.* New York: Schocken, 1972, p. 83. An old, but interesting, anthology about the impact of technology on our society.

6. Friedrichs, Guenter, and Adam Schaff, eds. *Microelectronics and Society.* New York: New American Library, 1983. An outstanding and well-written collection of essays that covers the impact of technology on the Third World as well as more developed societies.

7. Andrew, John. "As Computers Change the Nature of Work, Some Jobs Lose Savor." *The Wall Street Journal,* May 6, 1983, p. 1.

8. Miller, Michael W. "Productivity Spies." *The Wall Street Journal,* June 3, 1985, p. 1.

9. Vallee, Jacques. *The Network Revolution: Confessions of a Computer Scientist.* Berkeley, Calif.: And/Or Press, 1982, pp. 164–165. The most interesting and readable book about computers and society around even though it is now somewhat dated. Vallee discusses much more than networks: he is concerned with all the implications of the computerization of society and presents some amusing and interesting anecdotes.

10. Iida, Jeanne, "Computer Crime: MIS Confront a Cancer." *Information Week,* February 22, 1988, p. 24.

11. Pear, Robert. "Crime Panel Backs Broad Expansion of Computer File." *The New York Times,* June 11, 1987, p. 1.

RESOURCES

BOOKS

Brand, Stewart. *The Media Lab.* East Rutherford, N.J.: Viking Penguin, 1987. Mr. Brand, editor of *The Whole Earth Catalog* series, spent a year at MIT's Media Lab and documented most of the research projects going on there.

Dealing with Electronic Vandalism. Arlington, Va.: ADAPSO Software Industry Division, 1990. ADAPSO, a software industry association, has developed a comprehensive guide to help identify, eradicate, and prevent computer virus infections in computer systems and software.

Introduction to Computer Crime. Los Angeles, Calif.: National Center for Computer Crime Data, 1987. The National Center for Computer Crime Data is a Los Angeles research firm that studies ways to detect, investigate, prevent, and prosecute computer crimes. They also publish a variety of research papers.

Landreth, Bill, with Howard Rheingold. *Out of the Inner Circle.* Redmond, Wash.: Microsoft Press, 1985. An inside look at what inspires hackers to break into computer systems.

PC-SIG Encyclopedia of Shareware. A comprehensive directory of shareware computer programs. Available from the user group PC-SIG, 1030D East Duane Avenue, Sunnyvale, Calif. 94806.

Rozak, Theodore. *The Cult of Information.* New York: Pantheon, 1987. Mr. Rozak offers an unusually apocalyptic vision of the computerized society. Also included are a historical survey of attitudes toward computers and a counterpoint to almost every other author mentioned in this chapter.

Stoll, Clifford. *The Cuckoo's Egg.* New York: Doubleday, 1989. A true story of international computer espionage in which the author tracks an elusive computer hacker, sets up a sting operation, and uncovers a spy ring in West Germany.

Strassmann, Paul. *Information Payoff: The Transformation of Work in the Electronic Age.* New York: Free Press, 1985. The theme of this book is information technology but the focus is people. Looking at information technology from individual, organizational, and societal perspectives, Strassmann offers analysis and criticism on how information technology is changing our lives.

Toffler, Alvin. *The Third Wave.* New York: Bantam, 1980. Futurists are like historians. They give us an artificial vantage point from which to look backward. The study of the future has become a respected profession. Corporations employ futurists in their planning departments, and there is even a World Future Society in existence. Computers undergo such rapid technological change that anyone who is seriously interested in learning about them should be aware of the many books concerned with the social impact of computers and the future. This book contains several references you will undoubtedly choose for further reading.

Wilk, Charles K. *Defending Secrets, Sharing Data.* Washington, D.C.: U.S. Government Printing Office, 1987.

Wood, Fred. *Electronic Record Systems and Individual Privacy.* Washington, D.C.: U.S. Government Printing Office, 1986.

MAGAZINES

Business Week. New York: McGraw-Hill. This magazine is a good source of information about trends and developments in information processing and technology. It is written for managers and is in the same style as *Time* and *Newsweek.*

Research and Development. Chicago: Cahners. An interdisciplinary publication that covers all applied research and development. The magazine is a good source of information about computer trends.

Technology Review. Cambridge, Mass.: MIT. MIT publishes this bimonthly review of the uses of science and its impacts and consequences on society.

STUDY GUIDE

Match the following key terms to the appropriate definitions:

A.

1. ____ Computerization
2. ____ Information society
3. ____ Industrial work
4. ____ Information work
5. ____ Computerized information services
6. ____ Electronic data interchange (EDI)
7. ____ Automatic teller machine (ATM)
8. ____ Technology
9. ____ Microelectronics
10. ____ Telecommuters

a. Work that involves the production of goods.

b. A special-purpose computer that allows bank customers to perform routine banking transactions themselves.

c. The practical application of knowledge.

d. The restructuring of society by the widespread use of computers.

e. A person who works at home or in a satellite office and uses computers and telephones instead of physical transportation to commute.

f. The electronic logic represented as microscopic circuits on a chip.

g. A society structured around the principles of information as a commodity and as a strategic resource.

h. The computer-to-computer electronic transmission of documents such as invoices and purchase orders.

i. On-line databases to which subscribers can gain access via telephone lines.

j. Work that involves the delivery of services.

B.

11. ____ Worm
12. ____ Trojan horse
13. ____ Hackers
14. ____ Virus program
15. ____ Password protection
16. ____ Encryption
17. ____ Decryption
18. ____ Software piracy
19. ____ Copy protection
20. ____ Site licensing

a. Codes that are recorded on the disk and are designed to prevent people from copying disks.

b. A program that reproduces itself by creating copies of itself.

c. A contract in which the customer is allowed to make copies of a software package for use at one site.

d. People who gain access to computer systems without authorization.

e. Any program developed specifically to interfere with a computer's normal operation.

f. The illegal or unauthorized copying of software.

g. The reversal of a previous scrambling of data to make it intelligible.

h. The scrambling of data to render it unintelligible to an unauthorized recipient.

i. A software form of security that relies on the use of a code that the user must enter to gain access to a computer system.

j. An unauthorized program hidden inside or attached to a legitimate program.

True/False:

21. __T__ Before computers, information was considered to be limited, expensive, and hard to get.

22. __T__ Japan is looking for future economic growth by exporting the knowledge of their people.

23. __F__ Sending customers computerized bills is an example of a strategic use of information.

24. __F__ The trend toward electronic transactions in banking has reached its peak.

25. __T__ Using an automatic teller machine in conjunction with a bank card to withdraw cash from your account is an example of using a debit card.

26. __T__ The most dramatic example of the application of microelectronic technology is the microprocessor.

27. __T__ Microelectronic technology places a demand

for higher levels of skills in the work force.

28. T Electronic travel agencies are one example of a growing number of information services.

29. F According to workers, computer monitoring enhances the productivity of clerical office workers.

30. F Telecommuters are people who travel long distances to get to their jobs.

31. T Hourly connect charges can make on-line databases expensive.

32. F When you purchase software, the rights to that software are transferred to you.

33. F Copy protection is favored by most consumers.

34. T Software is licensed, not purchased.

35. F Information in computerized credit files cannot be obtained without the subject's consent.

Multiple Choice:

36. The major impact of the computerization of society is
    a. Widespread unemployment.
    b. The slowing down of technological change.
    c. Electronic sweatshops.
    d. Restructuring of work, education, and leisure.

37. In the 1950s, approximately what percentage of the work force was employed in factory blue-collar work?
    a. 40 percent.
    b. 50 percent.
    c. 60 percent.
    d. 70 percent.

38. Information workers do not include which of the following occupations?
    a. Assembly-line workers.
    b. Secretaries.
    c. Engineers.
    d. Clerks.

39. Which of the following is the reason why economists struggle with the concept of information as a resource?
    a. Information is like oil, steel, or food.
    b. There are limits on how much information an individual can consume.
    c. Information as an economic resource is similar to information as a political resource.
    d. Information does not go away when you consume it.

40. Which of the following is the most commonly used scheme to combat software piracy?
    a. Site licensing.
    b. Locking the computer.
    c. Copy protection.
    d. Shareware.

41. Which of the following is not an example of purchasing access to information as a commodity?
    a. Paying your cable TV bill.
    b. Subscribing to Prodigy.
    c. Renting computer time.
    d. Paying your electric bill.

42. Technology plays one role in obsolescence by
    a. Lengthening product life cycles.
    b. Making skilled work immune to obsolescence.
    c. Shortening product life cycles.
    d. Pointing out the similarities between parts of a system that move too fast and those that lag behind.

43. A travel agent's job could be made obsolete by
    a. Increasing high-tech jet travel.
    b. Access to a network of computers.
    c. Electronic publishing.
    d. Adding more computer technology to his or her job.

44. A good personal strategy for coping with obsolescence might be
    a. Training for a specific vocation.
    b. Playing your part within the established framework.
    c. Acquiring a specialized expertise in some field.
    d. Acquiring generalized work skills.

45. Some unions are interested in banning telecommunications because
    a. The benefits are on the company side.
    b. Too many people are telecommuting and not joining unions.
    c. The benefits are on the workers' side.
    d. Workers themselves do not want to telecommute.

Thought Questions:

46. Is the transition from industrial to information society easy to understand? Which aspects of the transition are not clear to you? Why?

47. We have been discussing the strategic uses of information in this chapter. Can you describe how information as a strategic resource is different from information as a commodity? Why or why not?

Projects:

48. Choose a task that you personally perform (i.e., banking, homework, job) that has been affected by computerization. Write a brief scenario describing how you accomplished the task before computerization and after computerization. Present your before and after scenario to the class.

49. Through your school library, find a newspaper or magazine article that discusses a specific computer-related crime. Write a paper that examines how the computer was used to commit the crime and how the crime might have been prevented. Present your findings to the class.

SOFTWARE EXERCISES

For this exercise, you are going to use your word processor to write a "state of security" report. Visit an organization in your community that uses computers. Find out as much as you can about their security strategies. Use the discussion in this chapter on security as your guideline. Make sure your report addresses the five nontechnical strategies:

• *Authenticate.* Always check who is accessing which information.

• *Authorize.* Make sure that the person who owns the information has given permission to use it.

• *Audit.* Keep records of who accesses what.

• *Supervise.* Most computer criminals are insiders. Make sure that the staff who use the computer are properly supervised when accessing critical systems.

• *Establish strict computer crime policies* and stick to them.

ANSWERS

1. d, **2.** g, **3.** a, **4.** j, **5.** i, **6.** h, **7.** b, **8.** c, **9.** f, **10.** e, **11.** b, **12.** j, **13.** d, **14.** e, **15.** i, **16.** h, **17.** g, **18.** f, **19.** a, **20.** c, **21.** T, **22.** T, **23.** F, **24.** F, **25.** T, **26.** T, **27.** T, **28.** T, **29.** F, **30.** F, **31.** T, **32.** F, **33.** F, **34.** T, **35.** F, **36.** d, **37.** c, **38.** a, **39.** d, **40.** c, **41.** d, **42.** c. **43.** b, **44.** d, **45.** a.

ESTHER DYSON

Profession: Editor and publisher of *Release 1.0*, a newsletter that analyzes the computer industry.

Profile: After graduating with a degree in economics from Harvard, Dyson worked as a reporter for *Forbes* magazine. She became interested in computers because she was attracted to the field's high concentration of intelligent people. Her newsletter is respected for its combination of witty commentary and industry insights.

Quote: *"We live in an information society in which computers are the fundamental capital. Computers are absolutely essential to our competitive edge in the world."*

CHAPTER 4

COMPUTERS AT WORK

PREVIEW

Just two generations ago, a high school education was considered unnecessary for most workers and a college degree was the sign of a doctor, professor, or lawyer. Today, practically all jobs require a college education, and even the least skilled jobs require a command of reading, computing, and thinking skills once required only by the professions. Just one generation ago, computers were considered high-technology luxuries reserved for the military, government, and big business. Today, computers are everywhere, and they have changed the way business is transacted, goods are designed and manufactured, medical problems are analyzed, and education is delivered.

Now, when you graduate from college and enter the workplace, computer and communication technology are very likely to play an important part of your job. Computers and communications have been gradually making their way into the work place since the 1950s. And every year that goes by, computers become more widespread. Today, everybody needs to be able to make the most of computer and communication technology. It has the potential to enhance and even revolutionize the way that you work.

To round out the big picture in Section One, this chapter surveys selected professions focusing on the diverse applications for computers, shows examples of people's effective use of computers, and discusses the technology and issues surrounding the use of computers on the job.

In this chapter, you'll learn

- How the nature of work is changing.
- How computers are used in manufacturing.
- How computers are used in retailing.
- How computers are used in health care and medicine.
- How computers are used in the arts and design.
- How computers are used in government, military, and law.
- How computers are used in education.
- Career options in the computer-related fields.
- Jobs, training, and the future.

THE CHANGING NATURE OF WORK

In Chapter 3, we presented a transformation in which the majority of jobs evolve from the manual labor of the industrial era to the knowledge work of the information era. We also said that computerization played a major role in that transformation. But why do people use computers? How does their use affect peoples' performance and productivity on the job? And what impact does new technology have on the workplace?

To answer the first question: Throughout this book you will see that computers have become more powerful, easier to use, and less expensive. Thus the effort required to apply computers in the workplace is much simpler than it was a decade ago. And as the cost of computing drops, even very small organizations can benefit from the use of computers.

Computers and technology have taken the tedium out of many jobs. As a result, they replace physical demands with mental demands. This, in turn, requires a broader set of problem-solving and analytical skills, more decision making, and more education. Like all revolutionary technologies, such as electricity, telephones, and automobiles, computers have been embraced by individuals and organizations rather quickly. Thus constant learning and adaptation are necessary to keep pace with rapid technological advances. Technology, although important, is not an end in itself. It is simply a tool. As you will see throughout this chapter, in the hands of creative and competent people, computer and communication technology can open up a new world of work and job opportunities.

COMPUTERS IN MANUFACTURING

Computer-aided methods have advanced to the point where computers handle nearly every aspect of a product's system development life cycle, from concept to completed product. It is possible to model, analyze, and test various designs on the computer. Making an actual product only needs to be done when the computerized design is complete and satisfactory.

COMPUTER-AIDED ENGINEERING, DESIGN, AND MANUFACTURING

Computers and technology are restructuring the process by which products are designed and manufactured. A good example of this is the growing use of computer-aided engineering (CAE), computer-aided design (CAD), and computer-aided manufacturing (CAM)—three interrelated systems that are used to take an idea from concept to design to finished product. Let us use a simplified example of before and after design and manufacturing in the automobile industry to show how computer-aided techniques affect the process. Keep in mind that no automobile manufacturers have completely automated the process.

Using manual methods, engineers sketch rough designs that represent new ideas for parts and components. Then draftspersons produce detailed drawings of the engineer's designs

Computer-aided engineering. *Graphic workstations help engineers visualize their designs in two and three dimensions.*

from which clay models and prototypes are produced. The models are analyzed and tested. Design errors and flaws are detected, and the drawings are revised. The drawings are then passed to manufacturing where shop-floor technicians interpret them, and decide how to make the part or component. The time from initial concept to completed automobile takes five years on the average.

Using computer-aided methods, engineers employ *computer-aided engineering (CAE)*—software for designing, analyzing, testing, and modeling parts and components. Engineers enter their assumptions about new ideas for better automobile designs, watch the computer instantly adjust the computer model, and see the consequences of their assumptions. Enough information can be obtained through modeling to eliminate design flaws and problems long before a real automobile is ever taken for a test drive.

Once the initial design is complete, draftspersons and technicians use *computer-aided design (CAD)*—a system that automates the drafting process. The design can be further analyzed, tested, and refined, and the output of CAD becomes electronic drawings and specifications that are used by manufacturing.

The information is fed into a *computer-aided manufacturing (CAM)* system, which permits computers to control and direct the manufacture and assembly of a product. Such a system might include the use of robots and other automatic machines to produce automobiles in a completely automated environment. Using these tools, the time from concept to completion is shortened to two years.

Automobiles are not the only products that benefit from computer-aided techniques. Computers, ships, airplanes, office buildings, nuclear reactors, and consumer electronic products are all products in which computer-aided techniques are playing an increasingly important role.

MANUFACTURING RESOURCE PLANNING

Material Requirements Planning (MRP) and Manufacturing Resource Planning (MRP II), collectively referred to as MRP, are the names for administrative software that help automate the production planning operation. They build a model of the manufacturing process, allowing managers to more effectively plan and control it. MRP systems can schedule deliveries of raw materials and coordinate manufacturing operations to produce products faster and more efficiently. In addition, MRP systems can integrate inventory, delivery dates, and sales forecasts to determine scheduling needs and coordinate accounts payable and receivable, shipping notices, billing, and time reporting requirements.

ROBOTS

The word robot was first used in 1923 by Czech playwright Karel Capek in his play *R.U.R. (Rossum's Universal Robots)* because at that time the word was used to mean slave labor. Then in 1936, the term *automation* (short for automatic operation) was coined by

Computer-aided manufacturing includes computer-controlled robots for welding.

Delmar Harder, a plant manager at General Motors. In those days, visions of a mechanized world in which humans were a mere cog in the industrial machine were very popular, and the terms robot and automation are having a difficult time shaking their negative connotations.

Actually, the vision that many people have of humanlike walking talking robots is far from the reality of the working robots in factories. A *robot* is a programmable, general-purpose manipulator. Robots in the factory are replacing *hard automation*, that is, dedicated equipment that can perform only a single operation under a carefully controlled set of circumstances. Hard automation equipment is very specialized and, therefore, not adaptable to a wide variety of tasks. The design challenge in robotics is now to make general-purpose robots that can easily be programmed to perform a wide variety of tasks, such as a painting machine that could adapt to painting an object of any shape.

FACTORY AUTOMATION

As you learned in Chapter 3, today's factories must be able to respond rapidly to changing consumer demand and economic conditions. In a highly competitive environment, such as the automobile industry, manufacturing must be more flexible and be able to switch easily from one model of car to another. Until recently, such flexibility could only be gained by adding more factory workers.

The situation has changed, however, thanks to computers, robots, and automation. *Factory automation* is characterized by three features: (1) flexibility, or the capability to perform different tasks; (2) ease of training, or the capability of people to program new tasks; and (3) the ability to perceive conditions that may be unpredictable and plan appropriate actions.

Now people are beginning to view robots not only as machines that replace people but as extensions of a company's information system, in which all aspects of manufacturing—materials handling, design, administration, production, assembly, quality control, packaging, and shipping—are automated and coordinated in one factory information system. The following sections present a hypothetical combination of many existing technologies integrated into one complete automated factory. This scenario shows the impact of computers and robots on factory automation.

Materials Handling

Materials handling refers to the moving and tracking of raw materials and parts into and through a factory. Materials handling benefits from robotics and automation because these technologies reduce costs and increase efficiency in a critical portion of the manufacturing process.

Robotics. A robot designed for materials handling.

For example, a relatively new approach to inventory control that has been adopted from Japanese automated factories is called the *just-in-time* approach. In this approach, just enough parts are received daily to meet the day's demands for producing goods. It is designed to reduce the expensive costs of storing and paying for inventory but also relies on (1) outside suppliers being able to supply the needs of the producing factory with parts that have no defects and (2) an automated system for materials handling. When a part comes into a factory, information about it gets entered into a materials-handling and tracking system. The technology of bar-code scanning that is so popular in supermarkets is playing an important part in factory automation. Every time a bar-coded part is moved or handled, its movement can be recorded and analyzed by computers.

Robots are beginning to play a major role in automated materials handling. One such device, called a bin-picking robot, combines a vision system and a touch-sensitive gripper. A *vision system* uses a television camera with image processing software. The robot is trained to recognize objects by presenting samples to the camera that are then stored and used for matching when the robot is in use.

Such systems are useful in applications where parts are stored randomly. Examples of bin picking include feeding machine tools, assembling products, sorting parts of similar size or shape, and loading or unloading materials from storage. Bin picking can eliminate the cost of machinery required to stack materials or feed them into the manufacturing process in some predetermined manner.

Also, robots could be used to carry parts in clean rooms where people might contaminate the air and in dangerous places, such as nuclear power plants.

Production and Assembly

During production, parts are stored in automated warehouse racks, where robots control scheduling and routing to assembly locations. Some factories consist of islands of automation with robotic workstations and automated storage and retrieval racks for parts. Mobile robots, technically called *guided vehicle systems*, have been designed to transport materials from the automated racks to the robotic workstations. These vehicles currently find their way around a factory by following sensing wires embedded in the factory floor, but they are starting to rely on vision processing techniques to see where they are going.

Assembly refers to the actual putting together of a product. An assembly line is where the classic techniques of hard automation have been used for many years. Examples can be found in any high-volume assembly line, where machines replace human workers. The choice between hard automation and robotics is leaning more and more toward robotics. High-technology products generally have shorter life cycles, and product improvements mean changes in manufacturing and assembly. Programmable robots can perform a wide variety of assembly tasks and, therefore, are more flexible and adaptable. Hard automation can usually perform only a single task, and when the product changes, the machinery becomes obsolete.

Several computer hardware companies have designed their factories with robots in mind. IBM, for example, builds its 3090 mainframes in a highly automated plant in Poughkeepsie, New York. There robots automatically assemble components on printed circuit boards and search for defects, while guided vehicle systems transport parts throughout the factory. Apple's Macintosh factory in Fremont, California, is similarly automated.

Inspection and Quality Control

Inspection can be accomplished by robots with vision systems. The current goal is to develop vision modules that can be integrated with existing robots. This offers greater flexibility as general-purpose vision systems are expected to expand inspection into all stages of the manufacturing process. In dramatic cases, inspection robots can go where it is impractical for people to go. For example, mobile robots are used to inspect radioactive areas of nuclear power plants.

Robotics. *Bin-picking robot at work.*

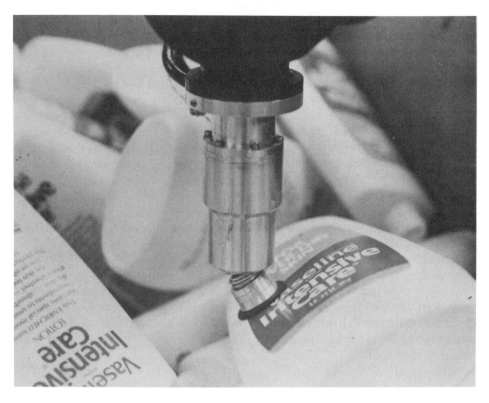

Robotics. *Robot arms can feel an object's shape and manipulate it.*

Computer-integrated manufacturing. *The IBM Automated Logistics and Production System is used by Ford to produce instrument clusters used in light trucks.*

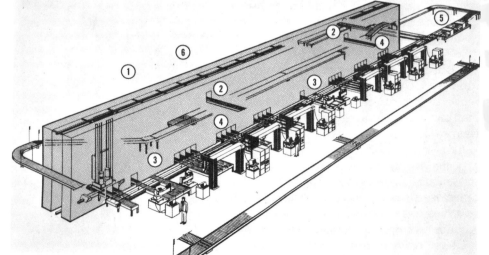

Packaging and Shipping

In the final stages of building products, automated materials handling robots count, package, and stack completed products. While the physical movement is occurring, information about the products is automatically entered into inventory, shipping, and ordering information systems.

Many companies have progressed to the stage where robots perform some of the work in a factory. Only a few companies, such as IBM and Apple, have specifically designed their products and factories so that robots and other automated systems do most of the work.

COMPUTER-INTEGRATED MANUFACTURING

When all the previously mentioned independent manufacturing operations are integrated, and the resulting factory automation system is linked to the design and administrative (e.g., cost accounting and project management) departments of an organization, the result is *computer-integrated manufacturing (CIM)*, that is, computer-based systems in different company departments that integrate independent design, manufacturing, and administrative functions. CIM coordinates all aspects of design and production, resulting not only in higher efficiency but better decisions. It makes no sense, for example, for a designer to design a product that cannot be produced by manufacturing. Nor does it make sense to try to manufacture a product that cannot be profitable.

CIM requires that the computers and machines within an organization be tied together in networks. But technology is simply a means to an end. CIM also requires an unprecedented degree of communication among designers, planners, shop-floor technicians, managers, and customers. In much the same way that the use of information systems in strategic ways has become the major goal of service organizations, CIM is playing a major role in attaining the strategic goals of a manufacturing organization.

COMPUTERS IN RETAILING

Almost all retailing organizations from department stores to supermarkets are extremely competitive. To meet the pressure of competition, organizations are changing their focus from the distribution of goods and service in which computer systems are used to keep track of inventories and business records, and to prepare reports, to organizations that are driven by customer demand. Computers and information systems are helping to accomplish that goal.

POINT-OF-SALE SYSTEMS

Increasingly, retailers such as department stores and supermarkets are using computer systems to collect data about their sales and customers at the point of sale. *Point-of-sale systems* are computer input devices located at the point at which goods and services are paid for. For example, supermarkets have long used scanners at checkout counters to record sales. In such an application, scanners reduce labor costs, make the checkout process more accurate by eliminating misreading of price tags and improper cash register reading, thus enhancing customer service.

Today, scanners serve as input devices to sophisticated information systems that identify best-selling products, eliminate less popular products, and provide electronic coupons for discounts on promotional items, and, if desired, subtract directly the amount of purchase from the customer's bank account. Scanners linked to warehouse systems identify the profit margins generated by individual products and trigger orders for more goods. Scanners linked to MIS systems track customer's purchase patterns, and forecast sales.

Traditionally, manufacturers have sold to wholesalers, who have sold to retailers, who have sold to final buy-

ers. Computers make possible the by-passing of many of the steps in this traditional chain. Manufacturers or distributors can advertise directly, and customers can use toll-free 800 numbers to place orders. Computer-controlled systems can custom package and label the goods and have them shipped directly to the customer's address. No warehousing or shelf stocking is required; the customer usually pays less for the goods, and the manufacturer makes a greater profit margin on the goods sold.

CUSTOMER SERVICE

The nature of customer service is not only changing, but it is becoming an ever-more-important part of the competitive retailing industry. Not only must a company have friendly people to handle customer service, they must leverage technology to deal with customers. Information systems help companies to get closer to their customer's needs and wants.

For example, in addition to salespeople listening to and reacting to complaints about merchandise, some company's information systems permit salespeople to consult a computer to while talking to a customer or drafting a letter of response. The system can

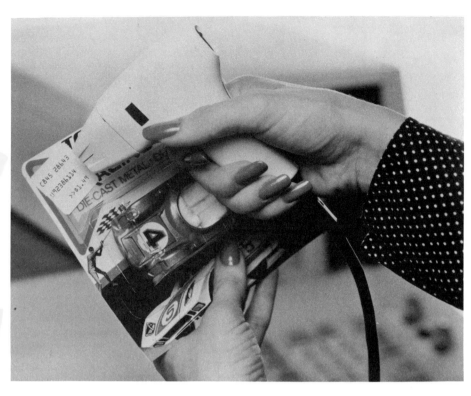

Scanning the price tag. Shown here is an optical character recognition wand that reads the inventory and price information from merchandise tags and relays it to a point-of-sale terminal.

determine whether correct items are in stock and how soon they can be delivered, and can answer questions about how to use specific products. By storing customer, inventory, and product information in a database, and making it accessible for viewing on a display screen, customer service is faster and more efficient.

On a nationwide scale, the General Electric answering center uses similar database technology to handle questions about the company's products, determine whether items are in stock, and give the customer delivery dates.

Some companies are experimenting with self-service customer information systems. Freestanding kiosks, equipped with computers and touch display screens, give a customer the ability to access do-it-yourself guidelines at a hardware store; electronic catalogs at a department store; or information about makes, models, and options at a car dealership. In addition, customer's often perceive the self-service approach as a value-added service.

Maintaining customer satisfaction is often as important as the initial sale. Existing customers and repeat orders usually require less time and resources than the initial sale and are inherently more profitable. Personal computer software vendors, for example, have found that their customer databases are indeed a valuable resource. Suppose a customer buys a software package and sends in the registration form. Because software is a highly competitive business, product upgrades are the norm rather than the exception. The customer can be offered a low-cost upgrade via direct mail, which is considerably cheaper for the vendor than a retail sale. The customer gets a low-cost upgrade; the vendor can sell additional products at a much higher profit margin because the vendor can bypass the wholesale and retail channels.

HOTELS, AIRLINES, AND RESTAURANTS

The retail industry is not the only one that uses information systems to get closer to their customer's needs and wants. In hotels, front-desk systems retrieve a guest record when a credit card is passed through a special reader. Some larger hotels keep guest preference profiles on computer. When the guest checks in, everything is already ready.

In most service industries, using the computer to automate the manual work makes it easier to provide more personalized service to the customer.

COMPUTERS IN HEALTH CARE AND MEDICINE

Computers play an important role in health care and medicine. Doctors, nurses, and other medical practitioners have adapted to computers because they already depend heavily on specialized information to perform their jobs. Having an information system to store and retrieve that information is a natural extension of an already complex and information-intensive process. In addition, with today's emphasis on government involvement and large-scale health care providers, controlling costs requires technology to improve the efficiency of administrative and patient record keeping and reduce expenses without sacrificing the overall quality of health care.

PATIENT MONITORING

Intensive care units are an early example of computer-controlled patient monitoring. At the bedside, critically ill patients are connected to a wide variety of sensors that measure vital signs such as heartbeat, breathing, and brain activity. If any of these vital signs change dramatically, an alarm is sounded and the appropriate life-saving techniques are administered.

Patient monitoring is not confined to the bedside however. Some persons with illnesses that require constant medication can benefit from portable or implanted monitoring and control devices. Diabetics, for example, can wear an implanted insulin pump that monitors the persons blood sugar and releases precise doses of insulin to control the blood-sugar level.

Computers in health care. Doctors, nurses, and other medical practitioners have adapted to computers because thay already depend heavily on specialized information to perform their jobs.

DIAGNOSTIC SYSTEMS

Doctors who are faced with specialized problems can consult experimental specialized programs that serve as a diagnostic assistant. Beginning in the mid-1970s, a class of computer programs known as *expert systems*— programs that serve as intelligent assistants to human experts—began appearing in medical schools and research centers. One such program, MYCIN, helps to diagnose certain classes of brain infections. A program called PUFF assists in diagnosing certain lung disorders. A program called ONCOCIN assists physicians in managing complex drug regimens for cancer patients. And a program called CADUCEUS simulates the diagnostic skills of an individual physician, Dr. Jack Meyers of the University of Pittsburgh.[1]

Such programs are still considered strictly experimental. But in test cases, the programs perform credibly, and many doctors are confident that these expert systems will eventually provide valuable assistance in areas in which specialized knowledge is a scarce resource. Such programs would be invaluable, for example, in the Third World, or in remote areas in which too few doctors must battle too many diseases, epidemics, and famines.

MEDICAL IMAGING

Traditional imaging systems such as X-ray machines and magnetic resonance imaging produce two-dimensional (2-D) photographs. By linking these devices to computers equipped with three-dimensional (3-D) modeling software, it is possible to convert 2-D images into 3-D images, and, in experimental systems, holographic 3-D images. Such systems show significant diagnostic promise. Accurate information is often hard to obtain from flat 2-D images. Three-dimensional images might allow surgeons, for example, to diagnose problems without resorting to exploratory surgery.

In a related application, prosthesis image systems are used to create accurate models and simulate reconstructive processes step by step so a surgeon can better plan his or her work. It is also possible to use computer-aided methods to design custom replacement parts.

Computers are also playing a role in medical education. In the future, health care teams composed of attending physicians, residents, and interns may use bedside personal computer-based systems that provide information for patient diagnosis and treatment. For example, if the patient has a bleeding ulcer, interns will be able to look up basic material on what causes this condition. They will also be able to consult specialized reference material for additional details about the condition.

While today, medical technology such as patient monitoring, expert diagnostic systems, and medical imaging systems are so experimental or expensive that they are limited to a few wealthy or well-insured patients, the potential cost of software-based personal computer systems is extremely low, and these systems may soon be widespread in nonindustrial nonurban cultures in which medical expertise is still a rarity.[2]

COMPUTERS IN THE ARTS AND DESIGN

Historically, the dubious aesthetic quality of computer-generated images coupled with high cost of computer graphic tools had been the primary barrier to widespread adoption of computers by artists and designers. The computer was often a high-priced specialized tool on which the artist or designer rented time or shared among a group of users.

But for many people, art and design are a business, not a hobby. The most widespread and rapid advances in using computers are in art and design made for commercial purposes. Commercial artists and designers quickly realized that technology is a powerful tool to reduce the cost and time involved in producing the medium in which they work. For example, the evolution of printing technology from movable type to computerized typesetting and imaging systems opened up myriad new cost-effective communication possibilities for graphic designers.

While few artists or designers have completely traded in their traditional tools for electronic tools, two trends are emerging: (1) Low-cost personal computers are performing many of the tasks once relegated to their larger special-purpose ancestors. (2) Some artists and designers are beginning to view the computer as a new medium that integrates print, television, music, and other communication media of the past and present. For example, presentations at meetings were once synonymous with slides and transparencies. The computer was simply a tool used to produce slides and transparencies. Today, complex computerized presentations that incorporate sound, animation, color, along with still images are an entirely new form of communication made possible by computer technology.

THE VISUAL MEDIA

The visual media, such as print, film, television, and photography, demand visual problem-solving skills. The tools to help solve problems visually can be grouped together under the broad term computer graphics. As you learned in Chapter 2, draw and paint programs form the foundation for creating a wide variety of digital images.

Art

Artists have always created images, even in ancient cultures. Because the computer is a tool that characterizes our contemporary culture, it is natural that some artists would gravitate toward using computers to experiment, explore, play with, and give shape to their subject matter and ideas.

Computer-assisted art takes many forms from replacing pen and pencil as the drawing tool to mixing colors by manipulating light on a display screen to creating many possible permutations of basic forms and shapes. In addition to computers, some contemporary artists use high-technology tools such as lasers, holograms, photocopiers, and facsimile machines to explore themes related to technology or employ that particular technology to help convey meaning.

Movies and Television

In science fiction movies and television shows, we are often treated to spectacular images of outer space and dramatic shots of distant worlds. Yet there is no navigation of outer space behind these images let alone a camera to photograph them. Today's graphic software makes imaginary scenes and realistic images indistinguishable from photographs, yet they exist only as binary digits in the memory of a computer.

A motion picture is made up of a series of still frames. To create the illusion of motion, the frames are displayed at a rate of 24 per second. During editing multiple images, such as a live actor superimposed over an artificial background, must be combined into each of the single frames. Computers can coordinate the editing and make it easier to manipulate and combine the images. The computer makes possible more precise positioning when fine-tuning, composing, or resequencing frames, thus simplifying a complex editing process and speeding it up dramatically.

Keep in mind that while computer-generated effects are indeed an extraordinary technical accomplishment, the more spectacular the effect, the more expensive it generally is to produce. This is the reason that the most impressive special effects are usually confined to high-budget movies and television commercials.

SOUND

Sound is a communication medium that expresses ideas in ways that cannot be approached by any of the other arts. Sound can include the human voice, music, nonmusical sounds such as those found in nature, or synthetic sounds such as the beep of a computer or home appliance to give you feedback. In entertainment, sound is essential to music, and is an important part of television and film. The ability to produce high-quality sound has always existed in musical instruments, but it has been only since the advent of the synthesizer that computers have played a dominant role in the production of music.

A *synthesizer* is a device that electronically generates sound instead of picking it up with a microphone. Most music synthesizers come with a pianolike keyboard. Some have guitar fret boards, drum pads, or wind instrument finger pieces. Most can play more than one sound at a time. Music synthesizers were once large devices relegated to music professionals, but today, you can buy high-quality inexpensive models in any consumer electronics store and add-in synthesizer boards can be found that plug into the expansion slot of a personal computer. When coupled with computers, synthesizers make the exploration, composition, and performance of electronic music an inexpensive art medium.

A technology called the *musical instrument digital interface (MIDI)* interconnects electronic music instruments and computers. When coupled with a *sequencer*—software that can capture, edit, and play back music—complex electronic arrangements are made possible through a wide variety of editing options. Just as a word processor can replace a writer's typewriter or pencil and paper, sequencer software can replace a composer's pencil and paper score.

In live performances, such as rock concerts, live and recorded sound are often indistinguishable, thanks to the use of computerized backing tracks. Promoters defend the use of preprogrammed music, arguing that fans want to see a perfect reenactment of an MTV video or a recording. However, some legislators believe the practice is deceptive and propose legislation that would require promoters to inform ticket buyers in advance whether preprogrammed music will be used in a live performance.

DESIGN AUTOMATION

Designers in professions such as clothing, publications, architecture, and industrial products use electronic drawing boards extensively to help automate the mechanics of creativity. Bor-

What computers do in the arts. *This musician is using his personal computer to compose, record, and play back music.*

Computer-aided design *helps this architectural firm solve design problems.*

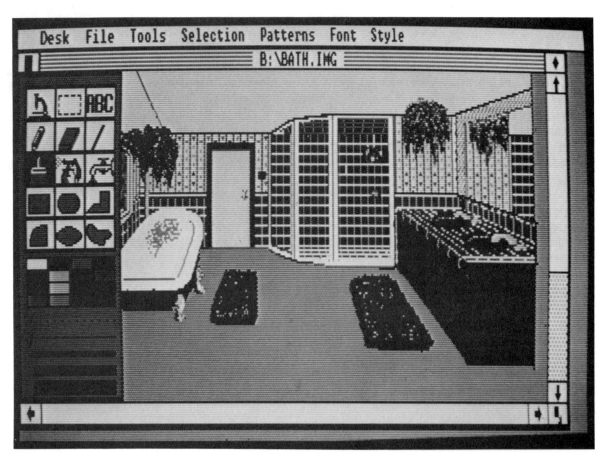

Computer-aided design. *Display produced by a draw program helps architect's visualize their proposed designs.*

rowing from the techniques of computer-aided design that were pioneered in the manufacturing disciplines, a variety of designers are using computer software to increase productivity and help speed up the design process.

Architects, for example, used to design buildings manually. The design process began when an architect drew a rough sketch, which is the high-level design of what the building is supposed to look like, and how it interfaces with the surrounding environment. Then, a scale model was hand built, critiqued, and modified. After client approval, blueprints and specifications were created for the contractor.

Today's architects use computer-aided design methods extensively. In much the same way that power tools increase the productivity of the carpenter, CAD increases the productivity of the architect. In addition to automating the drawing process, CAD enables the architect to build computer models of the building, rotate the de-

sign to view the building from various angles, allow the client to take a simulated walkthrough of the building, simulate its heating and cooling subsystem performance under various climatic conditions, and create blueprints and specifications for the building.

Clothes designers in large corporations such as Esprit, Levi Strauss, and Benetton use CAD to design patterns, colors, and clothing shapes. In addition, designs, patterns, and colors can be archived in databases. The designer can call up a previously designed pattern, for example, modify it slightly, and feed the design to automated machinery that cuts patterns out of fabric.

COMPUTERS IN GOVERNMENT, MILITARY, AND LAW

Professionals in government, military, and law have become some of the most sophisticated users of information systems. They quickly learn the importance of intelligent information gathering and manipulation and, as a result, information systems are the lifeblood of these professions.

GOVERNMENT

Federal, state, and local government professionals, as well as their adversaries (e.g., lobbying groups such as the National Rifle Association and the Sierra Club), are concerned with forecasting trends, planning services, developing public policy, enforcing laws, and protecting the welfare of citizens.

Politicians rely heavily on their constituent databases and lobbying groups on their membership databases to track people's profiles, contribution histories, topics of concern, and levels of experience with specific issues. In their effort to sway public policy, for example, special interest groups can extract specific members' names and addresses and send out letters to inform them of pending legislation.

In recent years, awareness has increased of the damage being done to the environment as a result of society's actions. This is, of course, a broad and complex set of problems that defies simple solutions. But one technology called a *Geographical Information System (GIS)* is lending a helping hand.

Geographical information system data include digitized maps and images of distributions of statistical data such as populations of humans, plants, and animals. Geographical databases can help planners set up displays of watershed areas, soil and water districts, property lines, school and tax districts, and zoning boundaries. For example, if planners need to know how a watershed area will be affected by new development, they can view the watershed area and zoning boundaries simultaneously, in order to make more informed decisions about the impact of the development on the environment.

Other GIS applications include viewing population and school district boundaries simultaneously to redraw district lines and plan school bus routes. Fire departments can study patterns of streets and traffic flows

along them at various hours of the day and plan the fastest route to a fire.

Government agencies, such as police departments, sheriff's offices, emergency medical services, and fire departments, leverage technology with computer-aided dispatch, communications, record keeping, and jail-management functions.

And technology is beginning to find its way into the legislative branch. Recently, the Michigan State Senate installed a legislative information system that puts a personal computer at every senators' desk. Using them, the lawmakers can review and vote on bills and, during slack periods, write letters and communicate with their offices via electronic mail.

MILITARY

Ever since the late 1950s, the U.S. military has used computers for defense. The nation's first air-defense system, a network of computers linked to radar stations, the Semi-Automatic Ground Environment, or SAGE, pioneered the use of real-time interactive graphics. (See Appendix A under "Whirlwind.") Today, the North American Aerospace Defense Command (NORAD) performs a similar defense function by guarding the United States against missile attack.

On the drawing boards is the Strategic Defense Initiative or SDI, a computer-controlled system that will use satellites to detect and lasers to destroy enemy missiles. SDI is very controversial, because it will be so complex and will rely so heavily on unproven untested hardware and software. Critics, for example, point out the possibility of a false alarm thus triggering a U.S. attack or even a nuclear war.

On a smaller scale, weapon systems, such as those found in submarines, tanks, and aircraft, use sophisticated technology for navigation, tracking, and control. The person using such systems has at his or her disposal graphic representations of landscapes with grids marking optimal paths to targets. Eye-tracking devices help aim the weapons at the target at which the person is looking.

One of the most impressive military computer applications involves train-

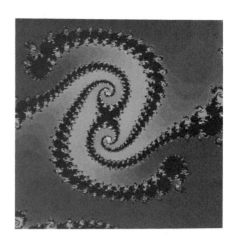

Computer-aided design. *Fractal (fractional dimension) curves and surfaces can be generated by computers. They are used to model natural objects, such as trees, mountains, and landscapes.*

Computers in government. *Incident reports and citation forms are stored electronically in the policeman's notebook-sized computer eliminating manual data entry.*

ing pilots with flight simulators. A *simulation* is a computerized representation of a real-world event or series of actions. Although flight simulators also help train civilian pilots, the most sophisticated versions can be found in the military.

A pilot, seated in a replica of a cockpit, views realistic simulated images displayed on the cockpit windows. As the pilot flies the simulator, the view changes immediately in response to altitude, speed, and position. Realistic special effects such as fog, airplane malfunctions, or enemy attack, can be added to the simulation. Such realism is made possible by drawing upon an immense visual database that contains data digitized from scale models, photographs, and topological maps. Special-purpose computers generate and display images in real time, in order to create the illusion of motion.[3]

Although the cost of military flight simulators is enormous, a simulation costs less than its real-world counterpart. By having pilots practice with simulators rather than real airplanes, the military avoids the risk of losing an expensive plane and worse, losing an irreplaceable life—that of the pilot. And, of course, without simulators, training astronauts for a space shuttle mission would probably be out of the question.

What does the military do to prevent the details of its newest Stealth bomber from being leaked to the KGB? Preventing compromises in national security and defense depends on limiting access by unauthorized people. Photographs, signatures, and fingerprints have been used for identification purposes long before the advent of computers. But the problem of verifying a person's identity has led to an interesting high-technology solution.

Biometric devices are instruments that perform mathematical analysis of biological characteristics. An individual's speech, handwriting, fingerprints, or even eye retina features can serve as a unique patterns for identification purposes. Biometric identification systems that can digitize, store, and compare these patterns can be used to verify a person's identity.

Biometric identification systems are still in the experimental stage, but when they become reliable enough, they are expected to provide a more accurate means of verifying peoples' identity at classified and secret locations throughout the military and government.

LAW

Today's law firms are characterized by the need to manage, process, and interpret large and complex amounts of information. Legal documents, such as briefs, transcripts, notes, laws, codes, and rules are increasingly available in electronic versions. Court reporters, for example, routinely make their transcripts available as text files that can be directly input to a word processor.

A wealth of historical legal data are available in the form of on-line databases. Law firms can subscribe to Westlaw and Lexis, firms that specialize in publishing precedents, decisions, administrative rulings, trade regulations, and laws governing securities and taxes. In addition, some information providers are starting to offer similar information on CD ROM databases.

Another type of database software that is particularly useful for attorneys and paralegal professionals is called *full-text retrieval software.* It allows text to be indexed, edited, annotated, linked, and searched for in an electronic document. In a trial, for example, attorneys may need to review, track, and cross-reference the testi-

Graphics. A U.S. Air Force F-15 flight simulator equipped with a real-time visual system enhances pilot training. High-resolution real-time animation (up to 50 frames per second) can be generated to provide realistic simulations.

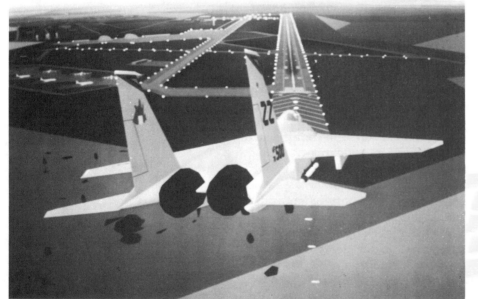

mony of witnesses. Using full-text retrieval software, the transcripts for the trial can be indexed, annotated, and searched to verify the consistency of a witnesses testimony right in the courtroom.

During the courtroom portions of trials, attorneys use desktop presentations to illustrate complex ideas to the jury in cases such as patent infringement or medical injury.

COMPUTERS IN EDUCATION

The intrigue of new computers and new software developments in education is highly compelling. Computers are one of the newest and most versatile tools of the teaching trade. Computer and communication technology are making possible imaginative approaches to teaching traditional subjects and are motivating teachers and students to try new ways of information gathering and learning.

LEARNING

The oldest instructional application of computers is *computer-assisted instruction (CAI),* which provides instruction and drill-and-practice in basic computation and language skills. The basic philosophy of CAI involves a direct link between student and software and the transfer of basic instructional decisions from teacher to curriculum developer.

Using CAI, information is presented on the computer's display, students are asked to respond, and their response is evaluated. If the student is correct, he or she moves on; if incorrect, similar problems are given until the correct response is elicited.

Advocates of CAI argue that students who have not mastered basic skills can benefit from drill and practice and that the computer helps to motivate students and frees the teacher to provide individual instruction. Critics of CAI argue that drill-and-practice tasks can be done just as easily without computers using, for example, flash cards or some other

form of drill. Hundreds of studies have been conducted to determine the effectiveness of CAI, and while the results concerning the effects of CAI are generally favorable, the research conducted provides little insight into how, what, and why students learn when they use CAI.[4]

In response to such criticism, educators have developed *intelligent CAI* programs in which students interact with the computer rather than respond to it in a predefined manner. Intelligent CAI can generate and solve problems, store and retrieve data, diagnose students' misconceptions, select appropriate teaching strategies, and carry on dialogs with students. Most of these programs incorporate simulations and games that allow students to try out their evolving models of knowledge in a particular area.[5]

ELECTRONIC BOOKS

New software tools and new ideas for user interfaces makes possible the presentation of materials that are manipulable in several different ways. One such example is the electronic book, in which the reader manipulates computer technology instead of printed pages.

For example, Sony Corp. of Japan uses a palm-sized CD player for reading books recorded on 3-inch compact disks. Each disk can store approximately 100,000 pages of text, the

Biometric devices. Shown to the left of the personal computer is IBM's signature verification hardware. A user seeking access to a secure system signs on with a biometric pen. The dynamics of the signature are compared with the authorized user's signature stored in the smart card. The system can detect differences in handwriting dynamics to deny unauthorized access.

Electronic books. *Guide allows the creation of electronic books complete with pictures, contents, and the means to navigate through pages.*

equivalent of 300 paperback books. The device, called the Data Discman, has a 10-line display screen and a small keyboard for selecting specific entries or portions of the text.

However, when an application involves presenting massive amounts of information on a computer screen, such as a reference work or computer-based training, a solution that allows the reader to interact with the document and adapt the document to his or her needs is particularly useful. The terms hypertext and hypermedia were coined in 1965 by designer and visionary Ted Nelson. *Hypertext* systems allow the creation of electronic books in which an author can link information and create nonlinear paths through related material. *Hypermedia* is an extension of hypertext that includes graphics, video, sound, and music.

One such hypermedia program, called Guide, is a software tool for creating and retrieving electronic documents. In its use, Guide bears some resemblance to an outliner program. In an electronic document, the first thing the user sees is the table of contents. Point and click on chapter one and more detailed information appears, the chapter contents for example. Point and click again and selected text in the chapter appears. Words or phrases in the chapter can be designated as but-

tons so that the reader can point and click and easily navigate through multiple layers or levels of information. And pointing and clicking can bring up a graphic or trigger a videodisk sequence as well. An electronic book can include full-motion color video, sound, color photography and line art. For example, Cornell University Medical College uses a videodisk, 18 networked Macintoshes, and Guide to teach a pathology class.

FUTURE DIRECTIONS

The future of computers in education is dependent upon developing highly productive information-rich models for learning. Classroom instruction is currently considered more effective than computer-based training, and there is no question that teachers are more valuable than computers. But in contrast to many less revolutionary technologies, the potential of new computer and communication technology is so great, that innovative educational applications are likely to continue to be rapidly developed. They include [6]

• Intelligent tutoring computer systems that can simulate and make the knowledge and services of an expert tutor available to the learner.

• Simulations and exploratory

laboratory experiments that build student understanding through exploration, manipulation, and guided discovery.

- Integrated tools that enable learners to concentrate on more cognitively demanding tasks.

- New assessment techniques that track learning, diagnose students' conceptual understandings, and evaluate the attainment of a range of skills.

- New design/knowledge kits that enable teachers to create their own teaching materials.

- New curricula based on a shifting emphasis from what to learn to how to learn.

COMPUTERS AND CAREERS

In the computer-related fields, there are a number of traditional occupations along with several emerging career opportunities. For example, as factory automation matures, new careers will open up for scientists, mechanics, and technicians who can work with robots. Similarly, the growth in sales of personal computers is creating opportunities in free-lance software design, computer consulting, and computer store management. The following is a sampling of several occupational descriptions.

COMPUTER OPERATIONS

Computer operators are the people who work with medium- to large-scale computer systems and direct and monitor the operation of the computer system; examples are librarians managing computer output and data-control clerks handling mistakes or corrections in computer-processed information and, more recently, backup, recovery, and security of databases. Also included in this category are data-entry clerks, such as key-to-disk or key-to-tape operators. However, as new ways of entering data into computers without human intervention are developed, these jobs will decline. These positions generally do not require a four-year college degree, but they do require specialized training on the equipment that is to be operated. The

best opportunities for such jobs are in corporations with mainframe computers and data processing departments.

SERVICE AND REPAIR

In this job category, people are often called service technicians; sometimes, in large corporations, they are called field engineers. Service technicians install equipment, perform routine maintenance, and repair faulty or malfunctioning equipment. They need a technical background in engineering or science obtained from a community college training program or a vocational program as well as specific training on the equipment they are going to be servicing. Four-year college degrees are generally not required.

PROGRAMMERS AND ANALYSTS

Applications programmers write general-purpose programs, such as spreadsheets and word processors, and vertical applications, such as accounting programs, inventory-control

Representative job opportunities for those interested in working with computers.

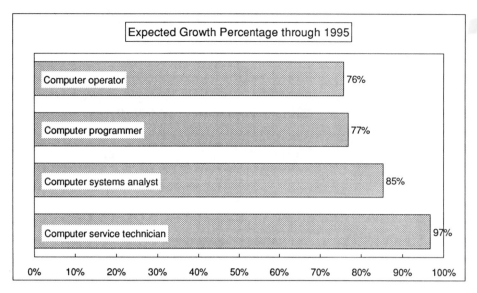

Expected Growth Percentage through 1995

Computer operator	76%
Computer programmer	77%
Computer systems analyst	85%
Computer service technician	97%

0% 10% 20% 30% 40% 50% 60% 70% 80% 90% 100%

The job outlook in brief. *Four computer-related job categories show some of the most dramatic growth potential over the next few years. (From* Employment Projections for 1995. *U.S. Bureau of Labor Statistics: April 1986.)*

programs, and other business programs. They fall into two categories: commercial or business application programmers and scientific or engineering programmers. A person in this category usually has a two-year or four-year college degree in business or science depending on the specific category.

Systems programmers write operating systems, compiler programs, database programs, and utility programs. In a medium- or large-sized organization, systems programmers will support the application programmers. Newer job trends include communication, network, graphic, and database specialists. The position requires a two-year or four-year college degree, and computer science is the preferred major.

Programmer analysts combine the functions of systems analysis and programming. A trend in large organizations is to combine the functions. A systems analyst performs analysis and design of new systems. A systems analyst usually has a four-year college degree and a knowledge of business, often obtained with a master's degree in business.

SUPPORT

The support category includes technical writers and editors, who are responsible for producing and maintaining all types of documentation, and database specialists, who design and control the use of an organization's

data resources. Technical writers and editors generally have English or journalism degrees and technical backgrounds. It is easier for a person with a writing background to move into technical writing and editing than it is for a person with a technical background to break into the technical writing field. Database specialists are often systems analysts who design and create the data structures. Skill requirements include knowledge of programming and systems methods. One interesting avenue for entry into the database specialist field is through library science. Many schools are revamping their library science programs by adding information science courses.

SALES AND MARKETING

Sales representatives can be found from large corporations to small computer stores. Sales is a unique profession and requires skills in detecting, analyzing, and satisfying customer needs and wants. Most organizations require employees to have some sales experience, so it is easier for a person with sales background in another field to move into computer sales than it is for a new person to break into computer sales. A four-year business or technical college degree is very helpful.

Marketing support people provide sales backup, training, and customer support. They need more specific or technical knowledge of the product or service than do the sales people, so often a two-year or four-year degree is preferred.

Rapid technological change creates many opportunities in public relations in which people must inform and educate the media about new products and services. This usually involves working with artists and designers to create new and innovative promotion materials and campaigns.

DESIGN AND ENGINEERING

Computer hardware engineers and designers generally have four-year college degrees or advanced degrees in electrical or electronic engineering. Software engineers usually have four-year or advanced degrees in computer science. Highly specialized professions, such as knowledge engineering, usually require doctoral-level degrees in computer science.

MANAGEMENT AND ADMINISTRATION

At the top management level, organizations often have a director of management information systems (MIS) or data processing who is in charge of all information-related resources in the organization. Large organizations often have multiple levels of management. For example, systems director, manager of programming, and manager of operations are all second-level titles. These people generally manage a specific department. A program manager, project supervisor, or software supervisor (a second- or third-level title) generally manages a specific group of programmers or analysts. Often, this involves a specific functional area such as accounting systems or inventory systems.

Management hires, fires, plans, budgets, and shapes organizational policy. This activity usually requires a specific set of skills coupled with experience. Most employers look for several years of experience before they will fill a management-level position. Middle managers often benefit from a technical background in the area they supervise. Frequently, managers combine a technical four-year college degree, such as engineering, with a master's degree in business (MBA).

JOBS, TRAINING, AND THE FUTURE

Steven Jobs, founder and chairman of Next, Inc., once said that "the college worker of today is the knowledge worker of tomorrow." As discussed in Chapter 3, the college degree has become the major form of job certification. Also, the restructuring of U.S. industry from blue-collar work to white-collar work means that several million older workers may have to be retrained. Some estimates show that the number of white-collar workers may

be as high as 80 to 90 percent of the work force by the year 2000. Your college degree, coupled with knowledge of computers and their applications, will be an asset in almost any type of job.

The number of young people entering the work force is declining because the average age of the population is getting older. Although this means less competition, in general, for younger college and vocational school graduates, it also means that more older workers will be in the market for training and retraining.

Larger numbers of women are entering the work force, and the proportion of women in the work force will continue to increase. One current issue in government jobs is the demand for "comparable worth." That means, for example, that a female data-entry clerk's job is comparable in worth and, therefore, in salary to a male truck driver's job. The issue is broader and more difficult to define than equal pay for equal work, but it will spread out of the public sector and into the private sector, with the result that women will be paid more for their work.

Minorities will be a larger share of new entrants into the work force. The task of improving the opportunities for minority workers will become more urgent because with fewer younger workers, employers will seek out and offer training to those they have traditionally ignored.

As mobility and communications become more widespread, more people will work at home. Also, people will spend less time at their jobs, and more people will work as the result of concepts such as job sharing and job rotation. Some companies are now experimenting with telecommuting and job sharing.

Communication skills and general problem-solving abilities will become more important as product life cycles shorten and retraining becomes a normal part of a job. In the electronics industry, for example, it is not uncommon to set up an assembly line and produce a product for a few months and then completely change the product that is being produced. Under such rapidly changing circumstances, companies prefer to retrain their employees because outside institutions cannot move fast enough to meet specific training requirements.

Despite the advances of technology and the importance placed on computer-related skills, people will still be the most important resource an organization possesses. The success of organizations will depend on how well they can utilize the talents and energy of their employees.

REVIEW

Computers and technology have transformed the workplace. They have taken the tedium out of many jobs, which in turn replaces physical demands with mental demands. People require more problem-solving and analytical skills and more education to work in such an environment. Computers and technology are tools and when applied properly, they can enhance work in many professions. In manufacturing, computer-aided methods assist in nearly every aspect of a product's system development life cycle. In retailing, computers are helping businesses meet the pressures of competition and customer demands. In health care and medicine information systems help manage the specialized information necessary for doctors, nurses, and other medical practitioners perform their jobs. In the arts and design, commercial artists and designers use computers as a cost and time saver as well as an aid to the mechanics of creativity. In government, military, and law, computers enhance the process of intelligent information gathering and manipulation. In education, computers have become one of the most versatile tools of the teaching trade. They make possible imaginative approaches to teaching traditional subjects as well as opening up new possibilities for learning. We surveyed traditional jobs in the computer-related fields, as well as presenting some emerging career opportunities. Regardless of which occupational area you choose to pursue, your college degree coupled with a knowledge of computers and their applications will be an asset.

REFERENCES

1. Rheingold, Howard. *Tools for Thought.* New York: Simon & Schuster, 1985. pp. 280-281.

2. Ibid., p. 280.

3. Conlan, Roberta, ed. *Computer Images.* Chicago, Il.: Time-Life Books, 1986. pp. 112-113.

4. U.S. Congress, Office of Technology Assessment. *Power On: New Tools for Teaching and Learning.* OTA-SET-379. Washington, D.C.: U.S. Government Printing Office, 1988. pp 45-47.

5. Ibid., p. 48.

6. Ibid., p. 26.

RESOURCES

BOOKS

Bellin, David, and Gary Chapman, eds. *Computers in Battle: Will They Work?* Orlando, Fla.: Harcourt Brace Jovanovich, 1988. No, say the authors, who argue that the military has placed too much faith in computers and who oppose the increasing computerization of the military. The authors are associated with a nationwide organization called Computer Professionals for Social Responsibility.

Goodman, Cynthia. *Digital Visions: Computers and Art.* New York: Harry N. Abrams, 1987. Although this book focuses on the fine arts as opposed to the commercial arts, it is an excellent survey of how computers are used in the arts. It also chronicles the names and works of most of the artists involved in computers for the last 25 years.

Stumpf, Stephen, with Celeste Kennon Rodgers. *Choosing a Career in Business.* New York: Simon & Schuster, 1985. This book covers commercial banking, corporate finance, accounting, product management, advertising, communications, public relations, sales, human resource management, systems analysis, and business consulting.

Workforce 2000: Work and Workers for the Twenty-first Century. Indianapolis, Ind.: Hudson Institute, 1987. A study commissioned by the U.S. Department of Labor that documents labor market trends and projects these trends to the year 2000. A good overview of the research used by the Department of Labor to determine potential policies and programs.

MAGAZINES

Occupational Outlook Quarterly, Bureau of Labor Statistics, U.S. Department of Labor, Washington, D.C. 20212. This magazine is published quarterly and is available for $9 per year. Write to Superintendent of Documents, U.S. Government Printing Office, Washington, D.C. 20402. ISSN 01994786.

Source Edp Computer Annual Handbook. This brochure surveys the computer related fields and provides updated salary data. For a complete copy of Source Edp's latest salary survey, write to Source Edp, Computer Annual Handbook, P.O. Box 7100, Mountain View, Calif. 94309.

STUDY GUIDE

Match the following key terms to the appropriate definition:

A.

1. ____ Computer-aided engineering (CAE)
2. ____ Computer-aided design (CAD)
3. ____ Computer-aided manufacturing (CAM)
4. ____ Robot
5. ____ Hard automation
6. ____ Factory automation
7. ____ Vision system
8. ____ Guided-vehicle systems
9. ____ Computer-integrated manufacturing (CIM)

a. Dedicated equipment that can perform only a single operation under a carefully controlled set of circumstances.

b. Software for designing, analyzing, testing, and modeling parts and components.

c. A system that uses a television camera with image processing software.

d. Computer-based systems in different departments that integrate independent design, manufacturing, and administrative functions.

e. A programmable, general-purpose manipulator.

f. A system that automates the drafting process.

g. Robots that can find their way around a factory either by sensing guide wires or through a vision system.

h. Flexible, easy-to-learn and easy-to-use, intelligent automation.

i. A system that permits computers to control and direct the manufacture and assembly of a product.

B.

10. ____ Point-of-sale systems
11. ____ Synthesizer
12. ____ Sequencer
13. ____ Simulation
14. ____ Biometric devices
15. ____ Full-text-retrieval software
16. ____ Computer-assisted instruction (CAI)
17. ____ Hypertext
18. ____ Hypermedia

a. Computer input devices located at the point at which goods and services are paid for.

b. Instruments that perform mathematical analysis of biological characteristics.

c. An extension of hypertext that includes graphics, video, sound, and music.

d. A device that electronically generates sound instead of picking it up with a microphone.

e. Software that allows text to be indexed, edited, annotated, linked, and searched for in an electronic document.

f. A computerized representation of a real-world event or series of actions.

g. Software that can capture, edit, and play back music.

h. Systems in which an author can link information and create nonlinear paths through related material.

i. Equipment that provides instruction and drill and practice in basic computation and language skills.

True/False:

19. F The effort required to apply computers in the workplace is much more complex than it was a decade ago.

20. F Faced with the choice between hard automation and robotics, industry is leaning more toward hard automation.

21. T Today's retailing organizations are primarily driven by customer demand.

22. F Traditionally, manufacturers have sold directly to final buyers.

23. T Repeat orders are inherently more profitable than the initial sale.

24. F Medical practitioners require little specialized information to perform their jobs.

25. F Expert diagnostic systems are replacing doctors in the process of diagnosing certain disorders.

26. F Among artists, the most widespread and rapid advances in using computers can be found in the fine arts.

27. F The ability to produce high-quality sound has existed only since the advent of the computer.

28. T Computer systems are advanced enough to allow politicians to use them to sway public policy.

29. F The most controversial aspect of the Strategic Defense Initiative is the fact that it will use satellites to detect enemy missiles.

30. F Biometric identification systems are widely used to provide an accurate means of verifying peoples' identity.

31. T Research into CAI provides little insight into how, what, and why students learn when they use CAI.

32. T The number of young people entering the work force is declining.

33. F Communication skills and general problem-solving abilities will become less important as retraining becomes a normal part of a job.

Multiple Choice:

34. Which of the following is not an example of why constant learning and adaptation are necessary to keep pace with rapid technological advances.

  a. As the cost of computing drops, very small organizations can benefit from the use of computers.
  b. Computers replace physical demands with mental demands.
  c. Computers have been embraced by individuals and organizations rather quickly.
  d. Technology is an end in itself.

35. Which of the following is the proper sequence of tools used to take an idea from concept to design to finished product?

  a. Computer-aided design, manufacturing, and engineering.
  b. Computer-aided engineering, design, and manufacturing.
  c. Computer-aided manufacturing, engineering, and design.
  d. None of the above.

36. Manufacturing resource planning or MRP is an example of

  a. Design software.
  b. Engineering software.
  c. Administrative software.
  d. Robotic software.

37. A robot is an example of

  a. Hard automation.
  b. Home automation.
  c. Office automation.
  d. Programmable automation.

38. In retailing, which of the following is not a use of computer systems to meet the competition?

  a. Collecting information at the point of sale.
  b. Advertising directly to final buyers.
  c. Keeping track of inventory.
  d. None of the above.

39. An early example of the role of computers in health care and medicine is a (an)

  a. Intensive care unit.
  b. Implanted monitoring and control devices.
  c. An expert diagnostic system.
  d. Medical imaging systems.

40. The future of computers in education is dependent upon

  a. More classroom instruction.
  b. Creating information-rich models for learning.
  c. Replacing teachers with computers.
  d. More traditional computer-aided instruction.

41. What percentage of the work force will white-collar workers most likely to be by the year 2000?

  a. 50 percent.
  b. 60 percent.
  c. 70 percent.
  d. 80 percent.

42. Why is the number of young people entering the work force declining?

  a. There is more competition for younger workers.
  b. The average age of the population is increasing.
  c. The average age of the population is decreasing.
  d. Fewer older workers are in the market for training and retraining.

43. The most important resource any company possesses is

  a. Factory automation.
  b. Information technology.
  c. People.
  d. Computers.

Thought Questions:

44. Is the prospect of using computers and their applications in your future job exciting? Why or why not?

45. Do you agree with the use of preprogrammed music in a rock concert to justify the claim that fans want a perfect reenactment of an MTV video or a recording. Why or why not?

Projects:

46. On page 96 future directions for computers in education were discussed. Pick one of the applications from the list, research the topic, then write a paper that examines the feasability of the application.

47. In your college or university find an example of a computer-assisted instruction program. Use the program, then write a paper that discusses the pros and cons of the program. Present your findings to the class.

SOFTWARE EXERCISES

Soon, you will be graduating from college and will begin the process of looking for your first full-time job. With a personal computer and appropriate application software, you can (1) create professional-looking documents, such as form letters and resumes, (2) analyze the advantages and disadvantages of various job offers, and (3) organize information about the job search.

Three general-purpose application programs—word processing, spreadsheet, and database—can be effectively used to make your job search more productive, professional, and organized. The following set of problems and procedures can be used in three different ways: (1) if you are using word processing, spreadsheet, and database programs as a part of your class, you can use those programs to hand in completed versions of the following assignments; (2) if you are studying these application programs, you can write the steps in the procedures and perform the exercises by hand; (3) you can also pick a specific word processor, spreadsheet, and database program, consult the documentation, and simulate the assignments.

A SAMPLE RESUME AND COVER LETTER

A resume is a general-purpose document that describes your credentials, experience, and background. Different resumes serve different purposes, so there is no one way to write a resume. However, in all cases a resume must communicate clearly, concisely, and effectively so that it is easy for a company to review your credentials quickly. Quantitatively, that means the resume should be neat, error-free, and formatted. Qualitatively, the resume should make a favorable impression on a prospective employer.

A cover letter is a special-purpose document that is addressed to a specific company or individual, states clearly the position for which you are applying, and might contain some additional information that is tailored to the specific company to which you are applying. The purpose of the resume and cover letter is to help you advance to the next step in the job-seeking process—the interview.

Assignment 1. Prepare a sample resume and cover letter for your own use in applying for a job. Use your own personal data in both documents, and address the cover letter to the fictitious company in the sample cover letter shown here.

Composing the Document

Gather the information you need for the resume. Then, type it and use the sample resume shown here as a format guide.

Revising the Document

Revising the resume means checking it for errors and polishing up the final draft. You can use the cover letter over by simply typing new names, addresses, and dates.

Filing the Document

Save a copy of both documents on your disk. Call them up as needed to produce a new "original" copy for each potential job.

Alternative Assignment 1. Choose a commercial word processing package and consult the documentation to find the commands in the program to accomplish the following tasks. List those commands below.

a. Create a new document titled Resume.

b. Boldface and underline specific words in the resume.

c. Move a paragraph from one location to another in a resume.

d. Search and replace a specific word in the resume.

e. Save the file onto a disk.

f. Print a copy of the document.

```
                        Resume

                  JOSEPH DOUGHERTY

                   1234 Any Street
                 Anytown, Calif. 90224
                   (213) 555-1212

                   Job Objective

         Computer Sales or Marketing Representative

                     Employment

Lab Assistant                              1988-1989
California College Computer Laboratory

Assisted students with programming and homework assignments
in the microcomputer lab.

Sales Clerk                                    1987
ComputerTown

A summer job in which I was responsible for counter and book
sales for a large-sized computer retail store.

Sales Clerk                                1985-1986
Easy Sell Department Store

Summer and part-time work in which I was a salesperson in
the Men's Clothing Department.


                      Education

BA--Business                                   1989
California College, Anytown, Calif.

Special emphasis on business data processing.

Prior to that I graduated from AnyHigh High School (1982) in
Anytown, Calif., where I was born and raised.

                 Student Activities

Student Member: Association for Computing Machinery.

My hobbies include, water sports and sailing; I also have a
Macintosh personal computer that I use for games, education,
and programming.
```

Sample resume.

ANALYZING ALTERNATIVE JOBS

Ideally, a job search involves making choices among several job offers. You will want to pick the best job. Accepting the highest-paying job offer is not the only way to choose between jobs. It also involves considering such factors as location, chances for advancement, and fringe benefits. One common analytical technique is to use some kind of weighing or scoring method for choosing among alternatives. In simplified form, the procedure for such a technique is as follows. You first list the alternatives or options from which to choose; then you define the criteria (in this case the indexed salary) for evaluating the alternatives; and, finally, you evaluate the alternatives to select the best one. For example, suppose that you have been offered jobs in several different cities around the country. Each city has a different cost of living, so you want to adjust the salary offers to reflect the higher and lower costs of living. The following hypothetical salary table shows you how to use such an analysis. Note that when the cost of living is higher than the average, the salary must be adjusted downward. This is done by dividing the average (100) by the cost of living index, then multiplying that by the salary amount.

```
                                        1234 Any Street
                                        Anytown, CA 90224
                                        May 1, 19XX

Mr. John Doe
Personnel Representative
Atlas Computer Corporation
55 Main Street
New York, N.Y. 10011

Dear Mr. Doe:

I am interested in applying for the position of _____
in response to your advertisement in _____. Please
find enclosed a copy of my resume for your consideration.

I have recently completed my degree program in _____
and will be graduating on June 1. I will be available for
employment anytime after that date.

I will be happy to supply you with names of references and
any other material you might need to help your evaluation. I
look forward to your reply.

                                        Sincerely yours,

                                        Joseph Dougherty
                                        Joseph Dougherty
```

*Sample
cover letter.*

Assignment 2. Use a spreadsheet program to construct an adjusted cost-of-living analysis for jobs in alternative cities. After you have finished building the model, use the spreadsheet to answer the following questions:

a. What appears to be the best salary offer based on the adjustment for cost-of-living index?

b. What if the salary offer in Boston was raised to $18,500?

c. What if the salary offer in New York was raised to $23,000?

d. What is the average salary offer?

Alternative Assignment 2. Choose a commercial spreadsheet package and consult the documentation to find the commands to perform the following tasks. List them below.

a. Create a new spreadsheet.

b. Define the formula to compute the average salary offer.

c. Save the file onto a disk.

d. Print a copy of the spreadsheet.

```
                    Cost of
      Alternative   Living    Salary    Adjusted
                    Index     Offer     Salary

      Chicago       120       20,000    16,600
      Boston         95       17,500    18,375
      Los Angeles   100       19,500    19,500
      Tampa          80       16,000    20,000
      Birmingham     80       15,500    19,375
      Minneapolis   110       18,000    16,380
      Seattle        90       18,000    19,980
      San Francisco 130       20,000    15,400
      Phoenix        95       18,500    19,425
      New York      140       21,000    14,910


      Average Offer           ******
```

Sample adjusted salary analysis.

ORGANIZING INFORMATION ABOUT THE JOB SEARCH

An effective job search involves making as many contacts as possible with potential employers. You might be scanning newspaper and magazine ads, checking listings in the placement office at your school, contacting employment agencies, and obtaining word-of-mouth tips from friends, relatives, and other people. It would be nice to have a means for consolidating and organizing this array of information, and a database program can assist you in organizing your list of potential employers.

Assignment 3. Use a database package to create a company contact database. Use the information in the sample data-base entry form shown here as a guide to structure the database.

Alternative Assignment 3. Choose a commercial database package and consult the documentation to find the commands to perform the following tasks. List them below.

a. Design the entry form.

b. Search the database for all companies located in California.

c. Design a report layout that includes position, company name, address, city, state, ZIP code, and telephone number.

d. Print a listing of the entire database.

```
    Company.........:_____
    Adddress........:_____
    City............:_____
    State...........:__
    Zip.............:_____
    Telephone.......:_____
    Extension.......:_____

    Job Applied For.:_____
    Date Contacted..:_____
    Person Contacted:_____
    Date of Reply...:_____
    Salary Offered..:_____
    Remarks.........:_____
                    :_____
                    :_____
```

Sample database entry form.

ANSWERS

1. b, **2.** f, **3.** i, **4.** e, **5.** a, **6.** h, **7.** c, **8.** g, **9.** d, **10.** a, **11.** d, **12.** g, **13.** f, **14.** b, **15.** e, **16.** i, **17.** h, **18.** c, **19.** F, **20.** F, **21.** T, **22.** F, **23.** T, **24.** F, **25.** F, **26.** F, **27.** F, **28.** T, **29.** F, **30.** F, **31.** T, **32.** T, **33.** F, **34.** d, **35.** b, **36.** c, **37.** d, **38.** d, **39.** a, **40.** b, **41.** d, **42.** b, **43.** c.

HARDWARE

PREVIEW

In Section One, you discovered that a computer was a system, an orderly arrangement of parts that work together to accomplish their intended purpose. This section groups the different components into the major functional categories: input, output, processor and memory, mass storage, and communications.

Computer systems come in a wide variety of makes and models, and there are a number of different devices that can be attached to them. A computer system can be put together in many different ways. It all depends on what you intend to do with it.

In any computer system there are choices that can be made about specific devices and components. These choices are influenced by cost, compatibility, function, and end use. To make informed decisions and choices, this section gives you more detailed information about these parts—what they are and for what they are used.

The major topics introduced in this section include

- Input.
- Keyboards.
- Pointing devices.
- Scanners.
- Sensors.
- Voice input.
- Computer system output.
- Impact printers.
- Nonimpact printers.
- Video-display technology.
- Specialized output systems.
- Voice output.
- The central electronic complex.
- Trends in the evolution of computer systems.
- Supercomputers.
- Parallel processing.
- Files and mass storage.
- Sequential, random, and index sequential files.
- Magnetic tape devices.
- Magnetic disk devices.
- Optical disks.
- The convergence of computers and communications.
- Communication channels.
- Computer networking.
- Communications industry issues.

CURTIS J. CRAWFORD

Profession: Vice president, national sales, AT&T Computer Systems, Morristown, New Jersey.

Profile: Mr. Crawford majored in computers and business in college. After graduating, he joined IBM as a marketing trainee and went on to hold several marketing and management positions before becoming a vice president at AT&T.

Quote: *"The future of computers is exceptionally bright. It's a world of opportunities that is only limited by our imagination."*

CHAPTER 5
INPUT

PREVIEW

From Chapter 1, recall the concept of an information system. Now consider the analogy between a human central nervous system and a computerized information system. Our input sense organs for sight, sound, touch, taste, and smell convey information to our central nervous system. Along the way, this information is encoded into a pattern that the brain can process. In an analogous way, keyboards, disk drives, scanners, sensors, cameras, and microphones are some of the ways computer systems receive information that is then encoded for processing.

Further insight can be gained by considering input as part of such an information system: input devices are then viewed as the sense organs of a computer system.

Input and output play key roles in information processing. A computer system will sit idle until input activates it for processing. Similarly, a computer system is not very useful if it cannot communicate results to the outside world. This chapter looks at input from a systems point of view. It describes the process of input, discusses the transition from older transcribed forms of input to newer direct source forms of input, and categorizes input by the type of technology. Comparisons and examples show the wide variety of these technical devices and their applications.

In this chapter, you'll learn

- The role and the process of input to a computer system.
- The function and operation of a keyboard.
- The use of various pointing devices.
- The function and operation of a mouse.
- The function and operation of a scanner.
- The process of optical character recognition.
- Ways that the human voice can be used as input.

COMPUTER SYSTEM INPUT

Generally, an information system is activated by the input of data or information. Input can also deactivate processing, just as a light switch can turn off a light as well turn it on. Thus the primary role of input is to activate or deactivate information processing.

Input is a process that involves the use of a device to encode or transform data into digital codes that the computer can process. For example, if you press the letter *A* on the keyboard of a terminal or personal computer, you activate an information processing cycle. The key is simply a switch that senses a finger touch and triggers a cycle to accomplish the following: (1) the keystroke is encoded, or converted into a machine-readable code, (2) the encoded piece of data is stored in a memory location for later processing, and (3) output is provided by displaying the letter *A* on the computer's monitor screen.

When learning about the process of input, it is useful to classify input into two broad categories: (1) *transcribed input*—data that are captured by transcribing from source documents onto another medium that is capable of being input to a computer system and (2) *direct source input*—data that are captured directly from their source without a separate transcribing step. As you will see in this chapter, advances in input technology are moving the process of input away from transcription toward the capturing of data directly from their source.

TRANSCRIBED INPUT

For many years, the most common method of preparing data for input to a computer system involved transcribing the data into computer-readable form. Often, data exist in a *source document,* a form that contains the data to be processed by a computer, such as a preprinted invoice. One of the earliest transcribing devices was the *keypunch machine.* Data were entered on a keyboard and transcribed by punching combinations of holes into specially designed cards. Keypunch machines have been replaced by *key-to-disk* or *key-to-tape* systems, devices through which data are entered on a keyboard and directly recorded on a disk or tape.

There are two major drawbacks to transcribed input. The first is that the process is time consuming. By the time data go through a transcribing process, it may take hours or even days before they are input to a computer system. The second is that the process is error prone. Human error is the single biggest cause of mistakes in data input.

Systems that use transcribed input data are often called *batch-processing* systems. A batch is a collection of data to be processed. For example, a common practice is to collect payroll data through the use of a source document called a time card. The time cards are

Computer system input. The diagram shows the different types of input devices. In addition, tapes, disks, and modems can all function to give input to a computer system.

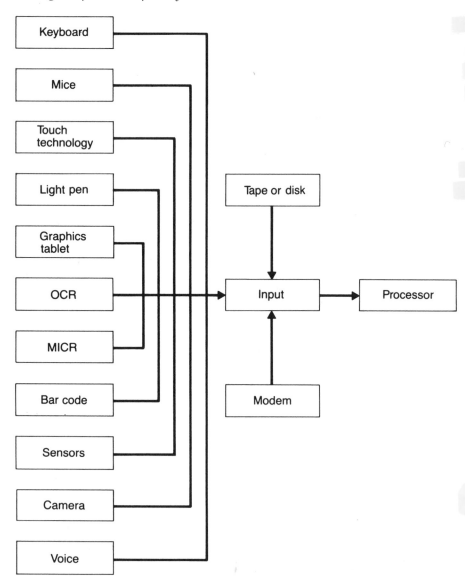

collected at the end of the pay period, batched together, and input to a payroll application program.

DIRECT SOURCE INPUT

Time-consuming and error-prone transcribing can be bypassed by entering data directly from their source. For example, the sale of merchandise at a clothing store is a transaction that might be input for computer processing. The actual data entry of the sale can be done in a variety of ways. An employee of the clothing store could press a series of keys on a cash register to activate processing. If the store's cash register is connected to a computer and the sales transaction immediately changes the inventory figure to reflect the sale, it is called *on-line transaction processing* because data enter the computer directly from the point of origin. If the item in the store has a specially coded price tag, processing could be activated by scanning the price tag with a special reading device known as a scanner. This saves time by eliminating the step of pressing cash register keys. Another advantage is that it is usually a more accurate way of entering data.

On-line systems use many different types of input devices. For example, modern office buildings have computer-controlled energy-management systems in which thermostats record changes in temperature and feed the data into a computer system. The computer outputs a signal to a regulator that controls a furnace or an air conditioner. In this particular type of application, the source data (temperature) do not exist in the form of a source document. Because the data cannot easily be keyed in, temperature sensors placed at various locations record the data directly.

At a computer-controlled traffic signal, an electronic sensor called a pressure transducer is buried under the street. It senses the flow of traffic and inputs that data to a microprocessor that controls the traffic lights.

Sensors can record changes in temperature, weight, pressure, light, and odor—all of which may be useful as input to a computer. It is even possible to record the human voice as input. Voice-input systems can be trained to respond to a set of simple spoken commands, such as "good" or "defective." You train them by recording the commands with your voice. The system then matches these stored voice patterns against spoken commands. For example, suppose a quality-control inspector is inspecting silicon chips under a microscope. The inspector's hands are occupied, so using a voice-input system he or she speaks directly to the system, which records the information for quality-control purposes.

Now that you have read a brief overview of the role and process of input, the next sections of this chapter will classify input devices by their type and discuss appropriate applications.

KEYBOARDS

Keyboards are the most widely used input devices. Like most input and output devices, keyboards are found as components in such input systems as computer terminals, key-to-tape or key-to-disk data-entry terminals, cash registers, and telephones.

CONSTRUCTION, USES, AND LAYOUT

In principle, the concept of a keyboard is straightforward, and they are fairly easy to design and implement. *Keyboards* consist of keyswitch technology coupled with electronic circuitry to encode the data that is entered by pressing keys. Electric typewriters and computers use electromechanical switches. Automatic teller machines often use membrane keyboards that have flat-sealed surfaces. Membrane keyboards are more suitable than switches for use in harsh environments. For example, such keyboards are used in fast-food restaurants, where dirt and grease might clog an ordinary keyboard.

Although the term keyboard might suggest images of typewriter-style keys, keyboards come in many varieties and can be found in telephones, calculators, cash registers, kitchen appliances, televisions, and burglar alarms.

Individual applications influence which type of keyboard to use. Entering only numeric data does not require a complicated keyboard. Word processing, on the other hand, might be enhanced by special function keys for adding and deleting characters or words or for rearranging paragraphs. Other specialized applications, such as an airline reservation terminal or a restaurant cash register, are enhanced by specially designed keyboards.

One major drawback of using a keyboard is lack of speed. Keyboarding requires manual labor; even a fast typist (85 words per minute) only enters data at an average rate of 7 characters per second. By contrast, a low-average human reading speed is 250 words per minute; the average college student reads 400 words per minute. Therefore, in a typical office, typing in information consumes a great deal of the time and effort of highly paid workers. One solution is to use faster input devices, such as scanners, which will be discussed in an upcoming section.

KEYBOARDS FOR PERSONAL COMPUTERS

In Chapter 1, you learned that keyboards for personal computers have several common characteristics; however, there is no standard layout for keyboards. On most of them, you will find the following:

- A typewriter layout.
- Function keys.

- Special control keys.
- Cursor movement keys.

Typewriter Layout

In the center of the keyboard is a typewriter layout for traditional entry of text and special characters. The most common layout for computers is called the ASCII (American Standard Code for Information Interchange) key layout. It differs slightly from the typewriter layout, which is called the Selectric key layout. For the novice, such as a child who has never learned to type, keyboards are often laid out with the keys in alphabetical order to make them easier to find.

Some computer and terminal keyboards come with removable keycaps and a switch that allows you to choose between the ASCII or Selectric key layout. For example, the Compucorp keyboard can be configured either way and includes special keycaps to meet the needs of French, German, Spanish, or Danish typists.

A computer keyboard needs more keys than the typewriter layout, and these are generally found surrounding the typewriter keyboard area. In addition to a numeric keypad, you will find (1) function keys; (2) special keys labeled [Ctrl] Control, [Alt] Alternate, [Esc] Escape, [Del] Delete, and Enter or Return; and (3) four cursor movement keys to move the cursor up, down, left, and right.

Function Keys

Function keys are keys labeled with the characters [F1] through [F10] or [F12]. The idea behind function keys is to simplify the use of application programs. For example, word processing software often uses the function keys to perform special commands, such as boldface, underline, or delete a sentence or a paragraph. Pressing the [F1] key brings up a help system in many applications.

A potential drawback is that each application program will use the given set of function keys differently. To compensate for this, either the application program will display the meaning of the function keys on the bottom line of the display screen or the program's

Keyboard. The IBM Enhanced Personal Computer keyboard features separate typing area, calculator-style keypad, and cursor- and screen-control keys.

documentation will provide a template that slips over and identifies the function keys.

Function keys can be used in conjunction with other keys. Holding down the [Alt] key while pressing [F1], for example, causes a different command to be executed than pressing the [F1] key alone. By combining the function keys with the [Ctrl], Shift, and [Alt] keys, up to 36 functions can be performed.

Special Control Keys

The Delete key [Del] is used to erase character by character. In some applications it can be used to erase a selected block of characters, such as a word, a sentence, a paragraph, or a group of cells in a spreadsheet.

The Escape key [Esc] is usually used to move from one mode of operation to another. For example, if you have instructed your word processing software to print a document and discover that you forgot to set your continuous-form-feed paper at the top of the form, you may be able to press the [Esc] key to stop the printing, correct the mistake, and then continue. However, different applications might have other uses for the [Esc] key.

The Enter key, sometimes called the Return key, fulfills two functions depending on the program with which it is used. The Enter key functions as a signal to continue in most programs. For example, suppose you are asked to respond to an operating system prompt, such as entering the time or date. The operating system will wait until the Enter key is pressed before continuing. After you type in the time or date, press the Enter key to continue. Pressing the Enter key also positions the cursor at the beginning of the next line, which is the electronic equivalent of pressing the carriage return key on a typewriter.

In word processors that feature word wrap, the carriage return function is handled automatically, so the Enter key is used to establish new paragraphs. In spreadsheet programs, the Enter key is used to enter a value into a spreadsheet cell.

The Control key [Ctrl] is always used in conjunction with one or two other keys to give instructions to a program. For example, when using a word processor, pressing the *D* key causes the character *D* to appear on the screen. If you hold down the [Ctrl] key while pressing the *D* key, the word processor might interpret the combination as an instruction to delete a character. The [Alt] key is used in the same manner.

The specific instructions that are implemented through the use of control keys are defined by individual programs. Like function keys, each application program will use the control keys differently. They are often used on keyboards without function keys. Control keys in conjunction with other keys enable you to perform complex operations with a minimal number of keystrokes.

Cursor Movement Keys

Moving the cursor around on the screen is one of the most common tasks in an application program. A cursor is a visual aid on a display screen. It may take the shape of a blinking box or underline, an arrow, or even a pointing finger. In word processing, for example, the cursor often blinks on and off and marks the location where the next character will appear on the screen.

You can move a cursor to any position on the screen by pressing the *cursor movement keys*, which are labeled with arrows. These keys can move the cursor up, down, left, or right. In fact, cursor movement is so important in an application such as word processing that it can usually be accomplished by additional key-driven commands. These commands might utilize function keys or control key commands to move the cursor forward or backward by word, line, sentence, or paragraph as well as to the beginning or end of a document.

POINTING DEVICES

Moving the cursor can also be accomplished with a *pointing device*—a device for interacting with a display screen. Some pointing devices with

Using a mouse. As the user rolls the mouse on the special grid pad, a pointer moves across the screen. The user can point to an object on the screen, press a mouse button, and select the object.

Mice. Shown here are one-, two-, and three-button mice. Advocates of the one-button mouse claim that it is less confusing to use. Critics claim that the two- and three-button mice offer the user more functionality.

which you may be familiar are the joystick and the trackball, which are often found in video and arcade games. Moving the handle of a joystick or spinning the ball on a trackball controls a corresponding cursor or pointer movement on the display screen. A more common pointing device is called a mouse.

THE MOUSE

The *mouse* is a pointing device that combines the traditional cursor movements—accomplished by pressing cursor movement keys—with the means to select an object on the display screen. For example, when confronted with choices on a menu, you point to the selection of your choice by positioning the cursor with the mouse, then you press a button on the mouse to select your choice. In word processing, a technique called pointing and dragging can be used to select a large block of text, such as a sentence or paragraph. This is done by pointing at the first character in the sentence or paragraph and keeping a mouse button depressed while you drag the pointer to the last character in the sentence or paragraph. The result is a highlighted block of text that can be manipulated with other commands, such as move or delete.

The original mouse was part of a research and development effort by Doug Engelbart at the Stanford Research Institute in 1967. He was working on ways to make computers easier to use and understand. The original mouse was about the size of a baseball, moved on large wheels, and had three control buttons. Its appearance led to its name. The cord looked like a tail, the three buttons looked like two eyes and a nose, and the wheels elevating the body looked like feet. Today's mice are smaller and more elegantly designed, but the name remains the same.

Engelbart's efforts attracted a great deal of attention at Xerox Corporation, where the mouse was tested and used extensively in-house before making its public debut in the Xerox Star office computer. A mouse is now offered as a standard feature of the Apple Macintosh and IBM Personal System/2, and as an optional feature for many other brands of computers. Many software packages incorporate optional mouse interfaces.

Mice are available in mechanical or optical versions. On the underside of the *mechanical mouse* is a ball that is similar to the trackball device found on many video games. As the mouse rolls up, down, left, and right across the flat surface, a signal is sent to the computer that drives the cursor up, down, left, and right, corresponding to the motion of the mouse. On the underside of the *optical mouse* is a photodetector. The mouse rolls over a special pad that has an optically detectable grid printed on it. The photodetector on the mouse counts the lines on the grid and translates them into cursor movement on the screen.

Advocates of mice claim that using a mouse is one of the fastest, simplest, and easiest-to-learn methods of manipulating a sophisticated computer program. It features more precise pointing than possible with the human finger as well as the ability to invoke action. Critics of mice claim that using a mouse becomes an unnecessary burden in applications such as word processing, spreadsheets, and databases that require extensive use of the keyboard. In addition to mice, there are other pointing methods.

TOUCH TECHNOLOGY

The most natural of all pointing devices is your finger. Pointing with a finger is used in two important pointing methods: touch screens and touch pads. The idea behind touch technology is to make a computer system easier to use. *Touch technology* senses the location of your finger as it nears or touches a screen or a touch-sensitive pad. For example, a touch screen might contain a menu with several selections. When you touch the part of the screen that corresponds to the selection of your choice, you activate the program that takes you to that selection.

One method for implementing touch screens involves crisscrossing the monitor screen with invisible beams of infrared light. When you touch a point on the screen, your finger interrupts the horizontal and vertical infrared beams. The Hewlett-Packard

Touchscreen option for personal computers uses this technology. Another method involves overlaying the screen with a thin layer of plastic that has the sensing grid built into it.

Citibank of New York uses touch screens for its automatic teller machines (ATMs). Touch technology allows the user to select the language (i.e., English, Spanish, or Japanese) in which he or she wishes to communicate with the ATM. Software can then switch the display to the language selected.

Touch screens are easy to use, especially in situations where you need information quickly. For example, Walt Disney's Experimental Prototype Community of Tomorrow (EPCOT) center combines infrared touch technology with color video monitors to create an easy-to-use interactive visitor information system. Visitors can gain access to a wide variety of information about the park, its attractions, and their locations by simply touching one of the many video monitors located throughout the center. The EPCOT system also displays video programs from a videodisk to create a more interesting and animated presentation.

Another touch technology is the touch pad. Presently, it is found prima-

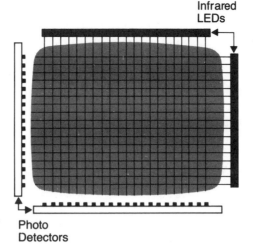

Touch screen. *One way of implementing touch-screen capability is by crisscrossing the screen with invisible beams of infared light. When your finger nears the screen, it interrupts the beams of light and the coordinate is sensed.*

rily in educational and entertainment applications. For example, the Koala touch pad can be used to control games, and it also allows you to "finger paint" graphics on the screen by touching the pad. One keyboard manufacturer incorporates a touch pad into one of its keyboards for finger control of cursor or pointer movement.

Touch technology is limited because of its poor resolution. Fingers are simply too large for great accuracy, so a *stylus* often has to be used to accomplish detailed work. Also, touchscreen systems are relatively expensive.

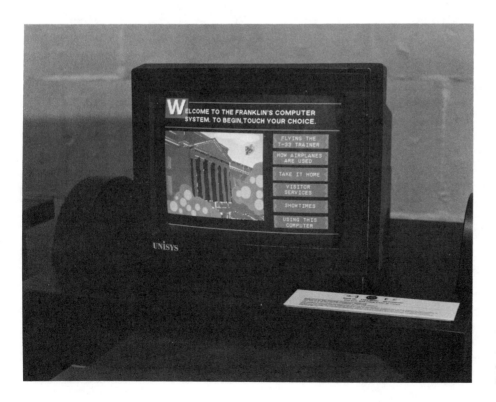

Touch screen. *The Franklin Institute Science Museum in Philadelphia provides access to exhibit information and visitor services through the use of touch screens.*

Touch pads use a pressure-sensative membrane that has a built-in grid of sensing wires.

the screen with much greater accuracy than can the human finger, and it can be used to draw on the screen. Consequently, it is used in such intricate applications as computer-aided design, where accurate drawing on the screen may be required.

DIGITIZER TABLETS

Electronic drawing is also possible on a sensitized surface, called a digitizer tablet. As the pen contacts the surface, a difference in electrical charge is detected and the drawn image is stored in the computer. This technique is actually a form of *digitizing.* The tablet contains a grid of sensor wires, and as the pen moves over the grid, it makes contact with specific points on the grid. In this way, continuous (or analog) movement of the pen is translated into discrete (or digital) signals.

LIGHT PENS

A *light pen* also utilizes the principle of touching the screen, but it does so with a hand-held pen that contains a light-sensitive tip. It can pinpoint a spot on

Touch screen. Visitors to the Franklin Institute obtain information about science by using touch-sensative screens.

SCANNERS

Scanners convert optically focused images, such as words, photographs, or drawings, into digital images that are suitable for computer processing. Images can then be processed like any other digital data. Scanners are commonly used where direct source input exists in the form of images, such as an existing book, with no convenient way to transcribe the data.

A photoreceptor device is required to convert reflected light into digital images. Desktop-publishing applications use scanners to capture images, and then retouch, crop, or resize them. Adding images to a printed page makes documents more comprehensible for the reader. Complex ideas can be better explained with the aid of pictures, graphics, and diagrams; some ideas are difficult to understand without them.

Most image scanners look like office copiers. A document is either placed on a glass plate and scanned by a moving photoreceptor or is fed through a device that contains a stationary photoreceptor. Some scanners are hand-held.

Digitized images require a great deal of disk storage. For example, an $8\frac{1}{2}$-by-11-inch page, scanned and digitized, could require up to 1 million bytes of storage. The best compression techniques available can reduce the

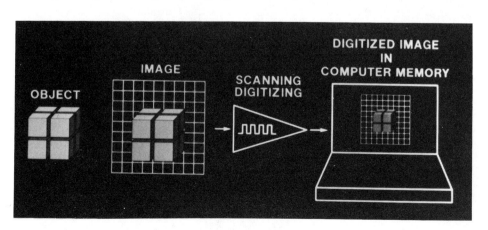

Scanners. *An optical lens scans an image, and software digitizes the image and stores it as a series of bits in memory. (Diagram courtesy of Datacopy Corporation.)*

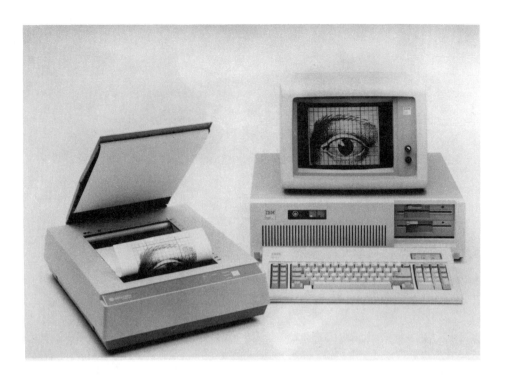

Scanners. *The scanner on the left has scanned and digitized the photo that is displayed on the monochrome display screen on the right.*

amount of storage required to about 120,000 bytes.

Image processing traces its roots to several scanning applications and devices, including magnetic ink character recognition, bar codes, and optical character recognition.

MAGNETIC INK CHARACTER RECOGNITION

The earliest form of scanner was the ***magnetic ink character recognizer (MICR),*** which is still predominantly used by the banking industry for pro-

---

SPOTLIGHT ON...
Scanner Applications

Scanners are frequently used in desktop-publishing applications. With the right software, a scanned image such as line art, an illustration, or a photograph can be scaled (reduced or enlarged), cropped (partially cut away), or enhanced. Doing this by computer instead of by hand saves time and money. However, to scan a continuous tone photograph and create a halftone (a type of photograph that can be reproduced by a printer) requires that the scanner have gray-scale capability to represent the varying levels of gray in a scanned photograph.

By adding optical character recognition (OCR) software, most scanners can be used for OCR applications. Such applications include converting paper-based documents to digital files, scanning forms to use as templates, and converting typewritten manuscripts into text files that can be edited with a word processor.

Scanners and facsimile or fax machines (discussed in Chapter 8) are another natural marriage. In fact, a scanner is an integral part of a fax machine. With the addition of a fax modem to your personal computer, you can send and receive digital images instead of mailing hand-written or printed copies.

The caveat: scanners, like ordinary copiers, make it easy to copy images and text, but that doesn't give you free reign. If the publisher, author, illustrator, or photographer owns the copyright to the image or text, honor the copyright and obtain permission before you publish.

To learn more, read The Scanner Book *by Stephen Beale and James Cavuoto. Illustrated with scanned images, 220 pp. Torrance, Calif.: Micropublishing Press, 1989.*

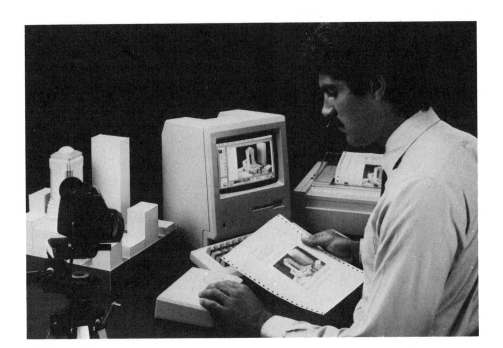

cessing checks. At the time MICR was developed, optical methods had not yet been developed. All checks contain a series of numbers printed in magnetic ink. The numbers identify the bank, the account, and the check number. Canceled checks also contain the amount of the check printed in magnetic ink. MICR makes check processing faster and more accurate by reading the magnetic ink numbers on the checks.

BAR CODES

Another form of scanning uses bar codes. Supermarkets use the Universal Product Code (UPC), which consists of a series of thick and thin **bar codes** that represent numbers. The code is quite precise and identifies both the manufacturer and the specific product (e.g., a 10-ounce can of Del Monte peaches versus a 6-ounce can of Del Monte peaches). Marking products this way greatly simplifies the information processing associated with the sale and restocking of products.

For example, a supermarket might have an inventory of 100 UPC-marked 8-ounce cans of Campbell's tomato soup. As cans of soup are sold, the supermarket must replenish its inventory or lose sales. When a product is coded, it is possible to activate information processing by simply scanning the code at the checkout counter. Scanning the code tells an on-line inventory control system to subtract one unit (-1) from the inventory amount of the item.

Bar codes. *Sample of the Universal Product Code.*

ROBERT H. BLISSMER
55 ADDINGTON ROAD
BROOKLINE, MA 02146

268

May 17 19 90

5-39
110

PAY TO THE ORDER OF Eileen Algaze

$ 50 00

fifty and 00/100 DOLLARS

BANK OF BOSTON
THE FIRST NATIONAL BANK OF BOSTON

Robert H. Blissmer

HARLAND BG6 10

⑆011000390⑆901⑈1641⑈   0268⑈   ⑆000000 5000⑆

Magnetic ink character recognition. *The use of magnetic ink characters on a check.*

Bar codes. *Bar-code readers are used extensively for remote data-collection applications, such as inventory control in a warehouse.*

It can also serve as input to a batch-processing program that generates daily storewide sales reports. In addition, it produces immediate output in the form of a product name and price printed on the customer's receipt.

Today, bar codes are used in factories and offices. They are useful in situations where a product needs to be tracked, such as in a materials-handling application in a factory, or where a product needs to be quickly identified, such as in an inventory-control application. In these applications, the bar code is used instead of a written or printed product number. Bar codes are even starting to show up on people. They can be found on patient identification bracelets and on employee badges in hospitals.

OPTICAL CHARACTER RECOGNITION

Optical character recognition (OCR) is the process of reading words in a scanned image and translating them into computer-readable codes. OCR was originally designed for input to typesetting machines for the newspaper industry. It was thought that relatively untrained typists could retype copy for OCR input and feed it into a scanner, thus cutting costs, reducing mistakes, and speeding up the newspaper composition process.

Early scanners could read only a few specially designed fonts. If you are not familiar with typesetting jargon, a font is the set of characters in a particular typeface and size. For example, the sentence you are now reading is set in a typeface called Palatino and its size is 10 points.

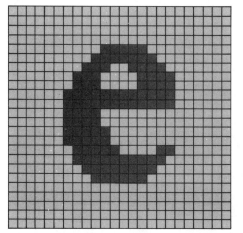

Optical chararcter recognition. *Some OCR devices use matrix matching techniques. Characters that are read are compared to the character patterns stored in memory and matched on the basis of their lightness and darkness values.*

Some OCR software works by a process known as *matrix matching*. As a typewritten page moves past the scanner, it optically scans each character and compares it with an existing character pattern stored in the OCR's memory. Matching patterns are encoded for storage and processing by a computer.[1]

Matrix matching is quite accurate, but storing the character patterns in memory often places limits on the number of fonts that can be recognized. To compensate for this, newer OCR software uses *feature analysis* techniques. By matching the shapes of characters (e.g., curves, straight lines, enclosed spaces, and so on) rather than the complete character pattern, such OCR software can recognize characters faster. It also requires less space to store the features rather than the complete character patterns.

CAN MACHINES REALLY READ?

Advances in OCR technology raise a provocative question: "When will a machine be developed that can read like a human being?" Such a reading device would have to understand what was being input and relate that information to particular processing tasks. In Chapter 12, you will read about programs that exhibit a limited understanding of what is being typed in at a keyboard, but this is still a long way from a true reading device. Today, however, software does exist that can recognize virtually any type of hand-produced or printed characters.

In the late 1970s, Raymond Kurzweil invented a reading machine to scan printed documents and, using electronic voice output, read them aloud to the blind or visually impaired. This OCR breakthrough technology combined the first version of feature analysis with software that could be trained to read the different fonts it encountered. But even for people with visual acuity, the machine posed a paradox. The machine stopped when it encountered a new font, and an operator had to identify the new font before the machine could proceed.

Despite its drawbacks, the reading machine's potential as a universal OCR device rekindled an interest in scanning documents that had already been typeset and printed, and the Kurzweil reading machine was refined and marketed as the Kurzweil data-entry machine.

Although the problems of reading already typeset material are still formidable, there are today a wide variety of low-cost OCR software interfaces between scanners and personal computers. These programs use various methods of character recognition to convert scanned text into an ASCII text file, suitable for import into a word processor, spreadsheet, or database program. They also interface with most popular scanners; are able to differentiate automatically among graphics, text, and multiple columns; and handle such nuances as regular text versus boldface, italic, or underlined text.

With such software, existing documents, books, manuals, or papers can be scanned and processed electronically, eliminating the manual process of retyping the information. For example, an old book that has never been part of a computerized information system can be scanned, revised, and typeset for a new edition.

IMAGE PROCESSING

Scanning documents is common in today's offices because scanners enable people to process documents more accurately and efficiently.

Federal Express Corporation uses a scanner in processing its air freight bills. The scanner reads the air bills and digitizes and stores the entire image. The OCR software in the scanner recognizes and encodes the air bill number only. Later on in the processing cycle, the digitized images can be sorted electronically by air bill number, which makes the application more efficient by eliminating sorting and reading the actual documents themselves.[2]

American Express also uses scanners to eliminate the costly practice of returning copies of all credit card receipts to the person who signed for them. American Express processes receipts by scanning them, digitizing the image of the receipt, and sending out customer statements that contain images of the receipts instead of the receipts themselves.

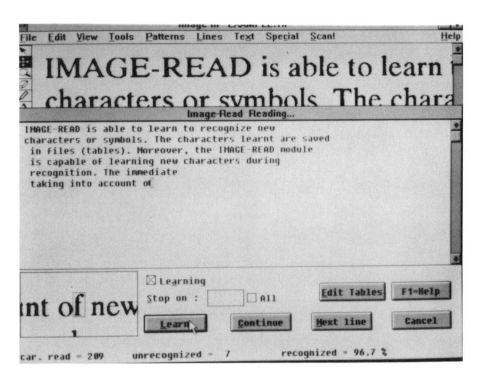

Optical character recognition. Software can be trained to recognize virtually any characters on a printed page.

The Eye of the Computer

On the *Voyager* space mission to Jupiter, Saturn, and beyond, the spacecraft was equipped with television cameras to scan the planets. Computers on board transformed the television images into digital signals that were then broadcast to Earth. A ground station on Earth picked up the digital signals and passed them to a computer at the Jet Propulsion Laboratory in southern California, where they were processed and converted back into pictures. The pictures look like newspaper wirephotos made up of millions of dots. Unlike wirephotos, however, each dot is a different shade of gray specified by the digital signal from the spacecraft. Later on, color can be added by the computer to enhance the picture. Approximately 40,000 photographs of the Jupiter region were taken in this manner.[3] Today, commercial satellites, such as the American *Landsats* and the French *Spot*, capture digital images of the Earth's surface, which are available for sale.

Electronic Photography

Electronic cameras, such as the Sony Mavica, store photographs not on film but as digitized images on a 2-inch magnetic disk inside the camera. Because the pictures are digital and don't have to be developed, they offer some

Can machines really read? The Xerox/Kurzweil Personal Reader is an optical scanner that reads typewritten and typeset text and turns it into synthetic speech. It provides blind, visually impaired, or dyslexic people with a means of accessing a wide range of reading material.

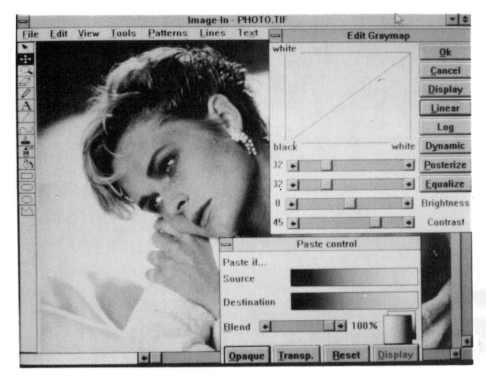

Image processing. *Photographs can be scanned, then reduced or enlarged, cropped, or enhanced with the proper software.*

interesting publishing alternatives. For example, a company photographer could take pictures of all the new employees. Then using a combination of a videocassette recorder (VCR) and a personal computer equipped with an add-in board called a frame grabber, the photographer edits, retouches, and manipulates the digital photographs, then transfers them into a computer-aided publishing program to publish the monthly company newsletter.

In the future, by using electronic photography, libraries of digital pictures could be created and electronically browsed through. The combination of picture images plus computer-generated text opens up more new applications. For example, just as music recording studios electronically mix sound tracks to produce record albums, desktop-publishing systems electronically mix text and photos to create electronic documents. Magazine and newspaper layouts can be entirely composed through electronic devices. This will be discussed in greater detail in Chapter 6.

Digitizing Audio and Video

In Chapter 2, you learned about desktop presentation programs that can produce text and graphics for presentation on 35-mm slides and over-

head transparencies. Today, tools are available that can add animation, audio, and video to presentations. In addition to software, adding sound such as voice or music to a presentation usually requires an *audio digitizer board*, which turns analog sound waves into digital files for playback, and a set of external speakers. Like images, digitized sound requires a great deal of disk storage space. One minute of uncompressed voice-quality sound can occupy one-half megabyte of disk space, and 1 minute of CD-quality music can take up to 5 megabytes (5 MB).

To digitize video from a VCR, camcorder, or television, requires a *video capture board*, which turns full-motion video signals into digitized files. Uncompressed full-motion video requires up to 1800 MB of disk storage space per minute.

Today, the only cost-effective way to store digitized audio and video on disk is to compress it. Several hardware techniques exist to compress, decompress, and play back digitized data. For example, a technique called digital video interactive (DVI) offers a 160-to-1 compression ratio. Using DVI, the 1800 MB of disk storage required for one minute of full-motion video could be reduced to slightly over 11 MB of disk storage space. You will learn more about DVI and disk storage space in Chapter 8.

Not all presentations require the level of sophistication that digitized audio and video offer, and the cost of producing such presentations is considerably higher than producing a slide show. But as hardware and software tools become less expensive, new presentation possibilities and opportunities will emerge.

SENSORS

Sensors (sometimes called transducers) are instruments capable of directly encoding a physical event into data. The term *data acquisition* is used to describe the special technology used in such systems as medical instrumentation, seismological analysis, ventilation and heating, and factory control. A continuous stream of analog data is collected by sensors and fed into an analog-to-digital converter for processing by computers. Other types of sensors include pressure sensors and photoelectric cells. Even microphones and video cameras can be used to encode events.

SMART SENSORS

The traditional method of using sensors involves connecting a sensing device to a computer system. A new technique combines the computer and the sensor on the same silicon chip because silicon is sensitive to the pressures, temperatures, images, sounds, and smells that must be sensed. The combined chips, called *smart sensors*, are capable of improving the performance of sensor applications because some of the data processing occurs directly in the sensor. Just as the human eye processes much information before it sends signals to the brain, a smart sensor monitors what is being sensed and only sends a signal to a larger computer when necessary.

Smart sensors are under experimental development for many medical, industrial, and defense applications. For example, one company is developing a military sensor that can stare at a target and transmit a signal if movement occurs. In medicine, a combined glucose sensor and microcomputer could be implanted in a diabetic person to monitor blood sugar levels and release exact dosages of insulin. A more elusive goal of smart sensor research is to produce robots with senses more similar to those of human beings. If such developments occur, robots would be a little more sensitive than they are today.

VOICE INPUT

Although voice input to a computer system is possible today, computers that can understand everything you say are still many years in the future. Most of what we know as voice input is in limited speech applications that in-

volve small vocabularies. There are two major categories of voice-input devices:

- *Word-recognition* devices that are capable of responding to individually spoken words or commands.

- *Speech-recognition* devices that are capable of recognizing connected words spoken in sentences or phrases.

WORD RECOGNITION

Most of the word-recognition systems now on the market rely on a technique known as *speaker verification*. When you talk into a microphone, your voice is converted into digital signals and is stored in the computer's memory. For the computer to recognize a particular voice, the user must first *train* the system by speaking the desired vocabulary. In this way, a *template*—the speech pattern against which future sounds are compared—is recorded in the system. Of course, the drawback to such a system is that it will respond only to the person who recorded the template. In addition, the vocabularies of such systems are generally limited to 100 to 200 single words. As the vocabulary of these systems increases, the amount of memory required to store the templates increases rather dramatically.

Applications for word recognizers include baggage handling systems, voice-activated military aircraft command systems for pilots, voice-activated door locks for automobiles, industrial inventory-control systems, and systems for verbally interacting with personal computer software packages.

Voice input. Block diagram showing the major functional components of a speech-recognition system. The system is trained by recording voice patterns that are stored in the template library and used for matching when the system is in actual operation.

Voice input. An operator trains a voice recognition terminal to recognize her voice.

SPEECH RECOGNITION

The goal of voice-input systems is to be speaker independent, that is, to recognize any person speaking phrases or sentences as opposed to isolated single words. Speech-recognition devices, nicknamed *talkwriters*—word processors that transform speech into text—have been developed that are capable of understanding 30,000-word vocabularies and that can recognize words at a rate of 15 to 60 words per minute. Instead of making individual templates for each spoken word, these devices use statistical techniques to record patterns of sound that can be matched against spoken words. Currently, the devices depend on costly special-purpose hardware, must still be trained to respond to an individual voice, and can only recognize words spoken slowly and carefully. It is predicted that when the cost of such devices drops, businesspeople will routinely dictate their memos and letters into talkwriters.

Although speaker-independent voice recognition has proved to be quite elusive, one technique that uses spectrograms—computer-enhanced voiceprints of the electrical wave forms of speech—appears to be most promising. Victor Zue, an MIT professor of electrical engineering, was the first to develop the ability to read spectrograms. He learned to identify words and phrases from spectrograms independent of who was doing the talking. Researchers now believe that if it is possible for a person to read spectrograms, then it is possible to program a computer to recognize the shapes and patterns of spectrograms, thus establishing a framework for true speaker-independent voice-input systems. In the long term, these devices may make a computer as easy and as interesting to talk to as another person.

REVIEW

Input was defined as being like the sense organs of a computer system. The process of input has evolved from transcribing data in an intermediate step to the direct input of data from its source. Input activates information processing. Keyboards are a major type of input device and are widely used in almost all applications. Pointing devices include the use of a human finger, a light pen, and a mouse to simplify the interaction with computers and to aid the input of drawings and graphics. Scanners can read and recognize a variety of images on the printed page, including characters and bar codes. Sensors are useful for the direct input of light, temperature, pressure, odor, and weight. Advances in technology are transforming sensors into smart systems that are capable of performing some processing before sending information to a larger computer system. Voice-input devices consist of word recognizers and speech recognizers. The vocabulary recognized by a voice-input device is usually very limited. The ability to recognize spoken sentences is just starting to become a reality, and true speaker-independent speech recognition is still an experimental venture.

REFERENCES

1. Brody, Herb. "Machines That Read Move Up a Grade." *High Technology,* February 1983, pp. 35-36.

2. Ibid., p. 37.

3. Sagan, Carl. *Cosmos.* New York: Random House, 1980. Although Sagan only skirts the computer issue in Cosmos, you can gain an interesting perspective on high technology by reading this and some of Sagan's other books.

RESOURCES

BOOKS

Beale, Stephen, and James Cavuoto. *The Scanner Book.* Torrance, Calif.: Micro Publishing Press, 1989. A guide to selecting, installing, and using desktop scanners. This book is a good overview of scanner applications and technology.

Bowe, Frank. *Personal Computers and Special Needs.* Berkeley, Calif.: Sybex, 1984. This is a fascinating book about computers for disabled people; it also covers many input and output technologies.

MAGAZINES

PC Magazine. New York: Ziff-Davis. This periodical contains business applications as well as reviews of new IBM Personal Computer and IBM-compatible hardware and software.

PC World. San Francisco, Calif.: PCW Communications. A monthly magazine of information about the IBM Personal Computer and the IBM-compatible market that provides you with coverage of new products and uses for personal computers.

Systems Integration. Newton, Mass.: Cahners. You will probably have to go to the library to find this magazine because it is not sold on newsstands. Its coverage of topics is somewhat more technical than that of *PC Magazine* or *PC World,* but it includes all the important areas of small computers.

STUDY GUIDE

Match the following key terms to the appropriate definition or application:

A.

1. ____ Input

2. ____ Transcribed input

3. ____ Direct source input

4. ____ Source document

5. ____ Keypunch machine

6. ____ Key-to-disk or key-to-tape systems

7. ____ Batch processing

8. ____ On-line transaction processing

a. A form containing data that are to be processed by a computer.

b. Systems in which data enter the computer directly from the point of origin.

c. Data that are captured by transcribing them from source documents onto another medium that is capable of being input to a computer system.

d. The use of a device to encode or transform data into digital codes that a computer can process.

e. A device in which data are entered on a keyboard and directly recorded on a disk or tape.

f. Data that are captured directly from their source without a separate transcribing step.

g. A device in which data are entered on a keyboard and transcribed by punching combinations of holes into specially designed cards.

h. Systems in which data are grouped together and input to a computer system at the same time.

B.

9. ____ Keyboard

10. ____ Function keys

11. ____ Cursor movement keys

12. ____ Pointing device

13. ____ Mouse

14. ____ Touch technology

15. ____ Light pen

16. ____ Digitizing

a. Positioning a blinking visual aid on a display screen.

b. Pointing to a tiny spot on the display screen.

c. Electronic drawing on a sensitized tablet.

d. Keys labeled with the characters [F1] through [F10] or [F12].

e. Typing a lengthy word processing document.

f. Pointing and dragging on a display screen.

g. An electronic "finger painting" system.

h. Generally interacting with a display screen.

C.

17. ____ Scanner

18. ____ Magnetic ink character recognition (MICR)

19. ____ Bar code

20. ____ Optical character recognition (OCR)

21. ____ Sensor

22. ____ Smart sensor

23. ____ Word recognition

24. ____ Speech recognition

25. ____ Talkwriter

a. Transforming speech into text.

b. Marking a product so it can be tracked in an inventory-control application.

c. Generally examining an image and translating the image into digital images that are suitable for processing.

d. Monitoring blood sugar levels in a diabetic person.

e. Reading typewritten characters on paper.

f. Responding to individually spoken words or commands.

g. Processing existing checks in the banking industry.

h. Generally encoding a physical event directly into data.

i. Recognizing connected words spoken in sentences or phrases.

True/False:

26. T The primary role of input is to activate or deactivate information processing.

27. F Input technology is moving toward more transcribed input.

28. F Transcribing data is a relatively error-free process.

29. T A major drawback to using a keyboard is lack of speed.

30. T Cursor movement is one of the most common tasks when interacting with an application program.

31. T Selecting choices from a menu often involves the activity called pointing.

32. F Word wrap eliminates the need for cursor movement keys.

33. F Touch screens rely on the use of a mouse as a pointing device.

34. F Light pens are not as accurate a touch method as using your finger.

35. F Digitizing involves translating digital signals into analog signals.

36. T Magnetic ink character recognition is an improvement on scanners.

37. T Bar codes are useful in inventory-control applications.

38. T Voice templates are digital signals stored in a computer's memory.

39. F The process of recognizing general human speech is called word recognition.

40. F Speaker-independent voice recognition has been achieved in many practical applications.

Multiple Choice:

41. One device that can eliminate the step of keying in data is called a (an)

   a. Key-to-disk machine.
   b. Optical scanner.
   c. Keypunch machine.
   d. Electronic cash register.

42. The single biggest cause of mistakes in data input is

   a. Point-of-sale terminals.
   b. Keying in the data.
   c. Source documents.
   d. Human error.

43. A computer-controlled traffic signal uses

   a. Sensing.
   b. Scanning.
   c. Thermostats.
   d. Training.

44. Optical character recognition (OCR) software can read

   a. Magnetically encoded numbers.
   b. Any combination of numbers or letters.
   c. Bar codes in supermarkets.
   d. Specially coded characters or patterns.

45. Electronic drawing on a graphics tablet is a form of

   a. Light pen.
   b. Touch technology.
   c. Digitizing.
   d. Dual-purpose input and output display.

46. The most widely used input device is a

   a. Mouse.
   b. Keyboard.
   c. Sensor.
   d. Camera.

47. Mice are used to replace

   a. Bar codes.
   b. Touch screens.
   c. Keyboards.
   d. Cursor movement keys.

48. A Kurzweil data-entry machine cannot read

   a. Typewritten material.
   b. Magnetic ink characters.
   c. Hand-produced characters.
   d. Existing books.

49. Which of the following is not a current application for image processing?

   a. Check processing.
   b. Desktop publishing.
   c. Satellite photography.
   d. Page composition.

50. The primary goal of voice-input systems is to

   a. Recognize isolated words.
   b. Recognize phrases or sentences.
   c. Improve voice templates.
   d. Improve voice training.

Thought Questions:

51. We have described various pointing devices as alternatives to using the keyboard for input. How might you use these devices in an application such as word processing?

52. Some experts argue that transcribed input is obsolete and will be replaced completely by direct source input. Do you agree or disagree? Why?

Projects:

53. Visit your local shopping mall and ask the merchants which types of input devices they use to record transactions. Prepare a report that covers four different types of devices and how they are used. Present your findings to the class.

54. Research advertisements for scanning devices such as optical character recognizers, bar code readers, or image scanners. Pick one technology and write a report on the advantages and disadvantages of the device. Present your findings to the class.

SOFTWARE EXERCISES

After reading this chapter, it might seem unlikely that the keyboard will soon be replaced as the primary means of data input. However, the increasing use of the mouse as a pointing device seems inevitable, given its important role in graphics-oriented interfaces. Since its beginning, the mouse has been misunderstood and maligned. Today, many people still question who should use the mouse and why.

Assignment 1. For this exercise, you are going to write a "State of the Mouse" report. This is a two-part exercise. First, you are going to use a word processor to write a survey. Second, after conducting the survey, you will write your report.

Each person is responsible for contacting five personal computer users. Note: You cannot use other members of the class or students taking computer courses as participants in your survey. You will interview those users and find out

- What kind of computer they use.
- Do they use a mouse?
- If no, why not?
- If yes, why?
- If no, do they think using one would be hard to adjust to?
- If yes, do they feel comfortable using it?
- If yes, how many buttons does it have?
- If yes, should a mouse have one, two, or three buttons, and why?

Use the information in the sample survey form shown here as a guide to creating your survey. Print a copy of your finished blank survey form to hand in to your instructor.

Based on tabulating the results of that survey, write your report. Make sure your report addresses the following questions:

```
Mouse Survey

Class: Introduction to Computers
Section: 2
Date: October 15, 19XX

1.  What kind of computer do you use at home or work?

2.  Do you use a mouse? (Yes or No)

3.  If no, why not?

4.  Do you think mice are hard to adjust to? (Yes or No)

5.  Do you feel comfortable using the mouse? (Yes or No)

6.  Should a mouse have one, two, or three buttons?

7.  Interviewer's remarks
```

Sample mouse survey.

- Is the mouse a popular device?
- Does mouse use correlate with the type of computer used (e.g., Macintosh or IBM)?
- What are the primary arguments given for not using a mouse?
- What are the primary arguments given for using a mouse?
- How many buttons should a mouse have?

Using the word processor, fill in one copy of your blank survey form and attach it to your report.

ANSWERS

1. d, **2.** c, **3.** f, **4.** a, **5.** g, **6.** e, **7.** h, **8.** b, **9.** e, **10.** d, **11.** a, **12.** h, **13.** f, **14.** g, **15.** b, **16.** c, **17.** c, **18.** g, **19.** b, **20.** e, **21.** h, **22.** d, **23.** f, **24.** i, **25.** a, **26.** T, **27.** F, **28.** F, **29.** T, **30.** T, **31.** T, **32.** F, **33.** F, **34.** F, **35.** F, **36.** F, **37.** T, **38.** T, **39.** F, **40.** F, **41.** b, **42.** d, **43.** a, **44.** d, **45.** c, **46.** b, **47.** d, **48.** c, **49.** a, **50.** b.

SUZANNE WATZMAN

Profession: Cofounder and chairman of Watzman+Keys, a graphic design and consulting firm based in Cambridge, Massachusetts.

Profile: After graduating from the Rhode Island School of Design, Ms. Watzman began her career in graphic design. Her firm assists clients in communicating more effectively in both print and electronic media. Ms. Watzman lectures frequently on the subjects of information technology and design. She is also a staff member of the MIT Technical Communication Program.

Quote: "*Technology is only a tool, not a solution. The effectiveness of the tool is dependent on the skills of the person using it. The most expensive, high-quality, computerized graphic design layout program will not turn anyone into a graphic designer.*"

CHAPTER 6
OUTPUT

PREVIEW

Like input, output also plays a key role in information processing. A computer system is useless if it cannot communicate the results of information processing to the outside world. This chapter looks at output from a systems point of view. It describes the function of output and categorizes output by the types of technology used to produce it.

The chapter begins by classifying, describing, and comparing the various types of printers. Then video-display technology, flat-panel display technology, and computer graphics are discussed. Specialized output systems are also examined. Finally, voice output is considered as an output medium. Comparisons and examples show the wide variety of these technical devices and their applications.

In this chapter, you'll learn

- Computer system output: types and devices.
- The differences among impact printers.
- The differences among nonimpact printers.
- Video-display technology.
- An overview of graphics.
- Uses for specialized output systems.
- Uses for voice output.

COMPUTER SYSTEM OUTPUT

Computer system output. *The diagram shows the different types of output devices. In addition, tapes, disks, and modems can all function to receive output from a computer system.*

In the early days of mass-produced automobiles, as long as you wanted a Model T Ford and you wanted it black, you could have a car. In the early days of computers, you could get output as long as you wanted it on 11 by 14-inch fan-folded paper. By contrast, today's computer output comes in many different sizes, shapes, colors, and even forms.

Information processing is complete when the results of processing are communicated. Remember the definition of communication in Chapter 1: the transfer of meaningful information. The information that a computer program produces is a stream of coded symbols. In most cases, it is the job of the *output device* to decode these symbols into a form of information that is easy for people to use or understand, such as text, pictures, graphics, or sound.

The exception to this rule arises when the output from a computer system is not intended directly for use by people. A good example of this is saving your files on a mass-storage device for later input to the computer. A more dramatic example is a factory computer system in which the output is destined for use by machines instead of people. One of the earliest examples of this, the numerically controlled machine, such as drill presses, lathes, and milling machines, uses the output of a computer program to control directly its own operation without human involvement. Today, factory assembly lines are run by robots. As you learned in Chapter 4, these robots are not the kind we see in science fiction movies, but rather programmable general-purpose manipulators that are capable of controlling and operating an entire assembly line.

TYPES OF COMPUTER OUTPUT

The four major types of computer output are

- Text, consisting of words, numbers, and other symbols in the form of a language.
- Images in the form of graphics or pictures.
- Sound that consists of music or voice.
- Machine-readable data, which are symbols in a form that other computer systems or machines can use.

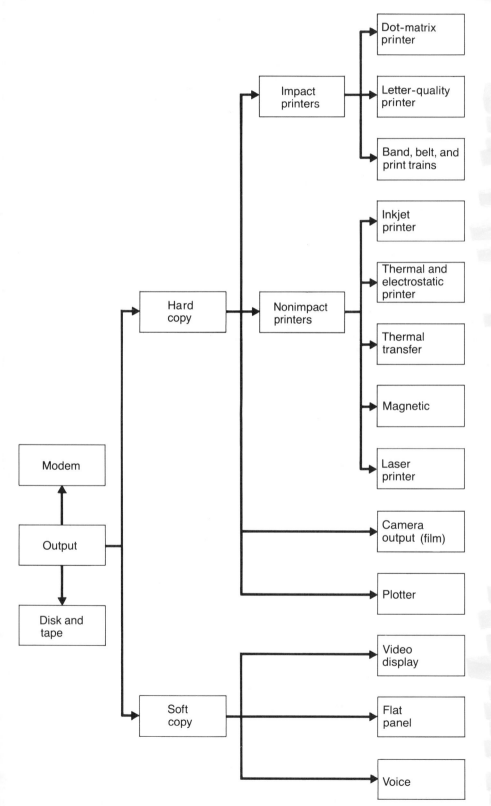

The first three categories are usually output to people; the fourth applies to output that is actually the input to another computer system or a machine. Of these four categories, text is still the most widely used type of computer output. This is because text is still a widely used medium of communication, and it is the easiest of the output technologies to implement. However, as technology advances, both input and output are becoming more varied.

DEVICES FOR PRODUCING OUTPUT

Although the information processing application itself determines what the content of the output will be, the format of the output depends, in part, on the output device. For example, in the case of generating a simple report, the choices include

- Printing or video display.
- Text and/or graphics.
- Black and white or color.

Which type of output to use is a decision that depends on the desired use of the information, the cost of producing that information, and whether the required technology is available. When selecting an output device, it is useful to understand the classifications of different output devices along with their capabilities and limitations.

Output from a computer system comes in hard copy, soft copy, or machine-readable form.

Hard copy refers to the recording of letters, graphics, or pictures on a hard medium, such as paper or film. Examples of hard copy include printing, drawing lines with a plotter, or photo-graphically recording an impression on film or microfilm.

Soft copy refers to the use of electronic signals to display a temporary image on a surface such as a video screen. Although this may seem to be a limitation, the image can quickly be changed. For example, graphic animation can be used to create movement.

Hard copy, on the other hand, is more permanent or fixed. The paper can be detached from the output device and carried or moved around. Also, paper is a familiar output medium. Working with printed material is well established; we generally know what a report or a book is and what conventions to follow in its preparation.

PRINTERS

The most common hard-copy devices are printers. There are a wide variety of printers that range in price from under $300 to specialty printers that can cost up to $50,000. Regardless of the price, there are some common characteristics that should be examined when matching a printer to an application. They include

- The ability to print images as well as text.
- The quality or resolution of the printed image.
- The speed of the printer.
- Whether the printer requires special paper.
- Whether the printer can print in color.

Printers. A laser printer can store the digital image of a form and print it on demand.

1040	Department of the Treasury—Internal Revenue Service	1988	
U.S. Individual Income Tax Return			

For the year January 1 – December 31, 1988, or other tax year beginning , 1988, ending , 198 . OMB No. 1545–0074

Use IRS Label. Other-wise, please print or type.	Your First name and initial (if joint return, also give spouse's name and initial)	Last name	Your Social Security Number
	Present home address (Number and street, including apartment number, or rural route)		Spouse's Soc. Sec. Number
	City, town or post office, State, and Zip code	Your occupation	
		Spouse's occupation	

| **Presidential Election Campaign** | Do you want $1 to go to this fund? | Yes | No | Note: Checking "Yes" will not change your tax or reduce your refund. |
| | If joint return, does your spouse want $1 to go to this fund? | Yes | No | |

Printers. Most letter-quality printers use shaped or fully formed character sets. Other printers use patterns of dots to create symbols. The higher the density of the dots, the closer the characters approach the appearance of shaped characters. Shown are enlarged illustrations depicting dot-matrix, inkjet, laser, and fully formed characters.

For example, suppose the application is to print a 1040 tax form. With some printers, the forms have to be fed to the printer before the actual printing cycle begins. With other printers, the image of the forms can be stored in the computer and printed along with the contents on plain paper.

The following section places printers in two broad categories; impact and nonimpact, describes the technology used when printing, and cites some advantages and disadvantages of each technology.

IMPACT PRINTERS

An *impact printer* gets its name from the method of creating characters on paper. Like a typewriter, a striking mechanism transfers a whole or partial character by striking a ribbon, which transfers the image onto the paper.

Letter-Quality Printers

Letter-quality printers are so named because their print quality is equivalent to that of an electric typewriter. In fact, the technology they employ evolved from the typewriter. They use cylinders, type balls, daisy wheels, or thimbles as type elements that contain a character set. Each character or symbol is transferred by impact.

For example, the daisy wheel print head is a spoked wheel with characters mounted on the tip of the spokes. The wheel is mounted in the printer and is spun by an electric motor to bring the desired character into print position. A single hammer then strikes the back of the tip and drives the character against a ribbon. The daisy wheel printer is the most popular letter-quality printer.

Although letter-quality printers produce high-quality output on plain paper, they cannot print images or color. Because of mechanical limitations, letter-quality printers can only print up to about 55 characters per second.

Dot-Matrix Printers

The most common type of impact printer is the *dot-matrix printer.* At the heart of a dot-matrix printer is a print

Dot-matrix printers. The Kodak Diconix 150 Plus is a portable dot-matrix printer.

THE IBM PROPRINTER

Dear Customer,
        Thank you for taking the time to view a demonstration of the
IBM PROPRINTER. The Proprinter is a versatile tool designed and
built by IBM for use with any of the IBM PC Family and many other
personal computers. Please review the features highlighted below.

Data-Processing Quality
        Printing Speed : 200 characters per second.
        Printing Sizes : 10 characters per inch / 80 characters per line.
                         12 characters per inch / 96 characters per line.
                         17.1 characters per inch / 137 characters per line.

Text Mode
        Printing Speed : 100 characters per second.
        Printing Sizes : 10 characters per inch / 80 characters per line.
                         12 characters per inch / 96 characters per line.

Near Letter Quality
        Printing Speed : 40 characters per second.
        Printing Sizes : 10 characters per inch / 80 characters per line.
                         12 characters per inch / 96 characters per line.

Download Fonts can be invoked in any combination of size and qualities :
For Example : Near Letter Quality   17.1 CPI (characters per inch)
        5 CPI, Near Letter Quality, Text

Use the TEXT mode to emphasize **important ideas** or,

Use the TEXT/Near Letter Quality combination to highlight **documents** !

Use the TEXT/Near Letter Quality/Double Wide combination for

Large, Pretty Printing

Utilize the subscript and superscript modes in math and science applications.

        H_2O $c^2 = a^2 + b^2$

Superscript or subscript with condensed (17.1 CPI)
              is great for printing contracts.

The UNDERLINE feature is great for **Titles** and **Headings**!

Dot-matrix printer. Sample output from the IBM Proprinter, a low-cost dot-matrix printer for personal computers.

head containing a column of steel pins. Images are formed by driving various combinations of pins against a ribbon and onto the paper. The two main advantages of dot-matrix printers are their relatively low cost and the flexibility with which they can produce images. A dot-matrix printer can print images as well as text. In an application you could, for example, copy a chart from Lotus 1-2-3, paste the chart into a document, and print the combination of text and graphics.

Because characters or images are produced by a selected pattern of dots, these printers can also change the size and style of characters and add emphasis such as bold, italic, or underlining. With the addition of multicolored ribbons, the printer can produce text and graphics in several colors.

Some dot-matrix printers use only nine pins in the print head; the quality of the print is poor because the dots are clearly visible. Newer printers have 24 pins and this improves the print quality considerably. Some dot-matrix printers offer near-letter-quality printing by moving the print head two or three times over each dot.

The speed of dot-matrix printers varies considerably depending on what is being printed and the model of the printer. When printing draft-quality text, some dot-matrix printers can operate in the range of 200 to 400 characters per second. When printing near-letter-quality text or graphics, low-cost dot-matrix printers slow down to a speed of 40 to 80 characters per second.

High-speed band printer. The IBM 4245 attaches to medium- and large-scale IBM computers and can print at speeds of up to 1200 lines per minute.

Inkjet printers. The IBM Color Jetprinter prints graphics or near-letter-quality text in up to seven colors.

Band, Belt, and Print Train Printers

Another class of impact printers is primarily used in large computer installations for high-speed printing of reports and forms. These impact printers are called band, belt, or print train printers. Unlike slower printers that print only one character at a time, these printers set up an entire line of print at once. Although they still print character by character or dot by dot, the process happens so fast that it seems to be printing one line at a time. Because of this, they are commonly referred to as *line printers*, regardless of the type of technology they use.

When the technology used for line printing is a band, belt, or print train, the printer contains one hammer or striking mechanism for each character position across the line. Several copies of the character set are stored on the band, belt, or train, which is in continuous movement past the bank of hammers. Hammer impact occurs at a given position when the correct character is rotated or spun to that position. This combination of multiple print-striking mechanisms plus multiple copies of the character set accounts for the ability to print at a fairly high speed. However, the combination of all this mechanical technology makes for very noisy printing (although soundproofing is available) and for poor-quality printing. Line printers are also far more expensive than character printers, are limited to printing text only, and cannot print in color.

NONIMPACT PRINTERS

Another category of printers is *nonimpact printers.* They operate on the same dot-forming principle as the

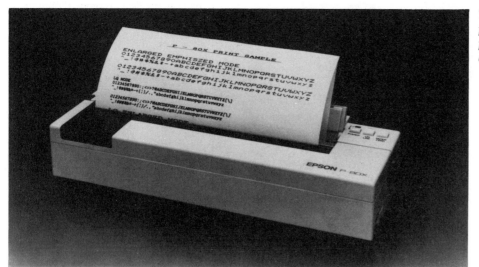

Thermal printers. *The Epson P-80X portable thermal printer features a 24-pin print head and a draft-quality speed of 45 characters per second.*

dot-matrix printer; however, instead of using an impact mechanism, they use nozzles, heat, electricity, magnetism, or optical methods to transfer an image onto paper.

Inkjet Printers

Inkjet printers form characters or graphics with a print head containing tiny nozzles or jets that spray drops of ink onto the paper. The effect is similar to dot-matrix printing.

An inkjet printer is capable of printing color images. By using a separate nozzle and ink cartridge for each of the three subtractive primary colors—cyan, magenta, and yellow—plus a fourth for black, up to six different hues can be printed. The color inkjet printer is an improvement over the problems of ribbons with multiple color bands that are required for color dot-matrix printers. Very expensive inkjet printers produce high-quality color that is well suited for low-volume publishing, proof copies, overhead transparencies, and camera-ready art.

Besides color, other advantages of inkjet printers include quiet operation and high reliability, thanks mainly to fewer moving parts. A possible disadvantage is the problem of nozzle clogging.

Thermal transfer printers. *The Okimate 20 is a low-cost color thermal-transfer printer that can be connected to personal computers.*

Magnetic printers. *With the Xerox 4060 ion printing system, users can create, modify, and store forms electronically as well as print at speeds of up to 60 pages per minute.*

Thermal and Electrostatic Printers

Thermal printers use heat and ***electrostatic printers*** use electricity to transfer an image onto specially treated paper. The process of thermal printing relies on a paper surface coated with a thin layer of chemicals that turn color when heat is applied. The output device's print head applies the heat in the shape of a dot-matrix or a character image without the use of a ribbon. Low-cost electrostatic printers operate the same way, except that the paper is coated with aluminum oxide and printing is activated by an electrical charge. Expensive large-format color electrostatic printers are available for printing drawings on continuous-roll 42-inch-wide paper.

Like the inkjet printer, an advantage of low-cost thermal or electrostatic printers is their quiet operation because of fewer moving parts. They can also be made less expensively than impact dot-matrix printers. Their major disadvantages are that the paper they use is expensive and difficult to find and fades quickly, they tend to operate at lower speeds, and they cannot print in color.

Thermal Transfer Printers

A thermal technology that can print in color is called thermal transfer printing. ***Thermal transfer printers*** heat a ribbon or color transfer sheet that contains particles of ink trapped in wax. When the wax melts, the ink is free to stick to the paper. Even with the added cost of a ribbon, color thermal transfer printers enjoy the benefits of quiet operation and simple design, which translates into lower cost and more reliability. Their main disadvantages are that they are slow and they work best with special smooth-surfaced paper. The surface of ordinary paper is too coarse to produce high-quality images.

Magnetic Printers

Because of the limitations on mechanical technology, such as movement of a print head mechanism or feeding paper through a tractor-feeding device, there is a limit to the printing speed of all the printers previously mentioned. To achieve higher print speeds, magnetic or optical technology is used to replace mechanical technology.

Magnetic printers, also called *ion printers*, create images by projecting a dot-matrix array of charged particles onto a drum. A magnetic toner then transfers and fixes the image onto paper. This technology was originally developed for tag and label printing. Because of its quiet operation, simple design, and high speed (60 pages per minute), magnetic printers can be used instead of line printers.

Laser Printers

Laser printers create images with a laser beam scanning across an electrically charged drum. As in a copier, toner or ink with an opposite charge sticks to the drum and is then transferred to paper by pressure and heat to create the finished image. In the past, laser printers were limited to minicomputer and mainframe applications that needed high-volume, high-quality printing. These high-cost laser printers will continue to be used for such applications. In the medium-cost range ($10,000) are color laser printers, and low-cost laser printers for under $1000 are now used for personal computer applications.

Laser printers offer near-typeset-quality text, medium-resolution graphics capabilities, and higher speed than conventional impact or nonimpact printers. For example, most of the low-cost laser printers can print eight pages a minute at a resolution of 300 dots per inch. They can mix type styles and sizes as well as graphic images on the same page.

Laser printers are quite different from conventional printers. They contain their own built-in microprocessor and RAM and ROM memories in order to produce high print speed and resolution. For example, to print one page of graphic images at a resolution of 300 dots per inch, each square inch requires 90,000 dots. An 8- by 10-inch piece of paper would require 7.2 million dots. If each dot is equivalent to a bit, it would take slightly under 1 megabyte of memory to store a single page. Because these printers process and print an entire page at a time, they are often called *page printers*.

A close cousin of the laser printer uses an array of light-emitting diodes (LEDs) instead of the beam of light emitted by a laser. *LED printers* feature a simpler design than laser printers, which translates into higher reliability and lower costs.

VIDEO-DISPLAY TECHNOLOGY

Video screen display is accomplished by a cathode ray tube (CRT). These are used in a wide variety of noncomputer applications, such as TV sets and video monitors, and in electronic test equipment, such as oscilloscopes.

Display on a CRT is accomplished by an electron beam that scans across a phosphor-coated surface, leaving points of light on the inside of the face of the tube. The entire screen is refreshed every 1/30th of a second. The beam current is either increased to make a lighter point or decreased to make a darker point along each of the scan lines. Each of these individual points is called a picture element. In the vocabulary of computers, this term has been shortened to *pixel*. This is very similar to the description of dot-matrix printing in which characters are formed by selecting dots to form characters. When used as a com-

Laser printers. *IBM's 3820 page printer can print at speeds of up to 20 pages per minute.*

![A] OUT IN THE [S] WILD! AFRICAN SAFARI

It's a jungle out there. Desktop publishing has evolved and proliferated so much that the peripherals which make it possible have to be tough to survive in this market. And the tougher the market, the more demanding the tests, the more savvy users turn to the OKI*LASER* 840 printer.

The OKI*LASER* 840 from OKIDATA provides high-speed performance, HP emulation, Adobe PostScript support, along with a choice of 35 fonts-each scalable from four point and up. Add 26 "true" HP bitmap

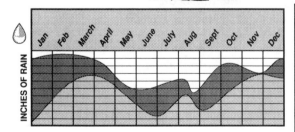

fonts, and you have a wide variety to choose from. Plus, character scaling, and 360 degree rotation. Its graphic capabilities are unlimited, and include pattern fill (greyscale) and shadow.

The OKI*LASER* 840 performs in the most demanding environments. And, its legendary OKIDATA quality and reliability make sure that it continues to perform, year after year.

Everyone seems to be into desktop publishing these days. But it takes a very special printer to enable you to realize the full potential of this rapidly expanding technology. The OKI*LASER* 840 is that special printer. As this page illustrates, the OKI*LASER* 840 offers a wide variety of fonts and shading capabilities, and can faithfully reproduce any image. And, as we all know, reproduction is vital to the survival of any species.

OKIDATA OKILASER 840

Output: 8 pages-per-minute

Resident Fonts: 35 Adobe scalable fonts, 26 "true" HP fonts

Additional Fonts: 2 slots

Page Description Language: PostScript controller board

Standard Memory: 2 MB expandable to 4 MB

Emulations: HPII, AppleTalk and Diablo

Paper Tray: one standard/one optional.

Laser printers. *Sample output from an Okidata laser printer showing the wide variety of graphics and text printing that is possible.*

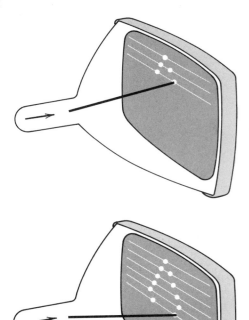

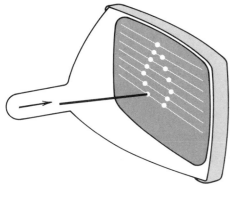

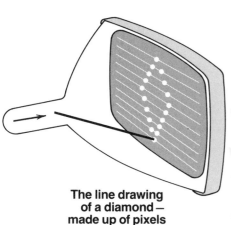

**The line drawing
of a diamond —
made up of pixels**

*Video display. Display on a cathode ray
tube is accomplished by an electron beam that
traces horizontal scan lines across a phospor-
coated surface. To form an image, such as the
simple diamond shown here, the beam is
intensified at each pixel in the image, leaving
a light point on the phosphor.*

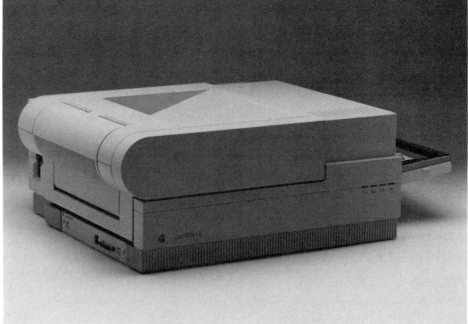

*Laser printers. Apple's LaserWriter II is a
desktop laser printer.*

puter-output device, the CRT divides
the screen image into a grid of rows
and columns.

CHARACTER MAPS VERSUS BIT MAPS

Display screens are divided into a grid.
This is accomplished by arranging a
part of memory, called video memory,
as a grid of rows and columns. There
are two primary techniques for displaying information on a screen.

Using a *character map*, video
memory is divided into a grid that is 25
rows high by 80 columns wide. Each
location on the grid can correspond to
a character, such as a letter, number, or
punctuation mark. A ROM stores each
character as a pattern of dots. To display the letter *A*, for instance, the processor simply sends the appropriate
code for *A* to the ROM, which copies
the pattern stored in the character map
and transfers that character's pattern
in the proper locations on the screen by
turning on the pixels. The main disadvantage to character mapping is that
the smallest piece of information that
can be displayed corresponds to the
grid size and the character set, and this

restricts both the kind and the detail
quality of the display. Character map
displays are used by the MS-DOS operating system and some of its applications.

Using a *bit map*, video memory and
the screen are divided into a much
finer grid of pixels than with character
mapping. On a Macintosh, for example, the 9-inch screen's grid size is
512 pixels wide by 342 pixels deep.
Like the area of a rectangle, multiplying the width times the depth gives
you the total number of pixels, which is
a measure of the *resolution* of the screen
(in the Macintosh case $512 \times 342 =$
175,104 pixels). In the case of one-color
displays, each bit in video memory
represents a pixel on the screen. If the
output is to a color screen, many bits
may be required for each pixel on the
screen because color displays require
more information than do simple one-
color displays.

Bit mapping offers a much higher
resolution and far greater diversity in
size and format when displaying images.
A disadvantage of bit mapping is that it
requires more complicated programming to manipulate or control all the
pixels and more memory to store them.

Summary of Printer Features by Printer Type

Printer Type	Print Graphics	Print Quality	Speed	Plain Paper	Noise	Color
Letter Quality	No	High	Medium	Yes	High	No
Dot-matrix	Yes	Medium	Medium	Yes	High	Yes
Band/belt/train	No	Medium	High	No	High	No
Inkjet	Yes	High	Medium	Yes	Low	Yes
Thermal	Yes	Low	Low	No	Low	No
Thermal transfer	Yes	Medium	Low	No	Low	Yes
Magnetic	Yes	High	High	Yes	Low	No
Laser	Yes	High	High	Yes	Low	Yes

High resolution is an important aspect of today's graphical user interfaces. In applications, such as desktop publishing, users need to see an accurate representation of how the image will look on the printed page. In addition, looking at a high-resolution screen will cause less eyestrain, and more information can be displayed.

MONOCHROME VERSUS COLOR CRTS

Both monochrome and color CRTs use the same basic technology. Color CRTs use three separate electron beams that represent the primary additive colors, red, blue, and green. The beams are focused so that their dot patterns slightly overlap on the screen to create the desired colors. Color is more expensive than monochrome because of the added circuitry and equipment needed to produce the color image.

There are two types of color CRT technologies. *Composite color CRTs* produce images the same way as an ordinary television set. *RGB* (short for red, green, blue) *CRTs* accept separate color signals and produce sharper, clearer images than a composite CRT.

Color does enhance the displayed image by providing

• Clarity and impact.

• More information than can be displayed in the same space as a monochrome display.

• A more aesthetically pleasing display.

Even though the software has to be more complex to produce this more complicated image, the bit-mapped color monitor can display multicolored drawings, graphs, charts, diagrams, and animation. However, in some low-resolution applications, color monitors have a serious drawback. Each point or pixel on the screen is formed by three overlapping dots, so that letters and characters often take on a fuzzy quality, creating serious eyestrain during extended use.

FLAT-PANEL DISPLAYS

For years, futurists have been telling us about the flat-panel TV screens

Flat-panel display. Because of their low power consumption, liquid crystal displays are popular for portable computers.

that hang on the wall like a picture. That technology is now beginning to appear and offers lighter weight, less bulk, and, usually lower power consumption.

One form of flat panel is the *liquid crystal display (LCD)*—a liquid-filled display surface that, when electrically charged, creates images using ambient light. Because LCDs have very low power consumption in comparison with video displays, they are now the most cost-effective displays for portable battery-powered laptop computers.

The historical drawback to LCDs has been their lack of clarity. Because early LCDs produced no light of their own but instead relied on reflected light for viewing, they had a very narrow range of viewing angles and could not be seen clearly if you did not look at them straight on. To compensate for this, manufacturers are dealing with the problem in two ways. The first is to backlight the LCD by adding lights that shine through the LCD screen from behind, thus providing a clearer image. The second is to build LCDs with *supertwist* crystals, which refract or twist the light to provide much higher contrast (e.g., darker characters against a lighter background). Higher contrast also makes possible a wider viewing angle when looking at the display. By adding color filter overlays to the LCD, multicolored display is possible.

Several laptop computers, such as the Tandy 1400 LT, the NEC MultiSpeed, and the Zenith TurboSport series, use backlighted supertwist technology in their LCDs.

The most mature, but least portable, flat-panel technology is the *gas plasma display.* In this device a gas, usually a mixture of neon and argon, is trapped between flat glass plates. A grid of electrodes permits the turning on and off of pixels. The IBM PS/2 Model P70 and the Toshiba 5100—portable computers that require ac power—use a gas plasma display screen.

The flat-panel technology that many experts predict will come closest to the capabilities of CRT display is the *electroluminescent display (ELD)*—a device that produces light through the application of electric current on a sensitive surface. One laptop computer that uses an ELD option is the Data General One. Like the LCDs, ELD panels for computer displays consume far less power and weigh less than CRTs. ELD panels are, however, still quite expensive and are used primarily by the military for portable terminals and computers in the field.

INTEGRATING FLAT-PANEL/ TOUCH-PANEL TECHNOLOGIES

An interesting combination of the technologies we have been discussing for input and output may soon appear on the market, packaged as an input/ output device in a lap computer. The idea was first tossed about by Alan Kay at Xerox's Palo Alto Research Center. The product (not completed) was to be called Dynabook, a personal device the size of a notebook that could, according to Xerox literature, handle "all your information-related needs."

In terms of technology, a flat-panel backlighted display would be connected to a *stylus*—an electronic pen with which the user could write on the display. For simplicity, the display itself would serve as both input and out-

Flat-panel display. The Toshiba T5200's gas plasma display screen.

put. The user interface would combine the normal conventions of pull-down menus for navigating through the system with handwriting recognition software. If you wanted to do word processing, for example, you would use the electronic pen to write on the display. Software would transform your handwritten words into text. Editing the text would be accomplished in much the same manner as is done today on paper. To insert a word, you simply draw a caret between two words and write in your insertion. Deleting text would be a simple as drawing a line through unwanted text. The system would be flexible and responsive to your needs and change its characteristics and display based on those needs.

Such a device could, in principle, eliminate the keyboard and the CRT screen of most of today's personal computers. This would eliminate a large part of the bulk and power requirements of present systems. The input and output systems of laptop computers are still limited to conventional keyboards and smaller LCDs. Flat panels combined with user interfaces capable of recognizing handwriting will be able to offer a larger lightweight, portable screen/keyboard combination and will revolutionize portable computers.

GRAPHICS: ANOTHER VIEW

In Chapter 2, the use of bar and line graphs, pie charts, and other diagrams for presentation graphics was discussed. These graphics consist of still images displayed on a bit-mapped screen or output to a hard copy device. More complex graphics incorporate movement, such as computer animation in a video game, interactively generated artwork in a computer-aided design application, or special effects in a flight simulation.

Three interrelated components are the keys to the trend toward more complex computer graphics:

• Graphics software.

• Video-display processors and other special graphics hardware.

• Color displays.

Graphics software provides a programmer or end user with instructions to accomplish such tasks as drawing lines and polygons, defining and changing colors and hues, moving images as in animation, and scaling an image (i.e., making an object appear larger or smaller on the screen). The most widespread example today is *Postscript*—a graphics programming language that provides an interface between application programs and printers, typesetters, and display screens. In addition to drawing and scaling, Postscript creates type faces or fonts from outlines stored in memory, which makes it extremely useful in desktop-publishing applications.

Even the simplest animated movements can require thousands of calculations, which can slow down the processor of any computer system and hinder the interactive capability of graphics software. To help accomplish such tasks, graphics systems usually incorporate video-display processors. These processors are *coprocessors*—separate processors that add additional functions to the central processor. In this case, they relieve the central processor of the tasks of updating video memory and converting image information into appropriate signals for the color monitor.

Color raster displays are the hardware component that allows the display of high-resolution flicker-free images. *Raster display* refers to the image-scanning technique used to display ordinary TV pictures, in which the electron beam continuously scans across and down the screen, then returns to the upper left-hand corner to repeat the process.

Computer graphics is an extremely broad topic, and the technical details of graphics are beyond the scope of this chapter. However, for overview purposes, we can group the major categories of computer graphics by their resolution, which is measured by the number of pixels on the display screen. The more pixels that can be displayed in the same area, the higher is the resolution.

Camera-output systems. High-speed computer-generated output on microfiche using laser imaging and dry-film technology.

Computer-aided publishing. The Xerox Documenter System lets users produce pages of text and graphics identical to the images on a desktop computer screen. In the foreground is the Xerox 6085 Professional Computer. In the background is a Xerox 4045 copier/printer.

LOW-RESOLUTION GRAPHICS

Low-resolution graphics are often found in arcade, simulation, and educational games. The resolution of these systems is approximately 250 by 250 pixels, very similar to the 279 by 191 pixels found in an Apple II. Applications that incorporate animated graphics, such as arcade video games, usually use a video coprocessor chip.

HIGH-RESOLUTION GRAPHICS

In personal computer systems, high-resolution graphics is provided in such applications as simulation; presentation graphics; and computer-aided publishing, design, and engineering. The resolution of the monitors of such systems ranges from 640 by 480 pixels up to 1280 by 1024 pixels. For example, the Macintosh II and IBM Personal System/2 color monitors offer a standard resolution of 640 by 480 pixels.

Today, the technology of high-resolution computer graphics is widely used for architectural, engineering, and design applications. Computer-aided engineering and design systems employ interactive graphics to design automobiles, houses, buildings, electronic components, and consumer products. Designers use *workstations*, which are powerful 32-bit desktop computers, that have evolved to meet the specific needs of engineers, scientists, and designers. The resolution of the monitors of these systems is often 1280 by 1024 pixels with the ability to display 256 simultaneous colors or shades of gray.

NEAR-PHOTOGRAPHIC-QUALITY GRAPHICS

Research at the frontier of computer graphics technology is beginning to achieve the goal of creating color images of near-photographic quality. To create these very-high-resolution (4000 by 4000 pixels) synthetic images, supercomputers and special processors are combined with sophisticated mathematical modeling software.

These advanced color graphics systems describe each pixel with 24 bits that specify the intensity of the three primary additive colors: red, blue, and green. By blending the colors, it is possible to achieve a realistic three-dimensional effect of shading, surface texture, and lighting effects.[1]

Computer animation of these highly realistic images is accomplished in the traditional filmmaking manner, that is, a series of still frames is displayed at 24 frames per second to create the illusion of motion.

The primary use for these advanced graphics is in special effects for television and movies. However, it is predicted that as the cost of the technology drops, the same high-quality effects will eventually be used for computer-aided engineering, computer-aided design, real-time flight simulation, and even video games.

SPECIALIZED OUTPUT SYSTEMS

Although printers and video displays are the most common output devices for computer systems, there are several applications that require highly specialized output devices. In the following, we describe the needs and requirements of these applications and the devices that are used.

CAMERA-OUTPUT SYSTEMS

In cases where high-volume printing is desired, another technique, called computer output to microfilm or microfiche (COM), can provide an alternative to high-speed impact or laser printing. Microfilm and microfiche are photographed documents or records in miniature form. Microfilm resembles a roll of conventional film and microfiche resembles a clear 4- by 6-inch card divided into frames. Because of their compact size, both microfilm and microfiche are ideal for storing lengthy printed reports. The disadvantage to their size is that they are not readable with the naked eye and require special equipment for viewing. A COM system can record computer output at speeds of up to 30,000 lines per minute, which is slightly faster than high-speed laser printing.

COMPUTER-AIDED PUBLISHING

In high-volume applications in which thousands of copies of the same material (e.g., magazines, newspapers, or books) must be printed, conventional offset printing is the least expensive method. Printing requires a *master* from which all copies are made. Typesetting is used in conjunction with output devices to make the master plates for the printing process. Years ago, typesetting was accomplished by hand setting pieces of lead type, but today laser printers and typesetters have replaced the hand labor of readying the written word for printing. A laser printer uses paper as its output medium whereas a typesetter uses photographic-quality film. Also, the resolution of a typesetter is considerably higher (1200- to 2400-dot-per-inch) than most of today's 300- to 400-dot-per-inch laser printers.

PLOTTERS

A *plotter* is an output device that produces an image on paper by controlling the motion of a pen carriage that draws lines. The plotter sees the output medium of paper as a series of *X, Y* coordinates. If you plotted similar coordinates on a piece of graph paper and drew lines connecting the points, you would have an approximate visual metaphor for how a plotter draws lines. The computer system sends the plotter a series of numbers representing *X, Y* coordinates in the desired pattern. The pen carriage then moves to the different positions while holding the pen on the surface of the paper. Curves are drawn by linking together a series of very short straight lines.

There are two major types of plotters: flat bed and drum. With some *flat-bed plotters*, the paper remains stationary while the pen carriage moves in both the *X* and *Y* directions. However, in recent years, moving-paper flat-bed technology has become a more prominent method. Some plotters employ a rotating *drum* that moves the paper in one direction while moving the pen carriage in the other direction. In either case, it is possible to specify and draw quite complex shapes in multiple colors by changing pens or by having the pen carriage hold several multicolored pens. In addition to small images, plotters are used to draw very large images at very high resolution, such as billboards and printed circuit art.

Plotters. *The Hewlett-Packard ColorPro plotter.*

VOICE OUTPUT

Because people develop the ability to speak so spontaneously and naturally, it is sometimes difficult for them to

Voice ouptut. *Digital's Dectalk has the capability of transforming most ordinary text files, such as documents stored in word processing files, into spoken output. It has variable speaking rates and a variety of voices.*

understand why simulating speech with a machine is so difficult. The growth of both voice input and output technology has been slowed by the fact that every individual perceives speech differently. Determining what constitutes high-quality synthesized speech is quite subjective.[2]

Voice output includes *speech coding*, which uses human speech as the source of the phrases and words to be synthesized, and *speech synthesis*, which produces basic speech sounds without the use of a human voice. Speech coding has found applications in games, toys, appliances, automobiles, and telephone voice mail. In some voice mail systems, for example, speech is digitized, compressed, and stored in memory or on disk. A user can retrieve selected portions of these digitized messages, send them to a routing list of recipients, or forward them to a third party. Voice mail will be discussed in greater detail in Chapter 10.

Speech synthesis has found applications in converting text into speech. For example, Digital Equipment Corporation's DECtalk system can read computer text, convert it to speech, and channel that speech through the telephone, thus providing a voice interface to existing applications. An electronic mail service could, for example, be equipped so that customers can call up and have their electronic mail read to them by telephone. Other possibilities include reading machines for the handicapped, stock and bank status inquiries, and flight-simulation equipment.

The goal of speech-synthesis systems is to create not only speech that is intelligible but also speech that sounds realistic. The problem involves electronically simulating a large vocabulary with a diverse set of linguistic rules in order to make the sounds seem natural. For example, when pronouncing the letter combination *gh*, it has no sound in the word *through*, is pronounced like an *f* in *enough*, and is pronounced like a *g* in *ghost*. The process of simulating such human effects on sound as the movement of lips and tongue, the vibration of vocal cords, and the reflection of sounds in the vocal tract is very complex.[3]

REVIEW

The four major types of computer output are text, images, sound, and data. The devices for displaying output include a wide range of printing techniques for producing hard copy images. Printers fall into two major categories—impact and nonimpact—and several of these printers can print in color. Video technology produces softcopy images in monochrome or color and more complex graphics can be produced by the technique known as bit mapping. The small size and low power consumption of flat-panel displays make them ideal for portable computer applications. Computer graphics is gaining in use because technology is pushing the resolution of display screens higher and higher. Camera systems can speed up the process of output by placing words and images on microfilm, and plotters can be used to draw effective black and white and color graphs and diagrams. Voice output consists of speech coding, using the recorded speech of humans, and speech synthesis, using the actual simulation of the human voice.

REFERENCES

1. Tucker, Jonathan B. "Computer Graphics Achieves New Realism." *High Technology,* June 1984, p. 42. This is an excellent but technical article on the graphics techniques that are used to create special effects in the movies.

2. Godin, Roger. "Sorting out Speech." *Electronics,* April 21, 1983, p. 135.

3. Kaplan, Gadi, and Eric J. Lerner. "Realism in Synthetic Speech." *IEEE Spectrum,* April 1985, p. 32. The *IEEE Spectrum* is a valuable magazine for overviews and updates on technology. It is expensive at $60 per year for a subscription; however, it can be found in most technical libraries.

RESOURCES

BOOKS

Bristow, Geoff, ed. *Electronic Speech Synthesis.* New York: McGraw-Hill, 1984. A technical reference book for those of you interested in the details of speech synthesis. The book also presents a less technical anthology of the history and technology of voice output.

Cavuoto, James. *Laser Write It!* Reading, Mass.: Addison-Wesley, 1986. An easy-to-follow guide to using the Apple Macintosh computer and LaserWriter laser printer to produce reports, resumes, newsletters, and business forms.

Rivlin, Robert. *The Algorithmic Image: Graphic Visions of the Computer Age.* Redmond, Wash.: Microsoft Press, 1986. A good book for the novice who wants to understand the ins and outs of computer graphics.

Scott, Joan, ed. *Computergraphica.* Houston: Gulf Publishing, 1984. This book is an anthology of essays and computer-generated illustrations divided into four sections: earth, life, invention, and imagination.

Seybold, John W. *The World of Digital Typesetting.* Media, Penn.: Seybold Publications, 1984. For anyone who is interested in the field of computer-aided publishing, this book is a comprehensive, complete, "must read" reference.

Sitarz, Daniel. *The Desktop Publisher's Legal Handbook.* Carbondale, Ill.: Nova Publishing, 1989. This book, written by an attorney, contains practical information on how to recognize and avoid legal problems such as avoiding copyright infringement, contract law, and legal forms.

Tufte, Edward R. *The Visual Display of Quantitative Information.* Cheshire, Conn.: Graphics Press, 1983. This book is a classic. It contains just about everything you'd like to know about computer graphics. However, be prepared for some heavy reading.

MAGAZINES

Computer Graphics World. Littleton, Mass.: Penwell Publishing. A monthly magazine devoted to the applications for computer graphics, along with the vendors and their products.

STUDY GUIDE

Match the following key terms to the appropriate definition:

A.

1. ____ Output device   **3.** ____ Soft copy   **5.** ____ Dot-matrix printer

2. ____ Hard copy   **4.** ____ Impact printer   **6.** ____ Letter-quality printer

a. A printer that uses a combination of a striking mechanism and a ribbon to transfer images onto paper.

b. A device that decodes coded symbols into a form of information that is easy for people to use or understand.

c. The recording of an image on a medium such as paper or film.

d. A printer that uses a cylinder, type ball, daisy wheel, or thimble to transfer formed characters by impact.

e. The recording of an image on a medium such as a display screen.

f. A printer that uses a selected pattern of dots transferred by impact.

B.

7. ____ Nonimpact printer   **10.** ____ Electrostatic printer   **13.** ____ Laser printer

8. ____ Inkjet printer   **11.** ____ Thermal transfer printer   **14.** ____ Desktop publishing

9. ____ Thermal printer   **12.** ____ Magnetic printer   **15.** ____ Plotter

a. A printer that uses a laser to record an impression on a drum.

b. A device that produces an image by controlling the motion of a pen carriage.

c. Printers that use nozzles, heat, electricity, magnetism, or optical methods to transfer images onto paper.

d. A printer that uses electricity to transfer images onto specially coated paper.

e. A printer that uses a selected pattern of dots transferred by heat.

f. Using personal computers to prepare and print a wide variety of typeset- or near-typeset-quality documents.

g. A printer that uses heat to melt wax containing particles of ink.

h. A printer that uses a selected pattern of dots transferred by spraying droplets of ink.

i. A printer that projects a selected pattern of charged particles onto a drum.

C.

16. ____ Pixel   **19.** ____ Liquid crystal display (LCD)   **22.** ____ Speech coding

17. ____ Character map   **20.** ____ Gas plasma display   **23.** ____ Speech synthesis

18. ____ Bit map   **21.** ____ Electroluminescent display (ELD)

a. A display that relies on reflected light for viewing.

b. A device that produces light through the application of an electric current on a sensitive surface.

c. Video memory that is divided into a grid 25 rows high by 80 columns wide.

d. A display that relies on a mixture of gases trapped between flat glass plates.

e. A technique that uses phonemes to synthesize voice output.

f. Video memory in which bits are used to represent pixels.

g. A technique that uses prerecorded human speech as the source of voice output.

h. A light or dark point on the surface of a display screen.

True/False:

24. F The information processing application determines the format of the output.

25. T The advantages of hard copy stem from our familiarity with paper.

26. T The most common form of printer is the dot-matrix printer.

27. T Nonimpact printers operate on the same dot-forming principle as dot-matrix printers.

28. F Because of more moving parts, inkjet printers are noisier and less reliable than dot-matrix printers.

29. T High-speed dot-matrix printers are an alternative to line printers.

30. F To achieve higher print speeds, magnetic or optical technology is used to replace mechanical technology.

31. T Laser printers are quite different from conventional printers.

32. T Cathode ray tubes (CRTs) are the most common form of video display.

33. F An alternative to laser printing is magnetic printing.

34. T A drawback of color displays is that letters and characters often take on a fuzzy quality.

35. F High-resolution graphics are on the order of 250 by 250 pixels.

36. T Video-display processors are a form of coprocessors.

37. F Creating near-photographic-quality graphics requires the use of special personal computers.

38. F Speech synthesis has found applications in converting speech into text.

Multiple Choice:

39. Which of the following is not a major type of computer output?
    a. Voice.
    b. Text.
    c. Images.
    d. Content.

40. An impact printer gets its name by
    a. Having the same print quality as an electric typewriter.
    b. Transferring a pattern of dots to the paper.
    c. Transferring a whole or partial character by striking a ribbon.
    d. Using heat to transfer an image onto paper.

41. Dividing an output screen into a grid of individual pixels is called
    a. Bit mapping.
    b. Character mapping.
    c. Selecting dots to form characters.
    d. Video-display technology.

42. Which of the following is not used in letter-quality printing?
    a. Daisy wheel.
    b. Inkjet.
    c. Type ball elements.
    d. Laser.

43. Thermal printers use which of the following methods to transfer an image onto paper?
    a. Applying heat.
    b. Melting wax.
    c. Spraying ink.
    d. Electricity.

44. One example of soft copy would be
    a. Drawing lines with a plotter.
    b. Recording an impression on microfilm.
    c. Graphic animation in a video game.
    d. Printing a copy of the CRT screen.

45. The technology of dot-matrix printing
    a. Gives the impression of printing one line at a time.
    b. Requires specially treated paper.
    c. Cannot produce graphics or pictures.
    d. Has few restrictions on the size of characters.

46. Nonimpact printing is an important technology because it
    a. Is primarily a high-speed method of printing.
    b. Is a lower-cost technology.
    c. Is the simplest way of color printing.
    d. Can produce output on microfiche.

47. Laser printing derives its flexibility from
    a. Transferring images onto specially treated paper.
    b. Its use of sophisticated mechanical technology.
    c. An embedded microprocessor in the printer.
    d. Its lack of moving parts.

48. The most cost-effective display for a portable computer today is
    a. Gas plasma.
    b. Cathode ray tube (CRT).
    c. Electroluminescent display (ELD).
    d. Liquid crystal display (LCD).

Thought Questions:

49. The printed word is by far the most popular type of computer output. Do you believe that any other form of output will, in the near future, surpass the printed word's popularity? Defend your position.

50. "When it comes to video-display technology, more resolution is better." Do you agree or disagree with this statement? Why?

Projects:

51. Choose one of the categories of printers mentioned in this chapter. Then visit a computer store and obtain information about two different printer's capabilities, limitations, and price in the category. Ask for samples of the two printer's output. Present your comparison to the class.

52. Prepare a research paper on the state of the art of flat-panel displays, including availability, price, and applications.

SOFTWARE EXERCISES

After reading this chapter, you no doubt are aware of the many comparisons of various output devices that have been made. People have devised many units and scales of measurement, but often there are differences from device to device and from system to system. By making comparisons you can evaluate the different characteristics of products, such as printers.

The speed of an output device is calculated by dividing a quantity measurement by a time measurement and is expressed in units that combine both these factors, such as characters per second. In this chapter we have also used the terms lines per minute and pages per minute to refer to a printer's speed.

For this exercise, you are going to use a spreadsheet to compare the output speed of several different categories of printers. You will convert the different speeds into one common denominator—characters per minute. Keep in mind that this common denominator is somewhat artificial. For example, it is not valid to compare printing a page of graphics with printing a page of text.

Use the following assumptions:

1 line = 80 characters

1 page = 5280 characters

Use the following conversion formulas:

multiply	by	to obtain
characters per second	60	characters per minute
lines per minute	80	characters per minute
pages per minute	5280	characters per minute

	A	B	C
1			
2			
3			
4			**Speed**
5	**Printer type**	**Printer name**	**(char/min)**
6			
7	Dot matrix	XXXXXXXXX	XXXXX
8		XXXXXXXXX	XXXXX
9			
10	Letter quality	XXXXXXXXX	XXXXX
11		XXXXXXXXX	XXXXX
12		XXXXXXXXX	XXXXX
13			
14	Inkjet	XXXXXXXXX	XXXXX
15			
16	Thermal transfer	XXXXXXXXX	XXXXX
17			
18	Line	XXXXXXXXX	XXXXX
19		XXXXXXXXX	XXXXX
20			
21	Laser	XXXXXXXXX	XXXXX
22		XXXXXXXXX	XXXXX
23		XXXXXXXXX	XXXXX
24			

Sample printer chart spreadsheet.

Assignment 1. Using data mentioned in this chapter, prepare a spreadsheet that lists printers and their speed in characters per minute in each of the following categories: (1) character printers, such as dot-matrix and letter-quality printers; (2) line printers, such as band or print train printers; and (3) page printers, such as laser printers. Use the sample spreadsheet shown here to format your output.

Assignment 2. Us
use the graphing
format the data ir

Assignment 3. Ol
ers from various r
spreadsheet that c
ters per minute as

ANSWERS

1. b, 2. c, 3. e, 4. a, 5. f, 6. d, 7. c, 8. h, 9. e, 10. d, 11. g, 12. i, 13. a, 14. f, 15. b, 16. h, 17. c, 18. f, 19. a, 20. d, 21. b, 22. g, 23. e, 24. F, 25. T, 26. T, 27. T, 28. F, 29. T, 30. T, 31. T, 32. T, 33. T, 34. T, 35. F, 36. T, 37. F, 38. F, 39. d, 40. c, 41. a, 42. b, 43. a, 44. c, 45. d, 46. c, 47. c, 48. d.

STEVEN P. JOBS

Profession: Founder and chairman of Next, Inc., Palo Alto, California.

Profile: Jobs is best known for cofounding Apple Computer, Inc., with Stephen Wozniak. In recognition of his pioneering work, Jobs was awarded the National Technology Medal by President Reagan in 1985. He left Apple in 1985 to found Next, Inc., a company that sells personal computer workstations for education and business.

Quote: "*The college worker of today is the knowledge worker of tomorrow.*"

CHAPTER 7
PROCESSORS AND MEMORIES

PREVIEW

The first part of this chapter takes you inside the world of the processor and memory. There you will find the miniature circuits that carry out millions of instructions per second and store thousands and sometimes millions of bits of information that can represent anything you can convert to the binary ones and zeros that the computer understands. Looking from the inside out, you will see that a computer's power largely depends on how many bits it can store and how fast it can manipulate them. This is accomplished by subsystems that are put together in a highly organized manner.

Learning how the subsystems of the processor are organized and used sets the stage for discussing the important trends that highlight the differences between computer systems. Looking from the outside in, you will see how computers are sorted out by size, design considerations, and the uses to which they are applied.

In this chapter, you'll learn

- What the central electronic complex of a computer is.
- What a processor and memory are.
- How the central electronic complex has evolved over the years.
- Trends in the evolution of computer systems.
- The differences among mainframes, minicomputers, and microcomputers.
- The role of the supercomputer.
- What parallel processing means.

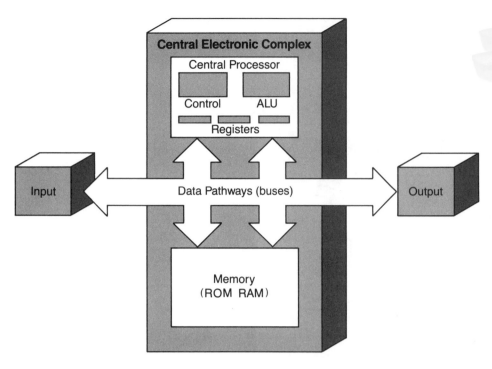

Central electronic complex. Block diagram showing the relationship of the major components of a computer system.

THE CENTRAL ELECTRONIC COMPLEX

At the center of every computer system lies a *central electronic complex,* a term coined by IBM. It consists of a processor, memory, and some paths for information to travel between the two. This is the central nervous system of the computer, and it is often contrasted to the devices that surround the processor and memory, such as keyboards, display screens, and disk and tape drives, which are known as *peripherals.*

The first half of the chapter describes the functional units that make up the complex and what they do. Then, the entire complex is described in terms of its evolution and the features that distinguish one computer system from another.

In many ways, a computer system is like a sound system. At the center of the sound system, an amplifier receives electrical signals from an input device, which may be a microphone, a tape deck, a phonograph turntable, an AM or FM tuner, a synthesizer, or some other specialized device found in a recording studio. An amplifier processes the stream of electrical signals and produces output signals, often to speakers, but also, when recording, to tape. A computer also receives electrical signals from an input device, which may be a keyboard, disk drive, mouse, or speech recognizer. It processes the stream of electrical signals and produces output signals to devices such as display units or printers.

Another similarity of sound systems and computer systems is the fact that both come in a wide variety of sizes, depending on their purpose. A sound system can be packaged in a

The central electronic complex of the Macintosh IIx computer. The large chip in the front center of the mother board is the Motorola 68030 microprocessor. To its right is the 68882 math coprocessor. On the upper right are the RAM and ROM single in-line memory modules. The other chips on the board perform special functions.

Processors. *Close-up photograph of the Motorola 68030 32-bit microprocessor. In actual size, the processor is $\frac{3}{8}$-inch square, the size of a small fingernail.*

small hand-held device (the Sony Walkman), as components for use in the home, as a small-sized system for use in a car, or as a large and powerful system, such as the sound systems used at outdoor concerts. Similarly, computer systems range from hand-held notebook sizes to large-scale supersizes, with a wide range of models in between.

The analogy ends with memory, which the sound system does not need. Memory is the part of the computer system where programs are temporarily stored while waiting to be processed and where data are retrieved and recorded. For the sequence of step-by-step operations of a computer to occur, memory and processor must work hand in hand.

WHAT IS A PROCESSOR?

A *processor*, also called a *central processing unit* or *CPU*, is a functional unit that interprets and carries out instructions. Every processor comes with a unique set of operations such as ADD, STORE, or LOAD that represent the processor's *instruction set.* Computer designers are fond of calling their computers machines, so the instruction set is sometimes referred to as machine instructions and the binary language in which they are written is called *machine language.*

An instruction is made up of *operations* that specify the function to be performed and *operands* that represent the data to be operated on. For example, if an instruction is to perform the operation of adding two numbers, it must know (1) what the two numbers are and (2) where the two numbers are. When the numbers are stored in the computer's memory, they have an address to indicate where they are, so if an operand refers to data in the computer's memory it is called an address. In the discussion "A Hypothetical Computer," you will see how an instruction uses addresses. The processor's job is to retrieve instructions and operands from memory and to perform each operation. Having done that, it signals memory to send it the next instruction.

This step-by-step operation is repeated over and over again at speeds measured in millionths of a second. A timer called a *clock* releases precisely timed electrical signals that provide a

Instruction set. *A sample generic machine language instruction set showing the different categories of instructions.*

Category	Example
Arithmetic	Add, subtract, multiply, divide
Logic	And, or, not, exclusive or
Program control	Unconditional branching, conditional branching, subroutines
Data Movement	Move, load, store
Input/output	Read, write

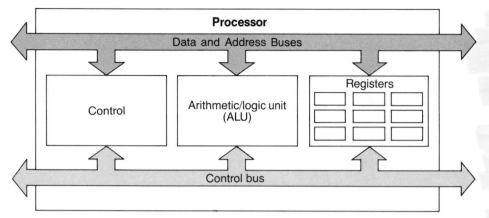

Processors. *Block diagram showing the functional components of a processor. They communicate with each other and with other parts of a computer system through electrical pathways known as buses.*

regular heartbeat for the processor's work. The term that is used to measure the computer's speed is borrowed from the domain of electrical engineering and is called a *megahertz (MHz)*, which means million cycles per second. For example, in an 8-MHz processor, the computer's clock ticks 8 million times every second.

A processor is composed of two functional units—a control unit and an arithmetic/logic unit—and a set of special workspaces called registers.

The Control Unit

The *control unit* is the functional unit that is responsible for supervising the operation of the processor. In some ways, it is analogous to a telephone switchboard with intelligence because it makes the connections between various functional units of the computer system and calls into operation each unit that is required by the program currently in operation. And like a switchboard with call waiting, the processor can be interrupted. An *interrupt* is a signal that tells the processor to put aside what it is doing and transfer control to another instruction. The processor resumes its original instruction when the interrupt is finished.

The control unit fetches instructions from memory and determines their type or decodes them. It then breaks each instruction into a series of simple small steps or actions. By doing this, it controls the step-by-step operation of the entire computer system.

The Arithmetic/Logic Unit

The *arithmetic/logic unit (ALU)* is the functional unit that provides the

computer with logical and computational capabilities. Data are brought into the ALU by the control unit, and the ALU performs whatever arithmetic or logic operations are required to help carry out the instruction.

Arithmetic operations include adding, subtracting, multiplying, and dividing. Logic operations make a comparison and take action based on the results. For example, two numbers might be compared to determine if they are equal. If they are equal, processing will continue; if they are not equal, processing will switch to another instruction.

Registers

A *register* is a storage location inside the processor. Registers in the control unit are used to keep track of the overall status of the program that is running. Control unit registers store information such as the current instruction, the location of the next instruction to be executed, and the operands of the instruction. In the ALU, registers store data items that are added, subtracted, multiplied, divided, and compared. Other registers store the results of arithmetic and logic operations.

An important factor that affects the speed and performance of a processor is the size and number of the registers. Technically, the term *word size* (also called word length) describes the size of an operand register, but it is also used more loosely to describe the size of the pathways to and from the processor. Currently, word sizes in general-purpose computers range from 16 to 64 bits. If the operand registers of a processor are 16 bits wide, the processor is said to be a 16-bit processor.

Specialized Processors

Some processors are designed to add additional functions to the central processor. For example, in Chapter 6, you learned that video display processors, also called graphics coprocessors, handle the tasks of updating video memory and converting image information into appropriate signals for the monitor. Math coprocessors relieve the central processor of the intensive numeric calculations required in scientific and technical applications. Digital signal processors (DSPs) are another example of specialized microprocessors. They assist the central processor in working with sound, speech, music, and image processing.

Other processors are designed to fill the specific requirements of an application. These processors are based on *application-specific integrated circuits (ASIC)*. An early example of a product that uses an ASIC is the digital wristwatch. The functions that a wristwatch performs are simple and easy to understand. Although a general-purpose processor could easily handle the functions of a watch, there is no need to do so, as it is much more economical to develop a specific integrated circuit chip to do the job. Another example of ASIC is the digital calculator. Today's specialized processor chips permit designers to build large amounts of computing power into all sorts of products, such as controller functions in appliances and automobiles, computer networking, speech recognition and synthesis, and graphics processing.

WHAT IS A MEMORY?

A processor cannot store all the information it needs while running a program; thus it depends on memory. *Memory* can be thought of as a series of cells, with each cell storing a piece of information. That piece of information is known as a byte, a number between 0 and 255. Memories are often rated in terms of their information storage capacity, which is usually measured in thousands of bytes. In Chapter 1, we saw that K is used as an abbreviation for 2^{10}, or 1024, bytes. If a computer has a 512K memory, it has 524,288 individual cells.

For the processor to reference memory, the cells must have addresses. The concept of an address is similar to the addresses found in the postal system, so it is useful to visualize a 512K memory as a large post office that contains 524,288 post office boxes. Just as the postal employee can refer to an address by specifying a post office box number, an instruction can refer to a particular cell in memory by specifying that cell's address as an operand. And just as a post office box may contain mail or instructions to go to a window to pick up mail, a memory cell may contain data or instructions.

Memories are generally classified by the nature of the accessibility of the information and are divided into two major categories: random-access memory (RAM) and read-only memory (ROM).

Random-Access Memory

Random-access memory (RAM) is a type of memory that can be read from or written to. Most RAM is actually *dynamic RAM* or DRAM (pronounced dee ram). It is dynamic because it is constantly being refreshed with electrical pulses. Recall from Chapter 6 that a video-display screen loses its image if it is not constantly refreshed. In the same way, dynamic RAM loses its contents without constant electrical refreshing. There is a type of RAM, called *static RAM*, that needs very little power for refreshing, but it is not as widely used because it is more costly to produce. Because most RAM is dynamic, it is said to be *volatile*; that is, it loses its contents when the electric power is shut off.

Memory. Each cell in memory is of fixed size and can store only one piece of information, whereas a mailbox is of variable size and can store many pieces of information.

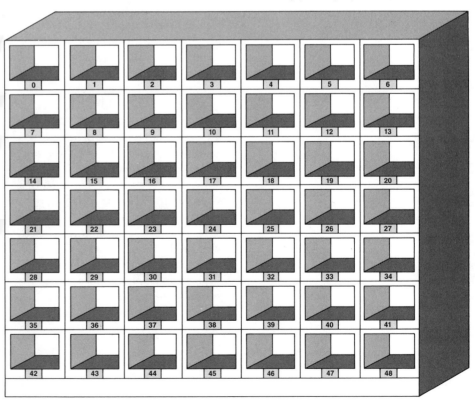

Random access means that the cells of a RAM memory are organized so that the access time for any one cell is the same as for any other cell. This is accomplished by arranging the memory cells in a two-dimensional array, in much the same way that a spreadsheet is arranged as a grid of rows and columns. Then a memory cell can be accessed by supplying an address that contains the row and column numbers of that cell.

Read-Only Memory

Read-only memory (ROM) is a type of memory that can be read from but cannot be written to or altered. ROM is static or *nonvolatile*; that is, it retains its contents when the electric power is shut off. ROM can be used as a specialized part of general memory, or it can be used to store parts of the operating system or small programs that per-

form specialized routines. For example, a portion of ROM might contain a program that performs division, so that when a program executes a DIVIDE instruction, it is actually executed using instructions in the ROM memory. In our discussion under "Microprogramming," you will see how ROM can be used to store the entire instruction set of a computer.

BUSES

A *bus* is a circuit that provides a path for transferring information between two or more devices. In a bus-oriented computer, processor, memory, and the input and output devices are connected by a set of three buses. When instructions and data share the same memory, they travel to and from the processor and memory over a common *data bus*. A second bus, called an *address bus*, connects memory cells that

Random-access memory. IBM's 16-megabit dynamic random-access memory (DRAM) chip shown on a postage stamp. The chip can store the equivalent of 1600 pages of double-spaced typewritten text.

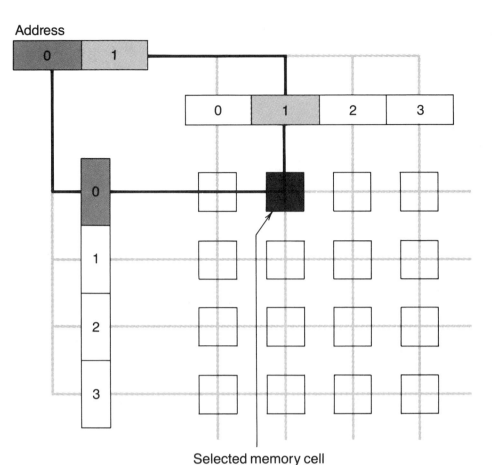

Memory. *Random access is achieved by arranging the memory into a two-dimensional array similar to a spreadsheet. The memory address contains the row and column numbers of the specified cell. Shown is a very small 4-by-4 array.*

Address

Selected memory cell

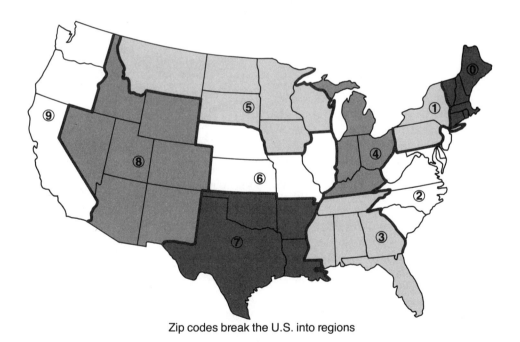

Zip codes break the U.S. into regions

Segment 1
Segment 2
Segment 3

Segments break memory into regions

Memory. *The technique of memory segmentation uses the first digit(s) of an address to divide memory into separate regions.*

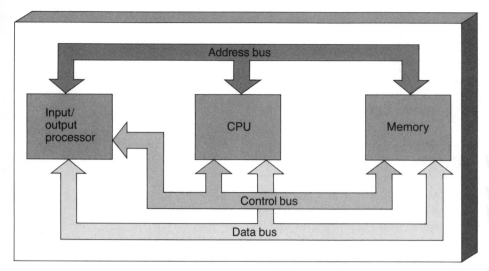

Buses. *Block diagram showing the various interconnections in a bus-oriented computer system.*

contain data needed for instructions to the processor. A third bus, called a *control bus*, is used to signal the various parts to transfer information and to signal the processor when the transfer is completed.

A HYPOTHETICAL COMPUTER

The best way to get a feeling for how the different components of a central electronic complex are interrelated is with a simplified step-by-step

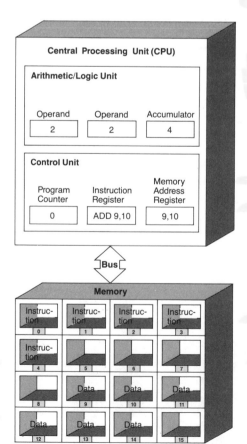

A hypothetical computer. At the end of one cycle, an instruction that specifies adding 2 + 2 has been fetched, decoded, and executed. The diagram shows simulated values in English and decimal form that would appear in each of the registers.

walkthrough of an instruction. However, keep in mind the analogy of looking at a single frame of a motion picture. When motion picture frames are looked at individually, no illusion of motion is given. The following assumptions will be made to simplify the example.

• Each complete instruction, that is, operation and operands, occupies one memory cell.

• Each data item occupies a single memory cell.

• The address- and data-bus pathways are the same size, as are the memory locations and the registers in the processor.

• Although program and data share the same memory, they are not intermixed. The instructions occupy one area of memory, and the data reside in another area.

The control unit starts things off by fetching the first instruction of the program from memory. It does this by placing the address of the instruction in a register called the program counter. From the program counter, the address is sent over the address bus to memory. At the same time, a signal to READ the memory is sent over the control bus. The instruction is retrieved, sent to the processor over the data bus, and placed in the instruction register. The program counter is then set so that it points to the next instruction in sequence and is ready to go on to the next cycle.

Now, the instruction in the instruction register is decoded to find out what it is. If data are needed, the address or addresses of the data are sent over the address bus, a signal to READ memory is sent over the control bus, and the data are retrieved and placed in a data register in the ALU.

Executing the instruction takes place in the ALU. For example, if the operation of the instructions calls for adding two numbers, the addition is performed and the results are stored in a register called an accumulator. The data in the accumulator are then sent to memory over the data bus along with a control signal to WRITE to memory. The process is then repeated by obtaining a new address from the program counter to see where the next instruction to be fetched is located. This step-by-step process is repeated over and over until execution of the program is complete.

THE EVOLVING CENTRAL ELECTRONIC COMPLEX

As the demand for computers with greater speed, memory, and sophistication grows, new techniques are constantly being developed to meet those demands. These techniques are based on the technology of microelectronics that we discussed in Chapter 3. They contribute to both improved performance and decreased costs. These techniques will be discussed in the context of microcomputers, where they are most pervasive.

INCREASE IN WORD SIZE

One of the most widely used terms to designate and measure the computing power of a microprocessor is word size. Two common word sizes are used in microprocessors: 16 and 32 bits, with a trend toward 32-bit processors.

Another important factor in comparing different processors is the size of the input/output data bus, which is the data pathway from RAM to input and output devices (such as disks), and vice versa. A 16-bit processor should ideally have 16-bit registers and 16-bit pathways to and from the processor. The same is true for 32-bit processors. For example, the Intel 8086, an early microprocessor used in personal computers, has a 16-bit internal data bus and a 16-bit input/output bus. The Motorola 68030, the microprocessor used in some Apple Macintosh IIs, is a 32-bit processor with a 32-bit internal data bus and a 32-bit input/output bus.

With a larger word size, a processor is capable of faster operation because its registers are larger. This simply means that it can handle larger instructions (which translates into more sophisticated instructions) and larger data items. With larger internal data

and input/output buses, processing speed can be increased because the processor can get more to work on each time an instruction or data item is retrieved from memory.

A term used to rate the speed of computers is *million instructions per second* or *MIPS*. It should be noted that manufacturers rate their computers in much the same manner as the Environmental Protection Agency (EPA) rates miles-per-gallon (mpg) figures for automobiles—under carefully controlled circumstances and peak conditions.

Another important difference among microprocessors is the amount of memory each can address. Larger word size translates into larger address-bus size; in turn, this means that the processor can address more memory. Very large computer memories are measured in millions of bytes. A commonly used term is *megabyte (MB)*, which is the equivalent of 2^{20} or 1,048,576 bytes. For example, both the 80286 microprocessor (used in some IBM PS/2 computers) and the 68000 microprocessor (used in early Macintosh computers) can address up to 16 megabytes (16 MB) of RAM. The 80386 and 80486 microprocessors can address up to 4 gigabytes of RAM. (A *gigabyte*, in which giga means billion, is the equivalent of 2^{30} or 1,073,741,824 bytes.) The ability to access a larger amount of memory has two important advantages: (1) it permits the use of more sophisticated and powerful programs, and (2) for the previously discussed reasons, it speeds up the rate at which the processor can run such programs. There are practical limits however. A program that used 4

Increases in word size. A comparison of several 8-, 16-, and 32-bit microprocessors showing differences among the buses, word sizes, and speeds.

		Word Size (Bits)	Address Bus (Bits)	I/O Data Bus (Bits)	Max RAM (bytes)	Max Speed (MHz)	Max Speed (MIPS)
Company	Processor						
Zilog	Z-80	8	16	8	64 KB	4	N/A
Mostek	6502	8	16	8	64 KB	4	N/A
Intel	8088	16	20	8	1 MB	8	0.3
Intel	8086	16	20	16	1 MB	12	0.3
Intel	80286	16	24	16	16 MB	16	2
Motorola	68000	32	24	16	16 MB	20	1.3
Motorola	68020	32	32	32	4 GB	33	7
Motorola	68030	32	32	32	4 GB	50	12
Intel	80386	32	32	32	4 GB	33	8
Motorola	68040	32	32	32	4 GB	33	17
Intel	80486	32	32	32	4 GB	33	20

Table title: Evolution of the Microprocessor to 1990

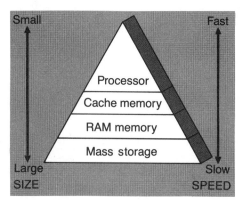

Small		Fast
↑	Processor	↑
	Cache memory	
	RAM memory	
	Mass storage	
Large		Slow
SIZE		SPEED

Advances in memory. In some computer systems, memory can thought of as a series of levels of memory ranked one above another on the basis of speed. When combined with virtual memory, a program is divided into pages. The most often used pages are stored in cache, and the least often used pages are stored on disk.

Reduced instruction set computers. The IBM System/6000 POWERstation 530 is a RISC-based workstation. It is used primarily for technical applications.

gigabytes of RAM, for example, would probably require at least the same amount of disk space. And, while the prices of memory and disks continue to drop, we are still talking about very large numbers.

MEMORY MANAGEMENT

In addition to physically larger and faster memories, several techniques permit memory to be used more advantageously. One such technique is virtual memory. *Virtual memory* techniques let you run a large program in a small real memory. Only the active parts of the program will be in memory, whereas the inactive parts reside on disk. For example, if a computer has 512K of real memory and the size of a program is 1 MB, the program is divided into pieces called *segments* and *pages*. A segment is a variable-length piece of memory that a program allocates, whereas a page is a fixed-length piece of memory.

Segmentation is a memory management technique for allocating and addressing memory. Segments also provide structure (a program can consist of a collection of segments) and protection (other programs can not access those segments). A segment is a convenient unit to swap into and out of memory, but because segments are of variable length, managing them in memory and on disk is complex and time consuming. To overcome these problems, an additional technique called paging is used. *Paging* is a memory management technique for mapping virtual addresses on disk to real addresses in memory. A program or segment that appears to be a single large piece of memory may actually be scattered throughout real memory in pages. The system handles segmentation and paging in such a way that the distinction between memory and the disk is invisible to the program.

A technique for executing large programs at very fast speeds combines the concept of virtual memory with the concept of a memory hierarchy, that is, a series of levels of memory ranked one above another on the basis of speed of access. Visualize a pyramid with a processor at the very top. At the next lower level of the hierarchy, some computer systems use a *cache memory,* which is a very-high-speed memory. Sometimes it is built into the processor to make it even faster. At the next lower level is normal RAM memory, and beneath that is slower external disk storage.

The memory hierarchy and virtual memory techniques are combined to work conceptually as follows. A large program is divided into pages. The cache memory will store the most often used pages, the RAM memory will store the next most often used pages, and the least used pages will be stored on disk. In effect, the combination of techniques can speed up processing because the number of times the program has to fetch instructions and data from RAM and disk memory is reduced.

Often, another level is added to the hierarchy in the form of a *RAM disk*—a reserved section of relatively slow RAM that is used to store information normally located on an even slower disk.

FASTER CLOCK SPEEDS

Another measure of processor power is the clock speed of the processor measured in megahertz (MHz). Recall that the processor's operation proceeds in fixed time intervals or cycles. Each operation, such as fetching an instruction, takes one or more cycles to complete. If the processor's clock is ticking at 16 million cycles per second (16 MHz) instead of 8 million cycles per second (8 MHz), the same operations would proceed twice as fast at the faster clock speed. By way of analogy, consider two cars making a trip between Los Angeles and San Francisco that leave at the same time. One is traveling at 40 miles per hour and the other is traveling at 60 miles per hour. Assuming that neither car receives traffic tickets or stops for lunch, which one will complete the trip first? If all other factors are equal, a processor with a faster clock speed, or higher megahertz rate, will complete a processing task faster than one with a slower clock speed or lower megahertz rate.

REDUCED INSTRUCTION SET COMPUTERS

In the 1970s, a team of computer scientists led by John Cocke at IBM were researching ways to develop very-large-scale telephone switching systems. They envisioned a high-speed controller as the heart of such a system. To achieve the desired performance, the controller would have to execute a few simple instructions at a very high speed. While researching conventional *complex instruction set computers (CISC)*, they discovered that a very small subset of instructions accounts for a very large percentage of all instructions executed. If the instruction set could be pared to a few simple instructions, then the majority of them could be executed in a single processor cycle.

The switching project was abandoned, but the computer scientists forged ahead in the belief that their ideas for a controller could be applied to a general-purpose computer. In 1980, the result was the 801 minicomputer, the first **RISC**, or **reduced instruction set computer.** RISC is a combination of hardware and software that reduces the number of instructions in a computer's instruction set and attempts to execute each instruction as quickly as possible.

Because the instruction set is so simple, a RISC processor can achieve very fast theoretical speeds. To achieve high-speed processing, a RISC processor needs two to three times as much memory as a CISC processor and a larger number of registers to hold information waiting to be processed. In addition, a program called an optimizing compiler analyzes logic operations and preloads the registers with instructions so the processor does not have to wait for them. You will learn more about compilers in Chapter 14.

TRENDS IN THE EVOLUTION OF COMPUTER SYSTEMS

The fundamental concepts that we have discussed set the stage for examining the differences among computer systems. The central electronic complex is only a small part of a computer system, but it plays a significant role in determining the computer system's capabilities.

One trend that overshadows everything else is the miniaturization of electronic circuits. Computers have become smaller, faster, more reliable, and incredibly less expensive. This is largely due to the evolution of microelectronic technology, in which electronic logic is represented as microscopic circuits. Computer circuits have progressed from vacuum tubes to silicon chips smaller than a fingernail, each containing over a million integrated circuits.

An important step in shrinking circuits involves integrating or combining several transistors and the circuits that connect them on one piece of semiconducting material. A *semiconductor* is a material whose electrical properties are less than a conductor such as copper and greater than an insulator such as glass. Because of the small size and thinness of the semiconductor, it came to be known as a chip. The semiconductor material most commonly used is silicon. This accounts for the term silicon chip—a major solution to the problem of making computers faster, smaller, cheaper, and more reliable.

The only way to make a computer circuit significantly faster with electronic technology is to make it smaller. Although electricity theoretically travels at the speed of light (186,000 miles per second), resistance in wires and circuits can cut that speed well below the theoretical limit. For example, an electrical signal will travel about 10 inches in one billionth of a second. The distance the signals must travel can be significantly reduced by packing the circuits closer together, which speeds up the operation of the computer.

The precision involved in making such small circuits is measured in *microns*, a micron being one-millionth of a meter. To get a feel for such a small dimension, look at the period at the end of this sentence. Its diameter is approximately 500 microns.

Very-large-scale integration (VLSI) packs 100,000 to 100 million switches

Level of integration	Switches per integrated circuit	Period
Small scale	10	Early 1960s
Medium scale	100	Late 1960s
Large scale	1000	Early 1970s
Very-large scale	1,000,000	Early 1980s
Ultralarge scale	100,000,000	Late 1990s

Mainframes. The Control Data Cyber 960 is a midrange mainframe computer.

Mainframes. The Amdahl 5990–1400 is an example of a large-scale mainframe computer.

on each chip. Examples of VLSI include the 16-megabit RAM chip, the 1.2-million-transistor Motorola 68040 and Intel 80486 CISC microprocessors, and the next generation of Intel i860 RISC processors, which contains 2.5-million transistors. Integrated circuit designers are routinely predicting that by the turn of the century *ultralarge-scale integration (ULSI)*—chips with 100 million to 1 billion components—will be possible. When such a high level of integration occurs, it will be possible to put the entire central electronic complex, including all processor and memory functions on a single chip.

Such very-large- and ultralarge-scale integration offers several benefits. Transistors are the fundamental building blocks of chips. The more transistors than can be placed on a chip the better because once the chip is mass produced, chip cost and reliability are similar regardless of the number of transistors. For example, one of the advantages of the 80486 microprocessor is that it combines the functions of the 80386 central processor and the 80387 math coprocessor along with extra cache memory on a single chip.

The performance characteristics of today's 32-bit CISC and 64-bit RISC microprocessors equals or exceeds the performance characteristics that are associated with medium- or large-sized computers. In the following we take a look at the differences among computer systems. By emphasizing an evolutionary view of their development we see how the needs of certain applications contributed to the design of the system.

MAINFRAME COMPUTERS

Computer builders first applied the concepts that we have discussed to the computers known as *mainframes*—large-scale computers used to process large volumes of data. The first mainframes were not the mass-produced computers that you know today. They were generally low-volume, handcrafted products, and as a result they were large, complicated, and expensive to purchase and operate.

When the experts looked at the few large computers that were built in the early 1950s, they did not have the slightest notion that an industry was in the making. In 1948 IBM declined even to enter the computer industry. Why? Its marketing research department had predicted that there would never be enough demand to justify entering the commercial market. Legend has it that experts of the time predicted that from 12 to 50 of these modern electronic computers would satisfy all the computing needs of the entire commercial marketplace for years to come. However, by the mid-1960s, thousands of government, business, scientific, and educational institutions had computers.

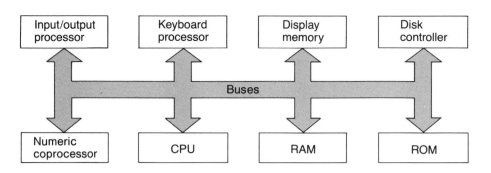

Specialized processors. Block diagram showing the bus interconnection of a computer system with several interrelated processors.

The applications for mainframe computers include the traditional data processing applications for business, such as payroll, billing, accounting, and inventory control—jobs that typically require intensive input and output. In scientific applications, mainframes are used primarily for simulation and modeling—jobs that require fast, accurate, and extensive calculations.

Channels

One of the first important breakthroughs in efficiency occurred with the discovery of how to make computers perform computations and input/output operations at the same time. The von Neumann computer is designed with a single central processor through which all operations must be funneled. All electronic computers are much faster than their slower input/output devices, which have to rely on the mechanical motion of a spinning disk or tape. Often, a processor has to wait while an input device, such as disk drive, reads data into memory. "Why not," reasoned the designers, "have the processor do something else while the data are being transferred to and from memory?" One way of doing this is to provide a separate processor

called a *channel* to handle the flow of data into and out of memory. Then, the channel can transfer data in and out while the processor performs calculation-intensive operations. The channel can inform the processor when its input or output task is complete. In this way, the processor gains the ability to execute instructions while input and output are occurring, which speeds up the overall operation of the computer.

Although channels are typically associated with mainframe computers, they can also be found in smaller computers such as the Next Computer System in which a specialized channel processor implemented on a chip enables input/output devices to move data in and out of memory without interrupting the central processor.

Time-Sharing

Another technique for increasing the overall efficiency of computer operations is *time-sharing*—the sharing of a single processor that switches back and forth among many separate programs in memory. An important application of time-sharing developed when owners of large computers wanted to share the processing power of their mainframes among many different users in different geographic lo-

Mainframes. The Unisys 2200/600 is an example of a very-large-scale mainframe computer with up to four processors.

Mainframes. The IBM System/390 is IBM's most powerful mainframe computer. Shown here is the ES/9000 Model 580.

cations. By connecting remote terminals to the time-shared mainframe, they allowed the central computer to service many users in a manner such that each person appeared to have complete use of the processor.

This is accomplished by a scheduling method known as time-slicing, in which many programs are each given a *time slice* during which a given program executes. During the heyday of time-sharing, it was not uncommon to find companies with a single mainframe connected to hundreds of terminals in different geographic locations. However, because of the popularity of personal computers and networks of computers, time-sharing is on the decline.

When the integrated circuit arrived in the late 1960s, the designing and building of computers changed in two major ways: (1) integrated circuits allowed more transistors to be used to construct more complex circuits, and (2) they allowed processors to be mass produced. Mass production has the additional effect of rapidly decreasing the cost of building integrated circuits,

so the two primary components, processors and memories, can be built much less expensively.

Compatibility

One of the biggest problems that a computer user faces is the problem of expanding or growing into a newer or more powerful computer system without losing the application programs that already exist.

Recall the discussion of instruction sets. A new computer system can be built with the same instruction set as the old one, or a completely different instruction set. If the instruction set is the same, then old applications can run without change. Often, computer makers evolve their instruction sets by making a *superset* of the old instruction set that retains all the old instructions, while adding new instructions.

In the 1970s, for example, IBM introduced a series of computers called System/370 that incorporated several new hardware and software features. It was to be a family of computers that ranged from very small business systems to the largest mainframes. One of the ideas behind the family was to promote upward migration. For example, a business first purchased a System/370 at the lower and less expensive end of the scale. As its business needs grew, the customer could purchase the next model up the scale, slightly larger, more powerful, and more expensive. As the customer's needs continued to expand, the business could eventually migrate all the way to the top-of-the-line models. The key to this strategy was the way IBM implemented compatibility. Compatibility allows easy transition between different computers because customers do not have to change their programs. An important key in the compatibility strategy is the concept of microprogramming, which was first developed by Maurice Wilkes in 1951.

Microprogramming

Microprogramming is a technique used by designers to implement the functions of a computer. The approach involves creating a computer within a computer, so that the processor has a microprogram operating within it. Contrary to what the name suggests, microprograms were first implemented on mainframes, then minicomputers, and finally microcomputers.

Microprogramming was commercially adopted with the introduction of the System/360 and its follow-up, the System/370. In microprogramming techniques, before a control unit of a processor begins to execute an instruction, it looks up the microprogram for that instruction in a special memory. It then executes the microprogram according to the microinstructions. Because the microprogram determines the instruction set of a computer, the instruction set can be changed by changing the microprogram. This is often done to add optional instructions to different models in a product family.

For example, the IBM System/370 series has a wide range of hardware differences, even in the CPUs. However, each model except Model 195 has a microprogram that interprets the IBM/370 conventional machine language instructions. In this way, a program written for any 370 model can be executed on any other model. The mi-

Minicomputers. *The NCR 32/800 high-end minicomputer.*

croprogram for every model emulates (imitates) the ideal 370 machine. Newer IBM machines such as the System/390 are still compatible with the System/370 through microprogramming.[1]

MINICOMPUTERS

The combination of the declining cost of integrated circuits and the change in how processors and memories were designed and built launched a new breed of computers called minicomputers. *Minicomputers* (also called *midrange computers*) are physically smaller and cost far less than their mainframe forerunners, yet they are still powerful enough to do many of the jobs that only the big mainframes could do before. Because they are smaller and cheaper, several new ways of using computers have become possible that were not attractive before the minicomputer.

Distributed Computing

One of the major contributions of the minicomputer was the widespread adoption of *distributed computing,* in

Distributed computing. *The IBM System/6000 provides a system for distributed applications and can support a mix of different types of computers.*

which a number of small computers can be distributed throughout an organization and take the place of one central computing facility. The lower cost of minicomputers made it possible to dedicate a computer to a single application.

Departments of large organizations as well as small businesses began to purchase minicomputers to use as departmental processors. For example, the branch office of a large corporation that had previously been sharing time on a mainframe could now use a mini-

computer to perform its record-keeping functions. The manufacturing department of a large organization could now use a minicomputer dedicated to running the factory. In the laboratory, scientists could use dedicated minicomputers to collect and analyze data gathered from experiments.

Multiuser Systems

Like mainframes, minicomputers were powerful enough to be used as time-sharing systems. For example, a medical clinic could use a minicomputer connected to several terminals to provide patient records to doctors, nurses, and administrative personnel. Similarly, a hotel could use a minicomputer system to connect terminals at the front desk, the manager's office, and in the accounting department. Large office buildings could use minicomputers to control ventilation and heating systems scattered throughout their premises.

All these systems offered features and performance that mainframe systems could not match in price. The cost of a minicomputer per unit of work performed (dollars per MIPS or dollars per MB) is less than that using a larger system. In many applications, minicomputers became cost-effective evolutionary replacements for mainframes. However, the continuing trend toward miniaturization was to have a large impact on the minicom-

Multiuser systems. *Shown here are a VAXstation 2000 workstation (foreground), a MicroVAX 2000 system (right background), and a VAX 8800 minicomputer (left background), which can be linked in a multiuser networked environment.*

puter. The minicomputer appeared in the mid-1960s, but by the late 1970s, the microcomputer was challenging the minicomputer in the same way that the minicomputer had challenged the mainframe.

MICROCOMPUTERS

A *microcomputer* is a computer with a CPU based on a microprocessor. The microprocessor was born in 1969 when a group of engineers at Intel Corporation were exploring how to produce a set of electronic components for a Japanese programmable desktop calculator. The person credited with the idea, Ted Hoff, decided that it might be possible to place all the arithmetic and logic circuitry on one chip, leaving input and output as separate chips. The group succeeded in placing almost all the components of a CPU on a single chip, and in 1971 Intel introduced the first general-purpose microprocessor chip.

Economic Feasibilities

The economic effect of microprocessors swept through the entire computer industry. At first, they fueled the development of microcontrollers (chips that could be placed in disk drives and input/output devices such as terminals) to make control of these devices intelligent. Microprocessors made widespread distribution of computing power economically feasible. Microprocessors and microcontrollers could be placed in homes, in appliances, in cars to control various mechanical devices, and in factories and offices to control specialized equipment.

This is the primary reason why the microprocessor enjoys its current competitive popularity. It is a standard general-purpose product that can be mass produced and, therefore, sold at low prices. Because it is programmable, it can be used in small quantities for any given application.

In many applications, microcomputers have become the cost-effective replacement for minicomputers. The reason: a microcomputer can now be designed to be as powerful as a larger computer by incorporating the same design concepts on a smaller physical scale.

Fault-Tolerant Computers

Microprocessors have also fueled the development of *fault-tolerant computers*—computers that use redundant components so that if one fails, a duplicate component can take over without interruption. Many of today's fault-tolerant computers are made by linking multiple microprocessors together.

Relying on a single computer or processor has its disadvantages. The term crash refers to a computer system that has become inoperable owing to an equipment malfunction or error in a program. The causes are varied. For example, (1) a logic circuit might fail or memory might fail, thus wiping out sections of a program or data, or (2) one altered instruction could cause the system to shut down suddenly or begin to process the wrong application or wrong information. In any time-sharing scheme, when the system crashes, all the users go down with it, and all must wait until the system is restored to resume work. A *fault* is similar to a crash and has become the standard term for the condition that causes a functional component to fail to operate in the required manner.

Any applications that are transaction and communication oriented are prime candidates for fault-tolerant computers. Examples include an on-line updating of a database found in an

Microcomputers. *IBM's Personal System/2 Model 55.*

Fault-tolerant computer. *The Tandem NonStop VLX is based on four central processing units.*

Smart card. *Experimental smart cards feature built-in microprocessors.*

airline reservation system or a stock quotation system. Interruption of service in these systems could mean costly delays and customer irritation. Other candidates for fault-tolerant computers include banks, which use them in their automatic teller machine (ATM) networks and offices and factory systems in which networks of computers rely on a central database.

Fault-tolerant computers also address the problem discussed earlier in which applications must grow and expand to meet user demands. For example, a bank might need to add more ATMs or a retail store might need to add more point-of-sale terminals. The traditional approach would be to buy a bigger computer to handle the increased work load. But a fault-tolerant computer already has the capability to link multiple processors together so that it is quite possible to add more processors in such a system to handle the increased work load. The concept of linking multiple processors together will be covered in our discussion "Parallel Processing."

Virtual Machines

The virtual memory techniques of microprocessors such as the Intel 80386 family, and the Motorola 68030 family, lend themselves to the implementation of a virtual machine. In a *virtual machine*, the user is provided with virtual memory, disks, consoles, printers, and other peripherals. A virtual machine permits multiple programs and operating systems to share the same computer while creating the impression of a dedicated stand-alone system. For example, VP/ix, an extension to the Unix operating system, provides a virtual environment in which Unix and MS-DOS applications can be run simultaneously. Multitasking (see Chapter 2) is accomplished by running a different application in each virtual machine. The virtual machines are protected from one another so that a crash in one does not crash the entire system.

Very Small Computers

One of the fastest-growing areas is small portable computers or *notebook* computers. A notebook computer re-

quires components that can be run from battery power, and the microprocessor manufacturers have responded with a process called CMOS (complementary metal oxide semiconductor). CMOS components require far less power and generate far less heat than do their corresponding non-CMOS components. This makes them ideally suited for battery-powered notebook computers, such as the Tandy, Zenith, Toshiba, and NEC.

Smart Cards

The smallest of all portable computers, the smart card, has neither power supply nor keyboard. These cards are the same size and thickness as today's credit cards and contain an embedded microcomputer. They are presently being tested in applications in which they provide a less expensive and easier to use alternative than a conventional computer. They should not, however, be confused with stand-alone computers. Smart cards simply contain programs and data that allow them to interact with an associated device or system. Their use would be similar to using today's ATM cards, in that you insert them into an input device, enter an identification number, and conduct your transactions.[2]

The Department of Agriculture, for example, conducted a test in which it replaced food stamps with smart cards. The test showed that it was feasible to use such a system to help regulate the misuse of food stamps. Smart cards might also be used to store medical profiles, personnel records, or automobile warranty information.

The application that is receiving the most attention is the use of smart cards for financial transactions. Smart cards could provide a unified method for interacting with a financial institution whereby one smart card would replace a credit card, a savings passbook, a checkbook, and an ATM access card.

SUPERCOMPUTERS

Despite the widespread trend toward smaller and smaller computers, there are still many tasks that require the processing of massive amounts of information at extremely high speeds. Examples include aircraft and automobile design, nuclear weapons development, weather prediction, computer animation, and many areas of basic scientific research. The computers that perform such tasks are called *supercomputers* because they are the fastest computers made and their performance far outpaces even the largest and most powerful mainframe computers.

Most of the supercomputers in existence are still in various government agencies, such as the U.S. Weather Bureau, or in federal laboratories, such as Los Alamos or Lawrence Livermore. In the United States, the main competitors are Control Data, with its Cyber series; Cray Computer Corp. with its Cray-2 and Cray-3; and Cray Research, with its Y-MP series. In the worldwide market, Hitachi offers a model called the S-810/20 and Fujitsu offers the VP-100 supercomputer.

Supercomputers are designed to perform different types of processing tasks than mainframes, so their speed is usually rated in gigaflops (A gigaflop is one billion floating point operations per second.) For example, today's Cray Research Y-MP has an 8-gigaflop rating and plans to introduce by the turn of the century a 64-processor supercomputer that will be rated at 100 gigaflops. In addition, the company has announced the teraflop (1 trillion floating-point operations per second) initiative. To achieve such processing speed, new processor technology, more processors, higher bandwidth, and improved input/output operations will all have to be pushed far beyond today's state-of-the-art supercomputers.

One key to the operation of high-speed supercomputers lies in the packaging techniques applied to the components. Very-large-scale integration makes possible the packing of hundreds of thousands of circuits on a single chip. The greater the density of the chip, the shorter the time electrical signals take to travel through it and the faster the chip can operate. The drawback to such dense packing is the heat that is generated by the circuits themselves. The speed improvement in the Cray-2 comes from immersing much of the computer in a liquid coolant bath of fluorocarbon, thus eliminating the heat buildup.

PARALLEL PROCESSING

As designers of supercomputers experiment with technologies such as shrinking the circuits smaller and smaller and immersing the components in liquid coolants to keep them from melting, they are beginning to run up against fundamental limits on the speeds that can be achieved by conventional single-processor computers. A problem occurs when the single channel between one processor and memory, along which data and instructions must flow, limits the speed of the computer system.

Multiprocessing is the simultaneous processing of two or more portions of the same program by two or more processing units. One way to speed up computers is to divide the labor among multiple processors rather than continue the quest for ever-faster single processors made with ever-more exotic materials and techniques. Many of today's large computers employ multiple processors.

Supercomputers. *This Cray 1S/2000 supercomputer is being checked for hot spots that would indicate that a fault or failure is beginning to appear.*

The IBM 3090 mainframe employs two to four processors. The Cray X MP 4 supercomputer uses four processors (the MP stands for multiple processors, and the 4 for the number of processors). But a new trend is emerging. *Parallel processing* combines multiple microprocessors with software techniques that facilitate executing parts of a program in parallel.

Various parallel-processing computers have been designed and built by incorporating multiple microprocessors. At the small parallel end of the spectrum, the Butterfly from BBN Advanced Computers combines from 2 to 256 Motorola 68020 microprocessors. In the middle, the experimental IBM RP3 combines 512 RISC processors. At the massively parallel end of the spectrum, the Connection Machine from Thinking Machines Corporation combines 65,536 (2^{16}) processors. In this approach, each processor performs the same task at the same time. Searching a database of 65,000 articles for a single key word, for example, could be speeded up considerably, if each article could be assigned to a single processor.

Although parallel-processor computers may eventually be more suitable than single-processor computers for many applications, the problem of using current software on parallel computers has yet to be solved. Simply throwing more processors at today's tasks does not mean that a job can be done better or faster. Software has to be changed to take advantage of parallel computers.

REVIEW

The central electronic complex contains both processor and memory that must work hand in hand to accomplish most processing tasks. A processor consists of a control unit, an ALU, and some pathways called buses to connect them to other functional units. Word size plays an important role in describing the power of a processor, memory is categorized into RAM and ROM, and the von Neumann approach is the classic approach for designing computers. A walkthrough of an instruction wrapped up the discussion on processor and memory concepts.

The differences among central electronic complexes can be characterized by looking at their size, speed, and instruction-set differences. The evolution of computers from mainframes through minicomputers to microcomputers also provides some clues to computer use. Even though computers are shrinking in size, they are becoming more powerful. Supercomputers and parallel-processor computers are on the technological frontier and are, therefore, influencing the way computers of the future will be designed.

Parallel processing computer. IBM's RP3.

REFERENCES

1. Giarratano, Joseph C. *Modern Computer Concepts*. Indianapolis, In.: Howard W. Sams, 1982, p. 87. An excellent but highly technical reference for up-to-date computer concepts.

2. Svigals, Jerome. *Smart Cards: The Ultimate Personal Computer*. New York: Macmillan, 1985, pp. 4-5. There is a definitive book on everything, and this is it on smart cards. The author led the team that developed IBM's magnetic-stripe cards and is now exploring standards for smart cards.

RESOURCES

BOOKS

Blotnick, Srully. *Computers Made Ridiculously Easy*. New York: McGraw-Hill, 1984. Although this book is easy to read and covers many computer principles quite well, I would suggest starting with Chapter 4 and reading the second half of the book before you read the first half.

Lorin, Harold. *Introduction to Computer Architecture and Organization*. New York: John Wiley, 1982. This book is packed with technical information and is somewhat hard to read, but it contains an excellent in-depth coverage of the organization of computer systems.

Norton, Peter. *Inside the IBM PC*. New York: Prentice Hall Trade, Simon & Schuster, 1987. A guide to the inner workings of the IBM Personal Computer.

Tannenbaum, Andrew. *Structured Computer Organization*. Englewood Cliffs, N.J.: Prentice-Hall, 1984. This book contains the best all-around technical coverage of computer systems: heavy reading, but excellent information.

MAGAZINES

Byte. Peterborough, N.H.: McGraw-Hill. After you understand hardware concepts, you may want to start reading *Byte*. It is technically oriented, but its articles and columns provide excellent coverage of current topics.

ComputerWorld. Framingham, Mass.: CW Communications. This weekly newspaper of the computer industry is not particularly oriented toward the novice, but it contains much news about developments in hardware and software.

STUDY GUIDE

Match the following terms to the appropriate definition:

A.

1. ____ Central electronic complex
2. ____ Peripherals
3. ____ Processor

4. __A__ Instruction set
5. __B__ Machine language
6. ____ Operation

7. __h__ Operand
8. ____ Clock
9. ____ Megahertz (MHz)

a. The part of an instruction that specifies the function that is to be performed.

b. The binary language in which a computer's instruction set is written.

c. The processor, memory, and some pathways for information to travel between the two.

d. A timer in a processor that releases precisely timed signals that provide a pulse for the processor's work.

e. A functional unit that interprets and carries out instructions.

f. Devices, such as keyboards and display screens, that surround the processor and memory.

g. A unique set of operations that comes with every processor.

h. The part of an instruction that tells where data that are operated on are located.

i. Million cycles per second.

B.

10. __a__ Control unit
11. ____ Arithmetic/logic unit (ALU)
12. ____ Register
13. ____ Word size
14. ____ Memory

15. ____ Random access
16. ____ Bus
17. ____ Cache memory
18. ____ Reduced instruction set computer (RISC)

19. ____ Semiconductor
20. ____ Very-large-scale integration (VLSI)
21. ____ Ultralarge-scale integration (ULSI)

a. The functional unit that is responsible for supervising the operation of the entire computer system.

b. A material whose electrical properties are less than a conductor and greater than an insulator.

c. A method of organization in which access time is the same for any location.

d. A functional unit that provides the computer with logical and computational capability.

e. A circuit that provides the pathway for the transfer of information between two or more devices.

f. A storage location inside the processor.

g. A technology that packs 100,000 to 100 million switches on each chip.

h. The term used to describe the size of operand registers and buses.

i. A high-speed memory that is sometimes built into the processor.

j. A series of cells, each of which can store a piece of information.

k. Hardware and software that reduces the number of instructions in a computer's instruction set and attempts to execute each instruction as quickly as possible.

l. A technology that packs 100 million to 1 billion switches on each chip.

C.

22. __d__ Mainframe
23. __b__ Channel
24. __g__ Time-sharing
25. __h__ Microprogramming

26. __j__ Minicomputer
27. __e__ Distributed computing
28. __a__ Microcomputer
29. __k__ Fault-tolerant computer

30. ____ Supercomputer
31. __f__ Multiprocessing
32. __c__ Parallel processing

a. A computer with a CPU based on a microprocessor.

b. A small processor in a computer designed to handle input/output operations.

c. The combination of multiple processors and software techniques to facilitate executing parallel instructions.

d. A large-scale computer used to process large volumes of data.

e. A number of small computers distributed throughout an organization.

f. The simultaneous processing of two or more portions of the same program by two or more processing units.

g. The sharing of a single processor switching back and forth among many separate programs.

h. A technique used by designers to implement the control functions of a computer.

i. The fastest computer made.

j. A medium-sized computer that is capable of many of the same functions as a mainframe computer.

k. A computer that uses redundant components to prevent failure.

True/False:

33. _____ Processors come with a unique set of operations called an instruction set.

34. _____ In an instruction, operands specify the function to be performed.

35. _____ A processor's job is to retrieve instructions from memory and perform step-by-step operations.

36. _____ The control unit is the functional unit that provides the computer with logical and computational capabilities.

37. _____ A logic operation is one that makes a comparison and takes action based on the results.

38. _____ The size of a computer's registers affects the speed and performance of a processor.

39. _____ A byte consists of 16 consecutive bits.

40. _____ Random access is accomplished by arranging memory in an array similar to a spreadsheet.

41. _____ The miniaturization of electronic circuits is an important trend in the evolution of computers.

42. _____ The early mainframe computers were high-volume, mass-produced computers.

43. _____ Microprogramming was first implemented on microcomputers.

44. _____ Microcomputers eventually became a cost-effective replacement for minicomputers.

45. _____ Applications that perform batch processing are prime candidates for fault-tolerant computers.

46. _____ One way to increase the speed of operation of a computer is to immerse its components in a liquid coolant.

47. _____ Newer designs for computers are incorporating a number of multiple processors linked together.

Multiple Choice:

48. Which of the following is not a part of the central electronic complex?

   a. Processor.
   b. Memory.
   c. Disk drive.
   d. Data pathways.

49. The arithmetic/logic unit is responsible for

   a. Decoding instructions.
   b. Adding.
   c. Fetching data from memory.
   d. Control signals.

50. ROM can be used to

   a. Store the results of processing.
   b. Store parts of the operating system.
   c. Store programs and data.
   d. Store any kind of data a program needs.

51. Which of the following is not a bus found in the central electronic complex?

   a. Instruction.
   b. Control.
   c. Address.
   d. Data.

52. Which of the following is not a common word size in microprocessors?

   a. 16 bits.
   b. 32 bits.
   c. 64 bits.
   d. 128 bits.

53. Compatibility means

   a. The use of different instruction sets.
   b. The use of subsets.
   c. Easy transition between different computers.
   d. Promoting downward migration.

54. One of the first breakthroughs in efficiency for mainframe computers was to

   a. Build fault-tolerant computers.
   b. Engage in multiprocessing.
   c. Engage in parallel processing.
   d. Build in separate processors for input and output.

55. Which of the following is not a technique for increasing com-

puter speed?

  a. Shrinking circuits.
  b. Fault-tolerant design.
  c. Cooling circuits.
  d. Parallel processing.

56. Which of the following did not have a direct impact on the introduction of the minicomputer?

  a. The declining cost of integrated circuits.
  b. Changes in how processors were built.
  c. The introduction of bus-oriented computers.
  d. IBM compatibility.

57. Supercomputers currently have speeds in the range of

  a. 1 to 9 million instructions per second.
  b. 10 to 49 million instructions per second.
  c. 50 to 100 million instructions per second.
  d. 100 to 999 million instructions per second.

Thought Questions:

58. As you learned in this chapter, the central electronic complex of a computer consists of many functional units. Which of these is most difficult to understand? Why?

59. If you carry the trend toward microprocessor-based computing into the future, it would appear that mainframes and minicomputers might be on the verge of extinction. Defend or attack this position.

Projects:

60. Apple Computer's latest generation of Macintosh computers uses Motorola 68030 and 68040 microprocessors. IBM's latest generation of Personal System/2 computers uses Intel 80386 and 80486 microprocessors. Prepare a report on the differences between these two families of microprocessors.

61. Much of today's computer research is focused on reduced instruction set computers. Consult your library and find articles describing the advantages and disadvantages of RISC processors. Write a paper describing what you find.

SOFTWARE EXERCISES

You can see from this chapter that there are a wide variety of makes and models of computers and we have only begun to scratch the surface in our discussions. For this exercise, you are going to create a personal computer comparisons database.

Assignment 1. Using the record structure shown here, create a personal computer comparisons database. Appendix C contains a noncomputerized database of personal computer hardware. Use that data as a starting point for entering your data. (Note: Chapter 7 also contains a table that lists various microprocessor speeds in MHz.) Once you have entered your records, perform the following exercises:

Field Name	Field Length	Example
Category	15	Home
Name	20	Apple IIe
Model	5	IIe
Company	25	Apple Computer Inc.
Microprocessor	5	6502
Clock speed (MHz)	2	4
Price	5	995
Company address	25	20525 Mariani Ave.
Company city	15	Cupertino
Company state	2	CA
Company ZIP	5	95014
Company phone	12	408-996-1010

Records for the computer comparison database.

• Sort the database in ascending order (lowest to highest) according to microprocessor speed.

• Search for, select, and print all 80286-based personal computer systems.

Alternative Assignment. For a group assignment you can split into groups, each taking one category listed in Appendix C. Gather data from trade magazines about personal computers in that category and enter it into the database.

ANSWERS

1. c, **2.** f, **3.** e, **4.** g, **5.** b, **6.** a, **7.** h, **8.** d, **9.** i, **10.** a, **11.** d, **12.** f, **13.** h, **14.** j, **15.** c, **16.** e, **17.** i, **18.** k, **19.** b, **20.** g, **21.** l, **22.** d, **23.** b, **24.** g, **25.** h, **26.** j, **27.** e, **28.** a, **29.** k, **30.** i, **31.** f, **32.** c, **33.** T, **34.** F, **35.** T, **36.** F, **37.** T, **38.** T, **39.** F, **40.** T, **41.** T, **42.** F, **43.** F, **44.** T, **45.** F, **46.** F, **47.** T, **48.** c, **49.** b, **50.** b, **51.** a, **52.** d, **53.** c, **54.** d, **55.** b, **56.** d, **57.** c.

HEIDI ROIZEN

Profession: President of T/Maker Corporation, Mountain View, California, a microcomputer software publisher.

Profile: A creative writing major at Stanford, Roizen has worked for Tandem Computer Corporation. She returned to Stanford to obtain an MBA, where she was inspired by personal computers and went on to found T/Maker with her brother.

Quote: "PCs are incredible tools; I see a limitless field with so many potential applications yet to be tapped."

CHAPTER 8
MASS STORAGE

PREVIEW

In the past, computer data were stored on punched cards, paper tape, and magnetic tape. Storage was bulky, and access to the data was usually slow and inefficient. But this situation has dramatically changed because researchers have continued to innovate in a quest for density—packing more and more data in less and less space. This chapter takes you through that quest for density. In the 1950s, magnetic tapes were refined and perfected and became capable of storing very large amounts of data in a small space. In the 1960s, disks were perfected, and the access to data was speeded up. In the 1970s and 1980s, the quest for density continued with the refinement and improvement of disk technology. And in the 1990s, optical disks continue to improve the capacity of mass-storage devices.

In this chapter, you'll learn

- How files and mass storage are related.

- The different types of file organization.

- The differences among sequential, random, and index sequential files.

- Characteristics of magnetic tape devices.

- Characteristics of magnetic disk devices.

- How data are stored in files on disk.

- Methods for improving a disk's capacity.

- An overview of optical disks.

FILES AND MASS STORAGE

The term *mass storage* is derived from the term *mass data*, which means a quantity of data larger than the amount storable in the memory of a computer at any one time. The purpose of a mass-storage device is to provide a permanent or nonvolatile medium for information so that it can be stored, retrieved, and manipulated. In effect, mass storage provides a place to store data and programs before and after processing.

Whether you are using application software or writing application programs in BASIC, Pascal, or one of the other programming languages, you may need to store your data in files. A *file* is an organized collection of information. Examples of files include documents used by a word processor, worksheets used by a spreadsheet program, and employee information files used by a database program. Even programs are stored in files called *program files*. In this chapter, a file will be examined from the viewpoints of what an application program "sees" and what a mass-storage device "sees."

Types of mass-storage devices.

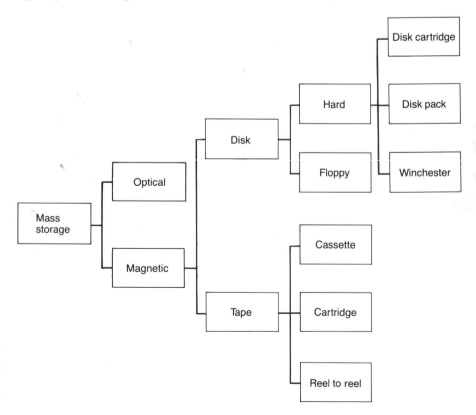

LOGICAL VERSUS PHYSICAL STRUCTURES

To an application program, a file has a *logical structure* that is defined according to its content or use. For example, a word processor sees a collection of characters and a series of pages within a document. A spreadsheet program sees a worksheet consisting of rows and columns of cells as its logical structure. Similarly, many database programs see a tabular row and column structure in which each row is a record and each column is a field. (As mentioned in Chapter 2, a field is the smallest unit of named data that has meaning in a record.)

To a mass-storage device, a file has a *physical structure* that consists of a collection of physical records with characteristics that depend on the form in which they are stored and retrieved. For example, an employee file, whose logical structure consists of all the information about an individual employee, might consist of a physical structure made up from several physical records. Programmers often use the term *mapping* to describe the correspondence between the logical and the physical structure of a file. For example, if a physical record and a logical record happen to be the same size, there is said to be one-to-one mapping. However, this is not usually the case.

The mapping between logical records and physical records is demonstrated by the following set of relationships:

• One physical record may equal one logical record.

• One physical record may equal a group of logical records.

• One logical record may equal a group of physical records.

For end users, logical structures are a convenient way to describe data. The operating system takes care of the details of storing and maintaining the physical structure of records in a mass-storage device. For example, the operating system is free to change the location of physical records as space requirements on the device may dictate. The end user gains a certain amount of independence from such physical storage details and need not concern himself or herself with how the mass-storage device and the operating system are taking care of such details.

Every mass-storage medium stores records in a slightly different manner. You will discover these differences as each device is discussed. For example, physical records on a disk have different characteristics than do physical records stored on a tape because the two media differ considerably in their physical form.

DEFINING A FILE

Defining a file is the process of creating the logical structure of the file. Word processing documents and spreadsheet files do not have to be defined because their logical file structure is predefined by the program (e.g., the fixed number of cells in a worksheet). The user of a word processor or a spreadsheet program needs only to name the file. A user of a database program has a more complicated problem because the logical structure has to be defined before processing can begin. Let us take a simple example of defining a file for use by a database application.

Suppose that you wanted to computerize your address book and create a People File. After thinking about the uses for such a file, you decide to subdivide it into friends, relatives, and professional contacts and to include birthdays for friends and relatives.

The process of defining a file for a database application involves specifying descriptive information about the logical records. At minimum, the descriptive information includes (1) naming the fields, (2) specifying a maximum length for each field, and (3) specifying the type of the field. To put it another way, deciding what your logical record will look like means deciding what the logical record's fields will look like. Because your application includes professional contacts as well as friends and relatives, you would probably like your records to contain the person's name, title, company, address, city, state, ZIP code, work phone, home phone, and birthday. You also need to specify whether the person is a friend, relative, or professional contact. For that you decide

to use a code, where 1 stands for friend, 2 stands for relative, and 3 stands for professional contact. You name this field your people code.

To finish the description of your logical records, you must also decide how many characters each field will contain. As shown in the accompanying table, the fields must be specified in terms of their maximum length. For example, you scan through your address book and discover that the person with the longest name is Theodore Benjamin, which is 17 characters long. You decide to add a few extra characters just in case and determine that the name field should be 25 characters in length.

To review, the set of fields equals the logical record. All the logical records taken together equals the file. It is possible to calculate the size of the file by summing the field lengths to obtain the logical record size and multiplying that length times the number of records in the file.

Establishing a file for such an application first involves defining the file and then entering data into the file. The application program has to provide a method for accessing the file. For example, you may want to retrieve individual records from the file by specifying a name. You may want to add records to the file, delete records from the file, access specific fields within each record, or access the entire file to prepare a mailing list.

SEQUENTIAL, RANDOM, AND INDEX SEQUENTIAL FILES

Most operating systems for personal computers support two types of files: sequential files and random access files. Both types of files contain records.

Sequential files can only be accessed from beginning to end sequentially. For example, to read or write the last record in the file, you must first read or write all previous records. A payroll file organized by employee number is a good example of a sequential file. As a general rule, large

Field Name	Field Length
Name	25
Title	10
Company	15
Address	20
City	20
State	2
ZIP	5
Work phone	8
Home phone	8
Birthday	8
People code	1
Logical record size	122

Defining a file. *Calculating the size of a logical record.*

Types of files. *Three common types of files for data storage.*

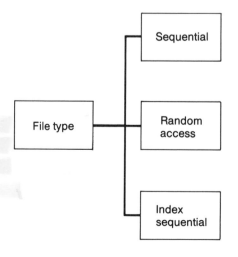

sequential files are sorted into an order: most often an ascending order, that is, starting with the lowest value and proceeding to the highest value.

There are applications, such as an airline reservation system, in which accessing the last record in a file needs to be just as fast as accessing the first or any record in the file. *Random-access files* allow you to read or write any record in the file without regard to its location. They are sometimes called *direct files* to distinguish them from random-access memory (RAM). Random access files require that you designate one of the fields to be a *key field* that denotes the record's position in the file. An inventory file made up of records using the part number as the key field or an airline reservation system using the flight number as the key field are examples of organizing random access files.

Most database systems use a variation of the sequential method called index sequential. An *index sequential file* is one in which an index is created to speed up access to records within the file. A useful analogy can be drawn between an indexed sequential filing system and a library. Just as each record in an indexed sequential file contains a key field, each book contains a number that identifies the book's position in the library. Both the records and the books are stored sequentially in ascending sequence. To access a record in an indexed sequential file, you first consult an index. To access a book in a library (assuming that you do not already know where the book is), you look up the book's number in a card catalog, then you consult the index numbers on the shelves that specify the beginning and ending numbers for books located on that particular shelf.

Both large indexed sequential files and large libraries have multilevel indexes. In the library, for example, you may need to consult a directory that tells you which floor contains what index numbers. Just as the operating system is free to change the location of physical records as space requirements on the device may dictate, the librarian is free to change the physical location of books, so long as he or she keeps the directory properly updated.

Files stored on mass-storage devices can be organized in a sequential, a direct or random, or an index sequential manner. The choice of an organization method is based on the way in which the records need to be accessed during processing. A payroll processing program that prints paychecks for each employee is ideally suited for sequential organization and access. Searching an inventory file for a specific part number to determine whether the part is in stock would lend itself to random organization and access. An employee file that is used for payroll processing and occasionally for changing the status of an employee, such as granting the employee a promotion or a raise, would lend itself to index sequential organization and access.

A disk can be used to store and retrieve data in a sequential, index sequential, or random manner, but magnetic tape can only be used to store and retrieve data in a sequential manner.

MAGNETIC TAPE DEVICES

Magnetic tape is coated with a film on which data can be magnetically recorded. It is a widely used storage medium for large computer systems. In the early 1950s, tapes were made of flexible metal coated with a thin film of

Magnetic tape devices. IBM's 3490 magnetic tape subsystem is a high-capacity cartridge tape drive.

iron oxide, but plastic Mylar proved to be a more cost-effective medium. Although the disk has replaced magnetic tape as the primary mass-storage medium, magnetic tape is still used for backing up disk files because it provides the lowest cost per bit of any magnetic medium.

To understand how data are stored on all magnetic media visualize the magnetic fields on the film as tiny magnets with north and south poles. It is possible to magnetize a field in one of two directions to record either a one or a zero. Once magnetized, the fields hold onto their data because they will all align themselves so that each field's north pole is next to another's south pole. In practice, what is actually recorded is a change in magnetic direction. For example, if a change from north to south represents a one, then a change from south to north represents a zero.

MAGNETIC TAPE AND SEQUENTIAL ACCESS

Recall for a moment the People File that was designed earlier. Could magnetic tape be used as a medium for the file? The answer is yes, but first look at some of the problems you would encounter in doing so. Assume that the people file is small, so you decide to arrange it in alphabetical order and store it sequentially on magnetic tape. In principle, its organization would be no different from a series of songs recorded on an audiocassette. Each song is stored sequentially, one after the other, and can only be accessed in sequential order. For example, to play the third song on a cassette, you have to forward the tape past the first two songs. To access a person whose name begins with the letter Z in your magnetic tape file, you would first have to read all the prior records in the file. Another constraint is the relatively slow input/output rate of the magnetic tape drive compared to magnetic disks; this would probably eliminate magnetic tape from consideration as a storage medium for your People File.

REEL-TO-REEL TAPE

Reel-to-reel tape is the oldest form of magnetic tape. It resembles reel-to-reel audiotape, except that it is wound on 1-foot-diameter plastic reels. The tape is typically $\frac{1}{2}$ inch wide and 2400 feet long. Each reel is capable of storing about 40 million bytes of information.

To read data from the tape, a read/write head detects the magnetic fields and converts them into electrical signal pulses. The pulses are transmitted by the tape drive to the computer for processing. To write data on a tape, the read/write head magnetizes fields on the tape as it passes beneath the read/write head. While reading, the write portion of the read/write head is inactive and vice versa. Some of the older tape drives could only read data from the tape when it was moving in the forward direction. The newer high-speed and high-capacity devices can read the data while the tape is traveling in either direction.

CASSETTE AND CARTRIDGE TAPE

Cassette tape is a relatively low cost medium for conveniently storing limited amounts of data. Cassette tapes have been used in applications such as intelligent terminals that batch and store data for later transmission to a central computer. In the past, cassette tapes were used extensively with smaller, inexpensive home-computer systems. The characteristics of cassette tapes are similar to those of reel-to-reel tape. Cassette tapes are inexpensive and primarily used for low-volume, low-speed sequential applications.

Cartridge or *streaming tape* is spe-

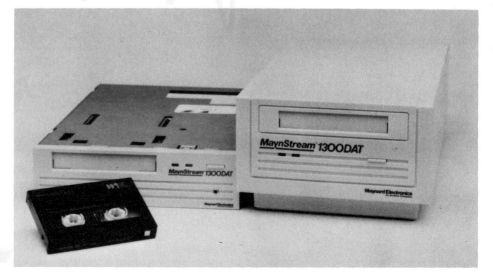

Cartridge tape units are designed to back up hard-disk drives. Shown here are internal (left) and portable (right) digital audio tape units with 1.3 gigabyte storage capacity on the 4mm digital audiocassette tape shown in the foreground.

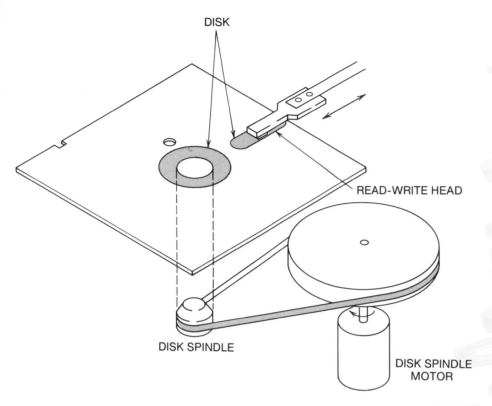

DISK

READ-WRITE HEAD

DISK SPINDLE

DISK SPINDLE MOTOR

Magnetic disk devices. In disk drives, the disk is mounted on a fixed spindle and revolves. The read/write head is mounted on an arm and is moved across the surface so it can be positioned over specific tracks.

Floppy disks. The $3\frac{1}{2}$-inch floppys are encased in a rigid plastic container and are less susceptible to damage by mishandling than the larger $5\frac{1}{4}$-inch floppy.

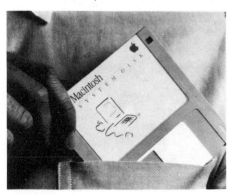

cifically designed to store backup copies of disk files. A *backup file* is a copy of a file made for possible later reconstruction in case the original file is lost or damaged. Because of their design, they are not a substitute for reel-to-reel tapes. They come in self-contained units like videocassettes.

Another technology that is gaining favor in the backup tape drive market is digital audiotape (DAT), which is based on similar consumer tape drives. DAT's primary advantage is its small cartridge size (2 by 2 by $\frac{3}{8}$ inches). Its disadvantage is a slower data transfer rate than comparable cartridge tapes.

MAGNETIC DISK DEVICES

The need for direct access to data stored in files was recognized as early as the 1950s (see Appendix A under RAMAC in 1956). Up to then, magnetic tape had proved to be quite adequate for systems using a batch-processing mode. However, applications that require a response in a short time period, such as airline reservation systems or inventory-parts-tracking systems, demand mass-storage devices that provide fast and random access to data.

The major difference between disk and tape is the disk's faster access time. A disk device can retrieve data in milliseconds (1/1000th of a second) compared with the minutes that might be required to access data on a magnetic tape. However, in backing up data, tape is the primary medium used because access time is irrelevant: the low cost of storing data on tape is the most important criterion.

The general characteristics and operation of all types of disks are the same. The *disk* consists of a platter on which a magnetic or reflective coating is applied. (Reflective-coated disks are used with optical disks, which will be discussed later.) The disk drive unit contains a read/write head on a movable arm and a motor and spindle assembly that rotates the disk. Data are recorded on the spinning disk on a series of concentric tracks. One way of classifying magnetic disks is by whether the disk is hard or flexible (floppy).

FLOPPY DISKS

In 1972 IBM introduced flexible disks as a medium for loading programs into mainframe computers. Because the disks were so flexible, they were nicknamed *floppy disks.* They are enclosed in a protective jacket that has openings for the drive spindle, the read/write head, the timing hole, and a write-protect notch that allows the user to prevent data from being written over inadvertently.

Floppy disks are the most popular storage medium for personal computers as well as for stand-alone data-entry systems, office word processing systems, and small computer systems. The disks are available in three standard sizes: $3\frac{1}{2}$ and $5\frac{1}{4}$ inches, and the now obsolete 8-inch size. The storage capacity of $3\frac{1}{2}$-inch disks is greater than that of $5\frac{1}{4}$-inch disks. This is because the smaller floppy disks have a higher data density.

The density of a disk is measured in two ways. First, the *track density,* or number of tracks on the disk, is measured in tracks per inch. Second, the bit or *linear density* is the number of bits per inch per track. Early floppy disks had a track density of 48 tracks per inch and a linear density of 2800 bits per inch and came to be known as single-density disks. Through technological improvements, the track and linear density of floppy disks has increased, and therefore the capacity of the disks has increased.

The early floppy disks were single sided. The addition of another read/write head created double-sided floppy disks and doubled the capacity of the disk. Today, all floppy disks are double sided.

Data are stored on a disk in *sectors*, which are segments of a circle, and *tracks*, which are circles of different radii on the disk. If you examine a $5\frac{1}{4}$-inch floppy disk, you will find a small timing hole next to the spindle hole in the center of the disk. A beam of light shines through the timing hole while the disk is rotating, and, on every revolution, the light beam marks the beginning of the disk so that electronic circuits can mark the relation of the read/write head to the sectors.

Even though floppy disks come in standard sizes and densities, different operating systems will store data on them differently (see Chapter 2). This means that one computer may not be able to read a disk created on another computer. For example, the IBM PC cannot read the data stored on a Macintosh floppy disk.

The advantages of floppy disks include the following:

• They have been standardized in their physical format and design.

• They are small and easy to handle, store, and send through the mail.

• They provide direct access to the data stored on them.

• They are relatively inexpensive.

However, there are some disadvantages that must be also be considered:

• They are easily damaged by heat, humidity, and surface contamination.

• The rate at which they transfer data into and out of main memory is very slow compared with hard disks.

• They wear out because the read/write heads touch the surface of the disk during operation. A floppy disk is usually good for about 2 million passes under the read/write heads.

HARD DISKS

Hard disks store data on rigid aluminum platters coated with a magnetic oxide material. Hard disks come in sizes of 14, 8, $5\frac{1}{4}$, and $3\frac{1}{2}$ inches. The $5\frac{1}{4}$- and $3\frac{1}{2}$-inch hard disks are found in desktop computers, portable computers, and small business computers. The larger-sized hard disks are found in mainframe and minicomputer systems. Hard-disk capacities currently range from 10 million bytes (10 MB) for personal computers to 1 billion bytes (1 GB) for large-scale computer systems.

To a personal computer user, the capacity advantages of hard disks over floppy disks offer access to hundreds of program and data files without the nuisance of swapping floppy disks. In addition, the maximum size of a single file is much greater on hard disks, and hard disks operate about 20 times faster than do floppy disks. The disadvantages are that most hard disks must be backed up regularly and are more sensitive to shock than floppy disks.

Because hard disks are rigid, groups of disks can be stacked on the same spindle. Such an assembly requires multiple read/write heads for each surface; these are attached to access arms that move the heads to the desired track. As with floppy disks, the number of tracks and the density vary from disk to disk.

The term *cylinder* is used to refer to the imaginary surface formed by all the tracks directly above and below one another. Accessing data on a disk requires the mechanical movement of the access arm and the time it takes for the desired data to rotate under the read/write head. The advantage of the cylinder approach is that data on several tracks can be accessed with one movement of the access arm. Once the access arm has positioned the read/write head over the desired surface, switching from one read/write head to another can be accomplished electronically. In this way, a hard disk can provide faster access to larger amounts of data with a single move of the access arm.

	5 1/4-inch	3 1/2-inch
Low density	360K bytes	720K bytes
High density	1.2M bytes	1.44M bytes

Floppy disks. Comparison of the relative densities of IBM and IBM-compatible personal computer floppy disks.

Floppy disks. A disk's surface is divided into a number of sectors. Each sector contains the same number of bytes regardless of its track location.

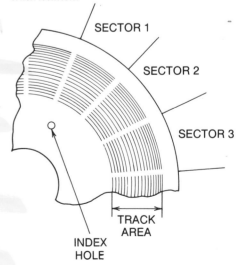

Hard disks. *Cutaway picture of a 14-inch Winchester disk with 635-MB capacity. Note the very small read/write head positioned on the right side of the disk platter.*

The use of the cylinder approach when organizing data is best shown when that approach is employed in conjunction with an index sequential file. At the lowest level, indexes point to a specific track on a disk. At the next higher level, indexes point to a specific cylinder. If an index sequential file is larger than one disk drive, a master index will point to specific disk drives.

Disk Packs

A *disk pack* is a stack of disks mounted on a common spindle that can be removed from a disk drive unit. The advantages include interchangeability of disk packs and transportability. However, the storage capacity of disk packs is limited compared to that of newer types of hard disks.

Hard disks. *An early 3 $\frac{1}{2}$-inch Winchester disk drive designed for portable computers.*

In a hard disk, the track and linear densities (discussed earlier when examining floppy disks) are directly related to the mechanical characteristics of the drive. Ideally, the closer the read/write head can be to the surface of the disk, the more data it can read from or write to the disk. However, the high-speed spinning of a hard disk (3000 to 5000 RPM) literally creates a miniature gust of wind at the surface of the disk. The read/write heads use that wind to float on a cushion of air, but if the head gets too close to the surface or a contaminant, such as a dust particle, gets blown in by the wind, the head can crash into the surface. One solution to this problem is to place both the read/write heads and the disks in a sealed, dust-free container.

Winchester Drives

Winchester drives are a class of hard-disk drives in which the disk and the read/write head are enclosed in a sealed container. The term Winchester comes from the code name for the IBM project that developed them.

By sealing the entire unit, the major source of contaminants—atmospheric pollution—is greatly reduced. Also, the read/write head can be made much smaller and can ride much closer to the surface of the disk.

In personal computers and small business systems, the trend is toward smaller and less expensive Winchester drives. In Chapter 7, the trend toward larger word sizes and memories was cited as a factor in broadening the range and sophistication of applications. Equally important is the fact that Winchester drives have been responsible for increasing the ability of small

systems to store relatively large amounts of data on-line and have thus made the development of sophisticated business application software practical for small computers.

Disk Cartridges

Disk cartridges are removable disks that are sealed in a container similar to a videotape cartridge. These disk cartridges offer the same amount of storage as many of the Winchester disks and can be inserted and removed in the same manner as floppy disks. They can be used as the primary storage medium or as a backup medium. A major drawback of any fixed disk is the need to make backup copies of files. Backing up is simplified in systems that have either two cartridge drives or one hard drive and one cartridge drive. Like the streaming tape discussed earlier, the contents of a hard disk can quickly be copied onto cartridge disks.

One such disk cartridge, found in a product called the Bernoulli Box, utilizes a flexible disk that is lifted up to the read/write head by circulating air once the cartridge is inserted into the drive. If a crash should occur, the disk simply falls away from the read/write head, minimizing the chance of losing data. Such disk cartridges can be easily taken out of the drive and transported to different locations.

Disk Arrays

Disk arrays combine and synchronize multiple disk drives into one self-contained unit. The advantages include faster data access, and higher data throughput than an equivalent-sized single-disk drive because switching from one read/write head

Disk packs. *The operator is about to insert a removeable 5-MB disk pack into its drive unit.*

Winchester disk size	Capacity	Applications
14 inch	150 megabytes to 1 gigabyte	Large-scale computers, large databases
8 inch	150 megabytes to 1 gigabyte	Minicomputers, small-scale business systems
5 1/4 inch	10 megabytes to 700 megabytes	Personal computers, workstations
3 1/2 inch	10 megabytes to 100 megabytes	Personal computers, portable computers

Winchester drives. *Comparison of the major types and capacities of Winchester drives.*

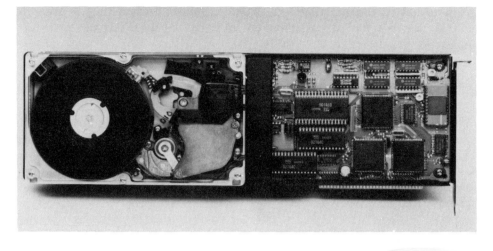

Hard disks. *The Hardcard, a 20-MB hard-disk drive, plugs into one of the expansion slots on an IBM or IBM-compatible personal computer.*

on one disk to one on another disk can be accomplished electronically. In experimental systems, researchers have combined thousands of disk drives into an array. However, software and data storage techniques have to be changed to take advantage of disk arrays. In a commercial system, the Compaq SystemPro computer uses an array of eight synchronized 212-MB disks to provide high data throughput in a 1.7 GB disk subsystem.

STORING PHYSICAL RECORDS ON DISK

As we have mentioned, each disk track is divided into regions called sectors. Depending on the disk, a sector may contain 128, 256, 512, 1024, or 2048 bytes, with the smaller numbers applying to floppy disks and the larger

numbers to hard disks. In effect, a sector is equivalent to a physical record on a disk. The operating system's job is to keep a directory to show which physical records are in use by which files.

In an earlier table you were shown the calculations for the logical record size for your People File. Recall that it was 122 bytes per record. Assume that you are going to store your file sequentially on a floppy disk that has 256-byte sectors. Therefore, each 256-byte physical record can contain two complete 122-byte logical records with 12 leftover bytes. If, for example, your file is to contain 100 records, then 50 sectors will be required to store your file.

Knowing these figures will allow you to calculate roughly the size of your files; that information, combined with an estimate of how many records

Disk cartridges. *Iomega's Bernoulli Box uses 5-MB removeable cartridges.*

are going to be in the file, allows you to estimate the disk space requirements for your application.

Storage of a random or direct file is different. If you described a random file whose logical record length totaled 122 bytes, some disks would store one logical record per sector. This makes it easier and faster for the disk drive to know where to access records in a random manner. Logical records whose length exceeds the sector size are often stored in adjacent sectors. For example, if the logical record size is 300 bytes and the sector size is 256 bytes, two adjacent sectors will be required per logical record.

In practice, today's sophisticated access software minimizes many of these problems by using cache memory, which was discussed in Chapter 7. Using such techniques, the "cost" of retrieving a logical record from physical sectors located anywhere on the disk is very low.

IMPROVING THE DISK'S CAPACITY

The trend in all disk technology is toward storing more data in less space. The method for increasing the density of a disk lies in shrinking the size of the magnetic fields. There are several ways of doing this: (1) placing the head closer to the surface of the disk, which has already been discussed; (2) using a smaller read/write head; (3) stacking the magnetized bits vertically rather than horizontally; and (4) improving the platter surface coating.

THIN-FILM READ/WRITE HEADS

A major change in disk read/write heads occurred in 1979 with the introduction of thin-film heads made with photolithographic techniques similar to that used in manufacturing integrated circuits. Smaller read/write heads translate into higher storage capacity because such heads allow the tracks on the surface of a disk to be closer together, which means greater track density. Also, a thin-film disk head is hardly bigger than the head of

a pin, and it floats within thousandths of an inch of the disk surface.

VERTICAL RECORDING

Recall that the magnetic fields on the surface of a disk lie horizontally like small north-south pole magnets. One promising technique, called *vertical recording*, is to stand the magnets on end so that the north-south poles point up and down or vertically toward the surface of the disk. This effectively increases the density of the disks because more magnetic fields can be packed into a given area on the disk. With vertical recording techniques, experts estimate that disk drives could store data at densities of 100 MB per square inch—100 times the density of current Winchester drives.

THIN-FILM DISKS

Thin-film disks are manufactured by plating the surface of the disk with a thin metallic layer instead of the ferric oxide layer that is commonly used on disk surfaces. The metallic layer allows the magnetic field to be smaller, which means more bits per inch on each track. In addition, it helps in packing tracks closer together, which means more tracks per inch on the surface.

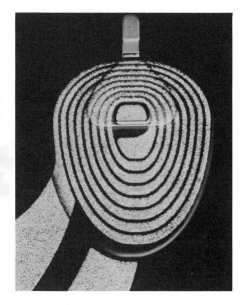

Thin-film read/write head. The IBM 3380 disk drive is a very-large-scale 14-inch Winchester drive with a capacity of 2520 MB. To achieve the density needed to store such large capacities, it uses thin-film heads as pictured in this enlarged photograph of the actual read/write head.

Thin-film disks. A diagram illustrating the low flying height of today's disk-drive heads. Shown are some possible contaminents relative to the flying height of the disk-drive head. (Illustration courtesy of Ampex Corp., Disc Media Operations. Reprinted by permission.)

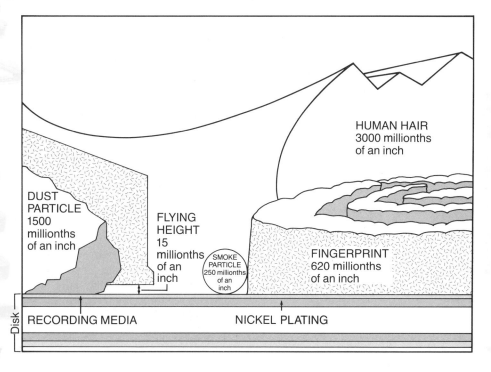

OTHER MAGNETIC STORAGE MEDIA

It is common practice to program ROM chips with application software and operating system software. This practice has given birth to the term *firmware*, that is, ROM computer circuits that perform the functions of program instructions. Examples of firmware can be found in some personal computer operating systems. Parts of the Macintosh operating system are found in ROM, and a ROM-based version of MS-DOS for portable computers is available. However, when the ROM becomes erasable and programmable, an entirely new medium for storing programs and data becomes possible.

PC CARDS

One such technology is the PC Card, a 2-inch by 3-inch by $\frac{1}{8}$-inch integrated-circuit card used as a removable data-storage medium for portable computers. The cards are based on a technology called erasable programmable read-only memory (EPROM) and currently have approximately 1 MB of storage capacity. Like $3\frac{1}{2}$-inch floppy disks, PC Cards can store data and programs, are erasable, and can be exchanged among dissimilar computer systems.[1]

PC Card technology is in its infancy, but it is expected eventually to replace floppy disks in portable computers. The advantages include faster access, smaller size, and less power consumption thanks to the lack of any moving parts. Disadvantages include the initial high cost of the cards and the reluctance of software vendors to make software available on PC Cards. However, as production volume increases and standards are adopted, both barriers are expected to disappear.

There are several other applications for PC Cards besides portable computers. Robots, laser printers, medical equipment, and digital still cameras that use PC Cards in lieu of film are already on the market. In Japan, software and traditional publishing companies are developing a system in which information such as stock data and news stories could be downloaded into PC Cards at vending machines in train stations or newsstands.

Eventually solid-state memory may replace rotating hard disks. One manufacturer is offering a prototype 20-MB solid-state device as a replacement for an equivalent-sized disk.

MASS-STORAGE CARTRIDGES

Storage systems have been developed to facilitate the storage and retrieval of the vast amounts of data that must be available for direct access processing. These storage systems are not practical for applications in which access time is critical; thus the best use of this technology is when large amounts of data must be directly accessed under relatively slow access time requirements.

To measure the capacity of such systems, the term terabyte was coined. A *terabyte* is roughly the equivalent of 1 trillion bytes of information. When referring to storage capacity, a terabyte is actually 2^{40}, which is 1,099,511,627,776 bytes. This staggering number can be appreciated more fully if we compare it to the storage capacity of other media.

One terabyte is roughly equivalent to

- 728,178 1.44-MB $3\frac{1}{2}$-inch floppy disks.
- 1024 1-GB disk drives.
- 7 IBM 3850 mass-storage systems.

Assume the average 300-page book contains approximately 750,000 bytes of text, so a terabyte could store approximately 1,466,016 of these books. The need for such huge quantities of storage arises from several sources:

- In scientific applications, for example, Landsat (land survey satellite), military command, and mapping, the computer produces huge amounts of data that must be stored, retrieved, and processed.

- In business applications, legal records retention requirements, such as storing old IRS and Social Security records, create the need to store vast amounts of data.

The IBM 3850 mass-storage system is an example of a very-large-scale

Mass-storage cartridges. This photo shows the inside of an IBM 3850 system, which stores data on 3-inch-wide magnetic tape cartridges. The mechanical unit in the center of the picture retrieves individual cartridges and positions them under the read/write head.

magnetic storage device. In this system, the storage medium is a 3-inch-wide, 770-inch-long strip of magnetic tape. Each strip is stored in a cylindrical data cartridge approximately 2 inches in diameter and 4 inches long. Each cartridge is designed to hold 50 million bytes of data in a format similar to that of some of IBM's disk packs. Each data cartridge is stored in a honeycomblike cell. The capacity of the system depends on the number of cells being used. However, the theoretical total capacity of the system is approximately 1.5×10^{11} bytes.

Data cartridges are retrieved by an electromechanical device that extracts the cartridge from the cell in which it is stored. Once a cartridge has been retrieved, it is placed in a read/write station and its contents are transferred to a magnetic disk for processing. The average time to retrieve a cartridge and begin transferring data to a disk is approximately 10 seconds.

OPTICAL DISKS

All the preceding technologies for improving the capacity of disks are pushing magnetic media to their density limitations. The optical disk, however, may be able to pick up where the high-density magnetic disk leaves off. An *optical disk* is a disk on which data are encoded for retrieval by a laser. Optical disks offer information densities far beyond the range of current magnetic mass-storage devices. Similar devices have been on the market for several years in the form of laser videodisks and audio compact disks for consumer use. These laser videodisks contain one spiral track, like the track on a phonograph record. Optical disks for computer applications store their information on concentric tracks, like their magnetic cousins.

Read-only optical disk. Personal computer users can connect their computers to CD ROM drives and read information from CD ROM disks.

Write-once optical disk. The Tab Optical Disk Filing System can store 60,000 letter-size pages on one optical disk. Data can be copied to optical disks and stored and retrieved electronically.

Currently, three versions of optical disk technology are competing for the mass-storage market: (1) read-only optical disks, (2) write-once optical disks, and (3) erasable optical disks.

READ-ONLY OPTICAL DISKS

Unlike conventional magnetic disks, **read-only optical disks** cannot be written on and so have the functional equivalency of read-only memory (ROM). In the early 1980s, experiments conducted by North American Philips produced the first commercial optical disk storage system based on a 12-inch videodisk. In the Philips system, data are recorded on 40,000 tracks per disk side for a total capacity of over 10 billion bits or approximately 1 GB per side.

The most popular version of read-only optical disks employs the same technology as the compact disk (CD) that has become popular for audio recording. The technology is digital and based on a $4\frac{3}{4}$-inch optical disk that can store 540 MB on a single side. The devices are called *compact disk read-only memories (CD ROMs)*.

Read-only optical disks are manufactured in a manner similar to that of conventional phonograph records. A master disk is first created and is then replicated by stamping out or pressing copies. Because read-only optical disks can be easily and inexpensively duplicated, they are a mass-distribu-

Erasable optical disks use a combination of lasers and magnetic surfaces to achieve erasability.

tion medium and can be used to store and distribute large library-type databases, software packages with accompanying interactive tutorials, and graphic image databases.

WRITE-ONCE OPTICAL DISKS

Write-once optical disks (also called write-once, read-mostly, or WORM) are blank disks that are recorded on by the user. To write data, a powerful beam of laser light burns tiny spots or pits into the coating that covers the surface of these disks. Once burned in, the spots are not erasable. To retrieve the data, a less powerful laser is used to read the pattern of spots.

Write-once optical disks are being used to replace microfilm storage and retrieval techniques in which high density is combined with a random-access retrieval. For example, Hitachi manufactures an optical filing system that could find application in banks, insurance companies, retail chains, and government agencies that have a need to copy and archive a vast number of documents. Because the optical disks have the ability to store images as well as sound, their use is quite versatile. Anything that can be digitized, such as documents, pictures, photographs, line drawings, and music, can

be recorded and stored on an optical disk.[2]

ERASABLE OPTICAL DISKS

Erasable optical disks use lasers to read and write information to and from the disk but also use a magnetic material on the surface of the disk and a magnetic write head to achieve erasability. To write on such as disk, a laser beam heats a tiny spot on it; then a magnetic field is applied to reverse the magnetic polarity of the spot. Because of this property, they are often called *magneto-optical* disks.

Erasable optical disk systems are still in the early stages of commercial development. They offer the same storage capabilities of the nonerasable optical disks along with the same reusability capabilities of conventional magnetic disks, such as Winchester systems; however, write and erase times are usually slow.

MULTIMEDIA APPLICATIONS

One of the most promising areas of optical disk applications is in the storage and retrieval of images and sound along with data. (Image processing was discussed in Chapter 5.) Storing images requires millions of bits of data.

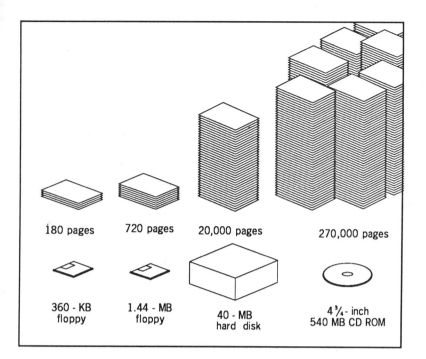

Comparing storage capacities. *Assume that one double-spaced typewritten page is the equivalent of 2K (2 kilobytes) of information. Shown here are the storage capacities in pages of the various types of mass-storage devices.*

animated graphics to complement the traditional forms of word and data processing.

The optical disk is the only medium that allows for the cost-effective, large-scale integration of graphics to complement traditional text and data. The graphic potential of an optical disk extends far beyond simple line drawings and includes pictures, the use of color, animation, and real-time video.

As optical disk technologies improve and the cost of the recording device drops, it is easy to imagine a videodisk system with read and write capabilities attached to a personal computer. Such a multimedia device would integrate video, audio, data, and text into a single medium and would provide the user with tremendous versatility in the form of music, video, picture communication, and

REVIEW

Mass storage provides a place to store programs and data before and after processing. Most computer users need to store data in files. Files are primarily of two types—sequential and random access—and a third type, indexed sequential, is used in cases where both types of access are required. Magnetic media are the dominant form of mass storage. Tapes played a prominent role in early computer systems, but today they are used primarily for backup and archiving. Specialized cartridge tapes are used to make backup files, and magnetic disks are the most important medium in mass storage today. Magnetic disks are categorized into floppy and hard. Floppy disks are a standard medium for small and personal computers, whereas hard disks have evolved from large, removable, multiplatter devices to smaller sealed devices. Researchers are exploring thin-film heads, thin-film disks, and vertical recording to improve the density of disks, and alternative magnetic recording media exist, such as integrated-circuit cards and mass-storage cartridges. Optical disks use lasers to read and write data and offer far greater densities than their magnetic predecessors.

REFERENCES

1. Lammers, David. "PC Standard in the Cards." *Electronic Engineering Times*, May 21, 1990, p. 1.

2. Davies, David H. "Developments in Optical Disk Recording." *Engineering Manager*, November 1984, p. 59.

RESOURCES

BOOKS

Brown, Robert E. *More than You Ever Wanted to Know About Hard Disks for Your IBM PC.* Sunnyvale, Calif.: Landmark Software, 1984. People who use their personal computer extensively will want to eventually add a hard disk. This book recommends ways to save money and gives tips and ideas for the hard-disk user.

Lambert, Steve, and Suzanne Ropiequet, eds. *CD ROM: The New Papyrus.* Redmond, Wash.: Microsoft Press, 1986. A fascinating tutorial on optical disk technology, CD ROM design, publishing, and applications and a great reference for text retrieval software, scanners, databases, user interfaces, and educational software design.

Ropiequet, Suzanne, ed., with John Einberger and Bill Zoellick. *CD ROM Volume Two: Optical Publishing.* Redmond, Wash.: Microsoft Press, 1987. A handbook for people who want to know about publishing on optical disks. Not as global as the first volume, but still a handy guide to this exciting new medium.

STUDY GUIDE

Match the following key terms to the appropriate definition:

A.

1. ____ Mass storage
2. ____ File
3. ____ Logical structure
4. ____ Physical structure
5. ____ Mapping
6. ____ Sequential file
7. ____ Random-access file
8. ____ Index sequential file

a. A collection of records whose characteristics depend on the form in which they are stored and retrieved.

b. A collection of records that can only be accessed by starting with the first record and proceeding through each record in the file.

c. A generic term for tapes and disks.

d. A file that contains a listing of key fields along with the location of the corresponding records.

e. A collection of records that is defined according to its content or use.

f. A description of the correspondence between the logical and physical structure of a file.

g. An organized collection of information about a specific topic.

h. A file that allows you to read or write any record in the file without regard to its location.

B.

9. ____ Magnetic tape
10. ____ Streaming tape
11. ____ Backup file
12. ____ Disk
13. ____ Floppy disk
14. ____ Track density
15. ____ Linear density
16. ____ Hard disk
17. ____ Cylinder
18. ____ Disk pack
19. ____ Winchester drive
20. ____ Disk cartridge

a. A removable disk in a cartridgelike container.

b. A tape with a surface on which data can be magnetically recorded.

c. A stack of disks mounted on a common spindle that can be removed from the drive unit.

d. A platter on which a magnetic or reflective coating is applied.

e. The number of bits per inch on a track.

f. A tape designed for the purpose of making backup files.

g. A copy of a file that is made for possible later reconstruction in case the original is lost or damaged.

h. A disk and read/write assembly that comes in a sealed container.

i. The imaginary surface formed by tracks that are directly above and below one another.

j. A platter made from ceramic or aluminum.

k. The number of tracks per inch on a disk.

l. A flexible disk.

C.

21. ____ Vertical recording
22. ____ Thin-film disk
23. ____ Terabyte
24. ____ Optical disk
25. ____ Read-only optical disk
26. ____ Write-once optical disk
27. ____ Erasable optical disk

a. Roughly the equivalent of 1 trillion bytes of information.

b. A disk that combines optical and magnetic techniques to record on the surface of the disk.

c. Disks that can be recorded on once by the end user.

d. A technique that places magnetic spots on a disk so that the north-south poles point up and down.

e. A disk that contains a metallic layer on its surface.

f. A disk on which data are encoded for retrieval by a laser.

g. An optical disk that cannot be written on.

True/False:

28. ____ The purpose of a mass-storage device is to provide a volatile storage medium for information.

29. ____ To an application program, a file can be viewed as a collection of physical records.

30. ____ To read or write the last record in a sequential file, you must first read or write all previous records in the file.

31. ____ Searching an inventory file for a specific part number would lend itself to sequential processing.

32. ____ Reading data from a tape is a nondestructive process.

33. ____ Cartridge tapes are specifically designed to store backup copies of disk files.

34. ____ A disadvantage of disk over tape is slower access time.

35. ____ A disk device can retrieve data in billionths of a second.

36. ____ Data are recorded on a spinning disk on a series of concentric tracks.

37. ____ Each disk track is divided into regions called sectors.

38. ____ By sealing the Winchester container, the read/write head can be made much smaller.

39. ____ Disk packs are removable disks in a sealed container.

40. ____ In effect, a sector is equivalent to a logical record.

41. ____ A gigabyte is much larger than a terabyte.

42. ____ Read-only optical disks are replacing microfilm for storage and retrieval of information.

Multiple Choice:

43. Which of the following is not involved in defining a file for a database program?

   a. Naming the fields.
   b. Specifying a maximum field length.
   c. Naming the physical records.
   d. Specifying the type of field.

44. The choice of an organization method is based on

   a. Whether the file is indexed, random, or sequential.
   b. The way the records need to be accessed during processing.
   c. The directory of the file.
   d. The key field of the record.

45. The oldest form of tape is called

   a. Cassette.
   b. Cartridge.
   c. Reel to reel.
   d. Backup.

46. Which of the following is not an advantage of floppy disks?

   a. Low cost.
   b. Small size.
   c. Direct access.
   d. Optical surface.

47. One of the main advantages of disk over tape is

   a. Sequential access.
   b. Faster access time.
   c. Larger capacity.
   d. Magnetic oxide coating.

48. One advantage of a disk pack is

   a. Transportability.
   b. Retractable read/write heads.
   c. Larger storage than the newer disks.
   d. Higher linear density.

49. A major drawback to fixed disks is

   a. They are removable.
   b. It is necessary to make backup copies.
   c. They operate at slow speed.
   d. They are rigid.

50. Which of the following is not used to shrink the size of the magnetic fields on a disk?

   a. Using predetermined record sizes.
   b. Using a smaller read/write head.
   c. Placing the head closer to the surface.
   d. Making the platter surface thinner.

51. A terabyte is equal to

   a. 2^{10} bytes.
   b. 2^{20} bytes.
   c. 2^{30} bytes.
   d. 2^{40} bytes.

52. Which of the following is not a promising area for erasable optical disk applications?

   a. Storing and retrieving micro-filmed documents.
   b. High-cost data storage.
   c. The archiving of data.
   d. Storing and retrieving images and sound.

Thought Questions:

53. Which of the two concepts, logical records or physical records, do you find hardest to understand? Why?

54. Some experts say that magnetic tape is already an obsolete storage medium and will disappear in a few years. Do you agree with this viewpoint? Why?

Projects:

55. CD ROM optical disks are rapidly becoming affordable storage devices for personal computer systems. Visit a computer store and find out for which applications CD ROM is useful. Present your findings to the class.

56. The storage capacities of Winchester disk drives vary considerably. Obtain the names of several different manufacturers of Winchester disk drives used with personal computers. Prepare a report on the storage capacities of each of the drives.

SOFTWARE EXERCISES

In this chapter we compared a terabyte to the storage capacity of other media. How were those numbers computed? By taking the capacity of a terabyte (1,099,511,627,776 bytes) and dividing it by the capacity of the various storage devices. You can do this by hand, but why not let a spreadsheet perform the calculations for you?

	A	B	C	D
1	Comparing Storage Capacities			
2	Assumptions: One CD ROM = 540 MB			
3				
4	One CD ROM disk is equivalent to			
5	xx	360 K floppy disks		
6	xx	1.44 MB floppy disks		
7	xx	20 MB cartridge tapes		
8	xx	40 MB hard disks		

For this exercise, you are going to use a spreadsheet to compare the capacity of a CD ROM disk to the capacity of several other mass-storage media. Assume that a CD ROM disk can store 540 MB of data (that's 540 times 1 MB). One CD ROM is equivalent to how many of the following?

- 360K floppy disks.
- 1.44-MB floppy disks.
- 20-MB cartridge tapes.
- 40-MB hard disks.

ANSWERS

1. c, **2.** g, **3.** e, **4.** a, **5.** f, **6.** b, **7.** h, **8.** d, **9.** b, **10.** f, **11.** g, **12.** d, **13.** l, **14.** k, **15.** e, **16.** j, **17.** i, **18.** c, **19.** h, **20.** a, **21.** d, **22.** e, **23.** a, **24.** f, **25.** g, **26.** c, **27.** b, **28.** F, **29.** F, **30.** T, **31.** F, **32.** T, **33.** T, **34.** F, **35.** F, **36.** T, **37.** T, **38.** T, **39.** T, **40.** F, **41.** F, **42.** F, **43.** c, **44.** b, **45.** c, **46.** d, **47.** b, **48.** a, **49.** b, **50.** a, **51.** d, **52.** b.

T. TRAVERS WALTRIP

Profession: Vice president of the Telecommunications Division of the Data Processing Department, The Travelers Companies, Hartford, Connecticut.

Profile: A recognized leader in the telecommunications industry, Mr. Waltrip was honored in 1987 as one of *Communication Week*'s "Top 25 Most Influential Figures in the Communication Industry."

Quote: *"The cardinal rule of telecommunications: if you can't measure it, you can't manage it."*

CHAPTER 9
COMMUNICATIONS

PREVIEW

For the past 100 years, we have been living through an invisible revolution. None of us has ever touched, smelled, heard, seen, or felt it, and yet we have rapidly learned to take it for granted. Right now, "invisible" information, traveling at 186,000 miles per second, is being communicated. Hundreds of thousands of telegraphs, telephones, radios, televisions, and computers, intricately networked together, are continuously talking and listening to one another. As computers and communications converge, their capabilities, power, and scope are transforming communications into one of the most powerful tools in human history.

This chapter will help you to understand how communications affects the field of computers, what concepts and technologies are involved in communications, and the extent to which you will be using the technology in the near future.

In this chapter, you'll learn

• How computers and communications are converging.

• The scope and history of communications.

• The concepts of communication channels.

• The differences among various hardware technologies.

• Types of computer networking.

• Several communications industry issues.

Scope of communications. *Dow Jones, publisher of* The Wall Street Journal, *transmits stories and advertisements to 17 regional printing plants via communications satellites.*

Computers and communications converge. *Major segments of the electronic communications industry. A large company, such as AT&T or GTE, will operate in virtually all segments; smaller companies will specialize. Note: Mass communications, such as radio and television broadcasting, are not included in the diagram.*

COMPUTERS AND COMMUNICATIONS CONVERGE

The field of communications is experiencing rapid and dramatic change. The communication of information is necessary in every aspect of business, government, education, and even the home. Traditionally, *telecommunications* has been the transmission of information over long distances by means of telephone, Teletype, radio, or television. *Data communications* has been the transfer of data or information between computer-related devices. Today, these distinctions have blurred as the two have been integrated into *information networks*, where information is processed and communicated electronically in the form of voice, data, and images over common media.

For example, telephone networks were once limited to providing voice services. As data communication technology advanced, telephone networks began providing data as well as voice transmission, and not long after that, image transmission services were added. Today, telephone networks have been transformed into highly distributed information systems, and they provide a variety of advanced communication and information processing services that go far beyond simply transmitting the human voice.

THE SCOPE OF COMMUNICATIONS

Businesses are especially dependent on the timely collection, analysis, and distribution of information to compete in a rapidly changing world. Today's businesses span the globe. For example, an international construction firm building an airport 10,000 miles from its headquarters would need communication among workers in the field, project managers at regional offices, and top management at corporate headquarters. Conventional telephone communication could take hours or days, and mail communication could take weeks. Another way to communicate over such long distances on a timely basis is to use data-communication capabilities. The following scenario is entirely within the realm of today's computer and communication technologies.

A supervisor for a construction firm is visiting a remote airport site deep in the heart of a Brazilian jungle. He discovers that there is a serious shortage of critical materials and that work is falling behind schedule. The supervisor begins solving the problem by using a company-supplied portable personal computer to determine the need for additional materials and to forecast the impact of delays on the completion of the project. To obtain additional needed information, he takes out a small box from the back of his jeep and

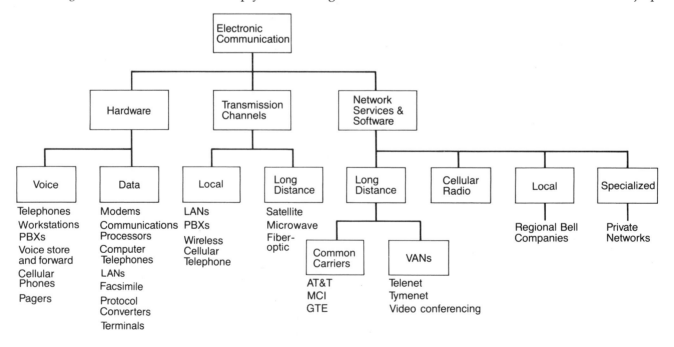

removes a small transmitting/receiving antenna in the shape of a 24-inch dish and connects it to the personal computer. He points the antenna dish north, initiates a communication program on the personal computer, and establishes a link with a communication satellite orbiting over the equator.

The supervisor checks the on-line inventory files to see if sufficient materials are on hand at project headquarters in Rio de Janeiro, Brazil. The system indicates that materials sufficient to meet the emergency need are not available within 2000 miles. The supervisor then prepares a project status report that includes a high-priority requisition for materials. He transmits the report to project headquarters via the satellite link.

The project manager reviews the status report and forwards the high-priority requisition to the firm's headquarters in the United States via another satellite link. At the firm's headquarters, a search is made of all construction sites within 5000 miles of the project site to determine the availability of the required materials. The search is made using additional computer-to-satellite-to-computer communication links, and the results are transmitted back to the supervisor at the project site.

The sequence of activities described may sound like something out of a science fiction novel, but every single piece of hardware and software necessary to implement this capability is currently available to us.

Today, modern newspapers and magazines disseminate information on a nationwide and even a global basis using data-communications technology. In 1983, for example, *USA Today* began using communication satellites to transmit stories, color graphics, and color photographs from headquarters to regional printing plants throughout the country.

HISTORICAL PERSPECTIVES

The communication of information via electronic means can be traced to several events in the 1800s and 1900s. In 1844 Samuel F. B. Morse (1791–1872), an American portrait painter, demonstrated his invention, the telegraph, by

sending the message "What hath God wrought!" from Washington, D.C., to Baltimore, Maryland. As you learned in Chapter 1, Morse established a basic principle of all data communications: the conversion of information into codes and then transmitting them as electric signals.

In 1876 Alexander Graham Bell (1847–1922) spoke the first sentence over a telephone. Prior to this, electronic messages were limited to the dots and dashes of the Morse code that could only be understood by trained telegraph operators.

In 1894 Guglielmo Marconi (1874–1937), an Italian inventor, demonstrated the first wireless transmission of an electric signal. The event marked the beginning of communication with electromagnetic waves. In 1901 Marconi traveled to Newfoundland, Canada, to receive the first wireless message from England—three dots—the Morse code for the letter *s*.

In the early 1900s the principles and devices that made possible radio and television broadcasting were invented and perfected. In 1919 the first radio station began broadcasting in Pittsburgh, Pennsylvania, and in 1936 the first public television service began in England.

The introduction of the computer as a component in a communication system occurred in 1940. In that year, Bell

Scope of communications. The Indonesian Palpa B communications satellite is about to clear the vertical stabilizer of the space shuttle Challenger *and begin its way toward its Earth orbital destination.*

Historical perspectives. The telegraph used by Samuel F. B. Morse to send the first telegraph message from Washington, D. C., to Baltimore, Maryland.

Historical perspectives. Alexander Graham Bell's first telephone.

Fiber-optic cable. On the right is a coaxial cable used to make local connections to a computer—typically 200 feet in length. On the left is a fiber-optic cable that not only replaces it, but extends the length of the connection by 6600 feet.

Laboratories demonstrated the capabilities of its "Complex Calculator" computer by Teletype between New York City and Dartmouth College in New Hampshire (see Appendix A for further description). Businesses, government, and industry did not begin to appreciate the importance and potential of linking computers with communication devices until the late 1950s. By 1964 American Airlines and IBM had completed the joint development of the first on-line passenger reservation system (Sabre), which linked over 2000 reservation terminals throughout the United States. The interest and activity in data communications have grown steadily since that time along with improvements in hardware, software, and communication channels.

The development of communication systems using satellites firmly established global communication networks. In 1957 the Russian *Sputnik 1* satellite became the first human-made device to transmit information from space. In 1962, President Kennedy signed the Communications Satellite Act designed to promote international communications. Also that year, the first communications satellite, *Telstar*, accomplished the first two-way transatlantic voice and video transmissions via an orbiting satellite. It was the first practical demonstration that satellites could compete with land-based forms of transmission. In 1963 the National Aeronautics and Space Administration (NASA) launched *Syncom II*, the first geosynchronous (22,300-mile orbit) satellite, demonstrating the soundness of the geosynchronous-orbit communications satellite concept in which the satellite travels at a speed that matches that of the Earth's rotation and maintains a constant relation to points on the Earth. And 1965 marked the beginning of commercial satellite communication service between North America and Europe with the launching of the *Early Bird*.

By 1976 the *INTELSAT II, III,* and *IV* series of satellites had been launched. By 1988 over 140 satellites had been placed in geosynchronous orbit.

Ground-based fiber-optic communications have evolved too, from the introduction of commercial fiber-optic cables in 1970 to today's transoceanic network of fiber-optic cables that link Asia, the United States, and Europe.

The evolution of communications has had a great impact on business, government, education, entertainment, and the individual. As a result, it is important to understand what communications is and the fundamentals of how it is accomplished. Recall from Chapter 1 that, in its simplest form, a communication system is made up of a sender (transmitter), a communication channel over which to send the data, and a receiver. Among other things, this chapter will expand on this definition and examine each of these components in detail, beginning with communication channels.

COMMUNICATION CHANNELS

A *communication channel* is a transmission path for electrical or optical signals. For two devices to communicate, such as two computers or a computer and a terminal, a channel must be established to link the two.

CHANNEL MEDIA

Several different types of physical media are commonly used to implement communication channels. The simplest and least expensive medium is called *twisted-pair wire*. The wires that connect your telephone to the local telephone office are an example of twisted-pair wires. Another common medium is the *coaxial cable*, which is wire surrounded by a flexible metallic shielding. A familiar example is found in cable TV connections. Coaxial cables are capable of much higher data transmission rates than are twisted-pair wires but are more expensive. The newest form of cable that is replacing coaxial cable is called a *fiber-optic cable* made of optical fibers. An optical fiber is a filament of glass about the same size in diameter as a human hair. It uses light instead of electricity to transmit information. Bundled together, fiber-optic cables provide a 25-to-1 weight advantage and a 10-to-1 capacity advantage over equivalent-sized coaxial cables. In theory, a fiber-optic cable can replace a wire in any application. Its high cost, which currently puts it at a competitive disadvantage, is dropping rapidly.

In addition to wires, some communication channels use the medium of electromagnetic radiation transmitted through open space. One common form uses microwaves to transmit data. The other major communication medium is the satellite system, which uses antennas to transmit and receive electromagnetic radiation to and from ground stations on the Earth. In addition, just as fiber-optic cables can replace coaxial cables, laser-based optical transmitters can replace microwave transmitters. Communication lasers use beams of light and the equipment used is similar to microwave transmission equipment.

Depending on its scope, the communication system may use several or all the types of communication media to send and receive data from one location to another. For example, our nationwide telephone system is made up of three main components: local loop, short-haul transmission, and long-haul transmission. The local loop, which links individual telephones to the local office, consists primarily of twisted-pair wires owing to the economics of installing and maintaining the local wires. The short-haul system, which spans distances of up to 250 miles, uses a combination of twisted-pair wires, coaxial cables, fiber-optic cables, and microwave transmission systems. Long-haul systems, which span the globe, use combinations of coaxial cable, microwave transmission, and, more recently, satellite and fiber-optic systems.[1]

BANDWIDTH

Another major concept in discussing communication channels is data capacity. **Bandwidth** refers to the amount of data that can be transmitted per unit of time, typically expressed as bits per second. You will also hear the term *baud rate*, which, in the context of low-speed data transmission, is synonymous with bits per second. The bandwidths of different communica-

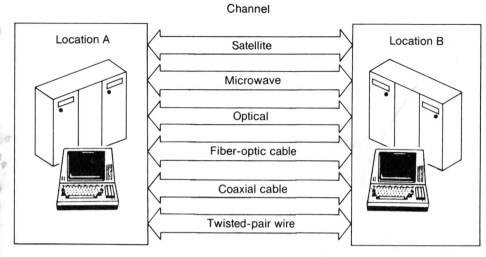

tion channels can vary greatly and are not directly related to the physical medium. A coaxial cable, for example, can have as high a bandwidth as a satellite channel.

Bandwidth is more closely tied to the needs of the data-communication application. For example, typing characters on a keyboard is limited by the typing speed of the user, so only a small bandwidth is needed for such an application.

In many communications applications, a small bandwidth is usually adequate. For example, when linking a personal computer to a time-sharing computer service, data are typically transmitted at 300, 1200, or 2400 bits per second. In communication terms, this is considered a voiceband channel. *Voiceband channels* are normally capable of transmitting data up to 9600 bits per second without special equipment.

On the other hand, the ability of the user to absorb information displayed on a video screen is much higher, so a

Data communication options. *Which option to use largely depends on the distance between location A and location B and the bandwidth requirements of the application.*

Bandwidth. *The capacity of a communication channel (bandwidth) is analogous to the capacity of a water pipe. The larger the pipe, the greater the amount of water that can flow through the pipe in any given unit of time. Broadband channels, such as those found in satellite systems, can be divided into thousands of voiceband channels.*

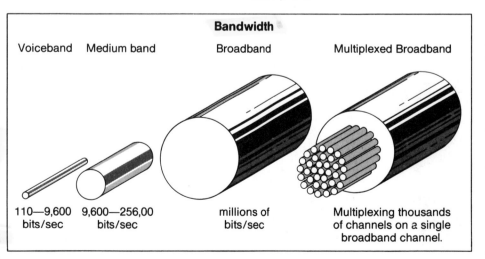

greater bandwidth is necessary. A good example is the large bandwidth needed to broadcast a television signal. Digitally transmitting a full-motion video and audio television signal requires a bandwidth of 45 million bits per second. A typical color television frame is made up of 1 million bits of information. To achieve the illusion of motion, individual frames are transmitted 30 times per second. Although it would be possible to send television picture frames over a 2400-bit-per-second channel, it would hardly make for an interesting television program, since the bandwidth of the channel would be too narrow to create the illusion of motion on the television screen. For example, it would take approximately 3 hours to transmit a single television frame at 2400 bits per second.

At the high end of the bandwidth scale, a nationwide retail chain such as Sears must transfer massive amounts of data (estimated at 1 billion bits of data daily) among various locations. For this type of application, high-bandwidth transmission is necessary. Telephone companies have channels available that are designed to carry data at 1.5 million bits per second. They are called *broadband* or *T1 channels.*

By using such a channel, the total time it takes for the retail chain to transmit the required data is significantly reduced. One publishing company uses a broadband satellite channel to transmit the copy for its magazine (including photos) from the composition site to an automated printing plant. With transmission at 1.5 million bits per second, the entire magazine is transmitted in less than an hour.

In between these two extremes lie many specialized *medium-bandwidth channels* that transmit data at 9600 bits per second to hundreds of thousands of bits per second. Telephone companies use such channels in their short- and long-haul systems. By using special techniques, several different voiceband channels can share one medium-bandwidth channel for efficiency of transmission. Other uses for medium-bandwidth channels include remote job entry to large mainframe computers, hotel and airline reservation services, banking and credit services, and company-to-company document distribution.

In the communications industry, bandwidth is a commodity that is sold, and channels are the method by which bandwidth is allocated. One high-bandwidth channel can be divided into many lower-bandwidth channels to meet the needs of specific applications, or many low-bandwidth channels can be combined into one high-bandwidth channel for efficiency of transmission. Which type of data-communication channel to use is primarily dependent on the bandwidth requirements of the application, the physical distance over which data has to travel, the required turnaround time, and, of course, the cost of purchasing the bandwidth.

Now that the basic concepts involved in communication channels have been examined, let us look at a few communication systems.

MICROWAVE SYSTEMS

Microwave systems use high-frequency microwaves to transmit and receive information. This type of system is capable of transmitting at higher bandwidths than are twisted-pair wires or most coaxial cables. However, microwave systems are expensive because they require relay stations with repeater antennas every 20 to 30 miles. Relay stations are needed because microwave systems can only transmit data on a "line-of-sight" path. Each station is placed in line with the next, amplifies the signal received, and transmits it to the next relay station in the chain.

SATELLITE SYSTEMS

A communication satellite acts as a relay station in outer space. It is placed in a geosynchronous orbit 22,300 miles above the Earth's surface, receives data beamed at it from a ground station, and relays that data to other ground stations. A single satellite in orbit at 22,300 miles can easily cover 40 percent of the Earth's surface. A network of three satellites can cover the entire world. In such a network, it is possible to relay data from satellite to satellite and then beam it to any

Microwave systems. An AT&T microwave relay station at Monticello, New Mexico. Another relay station would be located within a line-of-sight distance of approximately 30 miles.

ground station on the Earth.

Communication satellites are among the most expensive high-technology electronic devices ever assembled. They typically weigh between 300 to 4000 pounds and are assembled with the highest degree of precision to ensure long-term reliability. A typical communication satellite allocates its total bandwidth capability among 6000 to 12,000 voiceband channels in addition to several wideband video channels. Most satellites draw their power from the sun with large solar panels. The *INTELSAT V* satellite, for example, has a solar power wingspan of over 50 feet.

The biggest advantage of communication satellites is that they offer digital broadband communication services connecting remote locations, both within the United States and throughout the world. However, they are not without their problems. The most serious problem is losing the satellite, through either malfunctioning or having the satellite go out of its predetermined orbit. These problems could be solved only by redundant satellite facilities or the ability to repair the satellite while in space. Another problem is the half-second it takes a signal to make a round-trip from ground to satellite to ground. You may have experienced this delay when making long-distance phone conversations where the conversation seems to be out of synchronization. This can also cause problems in data communications where fractional-second response time is essential.

FIBER-OPTIC SYSTEMS

The development of fiber-optic technology combined with the invention of the semiconductor laser has created what AT&T researchers call photonics (or lightwaves), in which information is transmitted in the form of lightwaves instead of electric current. Currently, the largest growth area for fiber-optic systems is in replacing conventional copper wiring in telephone networks.

The advantages of fiber-optic cable over conventional cable are increased channel capacity and longer distances between amplifying stations. For ex-

ample, fiber-optic cables have transmitted data at 1 trillion bits per second in experiments in laboratories. As a signal travels over a cable, it eventually dissipates, so the phone company uses repeaters that pick up the signal, amplify it, and retransmit it to the next repeater. In a conventional cable, repeaters are positioned at 1-mile intervals. In fiber-optic cables, the repeaters can be positioned at 30-mile intervals.

Advocates of fiber-optic systems say that as costs of making fiber-optic cables decrease, satellite systems will become obsolete as ground-based communications become a more cost-effective alternative. For example, plastic optical fibers are starting to replace glass-based optical fibers. Plastic optical fibers are less expensive to manufacture than are glass optical fibers. In addition, plastic is ductable and bendable, whereas glass is brittle and nonflexible.

Some researchers are even predicting that photonic switching chips will eventually replace electronic integrated circuits in computers. AT&T researchers have built an experimental optical processor that employs photonic switches along with fiber-optic circuits and can switch on and off at speeds of a trillionth of a second, which is thousands of times faster than the fastest electronic switch.

Today's *photonic switches* are prototypes called Self Electro-optical Effect Devices (SEEDs) and are turned on and off by light beams, in much the same way that electronic transistors are turned on and off by electrical charges. And, like the evolution of the electronic integrated circuit, the number of components on a SEED may soon show a dramatic increase in density, and optical-based computers may then become a reality.

Semiconductor laser. *The output of this extremely small semiconductor laser can be tuned electronically from one ultrapure frequency to another.*

COMMUNICATION TECHNOLOGY

The earlier forms of data communications involved the simple hardware components of a central computer directly connected by wire or coaxial cable to one or more terminals. Since

Modems. *On the left is an internal modem that plugs into an expansion slot inside a personal computer. On the right is an external modem.*

that time, the applications of communications have expanded to include many different types of communications hardware.

MODEMS

The most common piece of data communication hardware in use today is the modem (short for *mo*dulator *de*modulator). Its popularity stems from the fact that the most convenient communication channel is the telephone line. The telephone system was designed for voice transmission long before the computer was invented. At that time, the analog method, in which information is represented by continuous smoothly varying signals, was most suitable for the needs of voice communication. As a consequence, when digital computers, in which information is represented by discrete on/off signals, are used in communication systems that employ telephone lines, the digital output of the computer has to be converted into an analog signal for transmission over telephone lines and then reconverted at the other end into digital form. A *modem* at each end of the channel performs the function of converting digital signals into analog signals and vice versa.

Several types of modems are commonly used. The earliest form is the acoustic modem. It consists of an acoustic coupler designed to hold the handset of an ordinary telephone and modem circuits to convert the signals and to interface with a terminal or personal computer. With the advent of the standard telephone jack connection, newer modems have taken on a slightly different form. They consist of the interface circuits along with a standard plug that the telephone jack can fit into. These newer modems are typically more reliable and convenient to use. Specialized modems designed for much higher transmission rates (up to 19,200 bits per second) are used in conjunction with communication channels that support the higher speeds. Today's electronic designers have built complete modems on a chip.

TERMINALS

Terminals are devices used in a communication system to enter or receive data. Some terminals are strictly limited to basic input/output functions and are known as *dumb terminals*. Others have built-in microprocessors and are known as *intelligent terminals*. Several common types of terminals include

Terminals. *On the left is a Digital VT330 monochrome monitor terminal. On the right is a VT340 color terminal.*

- Video-display terminals.
- Typewriterlike terminals.
- Transaction terminals.
- Remote-job-entry (RJE) terminals.

Video-display terminals use a keyboard in combination with a cathode ray tube display. The most common form of video-display terminal is becoming the personal computer, which, when connected to a communication line via a modem, can operate in terminal mode.

Typewriterlike terminals are useful when paper copy is desired. They employ a keyboard in combination with a printer.

Transaction terminals are specially designed for inquiry and response applications and capturing transaction-related data at the point of origination. Although any terminal can perform these functions, transaction terminals are often equipped with bar-code readers, magnetic strip readers, or other devices to bypass keying in the data. A few have been produced in hand-held versions. This type of terminal has found wide use in banks, retail stores, and supermarkets.

Remote-job-entry (RJE) terminals are primarily used in situations where large quantities of data are collected and batched for transmission to a central computer.

TERMINAL EMULATION

Today, it is possible to substitute a personal computer for a terminal in most applications. One technique is *terminal emulation*—personal computer software that emulates a remote terminal. Suppose a database application resides on a Digital VAX minicomputer and is designed to be accessed via terminals. It is possible to query the database application via a Macintosh, for example, by running a terminal emulation program. The software makes the personal computer look like a terminal, and the minicomputer thinks it is communicating with an ordinary terminal.

In the IBM world, software such as the IBM 3270 Terminal Emulation program provides a similar capability for IBM's personal computers. In addition, the user can switch back and forth between terminal emulation and personal computer applications quite easily.

One advantage to terminal emulation is the elimination of redundant equipment: a user does not have to have a terminal and a personal computer on his or her desk. Another advantage is that data can be *downloaded*—a method for sending data from a central location to a remote location and storing it there for future use. This makes it possible to copy in-

Terminal emulation. *Many terminals are limited to text-only displays as shown on th VT220 screen (A). Terminal emulators often use the graphics capabilities of the personal computer as shown on the Macintosh screen (B).*

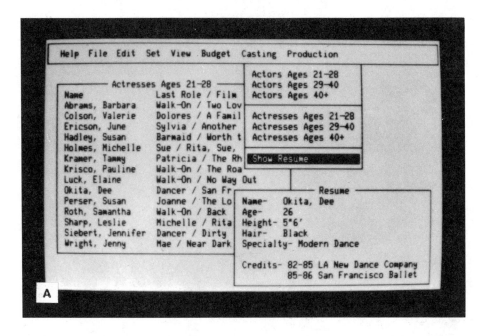

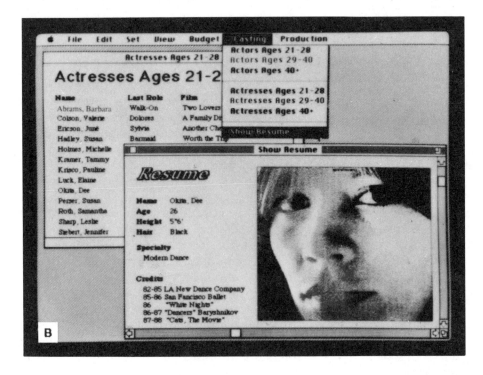

formation from a mainframe application and paste it into a personal computer application such as a spreadsheet or word processor.

One disadvantage of terminal emulation is that when personal computers operate in terminal emulation mode, they give up the normal capabilities of the personal computer. Another disadvantage is that the person using the emulated terminal must still learn the set of commands that goes along with accessing the minicomputer or mainframe. Using two different sets of com-

mands in two modes can be very confusing.

COMMUNICATIONS PROCESSORS

A *communications processor* is a device that interfaces a computer to a communication network. When these devices are employed in situations in which a large-scale central computer is used for data communications, they are called front-end processors. The communications processor is designed to perform a number of tasks, such as management of several communication channels and error detection and correction. The objective is to allow the central computer to perform its processing tasks without being burdened with these additional tasks. For example, communications processors can manage transaction processing, time-sharing, remote job entry, and distributed processing simultaneously.

FACSIMILE (FAX) MACHINES

Facsimile or FAX is a method for electronically copying and transmitting an image. FAX machines send and receive images over telephone lines. They scan documents, digitize the image, and transmit the information to another FAX machine, which reconstructs the image and prints it. Most FAX machines use thermal printers, but plain-paper FAX machines are becoming more common.

Using a FAX machine is similar to making a telephone call. To send a FAX, you first use the FAX's built-in telephone to dial the number of another FAX machine. After a connection is established, you insert your document into the FAX machine. When the transmission is successfully completed, the FAX machine provides feedback, and terminates the connection. Receiving a FAX is automatic. The FAX machine must, of course, be turned on and connected to a phone line. An incoming call triggers the FAX to begin receiving the document. This type of point-to-point communication requires the sending and receiving FAX machines to be connected simultaneously. In Chapter 10, we will discuss store-and-forward systems, such as electronic mail, in which the sender and receiver do not have to be connected simultaneously.

To make sure that FAX machines from different manufacturers can communicate with one another, all vendors have adopted standards from the Consultative Committee for International Telephony and Telegraphy (CCITT). The most common is called CCITT Group 3, a standard that provides a printing resolution of 203 by 193 pixels per inch. More expensive

Facsimile. The Murata facsimile machine shown on the right can double as a scanner and a printer.

FAX machines use the Group 4 standard, which offers 300-by-300 pixel resolution.

FAX machines can also be combined with other computer and communication technologies. FAX boards that contain a built-in modem and plug into one of the expansion slots inside of a personal computer enable facsimile transmission of word processing documents without first making a paper copy. By using communi-

Facsimile. Ricoh's MC50 portable copier can work as a scanner and a facsimile device with the appropriate attachments. Shown is the MC50 with the portable facsimile transceiver.

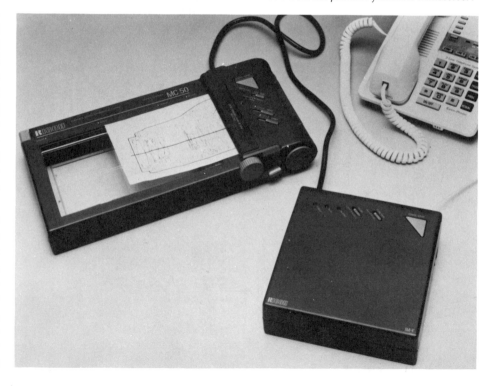

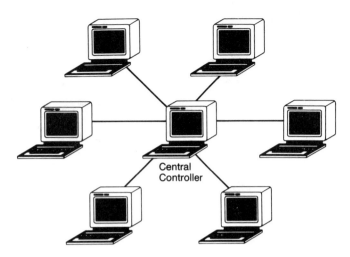

*A **star network*** *uses a central controller to which remote terminals or computers are attached. If the controller becomes inoperable, all terminals or computers on the network cease to function.*

*A **hierarchical network*** *is essentially a multilevel star network.*

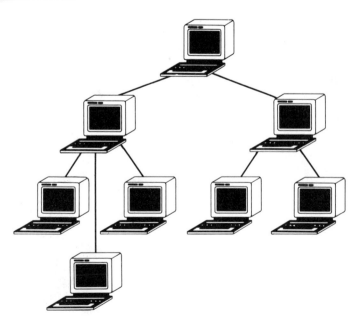

cation software, the document can be sent to a FAX machine or a comparably equipped computer.

COMPUTER NETWORKING

Computer networks can assume many forms. A network might be a time-sharing central computer connected to many terminals. The terminals might all be within the same building, or they might be geographically dispersed over a much larger area, in which case the computer network is called a *wide-area network*. A network might be a distributed processing system in which multiple computers are connected to each other. It might even be one in which data and voice are transmitted simultaneously. When the distance that a computer network covers is limited, it is generally called a local-area network.

LOCAL-AREA NETWORKS

A *local-area network (LAN)* is a communication channel that spans a limited geographic area. Data are transmitted digitally over the channel (twisted-pair wire, coaxial cable, or fiber-optic cable) at speeds currently ranging from 1 million to 16 million bits per second. A LAN is typically limited to a single building or a single department within a building. When the distance to be covered goes beyond several thousand feet (a few miles), LANs can be connected together for communications.

The uses for LANs will be discussed in Chapter 10. The following section describes several types of network configurations and how they function from a communication standpoint.

NETWORK CONFIGURATIONS

An important aspect of any network (wide or local area) is the path or route that the data take when they are being transmitted from one location to another. This is referred to as network configuration or topology. Several different network topologies exist, each with its own advantages and limitations.

Star Networks

Star networks derive their name from the fact that one central controller (usually a computer) has communication channels radiating outward, each one connected to a separate device, such as a terminal or another computer. For two devices to send or receive data from one another, the data must be routed through the central controller. Star networks are typically found in cases where a large-scale central computer is connected to many terminals, as in a time-sharing system. For example, some school systems have a large- or medium-scale computer that handles administrative tasks, class scheduling, registration, and grading and also have several terminals connected for instructional use.

The reliability of the central controller becomes the main issue in star networks, because when it goes down, the entire network fails.

Hierarchical Networks

Hierarchical networks, also known as tree-shaped networks, consist of a central computer to which several other computers or nodes are connected. Each node, in turn, has devices, such as terminals, connected to it. In concept, each node in a hierarchical network forms a star network, so that the problems of star networks are compounded by the additional layers of control.

Nationwide organizations with divisional and regional offices use hierarchical networks. In a sales application, for example, order-entry information is collected at the lowest levels and is passed along to departmental computers at the regional offices. There, regional customer and order databases are updated, accounts receivable records are processed, and salesperson performance data are collected. Regional sales information is passed to division offices for summary and analysis. Finally, summarized sales information is passed to the corporate office for inclusion in the corporate management information, financial modeling, or decision support systems.

Ring Networks

A *ring network* is a completely closed loop. A single communication channel, with devices connected to it, runs through a building or office until the end of the channel connects back to the beginning. There is no central controller. Each device on the ring (usually a computer) is equal in rank. The most popular type of ring network is called a *token ring network*, in which one token at a time passes from computer to computer and carries messages around the network. A *token* is the electronic equivalent of an envelope. It contains a destination address and a fixed amount of information.

This type of network could be used, for example, in a company where computers are located in the sales, account-

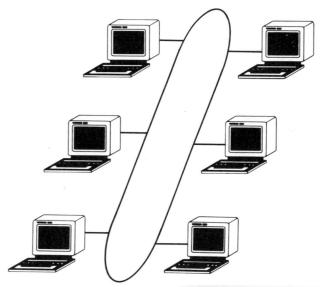

ing, production, and purchasing departments. Each computer would handle the applications unique to its department. When sharing of data is required, the computers pass data to one another over the ring network. For example, purchasing information must be passed to the accounting department for inclusion in the accounts payable system, or production-scheduling information must be passed to the purchasing department for use by the purchasing and inventory systems.

Bus Networks

A *bus network* is a single communication channel routed along a path in

A ring network is a completely closed communication channel with various devices connected to it.

A bus network is a common channel to which various devices can be attached. Attaching a new computer to the network or taking one away does not disturb the operation of the rest of the network.

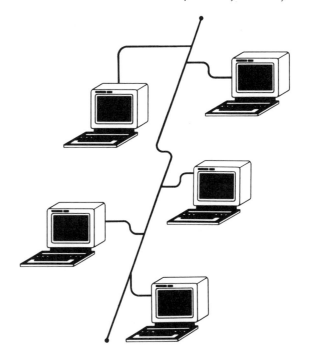

Private branch exchanges. The Dimension PBX telephone switching system.

the vicinity of each device that must be connected to it. The beginning and end of the network do not connect, so a terminator must be placed at each end of the bus. As in the ring network, no central controller is necessary. Each device on the bus has equal rank and can communicate with any other device on the network.

Bus networks are convenient where computers and devices are spread out through a building. A single communication channel can be run through rooms and offices and even span different floors of a building. In principle, it functions like a ring network in that each computer can handle independent processing tasks and can also communicate information to other computers.

PRIVATE BRANCH EXCHANGES

Another choice in communication networks is known as the **private branch exchange (PBX)**. The PBX is an electronic telephone switchboard. For example, in a large office with several hundred phones, connecting those phones together and to lines outside the office can be costly. When a PBX is used, it functions as a communications controller by handling and routing incoming and outgoing communications. A PBX can be programmed to perform the following functions:

• Handle thousands of communication lines.

• Handle automatic answering or outward calling to terminals via communication lines.

• Serve as a gateway to information networks outside a company.

• Log all message traffic, both incoming and outgoing.

• Provide communication capabilities for incompatible computers and other devices.

• Determine an alternative transmission path if an excessive error rate or heavy traffic is detected on a specific channel.

The newest generation of PBXs is digital and can carry both voice and data as digital bits at capacities measured in millions of bits per second. The ability to carry voice and data simultaneously makes PBXs an attractive alternative to separate phone and LAN systems. Also, because these PBXs are digital, modems are needed only to access telephone lines outside the office, so the digital PBX can function as a LAN as well as a voice telephone network.

WIRELESS COMPUTER NETWORKS

The Dick Tracy wrist radio of comic book fame may soon become a reality if cellular mobile radio systems become widespread. Cellular radio is made possible by dividing a geographical area into hexagonal-shaped cells, where adjacent cells have noninterfering radio frequencies. Instead of having one antenna broadcasting to a limited number of users, each cell, which ranges in size from 1 to 10 miles across, has its own antenna. The most popular application is for mobile telephones. For example, as the receiver of a phone call in an automobile advances from cell to cell, the call continues uninterrupted as a central switching facility automatically changes the frequency. In theory, cellular radio could make fixed wire-based phones obsolete.

Wireless computer networks. Cellular mobile radio divides a geographical region into hexagonal-shaped cells, each with its own small antenna. As a mobile user passes from one cell to another, calls are switched by changing frequency and calls continue uninterrupted.

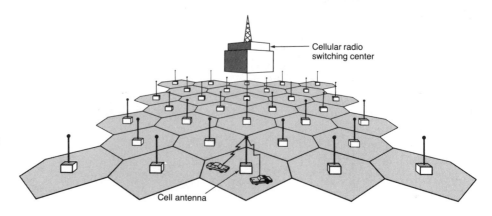

Cellular radio switching center

Cell antenna

On the computer front, cellular radio makes possible a mobile integrated voice-data network using radio waves. Such a system provides two-way communications between hand-held computers without the use of wires. For example, Motorola has developed a portable data-communications system called the PCX that provides real-time communications between people on the move. With this system, everyone can carry a pocket radio computer and have access to a wide variety of information.

COMMUNICATIONS INDUSTRY ISSUES

The tremendous nationwide and worldwide growth of data communications has raised a number of issues concerning the growth of the industry, regulation of the companies involved, and control over access to the data being transmitted.

GROWTH OF THE INDUSTRY

Communications could very well be the most powerful industry in the information society. The industry has grown to the point where it can be viewed as having four major subindustries: common carriers, manufacturers of interconnect de-

vices, value-added networks, and satellite transmission. The common carriers are already a multibillion-dollar industry. Each of the others has the potential to become a multibillion-dollar industry quickly.

The common carriers are what we

SPOTLIGHT ON...

ISDN Applications

Integrated Services Digital Network (ISDN) is the communication industry's vision of the public telephone network of the future. ISDN is an evolving body of international telecommunication standards being established by the CCITT (Consultative Committee for International Telephony and Telegraphy).

For users, ISDN will provide end-to-end digital access for all communication applications over existing phone lines without modems. More importantly, a new generation of software-based services will also become available. These will include the capabilities to simultaneously talk on the phone, watch a video program, and send and receive facsimile and electronic mail—all over the same phone line. When completed in the early twenty-first century, the digital network started in 1988 will be cheaper, smarter, and, like the difference between the "quiet" compact disk and the "noisy" record or tape, of higher quality than the current network.

To enable these new capabilities, ISDN turns an ordinary low-bandwidth telephone line into a high-bandwidth multiple-channel communication line. Basic access ISDN splits a phone line into two 64,000-bit-per-second B channels and a 16,000-bit-per-second D channel. This method is technically called 2B + D. For large-scale applications a primary access creates 23 B channels and one 64,000-bit-per-second D channel (23B + D). By creating multiple channels, ISDN frees the B channels for carrying more data and makes two-way transmission simpler.

Because ISDN is a worldwide standard, it also holds the promise of a universal telephone number. With your portable computer and your ISDN number/ID code, you'll be able to tap into the network from anywhere in the world, and gain access to computers as well as other people.

To learn more, read Business Telematics, *by Byron Belitsos and Jay Misera. Illustrated, 460 pp. Homewood, Ill.: Dow-Jones Irwin, 1986.*

Wireless computer networks. *Motorola's wireless PCX portable radio data terminal provides communication between a terminal and a host computer.*

normally refer to as the telephone company. Long-distance common carriers include AT&T, MCI, and General Telephone and Electronics (GTE). Local common carriers include the seven regional Bell operating companies, such as NYNEX (New York and New England) and US West. These companies provide image, facsimile, data, and various message services as well as traditional voice service.

The interconnect-device industry manufactures devices such as switching equipment, modems, multiplexers, private branch exchanges, and terminals. Major companies are Rolm, Northern Telecommunications, and Hayes.

The value-added networks (VANs) lease communication channels from the common carriers; add their own specialized services, such as facsimile transmission, electronic mail, or packet switching; and then sell the services to individual subscribers at a lower rate than would be possible if it were bought directly from the common carrier. In effect, VANs buy bandwidth in large quantities at wholesale prices from the common carriers, add value, and then repackage it into smaller products that are sold at retail prices.

The satellite industry manufactures satellites and related ground stations and sells high-bandwidth point-to-point communication services to major companies that need such high-capacity data transmission. Major companies in the satellite industry include Western Union, AT&T, and American Satellite Company.

INDUSTRY REGULATION

Regulation of the communication industry has existed since the late 1800s. Because radio communication is conducted over specifically allocated frequencies of the electromagnetic spectrum, two or more signals sent over the same frequency have a strong possibility of interfering with one another. To deal with this and other problems, the U.S. Congress set up the Federal Communications Commission (FCC) through the Communications Act of 1934. The FCC's charter is to perform the allocation function by regulating interstate and foreign communication facilities originating in the United States. This includes licensing and regulating radio, television, telephone, telegraph, facsimile, and transmission by wire, cable, microwave, and satellite systems. In addition, a Public Utility Commission (PUC) in each state regulates communication activities within its borders. The FCC works closely with the PUCs to grant and enforce monopoly rights and regulate the prices charged to users. Their joint objectives are to protect users from excessive charges while providing communications companies an opportunity to earn a fair rate of return on their investment.

Because of FCC policies, until the late 1960s prospective communication users had no choice but to go to their common carriers for all service and equipment. However, in 1968, the FCC made a ruling in the Carterfone decision that allowed independent equipment to be connected to the Bell System's telephone network. This decision heralded a gradual move toward deregulation of the industry and stimulated new technological developments outside the closed Bell System. The FCC handed down its Computer I decision in 1971. This allowed new firms to construct and offer land-based communication services and clearly distinguished between communication and computer-related activities. In 1972 another decision allowed new common carriers to launch and operate communication satellites.

In 1980 the FCC handed down the Computer II decision, which divided all telecommunication services into two categories—basic and enhanced—and required that common carriers furnish enhanced services through separate companies.

In 1983, the Department of Justice broke up the AT&T monopoly, which left seven regional Bell operating companies to provide local telephone services and AT&T to provide long-distance services.

Partially as a result of this move, and partially as a result of the trend toward integrating computer and information services into telephone networks, the FCC abandoned Computer II in favor of the Computer III Report and Order in 1986, which adopted a new framework for regulating the resulting integrated computer and communication network.

The Computer III decision legalizes competition among the providers of enhanced services such as electronic *Yellow Pages* and classified advertisements, home shopping, electronic and voice mail, and travel reservations. Prior to this decision, common carrier companies were prohibited from offering such services directly.

SECURITY AND CONTROL

In a communications environment, information is subject to exposure while in transit and when being accessed by a computer. This exposure raises the issue of privacy—the accidental or intentional release of personal information about an individual—and theft— the stealing of confidential information. The latter also includes the theft of information that is used to perpetuate embezzlement or fraud.

The issue of data loss or change refers to situations in which data are accidentally or intentionally lost or changed during transmission. The errors and omissions issue relates to inaccurate or incomplete data transmission whether accidental or intentional. Both issues are more related to data transmission accuracy than are the more sensitive issues of privacy, security, and theft. To address these concerns adequately, the local, state, federal, and international laws and regulations must be clarified and enforced.

OPTIONAL COMMUNICATION CONCEPTS

To understand communications completely, a number of additional concepts are included in this chapter. These concepts include

- Switching concepts.
- Multiplexers.
- Transmission modes.
- Transmission types.
- Protocols.

SWITCHING CONCEPTS

One way to establish a connection between two points on a communication network is known as circuit switching. In the case of making a telephone connection between Los Angeles and New York, the phone company uses circuit switching to find a free circuit among the many possible alternatives between the two cities and to keep that circuit open for the duration of the call. If the call consists of two computers talking to one another, they may only be exchanging short bursts of data and spending the majority of their time waiting for additional data. Regardless of whether transmitting or waiting, the circuit is still connected, and the user is paying for the connect time, which results in a very inefficient use of bandwidth.

While searching for a solution to the problems of developing technology that could assure the survival of military communication systems in the event of an attack, a method of transmitting data called *packet switching* was developed by computer scientist Paul Baran. Baran's idea was to break messages into smaller units called packets. Each packet contains the address of its destination and the data to be sent.

An analogy can be found in the postal system, where letters (data) are placed in addressed envelopes, sent by truck or plane through the mail (channel), and delivered to the proper receiving address. With packet switching, messages are broken into packets

Security of Transmission Systems				
	Satellite	Microwave	Coaxial	Fiber optic
Bandwidth	Very high	Very high	Low-medium	Very high
Security	Poor	Medium	Medium-high	Very-high

Security. Encryption and decryption techniques must be used to make any communication system secure. For example, any knowledgeable person can set up their own satellite antenna and intercept certain cable TV programs.

that are transmitted in short bursts over a communication network to the specified address, where they are reassembled into the original message.

Whereas circuit switching makes a physical connection between two points, packet switching makes a virtual connection. The concept is similar to virtual memory in which the computer appears to store an entire program in memory, when in fact the program is stored in virtual memory and only parts of it are actually in memory at any one time. By sending data in small packets, each with its own address, bandwidth can be allocated more effectively. A large number of packets can be multiplexed onto a single channel. Many small packets can be routed over many different paths on the network instead of large messages routed over a single path. If errors occur, usually only a single packet of data is lost instead of the entire message. If different paths in the network go down, packets can easily be rerouted because no physical connection has been established, only a virtual connection.

For example, GTE's Telenet is a packet-switched network that can be used to connect home computers to an information service such as The Source. To use the system, you dial a local Telenet number and make connection with a packet-switching controller. All data from that controller are sent in packets to The Source's central computer in Virginia. Since many different users are sharing the same line through packet switching, the cost to each individual user can be lowered. (You do not pay this bill directly; the cost is included in the hourly connect-time charges you pay to The Source.) Your alternative is to dial The Source directly in Virginia, which might entail a considerable long-distance phone bill in addition to your connect-time charges.

MULTIPLEXERS

A *multiplexer* is a device that allows multiple communication signals to share one communication channel. The objective of a multiplexer is to lower communication costs by allowing more efficient use of bandwidth.

Traffic over a communication channel is rarely smooth and continuous. Just as freeways are jammed during rush hour and empty late at night, or electrical consumption rises dramatically on a hot evening when air conditioners and appliances are turned on, communication channels also have peaks and valleys. Similarly, adding more lanes to already-crowded freeways does not necessarily solve the traffic problem, and adding more bandwidth in a communication system does not necessarily provide better communication capability. Another solution involves more effective utilization of the bandwidth that is already there. Multiplexing is accomplished in several ways.

Frequency-division multiplexing involves splitting the frequency range of the transmission channels into narrower bands. Data from each user are then sent over a specific band. This technique is used in the telephone long-haul system. A typical telephone coaxial cable, for example, is capable of carrying 10,000 simultaneous voice conversations simply by frequency multiplexing the signals that represent individual conversations. Also, the telephone company short-haul system transmits voiceband communication by multiplexing 12 to 24 voiceband channels into one larger channel.

Time-division multiplexing involves assigning a given channel to several different users at predetermined time intervals. In effect, each user takes a turn, during which a portion of his or her data is transmitted or received. This portion of data is referred to as a *frame*. With this method, the receiving multiplexer must reassemble all the frames for each user.

A *concentrator* is a device that combines individual messages into a single message for transmission to a processing unit. At the receiving end, a deconcentrator must extract the individual messages from the data sent in a single transmission. This is similar to the concept of blocking logical records into one physical record for storage, then breaking the block into logical records for processing, as was discussed in Chapter 8.

A *statistical multiplexer* allows several devices to share a channel by allocating time on the basis of the device's need to transmit data. For example, if two devices are competing for the same channel, the statistical multiplexer will bypass the inactive device and allocate the channel to the active device. If both are active, the statistical multiplexer will store data from one device until time on the channel is available for transmission.

TRANSMISSION MODES

The two most commonly used modes to transmit data are synchronous and asynchronous. *Synchronous mode* simply means that data are continuously transmitted against a common clock coordinated between the transmitting and receiving device. If no data are ready to be sent, idle characters are sent to keep the two devices in synchronization. This mode is used for transmission of large blocks of data. The receiving device and sending device must be operated simultaneously and are resynchronized by passing a predetermined group of synchronization characters between them.

Asynchronous mode refers to the transmission of data in which information is sent one character at a time. The transmitter may send characters at irregular intervals, hence the name asynchronous. Each character is transmitted as an independent entity, and because of this, asynchronous transmission systems are sometimes called start-stop systems in which each character is preceded by a start signal and is followed by a stop signal.

Synchronous transmission is more efficient because there are fewer control bits in proportion to the total number of bits transmitted. However, if an error should occur while a block of data is being transmitted, the entire block of data has to be retransmitted. In asynchronous mode, an error may only destroy a single character.

TRANSMISSION TYPES

In the telephone system, two-way communication is accomplished through a two-wire or a four-wire system. In the two-wire system, both transmitter and receiver of two separate telephones must share the line. There are two basic types of data transmission used in communications, half duplex and full duplex. The *half-duplex* method of transmission is used primarily with two-wire circuits and can only send data in one direction at a time. When using a half-duplex line, you must wait until the other party has finished sending data before you can transmit a response.

The *full-duplex* transmission type is used with four-wire circuits. This type allows signals to be sent in both directions at the same time. Most data-communication systems that use the telephone network transmit in half duplex. Sending data in full duplex requires a higher-grade line, such as a private or leased voice-grade line.

PROTOCOLS

A *protocol* is a formal set of rules for specifying the format and relationship when exchanging data among communicating devices. A good analogy is the diplomatic protocol used when exchanging information in meetings between people of two countries. A handshake is an example of protocol between two people. In computer terminology, *handshaking* refers to the protocol of exchanging information when two devices initially establish contact with one another to find out whether they are compatible. For example, the devices must determine whether they transmit data at the same rate, in the same format, in half- or full-duplex mode, and asynchronously or synchronously. If all conditions are compatible, the devices will be able to communicate. Protocols are also used to facilitate transfer of files between microcomputers and in LANs to determine when the network is available to send a message.

REVIEW

Communications and computers have converged into integrated digital networks. Communications involves the use of channels, which in turn need a medium for transmitting electromagnetic radiation. The four most common media are twisted-pair wire, coaxial cable, microwave transmission, and satellite transmission. Fiber optics and lasers will play more important roles in the future as light-based communication becomes more competitive. Bandwidth measures the capacity of a communication channel. Several communication technologies, including modems, terminals, terminal emulators, communications processors, and facsimile machines, were discussed. Computer networking was examined through the perspective of LANs, private branch exchanges, and wireless computer networks. Different sectors of the communications industry were explained along with the trend toward decentralization and the issues of security, privacy, and control. Finally, additional data-communication concepts, such as switching techniques, multiplexers, transmission types and modes, and protocols, were covered.

REFERENCES

1. Evans, B. O. "Computers and Communication." in *The Computer Age: A Twenty-Year View*. Cambridge, Mass.: MIT Press, 1980, pp. 350-351.

RESOURCES

BOOKS

Belitos, Byron, and Jay Misera. *Business Telematics*. Chicago, Il.: Irwin, 1986. If you need a comprehensive overview of communications, complete with case studies, this book provides an up-to-date, in-depth treatment of every topic covered in this chapter and more.

Martin, James. *Networks and Distributed Processing*. Englewood Cliffs, N.J.: Prentice-Hall, 1981. James Martin has become an industry guru through the many books he has written and the seminars he teaches. Most of his books are worth reading for their excellent explanations of the subjects.

Williams, Frederick. *The Communications Revolution*. New York: New American Library, 1983. A highly readable, nontechnical introduction to communication industry issues and future topics.

STUDY GUIDE

Match the following key terms to the appropriate definition:

A.

1. _b_ Telecommunications
2. _e_ Data communications
3. _f_ Information networks
4. _a_ Communication channel
5. _d_ Bandwidth
6. _g_ Modem
7. _c_ Terminal
8. _h_ Terminal emulation

a. A transmission path for electrical or optical signals.

b. The transmission of information over long distances by means of telephone, teletype, radio, or television.

c. A device that is used in communication systems to enter or receive data.

d. The amount of data that can be transmitted over a given unit of time.

e. The transfer of data or information between computer-related devices.

f. Electronic processing and communication of information in the form of voice, data, and images over common media.

g. A device that converts digital signals into analog signals and vice versa.

h. Personal computer software that emulates a remote terminal.

B.

9. _d_ Communications processor
10. _f_ Facsimile
11. _a_ Local-area network (LAN)
12. _c_ Star network
13. _g_ Hierarchical network
14. _e_ Ring network
15. _b_ Bus network
16. _h_ Packet switching

a. A communication channel that covers a limited geographical area.

b. A communication channel routed along a path in the vicinity of each device connected to it.

c. A central controller with one communication channel attached to each device connected to it.

d. A device that interfaces a computer to a communication network.

e. A closed-loop communication channel.

f. A method for electronically copying and transmitting an image.

g. A central controller with a series of nodes, each connected to several terminals.

h. A method for breaking messages into smaller units that can be transmitted separately over communication networks.

C.

17. _d_ Multiplexer
18. _b_ Frequency-division multiplexing
19. _c_ Time-division multiplexing
20. _a_ Concentrator
21. _j_ Statistical multiplexer
22. _f_ Synchronous mode
23. _h_ Asynchronous mode
24. _e_ Half duplex
25. _i_ Full duplex
26. _k_ Protocol
27. _g_ Handshaking

a. A device that combines individual messages into a single message for transmission to a processing unit.

b. Assigning a channel to several users by splitting the frequency into narrower bands.

c. Assigning a channel to several users on the basis of fixed time intervals.

d. A device that allows several communication signals to share the same channel.

e. Two-way communication in which data are sent in one direction at a time.

f. A method in which blocks of data are transmitted by coordinating them against a clock common to the sender and receiver.

g. The exchange of information when two devices initially establish contact to determine whether they are compatible.

h. A method in which individual characters are sent at irregular intervals.

i. Two-way communication in which data are sent in both directions at the same time.

j. A device that assigns a channel to several users by allocating time on the basis of a device's need to transmit data.

k. A formal set of rules for specifying the format and relationship when exchanging data between communicating devices.

True/False:

28. _____ The distinction between telecommunications and data communications has become much clearer with the advent of information networks.

29. _____ Global communication networks were firmly established by the development of communication systems using satellites.

30. _____ In theory, a fiber-optic cable can replace a wire in any application.

31. _____ Twisted-pair wires are the simplest and least expensive media for communication channels.

32. _____ The term bits per second is a measure of the speed of a communication channel.

33. _____ Channels that are designed to carry data at millions of bits per second are called voiceband channels.

34. _____ Channels are the method by which bandwidth is allocated.

35. _____ The most convenient communication channel in use today is the telephone line.

36. _____ The reliability of the central controller is a primary issue in a bus network.

37. _____ Microwave systems require relay stations with repeater antennas every 1 to 10 miles.

38. _____ Modems can handle simultaneous voice and data transmission.

39. _____ A major goal of local-area networks is to be able to connect equipment from different vendors on the same network.

40. _____ In asynchronous mode, the transmitter may send characters at irregular intervals.

41. _____ In the communications industry, the telephone company is called a common carrier.

42. _____ Value-added networks buy bandwidth in large quantities at wholesale prices and sell it in smaller quantities at retail prices.

Multiple Choice:

43. A wire surrounded by a flexible metallic shield is called a
   a. Twisted-pair wire.
   b. Fiber-optic cable.
   c. Coaxial cable.
   d. Telephone wire.

44. Voiceband channels normally operate at
   a. 110 to 300 bits per second.
   b. 300 to 2400 bits per second.
   c. 1200 to 2400 bits per second.
   d. 2400 to 9600 bits per second.

45. Multiplexing allows several users to share a
   a. Central computer.
   b. Local-area network.
   c. Communication channel.
   d. Satellite.

46. A front-end processor is ideally suited for
   a. Local-area networks.

   b. Time-sharing systems involving a large-scale computer.
   c. Microwave transmission systems.
   d. Combining data from several sources into a single channel.

47. A satellite in orbit 22,300 miles in space can cover what percentage of the Earth's surface?
   a. 20 percent.
   b. 30 percent.
   c. 40 percent.
   d. 50 percent.

48. Which of the following network types does not need a central controller?
   a. Star network.
   b. Ring network.
   c. Hierarchical network.
   d. Packet-switched network.

49. More effective use of existing bandwidth can be accomplished by

   a. Full duplexing.
   b. Broadband channels.
   c. Circuit switching.
   d. Packet switching.

50. The most common mode used for transmitting large blocks of data is called
   a. Asynchronous.
   b. Half duplex.
   c. Synchronous.
   d. Full duplex.

51. The function of a public utility commission is to
   a. Allocate frequencies of the electromagnetic spectrum.
   b. License satellite communication systems.
   c. Regulate interstate and foreign communication activities.
   d. Regulate communication activities within a state.

52. The 1968 Carterfone decision moved the communications industry toward

    a. Launching and operating communication satellites.
    b. Less regulation.
    c. Distinguishing between communication and computer-related activities.
    d. More regulation.

Thought Questions:

53. If computers and communications are converging what will the computer systems of the future look like?

54. In the communication industry, all trends point toward less government regulation. Do you think deregulating the communications industry is a good idea? Defend your answer.

Projects:

55. Make a list of all the communication facilities at the school you are now attending. What are they used for? Prepare a report and present it to your class.

56. Visit an office that has connected several personal computers with a local-area network. Find out what the LAN is used for and how it differs from a stand-alone personal computer installation. Present your findings to the class.

SOFTWARE EXERCISES

Have you considered using personal computers as communication tools? Just as they can simplify tasks such as writing, record keeping, and analysis, computers can help simplify communication. How are they used for communication at your college or university?

Use your word processor to prepare a report that surveys the different computer/communication uses at your school. The class can be divided into teams. Each team can focus its report on one of the following topics:

- On-line services or information utilities. Examples are The Source, CompuServe, and Prodigy.

- On-line databases. Examples are Dialog, Nexis, Lexis, and Bibliographic Research Services.

- Public electronic mail services. Examples are MCI Mail, Western Union EasyLink, and CompuServe.

- Public bulletin boards. Examples are Usenet and Bitnet.

ANSWERS

1. b, **2.** e, **3.** f, **4.** a, **5.** d, **6.** g, **7.** c, **8.** h, **9.** d, **10.** f, **11.** a, **12.** c, **13.** g, **14.** e, **15.** B, **16.** h, **17.** d, **18.** b, **19.** c, **20.** a, **21.** j, **22.** f, **23.** h, **24.** e, **25.** i, **26.** k, **27.** g, **28.** F, **29.** T, **30.** T, **31.** T, **32.** F, **33.** F, **34.** T, **35.** T, **36.** F, **37.** F, **38.** F, **39.** T, **40.** T, **41.** T, **42.** T, **43.** c, **44.** b, **45.** c, **46.** b, **47.** c, **48.** b, **49.** d, **50.** c, **51.** d, **52.** b.

INFORMATION

SYSTEMS

PREVIEW

A credit-card purchase in a department store is validated immediately. A telephone call to a travel agent allows you to reserve a rental car in a city 3000 miles from home. A card placed in an automated teller machine (ATM) yields accurate information about the status of your account. A computer-developed part design is fed directly to the machine that is making the part. Each of these examples illustrates the changing nature of computer-based information systems.

This section will describe the relationship between information technology and organizations, and how that technology influences the process of change in organizations.

Chapter 10 first looks at the components and structure of management information systems. Then it explains three general-purpose information technology tools—personal computing, workgroup computing, and network computing—that are changing the role of management information systems. Chapter 11 discusses how improvements in database technologies and methods provide management with decision-making information and how to keep one step ahead of the competition. Chapter 12 explores artificial intelligence (AI), expert systems, and neural networks, and we look at applications in which these techniques are successfully used.

The major topics introduced in this section include

- Management information systems (MIS).
- The components of MIS.
- The structure of MIS.
- Information technology tools.
- The implications of information technology.
- Database management systems (DBMS).
- Airline reservations: a DBMS application.
- Components of a DBMS.
- Database management issues.
- Artificial intelligence.
- Natural language processing.
- Expert systems.
- Neural networks.

MARY JO BURNES

Profession: Director, Corporate Information Systems, Cincinnati Milacron, Inc., a manufacturer of machine tools and plastics machinery in Cincinnati, Ohio.

Profile: Burnes graduated with a B.S. degree in 1971 from Miami University in Ohio, where she majored in systems analysis. She joined Cincinnati Milacron in 1974 as a programmer/analyst, moved up to project leader, then into management. In 1988 she was promoted to MIS Director, the first person in the company to have "come up through the ranks" to fill that position.

Quote: "We are long past the day of only technical specialists using computers. Today, almost all business professionals must know how to make effective use of computer technology."

CHAPTER 10

MANAGEMENT INFORMATION SYSTEMS

PREVIEW

Computers and information systems play critical roles in the operation of many organizations. All organizations, from factories to banks, are highly dependent on information for their day-to-day operations. The vast quantity of information that large corporations and government agencies need to operate, and the speed with which that information is created and used, makes computer-based management information systems (MIS) critical to such operations.

In organizations where computers are vital to operations, MIS departments are hard at work trying to understand the nature of the organization's business and to improve it with information technology. They accomplish this by carefully tailoring information technology to meet the needs of managers and other users throughout the organization.

This chapter will introduce the concepts, applications, and technology associated with MIS. First, it looks at the background, components, and structure of MIS. Then it explains three general-purpose information technology tools—personal computing, workgroup computing, and network computing—that are influencing the role of MIS. Finally, the chapter explores the impact of information technology on people. In Section Four, we will describe the process by which these systems are developed.

In this chapter, you'll learn

- What MIS means.
- The components of MIS.
- The structure of MIS.
- The importance of information management.
- The information technology tools of personal, workgroup, and network computing.
- Local- and wide-area networks.
- The effect information technology has on management and organizations.

WHAT IS A MANAGEMENT INFORMATION SYSTEM?

The term *management information system,* or *MIS,* refers to a system that gathers, condenses, and filters data until it becomes information, and then makes it available on time, and in a useful form, for use in decision making at various levels of management within an organization.

Of course, an information system does not necessarily imply the use of a computer. Many businesses, for example, employ people to peruse news services and newspapers, select articles that are of interest to the business, and edit them into a daily report for management.

However, as the scale and complexity of a business grow, its managers can unquestionably take advantage of information technology to make their people more productive and their businesses more efficient. For example, the previously mentioned articles could be captured using a scanner and optical character recognition software, edited with a word processor, and fed to management via the company's electronic mail system. And as the cost of computer technology drops, even very small organizations can begin to benefit from computer-based MIS tools.

THE FOUNDATIONS OF MIS

MIS can trace its roots to several historical management theories. Standardization and mechanization were the dominant management ideas of the first half of the twentieth century,[1] and the first computerized information systems of the late 1950s and early 1960s simply mirrored these management theories. The role of MIS involved automating the basic business transactions such as order entry, inventory control, and accounts payable and receivable, and then processing them. Feedback on the operation of the system came to management via reports.

The culmination of these theories came in the late 1960s with the *total systems concept,* in which a single centralized repository of information would represent all the organization's activities. It was soon discovered, however, that such a system would be a compromise. No one system could be all things to all people.

The total systems idea was augmented in the early 1970s with *decision support systems (DSS)*—applications within MIS that directly support specific decision making. DSS grew out of the recognition of the manager as a decision maker, not as a caretaker. Information was needed to evaluate alternatives and to project and estimate probable outcomes and consequences of various decisions.

Both of these ideas can still be found in MIS today. The idea of managing the transactions of a large corporation with thousands of customers and employees without the aid of an MIS, for example, would be unthinkable. Supporting decision making with the help of computers is still an important class of applications within an MIS.

But as corporations and governments evolved, increasing complexity and competition placed new demands on management. To cope successfully, management had to place more emphasis on formulating, planning, and executing *strategies,* plans of action designed to cope with change, competition, and uncertainty. As a result, strategic management has become an important theory that guides organizational thinking and behavior, and the use of information and information systems in strategic ways has become the new, and important, role of MIS in the organization.

Using information strategically requires managers to think about (1) where the organization is heading, (2) how the competitive environment in which the organization operates is changing, and (3) the consequences of those changes to the organization.

Major movie studios, for example, have to gather and respond to information very quickly. When a new film opens in theaters, it is in competition with many films. The studios cannot wait weeks or months to find out how the film is faring. They need a strategy. Studios use MIS to collect box office receipts daily from theaters around the world. The data are compared with the results of other films and are fed into advertising systems that help management make immediate decisions on whether to increase or decrease advertising and promotion expenses and theater bookings.

Using information strategically has long-term implications too. For example, in the early 1970s, Citibank saw that its administrative costs were rising without a corresponding increase in services to customers. Faced with the possibility of costs exceeding revenues, Citibank decided to install automatic teller machines (ATMs) throughout the highly competitive New York metropolitan area. It was a strategic move that resulted in a substantial increase in Citibank's market share and forced the competition to play catch-up.

THE COMPONENTS OF MIS

A management information system consists of two major components. First is *information technology*—a collective term for the computer and communication hardware and the system and application software that we have been discussing throughout this book. By assembling, storing, transmitting, processing, and retrieving data, information technology helps make information more accurate and useful, and makes it available when and where it is needed.

Second are the human resources and procedures needed to help people within the organization put that information to work. To accomplish this, an organization will set up a group or computer facility called the *MIS department*. A typical MIS department of a medium- or large-scale organization is composed of five functional units:

• An *information center* that provides liaison between the MIS department and computer users. The center is the place where users can turn for help in solving technical problems, finding corporate data, buying hardware and software, and getting started with computers.

• An *applications development group* in which programmers develop new application software for the company's computers.

• A *systems group* in which systems

analysts develop new systems and work with the users of the information systems to ensure that the applications are meeting their needs.

• An *operations group* that tends to the day-to-day care and feeding of the many computers in the organization.

• A *technology planning group* to ensure that information technology is used to further the strategic goals of the company, and to ensure that opportunities to apply that technology creatively are not overlooked.

You will learn more about how an MIS department develops new systems in Section Four.

Although the term management information system or MIS is a widely used title for both the system and the department that administers, develops, and dispenses the services, some organizations choose to use a different title. You will often hear terms such as data processing (DP), electronic data processing (EDP), information services (IS), or computer information systems (CIS) to describe MIS. These terms are used interchangeably.

THE STRUCTURE OF MIS

The structure of MIS parallels the structure of the organization. An organization is often divided into functional units such as marketing, finance, administration, and manufacturing. There are management information systems for each functional unit as well as systems common to all functional areas. For example, a factory-floor monitoring system would only

Organization of the MIS department.

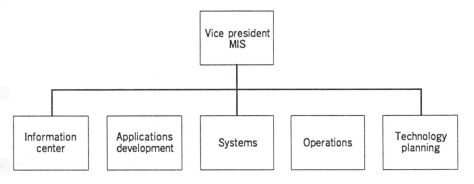

be used by manufacturing, whereas a sales system might be used by marketing, administration, and manufacturing.

Within each functional unit there are usually three levels of management whose needs an MIS must address. They are

• The *operational level*, which is concerned with the day-to-day management of the organization. For example, the assistant manager of a bookstore works at the operational level. His or her responsibilities might include verifying the cash register totals that record the daily transactions and monitoring employee performance.

• The *tactical level*, also known as middle management, which is concerned with achieving goals and correcting specific exceptions. Middle managers are usually responsible for more than one group of employees. For example, suppose a bookstore is part of a nationwide chain. A middle manager might be responsible for the 10 stores in the Southern California region. He or she is concerned with whether individual bookstore sales are meeting preset targets and ordering books to meet the consumer preferences of the region.

• The *strategic level*, associated with top management, is concerned with the long-range goals of the entire organization. The president of a chain of bookstores needs to perform such tasks as prepare budgets for the coming year, analyze opportunities for new bookstore locations, make appropriate decisions, and analyze the competitive environment in which the bookstores operate.

However, because no two organizations have exactly the same needs, MIS solutions are not generic. An organization's approach to MIS depends on a number of factors:

• Size and number of facilities. Small companies may only need a few personal computers, whereas very large organizations may need to manage a complex network of thousands of computers located throughout the world.

• The kinds of arrangements an organization has with customers and suppliers. A company that builds products to custom orders has different MIS needs than a company that mass produces consumer goods. For example, a company that assembles airplanes to order does not want to keep an inventory of parts on hand and would prefer that parts be delivered just in time to assemble the airplane. On the other hand, in the food-canning industry, crops are seasonal, so there is a short time period in which food can be canned. But demand is year round, so the food canner must keep a large inventory on hand to keep pace with supermarket demand.

• The type of industry the company is in. Creating a financial instrument, such as an insurance policy, requires quite a bit of information and a few workers to assemble the finished product. An assembly line for manufacturing transistor radios is far more capital and labor intensive.

• The speed with which the market changes. A consumer-goods company needs to gather information about the retail sales environment weekly or even daily to assess the impact of changing consumer preferences and the effects of the competition. An oil exploration company has a much longer planning horizon and needs to concentrate more on the task of finding new sources of oil.

ORGANIZATIONAL PERSPECTIVES

The environment in which organizations operate is rapidly changing. For hundreds of years, organizations have relied on paper to store data, transactions, procedures, and correspondence. Processing and storage were accomplished manually. Then the telephone began to play an important role in organizational communications. But in today's information-rich environment, these manual systems have become inadequate except in the smallest organizations.

All organizations from factories to banks are highly dependent on information. The people who work in these organizations need to analyze, interpret, and communicate this information productively to solve problems, formulate strategies, and make decisions. Furthermore, technology is having a major impact on the structure of the organization and its people. All these factors must be taken into account if the MIS is to be employed effectively.

THE INFORMATION EXPLOSION

The term *information explosion* refers to the growing volume of information created by the increasingly complex society in which we live. There are several reasons for calling it an explosion. The growth in the number of information workers that was discussed in Chapter 3 is responsible for creating new levels of paperwork and bureaucracy. Management reporting requirements and government regulations add enormously to the paperwork burden placed on organizations. The widespread adoption of computers for transaction processing sometimes generates increasing quantities of unnecessary paperwork. The growth of communications also adds to the quantity of information that is available for businesses.

All these factors create a complex information environment that affects the performance of organizations and directly translates into an increased cost of doing business. For example, suppose a department store receives a shipment of merchandise and does not receive the accompanying paperwork. The failure of the paperwork to arrive ahead of the shipment can cause costly delays in receiving, unpacking, processing, and selling the merchandise. In most organizations, the flow of information is as important as the flow of goods or services.

PRODUCTIVITY

One major reason for implementing an information system is to increase the productivity of workers. In the factory, productivity can be measured by such simple concepts as units of output produced per unit of time. In most cases, productivity can be raised by a time-tested method: use technology, primarily in the form of new machines that require fewer workers, lay off the displaced workers, and reduce the skill levels of the remaining work force. This strategy has indeed raised the productivity of the remaining factory workers.

But in the office, measuring productivity is much more complicated because no one has yet devised a clear and accurate way to measure information worker productivity. Although most people would agree that information technology increases productivity, it is arguable whether productivity increases in proportion to the level of investment an organization makes in information technology.

Clerical Worker Productivity

In the period from the 1960s to the present, offices have expanded so rapidly that it was assumed that more productive ways of producing and distributing paperwork became necessary. Attention began to focus on applying information technology to the repetitive tasks of clerical workers such as secretaries, and the result was the evolution of word processing.

Word processing, as you learned in Chapter 2, is software that handles a standard set of office activities—composing, revising, printing, and filing written documents. Word processing had two initial impacts on offices. The first was an apparent increase in the productivity of secretaries, measured by the number of pages typed per hour. The second was an organizational change in work classifications and responsibilities of clerical workers.

When manual typewriters were replaced by electric typewriters, typing speed increased, so productivity went up. Then electric typewriters with memories, such as the IBM MTST, were introduced, and the ability to edit and revise documents much faster helped to increase productivity further. Finally, the introduction of the video-display-based word processor further speeded up the document preparation and revision process.

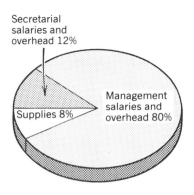

Productivity. *Breakdown of total costs in a typical office. (Data from Xerox Corporation estimates.)*

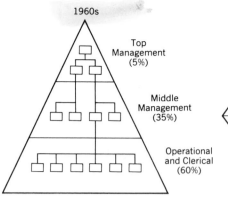

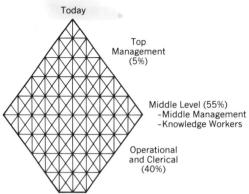

The transition of organizational structure from hierarchical pyramid forms to networked diamond forms is the result of investment in information technology tools. (From Stage by Stage, *Copyright (c) 1986, Nolan, Norton & Company. Reprinted by permission.)*

Because these word processors were considerably more expensive than manual or electric typewriters, it was thought that the best way to utilize them was to create a centralized word processing department where this equipment could be utilized for as many hours per day as possible.

Companies that tried this approach experienced extremely undesirable side effects: as some clerical and secretarial personnel were shifted into the centralized word processing department, automation began to be associated with losing secretaries. Also, the secretaries who had to work in the word processing department often experienced little variety, strict monitoring, and minimal responsibility in their jobs. They became the victims instead of the beneficiaries of information technology. Implementing any form of information technology must take these human factors into account. On the other hand, as the cost of word processing began to drop, the centralized word processing department was gradually eliminated.

Professional and Managerial Productivity

The focus of information technology has changed from augmenting the work of clerks and secretaries to augmenting the work of professionals and managers, but the major problem with this strategy is finding out how to measure nonclerical worker productivity. Whereas clerical tasks are usually highly structured, managerial and professional work is characterized by informal, unstructured, and creative tasks.

In the past, efficiency experts sug-

gested that a good work system was one in which work was broken into individual tasks, with one person performing each task. But managerial and professional work activities involve judgment, creativity, knowledge, and experience, and the productivity of these activities cannot be measured by traditional time-and-motion studies.

CHANGING ORGANIZATIONAL STRUCTURE

The pyramid has been widely used as a symbol of an organizational structure. The pyramid organization chart, for example, shows a few senior managers on top, more tactical managers in the middle, and quite a few operational managers at the bottom. Communication in such a structure is hierarchical and vertical: it flows up and down the pyramid. The pyramid evolved because bosses could communicate with only a few people at a time. They had to pass information to a few subordinates, who in turn passed information to their subordinates, and so on.

Today's organizations, however, are shifting from vertical hierarchical pyramids to a much broader and more horizontal structure. This is due to several factors, one of which is the trend toward more information workers that we mentioned in Chapter 3. For example, in the 1970s two-thirds of the Travelers financial services company's work force were clerical and one-third were information workers. In the 1990s one-third are clerical and two-thirds are information workers.

Another factor that is helping to change organizational structure is the evolution of communication technology. New technologies, such as voice and electronic mail, facilitate horizontal as well as vertical communication and permit groups of people to exchange information. Using such technology, it becomes feasible to bypass the pyramid-shaped chain of command. We will discuss voice and electronic mail in detail in the next section.

The structure of such organizations resembles a diamond, with many information workers in the middle, fewer operational people at the bottom, and the ability to communicate horizontally as well as vertically.

INFORMATION TECHNOLOGY TOOLS

What does this mean for an MIS department? Work evolves as new possibilities become apparent. MIS has to take advantage of information technology to help make information more accurate and useful, and make it available when and where it is needed. This includes tending to the transaction-based systems that make sure that important data about operations are electronically captured and stored in an organized way, as well as maintaining the strategic role of helping people within the organization put information to work.

Today's MIS departments employ three basic types of information technology tools to help an organization's employees perform more productively on their jobs. They are

- Personal computing.
- Workgroup computing.
- Network computing.

To help you understand the roles that information technology plays, we will describe the functions these technologies perform in an organization, their applications, and how they can be used to change the nature and character of work itself.

PERSONAL COMPUTING

Personal computers have recently assumed a very strategic role in most MIS departments. The historic trend in hardware development, as discussed in Chapter 7, has been to shift more and more computer resources to individual users. This trend occurs because the cost of computing continues to drop. In the beginning, large-scale computers were single-user resources. Then batch systems were developed to take better advantage of the computing resources. Next came time-sharing, which allowed large numbers of users to interact with the computer through terminals. In the 1980s, personal computers became powerful enough to assume a significant portion of the information processing work

load. Later in this chapter, we will discuss the next phase of this evolution, network computing.

Traditionally, MIS provided large-scale shared information systems resources to solve information workers' day-to-day problems. The advent of personal computing changed this situation. Personal computing offered workers a way to work more productively and become more sophisticated in performing their jobs. Of course, large-scale systems have not disappeared and are still critical to the operation of most organizations. But what has changed is the fundamental way workers interact with computers. Consider the following scenario.

A brand manager for a nationwide consumer-goods company has to evaluate the effects of a sales promotion on last week's sales of orange juice in supermarkets. His boss wants a summary report on her desk by the

Personal computing. The way in which workers interact with computers has changed because of personal computers.

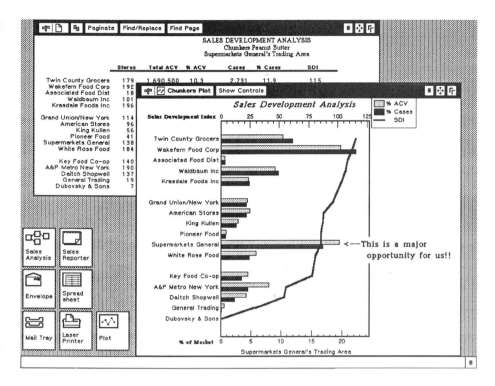

Personal computing. Personal computers connected to mainframes can easily track production, inventory, and sales, and display text and graphics to help create reports. (Courtesy Metaphor Computer Systems.)

New applications. Datapoint's MINX features a two-way video interface built into the monitor of a personal computer.

end of the day. The report must include estimates of how sales of competitive brands of orange juice fared during the promotion.

The manager uses a personal computer on his desk. As in most organizations, the personal computer does not stand alone, but is connected to the corporate mainframe and other computers that provide access to the mil-

lions of transaction records that track production, inventory, and sales. In fact all the company's computer facilities around the country are electronically linked to increase computing capacity and to allow information to be shared.

The manager also uses his system to access commercial on-line databases to obtain intelligence, such as information about the competition, from outside the company. As he does with the corporate databases, he can move data from the commercial databases into spreadsheets for analysis or into documents to produce reports.

Personal computer applications are often used in creative combinations. For example, to produce a monthly report for top management, the manager accesses the corporate and commercial databases, downloads data to the personal computer, and uses a spreadsheet program to analyze the data, a graphing program to produce the charts and graphs for his report, and a word processor to write the report. He then transfers the finished report to a desktop-publishing program for final sprucing up and then prints the report on one of the marketing department's laser printers.

NEW APPLICATIONS

What happens when the busy professional or manager has to leave his or her desk to travel or meet with other people? What happens when a person is granted maternity or paternity leave but must finish an important project? Portable computers have taken over some of the work once done on the desktop. Today's notebook-sized personal computers (8 $\frac{1}{2}$ by 11 by under 2 inches) and their applications—word processing, spreadsheets, and databases—are simply a portable substitute for desktop personal computing.

Tomorrow's notebook computers will incorporate features that will make them an electronic substitute for paper notebooks. In Japan, for example, Sony sells the PalmTop PCT-500, a hand-held computer that can recognize handwritten Japanese characters drawn on its screen with a stylus. In the United States, the GridPad notebook computer features a stylus for writing hand-printed characters on an LCD screen. Although the GridPad's current applications are limited to an electronic clipboard for data entry, it points the way toward notebook computers that can recognize any type of handwriting and, in turn, new interfaces that would make using such a device more like using a notebook than a computer. However, similar to the case of voice input (discussed in Chapter 5), computers that can recognize and understand everything you write are still in the future.

Through the use of digital cellular radio communications, the portable computer can be linked with a base-station computer in the office. Perhaps when this happens, personal computers will be as easy to use as notebooks and telephones.

WORKGROUP COMPUTING

Stand-alone personal computers can perform many useful services, but their capability changes dramatically when they can share information with one another. Personal computers have traditionally been thought of only as computational engines. Now the communications function is starting to share the limelight, and personal computers are becoming personal communicators.

This is because one of the key aspects of any organization is communication. Viewed as a system, an organization is not merely a group of individuals, but a network of relationships among communicating individuals. For this reason the telephone has become one of the most productive tools in today's organizations. A great deal of communication crisscrosses every organization. Its two primary forms are (1) documents that contain text and graphics and (2) voice communication. Individuals produce this communication to enable others to perform their jobs. Communication is the metabolism of any organization. If it slows down, the result is usually a sluggish bureaucracy. If it speeds up, organizational efficiency improves dramatically.

Workgroup computing facilitates the process of people working together in groups that are electronically connected. It is a concept that electronically encompasses the following:

- Accessing and collecting information.

- Sharing common resources, such as printers and disks.

- Distributing tasks across a network.

- Collaborating with other information workers.

- Planning and holding conferences and meetings.

- Communicating the results.

Workgroup computing may be as simple as a message system that links people throughout an organization, or it may entail software that facilitates people working together electronically as a team to produce proposals or other documents.

In most organizations, messages often pass back and forth between desks. A message may be in several forms, such as a telephone message, an interoffice memo, a letter, an invoice, a proposal, or a newsletter. A message can also include graphic or pictorial elements and should not be thought of as merely a written note. Most messages

Workgroup computing. *The Xerox XC 24 network provides printing, filing, and communication among personal computers.*

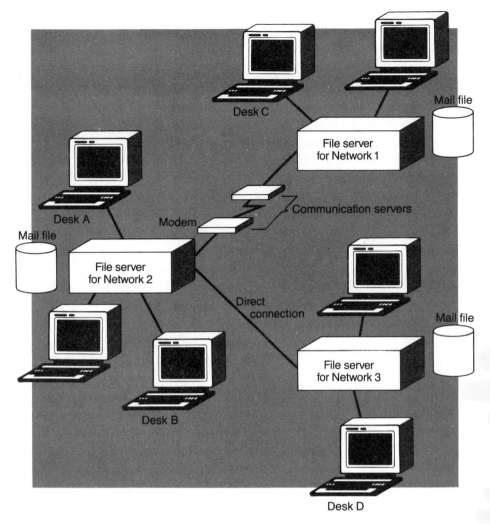

Desk C

Mail file

File server
for Network 1

Desk A

Communication servers

Mail file

Modem

File server
for Network 2

Direct
connection

Mail file

File server
for Network 3

Desk B

Desk D

Electronic mail can be transmitted among several networks. Desk A sends a message to desks B, C, and D. Each recipient files the message, and can answer, forward, temporarily store the message on disk, or direct it to a printer. Networking software takes care of creating, deleting, and copying messages on the disks.

are composed on paper or are spoken into a device, such as a telephone or a dictating machine. Messages are often transmitted via telephone, Telex, interoffice delivery systems, the postal service, or overnight delivery service such as Federal Express.

VOICE MAIL

The simplest message system relies on the combination of telephones and computers. *Voice mail*—in which spoken messages are digitized, stored in computers, and later retrieved by the recipient—enhances communication and saves time and money. A companywide voice-mail network can improve communication and raise the productivity of managerial, administrative, and professional workers. How does voice mail do it? By eliminating telephone tag among their employees. For example, studies show that when placing a telephone call, 75 percent of the time you don't get to talk

with the person you called. By utilizing voice mail, the telephone tag problem can be eliminated.

In most voice-mail systems, voice messages can be sent to groups of recipients. By doing so, problem-solving teams can be created "on the fly." For example, a typical problem-solving team might include people from administration, marketing, research, and sales who are in different geographic locations. Each member of the team will work at his or her desk and an ad hoc electronic voice-mail network will be established to interconnect the members of the team. This speeds up the flow of work and makes it faster and easier to solve a problem.

ELECTRONIC MAIL

Another valuable workgroup computing tool is *electronic mail*—an electronic technology that handles the sending and receiving of written messages.

The key concept in understanding how electronic mail can serve as the foundation for a workgroup computing system is the electronic mailbox. *Electronic mailboxes* are files stored on disk, in which each message in the mailbox corresponds to a record in the file. The electronic mailbox provides a communication interface in that mail can be sent to and read from mailboxes as well as being stored there. People use electronic mailboxes to communicate by processing electronic mail on a message-by-message basis, reading messages, and, in turn, acting on them. A personal computer uses word processors, spreadsheets, and the creation of graphics to compose messages. The electronic mailbox is used to store and distribute messages, and, with the proper interface, it can link into a larger communication system.

Recall the discussion of facsimile (FAX) technology in Chapter 9. It too can handle the sending and receiving of written messages, but its historical disadvantage has been the fact that the sender and receiver must be connected simultaneously. Today, telephone companies are offering the FAX equivalent of electronic mailboxes to store FAX messages so they can be distributed at a later time. Also using such store-and-forward services, it is possible to use electronic mail to send a message to a FAX machine.

Electronic mail has an advantage over voice mail when it is necessary to communicate complex data such as a document. Voice mail has an edge in that any telephone can become a terminal. It is possible to combine the two into an integrated system that reads your electronic mail using voice synthesis.

ELECTRONIC CONFERENCING

For a workgroup to be truly effective, its members should not have to be in the same place at the same time to do their work. The electronic mail model serves as a starting point, but it needs to be augmented to support not only the delivery of messages between people, but the management of conversations and discussions between several people.

The model for this type of interaction is the development of *electronic conferencing systems*. This involves groups of people who meet by communicating with one another via personal computers. It uses the same technology as electronic mail, but whereas electronic mail is associated with one-to-one communications, electronic conferencing is associated with many-to-many communications. For example, suppose 10 people wanted to set up an electronic conference. In a face-to-face conference, the participants need to meet simultaneously, whereas the electronic conference eliminates the need for simultaneous participation. Electronic conferences can extend over a period of days or weeks, and are also effective for holding a meeting in which the people are not located in the same area. Several commercial conferencing services are available. EIES, Participate, Notepad, Confer, and Hub can all be subscribed to for a monthly fee plus an hourly charge for the time you are connected to the service.

COLLABORATIVE WORK

The examples of collaborative work we have cited span a wide range, from a manager and his or her subordinate working together to create a proposal to the large teams of people required to take a major new product from concept to design to manufacturing. In all cases information must be integrated from many sources.

One technology that makes collaborative work possible is the local-area network (LAN). As discussed in Chapter 9, a *local-area network* is a communication channel and appropriate interface devices that connect personal computers, mass-storage devices, and output devices.

At Xerox Corporation, meetings have been augmented with LANs and special software. Xerox uses its network of computers to help facilitate face-to-face meetings. An agenda is sent electronically to all participants' electronic mailboxes before the meeting. During the meeting, one person electronically records minutes and notes. Then follow-up activities are electronically scheduled, and the results of the meeting are automatically posted in the participants' electronic mailboxes. Xerox claims that the system makes communication more effective, permits better use of people's time, and helps to resolve issues much faster than older manual methods.

Application software that supports true collaborative work is still in its infancy. Most of today's workgroup software simply supports the sharing of common files over a LAN. The key to developing collaborative software involves *cooperative processing* among multiple applications.

Researchers at Xerox Corporation's Palo Alto Research Center (PARC) are working on an experimental electronic meeting system called Colab in which six personal computers and a large-screen projector are connected over a local-area network. The large-screen projector functions as a chalkboard, and the results are simultaneously displayed on each personal computer. People can converse during the meeting via their computers and one window on each screen keeps track of the conversation. At the same time, people can work individually: they can call up information from previous meetings, access other files, or work on parts of a group project.

Sometimes meetings cannot be held

Video conferencing. Participants in a video conference meet with another group at a remote location via two-way television.

Videotex. Digital's VAX VTX is a videotex system that provides an alternative to traditional paper-based methods of distributing information, such as price lists, directories, and travel and activity schedules.

face to face. For example, managers need to be in contact with other managers, companies, suppliers, and customers, and these people usually are widely separated by time and distance. The addition of a *communication server* (sometimes called a gateway or a bridge) links the local network into wide-area telecommunications networks for long-distance interaction.

NETWORK COMPUTING

Network computing involves technology that combines geographically dispersed office workers, computing resources, and information into a single integrated environment. Network computing builds on personal computing, which provides the means to put computing power on the desktop, and workgroup computing, which provides communication and resource sharing across a network.

VIDEO CONFERENCING

Video conferencing involves the linking of remote sites by one-way or two-way television. A common example of a one-way video conference is when a television newsperson conducts a video interview. The person being interviewed appears on a video screen in front of the interviewer, but that person cannot see the interviewer. There is, of course, a two-way audio connection.

If meeting rooms or conference rooms in offices can be equipped with the necessary audiovisual facilities, travel time and money can be saved by holding a teleconference instead of a face-to-face conference. Many businesses are experimenting with sales and board meetings through video conferencing. The cost is still high, especially if the video conference involves a direct two-way video connection. Although video conferences do eliminate the distance barrier, two-way conferences still require that the participants meet at the same time. This problem can be made more difficult when the distance spans several

time zones.

It is interesting to note that video conferencing technologies are changing the way hotels do business. Have you noticed the satellite dishes outside many Holiday Inns? Most major hotel chains now offer video conferencing services. For example, a group of people could meet in a specially equipped room at the New York Hilton while another group could meet in a similar room at the Chicago Hilton. The two meetings could then be interactively linked by video conferencing. The hotels are hoping that if business travel is on the decline, electronic meetings might be on the rise.

VIDEOTEX

Videotex is a form of electronic publishing that consists of a database connected to terminals or personal computers. It stores and displays information in units called frames or pages. Videotex offers an easy way for an untrained user to access one or more databases of information.

Offices using videotex can electronically publish standard operating procedure manuals, sales literature, in-house newsletters, companywide phone lists, and other information that is subject to periodic change. Some videotex systems permit users to conduct electronic transactions. For example, an office worker might view an inventory database of office supplies and then electronically place an order for various supplies. Commercial systems, such as Prodigy from IBM/ Sears, offer publicly available videotex services.

WIDE-AREA NETWORKS

The networks we have been focusing on are primarily intended to solve problems internal to organizations, but when such networks are expanded to include a business organization's suppliers and customers, they have the potential to be used as a strategic as well as a productivity-increasing tool. Examples are the following;

• General Motors (GM) has begun a plan to automate the exchange of information between it and its suppliers. For example, GM can now electronically receive an invoice, match it to a purchase order, and trigger an electronic payment to the supplier.

• Levi Strauss can electronically link to its retailers. Through the system, the retailer can receive electronic invoices and shipping notices as to when merchandise will arrive. The retailer can then better coordinate its shipments of goods, carry just enough inventory to satisfy its customers, and avoid costly over-stocking and returns.

• American Hospital Supply Corporation uses computers and networks to strengthen relationships with existing customers and increase business. Hospitals can electronically link directly to the American Hospital Supply order-entry computer system, which helps a hospital manage costly inventory and speeds the delivery of critical medical care supplies. This system also improves the chances that a hospital will order from American Hospital Supply instead of from a competitor.

• Several insurance companies link independent agents into their information system and are able to offer a wider variety of services and shorten the time it takes to process new policy requests.

In these cases, clients and customers have more direct contact with an organization's management information systems. As these systems become more widespread and easier to use, clients and customers will have much more contact with computers. If the systems are properly designed, the organization will save money, and the client or customer will receive faster and better service.

Such networking makes possible an increase in the time available to serve clients and customers responsively. The improved flow of communications and the accessibility of corporatewide information at a single personal computer should make it possible for one person to provide most of the services required by a client or customer. This direct contact

with clients offers many opportunities to circumvent an ineffective bureaucracy. Have you ever called an organization for information only to be placed on hold, transferred to different departments, or told to call back? Perhaps you were simply unable to get your inquiry answered. The people at the other end of the line may be just as frustrated as you because they don't have the information technology tools to enable them to do the job or handle the request. The ability of information technology to coordinate information will eventually make this current feature of bureaucracy seem archaic.

In the case of the financial services industries like investment banking and brokerage, information technol-

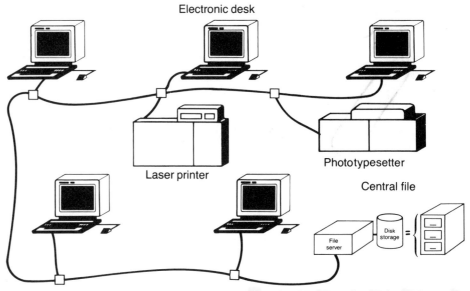

Electronic desk
Laser printer
Phototypesetter
Central file
File server
Disk storage

A local-area network can also connect to specialized devices such as a laser printer or phototypesetter.

A communications server (also called a bridge or gateway) connects one local-area network to any other network, terminal, or computer through wide-area networks such as the telephone system.

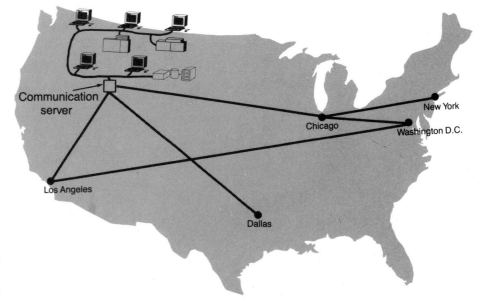

Communication server
New York
Chicago
Washington D.C.
Los Angeles
Dallas

ogy has created a cashless financial system that interconnects the buyers and sellers of financial instruments into a single marketplace. Networking technology has allowed this marketplace to span the entire globe, creating new and important interdependencies between nations.

THE EFFECTS ON PEOPLE

Even though we have been discussing technological solutions throughout this chapter, we cannot ignore the effects of MIS and information technology on people. Most work relies on a simple principle: communication among managers, clerical and factory workers, suppliers, and customers. Even the most ingenious technological solutions to problems do not always create harmonious results. Information technology alters the nature of work, but people must change the way they approach such basic tasks as gathering data, writing, and communicating if they are to adapt successfully to information technology.

One of the more interesting aspects of information technology is that everything becomes more abstract. For example, going to work and handling paperwork are very real and concrete. They are tangible things to which people can easily relate. All the infor-

mation technology trends, however, point to less tangibility. From pictures on a computer screen that replace physical objects to electronic communications that replace meetings and travel, the form and substance of business organization and work are changing. Although it is too early to tell whether or not this will have negative effects, it certainly will be different.

In 1910 the architect Louis Sullivan developed the influential design principle "form follows function." When this principle is applied to an office it follows that the physical layout of the office is determined by its chain of processes, that is, the documents and voice communications being sent, received, held, filed, referred to, and copied. As electronic technology replaces manual technology, information and communication become more and more "invisible." What happens to our notion of a desk when all notes, memos, calendars, and files are just data in a computer network? What happens to our notion of a letter when messages are composed, transmitted, and received electronically? What happens to our notion of an office when a portable computer in an attache case can communicate by radio?

We will also see communication become increasingly more important in acting like the "metabolism" of an organization. This will change the dynamics of the interaction between people and may eliminate some of the sluggishness of corporate bureaucracy. Workgroup and network computing makes it possible to bring people together who are normally separated by travel time, time zones, and conflicting schedules. As a result, collaboration may become an important feature of work in the future. In theory, this should speed up the flow of work by making it faster and easier to accomplish the goals of the organization.

Once information technology makes mobility and communication easier, the time previously spent scheduling and coordinating people's time and their face-to-face interactions can be spent more creatively. Electronic calendars can simplify scheduling meetings, conferences, and ap-

The effects on people. Software versions of a Rolodex, memo pad, and organization chart.

File   Edit   Window   View   Reorganize   Templates   Formats

Status Center

+ **Doug Castle, VP Marketing**
  + **Action Items & Things To Do**
    - call all names in rolodex, re new produ·
    - name new National Sales Manager
    - buy gift for vi∙
    - speech outline∙
  + **Memos & Lette**
    ▫ Rollout Memo
    ▫ Resignation Le
    ▫ Termination L
  + **Daily Appointm**
    + Monday, June
    + Tuesday, June

rolodex

+ Alsop, Stewart
+ Bobker, Steve
+ Brothers, Dennis
+ Dvorak, John
+ Dyson, Esther
+ Gassee, Jean-Louis
  - 408-555-1500
+ Kawasaki, Guy

Sales Territo

3   4

NATIONAL
SALES
MANAGER

Jack Hardy

EASTERN REGION	SOUTHERN REGION	WESTERN REGION
New York	Atlanta	Seattle
John Mynatt	Nancy Tamier	Art Hopper

pointments. In the long term, the whole concept of the static organizational structure may disappear and be replaced by more dynamic workgroups that are created and dissolved to meet the needs at hand. The organization may even become "located" in electronic networks and databases. Instead of a physical place where you work, it becomes a "virtual" place where you work—you could be anywhere.

Such structural changes will stimulate corresponding social changes in the organization. For example, all the information technologies discussed are far more than substitutes for manual systems. As they free us to do things in new ways, new skills will be required to adapt to the changing structure. The management function of supervision and control may take on an entirely new meaning as workers shift from being together in physical offices to being together in logical networks.

Information technology is being rapidly developed. But as has been the case with most technology, factors such as laws, social structures, habits, and communications will determine how fast the changes will take place.

REVIEW

A management information system gathers data, turns it into information, and makes it available to those who are managing the organization. Recently, attention has begun to focus on the strategic uses of information technology. Most organizations have an MIS department to help put information to work. The structure of an MIS parallels the structure of an organization. It encompasses the functional units of an organization as well as the different levels of management. The evolution of MIS is motivated by the information explosion and the need to make workers more productive. In addition, organizational structure itself is changing from a pyramid- to a diamond-shaped structure. The technologies that have the most impact on MIS are personal computing, workgroup computing, and network computing. Most work originates at the personal computer on the desktop. To share and communicate the results of that work with others, personal computers are linked by local- and wide-area networks. The effects of technology advances on people may result in a potential restructuring of both their workplaces and work habits and patterns. But our laws, social structures, habits, and customs will change more slowly than information technology.

REFERENCES

1. Strassman, Paul A. *Information Payoff: The Transformation of Work in the Electronic Age.* New York: Free Press, 1985, p. 25.

RESOURCES

BOOKS

Diebold, John. *Business in the Age of Information.* New York: AMACOM, a division of American Management Association, 1985. This is a series of essays devoted to information resource management and is interesting because it focuses on information technologies as business resources.

Gerstein, Marc S. *The Technology Connection.* Reading, Mass.: Addison-Wesley, 1987. This book surveys several areas of information technology. Although it is written for managers and professionals, its small size and writing style make for interesting reading for anyone.

Zuboff, Shoshana. *In the Age of the Smart Machine: The Future of Work and Power.* New York: Basic Books, 1988. An enormous treatise on the impact of computers on business. Ms. Zuboff argues for a restructuring of work patterns and roles so that organizations can catch up with the explosion in information technology.

MAGAZINES

Seybold Publications, Inc., P.O. Box 644, Media, Penn. 19063. This company publishes several newsletters, including *The Seybold Report on Desktop Publishing* and *The Seybold Report on Professional Computing,* which cover all the advances in information technology as they happen. Check in your library for copies as these publications are quite expensive.

CIO. Framingham, Mass.: International Data Group. CIO stands for chief information officer, a title that is becoming more popular in MIS departments today. This monthly magazine is an excellent source for stories about MIS departments and strategies.

STUDY GUIDE

Match the following key terms to the appropriate definition:

A.

1. _b_ Management information system (MIS)
2. _h_ Total systems concept
3. _e_ Decision support system (DSS)
4. _i_ Strategies
5. _d_ Information technology
6. _c_ MIS department
7. _f_ Information explosion
8. _a_ Workgroup computing
9. _g_ Voice mail

a. A concept that facilitates the process of people working together in groups that are electronically connected.

b. A system that gathers, condenses, and filters data until it becomes information, then makes it available on time, and in a useful form, for use in decision making at various levels of management within an organization.

c. A group or computer facility that helps people put information to work.

d. A collective term for computer and communication hardware and system and application software.

e. Applications within an MIS that directly support specific decision making.

f. The growing volume of information that is created by an increasingly complex society.

g. A technology in which spoken messages are digitized, stored in computers, and later retrieved by the recipient.

h. A system in which a single centralized repository of information would represent all the organization's activities.

i. Plans of action designed to cope with change, competition, and uncertainty.

B.

10. _b_ Electronic mail
11. _e_ Electronic mailbox
12. _c_ Electronic conferencing system
13. _h_ Video conferencing
14. _f_ Videotex
15. _a_ Network computing
16. _g_ Local-area network (LAN)
17. _d_ Communication server

a. Technology that combines geographically dispersed office workers, computing resources, and information into a single integrated environment.

b. An electronic technology that handles the sending and receiving of messages.

c. A meeting that is conducted over an electronic network using terminals or personal computers.

d. A device that connects telecommunication networks to the local-area network.

e. A file stored on disk in which records represent messages.

f. A form of electronic publishing.

g. A communication channel that connects devices within a limited geographic area.

h. A meeting held between remote sites linked by two-way television.

True/False:

18. _____ Historically, the role of MIS has been to use information in strategic ways.

19. _____ An example of the strategic use of information involves automating transaction-processing systems.

20. _____ Human resources and procedures are an important component of an MIS.

21. _____ Because no two organizations are the same, MIS solutions are not generic.

22. _____ Within MIS, the technology planning group helps to further the strategic goals of the company.

23. _____ The widespread adoption of computers is creating a paperless society.

24. _____ In most organizations, the flow of information is as important as the flow of goods or services.

25. _____ Measuring information worker productivity is an exact science.

26. ____ In the office, productivity correlates with the level of investment an organization makes in computer technology.

27. ____ Personal computers do not play a strategic role in most MIS departments.

28. ____ An office is a network of communicating individuals.

29. ____ Local-area networks are used as a gateway for long-distance interaction.

30. ____ A local-area network can span the country.

31. ____ Videotex is available as a public service.

32. ____ The technological factors will determine how fast changes in the office will occur.

Multiple Choice:

33. Which of the following is not a level of management mentioned in this chapter?

  a. Operational.
  b. Tactical.
  c. Strategic.
  d. Procedural.

34. Which of the following is not a factor that contributes to the information explosion?

  a. Adopting computers.
  b. Growth in people.
  c. Growth of communication.
  d. More management reporting requirements.

35. Word processing increased the productivity of secretaries by

  a. Changing the work classifications of clerical workers.
  b. Lowering the cost of office technology.
  c. Eliminating the need for paperwork.
  d. Increasing the number of pages typed per hour.

36. Which of the following types of computing is not an information technology tool?

  a. Personal.
  b. Workgroup.
  c. Network.
  d. Organizational.

37. As organizations shift from vertical hierarchies to more horizontal structures, the shape of their structure more closely resembles a

  a. Square.
  b. Pyramid.
  c. Diamond.
  d. Rectangle.

38. Personal computers that can communicate with each other are important because

  a. Professionals spend most of their time communicating.
  b. Communication is a key aspect of any office.
  c. The telephone is the most important tool in the office today.
  d. An office is a group of individuals.

39. Which of the following is not a type of server that can be found in networks?

  a. File.
  b. Communication.
  c. Personal.
  d. Database.

40. One of the benefits of video conferencing is

  a. Specially equipped conference rooms.
  b. Saving travel time.
  c. Lower communication costs.
  d. Linking of local sites.

41. Videotex provides a means for individuals to become information providers by

  a. Offering a simple user interface.
  b. Publishing companywide phone books.
  c. Displaying pages of information.
  d. Offering a standard method for producing frames of information.

42. Which of the following can an electronic calendar not simplify?

  a. Meetings.
  b. Voice mail.
  c. Appointments.
  d. Conferences.

Thought Questions:

43. We have discussed the transition of MIS from an administrative to a strategic role in organizations. What factors account most for this trend?

44. How might some of the information technologies discussed in this chapter be applied to education?

Projects:

45. Visit an organization in your area and interview an MIS director. Find out whether the organization uses information technology in strategic ways. Write a brief report that summarizes the organization's stance on management information systems.

46. Visit your school's administrative computer center. What kinds of technology do they use for managing information? Where might they apply information technology strategically? Report your findings to the class.

SOFTWARE EXERCISES

One of the most difficult problems facing an organization that wants to establish workgroup computing is choosing the best local-area network to tie its personal computers together. A LAN is a complex beast—at least an order of magnitude more complex than stand-alone personal computer systems. Although we don't expect you to become an expert on LANs, an interesting exercise is to investigate what it takes to purchase a LAN versus purchasing a stand-alone personal computer system.

• Use your word processor and the chart shown here to create a request for a proposal letter to mail out to computer stores that sell LANs.

• Create a database to store information about the LANs for which you receive information.

• Use your spreadsheet to create a cost-comparison chart similar to the one shown here. Use the graphics program to create a graph comparing total cost and cost per workstation for alternative networks.

• Use your word processor to create a report to management that justifies which local-area network system should be purchased.

Comparing LAN costs.	Network A	Network B	Network C
File Server			
With 40 MB hard disk	_____	_____	_____
Network cabling	_____	_____	_____
Five System units			
Unit price	_____	_____	_____
Total price	_____	_____	_____
Network adapter cards	_____	_____	_____
Color displays	_____	_____	_____
Shared laser printer			
printer cable	_____	_____	_____
Other			
File server software	_____	_____	_____
Shared word processor	_____	_____	_____
One year service	_____	_____	_____
Sales Tax	_____	_____	_____
Total	_____	_____	_____
Price per workstation	_____	_____	_____

Comparing LAN costs.

ANSWERS

1. b, **2.** h, **3.** e, **4.** i, **5.** d, **6.** c, **7.** f, **8.** a, **9.** g, **10.** b, **11.** e, **12.** c, **13.** h, **14.** f, **15.** a, **16.** g, **17.** d, **18.** F, **19.** F, **20.** T, **21.** T, **22.** T, **23.** F, **24.** T, **25.** F, **26.** F, **27.** F, **28.** T, **29.** F, **30.** F, **31.** T, **32.** F, **33.** d, **34.** b, **35.** d, **36.** d, **37.** c, **38.** b, **39.** c, **40.** b, **41.** d. **42.** b.

ROBERT CARR

Profession: Vice president of software, Go Corporation, Foster City, California.

Profile: Carr founded Forefront Corporation in 1983 and developed Framework, an integrated software package for personal computers. When the company was acquired by Ashton-Tate, Inc., in 1985, Carr served as Ashton-Tate's chief scientist. In 1987, he joined Go.

Quote: "Writing English and software are far more than just acts of capturing something in code or on paper. They are processes that help evolve your thinking tremendously. When you're forced to write something down, you think the idea through two or three steps further."

CHAPTER 11

DATABASE MANAGEMENT SYSTEMS

PREVIEW

In any information system, data are the raw material from which information is produced. Storing data is useful only if organizing and retrieving it can be accomplished quickly and efficiently. Mass-storage devices have made practical the low-cost storage of vast amounts of data. Finding ways to manage that data, provide up-to-date access to it, and develop new applications around it have been major concerns of MIS organizations for the last two decades. The recognition of the strategic value of information has made databases and their management even more important.

In the 1960s, computer scientists began to develop new software for organizing and retrieving data, and the field of database management was born. Today, database management plays a critical role in most management information systems. You should review the material on database software in Chapter 2 and the material on files and logical structures in Chapter 8 before reading this chapter.

In this chapter, you'll learn

- The basics of database management systems (DBMS).

- The major database models.

- The functions of query languages.

- The functions of report generators.

- Uses for application-development tools.

- The meaning of data independence, integrity, and security.

- Trends in distributed databases.

- Additional technical database concepts.

DATA BASICS

As you learned in Chapter 2, *database software* is used for computerized record keeping. All organizations record, organize, and store data. Some use paper documents organized in file folders, file drawers, and filing cabinets. Important data are often stored in Rolodex files and manual accounting ledgers. Changing applications, such as keeping track of orders, raw materials, inventory, customers, payables, and receivables, often rely on these manual accounting ledgers that provide the basis for most of the record keeping.

THE NEED FOR DBMS

When organizations grow in size or complexity, so do the problems of managing a large amount of complex, changing data. Suppose, for example, that a mail-order business quickly grows from having 200 customers to having 2000 or even 20,000 customers. It becomes more difficult to know where to find the data, whether the data are up to date, and whether appropriate people have access to data about those customers and their orders.

One solution to such problems is to gather and enter data into computer-based files. A collection of one or more files treated as a whole unit makes up a *database*. A *database management system* is software that organizes, manipulates, and retrieves data stored in a database.

Size and complexity are not the only reasons why organizations need DBMS. Several major trends are emerging that enhance the value and usefulness of database management:

• Managers who require more up-to-date information to make effective decisions.

• Customers who demand increasingly sophisticated information services and more current information about the status of their orders, invoices, and accounts.

• End users who find that they can develop custom applications with database programs in a fraction of the time it takes to use traditional programming languages.

• Organizations that discover information has a strategic value and utilize their database systems to gain an edge over their competitors.

Database management spans a broad range of information systems and needs. Some are based around a single personal computer and are used in an ad hoc fashion to support decision making. A small retail store, for example, might collect names and addresses of customers and use that data to mail an advertisement for a special sale or promotion. Others are based around several interconnected mainframe or minicomputers and are used to support large-scale transaction-processing systems. A spare parts inventory-control system for a commercial airplane manufacturer, for example, needs to keep track of up to 300,000 parts per aircraft.

A DBMS need not be confined to storing words and numbers. Manufacturing organizations use DBMS to store engineering drawings, sometimes storing millions of drawings on optical disk systems that resemble jukeboxes.

Also, some applications may require quite specialized databases. For example, a *text database* is a collection of words such as articles in *The Wall*

Document management systems combine drawings with words and numbers.

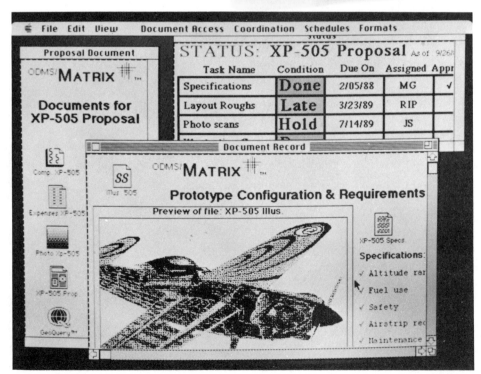

Street Journal or a series of legal abstracts. Such databases are either stored on-line or on CD ROM optical disks and include the means to search through massive amounts of data to answer specific questions.

AIRLINE RESERVATIONS: AN APPLICATION

To illustrate the concepts and uses of a DBMS, let us examine the case of an airline reservation system. Although you should be aware that several other important concepts are required to implement such a system (i.e., an on-line system with fast response time, a transaction-processing system connected to remote terminals or personal computers, and fault-tolerant computers), we have covered these in earlier chapters and will now focus on the database management aspects of an airline reservation system to highlight our points.

In the 1960s, one of the first commercial applications for database management was computerized reservation systems for the airlines. In fact, the airline industry pioneered many database and on-line information system concepts. Recall from Chapter 9 that in 1964 IBM and American Airlines jointly developed the Sabre on-line reservation system. The goal was to provide a reservation system that would allow passengers anywhere in the country to make or change reservations at any time through a centralized computer system.

A significant aspect of this system involved designing a database that could store the name and other information about the passengers and link that information to the time, date, and flight number of the reservations. Other requirements included providing agents and passengers with information about all the flights and their schedules, the seat inventory and availability of each flight, and passenger name lists.

Of course, on-line airline reservation systems have been quite successful, and they have changed the way the travel industry does business. Hotels, motels, car rental companies, and travel agencies were forced to follow

suit by buying or developing similar systems.

Now, airlines use DBMSs as strategic competitive weapons in the battle to win passengers and keep their planes as full as possible. They have expanded their customer-based services by competing with strategies based on on-line database systems.

For example, People Express, the popular no-frills airline of the 1980s, was put out of business by the power of the major airlines' internal reservation systems, according to its owner Donald Burr. Burr and his manage-

```
Enter departure city or code.
 >BOS
Enter destination city or code.
 >SFO
Enter departure date
 >01MAR
Enter departure time
 >10A
Enter number of seats required
 >2

01MAR/SAT       Leave: BOSTON
                Arrive: SAN FRANCISCO

#  Flight  Leave      Arrive    Eqp Stop
1  UA  95  BOS- 900A  SFO-1214P D10  0
2  UA 861  BOS-1000A  SFO- 257P D8S  1
3  AA 117  BOS- 900A  SFO- 125P D10  1
4  TW 177  BOS- 855A  SFO- 205P L10  1
5  CO  15  BOS- 850A  SFO- 135P D10  1
```

Airline reservations. Behind every airline reservation system is a high-performance database containing a wide variety of flight information.

Airline reservations. Once enough information is known, a reservation can be booked.

```
        FARES/FARE RESTRICTIONS
 AA  Fares for 01MAR - SEE RESTRICTIONS
From: BOSTON          MASSACHUSETTS
  To: SAN FRANCISCO   CALIFORNIA
Fare Class of                    Fare
#    Service    OW Amount RT     Code
1 First     $632.00 $1264.00     F
2 Coach     $486.00  $972.00     Y
3 Nite First $510.00 $1020.00    FN
4 Nite Coach $416.00  $832.00    YN
5 Special            $258.00     QSALE
6 Special            $318.00     QE30X23
7 Special            $278.00     QE30Z23

Fare #:  5  Must book round trip
TYPE OF FARE:ADULT
EARLIEST TRAVEL DATE:  8JAN
LAST TICKETING DATE: 20MAR
MUST START TRAVEL BY: 20MAR
BOOKING CODE: Q QN
SURCHARGE:   2MON THRU SUN
MAXIMUM STAY:  30 DAYS
```

ment had decided not to invest in a full-featured reservation system, and the major airlines decided to underprice People Express, but on a selective basis with ultrasuper-saver fares. The major airlines' on-line databases were what enabled them to offer just enough low-fare seats to fill planes while selling the great majority of seats at a profitable level. Overnight, People Express was empty, claimed Burr.[1]

Each airline uses its own internal DBMS in addition to the shared reservation systems that are accessible to all airlines and travel agents. Airlines gather information from their databases to track travel patterns, and with the information they can apply lower fares to selected cities and to limit those lower fares to fewer numbers of seats on those flights. Not only can the airlines more accurately keep track of passengers on their flights, but they can also adjust fares and the number of low-priced seats offered on a daily basis. The airlines gain flexibility and higher loads, and the customers may benefit by paying lower airfares.

All progressive industries use their database systems to provide customer services and gain a competitive advantage. For example, banks offer automatic teller machines and electronic fund transfers, whereas financial service companies such as Merrill Lynch compete with banks by offering cash-management services. Package-delivery services such as Federal Express use their database systems to route and deliver packages overnight.

CHARACTERISTICS OF A DBMS

Although every application has specific and individual needs, there are characteristics that are common to all DBMS. They include the capability to

- Design and create the database.
- Manipulate the data.
- Make up-to-date information available to users.

- Provide application-development tools to meet the needs of changing requirements.
- Protect the database against inconsistency and errors.
- Safeguard the database against unauthorized access.

Keep in mind that the purpose of this chapter is to illustrate the scope and various styles of DBMS. If you combine this with the material in Chapter 13, you will have a more complete understanding of the process of designing a DBMS.

DATABASE MODELS

There are many different ways to structure and organize the relationships among data in a database. The first step in creating a database is to choose the model with which to represent the data. Recall from earlier discussions the terms *files*, *records*, and *fields*. These are the building blocks that are used to construct more complex database models.

A model, often called a *schema*, is used to describe the overall characteristics of a database. Like the table of contents for a book, a **database model** identifies the major parts (e.g., files, records, and fields) of a database and illustrates how these parts fit together.

Database models include flat file, relational, hierarchical, network, object oriented, and text.

FLAT FILE

The simplest of all database models is the flat file, also called a table. The **flat file** is a single file consisting of rows (records) and columns (fields) of data that resemble a two-dimensional spreadsheet. For example, suppose you want to create a customer file for your mail-order business. You can use a flat-file model with one record per customer, use the names and addresses of your customers to create individual fields, and combine those data with a unique customer identification (ID) field. The ID field is a **key field** that eliminates the problem of

Flat files. A customer file in which a row is the equivalent of a record and a column is the equivalent of a field.

Cust. ID	Name	First	Address	City	St	ZIP
101	Smith	Mark	656 246th St.	Roslyn	NY	11576
102	Dabolt	Shelia	12 Windsong Dr.	Arlington	VA	22201
103	Nasser	James	123 Watercress Ln.	Midvale	UT	84047
104	Hernandez	Enrique	1733 Monrovia Ave.	Irvine	CA	92714
105	Smith	Mark	807 W 19th St.	Seattle	WA	98168

duplicate customer names (e.g., Mark Smith in Seattle and Mark Smith in New York). In the next section, you will see how key fields provide links to other parts of the database model.

Whereas a single flat file such as a customer file is useful for keeping track of customers and preparing mailing lists, it cannot create a complete mail-order application. For that a different database model is needed.

RELATIONAL

In 1970, E. F. Codd, who was working for IBM at the time, published a paper titled "A Relational Model of Data for Large Shared Data Banks." That paper is now credited as the origin of the entire field of relational database technology.

The **relational model** uses one or more flat files or tables and creates relationships among the tables on the basis of a common field in each of the tables. Each flat file or table is called a **relation**. For example, a mail-order application must organize the customers as well as the products for sale, so what is needed is an inventory file. The inventory file describes each item for sale, and its key field is a unique item number.

The other components of our mail-order application are taking orders and billing customers. For taking orders, an order file would consist of an order number, order date, customer number, item number, and quantity ordered. To generate bills or invoices, an invoice file would contain invoice number, customer ID, date, items and quantities ordered, prices, and whether the invoice has been paid.

The database now consists of four flat files: customer, inventory, order, and invoice. Note that there is little *redundancy* or duplication of data among the relations. Now we are ready for the data manipulation operations.

Filling an order would proceed somewhat as follows. A customer sends in an order for merchandise. That order is assigned a unique order number. The order file is updated by relating the data in the customer file with the data in the inventory file. Similarly, the invoice is generated by

relating the inventory file, the order file, and the customer file on the basis of the common fields among the files.

In relational terminology, what has been happening is that a set of operators, known as *relational algebra*, has been applied to the relations or files. The operators take data in existing files and produce the desired results. Common operators are the *join* operator, which combines two separate files using a common field, and the *project* operator, which creates a new file by selecting fields from an existing file.

Examples of products that use the relational model are IBM's DB2, Oracle Corporation's Oracle, and Sybase, Inc.'s Sybase DBMS.

HIERARCHICAL

The **hierarchical model** is older than the relational model. It creates relationships among data by structuring data into an inverted tree in which records contain (1) a single root or master key field that identifies the type, location, or ordering of the records and (2) a variable number of subordinate fields that define the rest of the data within a record.

The hierarchical model was developed because hierarchical relationships are commonly found in business applications. As you learned in Chapter 10, an organization chart often describes a hierarchical relationship: top

Item No	Description	Price	Qty
903	Toshiba T1600	$4,999	4
905	Compaq SLT/286	$5,399	7
911	Zenith TurboSport 386	$7,999	3
954	GridCase 1520	$3,495	5
922	Tandy 1400	$1,599	10

The relational model. Each flat file is a two-dimensional table. Tables are logically linked by having a field in common.

Order No.	Order Date	Cust ID	Item No	Qty Ordered
1	23-May	101	903	1
2	24-May	104	922	2
3	1-Jun	105	903	1

The inventory file.

Invoice No	Cust ID	Date	Qty Ordered	Item No	Price	Paid
111	101	24-May	1	903	$4,999	No
112	104	25-May	2	922	$3,198	Yes
113	105	3-Jun	1	903	$4,999	No

For taking orders, an order file is updated by relating data in the customer file with data in the inventory file.

An invoice is generated by relating the inventory file, the order file, and the customer file.

Sold To:	Enrique Hernandez 1733 Monrovia Ave. Irvine, CA 92714		
Date:	May-25	**Invoice No.**	112
Quantity	**Description**	**Price**	**Amount**
2	Tandy 1400	$1,599.00	$3,198.00
		Sub Total	$3,198.00
		Tax	$191.88
		Total	$3,389.88
Terms:	Prepaid Visa No 1111 0022 3344 5566	**Amt Due**	$0.00

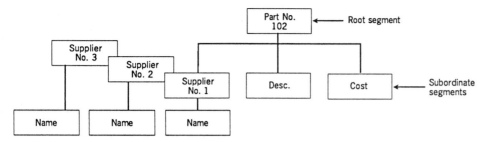

The hierarchical model. *With this model, the file is designed like an inverted tree, with the root at the highest level. Shown here is a simplified airplane spare parts database.*

management is at the highest level, middle management at lower levels, and operational employees at the lowest levels. Note that within a strict hierarchy, each level of management may have many employees or levels of employees beneath it, but each employee has only one manager. Hierarchical data are characterized by this one-to-many relationship among data.

As another example, consider a simplified airplane spare parts database. An airplane, like most systems, is made up of a set of assemblies that are made up of subassemblies and so on. Using a hierarchical approach, the relationships between records and fields might be established as follows: the first or highest level would contain the major assemblies, such as wings, fuselage, and cockpit; the second level of the hierarchy would contain subassemblies for each major assembly; and the levels farther down would include the specific part numbers and part information.

This approach would be very convenient for answering customer inquiries about parts and their availability, but it would be less convenient for making an inquiry about what parts

are on what planes. Before information about specific parts and planes can be obtained, each major assembly must first be retrieved, and several levels of the hierarchy must be navigated to obtain the part information.

In the hierarchical approach, each relationship must be explicitly defined when the database is created. Each record in a hierarchical database can contain only one key field and only one relationship is allowed between any two fields. This can create a problem because data do not always conform to such a strict hierarchy. The rivets in a wing, for example, might be identical to the rivets in the fuselage.

Examples of commercial database products that use the hierarchical model are IBM's IMS and Cullinet's IDMS.

OTHER DATABASE MODELS

There are several other database models that are worth a brief mention. We have already mentioned the text model.

The *network model* creates relationships among data through a linked-list structure in which subordinate records can be linked to more than one parent record. This approach combines records with links, which are called *pointers*. The pointers are addresses that indicate the location of a record. With the network approach, a subordinate record can be linked to a key record and at the same time itself be a key record linked to other sets of subordinate records. The network model historically has had a performance advantage over other database models. Today, such performance characteristics are only important in high-volume, high-speed transaction processing such as automatic teller machine networks or airline reservation systems.

The *object-oriented model* groups data into collections that represent some kind of object. For example, all the data that relate to the wing of an airplane. More important, the object-oriented model also allows records to inherit information from ancestor records. In the mail-order application; for example, an order for shoes would inherit information such as the

The network model. *With this model, occurrences of records are linked via pointers (addresses that specify the location of data in the file) to other occurrences of records in the database.*

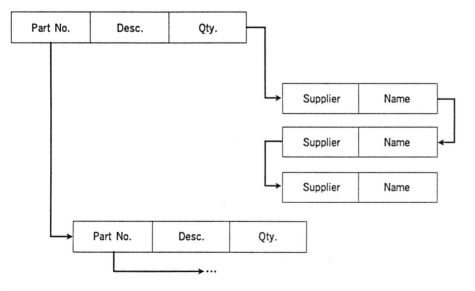

customer's name and address from the order file.

DIFFERENCES AMONG THE MODELS

The flat file model is used widely because of its simplicity, and many problems can be solved by using this model. The relational model is currently the most popular approach because of the simplicity of file creation and data manipulation operations. Relational DBMS can be found on personal computers to mainframe systems. However, the term has come to mean any DBMS that can relate files to one another in any way. Systems that adhere strictly to relational algebra as defined by computer scientists are quite rare. The hierarchical model was the earliest of the database models and has been refined over the years. However, it requires considerably more thought and design to implement a hierarchical DBMS than a relational DBMS. The network model is the most complicated type of database to design. Once established, however, it is the highest performing database for specialized applications such as reservation or transaction-processing systems. The object-oriented model is relatively new and only a few examples of object-oriented databases exist. It is gaining popularity as object-oriented programming gains popularity.

DATA MANIPULATION

As you have seen from our examples, a DBMS provides the means with which to add, delete, display, maintain, print, search, select, sort, and update the data. Users of database systems are mostly concerned with four basic data manipulation operations:

- Retrieve or select information.
- Modify or update the database.
- Delete old or obsolete information from the database.
- Insert or add new information to the database.

The following examples use the mail-order application for the four basic operations.

- *Retrieve* or *select*. Example: Select all customers whose invoices have not been paid.
- *Modify* or *update*. Example: Change Mark Smith's address in the customer file.
- *Delete* or *remove*. Example: A line of merchandise is no longer available. Remove the products from the inventory file and notify the customer that the order is impossible to fill.
- *Insert* or *add*. Example: A new customer has placed an order. Add the customer to the customer file.

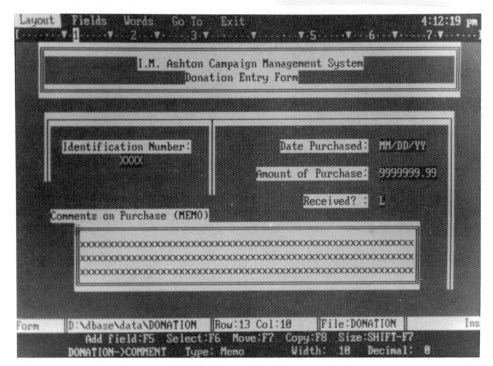

On-screen form. *Data-entry forms simplify the task of entering new information or updating information.*

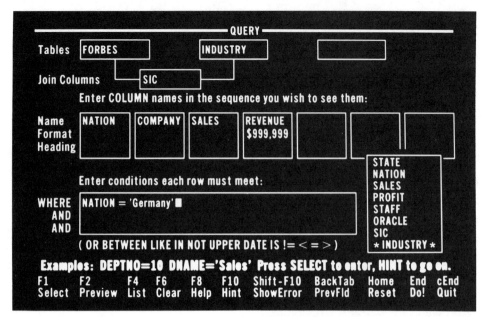

```
┌─────────────────────── QUERY ───────────────────────┐
  Tables  [FORBES]              [INDUSTRY]        [          ]

  Join Columns    [  SIC  ]

        Enter COLUMN names in the sequence you wish to see them:

  Name    [NATION ] [COMPANY] [SALES ] [REVENUE ] [      ] [      ] [      ]
  Format                                 $999,999
  Heading                                          ┌──────────────┐
                                                   │ STATE        │
                                                   │ NATION       │
        Enter conditions each row must meet:       │ SALES        │
                                                   │ PROFIT       │
  WHERE   [NATION = 'Germany'■                   ] │ STAFF        │
  AND                                              │ ORACLE       │
  AND                                              │ SIC          │
        ( OR BETWEEN LIKE IN NOT UPPER DATE IS != < = > ) │ ★ INDUSTRY ★ │
                                                   └──────────────┘
  Examples:  DEPTNO=10  DNAME='Sales'  Press SELECT to enter, HINT to go on.
  F1       F2       F4    F6    F8    F10    Shift-F10  BackTab  Home  End  cEnd
  Select   Preview  List  Clear Help  Hint   ShowError  PrevFld  Reset Do!  Quit
```

Structured query language front end. *In this example, the user is specifying that information about German companies is to be retrieved. An SQL front end enables users to construct complex requests for information without having to learn relational algebra.*

Note the distinction in these examples between modifying, which usually refers to changing, adding, or deleting information within a particular record, and deleting or inserting, which refers to an entire record.

Many database management systems assist the user when adding or updating data by providing a *form* that identifies the names and characteristics (i.e., the width of the field and whether the field is text or numeric) of the fields within a record. A form simplifies data entry because it is displayed on the screen and the user can fill in the blanks. In addition to being an efficient aid when adding new records, forms are commonly used to update records in a database. Suppose, for example, the mail-order business takes orders by phone. When a customer calls in an order, the order-entry person uses an order-entry form on a display screen to enter information about the order.

Another data manipulation feature is the user's ability to sort a database. *Sorting* means rearranging the records in a database according to a set of predefined criteria. Sorting can be done in ascending or descending order. For example, the marketing department might want to mail certain customers an announcement of a sales promotion. They might need a list of names and addresses of customers sorted in ascending order by ZIP code and, within that ZIP code, in ascending al-

phabetical order by name.

DBMSs can also perform calculations. For example, the invoice that accompanies the order contains price multiplied by quantity for each line item, a subtotal field, a tax amount if applicable, and a total amount. Most systems support mathematical functions, such as average, minimum, maximum, net present value, and rate of return.

QUERY LANGUAGES

Obtaining information from a database is the most commonly performed operation. A *query language* is a set of commands that permits the user to retrieve information from a database. The simplest example of a query, or question, is to request that the contents of a single record be listed on the display screen. DBMSs also provide the ability to search for and select specific records within the database. To do this, the user enters one or more search criteria, and the DBMS then searches the database to retrieve records that match.

Query languages can perform quite complicated searches. Standard matching conditions include equal to, not equal to, greater than, greater than or equal to, less than, less than or equal to, range equal, and range not equal. The user can usually combine selection criteria for several different conditions by using *and* and/or *or* to produce a complex query. There are several types of query languages.

Structured query language or *SQL*, is a query language for manipulating data in a relational database. It was originally developed for internal use at IBM, but as relational databases grew in popularity, it was turned into an official standard by the American National Standards Institute (ANSI).

It is unlikely that an end user would encounter SQL directly. Like an operating system, much of SQL's work is done behind the scenes and is therefore transparent to the end user. It is more likely that an end user would formulate a query in English-like statements and let the DBMS translate that query into a formal SQL query.

Query by example or *QBE* is a fill in the blanks approach to questioning a

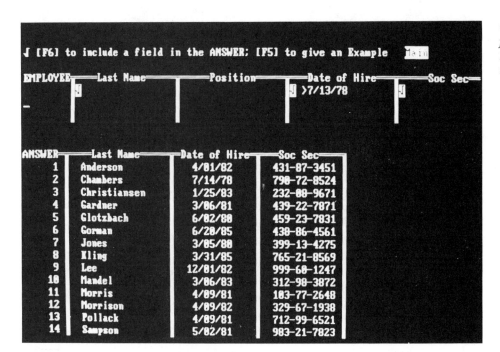

```
EMPLOYEE══Last Name══════════Position═══════Date of Hire═════Soc Sec═══
         9                                  9 >7/13/78        9
_


ANSWER══════Last Name═══════Date of Hire═════Soc Sec═══
    1      Anderson           4/01/82        431-87-3451
    2      Chambers           7/14/78        798-72-8524
    3      Christiansen       1/25/83        232-88-9671
    4      Gardner            3/06/81        439-22-7871
    5      Glotzbach          6/02/80        459-23-7831
    6      Gorman             6/20/85        430-86-4561
    7      Jones              3/05/80        399-13-4275
    8      Kling              3/31/85        765-21-8569
    9      Lee                12/01/82       999-60-1247
   10      Mandel             3/06/83        312-98-3872
   11      Morris             4/09/81        103-77-2648
   12      Morrison           4/09/82        329-67-1938
   13      Pollack            4/09/81        712-99-6521
   14      Sampson            5/02/81        983-21-7823
```

Query by example. Shown here is a search for employees who were hired after July 13, 1978 (date of hire greater than 7/13/78), using the database program's query by example.

database. With QBE, the user searches for information by filling out a query form on the display screen. This can be done by (1) checking off columns and rows that match the search criteria or (2) defining the table, the fields, and the search conditions. Although QBE was originally designed at IBM, variations of QBE have become popular in personal computer databases because they are relatively easy to use and do not require detailed knowledge of the syntax and grammar of a specific query language.

A *natural language interface* allows the user to question the database in free-form English. To translate the user's English question into a request for information from the database, natural language interfaces contain a specialized vocabulary and rules for putting together queries using the vocabulary. Often, the user must train the natural language system just as a user must train a voice-recognition system.

The advantage of such systems is that they can provide novice or casual users with simple tools with which to access a database. The disadvantage is that natural language interfaces have to be tailored specifically to the database being questioned. For example, English questions to a flight-reservation database would have no meaning

```
                    ═Current Query Context═
       │ list the salespeople with salary greater than average      │

       salespeople            salary
       ────────────────       ──────────
       LAKE                   $30,000.00
       WALSH                  $33,000.00
       BLAKE                  $32,000.00
       TAYLOR                 $33,000.00
       MITCHELL               $33,000.00
       JAMES                  $30,000.00
       BOSLEY                 $30,000.00
       SMITH                  $30,000.00
       BERRY                  $31,000.00

        average: $29,600.00
       Enter query or [ESC] to return to main menu.
       R>_
```

A natural language interface allows you to enter general requests in English or questions as shown here.

PAGE 1				14:35	1 JAN 1985		
CUST.	COMPANY....	ADDRESS.........	CITY............	ST.	ZIP.	BALANCE	
A104	AFCO INC	4401 FRONT S.	SAN DIEGO	CA	99380	135.15	
C567	CANDI INC	147 TIGER MT	LOS ANGELES	CA	99090	219.50	
G543	GRUBB INC	12 REDWOOD RD	SAN DIEGO	CA	99495	1139.12	
H453	HOLIDAY CO	60 NE DOGWOOD	SAN JOSE	CA	99345	59.01	
P678	PORT CALLS	98 CAPPELLA CT	SAN JOST	CA	99455	66.60	
S433	SAVE-IT	2507 MEDINA	SAN CARLOS	CA	98766	211.20	
S789	SMITH BROS	105 MAIN	SAN DIEGO	CA	99494	96.39	
						1926.97	
F590	FOGHORN	10 LAKE ST	BOCA RATON	FL	04533	11.47	
L987	LIQUID SUN	42 VINEYARD ST	MIAMI	FL	04452	298.16	
						309.63	
C791	CALMA CO	3350 151ST SE	COUER D'ALENE	ID	83817	19.99	
D445	DACEL CTR	67 HILLTOP RD	KELLOG	ID	83313	111.49	
L234	LCI	34 NE HAYS	BOISE	ID	83704	204.14	
M102	MAIN TAMER	14 NE 1ST	BOISE	ID	83705	886.77	
						1222.39	
					GRAND TOTAL	3458.99	

A report generator produces hard-copy output.

Program generator. dBase III Plus contains a built-in program generator so that users can develop applications without programming.

displaying the results of a query on a computer display screen. Printed reports give management and analysts the opportunity to study, analyze, and interpret data more thoroughly. Report generators provide the capability to summarize data, perform mathematical calculations—such as totals, subtotals, counts, and averages for the report—and even print graphs and charts of the data.

Suppose, for example, that the management of an airline wants to identify what types of passengers are responding to certain promotional fares, so that future promotions can be more closely tailored to these passengers. A report generator could produce a detailed report for management so that it could be passed around to colleagues and studied, questioned, and challenged.

when asked of an inventory-control database. Natural language interfaces will be discussed in greater detail in Chapter 12.

There are other specialized query languages that perform specific functions. For example, the airlines employ a system called Soundex to match airline passenger names with reservations. Soundex stores the passenger names phonetically and allows a name to be found even if the correct spelling is not known.

REPORT GENERATION

Although data manipulation and query are important, it should also be possible to print a report instead of

APPLICATION-DEVELOPMENT TOOLS

Early DBMS end-user tools were limited to query languages and report generators. Applications could only be developed with traditional programming languages, such as COBOL or Pascal. One major advantage of newer DBMSs is that the user can use the DBMS *program-generator* facilities to customize a system to meet specific needs without having to write programs. After the preliminary design steps, developers can often perform tasks such as defining files and fields, building menus, formatting data-entry screens, specifying complex queries, and creating reports without writing code in conventional programming languages.

Once the application is designed, it can be run as is or converted into a program that can be modified and customized to fine-tune the application. Advocates of DBMS application-development tools claim that complete applications can be developed by both experienced programmers and novice end users in far less time than it takes to develop an equivalent application using a traditional programming language, such as COBOL, C, or Pascal. More information about program generators and other end-user tools will be provided in Chapter 15.

DATA INDEPENDENCE

An important point about database systems is that the database should exist independently of specific applications. Traditional data processing applications are data dependent. COBOL programs contain file descriptions and record descriptions that carefully describe the format and characteristics of the data.

It should be possible to change the structure of a database without affecting applications that use it. For example, suppose that the requirements of an application change. An example would be expanding ZIP codes from five digits to nine digits. In the traditional approach using COBOL, a COBOL application program that used that particular field would have to be changed, recompiled, and retested. Other programs that had not been changed would no longer be able to recognize or access the file that had been changed; this, in turn, might cause massive disruption in processing unless the change were carefully planned.

Most database programs provide the ability to change the database structure by simply changing the ZIP code field and the data-entry form. In this case, data independence allows for minimal disruption of current and existing applications. Users can continue to work and can even ignore the nine-digit code if they choose. Eventually, all records in the file will be converted to the new nine-digit ZIP code, but the ease with which the changeover takes place emphasizes the importance of data independence.

DATA INTEGRITY

Data integrity refers to the accuracy, correctness, or validity of the data in the database. In a database system, data integrity means safeguarding the data against invalid alteration or destruction. For example, in a relational database it is possible to join two tables to create a third table. Suppose someone alters one of the original tables. The changes will not be reflected in the third table unless some form of mechanism for maintaining the *referential integrity* of the database is in place.

In large on-line database systems, data integrity becomes a more severe problem and two additional complications arise. The first has to do with many users accessing the database concurrently. For example, if thousands of travel agents and airline reservation clerks are accessing the same database at once, and two agents book the same seat on the same flight, the first agent's booking will be lost. In such cases the technique of locking the record or field provides the means for preventing one user from accessing a record while another user is updating the same record.

The second complication relates to hardware, software, or human error during the course of processing and involves database transactions to keep the database in a consistent state of integrity. A *database transaction* is a group of database modifications treated as a single unit. For example, an agent booking an airline reservation involves several database updates (i.e., adding the passenger's name and address and updating the seats-available field), which comprise a single transaction. The database transaction is not considered to be complete until all updates have been completed; otherwise, none of the updates will be allowed to take place.

In a banking example, suppose a teller wanted to transfer $100 from account *A* in California to account *B* in New York. If a computer or communications malfunction should occur during the time it takes to send the information across the telephone lines from California to New York, the integrity of the bank's database would be vio-

A database transaction consists of several events or actions but is viewed as a single operation by the user. If a bank clerk initiated this sample database transaction, it would not be complete until the deposit to account B was confirmed; otherwise none of the events would be allowed to take place.

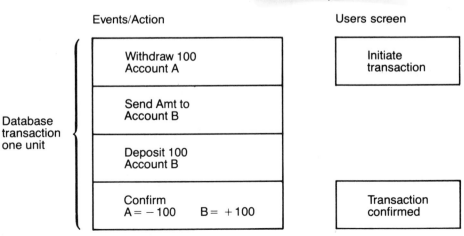

Data security through password protection.

lated. Account *A* might have $100 debited while account *B* might not have been properly credited. A database transaction solves this integrity problem by treating the transfer as a single operation consisting of withdrawing $100 from account *A* in a branch in California and depositing $100 to account *B* in New York. In this case, the database transaction would not allow the initial transfer from account *A* to take place until the deposit had occurred in account *B*.

DATA SECURITY

Data security refers to the protection of a database against unauthorized or illegal access or modification. This usually involves one or more levels of password protection that are specified in the data dictionary. For example, a high-level password might allow a user to read from, write to, and modify the database structure, whereas a low-level password might only allow a user to read from the database.

Often an *audit trail*—the recorded history of the modifications to a database—can be used to identify where and when a database was tampered with, and it can also be used to restore the file to its original condition.

DISTRIBUTING DATABASES

Recall from Chapter 7 the discussion of *distributed computing* in which a number of computers can be distributed throughout an organization and take the place of one central computing facility. Similarly, a *distributed database* is one in which different parts of

the database reside on physically separate computers. One goal of distributed databases is the access of information without regard to where the data might be stored. Keep in mind that once the users and their data are separated, the communication and networking concepts that were discussed in Chapters 9 and 10 come into play.

Distributed databases require software that resides partially in the personal computer and partially in the larger computer. This software bridges the gap between personal and larger computers and resolves the problems of incompatible data formats. Ideally, it would make the mainframe databases appear to be large libraries of information, with most of the processing accomplished on the personal computer.

As an example, suppose a person wants to obtain some financial data from a corporate database to use in a spreadsheet program. Software would allow the user to formulate a query by example. Then the program establishes contact with the database, translates the user's request into SQL, downloads the requested data to the personal computer, terminates the link to the database, and transfers the data directly into the format needed by a spreadsheet program. All this is accomplished without the user having to understand the "behind-the-scenes" details of the process involved.

A drawback to some distributed systems is that they are often based on what is often called a *mainframe-centric model*, in which the larger host computer is seen as the master and the terminal or personal computer is seen as a slave. There are some advantages to this approach. With databases under centralized control, many of the problems of data integrity and security that we mentioned earlier are solved. But today's personal computers, departmental computers, and distributed processing require computers and their applications to communicate with each other on a more equal or peer-to-peer basis.

THE CLIENT/SERVER MODEL

One way to take advantage of many connected computers running database applications is to distribute the application into cooperating parts that are independent of one another. A *client* is an end user or computer program that requests resources across a network. A *server* is a computer running software that fulfills those requests across a network. When the resources are data in a database, the *client/server model* provides the framework for distributing databases.

File Servers

A *file server* is software that provides access to files across a network. A *dedicated file server* is a single computer dedicated to being a file server. This is useful, for example, if the files are large and require fast access. In such cases, a minicomputer or a mainframe would be used as a file server. A *distributed file server* spreads the files around on individual computers instead of placing them on one dedicated computer.

Advantages of the latter server include the ability to store and retrieve files on other computers and the elimination of duplicate files at each computer. A major disadvantage, however, is that individual read/write requests are being moved across the network and problems can arise when updating files. Suppose one user requests a record from a file and changes it while another user requests the same record and changes it too. The solution to this problem is called *record locking*, which means that the first request for a record locks the record to other users, making them wait until the first request is satisfied. Other users may be able to read the record, but they will not be able to change it.

Database Servers

A *database server* is software that services requests to a database across a network. For example, suppose a user types in a query for data on his or her personal computer. If the application is designed with the client/server model in mind, the query language part on the personal computer simply sends the query across the network to the database server and requests to be notified when the data are found.

Examples of distributed database systems can be found in the engineering

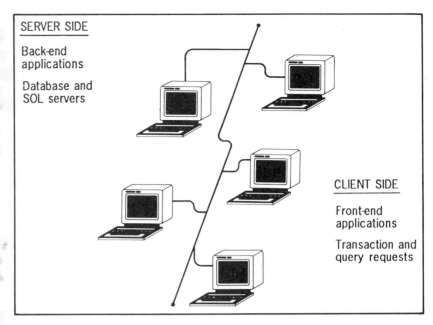

SERVER SIDE

Back-end applications

Database and SOL servers

CLIENT SIDE

Front-end applications

Transaction and query requests

Client/server model. System software makes possible cooperative processing in which some parts of an application run on a client and other parts run on a server.

world. Sun's Network Filing System (NFS), for example, is used in computer-aided engineering applications to distribute data among the hard disks in a network of Sun workstations.

Distributing databases is an evolutionary step because it is logical that data should exist at the location where they are being used. Departmental computers within a large corporation, for example, should have data reside locally, yet those data should be accessible by authorized corporate management when they want to consolidate departmental data. DBMS software will protect the security and integrity of the database, and the distributed database will appear to its users as no different from the nondistributed database.

OPTIONAL DATABASE MANAGEMENT CONCEPTS

For a more complete understanding of DBMS, additional technical material is included in this chapter. Although these concepts are optional, understanding them will enhance your knowledge of how databases work.

Adequate planning and knowing the capabilities and limitations of DBMSs are a prerequisite for successful implementation. The database structures described in the last section are high-level models of data and their relationships. They allow people to design and use a database by employing models with which they are familiar and comfortable. When designing a database, however, it is necessary to keep in mind several concepts to achieve the best operational results. The following is an overview of several of these operational concepts.

PHYSICAL FILES

The term *physical files* refers to how the actual data are stored and accessed on a medium such as a disk. Recall from Chapter 8 the direct or indexed methods of storing data on a disk. These are the most commonly used methods for storing physical files. Sequential media, such as tape, are usually not considered appropriate for physical files in a database system. The inability to access a physical record randomly on a sequential tape is too limiting for large-scale database applications.

The method used for retrieving records on a disk must be taken into consideration when designing a database. Regardless of the database model (i.e., flat file, relational, hierarchical, or network), the same techniques for arranging and retrieving records can be used in all cases.

If the database is small, rearranging the physical records is unnecessary. When a record is to be retrieved, a simple sequential search is performed until a match is found. As the database grows larger, however, retrieval becomes very slow.

INDEXING

Often it is more practical to keep a separate *index file* to keep track of the addresses of each record. In Chapter 8, we mentioned the library and its card catalog as an example of indexing. Libraries also contain an author index and a subject index, which allow you to find a book by either its subject or author. Similarly, an indexed database can provide different key fields to access data that can greatly improve the speed of retrieving data from a disk.

Because an index is in sorted order, it can be searched rapidly using a technique called a *binary search*. For example, suppose a list is sorted alphabetically by name, and the name "Randolph, John" is sought. A binary-search technique would first divide the list in half by identifying the midpoint name in the list and then determine which half of the list contains the name sought. By first identifying the midpoint name in the list, which might turn out to be "Morrow, George," and comparing the first letter of Randolph with the first letter of Morrow, the binary-search technique discovers that Randolph is in the second half of the list. By dividing the remainder of the list in half and continuing through the sequence of midpoints, the name Randolph would be found much quicker than if a sequential search were performed. Binary searches are very fast when the list is in memory, but if the index is a file on disk, binary searching may take too long.

A balanced binary tree in which each parent node has two child nodes. In a balanced tree, the height of the right subtree of every node should never differ by more than one level from the height of its left subtree.

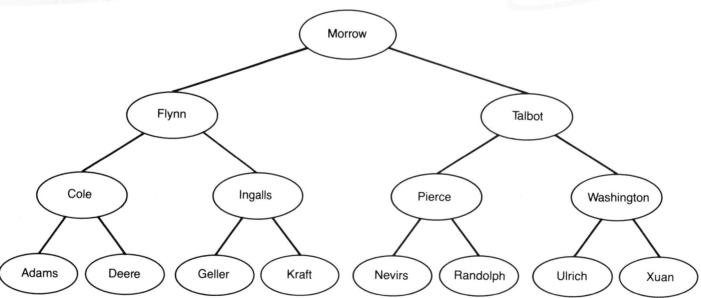

B-TREES

To utilize the binary technique on a disk, a structure for storing and retrieving data called a *B-tree* or balanced tree is used. A B-tree file is similar to a hierarchical organization in which a group of records is structured into an inverted tree based on a series of midpoints. For example, the root of the tree is the midpoint of a file, at the second level are more midpoints, and so on. Many database programs use B-tree structures for their index files because they permit fast disk retrieval.

HASHING

Hashing is another retrieval technique in which a unique number is assigned to each record and used as an address on the disk. Each time a record is needed, a mathematical operation called a hash function is used to compute the number, and the corresponding record is retrieved from the disk without a search. Hashing works best when a reasonable maximum size for the file is known in advance.

```
BUD                    BUILD DICTIONARY ITEMS

01  File Name      CUSTOMERS
02  Field Name     PHONE
03  Single/Multivalued    M1.1
04  Field Type   (F, S, G)   F
05  Field Number      10        06  Which Part of Key  0
07  Output Conversion
    (MONEY, DATE, TIME)

08  R/BASIC Formula

09  Justification    L          10  List Display Length  12
11  Edit Patterns
12  Bottom Screen Prompt    TELEPHONE NUMBERS
13  LIST Column Heading      PHONE
14  Source of Information
15  Description   ENTER ALL THE PHONE NUMBERS FOR THIS CUSTOMER
```

A data dictionary can store field-structure definitions entered by the database.

DATA DICTIONARY

The DBMS creates a logical collection of data out of physical files. It knows where records are stored within the physical files by creating and maintaining a *data dictionary*, a database

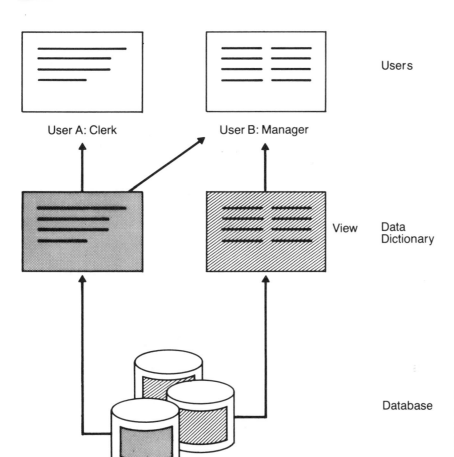

Users

User A: Clerk   User B: Manager

View   Data Dictionary

Database

Views are data descriptions that exist in the data dictionary. They simplify a user's perception of a complex database and can also provide a measure of security by hiding data from certain users. Note that one user may have access to two or more views.

```
┌─────────────── File Type Selection Menu ───────────────┐
│  1) DIF file (from VISICALC, or others) .................(1)  │
│  2) SYLK file (from MULTIPLAN, or others) ...............(2)  │
│  3) ASCII file with data fields in fixed locations.......(3)  │
│  4) ASCII file with data fields separated by delimiters .....(4)  │
│  5) LOTUS 1-2-3 worksheet files .........................(5)  │
│  6) dBase II files ......................................(6)  │
│  7) PFS:FILE files ......................................(7)  │
│  8) Exit ................................................(8)  │
└─────────────────────────────────────────────────────────┘

┌─────────────────────────────────────────────────────────┐
│  Enter number corresponding to selection or ? for help:........( )  │
└─────────────────────────────────────────────────────────┘
```

Utilities. *Many DBMSs provide an import utility that converts existing files into a format that the DBMS can use.*

within a database that contains descriptions of the fields, records, files, and their relationships. In large-scale systems, a data dictionary also includes provisions for assigning levels of security for database access, for validating data, and for cross-referencing information.

Besides the accessing and storage methods employed by the physical files, the data dictionary supplies multiple views of the database. In this context, a *view* consists of all the fields that can be accessed by a specific user. A view makes the user unaware of the rest of the data in the database, which improves security.

For example, in an airline database, the reservation agent's view of the database might be restricted to only the information related to the number of available seats and price of a flight, whereas management's view might include the information related to the number of discounted seats allowed and the cost of a ticket. These two views of the same database can be specified through the data dictionary.

UTILITIES

Utilities are programs that allow a user or programmer to create and maintain the database. If a database constantly has new records added and old records deleted, it may be necessary to reorganize the physical storage of the database. For example, the addition of new records usually occurs at the end of a physical file, whereas the deletion of old records tends to leave gaps in the physical file. These additions and deletions to files can affect access time to the file and the efficiency of disk storage utilization, so reorganization becomes an important maintenance task.

Data entry commonly takes place by keying in the data, but often the data already exist in another format, such as in an existing file. Most DBMSs provide a utility program that can *import* data by copying and converting it from existing files, as well as *export* data from the particular DBMS to other application programs such as spreadsheets or word processors.

REVIEW

Database management systems have evolved from a highly specialized programming technique requiring its own set of skills and activities into an end-user-oriented activity. Database systems can range from the large-scale corporatewide systems to small systems designed to run on personal computers. Database systems can use the flat-file, relational, hierarchical, or one of several other models to structure data. Users of database systems are most concerned with retrieving, modifying, and deleting information from a database, and with adding information to a database. The future trend is toward a distributed network of personal computers, each able to access databases across the network. For a complete understanding of databases, it is important to understand principles such as physical files, indexing, B-trees, hashing, data dictionary, and utilities.

REFERENCES

1. Freedman, David H. "Cancelled Flights." *CIO*, April 1989, pp. 48-50.

RESOURCES

BOOKS

Banet, Bernard, Judith Davis, and Ronni Marshack. *Data Base Management Systems: The Desktop Generation*. New York: McGraw-Hill, 1985. An excellent but somewhat dated survey of eight popular personal computer database management systems along with some tips for analyzing database requirements and needs.

Date, C. J. *A Guide to the SQL Standard*. Reading, Mass.: Addison-Wesley, 1987. This book is not for the squeamish. However, relational databases and Structured Query Language have become standards, so those who wish to find more detail in a short book will find it here.

Kruglinski, David. *Data Base Management Systems: A Guide to Microcomputer Software*. New York: Osborne/McGraw-Hill, 1986. A good survey of personal computer database management systems with extensive coverage of concepts.

MAGAZINES

Data Based Advisor. San Diego, Calif.: Data Based Solutions. A monthly magazine dedicated to personal computer database systems. Contains product reviews, tips, and technically oriented feature stories.

DBMS. Redwood City, Calif.: M & T Publishing. A monthly magazine that covers database-related trends, issues, and products. The magazine has more of a management than a technical orientation.

STUDY GUIDE

Match the following key terms to the appropriate definition:

A.

1. __C__ Database
2. __f__ Database management system (DBMS)
3. __a__ Text database
4. __g__ Database model

5. __k__ Flat file
6. __i__ Key field
7. __h__ Relational model
8. __b__ Relation

9. __l__ Hierarchical model
10. __e__ Network model
11. __j__ Object-oriented model
12. __d__ Form

a. A collection of words such as a series of legal abstracts.

b. Each table in a database.

c. A collection of one or more files treated as a whole unit.

d. Identifying the names and characteristics of fields in a record.

e. A model that creates relationships among data through a linked-list structure.

f. Software that organizes, manipulates, and retrieves data stored in a database.

g. Identifying the major parts (e.g., files, records, and fields) of a database and illustrating how these parts fit together.

h. A model that creates relationships among tables on the basis of a common field in each of the tables.

i. A unique identifier that eliminates duplicate records.

j. A model that groups data into collections that represent some kind of object.

k. A single file consisting of rows (records) and columns (fields) of data that resemble a two-dimensional spreadsheet.

l. A model that creates relationships among data by structuring data into an inverted tree.

B.

13. __e__ Sorting
14. __g__ Query language
15. __f__ Structured query language (SQL)

16. __j__ Query by example (QBE)
17. __d__ Natural language interface
18. __h__ Data integrity
19. __a__ Database transaction

20. __b__ Data security
21. __c__ Distributed computing
22. __i__ Distributed database

a. A group of database modifications treated as a single unit.

b. Protection of a database against access or modification without authorization.

c. A number of computers distributed throughout an organization that take the place of one central computing facility.

d. Software that allows a user to interact with the database system in free-form English.

e. A technique for rearranging data according to pre-defined criteria.

f. A query language for manipulating data in a relational database.

g. Software that permits a user to retrieve information from a database.

h. The accuracy, correctness, or validity of the data in the database.

i. A database in which different parts of the database reside on physically separate computers.

j. A fill in the blanks approach to questioning a database.

C.

23. __j__ Client
24. __m__ Server
25. __i__ Client/server model
26. __k__ File server
27. __l__ Database server

28. __d__ Physical file
29. __a__ Index file
30. __f__ Binary search
31. __c__ B-tree
32. __b__ Hashing

33. __h__ Data dictionary
34. __g__ View
35. __e__ Utilities

a. A file that keeps track of the addresses where records can be found.

b. A mathematical technique for assigning a unique number to each record in a file.

c. A structure in which a group of records is divided into an inverted tree based on a series of midpoints.

d. The way in which the actual data are stored and accessed on a medium such as a disk.

e. Programs that allow a user or programmer to maintain a database.

f. A search method in which a list of items is successively halved until the sought item is located.

g. In a database, a group of data associated with a specific user.

h. A file that contains descriptions of fields, records, files, and their relationships.

i. A model that provides the framework for distributing databases.

j. An end user or computer program that requests resources across a network.

k. Software that provides access to files across a network.

l. Software that services requests to a database across a network.

m. A computer running software that fulfills requests across a network.

True/False:

36. _____ The emerging recognition of the strategic value of information will make databases obsolete.

37. _____ Database management spans a broad range of information systems, from those that are based around personal computers to those that are based around mainframe computers.

38. _____ The discovery by end users that they can develop applications faster with databases than with traditional programming languages is enhancing the value of DBMS.

39. _____ Relational databases were developed before hierarchical databases.

40. _____ The network approach provides the most flexibility in allowing new kinds of questions to be asked of the database.

41. _____ Using indexing slows down retrieval of records in a database.

42. _____ A view makes a user aware of all the records and fields in a database.

43. _____ A query language is a set of commands that allows a user to add and change records in a database.

44. _____ In theory, databases should exist independently of the specific applications.

45. _____ Data integrity provides a method for locking out one user while another is updating the database.

46. _____ A goal of distributing databases is accessing information without regard to where the information is stored.

47. _____ Password protection can prevent an unauthorized user from writing to a database.

48. _____ Data should not exist at the location where they are being used.

49. _____ The client/server model takes advantage of computers on a network.

50. _____ Distributed software works across all brands of personal computer and mainframe database software.

Multiple Choice:

51. Which of the following is not a trend that is enhancing the value and usefulness of database management?

   a. Managers who need more up-to-date information.
   b. Customers who demand sophisticated information services.
   c. End users who find traditional programming to be faster.
   d. Organizations that discover the strategic value of information.

52. The flat file

   a. Is the basis for hierarchical databases.
   b. Resembles a two-dimensional spreadsheet.
   c. Does not use key fields.
   d. Is all that is needed to create a mail-order application.

53. The hierarchical model creates relationships among data by

   a. Creating linked lists with pointers.
   b. Creating two-dimensional tables.
   c. Structuring data into rows and columns.
   d. Structuring data into an inverted tree.

54. The most popular database model today is

   a. Relational.

b. Hierarchical.
c. Network.
d. Object oriented.

55. Storing individual views occurs in

    a. Report generators.
    b. Query languages.
    c. Data dictionaries.
    d. Data security.

56. Entering or updating data is often accomplished with the use of a

    a. Data dictionary.
    b. Form.
    c. Natural language interface.
    d. Query language.

57. Keeping track of the physical location of records in a database is often accomplished with a(n)

    a. Data dictionary.
    b. View.
    c. Binary search.
    d. Index.

58. In the relational model, fields are represented by

    a. Linked lists.
    b. Pointers.
    c. Vertical columns.
    d. Horizontal rows.

59. The network model for database design is

    a. The most complicated type of database.
    b. The least powerful approach.
    c. Used extensively with personal computers.
    d. The simplest type to understand.

60. A retrieval technique in which a unique number is assigned to each record and computed each time a record is sought is called

    a. Hashing.
    b. Indexing.
    c. Binary searching.
    d. Pointing.

Thought Questions:

61. Of the types of databases—relational, hierarchical, network, and object oriented—which is the easiest to understand? The hardest? Why?

62. If you were a salesperson for an organization with a DBMS, how would you use the DBMS to help you perform your job?

Projects:

63. Visit a car-rental agency or major hotel that uses a computerized reservation system in your area. Find out how its reservation system is similar to the airline reservation system described in this chapter. Prepare a report for your class.

64. Research books, magazines, or personal sources to find a unique use for a natural language interface. Make a presentation to your class concerning what you find.

SOFTWARE EXERCISES

For this exercise you will use a database program to create a database consisting of all the magazines referenced at the end of each chapter. You don't have to include the descriptive information, but do check with the library so you can include publisher addresses and subscription prices. Your output will be a printed report sorted in alphabetical order.

ANSWERS

1. c, **2.** f, **3.** a, **4.** g, **5.** k, **6.** i, **7.** h, **8.** b, **9.** l, **10.** e, **11.** j, **12.** d, **13.** e, **14.** g, **15.** f, **16.** j, **17.** d, **18.** h, **19.** a, **20.** b, **21.** c, **22.** i, **23.** j, **24.** m, **25.** i, **26.** k, **27.** l, **28.** d, **29.** a, **30.** f, **31.** c, **32.** b, **33.** h, **34.** g, **35.** e, **36.** F, **37.** T, **38.** T, **39.** F, **40.** F, **41.** F, **42.** F, **43.** F, **44.** T, **45.** T, **46.** T, **47.** T, **48.** F, **49.** T, **50.** F, **51.** c, **52.** b, **53.** d, **54.** a, **55.** c, **56.** b, **57.** d, **58.** c, **59.** a, **60.** a.

NICHOLAS NEGROPONTE

Profession: Founder and director of the Media Laboratory at MIT, Cambridge, Massachusetts.

Profile: After graduating from MIT with a degree in architecture, Negroponte founded and directed an MIT research project on computer-aided design called the Architecture Machine Group. Following that, he pulled together a dozen scattered MIT research groups to found the Media Laboratory in 1984.

Quote: "*Newspapers as we know them won't exist. They will be printed for a readership of one. Television won't simply have sharper pictures. You'll have one button that says tell me more, and another button that says tell me less.*"

266

CHAPTER 12

ARTIFICIAL INTELLIGENCE AND EXPERT SYSTEMS

PREVIEW

The idea that a computer can exhibit humanlike intelligence is both interesting and challenging to the imagination. In research laboratories, computer systems are being developed that challenge traditional theories about behavior and thinking, and now products are moving from the laboratories into commercial applications.

Artificial intelligence (AI) has practical applications in both the office and the factory. In the office, AI techniques are paving the way toward more advanced problem-solving computer systems called expert systems. In the factory, the term artificial intelligence has largely been replaced by the terms robotics and programmable factory automation. Although these systems are generally thought of as machines programmed to repeat the same tasks over and over, robots are now exhibiting the kind of intelligent behavior that allows them to adapt quickly to new tasks and to react with some degree of spontaneity to errors and changing conditions.

In this chapter, you'll learn

- If machines can really think.
- How playing games with computer programs has provided valuable insight into AI.
- Examples of natural language processing.
- What expert systems do.
- How expert systems work.
- What neural networks do.

CAN MACHINES REALLY THINK?

Artificial intelligence (AI) is the branch of computer science that attempts to (1) understand the nature of intelligence and (2) produce new classes of intelligent machines by programming computers to perform tasks that require humanlike qualities, such as reasoning and perception. Intelligent machines are now being applied to problems that were formerly considered the domain of human intelligence.

What is intelligence? According to author Christopher Evans, the most basic and fundamental definition of intelligence is the ability of a system to adapt appropriately to a changing world: the more capable it is of adapting—the more versatile its adaptation power—the more intelligent it is.[1]

This definition condenses two very important aspects of human adaptation: self-programming, the skills people use to build other skills, and the ability of intelligent human beings to solve problems quickly. Yet when it comes to thinking, psychologists and computer scientists alike are in agreement that science does not yet understand how the human mind works. For example, the process of storing and retrieving information in the brain is still the subject of intense research.

Ever since the eighteenth century, philosophers have debated the question of whether it is possible for a machine to think. In the 1930s, mathematicians Alonzo Church and Alan Turing independently formulated the hypothesis, known as the Church-Turing thesis, that mental processes of any sort can be simulated by a computer program. Author Douglas Hofstadter restated the hypothesis as follows: "As the intelligence of machines evolves, its underlying mechanisms will gradually converge to the mechanisms underlying human intelligence." In other words, to create intelligence, AI researchers will have to keep pushing to ever more fundamental levels of intelligence, closer and closer to the unknown workings of brain mechanisms.[2]

THE TURING TEST

In 1950 Alan Turing published a paper titled "Computing Machinery and Intelligence," in which he sought to answer the question: Can machines think? If a machine were created that could think, how would one go about testing it? Turing proposed a method of testing a machine for thinking ability, originally called the imitation game, but now known as the Turing test. In its simplest form, the Turing test can be described as follows. An observer is put in a room where there are two terminals, one connected to a computer program and the other connected to a person. The observer does not know which is which, and the test is to find out which is the person and which is the computer program by carrying on a conversation through the terminals. The observer is allowed to converse with either terminal on any topic of his or her choosing and to try to gain clues that will force the computer to expose itself. Of course, the computer can lie in its attempts to fool the observer, so questions such as, "Are you the computer?" will do little good.

The computer would have to have considerable knowledge at its disposal to pass the Turing test. Surprisingly, a few programs have passed variations of the Turing test. One program called Parry was designed to simulate the belief structure of a paranoid person. Parry's creator, Dr. Kenneth Colby, performed his own Turing test by sending transcripts of one of Parry's conversations along with transcripts of an actual interview with a paranoid patient to a number of psychiatrists in the United States. He asked the psychiatrists to determine which was the real patient and which was the program. Only 51 percent picked the right transcript, which is no better than if the psychiatrists had picked the transcripts at random.[3]

In 1980 chess grand master Helmut Pflager played 26 games of chess simultaneously. Unknown to him, 3 of the games were being played by computers. The human players were actually receiving radio signals telling them to move according to the com-

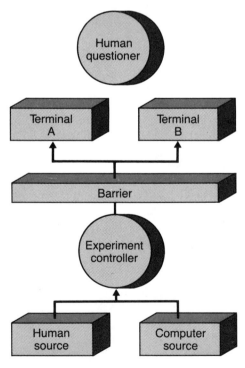

The Turing test. Which one is the computer? With a literal interpretation of the Turing test, an observer tries to guess which input is coming from a computer and which is coming from a human source. Actual variations of the test have included playing games against a computer opponent and trying to determine whether a written transcript of a conversation was produced by a human or by a computer.

puter-generated moves. One computer, called Belle, beat Pflager, who could not tell the difference between the human and computer play. Nor could any of the chess experts who later examined the game's moves. Pflager was furious when he found out "who" had defeated him.[4]

It should be pointed out that it is still uncertain whether any form of the Turing test actually tests for intelligence, but the power of computers to mimic certain human behaviors has increased dramatically over the last 30 years.

THINKING ABOUT THINKING

Perhaps the most profound implication of AI is that it suggests the possibility of new ways of viewing behavior and thinking. Some people would argue that artificial intelligence is a matter of degree not kind. According to Seymour Papert,

People are biological. When we ask if a machine thinks, we are asking whether we would like to extend the notion of thinking to include what machines might do. This is the only meaningful sense of the question: Do machines think?[5]

Without getting into too much detail, scientists call this a paradigm shift—the rejection of one time-honored scientific theory in favor of a newer and more satisfactory theory.

For example, today's physics textbooks teach students that light consists of photons—entities that exhibit some of the characteristics of waves and some of particles. However, before that theory was developed by Einstein, Planck, and others at the turn of the century, physics texts taught students that light consisted of wave motions.[6]

Today, we view our behavior and thinking through the time-honored theories of psychology. In the future, AI research may provide a new way of looking at behavior and thinking and, therefore, create a paradigm shift in the way we view ourselves.

Using AI techniques, theories can be formulated and tested with the aid of computers, but one paradox still confronts all AI research. Once a task is programmed to be performed by a

computer, people generally no longer think of it as an intelligent task. For example, consider the problem of finding the square root of 345.78. Before computers, anyone who could solve that problem would have been said to be very intelligent, yet today any schoolchild can solve the problem immediately with an ordinary pocket calculator. Today, people are less impressed with the ability to perform complex calculations. You should be careful not to confuse getting the right answer with intelligence.

FROM THINKING TO INTELLIGENT BEHAVIOR

Although no one has yet developed a program that even comes close to transforming a computer into an intelligent entity, some of the most successful efforts of AI research have been programs that play games, such as chess, checkers, or backgammon. Games have clear-cut and limited rules that make them easy to simulate on computers; therefore, much of the research in AI has been accomplished using such games.

The evolution of chess-playing computers offers some insight into AI research. The computer Belle, mentioned earlier, was until 1983 the world's most powerful chess machine. It started out at AT&T's Bell Laboratories in 1973 as a program that could evaluate approximately 200 moves per second. Belle uses a brute-force method for playing chess: the program reaches its conclusions by searching for as many possible alternative moves as it can during a game. Its inventors thought that the original program was too slow, so they built a special-purpose computer optimized to calculate chess moves. The computer now has the ability to examine 160,000 possible moves per second. In the 1982 U. S. National Open, Belle tied for second place in speed chess, in which players are required to play a complete game in 5 minutes.[7]

The program points out one of the problems with early AI work, namely,

Artificial intelligence gives a radar target classification (RTC) system the ability to recognize what the radar "sees." The RTC system extracts features from radar imagery and associates them with high-level models of possible ship classifications stored in the system's knowledge base. Shown here is a picture of a Belknap-class cruiser.

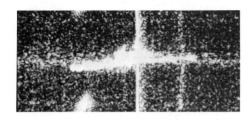

Shown here is the initial radar image of the ship on the previous page.

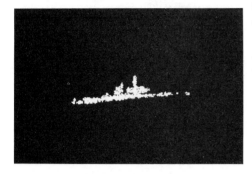

The image is processed to obtain low-level image features, which are matched against data stored in the knowledge base. It employs a matching process that uses rules obtained from human experts.

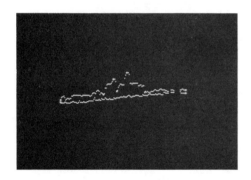

After further processing, such information as ship length, antenna locations, and deck and superstructure locations are determined, and the system calculates a probability match for each ship model in the knowledge base.

The RTC system decided that the image is not that of an aircraft carrier and probably not a destroyer. It identified a Belknap-class cruiser as the highest probability based on the image features.

that it runs up against the problem known as the *combinatorial explosion,* in which the number of possibilities becomes too vast for the program to calculate or compare in a reasonable amount of time. For example, Claude Shannon, formerly of MIT, once calculated that a chess program that examined every move would have to analyze 10^{120} possible moves. (By comparison, the estimated number of atoms in the universe is 10^{80}).

Such programs also point out that AI researchers do not always have a clear understanding of how people think, learn, or solve problems. Clearly, a master chess player does not examine every possible move before actually making a move, and other game-playing programs have been developed that use different search methods to narrow the number of possible moves.

According to John Anderson, professor of psychology and computer science at Carnegie-Mellon,

In chess, for instance, there isn't much difference between the duffer and the master in overall intelligence, and both will consider the same number of moves. What distinguishes the master is that he has committed to memory the appropriate analysis of the tens of thousands of patterns that possibly could occur on the chessboard. It seems that a major component of being intelligent is based on this ability to convert as much of one's knowledge into knowledge that can be used in pattern matching. This is what we think happens when someone becomes an expert in a field.[8]

In 1989, a chess-playing computer called Deep Thought, tied for first place in a tournament featuring a mixed field of human grandmaster players and computers. Deep Thought can examine 720,000 possible moves per second, thanks to two special-purpose chess-playing processors. But Deep Thought goes far beyond the brute-force method of playing chess. It can evaluate chess pieces and positions relative to other pieces. And it determines its moves by narrowing down the choices, thus enabling it to look many moves in advance along a line of strategy and avoid moves that would be poor or nonsensical. Although Deep Thought cannot always beat a human grandmaster, its evalua-

tion capabilities are being improved continuously. The computer plays conservative chess, makes very few errors, and is quick to pounce on opponents mistakes.[9]

In October 1989, World chess champion Gary Kasparov handily beat Deep Thought. But Deep Thought's inventors were not discouraged. According to Murray Campbell, one of the five scientists who developed Deep Thought, "Who knows what intelligence really is? Whatever it is, there are two ways for a computer programmer to try to go about it. One is to create a machine that will emulate human intelligence. The other is to make a machine that will produce intelligent behavior. Deep Thought is of the latter variety, and it uses different search methods than humans do. We think it produces intelligent behavior. It's up to the philosophers to decide if it is intelligent."[10]

NATURAL LANGUAGE PROCESSING

Natural language processing involves understanding and responding to commands that are given to a program in a natural language such as English. The earliest attempts at natural language processing involved U.S. Defense Department research into computer translation, in which documents in one language were converted to equivalent documents in another language. The Defense Department wanted to translate Soviet technical documents into English, but researchers were unable to solve the problems of ambiguous usage of natural languages.

Two humorous stories point out the problems of this type of translation. A computer translation program translated the English phrase "hydraulic ram" into Russian, then retranslated into English, and came out with "water goat." The English phrase "The spirit is willing, but the flesh is weak" was translated into Russian and then retranslated as "The vodka is strong, but the meat is rotten." Today, low-cost, hand-held, special-purpose com-

puters can translate foreign language words into English words.

UNDERSTANDING NATURAL LANGUAGE

Parry, the program that passed the Turing test, was indeed a clever program, but it only pretended to understand what was being typed in at the computer's keyboard. In recent years, a number of programs have been written that do exhibit understanding. But their domain, or the range of subjects about which they can converse, is very limited. The best-known question-answering program was SHRDLU, named after the Linotype operators' code ETAOIN SHRDLU, a set of nonsense symbols that is used to mark typographical errors in newspaper columns. SHRDLU was completed in 1971 as a thesis project at MIT by Terry Winograd. The research centered on "blocks world," a simulated table with toylike blocks of varying sizes, shapes, and colors.[11]

Winograd's research was directed toward getting the computer to understand questions in English about the blocks. With SHRDLU, the user types in commands to move blocks on a display screen. The user can also ask questions about the new positioning of the blocks, and the program will answer the questions by describing its action in English. The ability to answer these questions is a demonstration that the program understands what is being asked.

To accomplish understanding, natural language systems contain knowledge about (1) *syntax*, the rules needed to make judgments about language; (2) *semantics*, the meaning of a phrase or expression; and (3) *pragmatics*, the meaning of words in a context. Natural language systems use these three types of knowledge in a two-step process. First, the language statement is parsed. The word *parse* comes from the linguistic method of breaking a sentence into subject, predicate, and object. Second, after the phrase has been parsed, an interpreter uses semantic and pragmatic knowledge to match the phrase to the internal problem-solving database.[12]

APPLICATIONS FOR NATURAL LANGUAGE PROCESSING

Conversational programs have paved the way for more intelligent computer system interfaces. Natural language processing products have made an appearance in the office in the form of natural language interfaces to database systems. The first of these systems was called Intellect, from Artificial Intelligence Corporation. It allowed questioning of a database in ordinary English and was quite powerful in certain applications.

When a natural language system, such as Intellect, is linked to a database application, it has to be tailored to the database with which it will interface. This is necessary so that it can understand expressions that solely relate to

Natural language. A sample dialog with Winograd's SHRDLU system.

> Pick up a big red block.
>
> *OK.*
>
> Grasp the pyramid.
>
> *I don't understand which pyramid you mean.*
>
> Find a block that is taller than the one you are holding and put it in the box.
>
> *By "it" I assume you mean the block that is taller than the one I am holding.*
>
> What does the box contain?
>
> *The blue pyramid and the blue block.*
>
> What is the pyramid supported by?
>
> *The box.*
>
> How many blocks are not in the box?
>
> *Four of them.*

Natural language processing. Intellect's data-flow diagram illustrates the processing steps through which each user request passes. (1) The request character string is broken into word pieces by the scan function. (2) The parser takes these words and grammatically diagrams the sentence. (3) Weed, the first step in determining the correct interpretation, attempts to fill in the holes of the partial interpretations. (4) Decide attempts to choose the proper interpretation based on preference values that have been generated for each thought. If decide has difficulties with the interpretation, it queries the database to resolve the question. If this approach fails, it queries the user for additional information. (5) Once the interpretation is processed, the requested data are retrieved from the database, organized, and displayed to the user.

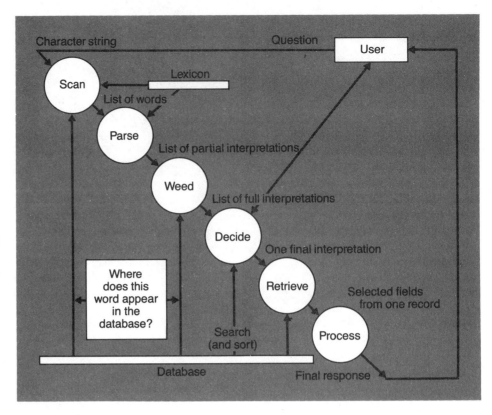

Expert systems. A mechanic's expert system can help diagnose automotive problems.

the database being questioned. For example, a flight-reservation database might use expressions that are entirely different from those used by a sales-order database.

Eventually, it is expected that natural language processing will combine with speech recognition to create very powerful and easy-to-use office and factory products. One example of such research is Toshiba Corporation's office automation systems that include an experimental voice-activated word processor, an optical character recognition system that reads hand-printed Japanese characters, and a word processor that converts Japanese to Chinese. The voice-activated word processor contains a base of 30,000 words.[13]

EXPERT SYSTEMS

Another practical application of AI has been in the area of expert systems. An *expert system* is a computer program that solves specialized problems at the level of a human expert. For example, Ford Motor Company and Hewlett-Packard have developed the Service

Bay Diagnostic System (SBDS), an automotive service bay that incorporates a mechanic's expert system.

To use the system, the mechanic plugs the SBDS sensor unit into a special port built into the car. For difficult problems, the expert system takes input directly from the car, as well as from observations supplied by the mechanic. It searches through its on-line manuals, makes inferences, may ask for more sensor readings, and guides the mechanic to a diagnosis of the problem.

FROM DATABASES TO KNOWLEDGE BASES

The preceding example points out some of the requirements for building an expert system. First, an expert system is developed by creating a knowledge base that is required for the application. A *knowledge base* contains (1) facts and data that are specific to a particular problem area and (2) rules that tell how to manipulate the facts or data stored. Unlike a conventional database, a knowledge base may include facts, assumptions, beliefs, expertise, and *heuristic methods*, which are exploratory methods for solving problems on an intelligent trial-and-error basis.

Creating a knowledge base requires that the system designer consult with a human expert. A person who creates an expert system is called a **knowledge engineer**—a computer scientist who designs and builds expert systems. The field of knowledge engineering grew out of the realization that building the knowledge base is one of the most important parts of an expert system. For example, obtaining knowledge from an expert is as important as actually developing the system itself, so a knowledge engineer must be trained in interviewing experts and in finding and developing reasoning procedures that match the expert's thought pattern.

After formulating the preliminary requirements and specifications of the expert system, a knowledge engineer has to develop two things: (1) the knowledge representation and (2) the reasoning strategies. The **knowledge representation** is the formal method for representing facts and rules about the area under consideration. A **rule** is a statement about the relationship of various facts or data.

For example, the first expert system, DENDRAL, helps chemists to identify the molecular structure of chemical compounds after they have obtained laboratory data using a tool called a mass spectrograph. Researchers know that the structure of a compound depends on a set of rules for chemical bonding. The knowledge engineer's job is to translate those rules into a set of rules that are used in the knowledge base.

The reasoning strategies are sometimes called an **inference engine**. An expert system reasons by processing symbols that represent objects. For example, when chemists make or discover a new compound, they can analyze it with a mass spectrograph, but they still need to figure out the specific shape that the compound's molecules will take. Even though the rules for chemical bonding are finite, there are millions of possible combinations based on a simple set of rules. The knowledge engineers involved in creating DENDRAL interviewed many chemists to find out their reasoning strategies for determining molecular structure from mass spectral data.

By combining a knowledge base that consists of a number of facts about chemistry with a reasoning capability similar to that of a chemist, DENDRAL is able to outperform a human chemist in the specific task of narrowing down the choices of possible structures of a compound.

HOW EXPERT SYSTEMS WORK

Expert systems currently work like an advisor on subjects such as science, medicine, oil and mineral exploration, sales, faulty equipment diagnoses, education, and computer system configurations. They are used interactively; the system prompts a user for information about a problem and then solves a problem, draws a conclusion, suggests a treatment, or makes a prediction and, if asked, can explain its line of reasoning along the way.

For example, at General Electric's steam turbine division, expert systems are used to help engineers design custom turbines. A generic set of rules, requirements, and design logic are captured in the expert system. When an engineer wants to design a specific turbine, he or she gives the expert system the needs and requirements. The expert system puts together the standard parts of the design, which the engineer can then customize.

By using the reasoning capability of the inference engine, a knowledge base, containing data and rules, can be searched. Some expert systems are data driven: when supplied with a problem in the form of a series of facts, the system attempts to deduce a solution along with the line of reasoning that was used to determine the solution.

For example, the DENDRAL expert system was used to determine the structure of the compound $C_{12}H_{44}S_2$. DENDRAL started its search for a structure by first checking its mathematics knowledge base. The program discovered that there are 43,867,912 possible structures for the compound. Then the program consulted rules about chemical topology, which reduced the number of possibilities to 14,715,814. Adding in mass spectral data further reduced the possibilities to 1,284,792. Rules from chemistry reduced the number of possibilities to

Expert systems. At General Electric, an expert system helps repair diesel locomotive engines.

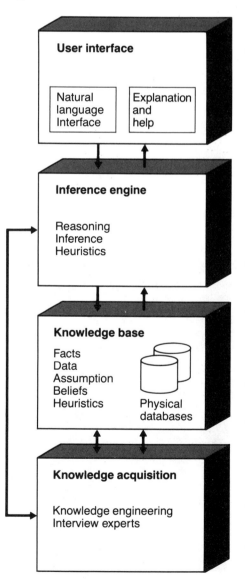

User interface

| Natural language Interface | Explanation and help |

Inference engine

Reasoning
Inference
Heuristics

Knowledge base

Facts
Data
Assumption
Beliefs
Heuristics

Physical databases

Knowledge acquisition

Knowledge engineering
Interview experts

Data Processing System	Expert System
Uses *algorithms* or problem solving in a predetermined finite number of steps.	Uses *heuristics* or rules of thumb that guide or lead to a likely satisfactory solution.
Uses *processing* in searching for or calculating answers.	Uses *inferencing* to reason toward a hypothesis.
Uses *databases* or files of predetermined facts.	Uses *knowledge bases* that include beliefs and assumptions gathered from humans.
Processes at a *raw data level* of a problem.	Processes at a *semantic* or *pragmatic level* of a problem.
Data *retrieval* follows a Boolean matching of patterns.	Data *retrieval* follows a rule-based matching based on threshold probabilities.

Expert systems. At General Electric, an expert system helps repair diesel locomotive engines.

1,074,648, and finally rules from the knowledge of nuclear magnetic resonance reduced the possibility to 1. By reasoning through the rules, DENDRAL was able to avoid considering millions of possibilities in deducing the structure of the molecule.[14]

DRAWBACKS TO EXPERT SYSTEMS

The major drawback to current expert systems is that they can only function in limited domains where accumulated experience can be easily translated into a knowledge base. For example, medical diagnostic expert systems have worked well because diagnostic skills are largely the result of accumulated experience with many cases in the field. These experiences can be described and translated into a knowledge base. Even so, expert systems are still no match for human experts, although DENDRAL is widely used by academic and industrial researchers because it can actually outperform a human chemist at one very specific task.

Another major problem with expert systems is their inability to handle novel or unique situations. Because of the complexity of building the knowledge base, general-purpose expert systems do not currently exist.

PROSPECTS FOR EXPERT SYSTEMS

Most optimists see a bright future for expert systems. They see expert systems applied in situations where there are a limited number of human experts in a field and where training people would be expensive and time consuming. Some people predict that expert systems will soon be used in organizations to disseminate to employees corporate information, such as office procedures, company policies, and employee review procedures. On the technical side, expert systems might be used for developing software and for designing very-large-scale integrated circuits. Also, expert systems are a focus of Japan's fifth-generation computer project in which expert systems are to be combined with a new advanced generation of computer hardware.

EXPERT SYSTEM SHELLS

Most companies that sell expert system software and consulting services offer versions of their expert system development packages that run on personal computers. An intermediate step between buying a ready-made expert system and building one from scratch is the *expert system shell*—a development environment that uses rules and examples as its input, but minimizes the need for programming. These shells combine knowledge, such as plans, goals, decision-making criteria, and values, with the ability to act on that knowledge, such as triggering a response or choosing a course of action. These application-style shells allow users to enter rules and data and build their own *decision support systems*.

For example, a manager might use such a shell to build a simple decision-support system to help prioritize a list of employees up for review. First, the manager lists the employees. Second, the manager assigns criteria for each category, such as salary level and job qualifications. Third, the manager weighs the alternatives, such as diversity of experience compared to length of employment. The program assigns numerical values to the criteria and alternatives and produces a recommended course of action.

Computer scientists would say that these are not true expert systems because they do not contain a formal knowledge base or an inference engine that can reason to a conclusion. Also, unlike true expert systems, decision-support software does not make decisions; it simply provides information to aid people in the decision-making process. But these programs do contain the ability to store and disseminate knowledge (i.e., the criteria, goals,

and values) that has been entered into the system, and are paving the way for a new generation of packaged application software for personal computers based on expert systems.

NEURAL NETWORKS

AI research is usually focused on attempts to develop software based on specific concepts that imitate specific mental qualities, such as expert systems. There are almost no efforts to develop a general humanlike intelligence that we would characterize as being a well-rounded human with a wide range of skills, knowledge, interests, and modes of thinking. In many cases, AI researchers are exploring intelligence and learning at the level of single-cell life forms and insects. Very advanced and ambitious research projects are attempting to develop systems that can take telephone calls from people and answer simple questions.

For example, a computer called a **neural network** has a memory that is modeled on the human brain. The memory of a neural-network computer consists of thousands of interconnected "neurons" that receive input from their neighboring neurons.

Expert systems. *Personal Consultant Plus—a personal computer-based expert system development tool—can use graphics to represent the questions in its knowledge base.*

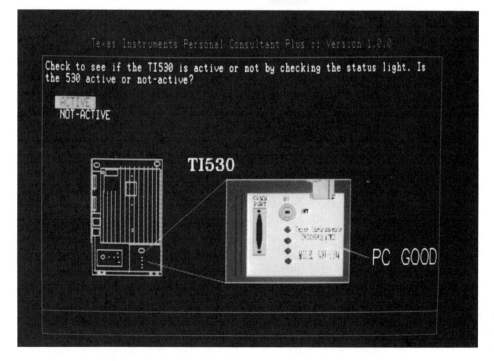

Expert systems. *Shown here is an expert system software toolkit for building expert systems.*

eventually prove to be a fruitful union. If neural networks are made of cooperating interconnected processors, each processor could function as a neuron, and the entire system of processors could function in parallel. The advantage of this scheme would be that a neural network application could be made to run extremely fast.

However, the analogy between the neural network and the human brain should not be carried too far. The largest parallel processing computers currently employ 65,536 processors. Scientists estimate that there are over 100 trillion individual connections between neurons in the brain. And scientists have not yet succeeded in mapping a single complex human neuron, let alone all of them.

NEURAL NETWORK APPLICATIONS

Neural networks may not be adept at certain kinds of intelligence based on formal reasoning, and they are no good at arithmetic, a task that conventional computers handle easily. But they do appear to be good at the kinds of pattern-recognition solutions needed to build the sensory input systems for certain kinds of intelligent machines.

For example, neural-network-based bomb detectors are being installed at major airports to screen baggage. The neural network is trained to recognize the characteristics of explosive material by identifying patterns of gamma-ray emissions. These bomb detectors eliminate the need for an operator to watch and listen to feedback from a scanning device.[15]

Neural networks have also been employed in process control applications. In an oil refinery, for example, a neural network was trained to help monitor temperature, pressure, and flows to help ensure product quality under fluctuating conditions. And on a loudspeaker assembly line, a neural network was trained to classify loudspeaker defects. Audible defects in the speakers had been detected by human operators, which introduced a great deal of subjectivity and human error into the testing. The neural network, in combination with audio-test software,

They can perform very simple processing based on patterns of input, and then produce results by sending their output back to neighboring neurons.

The neural network acts as a memory that continuously responds to simultaneous input in the form of a pattern, such as speech or visual information. The neurons can process information in parallel, and they can change their behavior based on previous input. This behavior interests researchers because it mimics learning. The neural network can get better at a task over time if, as a by-product of its processing, it receives feedback. For example, in the case of speech recognition, the neural net receives sound patterns as input and attempts to recognize them. The net will slowly remember patterns that it recognized correctly and forget patterns that are meaningless.

Today, neural networks simulate the interconnections of neurons on single-processor conventional computers. However, neural networks and parallel processing, the technology that was discussed in Chapter 7, may

solves the subjectivity of the testing by accurately classifying speaker defects.[16]

FUZZY SET AND LOGIC SYSTEMS

One area of experimental research combines expert system with neural networks into *fuzzy set* and *logic* systems. Fuzzy sets are sets in which objects do not exhibit a clear-cut yes-or-no condition. For example, the set of music a person likes is usually a fuzzy set. You may love rock music, tolerate jazz, and dislike classical music. But what do the words love, tolerate, and dislike mean? By arbitrarily assigning a number value to the members of the set (e.g., 0.8 for rock, 0.5 for jazz, 0.1 for classical), a fuzzy set establishes a gray-scale value for the set. While a detailed discussion of fuzzy logic is beyond the scope of this chapter, fuzzy systems are best for problems in which no distinct right or wrong answer exists or in which the opinions of people vary dramatically. For example, a fuzzy system might be useful for analyzing the complex problem of exploring the various impacts of human exploration of space on the U.S. economy.[17] Whereas an expert system would be very good at incorporating the knowledge of a single expert or a group of experts in a very specific problem domain, a fuzzy system could, in theory, be better at incorporating the knowledge of many different experts of varying believability and skills in different areas.

There is still debate whether computers will ever exhibit intelligence equivalent to that of a human being. Certainly, few would argue that computers are good at manipulating symbols and arithmetic, often exceeding human capabilities when solving specific problems in these areas. However, computers that can exhibit intuition, understanding, insight, or common sense are still far in the future.

REVIEW

Artificial intelligence is a research effort, but practical applications have appeared. The notion of thinking machines has been with us for decades, and the Turing test can be used as a conceptual tool for measuring a computer's ability to think. You saw that AI is being applied to theories about thinking. Computer games were the result of some early efforts in AI, and programs that could beat people at games became a routine development. Natural language processing was discussed: its primary application is in the development of user interfaces to database systems. One very practical development of AI is expert systems, and we explored what they are and how they work. Neural networks are computer systems modeled on the human brain. Their memory consists of thousands of interconnected neurons, and they are starting to be used for pattern-recognition tasks in applications that need a sensory input system to an intelligent machine.

REFERENCES

1. Evans, C. *The Micro-millennium*. New York: Pocket Books, 1979, p. 182. See Chapter 1, "Resources," for the description of this book.

2. Hofstadter, D. R. *Godel, Escher, Bach: An Eternal Golden Braid*. New York: Random House, 1980, p. 579. This book is not for the fainthearted; however, Chapters XVII and XIX contain much useful information on AI. Also, see pages 597-599 for a summary of the storm of opposition Turing expected and received.

3. Krutch, J. *Experiments in Artificial Intelligence for Small Computers*. Indianapolis, Ind.: Howard W. Sams & Co., 1981, pp. 89-90. This is an especially good book because it contains sample programs in BASIC that you can write and that enable you to experiment with artificial intelligence ideas.

4. Rochester, J., and J. Gantz. *The Naked Computer*. New York: William Morrow, 1983, pp. 300-301.

5. Huyghe, Patrick. "Of Two Minds." *Psychology Today*, December 1983, p. 28.

6. Kuhn, T. *The Structure of Scientific Revolutions*. Chicago, Ill.: University of Chicago Press, 1970, p. 12. A good but dense explanation of paradigm shifts and scientific revolutions.

7. Bernstein, Jeremy. *Three Degrees Above Zero*. New York: Scribner, 1984, p. 30. History buffs will find this book a particularly good overview of AT&T's Bell Laboratories.

8. McCarthy, J. "The Little Thoughts of Thinking Machines." *Psychology Today*, December 1983, p. 53.

9. Byrne, Robert W. "Chess-Playing Computer Closing in on Champions." *The New York Times*, September 26, 1989, p. B5.

10. Schonberg, Harold C. "Kasparov Beats Chess Computer (for Now)." *The New York Times*, October 23, 1989, p. 1.

11. Hofstadter, D.R. *Godel, Escher, Bach*. p. 628.

12. *Artificial Intelligence: Impact on the Office*. Boston, Mass.: The Yankee Group, 1984, p. 47.

13. Bolger, C. Jr. "Assessment of Artificial Intelligence: Development, Usage and Impact on Business." *Interface 1984 Proceedings*, New York: McGraw-Hill, 1984, p. 228.

14. Ham, M. "Playing by the Rules." *PC World*, January 1984, pp. 38-39.

15. Johnson, Colin. "Neural Nose to Sniff Out Explosives at JFK Airport." *Electronic Engineering Times*, May 1, 1989, p. 1.

16. Kestelyn, Justin. "Neural Networks Today." *AI Expert*, June 1990, p. 71.

17. Caudill, Maureen. "Using Neural Nets: Fuzzy Cognitive Maps." *AI Expert*, June 1990, pp. 49-53.

RESOURCES

BOOKS

Feigenbaum, E., and P. McCorduck. *The Fifth Generation*. Reading, Mass.: Addison-Wesley, 1983. This book explores the Japanese efforts to develop a fifth generation of supercomputers that incorporates new hardware and artificial intelligence software. A good overview of an emerging area.

Hayes-Roth, F., et al. *Building Expert Systems*. Reading, Mass.: Addison-Wesley, 1983.

Lewis, Cortland S. *Computerized Manufacturing Automation: Employment, Education, and the Workplace*. Washington, D.C.: U.S. Congress, Office of Technology Assessment, OTA-CIT-235, 1984. A good primer on automation and the work force, but like many government publications, packed with information that must be sorted and sifted through.

Minskey, Marvin, ed. *Robotics*. Garden City, N.Y.: Doubleday, 1985. A good starting point for a person who wants to know all about robots. Edited by one of the artificial intelligence pioneers.

Wright, Paul, and David Bourne. *Manufacturing Intelligence*. Reading, Mass.: Addison-Wesley, 1988. Whereas most academic books on artificial intelligence tend toward theory, the authors take us on a journey through a factory and describe problems of and practical applications for AI, robotics, and machine vision. This book bridges the gap between computer science and manufacturing.

MAGAZINES

AI Expert. Des Moines, Iowa: AI Expert. A monthly magazine devoted to the commercial and practical applications of artificial intelligence.

STUDY GUIDE

Match the following key terms to the appropriate definition:

A.

1. ____ Artificial intelligence (AI)
2. ____ Natural language processing
3. _K_ Expert system
4. ____ Knowledge base

5. ____ Heuristic methods
6. ____ Knowledge engineer
7. ____ Knowledge representation
8. _f_ Rule

9. ____ Inference engine
10. ____ Expert system shell
11. _c_ Neural network

a. The collection of facts, data, beliefs, assumptions, and heuristic methods about a problem area.

b. Programs that can understand and respond to commands that are given to them in a language like English.

c. The branch of computer science that attempts to understand the nature of intelligence and produce new classes of intelligent machines.

d. The formal method for representing facts and rules about the area under consideration.

e. A computer in which the memory is modeled on the human brain.

f. A statement about the relationships of various facts or data.

g. The reasoning mechanism of an expert system.

h. A development environment that uses rules and examples as its input, but eliminates the need for programming.

i. A systems designer who develops expert systems.

j. Exploratory methods for solving problems on an intelligent trial-and-error basis.

k. A computer program that solves specialized problems at the level of a human expert.

True/False:

12. ____ In artificial intelligence research, the computer is proving itself a valuable tool in simulating intelligent human behavior.

13. ____ Computers are now routinely passing the Turing test.

14. ____ Neural nets can perform very simple processing based on patterns of input.

15. ____ A combinatorial explosion occurs when the number of possibilities becomes too vast for a program to calculate in a reasonable amount of time.

16. ____ Chess-playing programs can consistently play chess at the master level.

17. ____ The earliest attempts at natural language processing involved research into language translation.

18. ____ A number of programs have been developed that exhibit an understanding of what is being typed at a keyboard.

19. ____ AI researchers are exploring intelligence and learning at the level of complex life forms.

20. ____ Scientists have succeeded in mapping complex human neurons.

21. ____ Neural networks are good at arithmetic.

22. ____ Developing an expert system requires that the knowledge engineer consult with a human expert.

23. ____ A rule is the formal method for representing facts and rules about the area under consideration.

24. ____ Expert systems work well in novel situations.

25. ____ Many general-purpose expert systems are now in use.

26. ____ Expert systems currently work like an advisor on various subjects.

Multiple Choice:

27. Psychologists and computer scientists feel that science has
   a. A good understanding of how the mind works.
   b. An almost complete understanding of how the mind works.
   c. Partial understanding of how the mind works.
   d. Very little understanding of how the mind works.

28. One of the first natural language systems was called

- **a.** Parry.
- **b.** SHRDLU.
- **c.** Belle.
- **d.** DENDRAL.

29. Which of the following does a natural language system not need to accomplish understanding?

- **a.** Syntax.
- **b.** Semantics.
- **c.** Grammar.
- **d.** Pragmatics.

30. Neural networks are good at

- **a.** Arithmetic
- **b.** Formal reasoning.
- **c.** Common sense.
- **d.** Pattern recognition.

31. Which of the following is a characteristic of today's computer systems?

- **a.** Arithmetic.
- **b.** Intuition.
- **c.** Understanding.
- **d.** Insight.

32. Scientists and researchers find neural networks interesting because they

- **a.** Solve problems at the level of a human expert.
- **b.** Can mimic learning.
- **c.** Are analogous to the human brain.
- **d.** Can perform complex processing tasks.

33. An expert system does not

- **a.** Solve problems at the level of a human expert.
- **b.** Contain expert knowledge about the subject under consideration.
- **c.** Require a knowledge base.
- **d.** Translate rules into another set of rules that are used in the knowledge base.

34. Which of the following is not a part of a typical knowledge base?

- **a.** Facts.
- **b.** Beliefs.
- **c.** Assumptions.
- **d.** Knowledge engineering.

35. Reasoning strategies are sometimes called

- **a.** A knowledge base.
- **b.** Rules.
- **c.** An inference engine.
- **d.** Facts and data.

36. A drawback to expert systems is their inability to

- **a.** Handle novel situations.
- **b.** Mimic a human expert.
- **c.** Store and disseminate knowledge.
- **d.** Be used by nonprogrammers.

Thought Questions:

37. What is your answer to the question: "Can machines really think?" Defend your answer.

38. How is a knowledge base different from a database?

Projects:

39. Every year a computer chess championship is held. Research magazines, newspapers, or books to find out the current winner and runners up, and write a paper comparing the various chess-playing programs.

40. Visit an organization in your area to find a use for expert systems. Prepare a report for your class.

SOFTWARE EXERCISES

For this exercise you are going to use your word processor to write an AI intelligence report that uncovers the opportunities and challenges of AI. Make sure your report addresses the following questions:

- How should a layperson go about exploring the possibilities for expert systems, natural language interfaces, or other AI technology?
- What special personnel, software, hardware, and other resources are needed?
- What has already been accomplished?

ANSWERS

1. c, **2.** b, **3.** k, **4.** a, **5.** j, **6.** i, **7.** d, **8.** f, **9.** g, **10.** h, **11.** e. **12.** T, **13.** F, **14.** T, **15.** T, **16.** T, **17.** T, **18.** T, **19.** F, **20.** F, **21.** F, **22.** T, **23.** F, **24.** F, **25.** F, **26.** F, **27.** d, **28.** b, **29.** c, **30.** d, **31.** a, **32.** b, **33.** d, **34.** d, **35.** c, **36.** a.

DEVELOPING

APPLICATIONS

PREVIEW

It is much easier to understand the capabilities and limitations of a computer application if you understand how it was developed. This section presents three interrelated perspectives on the process of developing computer applications.

Chapter 13 discusses the role of the systems analyst and describes a typical systems development life cycle, showing how developing computer systems consists of a systematic problem-solving effort.

Chapter 14 discusses the relationship of the computer programmer to his or her product—the computer application—and the evolving tools and techniques used to develop those applications.

Chapter 15 explores the continuum between traditional programming and newer application development alternatives and shows why particular choices among the alternatives are made. The chapter also discusses the diversity of end-user tools and explains some of the newer trends and tools in application design.

The major topics introduced in this section include

- The role of the MIS department.
- The systems life cycle.
- The definition phase.
- The design and development phase.
- The implementation phase.
- The evolution of software development.
- Structured program design.
- The phases of software development.
- Object-oriented programming.
- A comparison of COBOL, FORTRAN, BASIC, Pascal, C, and Ada.
- Alternatives to traditional programming.
- Macro languages.
- Program generators and database programming languages.
- Interface builders.
- Authoring systems.
- Object environments.

SANDRA KURTZIG

Profession: Founder, chairman, president, and Chief Executive Officer (CEO) of ASK Computer Systems, Inc., a supplier of information systems for manufacturing companies.

Profile: Kurtzig has an M.S. degree in aeronautical engineering from Stanford University. In 1972, she quit her job as a marketing specialist with General Electric and founded ASK at the age of 24. Her intent was to start a custom programming business in her home while raising a family. But the company took off, and she became the first woman to head a major high-technology concern. Today she is working on ASK's next generation of products, reviving the entrepreneurial climate in the company, and raising her teenage sons.

Quote: "When I started ASK, a woman heading a technology company wasn't the norm. Back then when I said I was in software, people thought I was selling lingerie."

CHAPTER 13

SYSTEMS ANALYSIS AND DESIGN

PREVIEW

Recall from Chapter 1 that a system is a set or arrangement of parts that act together to perform a function. Systems analysis is the study of systems in order to understand them better. In this chapter, systems analysis refers to the study of the real-world system that the computer system will attempt to automate or augment. However, you should keep in mind the fact that a computer is not always the solution to a problem.

Ideas for computer systems come from many places, but at the core of most ideas is the recognition that a system is not operating as effectively as possible. And, of course, a computer system may offer a solution.

This chapter explores a formal approach to the process of defining, designing, and implementing new computer systems. It concludes with an informal approach to the process of selecting a personal computer system.

In this chapter, you'll learn

- The role of the MIS department.
- The role of systems analysis.
- The phases of the systems life cycle.
- The definition phase of systems analysis.
- The design and development phase of systems analysis.
- The implementation phase of systems analysis.
- How to apply systems analysis techniques to selecting a personal computer system.

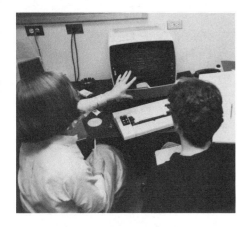

Programmer/analysts perform both programming and systems analysis.

Computer system analysts work in the MIS department and are concerned with the technical aspects of systems design.

THE MIS DEPARTMENT

Recall from Chapter 10 that an MIS department is composed of five functional units: an information center, an applications development group, a systems group, an operations group, and a technology planning group.

If an organization wants to computerize an existing manual system or develop a new system, it calls upon the services of the systems group and applications development group to define, design, and implement that system. For example, the systems group of a bank might work with the finance department to develop a system that lets customers have instant access to their accounts through automatic teller machines. Larger banks, like Citibank of New York, have used MIS to expand their customer base far beyond the geography of their home states.

The systems group of an MIS department has a staff that includes managers, programmers, and systems analysts.

THE ROLE OF SYSTEMS ANALYSIS

Systems analysis is the process of understanding a user's needs and, from those needs, deriving the functional requirements of a system. The role of the systems analyst is that of a problem solver who can start with complex problems and break them into reasonable solutions. He or she does this by talking to the user and discovering what the user wants and needs. Then, the systems analyst expresses those needs in well-organized terms so that an appropriate computer system can be developed.

In small- and medium-sized organizations, one person may perform the functions of systems analysis and programming; this person is called a *programmer/analyst.*

In large organizations, the tasks of systems analysis are often divided into specialized jobs handled by *computer systems analysts*—persons assigned to the MIS department who are concerned with the technical aspects of system design—and by *business systems analysts*—persons assigned to

an organizational department other than the MIS department.

Business systems analysts, often called user analysts, act as contacts between their department and an MIS department. Because of their familiarity with the department, business systems analysts can identify problems and opportunities more quickly to improve the effectiveness of existing systems. Usually, they can define functional requirements in practical user-oriented terms. In such situations, computer systems analysts, often called data processing analysts, limit the scope of their activities to the technical design of a system that will meet the requirements specified by business systems analysts.

THE PROCESS OF SYSTEMS ANALYSIS

Systems analysts must approach problems using a problem-solving process that contains several useful principles. The first principle is a *top-down approach,* starting with the whole problem and developing more and more detail as the solution evolves. The second is a *life-cycle approach,* proceeding from definition to design and development to implementation and the eventual retirement and replacement of a system. Third, many of the important and creative decisions occur early in the definition and design stages of the life cycle. Fourth, because the approach is a *process,* it consists of a systematic series of actions directed toward a goal.

THE SYSTEMS LIFE CYCLE

Although MIS professionals such as systems analysts agree on using a phased approach to describe the systems life cycle, there is considerably less agreement on what the phases are, how they are described, and how they are applied. To introduce the concept of a phased approach in which each phase has a starting and ending point, the systems life cycle will be viewed as having three broad phases:

- Definition.
- Design and development.
- Implementation.

Each phase is made up of systems analysis tasks that involve several activities. The phases will be discussed in sequence, but keep in mind that these activities proceed in an iterative cycle; that is, they are often done over and over again. For example, suppose a systems analyst is in the early stages of the design phase and, through questioning the user, discovers new information that sheds light on a problem. The analyst should go back to the definition phase and incorporate that information into the requirements.

PHASE I: DEFINITION

In this chapter, problems will be viewed as unmet needs. Thus they can be seen as opportunities to develop new and better methods, procedures, and, if appropriate, computer systems. The definition phase should be used to examine all aspects of the problem and to come up with a definition of the problem. The scope of a problem definition varies. In an informal setting, simply specifying business application requirements is often sufficient. In a formal setting, the product of the definition phase is a *functional specification*—a precise description of the functional requirements of a computer system.

The definition phase can be viewed as a series of steps that consist of

- Getting to know the application.
- Deciding whether a computer system can meet the application's requirements, and how it will do so.
- Defining processing requirements, constraints, costs, and benefits.
- Developing functional specifications and prototypes.
- Reviewing the specifications and prototypes.

In some instances, the steps leading up to the functional specification and evaluation might be quite informal. In these cases, the systems analyst uses the simple techniques of questioning and comparison. By asking questions, the analyst can consult references that have already addressed the problem

or can talk to people with more experience in the problem area under consideration. By making comparisons, the analyst will be able to recognize and isolate those parts of the problem that are familiar.

In other instances, as in a large organization where many projects are in competition for management's attention, more formal analytical techniques, such as feasibility studies, top-down design, and structured analysis, are required. A good rule of thumb is: The more people that need to interact in the decision-making process, the more formal the analysis and specification of the functional requirements will have to be. One important aspect of functional specifications is their value as a communication tool between various people in an organization.

REQUIREMENTS ANALYSIS

The first questions a businessperson, such as the manager of a department, should consider are: "What needs to be done better in my business?" and "Will a computer help?" Of course, that person might have a difficult time answering those questions exactly. And there are cases where managers introduce computers into their departments without understanding their applications. For example, suppose a small firm does not have a working manual accounting system but contracts the job to an accounting service because no one in the firm really understands accounting. In this case, a computerized accounting system might be difficult to implement or, worse yet, might create new problems.

However, thinking about a new computer system is an ideal opportunity for businesspeople to reexamine their business and the manner in which it is operated. The starting point for the requirements analysis is a review of the potential applications. A review of the application areas covered in Chapter 2 will give you an overview of these areas.

Making a requirements list of your applications can be done in a simple, nontechnical way. First, make a list of potential applications. Then, write a description of each application and decide whether it can justify needing a computer system. Also, include in the

Business systems analysts work in various departments throughout an organization.

The systems life cycle, as defined in this chapter, proceeds through a series of systematic phases, but it is also iterative so that revisions or changes become a natural part of the process.

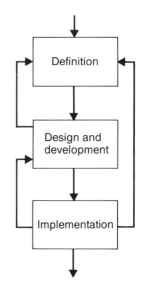

description how much time will be spent using the application. When people begin to describe their applications, it becomes easier to picture more concrete uses and functions for computer systems. The descriptions will serve as guidelines in later phases of the life cycle.

For example, let us examine the case of two secretaries: one is an executive secretary for the president of a firm and the other is a legal secretary for a law firm. The executive secretary is primarily interested in a word processing application to handle business correspondence, which consists of letters, memos, and brief proposals that flow through the office. The secretary will use word processing on a daily basis, but only for brief periods during the day. As the secretary begins to describe the applications, he finds out that most of the documents are under three pages and that a word processing package that is easy to learn and use will satisfy most of his needs.

On the other hand, the law firm's secretary needs a word processing application to process the legal contracts and other documents that flow through the law firm's office. In this case, the documents are lengthy, contain numerous footnotes, and require extensive revisions. The word processor plays a central role in this secretary's work, and it is used extensively. The simple, easily learned word processing software might suffice for the executive secretary, but the legal secretary needs word processing software geared to the legal profession that may be harder to learn but, in the long run, will be a more effective tool.

The requirements analysis is important because it will play a major role in determining the design of specific soft-

Field Name	Field Length	Field Type
Part number	10	Numeric
Part description	30	Text
Manufacturer	40	Text
Quantity in stock	6	Numeric
Unit price	6	Numeric
Reorder point	6	Numeric
Units of Issue	2	Text
Total	100	

Requirements planning. Sample logical-record layout and size calculations.

ware and hardware systems.

Often, systems analysts in medium- and large-scale organizations must use an existing system on which they base their requirements analysis. In this case, gaining an understanding of the existing system can be viewed as a *background study* that is a preliminary phase to the definition phase. A systems analyst would analyze an existing system and produce a written document that would identify the following:

- Exactly what the system is doing.
- What it is doing well.
- What it is doing poorly or not at all.

Once the analyst understands the existing system, he or she can develop a detailed functional specification in which problems and opportunities to improve effectiveness are identified and communicated to others. The analyst should always examine the existing system to see if needs can be met without a new system.

Another task in the background study is to collect information about alternative solutions and their feasibility. The systems analyst works with users to analyze the alternatives. In this case, the goal of the background study is to

- Identify and prioritize system-related problems and costs.
- Identify opportunities for improvement.
- Produce a functional specification.

In many cases a system must be designed to fill a need that did not exist beforehand. New computer systems are often technology driven, that is, as a technology becomes feasible to implement, it presents new business opportunities. For example, the automatic teller machines (ATMs) that were described in Chapter 3 presented the banking industry with a new opportunity. In that case, the process did not start with a request from a user, but as an opportunity created by new computer software and hardware.

The requirements analysis should answer such questions as:

- What is the problem?
- Will a computer help?

- What is the system required to do?
- What are some preliminary approaches to the problem?

After initial analysis, you should study the requirements, make sure you understand them, and then proceed to more specific planning.

REQUIREMENTS PLANNING

In the definition stage, *requirements planning* is a broad term that includes planning for outputs, inputs, and file/storage and processing requirements. Requirements planning also includes specifying any constraints and the costs and benefits associated with the system.

Sometimes the outputs are defined by the needs of the people using the system; other times the outputs are input to another system.

Output Requirements

Planning for output requirements answers some of the following questions:

- Who is the output for and why?
- What specific types of outputs are needed?
- What is included in the output?

For example, assume the systems analyst has an existing accounting system against which he or she can compare the output requirements of the computerized accounting system and estimate the output needs. The analyst knows the department will need financial reports (e.g., daily sales or current receivables) required for the day-to-day operation of the business as well as statements for government agencies (e.g., the IRS) and for the bank.

Each output, regardless of form, is broken down into a list of data elements or fields. For example, a customer invoice might contain an invoice number; invoice date; customer number, name, and address; product number; quantity ordered; unit price; extended-line-item total (i.e., quantity ordered multiplied by unit price); the sum of the line-item totals; tax; and the total invoice amount.

Each field of an output report or display is then evaluated in terms of its origin, or where it will come from when the output is produced. There are three points from which the fields can originate: (1) from an input file or from a person entering the data, (2) from a previously defined file, or (3) from a computation during processing, as in the case of the line-item and final totals.

Once the output fields have been identified and classified as to origin, they are grouped to form logical records. For example, a collection of fields pertaining to an inventory-control system might be grouped into a logical record as follows: part number, part description, manufacturer, quantity in stock, unit price, reorder point (i.e., the point at which quantity in stock is low enough so that more parts should be ordered), and unit of issue (e.g., each, dozen, gross, case).

Input Requirements

Inputs are the raw material of the proposed system. The requirements should include the amount of data and timing. For example, suppose that the input to a proposed accounting system consists of data that are entered at a keyboard. Requirements planning should answer such questions as

Requirements planning. A sample form for calculating the total time to process input transactions.

Day of Month	Average Daily Number of Transactions (checks received)	Time per Transaction (minutes)	Total Time Requirements (rounded up hours)
1	120	7	14
2	100	7	12
3	115	7	13
4	100	7	12
5	50	7	6
6	40	7	5
7	30	7	4
8	30	7	4
9	20	7	3

- How long does it take to enter a transaction?
- How many transactions are handled daily by the system?
- Are there any peaks and valleys?

By asking questions, a systems analyst estimates the total work flow for the system by estimating the number of transactions needed daily. He or she also discovers that early in the month, the volume of transactions (the number of checks received) goes up considerably. On the basis of that estimate, the analyst discovers that the job of entering data into the system would take 15 hours a day. The analyst must then decide if operating the system for two 8-hour shifts per day is viable or if the capacity of the system must be increased so that the data can be entered in less time.

File and Storage Requirements

Once the output and input requirements have been estimated, the files and storage requirements must be defined. The first thing that the systems analyst needs to consider is the volume of data—including projected growth—to be stored. For purposes of planning, the analyst should determine the following:

- The program and data files that are to be stored on disk
- The size of the data files
- Estimated expansion, or the growth factor during the life cycle of the system
- The accessibility of the programs and data for processing (e.g., is the

system batch or on-line)
- Backup requirements

In most instances, the structure of the file or files must be defined. To do this, the logical records and the file organization must be defined. And, finally, the methods of entering, deleting, and updating logical records must be considered.

Processing Requirements

Processing requirements are determined once the essential outputs, inputs, and file/storage requirements have been estimated. One method that has gained popularity is called the data-flow method. The steps in the data-flow method are (1) data-flow diagram, (2) data dictionary, (3) structure charts, (4) pseudocode, and (5) structured program code. The last three steps apply to individual program design and will be discussed in Chapter 14.

A *data-flow diagram* consists of a series of blocks connected by flow lines. Each block represents a process or a transformation of data in the system, such as an update or the production of a report. The flow lines are labeled with the data that are flowing between processes. Once an overall data-flow diagram has been developed, the analyst then checks to see where the center of the diagram is. All processes that flow into the center are related to the input part of the system. The center of the system becomes the top level of a structure chart that will be developed from the data-flow diagram and used to isolate individual programs.

A *data dictionary* is simply a listing of all the data elements and data structures within the system along with the data attributes, such as field length and type. The data dictionary is sorted into alphabetical order to provide a master index and specific information about all the data elements and data structures in the system.

Constraints are a necessary part of requirements analysis and planning. An important task of systems analysis is to discover the constraints as early as possible so that the proposed system

Requirements planning. A sample form for calculating disk storage requirements.

File	Average Characters per Record	Number of Records	Growth in One Year	Total Bytes Required
Customer list	100	1000	+15%	110,000
Accounts receivable	150	1000	+25%	187,500
Accounts payable	130	1000	+25%	162,500
• • •	• • •	• • •	• • •	• • •

has a chance of success. Some specific examples of constraints are

- A budget limit of $10,000.
- Training people who have never before worked with a computer.
- Enhancing a system that must remain compatible with the existing system and files.

An estimate of costs and benefits should be included as a part of any plan. An organization considers a computerized system because it benefits the organization (1) by improving productivity or profit margins or (2) by providing the capability to handle new business. Both should result in increased profits. When the benefits are tangible, they can be calculated. For example, productivity is output divided by input. If two (2) secretaries produce 40 memos per day with a typewriter, the output (40) is divided by the input (2) to yield 20 memos per day. If the same two secretaries can produce 60 memos per day with a word processing system, then their productivity has increased by 50 percent. However, the benefits of a computerized system are not always so tangible, and coming up with hard numbers is often quite difficult. For example, how much is it worth to have a computer system respond to customer inquiries within an hour instead of within a day?

The costs of a new system are often estimated and compared to those of the old system to determine the estimated development costs. For example, suppose that a new system is estimated to cost $20,000 to develop. Also, it is estimated that an existing system costs $10,000 per year to operate and a new system will cost $5000 per year to operate. The development cost of the system can be divided by the yearly savings ($20,000/$5000) to show that the new system will pay for itself (the payback period) in four years.

FUNCTIONAL SPECIFICATIONS

The formal output of the requirements analysis and planning step is often called a functional specification. It is a technical report prepared for the system designers, often titled "Specification of Requirements for _____" or simply "Functional Specifications for _____." The report contains an overall picture of the proposed system in terms of the requirements of and the constraints imposed on the system solution. The requirements provide the guidelines on which the systems design process will proceed.

In large organizations, the completed functional specification is presented to the organization's management in the form of a written proposal. The functional specification provides management with sufficient information to make a decision about approving the new system for development, approving some portion of the system for development, or leaving the existing system alone. Ideally, the information presented to management should

- Define the existing problems and present opportunities for improvement.
- State the scope and objectives of the new system.
- State the total cost of the new system.
- Describe the new system requirements.
- Compare projected alternative solutions, including anticipated costs and benefits.

EVALUATION

The definition phase is not complete when a functional specification is developed. The final step in the process is the evaluation and challenge of the specifications. Systems analysts are not always the best people to evaluate their own specifications. The user is the first good source for evaluating the functional specifications because he or she will challenge any wrong assumptions that have been specified. Review is often accomplished by a peer review, called a *structured walkthrough,* in which the proposed specifications are presented to other analysts, programmers, or system developers for feedback, comments, and criticism.

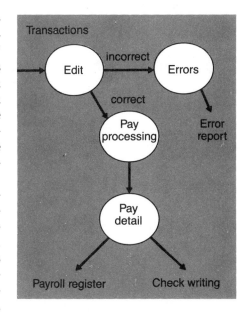

Data-flow diagram. *The technique of data-flow diagramming is informal and does not require any predefined symbols, as does flowcharting.*

PHASE II: DESIGN AND DEVELOPMENT

The design process for a new system begins after the requirements have been defined and the proposed system has been evaluated and approved. The functional specification, whether informal or formal, serves as the starting point for the design and development phase. Although guidelines have been established, no specific design decisions should be made in the definition phase. At this point, it is up to the person who is performing the systems analysis tasks to perform the following design tasks:

- Match software to the requirements.
- Match hardware in the appropriate price range with the software needs.
- Consider the technical features of the computer system.
- Consider the source (i.e., computer store, dealer, direct mail, or the follow-up service).

ALTERNATIVES TO PROGRAMMING

The analyst performing the design and development phase should determine if software already exists to solve the problem called for in the functional specification. When evaluating application software, a rule of thumb to consider is the following: Either the requirements will have to adapt to fit the package or the package will have to be adapted to meet the requirements.

With this in mind, there are several options that should be pursued when evaluating software. (1) Investigate special-purpose application software. Often, this kind of software is already custom-tailored to the proposed application. (2) Investigate general-purpose software, for example, a database management program. Such software can often be easily tailored to meet the functional specifications. (3) Consider developing the software from scratch, in other words, writing specific programs to accomplish the tasks.

A software package that meets the requirements of the functional specification offers several advantages. First,

a new system can be acquired and implemented much faster than developing one from scratch. Second, given the high cost usually associated with software development, buying software may be the most economical choice.

One must identify how closely each potential software package comes to meeting input, storage, processing, and output requirements. Areas where requirements differ from package capabilities must be evaluated in terms of the importance of the differences and the ability (including cost) to modify the package to meet the requirements.

PROTOTYPING

Software development will be discussed in detail in Chapter 14. From a systems design point of view, the process of developing software has traditionally required a programming staff qualified in writing high-level language programs. There is, however, one technique that is gaining popularity among system designers that is preliminary to software development. *Prototyping*—the process of building working models of system inputs, outputs, and files—is often used to speed up the design process. With a prototype of the system, users can gain hands-on working experience with the model and more quickly evaluate the ability of the system to meet their needs. Advocates of prototyping claim that giving the user a live demonstration of how the system looks and works is better than giving the user a functional specification to evaluate. A prototype may be used as a simple demonstration, or it may be possible to continue refining the prototype until it becomes the actual system.

DOCUMENTATION TECHNIQUES

At the completion of the design process, a comprehensive package of documentation is assembled. It is important to note that the system documentation is assembled at this time—not created! Detail documentation of the system should be created during each phase of the design process. The package should contain a clear description of every facet of the new system in sufficient detail to support its development, including these aspects:

- Examples of output.
- Descriptions and record layouts of each file.
- Data-flow diagrams.
- A data dictionary.
- Identification of individual programs.

A *design review* is the process of carefully reexamining the proposed design with the intended users and other systems analyst and programming professionals. It is similar to the review of the requirements and specifications mentioned earlier in the chapter. This is the point at which it is necessary to obtain final user approval to develop the system exactly as designed. If this review is not carried out carefully, there is a possibility that the system will not meet the needs of its users. This can lead to dissatisfaction and may require that portions of the system be redesigned and redeveloped.

High-level documentation provides a picture of the overall structure of the system, including input, processing, storage, and output. The general flow of information throughout the major processes of the system can be depicted in either a data-flow diagram or a systems flowchart. In addition, structure charts, which will be discussed in Chapter 14, should be used for individual programs.

The purpose of *detail documentation* is to provide a programmer with sufficient information to write the program. The documentation should include report layouts for input and output, record layouts that define the files, and structure charts that define the relationship among the components of the programs.

COMPUTER-AIDED SOFTWARE ENGINEERING

Computer-aided software engineering (CASE) is a set of tools to automate the tasks involved in designing and developing large-scale or complex software projects. Software engineering will be

defined and discussed in detail in Chapter 14. However, systems analysts often use CASE to apply the computer to the tasks of defining, designing, and developing software. The basic components of a CASE system are

A *data dictionary* to store all the information relevant to the software project.

Diagram generators for creating flowcharts and data-flow diagrams that use the data dictionary to coordinate input, output, and processing requirements and automate the process of designing these diagrams.

Prototyping tools that generate demonstration versions of the application early in the life cycle.

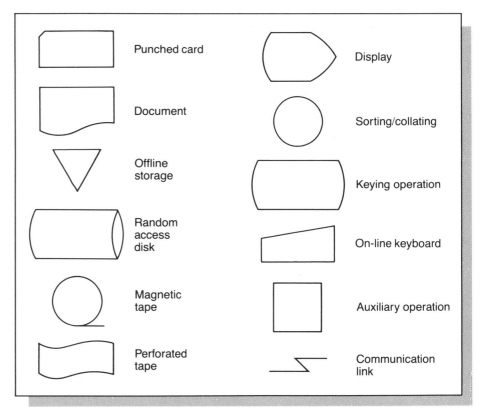

Documentation. *System flowchart symbols.*

Documentation. *Structure diagram of a sales system.*

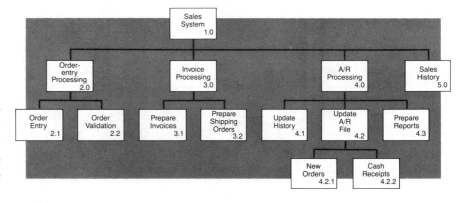

Consistency checking tools that make sure that the design is consistent with the specifications and code is consistent with the design.

Used together, these CASE tools can provide a complete development environment that can span the entire application development life cycle.

PHASE III: IMPLEMENTATION

The purpose of the implementation phase is to install the computer system and make it operational. This involves physically installing the system, testing the system, documentation and training, conversion, and evaluating the performance of the system. Keep in mind that the larger the system, the more rigorous the implementation phase. Implementing a personal computer-based system usually requires far less testing, training, and evaluation than does a mainframe-based system.

Computer-aided software engineering. CASE tools, such as Excelerator, allow analysts to interactively create data-flow diagrams.

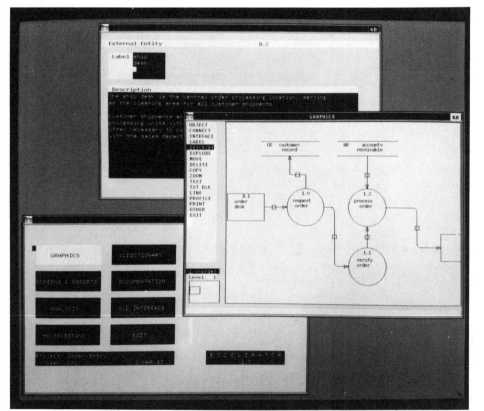

INSTALLATION

Installation involves preparing the site for the arrival of the hardware. Factors such as space for the computer systems, storage space for additional supplies, special power, and cabling and telephone jacks must be considered.

TESTING

Initial testing consists of **user diagnostics**—a series of test programs designed to determine where problems might exist in the hardware. When a computer is first installed, the user, the analyst, or the vendor should make sure that there are no physical problems by running the diagnostic tests.

In testing the new system (i.e., the application programs), the following activities should be completed:

• All programs must be tested, both individually and in their related groups.
• Technical documentation and user operating procedures must be completed.
• All personnel involved in the day-to-day operation of the system must be trained in their individual job-related procedures.

After all the prerequisite activities have been completed, the system's testing phase can begin. This phase requires a cooperative effort among user personnel, systems analysts, and the technical staff. Together, they design a comprehensive test of all facets of the new system. A base of test data is prepared and the expected results from processing are determined. The systems test is then conducted, and the results of the test are evaluated to determine if they are correct. If problems are detected, they must be identified and corrected. The systems test allows the users a final opportunity to walk through their new system's operating procedures.

USER DOCUMENTATION AND TRAINING

After the systems design and development phase is completed, the final technical and user documentation is assembled. The technical documentation will be used for maintaining the system once it is in operation. It also serves as a basis for planning any new system enhancements. The user documentation is used to train personnel who must be able to perform system-related input, processing, and output procedures. It is important for each individual to understand what to do, when to do it, how to do it, and where to do it.

Training can be accomplished in several ways. One way is to simply spend time with the system, read the documentation, and experiment with the software features. Another help is to join a user group in your local area, where you will meet people who have purchased similar systems and who are willing to discuss problems and swap software. Learning through a tutorial is still another approach. Today, most major programs include a tutorial as a part of the package.

CONVERSION

Implementing a new system often involves *conversion*—the process of changing from one method of operation to another or from one computer system to another. The planning for this phase involves two distinct steps. The first is to plan and carry out the initialization of all computer-based files in the new system. Some files may need to be created from scratch; others may be constructed by importing data currently stored in the system's files. The second step involves planning the start-up of the new system.

There are four basic approaches to the conversion. (1) The *direct conversion method:* The old system is simply stopped and the new system is started up in its place immediately. (2) The *parallel conversion method:* The organization operates both the old system and the new system in parallel until it is clear that no operating problems are occurring in the new system. (3) The *pilot test conversion method:* One or two key units are converted first and are allowed to operate for a period of a few weeks to a month. After this shakedown period, in which problems are identified and solved and implementation procedures are refined, the rest of the organization is converted to the new system. (4) The *modular conversion method:* The system is divided into modules. Once a module is converted and running smoothly, then the next module is converted. For example, in a project in which a complete financial accounting system is to be implemented, selected portions (e.g., the accounts payable portion of a total accounting system) are converted one at a time.

EVALUATING PERFORMANCE

After the system has been installed, the analyst should keep in touch with those who are using the system. The purpose of this is to uncover any problems with the hardware, the software, the operating procedures, or the training. Also, a postimplementation study is often undertaken from three to six months after the new system is installed. This gives the users a chance to become familiar and comfortable with the new system before the analyst evaluates the impact of the system and assesses the need for any changes.

A CASE STUDY: SELECTING A PERSONAL COMPUTER SYSTEM

A systematic problem-solving process, similar to the one that the systems analyst uses, is a useful technique for any person who is contemplating the purchase of a computer system.

This section will explore some factors that potential users should consider when trying to decide how to select a personal computer system. When combined with the chapter's sections on systems analysis, it provides a complete guide to selecting a personal computer system. As a stand-alone section, it provides a useful overview for potential purchasers. Consider the following scenario.

Daryl Duemore, a businessperson, is concerned about financial planning for his small business. Most of Mr. Duemore's competitors have computers, and it seems that today everyone has a small business computer in his or

Ready-made programs, *such as Paradox (a database management program), can often be tailored to create custom applications.*

Selecting software. *Sample software evaluation checklist.*

Criteria	Package 1	Package 2	Package 3
User interface			
Ease of use			
Help screens			
Entering data			
Editing data			
Prompts			
Error messages			
Consistency			
Ease of installation			
Instructions			
Making back-up copies			
Hard-disk capabilities			
Performance			
Maximum records			
Printer support			
Recovery from errors			
Documentation			
Index			
Technical appendix			
Commands			
Error messages			
Ease of learning			
Examples			
Tutorial disk			
Illustrations			
Support			
Availability			
Cost			
Rating: 4 = A, 3 = B, 2 = C, 1 = D, 0 =F.			

salesperson is correct in suggesting a personal computer, what should Daryl Duemore do?

SELECTING SOFTWARE

The process of selecting software proceeds as follows:

- Gather information (including price) about available packages.
- Narrow the field by rejecting unsuitable packages.
- Evaluate and compare the remaining packages.
- Talk to other users.
- Conduct a hands-on test.

When matching software to your application needs, a useful technique involves making lists of questions and answers to organize your evaluation. For purposes of narrowing our presentation, the following discussion assumes you have completed the preceding four steps and are ready to conduct hands-on testing. It offers a set of preliminary guidelines that can get you started when conducting hands-on evaluations. You should supplement these guidelines with specific questions regarding the proposed application.

User Interface

Two programs with identical capabilities may present themselves to the user in very different ways. For example, one may be graphically oriented and present pull-down menus of commands and explanations. Another may be command driven and simply assume that you know or have access to the available commands.

Ease of use is an important part of evaluating the user interface. Even when software is complex, the ease with which you can begin using the software and the number of things you can accomplish without having to look in the manual are a good indicator of a program's ease of use. Do help screens exist in the program? Do they actually provide specific information? How easy is it to enter and edit data? Does the software prompt you in a clear and consistent manner? Does the software provide error messages when you enter the wrong data (e.g., entering al-

her office. Armed with an advertisement that describes a new powerful personal computer system, Mr. Duemore visits a local computer store. The salesperson suggests that with the right spreadsheet, purchasing the personal computer is the solution to Mr. Duemore's problems. Assuming that

phabetic data into a numeric field)? How does the software present the error messages (e.g., "Sorry, the disk is full, please insert a blank formatted disk" versus "Disk Error 217")? Is the software consistent (i.e., Does it always present you with similar choices no matter what part of the program you are in)? Is it easy to modify the application once created? For example, suppose you invested a great deal of time and energy designing and creating a file for a packaged database management program. Later, it is discovered that an additional field needs to be inserted into the file. Can the program in question handle that modification?

Ease of Installation

An important evaluation step is to test the installation of the software. A software package that is already running on a demonstration computer does not tell you how difficult it is to take it out of the package and get it up and running on your own computer. Is it difficult or impossible to make backup copies? Can it be installed on a hard disk? Follow the installation procedure. This will give you the first clue to how well the software's user interface and documentation have been designed.

Performance

Test the software under maximum conditions. For example, if you plan to implement a system that requires 1000 records on disk, make sure that the software can support that many records; then, test the system with 1000 records. A demonstration program that is processing 10 or 15 sample records may perform quite differently from a program that is processing 1000 records. Also, consider the equipment on which you are performing the test. For example, are you testing the program with a hard disk and/or a RAM disk? These devices can make a program run much faster; if you are not aware that they are being used, you may be in for a surprise when you run the program under different conditions. Always test the software's ability to print something. Observe how the software handles the printing func-

tion and whether it is capable of implementing any special features, such as different type styles and sizes, boldfacing, or underlining.

When testing software, try to make the program fail or crash; then, observe how it allows you to recover. Some tests you can use are (1) see what happens when you remove a disk before issuing a command to read or write from that disk, (2) try to print a sample report when the printer is not turned on or connected, and (3) deliberately press the wrong key when you are asked to press another. Does the program inform you of the mistakes and suggest a correction, or does it simply stop working and require you to restart the system?

Documentation

The quality and style of the printed manuals show how much thought (and money) was put into the product. Good documentation achieves two different, and often conflicting, goals: (1) it must inform and serve as an easy reference guide, and (2) it must teach the fundamentals of how to use the program.

Evaluate the documentation's usefulness as a reference manual. Does it have an index? How comprehensive and well organized is the index? Does it contain technical appendixes? Does it contain a separate alphabetic listing

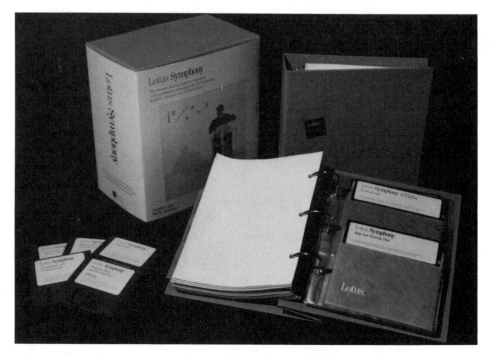

Documentation. *Evaluate the documentation of a program as a reference guide and as a teaching tool.*

of the commands and their functions? Does it explain error messages?

Evaluate the documentation as a teaching tool. Is it possible to read through the manual to pick up the basics first and then to learn the more complex functions? Are there examples? Is the documentation accompanied by a tutorial disk? Does the documentation have disks with sample files? Does the documentation contain illustrations or screen shots? Effective documentation minimizes the need for lengthy instructions, and it answers your questions while you learn to use the software.

Compatibility

Does the software integrate with other applications? Does the ability exist to transfer data to and from other programs? For example, a user has an existing database application running under a program called dBase III and wishes to convert the files to run under a different database program called Paradox. Does the program have utilities or functions that can import the data? If not, the user will have to enter the data by hand.

Support

It is important to establish a clear understanding of what the dealer and the vendor will do for you if you buy a software package. Find out how much initial instruction will be provided. Will the dealer answer your questions after you begin to use the program, or is that covered under a separately priced training package? Talk to other people who have bought from the dealer in question.

Does the software vendor support the product? Good vendors have clearly stated policies that cover replacing damaged disks, updating the software, providing existing users with free or discounted upgrades, and customer-support telephone hot lines.

Price

The price range of personal computer software can vary enormously. Higher-priced packages can cost more than $1000. Lower-priced packages (under $100) may appear to be the better bargain, but this is not necessarily so. In a detailed evaluation of two or more packages, you may want to make a list of essential features and then derive a feature-price ratio with which to compare the packages.

It is probably best to evaluate the software independently of the hardware because a good or popular software package is available for a wide variety of computers. Evaluate the software in terms of how it can meet specific needs. The more you know exactly what it is you want to do, the better you will be able to find the right software.

Operating System

The operating system plays a key role in how the system will work. The most popular personal computer operating system is MS-DOS. Also, Unix, originally developed for minicomputers, is available on 16- and 32-bit personal computer systems. Some computers (e.g., those in the Apple Macintosh family) are sold with their own proprietary operating systems. With the exception of Apple, such computers are generally limited in the kind of software that can or will be developed for them. Most large software developers write programs for MS-DOS, OS/2, and the Macintosh.

SELECTING HARDWARE

Matching hardware in the appropriate

Shopping for software and hardware. Many computer stores focus on the small business customer and provide a wide variety of training and consulting services.

price range to your software needs can be a difficult task. For purposes of narrowing this presentation, the following discussion will highlight some of the technical differences found among various personal computer hardware components. Don't forget that price is an important consideration too.

There are many technical differences among personal computer systems. You should be aware of some of these technical factors because there are no ready-made personal computer solutions that will satisfy all requirements. The design of individual personal computers is influenced by a number of factors.

Processor

The term processor refers to the particular brand of microprocessor chip (CPU) that is found at the heart of every personal computer. A common selling feature is word size—the number of bits that the CPU operates on at one time. For example, a salesperson may state that brand X computer has a 32-bit processor, implying that it is better or faster than brand Y computer with a 16-bit processor. This can be misleading, because you should look at the total system, not simply the processing power of a particular CPU. A faster processor will not necessarily decrease the total time it takes to access and process 1000 records on a disk. Also, you should be aware that software designed to run on one processor will generally be incompatible with other processors.

Memory Capacity

A very important advantage of the 16- and 32-bit personal computers is the greatly expanded memory capacity that they offer. However, early generations of operating system and application software are unable to take advantage of large memory. Expanded memory is available that can boost a computer's memory capacity, but its use is limited by the technique called bank switching. Operating systems, such as OS/2 and Unix, are designed specifically to use larger memory.

Display Capability

Smaller, less expensive personal computers require that you connect them to an ordinary TV receiver or CRT display. Some can even display high-quality color images. The laptop computers come with their own built-in LCD displays. The home, transportable, and desktop computers have more display options. If you have an application that primarily involves the display of text, such as word processing, and some business applications, a monochrome monitor is acceptable. Other applications (e.g., business graphics and educational games) can benefit from a color display. The internal component that determines what the output will look like is the graphics adapter. Generally, you want to find out whether the system has a monochrome adapter, a color adapter, or both. When the monitor is sold as a separate component, matching the monitor to the system becomes more expensive as the color quality increases.

Keyboard

A good keyboard is as essential as a good monitor. Detachable keyboards offer the greatest flexibility. In addition, a good keyboard should give you either tactile or audible feedback when you press the keys. There are many arguments in favor of a standard keyboard. Although most keyboards use the QWERTY design for the alphanumeric portion of the keyboard, the control keys and function keys occupy different positions depending on the manufacturer. Devices that complement the keyboard, such as mice and touch screens, are becoming very popular.

Mass Storage

Disks are the most common, versatile, and flexible mass-storage devices. Although the size and media have been standardized, data recorded under one operating system or program are generally incompatible with data recorded under another operating system or program. For example, if you have existing data on a Macintosh $3\frac{1}{2}$-

inch disk and you want to transfer it to an IBM PS/2 $3\frac{1}{2}$-inch disk, you have to find a program that can perform the conversion. Also, the capacity of the same $3\frac{1}{2}$-inch floppy disk will vary depending on the operating system's capabilities. Winchester disks are starting to be built into the more expensive personal computers; they offer far more storage capacity (typically 20 to 80 megabytes) than floppies. Winchester disks are a good choice when either data for an application are going to require a large file or fast access to data is a requirement. The size of files should be a part of your requirements and needs analysis.

SHOPPING

There are several places to shop for software and hardware. If you are a first-time purchaser or you want the personal touch of a salesperson, shop at one of the many computer specialty stores, such as Computerland, Businessland, or Sears Business Centers. Office products dealers might carry systems, and Tandy (Radio Shack and Grid Systems) operates its own chain of product centers. If you are reasonably sure about what you want, you can buy either direct from some companies or through mail-order outlets. Not all companies, however, will sell direct or through mail-order outlets because they have restrictive agreements with dealers.

Locating a source is an important part of the selection process. For a personal computer system to be tailored to your specific requirements, the assistance of a salesperson at a dealer will probably be necessary. You should shop around and find a store and salesperson with whom you feel comfortable. You should start this task early. When you are armed with your list of requirements and applications, you can then begin to ask for hands-on demonstrations of specific software and hardware products.

REVIEW

Most problems can benefit from a systematic, step-by-step approach to a solution. This process applies directly to systems analysis. The systems life cycle is a phased approach in which each phase has a beginning and ending point. In the first phase, requirements are analyzed and functional specifications are written. In the second phase, design and development, specific design decisions are made. The design process also focuses on the more technical aspects of developing new systems and includes the tasks of selecting software and hardware. Documentation, which is assembled at the completion of the design process, is created throughout the life cycle. The implementation phase involves installing and operating the system. Evaluation of the system, once it is in place, provides designers with feedback concerning changes and/or new systems and procedures.

RESOURCES

BOOKS

Dayton, Doug. *Computer Solutions for Business*. Redmond, Wash.: Microsoft Press, 1987. A simple step-by-step guide to automating an office or small business.

Glasson, Bernard C. *EDP System Development Guidelines*. Wellesley, Mass.: QED Information Sciences, 1984. A highly technical but useful set of guidelines for the development of medium- and large-scale computer-based systems.

Seybold, Patricia B. *The Seybold Series on Professional Computing*. New York: McGraw-Hill, 1985. These books are quite useful for someone who wants guidelines for evaluating and purchasing packaged application software. Book titles in the series include *Integrated Spreadsheet Software, Word Processing Software for the IBM PC,* and *Data Base Management Systems*.

Walters, Roger E. *The Business Systems Development Process*. New York: Quorum Books, 1987. A nontechnical, step-by-step description of the system development life cycle. If you are interested in delving into the process, this book examines the areas that should be evaluated during planning and executing a large-system development project.

STUDY GUIDE

Match the following key terms to the appropriate definition:

A.

1. ____ Systems analysis
2. ____ Computer systems analyst
3. ____ Business systems analyst
4. ____ Top-down approach

5. ____ Life-cycle approach
6. ____ Process
7. ____ Functional specification
8. ____ Background study

9. ____ Requirements planning
10. ____ Data-flow diagram
11. ____ Data dictionary

a. Considering and estimating the inputs, outputs, filing, storage, processing, constraints, costs, and benefits of a system.

b. An analyst who is in an organizational department other than the MIS department.

c. Starting with the whole problem and developing more and more detail as the solution evolves.

d. A process that proceeds from definition to design and development to implementation.

e. A listing of all data elements and data structures within the system.

f. A series of blocks connected by flow lines.

g. A precise description of the functional requirements of a computer system.

h. A systematic series of actions directed toward a goal.

i. An analysis of an existing system.

j. A process of analyzing a user's needs and then deriving the functional requirements of a system from those needs.

k. An analyst who is in the MIS department and is concerned with the technical aspects of system design.

B.

12. ____ Structured walkthrough
13. ____ Prototyping
14. ____ Design review
15. ____ High-level documentation

16. ____ Detail documentation
17. ____ Computer-Aided Software Engineering (CASE)
18. ____ User diagnostics

19. ____ Direct conversion method
20. ____ Parallel conversion method
21. ____ Pilot test conversion method
22. ____ Modular conversion method

a. The process of breaking down a new system into smaller units and operating each of those units consecutively.

b. A picture of the overall structure of a system.

c. The process of operating a test version of a new system on a small scale.

d. The process of reviewing a proposed specification to evaluate its feasibility.

e. A series of test programs designed to determine where problems might exist in hardware.

f. A specific set of specifications that enables a programmer to write software.

g. The process of building working models of a system's inputs, outputs, and files.

h. The process of stopping an old system and immediately starting up a new system in its place.

i. The process of reviewing a proposed design to evaluate its feasibility.

j. The process of operating an old system and a new system simultaneously.

k. A set of tools to automate the tasks involved in designing and developing large-scale or complex software projects.

True/False:

23. ____ When you use a systematic problem-solving approach, most creative decisions occur in the implementation phase.

24. ____ Often a systems analyst consults with other systems analysts to discover what the user wants or needs.

25. ____ In large organizations, the tasks of systems analysis are often divided into specialized job categories.

26. ____ The process of developing a new computer system usually proceeds in an iterative cycle.

27. ____ The purpose of the definition phase is to come up with a detailed development plan for the system.

28. ____ Getting to know the application is the first step in the definition phase.

29. ____ Thinking about a new computer system is an opportunity to reexamine a business and the manner in which it is operated.

30. ____ Input requirements should include the amount of data and timing.

31. ____ When the proposed benefits of a system are intangible, they can be calculated.

32. ____ The systems analyst who developed the functional specification is always the best source of information for evaluating the specification.

33. ____ In the design and development phase, specific design decisions about the new system are made.

34. ____ General-purpose software is already tailored to meet the specific needs of an application.

35. ____ Selecting packaged software is usually the least expensive way to develop a system.

36. ____ A systems analyst should first select hardware, and then match software in the appropriate price range to the hardware needs.

37. ____ The systems development cycle ends when the new system is installed.

Multiple Choice:

38. Which of the following is not a useful principle in a systematic problem-solving process?

   a. A top-down approach.
   b. A bottom-up approach.
   c. A life-cycle approach.
   d. A process approach.

39. In small organizations, the tasks of systems analysis are

   a. Delegated to business systems analysts.
   b. Performed by programmers.
   c. Delegated to computer systems analysts.
   d. Performed by one person.

40. By making comparisons, the person performing the initial analysis can

   a. Consult references that have already addressed the problem.
   b. Talk to people with more experience.
   c. Recognize parts of the problem that may be familiar.
   d. Develop a rich variety of alternatives.

41. One of the most important questions to ask during the definition phase is

   a. What is the problem?
   b. What can I do about the problem?
   c. Have I done it before?
   d. Who can I talk to?

42. The starting point for requirements analysis is

   a. Functional specifications.
   b. A structured walkthrough.
   c. A review of potential applications.
   d. Design reviews.

43. Which of the following does not apply to gaining an understanding of the existing system?

   a. Understanding the flow of information between decision points.
   b. Determining a detailed problem definition.
   c. Meeting needs without a new system.
   d. Filling a need that did not exist before.

44. In a data-flow diagram, all processes that flow toward the center of the diagram are related to

   a. The input part of the system.
   b. The output part of the system.
   c. The processing part of the system.
   d. The storage part of the system.

45. In the system design process, the analyst is more likely to need

   a. The implementation process.
   b. Specific problem-solving skills.
   c. Knowledge of hardware and software capabilities.
   d. Knowledge of interviewing techniques.

46. When evaluating package software in the design and development phase, the first option to consider is

   a. Special-purpose application software.
   b. General-purpose application software.
   c. Developing the software from scratch.
   d. Prototyping.

47. Which of the following is used to train personnel on a new system?

   a. User diagnostics.
   b. High-level documentation.
   c. Detail documentation.
   d. User documentation.

Thought Questions:

48. Why do systems analysts use a systematic step-by-step approach to problem solving?

49. If you were given the assignment of determining the best accounting application for your organization, what would be your alternatives?

Projects:

50. Obtain a copy of the documentation for an application program. Using the criteria outlined in the chapter, evaluate the documentation and rank it as poor, average, or superior. Defend your answer.

51. A new system will cost $50,000 to design, develop, and implement. It is estimated that yearly savings of $2000 will occur as a result of implementing the system. Is the system feasible? Should the system be implemented? Defend your answers.

SOFTWARE EXERCISES

Daryl Duemore definitely needs help selecting a personal computer system, but first he will need help selecting a spreadsheet package. Using the sample software evaluation checklist on page 294, evaluate the spreadsheet program you are using along with two other spreadsheet programs.

Use your spreadsheet program to create an evaluation checklist. Add a row at the bottom of your spreadsheet to contain the average score for each package.

Use your graphics program to create a bar graph that compares ease of use and help facilities for each of the three packages.

Use your word processor to write a report to Mr. Duemore that justifies your selection of the best spreadsheet package.

ANSWERS

1. j, **2.** k, **3.** b, **4.** c, **5.** d, **6.** h, **7.** g, **8.** i, **9.** a, **10.** f, **11.** e, **12.** d, **13.** g, **14.** i, **15.** b, **16.** f, **17.** k, **18.** e, **19.** h, **20.** j, **21.** c, **22.** a, **23.** F, **24.** F, **25.** T, **26.** T, **27.** F, **28.** T, **29.** T, **30.** T, **31.** F, **32.** F, **33.** T, **34.** F, **35.** T, **36.** F, **37.** F, **38.** b, **39.** d, **40.** c, **41.** a, **42.** c, **43.** d, **44.** a, **45.** c, **46.** a, **47.** d.

WILLIAM H. GATES

Profession: Founder, chairman, and chief executive officer (CEO) of Microsoft Corporation, Redmond, Washington.

Profile: Gates is one of the driving forces behind the personal computer software industry. He started his career in computing as a computer consultant in high school, and while an undergraduate at Harvard University, developed a version of BASIC for microcomputers. Shortly thereafter, he dropped out and started Microsoft.

Quote: "Icon-driven interfaces will soon be the rule in personal computing. Within three years, 80 percent of all PCs will use a graphical user interface, compared to less than 10 percent today."

programmer when designing a graphical user interface for a program. Used interactively, the programmer can generate the screens, prototype the application, and have the CASE tool generate the program.

New tools and techniques allow programmers and software engineers to achieve the following objectives:

• Produce reliable, error-free software.

• Produce software that is easy to change and correct when errors are found.

• Modify the programs to satisfy new requirements.

• Produce parts of programs that will work with parts produced by other programmers.

• Produce software that is reusable.

In addition to productivity-enhancing tools, there are two fundamental approaches for realizing these objectives: structured program design and object-oriented programming.

STRUCTURED PROGRAM DESIGN

New tools and techniques. CASE:W, a computer-aided software engineering tool, helps programmers create a graphical user interface for Microsoft Windows applications.

Structured design is the process of designing the components of a computer program and their interrelationships

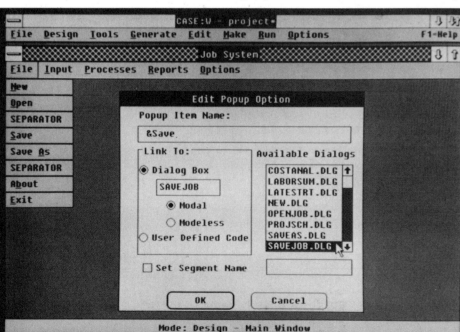

in the best possible way. It can help to formalize design activities and decisions so that teams of programmers can work together on software development projects. Three interrelated concepts form the basis of a structured approach to program design: top-down design, modularization, and the standardized control structures.

TOP-DOWN DESIGN

One popular technique for structured design is called the **top-down design** method. It consists of, first, specifying the solution to a problem in general terms and, then, breaking the solution down into finer and finer details. Top-down design is similar to creating an outline and later filling it in. It is often contrasted to bottom-up design. Top-down design refers to starting with the whole and working toward the parts whereas **bottom-up design** refers to starting with the parts and trying to build a whole, and it is generally used when coding a program. Often, the bottom or lower-level functions (i.e., input such as accessing a file or output such as printing a report) are known early in a project along with the top-level objectives.

A tool that is often used in top-down design is a **structure chart**, sometimes called a hierarchy chart, which, like a blueprint, is a diagram that shows the components of a program and the interconnection between components. The programmer analyzes the problem by starting at the top or the most general function and carefully works down to the lower-level functions. The programmer need not look at any details of the processes involved. The task is to determine what needs to be done, isolate the processing steps, and break the program into a set of interrelated modules. The resulting diagram of modules becomes a useful visual method for checking the design logic.

MODULARIZATION

The concept of modularization helps a programmer to divide a complex program into smaller subprograms. A **module** is a set of instructions that can be tested and verified independently

CHAPTER 14

PROGRAMMING

PREVIEW

Software is the term for programs that control the functions of computer systems. *Software development* is the process of analyzing the requirements of a system, and then designing, writing, and testing the software. In this chapter, we discuss software development from the following perspectives: (1) the evolution of programming, (2) the actual programming process and how it is structured into well-defined phases, and (3) a comparison of different programming languages. You do not have to know anything about a specific programming language to understand this chapter. After reading this chapter, however, you should have a better understanding of the concepts and techniques of software development.

In this chapter, you'll learn

• The evolution of programming.

• Structured program design.

• The phases of software development.

• An overview of object-oriented programming.

• An overview of COBOL, FORTRAN, BASIC, Pascal, C, and Ada.

Evolution of programming. The earliest programming involved hand wiring patch panels each time an application was changed. Shown here is a patch panel for an early Sperry Univac card sorter.

Evolution of programming. By the 1960s, programmers had begun to develop general-purpose programs for business and scientific applications.

THE EVOLUTION OF PROGRAMMING

The first programmers were scientists, technicians, and mathematicians who were intrigued by the idea of using computers as tools to solve some of their problems. They viewed computers as they would any other laboratory instrument: when an experiment was to be performed, a hypothesis tested, or an equation solved, programmers generally hand wired some circuits together or developed a set of instructions that could be input to a computer (usually by punched cards or tape) and produced an answer to their problem. This software was usually one of a kind—unique to the problem that was being solved—and was typically discarded after being used once. It was not until the advent of commercial computers in the early 1960s that software development started to become a distinct profession. The initial applications for these computers tended to be in areas that already had standardized manual procedures. The neat and efficient procedures in areas such as payroll, invoicing, and order entry provided "ready-made" models for the transition to computers. Procedures contained in written documents, such as accounting ledgers and manuals, were easily transformed into procedures for computer programs.

In the 1970s and 1980s, it became clear that software development was becoming much more complex. The software that was being created was quite different from that used in earlier, straightforward business and scientific applications. The steady drop in computer prices had put computers into the hands of millions of new users, who needed various kinds of software. This fueled an amazing demand for software. Whereas software development was once associated with individual programmers working on individual problems, now teams of programmers were needed to tackle larger and more complex software development problems.

THE BEGINNINGS OF SOFTWARE ENGINEERING

The process of programming is very effective when one person is responsible for all aspects of a specific program. However, this one-on-one relationship between programmer and program can produce some negative results. Because programming languages are general-purpose tools, there is no "one way" to do something in a program. Although each individual instruction in a programming language must obey certain rules and the overall program must be logically structured to accomplish the task or set of tasks, instructions can be combined in a variety of ways to produce a solution to a problem. We only have to look at the numerous solutions to a simple assignment in a programming class to verify this. In a work environment, two programmers who "speak" the same programming language can be totally confused by each others' programs.

It is useful to distinguish between a programmer who is writing a program for his or her own enjoyment or benefit—one creating a video game or a personal telephone directory—and a programmer who is working in a professional environment—such as the MIS department of a large company. In the large company, there are many programmers and many programming tasks or jobs. Other departments or groups within the company are constantly requesting new computer applications. Sometimes a large backlog can occur that may result in a delay of months or even years.

With this kind of environment, existing applications will be constantly changing. When an application works well, the users tend to want new additions, new features, and expanded capabilities. When an application goes wrong and does not work well, users want the application fixed. In either case, changes to existing programs are the rule and not the exception. The process of changing an existing program, known as *program maintenance,* continues throughout the life of the program, until it is retired or replaced by a new generation of software technology.

As is the case with many occupations, a programmer may not stay on the job for a long period of time, so new people must constantly be trained. Programmer turnover produces programs that are only partially complete and must be completed by another programmer.

The tendency toward more complexity in software development led to the need for *software engineering,* which is the application of scientific and mathematical principles to the design and development of producing software. This, in turn, led to the development of new tools and techniques for developing software.

NEW TOOLS AND TECHNIQUES

With the advent of software engineering as a profession, it was only natural that people began to look for ways to make the job of program writing easier and more productive. For example, with today's emphasis on graphical user interfaces, programmers must master the intricacies of programming for them. Several CASE tools (which were discussed in Chapter 13) assist a

A programming environment, such as in large company.

of its use in a larger program. In other words, it can be coded, debugged, and tested without having to write an entire program. It is much easier to write a small module, test and verify it, and then combine it with other modules to form a program than it is to write and test an entire large program from beginning to end.

How do independent modules work as part of a larger program? Just as programs accept input, process it, and produce output, modules perform similar functions. Modules communicate to one another by passing data back and forth. Inputs specify the information needed for the module to do its task. The output is the result of the processing done by the module. In this way, a module becomes a well-defined processing task that can be developed and then tested separately.

Modern programming languages support modularization directly through features called units, packages, functions, procedures, and even modules. Large software development projects are so complex that modularization is a necessity. When a team of programmers is working on a project, modularization not only allows dividing the task into smaller units but also provides a formal means for team members to communicate with one another.

Let us examine how a programmer might use top-down design and modularization to structure the problem of how to plan and carry out a dinner party. The structure chart will start with a single block at the top that becomes the control function or control module.

The next step in the process is to determine what specific tasks will have to be performed. First, there is the task of planning the evening. A programmer might call this the initialization module. The opposite of this is the ending module, which consists of the activity after dinner, such as cleaning up. In between are the main processing modules that deal directly with preparing and serving the dinner.

One of the major advantages of modularization is that the modules can be verified for correctness as you proceed with the design. The design at this stage consists of dividing the

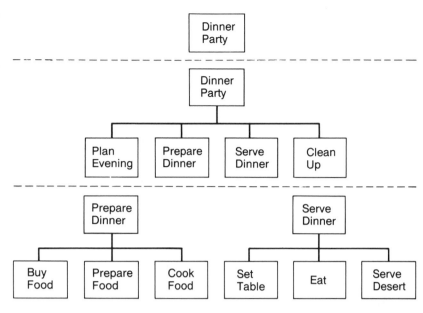

Top-down design using structure diagrams. *This series of diagrams shows how the problem of planning a dinner party is broken into smaller modules as the process proceeds.*

problem into smaller modules, each one encompassing a single task. Looking at our example, preparing dinner consists of buying, preparing, and cooking the food. You can continue to divide the whole into parts by isolating all the tasks that are related to serving dinner. Note that a structure chart works from top (most general functions) to bottom (most specific functions) and from left (first thing that needs to be done) to right (last thing that needs to be done).

The task of dividing the program into modules is finished when the programmer is sure there is no misunderstanding about what task or function is performed by each module. Our example illustrates how to simplify a problem by dividing it into modules using top-down design.

ALGORITHMS

An *algorithm* is a step-by-step set of instructions for solving a specific problem. A recipe is an algorithm; so are the instructions for putting together an assemble-it-yourself toy. In the context of computers, algorithms are sets of instructions for computational problems. There are problems for which no known algorithms exist, for example, getting a computer to play a perfect game of chess. This problem is so complicated that complete algorithms for "processing" chess moves have yet to be discovered. There are also problems for which an algorithm exists, but the

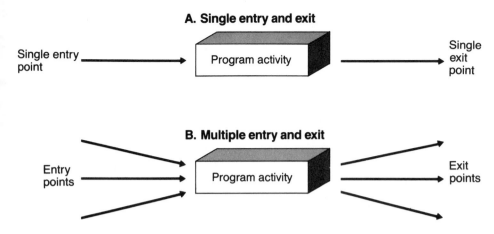

A. Single entry and exit

Single entry point → Program activity → Single exit point

B. Multiple entry and exit

Entry points → Program activity → Exit points

Control structures. When drawing a flowchart or block diagram, the recommended structured approach is to have one entry point and one exit point. Multiple entry and exit points are not allowed.

computer time needed to solve it grows exponentially with the size of the problem. Such problems are called *intractable.*

For example, consider the legendary Towers of Hanoi puzzle. It has three pegs. On the first peg are 64 rings; the largest on the bottom, the smallest on the top. Rings are to be moved one ring at a time, and a larger ring may not be placed on top of a smaller one. The goal is to stack all 64 rings correctly on the second peg. Several algorithms (the details of which are unimportant) exist to solve this problem. And if there are only 3 or 4 rings on the first peg, the time required to achieve the goal is trivial. However, in the 64-ring problem, if you were capable of moving 1 million rings per second, it would take more than a half a million years to complete the process.[1]

There are also problems for which both an algorithm and a reasonable

time-solution exist. For example, using the binary search technique that was discussed in Chapter 11, how many comparisons would it take in the worst case to find a name in a 1-million-name telephone directory? (In the worst case of a sequential search, 1 million comparisons would be required.) The answer is 20. Also, as the telephone directory grows exponentially larger, the number of comparisons required does not increase at a similar rate. A 1-billion-name telephone directory would, in the worst case, require only 30 comparisons.[2]

Many algorithms exist for sorting, searching, statistical calculating, and other mathematical procedures. If you need to sort some data quickly, for example, you can look up a published algorithm for fast sorting, copy it, and incorporate it into your program. These published algorithms are an excellent source of problem-solving information, and if they fit the problem, they can easily be adapted by the programmer.

CONTROL STRUCTURES

Structured programming refers to the application of top-down design methods to programming. One basic premise of structured programming is that all programs can be written using three basic *control structures,* which are statements in the program that control the order in which the instructions are executed. The basic control structures are *sequence, selection,* and *looping*—the process of repeating the execution of a set of instructions. A fourth control structure, called the *case* control structure, is often included in structured discussions. These control structures are designed to help maintain the modular program structure. To illustrate the concepts, consider the accompanying diagrams in which each box represents a program activity. In structured programs, each box has only one entry point and one exit point.

Sequence control structures consist of a sequence of two or more program statements that are executed in the same order in which they appear in a program.

Selection and case control structures choose from two possible paths

Control structures. Sequence control structure (left). Selection control structure (right).

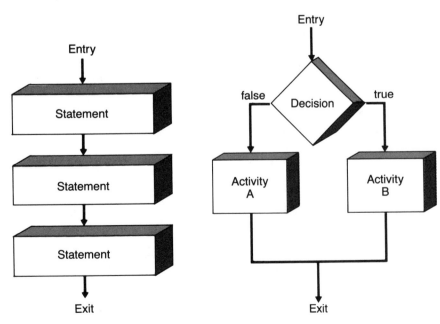

Entry → Statement → Statement → Statement → Exit

Entry → Decision — false → Activity A / true → Activity B → Exit

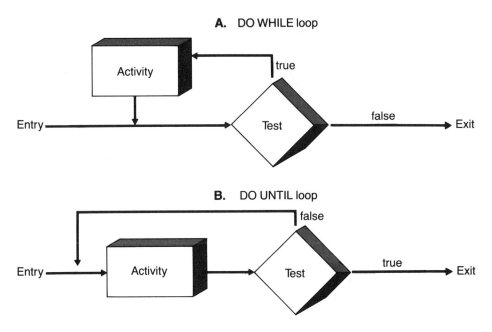

A. DO WHILE loop

Activity

Entry — Test — false — Exit

true

B. DO UNTIL loop

false

Entry — Activity — Test — true — Exit

Control structures. *Looping control structures.*

based on the evaluation of an expression that can be true or false. Any programming language that provides the IF THEN ELSE statement can directly implement structured selection.

Looping control structures take on two forms. One type, called the DO WHILE, evaluates a test expression first, and if true, the programming activity defined is executed once. Then the test expression is evaluated again, and if still true, the activity is executed again. This loop continues until the test expression is evaluated as false. In the DO UNTIL, the activity specified is first executed, then a test expression is evaluated, and if false, the activity is executed again. The loop continues until the test expression is evaluated to

be true. In effect, the DO UNTIL is a mirror image of the DO WHILE.

THE PHASES OF SOFTWARE DEVELOPMENT

Software development consists of a sequence of activities or phases necessary to design, code, test, and document the software. Regardless of the programming language or the nature of the problem to be solved, the process of creating software or programs consists of the following phases:

• Define the problem.

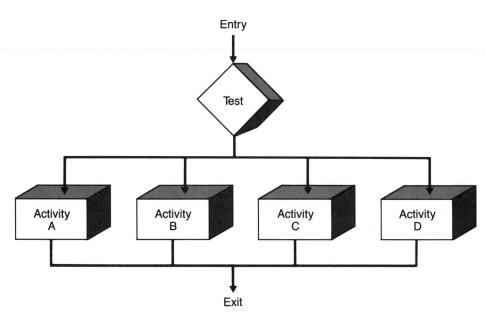

Entry

Test

Activity A | Activity B | Activity C | Activity D

Exit

Control structures. *Case control structure.*

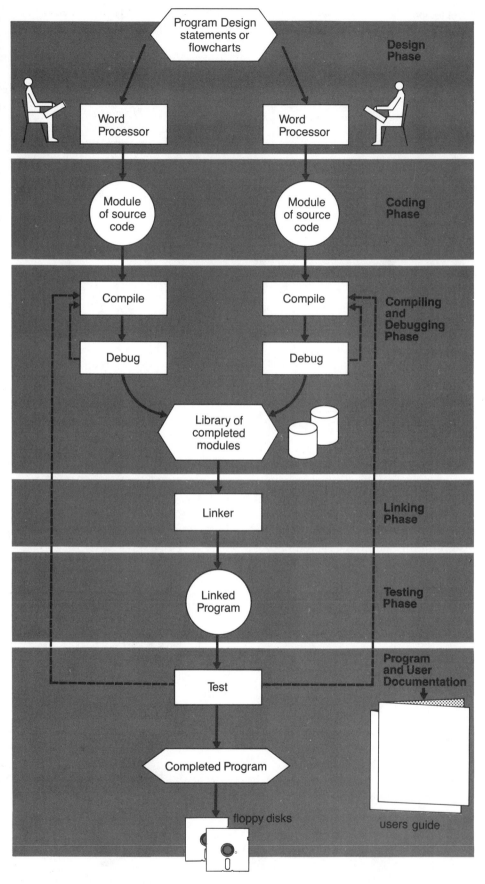

The phases of software development. In this figure, two programmers are working in parallel on the same program. Each programmer takes a module of the whole program and enters source code with a word processor.

- Plan the solution.
- Code the program.
- Translate the program.
- Link the program.
- Test the program.
- Assemble the documentation.

These phases will be discussed in sequence in the following sections. Keep in mind, however, that many of these phases proceed simultaneously and that the activities overlap when actually creating software. For example, testing occurs at several points in the process as well as a final test of the completed software. Documentation starts at the beginning of the software development process and continues through the end. New or additional program design may occur in the middle of the process. Coding, translating, testing, and linking are also overlapping activities.

DEFINE THE PROBLEM

Two things must happen in the program design phase: (1) the problem must be understood and defined, and (2) a solution must be engineered. Some of the understanding can be derived from the *requirements list*, which is a written set of statements that specify what the software must do or how it must be structured.

These requirements are specified by a systems analyst or a software engineer. In addition to the requirements, the problem should be studied in an actual situation to understand how people use the system, the data the system processes, the hardware used to implement the system, and any other factors that might affect the performance of the system. These factors should then be compared to the requirements. This process generally produces a completed program or system that is more naturally organized than if the requirements alone drove the initial design.

PLAN THE SOLUTION

The second major step in the program design process is the engineering of a solution. The top-down strategy—starting with the whole and working toward the parts—is a fundamental

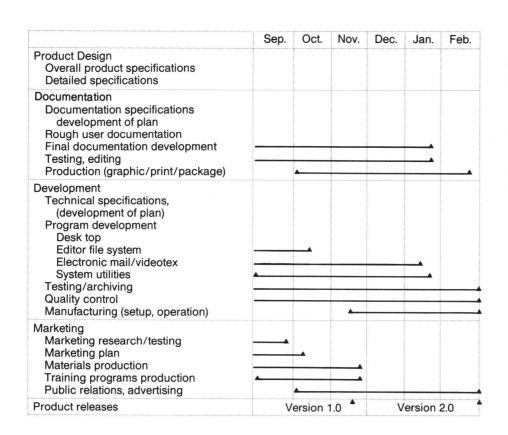

	Sep.	Oct.	Nov.	Dec.	Jan.	Feb.
Product Design						
Overall product specifications						
Detailed specifications						
Documentation						
Documentation specifications						
development of plan						
Rough user documentation						
Final documentation development	●————————————▲					
Testing, editing	●——————————————————————▲					
Production (graphic/print/package)		●————————————————————————————▲				
Development						
Technical specifications,						
(development of plan)						
Program development						
Desk top						
Editor file system	●————————▲					
Electronic mail/videotex	●————————————————————▲					
System utilities	●————————————————————————▲					
Testing/archiving	●————————————————————————————————▲					
Quality control	●————————————————————————————————▲					
Manufacturing (setup, operation)			●——————————————————————▲			
Marketing						
Marketing research/testing	●————▲					
Marketing plan	●————————▲					
Materials production	●————————————————▲					
Training programs production	●————————————————▲					
Public relations, advertising		●————————————————————————————————▲				
Product releases	Version 1.0 ▲			Version 2.0 ▲		

The phases of software development in schedule form. Another way of looking at the phases of software development is to create a schedule. Although estimates vary, coding—the easiest task—typically takes one-sixth of the total time, whereas testing takes over one-half of the total time. Generally speaking, it is much better to spend more time in the beginning design phases. It is much more costly to fix an error that is found in the latter stages than to fix an error that is found in the beginning phases.

principle in all program design and allows the programmer to analyze a complex problem by breaking it down into simple functions.

For example, assume that a computer game to teach math needs to be written. It should provide the student with practice problems in addition, subtraction, multiplication, and division as well as the choice of which type of math problem he or she would like to try. The program should keep track of the score (the number of right problems answered) and display that information to the student on completion of a session.

After analyzing the requirements, the programmer begins the task of putting the solution down on paper. Our example might produce a simple hierarchical structure chart, in which each function (or module) appears as a block and its interaction with every other function is shown. After an initial breakdown of the program, the programmer can then concentrate on more detailed design of each function.

Flowcharting

Once a preliminary solution is engineered, the programmer must begin to design the program. What tools does the programmer have to help design the program? One of the earliest tools was the flowchart. A program *flowchart* is a graphic way to represent the thinking that goes into designing a program or module. It is made from standard symbols that indicate types of operations: ovals indicate the starting and ending points, parallelograms indicate input or output operations, diamonds stand for decisions, rectangles represent all other processing operations, and arrows indicate the flow of control. A flowchart for a simple program that converts a number representing degrees Celsius into degrees Fahrenheit, for example, would contain an oval start symbol, a parallelogram for input, a rectangle for processing, another parallelogram for output, and an oval end symbol.

Structure diagram of a math game. Breaking a math game into its basic functions (modules) so that each can be designed in detail.

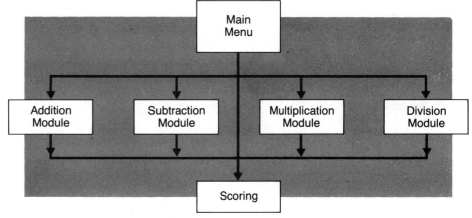

Program flowchart symbols.

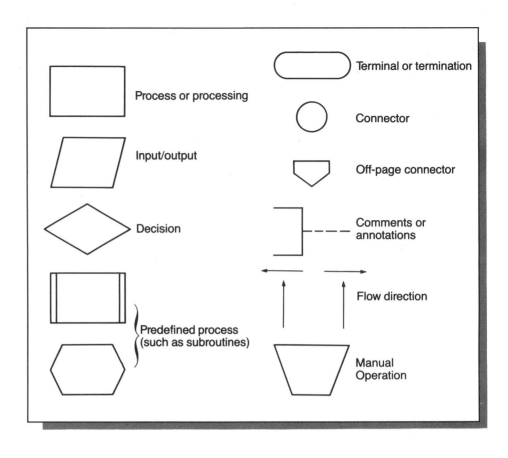

Process or processing

Input/output

Decision

Predefined process (such as subroutines)

Terminal or termination

Connector

Off-page connector

Comments or annotations

Flow direction

Manual Operation

A program flowchart where symbol (1) represents an input or output operation and symbol (2) represents a processing operation (in this case, a calculation). Arrows indicate the direction of flow in the program.

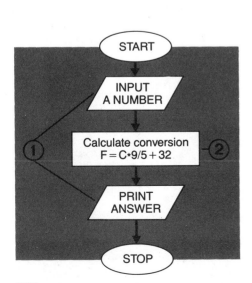

START

INPUT A NUMBER

① Calculate conversion $F = C*9/5 + 32$ ②

PRINT ANSWER

STOP

Pseudocode

One alternative to the flowchart is called *pseudocode*—a written description of a program using English statements. The idea behind pseudocode is to write English-language statements that are almost as specific as the code itself but flexible enough to be written in more than one programming language. For example, assume that the requirements for a simple program are as follows: A bucket contains 16 Ping-Pong balls that are colored red, blue, and green. Separate the Ping-Pong balls into piles according to color. Later, a flowchart and a pseudocode description of this problem are compared. At the end of the chapter, this example is coded in six different programming languages and used to compare those languages.

Designing a large flowchart is a time-consuming process, and modifying one is even more difficult. Programs do exist that can read a written program and produce a flowchart, but they are only useful for documenting the program after it is written. On the other hand, pseudocode is usually easier to work with. Programming aids, in the form of specially designed word processors, help the programmer to enter the pseudocode statements, indent them properly, and cross-reference the statements.

CODE THE PROGRAM

Coding a program means writing that program in a specific programming language. Normally this is done with a program editor, which is a special-purpose word processor that allows the programmer to enter, edit, change, add, and delete programming language statements.

When a program is large, the program is broken into smaller, more manageable modules. This strategy makes coding, compiling, and debugging easier. If the application has been properly broken down into good workable modules, it is quite possible that several programmers may be working on different modules of the same program in parallel.

Another tool that is becoming more and more available to the programmer is a good structured programming language. Basically, a *structured programming language* facilitates breaking the program into smaller units or modules and allows clearer expression of the problem and simpler organization. Pascal is a good example of a structured language. Other examples include C, Ada, and Modula-2. There have also been modifications of older languages, such as BASIC, COBOL, and FORTRAN, into versions that allow for structured programming techniques.

LANGUAGE TRANSLATION

The program coded by the programmer cannot be directly executed by a computer unless it is coded in machine language. The program written in a programming language such as BASIC or Pascal is called a *source program* or simply source code. It must be translated into machine language, which is called an *object program* or object code. The translator program is called a compiler or interpreter. Both compilers and interpreters perform the functions of (1) checking program instructions for correct spelling and grammar and then (2) translating correct program instructions into a machine language, but they work slightly differently.

Compilers Versus Interpreters

An *interpreter* is designed to translate interactively each programming statement into an immediately usable sequence of machine language instructions. For example, when you write a BASIC program on most personal computers, you type in the program statements and then run the program. The BASIC interpreter translates the first statement in the program, then executes it, then it translates the second statement and executes it, and so on, until the program is finished.

On the other hand, a *compiler* spends some time evaluating the entire program and then translates all the programming statements into a machine language program that is executed at once. If you were using a compiler version of the BASIC language, you would type in your programming statements and compile the program. The entire program would then be executed without the line-by-line translation steps. Any language can be either interpreted or compiled.

Interpreting each program statement before it is executed considerably slows down the execution speed of a program, but it does not require extra steps to compile and link. This is useful in certain environments, such as an educational institution where the goal is to teach the language, not optimize program throughput. In cases where programs are run in a production environment and throughput is more critical, a compiled language is preferred. A program that has been correctly designed need only be compiled once. Then the executable machine language program can be run over and over.

Syntax Errors and Logical Errors

You will often hear the term *debugging.* Bugs are another name for errors. A program will not work properly—do the task for which it was intended—until it is error free or debugged. The initial debugging step consists of using the compiler to uncover spelling and grammar errors. Programming languages require such preciseness that it is impossible for even experienced programmers not to make mistakes. No matter how careful the programmer is, there will be errors in all but the simplest programs. However, because the rules for writing programs are so rigid, it is quite easy to make the compiler or the interpreter do the work for many kinds of errors.

Generally, the compiler or interpreter will point out what error occurred and where it occurred, but not always. Sometimes the error message only points to a general area in which the error occurred. Error messages tend to be cryptic, so the programmer must have a good working knowledge of the compiler to discover the cause of the error. The initial debugging is greatly enhanced by the interactive use of a program editor. Using a good program editor, a syntax error can be detected and corrected and the program or module recompiled in a matter of minutes.

On the other hand, logical errors are indicators that the logic the programmer used when coding the program failed to solve the problem. Logic errors do not produce error messages. The only clue to their existence is that

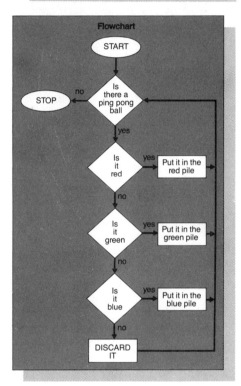

Pseudocode versus flowcharting. The same sample problem written in pseudocode and with flowchart symbols. The diamond symbols of the flowchart that indicate a decision point are the equivalent of the if/else combinations in the pseudocode.

Testing for errors. *The purpose of testing a program is to find errors. A program should never do something it is not supposed to do. For example, testing the menu part of this program should include seeing what happens when a key other than 1, 2, 3, 4, or 5 is pressed. Ideally, the program would notify the user of an invalid entry, then return the user to the main menu for another try. Note that just because the program works when a 1, 2, 3, 4, or 5 key is pressed does not mean that the program is error free.*

they produce wrong solutions, but this can be very subtle. For example, suppose a programmer coded the computer-aided math drill program and made a logical error in designing the part that counts the number of correct answers but did not violate any spelling or grammar rules. The error would not show up as a syntax error when the program was compiled or interpreted and would only be discovered after carefully testing the program.

LINK THE PROGRAM

When a module is completely debugged, it is usually given a name and stored in a library file on a disk. Because modules are stand-alone entities, there must be a way to combine two or more modules to form a whole program. This is the job of a linker.

A *linker* is a program that links modules together and produces a single program. The linker's output is an "executable" program that can be tested for (1) the modules' ability to communicate properly with one another and (2) the modules' ability to cooperate to perform the program's intended function.

A *loader* is a program that brings programs stored on a disk into memory for execution. An example of a loader is a program called the bootstrap loader that brings the operating system from disk and loads it into memory.

TEST THE PROGRAM

Just because a program or module has been debugged does not mean that it works properly. Debugging refers to the process of finding errors in an individual module or program by the programmer who wrote it. *Program testing* refers to a more comprehensive set of criteria against which the program can be evaluated and verified. It is analogous to an independent laboratory that tests a consumer product. The goal of testing is to find errors. A major form of testing involves running the program using different sample sets of data and simulating the conditions under which the finished program will be run. The testing phase involves working out all the logical errors in the program, the kind that a compiler can-

not detect. It is best to test all the possible conditions that can occur in a program, both expected and unexpected.

Of course, to meet the requirements, the program must work. Good testing is especially dependent on understanding the inputs and outputs discussed in the program design phase. A test usually consists of a series of test cases, each of which specifies a set of data inputs along with the expected results or outputs. When a program is divided into modules, each module can be exhaustively tested, then combined with other modules, and tested together until the final program can be verified. A completed program should not only do what it is supposed to do (i.e., perform its intended function), but it should also not do anything that it is not supposed to do.

ASSEMBLE THE DOCUMENTATION

Documentation falls into two categories: program documentation and user documentation. *Program documentation* is the written information necessary to support the software. All software has a life cycle in which it must be maintained. Some of the maintenance involves fixing any errors that might have slipped through the testing phases and other maintenance involves additions or enhancements that might have to be incorporated into the program. Ideally, the computer programs themselves should be their own best documentation. If proper procedures have been followed, programs should be readable to the extent that any programmer can understand them. In most cases, however, program documentation also includes a pseudocode listing or a flowchart and formal specification of the inputs, control data, and outputs.

For the software user, the documentation that matters is the set of user or instruction manuals. These documents should (1) explain how to use the software and (2) cover everything that can possibly happen while the software is being used. It is a good software design practice to complete a preliminary user's manual at the same time the requirements are being prepared. Then, as the development proceeds, the user manual helps to point out any difficulties that might arise for a person who is unfamiliar with the inner workings of the software.

OBJECT-ORIENTED PROGRAMMING

Object-oriented programming is a technique in which the programmer works with predefined objects. It is characterized by the following concepts.[3]

• *Objects.* Data and the operations on the data are grouped together and treated as objects. This is the opposite of procedural programming in which data and instructions are always separated.

• *Class.* Objects are classified, that is, they belong to a class or are instances of a class. The class contains the characteristics that are common to all objects in the class and the shared procedures available to objects. A collection of classes associated with a particular environment is called a library. As in biology, objects are organized in a hierarchy of classes. The unit of modularity in an object-oriented system is the class, so programmers often speak of developing classes rather than programs.

• *Inheritance.* Each object knows its class membership and inherits (i.e., receives a copy of) from this class and its ancestors all of its behavior and structure. Inheritance also allows new classes to be built on top of older classes instead of being rewritten from scratch. Unlike biological inheritance, however, the classes ancestors have not died. They are "alive" and "well."

• *Messages* are requests for an object to perform one of its operations. Programming is done by sending messages from one object to another describing what is to be accomplished. Objects, in turn, decide once they have received a message, how to process it.

• *Dynamic binding.* The ability of a program to determine at run time which procedure to run in response to a message.

Recall the mail-order application that was discussed in Chapter 11. Analyzing the application in terms of objects, we can see that the system will include customer objects and order objects. Customer objects belong to a class—a collection of characteristics that are common to all objects that belong to the class. In describing the customer file, for example, we are really describing the customer class, that is, the attributes such as name and address, that characterize the class of objects we call customers. In object terminology, each customer is an instance of the customer class.

Similarly when a customer buys products, there must be an order, and we can call that an order object. The order object for each customer belongs to an order class. To create an invoice, the invoice object must contain unique procedures. For example, it knows how to print itself and will perform that behavior when asked to do so. But it also inherits characteristics and procedures from the customer and order objects.

Classes describe what objects can exist, the characteristics of those objects, and what kinds of procedures can be performed with the objects. Classes and inheritance allow new system elements to be defined by leveraging the specifications of existing classes. For example, if we wanted to show our invoice on a display screen as well as print it, we could add a new "display invoice" object that inherits the general characteristics of invoices from an invoice class. A software developer would create the display invoice object by programming the differences between the print invoice object and the display invoice object. In the process, previously defined characteristics are used when appropriate.

Objects and their classes provide another technique for understanding and defining a problem phase in the process of designing a program. Perhaps what is more important, the object model is very accommodating to engineering a solution. In most cases, the object model can be used directly as a blueprint when creating an object-oriented program.

Advocates view object-oriented programming as a paradigm shift (i.e., the rejection of one time-honored tech-

Procedural Style	Object Style
Data and procedural declarations are only coincidentally related.	Data and procedural declarations are combined into one object declaration.
Data types can be exposed.	Data are usually hidden inside an object implementation.
Specific procedures and the data they operate on are explicitly combined by the programmer.	The programmer specifies procedures in a general way: specific procedures are chosen by the object itself.
Flow of control is explicitly stated by the source code, and is fixed when the program is compiled.	Flow of control is decided by the objects themselves while the program is executing.

nique in favor of a newer and more satisfactory technique) in the software development process.

The classic example of an object-oriented programming language is Smalltalk-80, which was developed by Alan Kay in the 1970s at Xerox's Palo Alto Research Center. Today, hybrid languages such as Objective-C, C++, and Turbo Pascal 5.5 incorporate object-oriented concepts and tools while retaining the conventional features of the language.

COMPARING PROGRAMMING LANGUAGES

Programming languages are the primary tools for creating software. There is a great deal of competition among programming languages, with hundreds in existence and about ten in widespread development use. There is an ongoing argument over which is the best language, and each language has its advocates and its critics. To prove their point, some critics even develop new programming languages.

The differences among programming languages often arise from the differences in what defines good software. Likewise, traditional patterns of programming are constantly challenged, as are long-ingrained beliefs about the proper tools and techniques

for software development. Whenever new programming languages are introduced into the software development community, a large-scale effort is required to test and validate the new language.

Although assembly language still plays a role in application programming, the following discussions are confined to high-level languages.

COBOL

COBOL, an acronym for COmmon Business Oriented Language, was introduced in 1960. In the 1950s, the U.S. government was the largest buyer of computers in the world. To help the fledgling computer industry, government policy encouraged competition by buying from several manufacturers. Unfortunately, in those days each computer had its own unique computer language. The government began to realize that it might have a massive compatibility problem on its hands, so in 1959 a committee was formed to develop a standard programming language that was not identified with any one manufacturer. One of the most influential people on the committee was Grace Hopper, who also wrote the first practical compiler program and was a pioneer in the field of computer languages.

By 1960, the standard had become the first version of the COBOL language. Because it was required for all government contracts, it quickly became a widely accepted language, and all computer manufacturers had to offer it. Then it was standardized by the American National Standards Institute (ANSI), which led to agreement on what a COBOL program should look like.

COBOL is written in English-like statements, so it is fairly easy to understand parts of the language. COBOL is specifically designed for business applications. Some versions include a built-in SORT feature, which enables programmers to easily rearrange files, and a REPORT WRITER feature, for producing complex reports.

COBOL takes longer to learn than other languages because its English-like statements make writing a simple program a lengthy and tedious task.

COBOL's primary control structure is the PERFORM statement. A COBOL program can be structured into paragraphs that function like modules and can be called on by PERFORMing the paragraph. Exclusive use of PERFORMs can result in a structured COBOL program. IF THEN ELSE statements in conjunction with PERFORM allow conditional execution of paragraphs, and PERFORM WHILE causes conditional repetition.

COBOL is primarily a business application language that deals with processing files and records and producing reports. For example, a person in the payroll department of a company might have an employee master payroll file in a file cabinet. COBOL is designed to allow programmers to express data structures in the same vocabulary as the payroll department employee. For the payroll application, a FILE DESCRIPTION exists for the payroll file, a RECORD DESCRIPTION exists for each type of payroll record in that file, and temporary WORKING STORAGE areas exist for holding the results of calculations. Great care was taken when designing COBOL so that it would allow data structures to be described in a manner similar to the application areas that were being programmed.

FORTRAN

In 1954, John Backus and a team of designers at IBM began to formulate a high-level programming language to solve scientific, mathematical, and engineering problems. FORTRAN (FORmula TRANslation) was introduced in 1957, and until 1960 it was the only alternative to programming in machine-level or assembly-level languages, and because scientific programming was more predominant than business programming, FORTRAN developed a wide following among technical people.

FORTRAN has remarkable staying power. It was standardized in 1966 and again in 1977. One of its major strengths is its widespread use and sharing among the scientific and engineering communities. It is quite easy, for example, to obtain prewritten FORTRAN subroutines for a wide variety of tasks.

Because it has been around for so long, FORTRAN is widely accepted and understood. With prior knowledge of algebra, (1) it is very easy to write a simple FORTRAN program, and (2) the full capabilities of the lan-

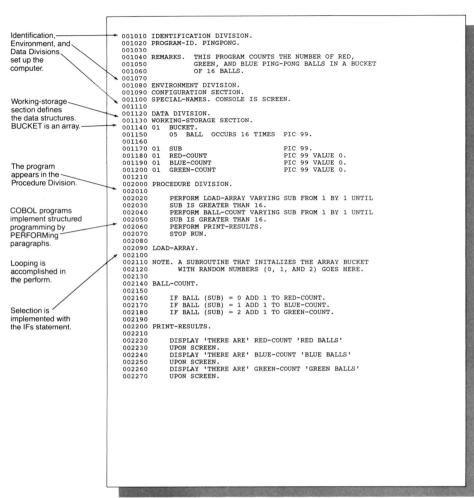

Identification, Environment, and Data Divisions set up the computer.

Working-storage section defines the data structures. BUCKET is an array.

The program appears in the Procedure Division.

COBOL programs implement structured programming by PERFORMing paragraphs.

Looping is accomplished in the perform.

Selection is implemented with the IFs statement.

```
001010  IDENTIFICATION DIVISION.
001020  PROGRAM-ID. PINGPONG.
001030
001040  REMARKS.   THIS PROGRAM COUNTS THE NUMBER OF RED,
001050            GREEN, AND BLUE PING-PONG BALLS IN A BUCKET
001060            OF 16 BALLS.
001070
001080  ENVIRONMENT DIVISION.
001090  CONFIGURATION SECTION.
001100  SPECIAL-NAMES. CONSOLE IS SCREEN.
001110
001120  DATA DIVISION.
001130  WORKING-STORAGE SECTION.
001140  01  BUCKET.
001150      05  BALL   OCCURS 16 TIMES  PIC 99.
001160
001170  01  SUB                        PIC 99.
001180  01  RED-COUNT                  PIC 99 VALUE 0.
001190  01  BLUE-COUNT                 PIC 99 VALUE 0.
001200  01  GREEN-COUNT                PIC 99 VALUE 0.
001210
002000  PROCEDURE DIVISION.
002010
002020      PERFORM LOAD-ARRAY VARYING SUB FROM 1 BY 1 UNTIL
002030      SUB IS GREATER THAN 16.
002040      PERFORM BALL-COUNT VARYING SUB FROM 1 BY 1 UNTIL
002050      SUB IS GREATER THAN 16.
002060      PERFORM PRINT-RESULTS.
002070      STOP RUN.
002080
002090  LOAD-ARRAY.
002100
002110  NOTE. A SUBROUTINE THAT INITALIZES THE ARRAY BUCKET
002120       WITH RANDOM NUMBERS (0, 1, AND 2) GOES HERE.
002130
002140  BALL-COUNT.
002150
002160      IF BALL (SUB) = 0 ADD 1 TO RED-COUNT.
002170      IF BALL (SUB) = 1 ADD 1 TO BLUE-COUNT.
002180      IF BALL (SUB) = 2 ADD 1 TO GREEN-COUNT.
002190
002200  PRINT-RESULTS.
002210
002220      DISPLAY 'THERE ARE' RED-COUNT 'RED BALLS'
002230      UPON SCREEN.
002240      DISPLAY 'THERE ARE' BLUE-COUNT 'BLUE BALLS'
002250      UPON SCREEN.
002260      DISPLAY 'THERE ARE' GREEN-COUNT 'GREEN BALLS'
002270      UPON SCREEN.
```

COBOL listing of the Ping-Pong ball problem.

FORTRAN program.
Sequence goes from
beginning of program
to END of statement.

The bucket of
balls is an array
data structure.

Looping implemented
with DO loops.

Selection structure
implemented with
FORTRAN's IF
statement.

```
C     THIS PROGRAM COUNTS THE NUMBER OF
C     RED, BLUE, AND GREEN PING-PONG BALLS
C     IN A BUCKET OF 16 BALLS
      INTEGER BALL, SUB, RCNT, BCNT, GCNT

      DIMENSION BALL (16)

      DO 400 SUB = 1,16
      CALL RND(I)
      BALL (SUB) = RND(I)
400   CONTINUE

C     IN THE PREVIOUS DO LOOP, RND IS A SUBROUTINE THAT
C     RETURNS A RANDOM NUMBER FROM 0 TO 2

      DO 500 SUB = 1,16
      IF (BALL(SUB) .EQ. 0) RCNT = RCNT + 1
      IF (BALL(SUB) .EQ. 1) BCNT = BCNT + 1
      IF (BALL(SUB) .EQ. 2) GCNT = GCNT + 1
500   CONTINUE

      WRITE (6,100) RCNT
      WRITE (6,200) BCNT
      WRITE (6,300) GCNT

100   FORMAT ('THE NUMBER OF RED BALLS IS', I2)
200   FORMAT ('THE NUMBER OF BLUE BALLS IS', I2)
300   FORMAT ('THE NUMBER OF GREEN BALLS IS', I2)

      STOP
      END
```

FORTRAN listing of the Ping-Pong ball problem.

guage can be learned easily. FORTRAN includes a number of built-in mathematical functions that are useful for solving problems. FORTRAN-77 has been extended to allow structured programming techniques by adding new features to the language.

FORTRAN's specific purpose is in scientific and engineering applications, and using it for other applications becomes quite difficult. Input and output operations cannot be accomplished easily because FORTRAN's file-handling capabilities are not as well defined as are COBOL's. FORTRAN is best for number crunching, but processing character-type data takes much more work in the language. Creating easy-to-read reports or screen displays is also a cumbersome task.

FORTRAN has a more limited variety of control structures. IF GO TO allows for conditional execution of statements. DO statements allow repetition. FORTRAN's concept of modularization is limited to the sub-

routine. A subroutine is a set of statements that can be executed from any point in the program by using a CALL statement.

Because of its mathematical nature, FORTRAN limits its expression of data structures to simple variables and arrays (tables), the latter being the only real structure that allows a programmer to organize complex data. Integers, single- and double-precision floating-point numbers, complex numbers, and Boolean (logical) expressions are all oriented toward giving the technician, scientist, or mathematician an easy way to express data for solving problems. When it comes to handling characters in a FORTRAN program, the programmer must be aware of many limitations. FORTRAN is not optimized to handle input or output as is COBOL, so describing records or files becomes much more difficult than in other languages.

BASIC

BASIC (Beginner's All-purpose Symbolic Instruction Code) was developed at Dartmouth College in 1964 by John G. Kemeny and Thomas E. Kurtz, who were working on a project to perfect a programming language that would be suitable in a time-sharing environment and could be used as a teaching tool. The idea was innovative at the time, and BASIC quickly drew attention in the academic world, where, because of its ease of learning, it became a popular language.

BASIC may well be the easiest of all the programming languages to learn. It is easy to create simple programs, especially in a programming class environment. Because it is so popular with microcomputers, many books, self-teaching manuals, and tutorials exist to help you learn the language. Many versions have been extended to include the ability to use structured techniques, but these versions start looking more like Pascal than BASIC.

In terms of sheer numbers, BASIC is the most widely used programming language, thanks to the millions of BASIC-speaking microcomputers that have been sold in the last several years. It is available for every personal computer, is usually provided free, and is occasionally imbedded in the read-only memory (ROM) of the system.

BASIC's popularity has allowed it to spread extensively without ever being standardized. There are many different versions of BASIC, ranging from simple versions available on Commodore, Apple, and IBM computers to structured BASIC and business BASIC versions available on larger computers. Unfortunately, each one is different, so little compatibility exists. The smaller, earlier versions are limited in their handling of character-type data and input and output. They do not allow for structured programming techniques. Computer purists will claim that learning BASIC as the first language only incubates bad programming habits.

BASIC's control structures use simple cases of IF THEN ELSE in combination with GOTO and GOSUB. GOTO branches to specific statements within a program, whereas GOSUB branches to a subroutine then returns control to the statement immediately following the GOSUB statement. BASIC also has FOR NEXT statements (similar to FORTRAN DO statements) that allow a group of instructions to be repeated a specified number of times.

BASIC handles data structures in much the same way as FORTRAN, perhaps in an even more limited manner. Variable types can include integers, real numbers, arrays, and strings (characters). Except in some newer versions of BASIC, describing a file or a record must be done with great care because the language is not designed to handle anything more than simple input or output.

PASCAL

In the late 1960s, computer science began to achieve the status of a formal discipline. With that status came scientific and mathematical concepts about the "correct" way to write a program. The existing languages seemed inadequate to many of the computer scientists, and in 1971 a Swiss computer scientist named Niklaus Wirth announced Pascal. It was designed to teach the emerging concepts of structured programming.

Pascal is now the preferred teaching

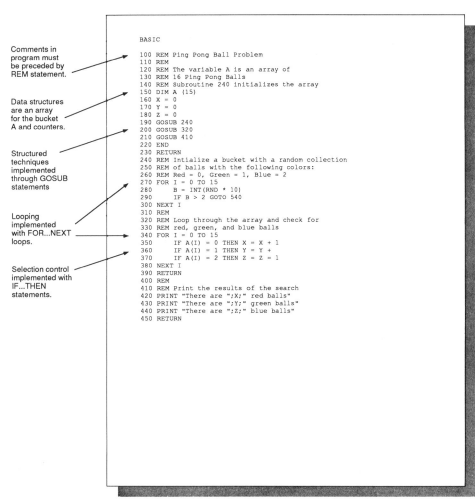

Comments in program must be preceded by REM statement.

Data structures are an array for the bucket A and counters.

Structured techniques implemented through GOSUB statements

Looping implemented with FOR...NEXT loops.

Selection control implemented with IF...THEN statements.

```
BASIC

100 REM Ping Pong Ball Problem
110 REM
120 REM The variable A is an array of
130 REM 16 Ping Pong Balls
140 REM Subroutine 240 initializes the array
150 DIM A (15)
160 X = 0
170 Y = 0
180 Z = 0
190 GOSUB 240
200 GOSUB 320
210 GOSUB 410
220 END
230 RETURN
240 REM Intialize a bucket with a random collection
250 REM of balls with the following colors:
260 REM Red = 0, Green = 1, Blue = 2
270 FOR I = 0 TO 15
280     B = INT(RND * 10)
290     IF B > 2 GOTO 540
300 NEXT I
310 REM
320 REM Loop through the array and check for
330 REM red, green, and blue balls
340 FOR I = 0 TO 15
350     IF A(I) = 0 THEN X = X + 1
360     IF A(I) = 1 THEN Y = Y +
370     IF A(I) = 2 THEN Z = Z = 1
380 NEXT I
390 RETURN
400 REM
410 REM Print the results of the search
420 PRINT "There are ";X;" red balls"
430 PRINT "There are ";Y;" green balls"
440 PRINT "There are ";Z;" blue balls"
450 RETURN
```

language in computer science and is considered the model for structured programming concepts in the computer science literature. In addition, it has proved quite successful for the creation of large-scale programs, and the international committees have standardized the language. Many versions are available for personal computers.

Pascal has become the language of computer science. Using it as your first programming language will reinforce the principles of structured programming more than any other language. Its general-purpose capabilities do not limit it to business or scientific applications.

Although Pascal is popular as a teaching tool, many different versions and extensions have not obtained the sanction of an official standards organization such as ANSI or ISO.

Pascal control structures include IF THEN ELSE statements and CASE statements for conditional execution. WHILE DO, REPEAT UNTIL, and FOR DO statements allow conditional repetition. Modularization is accom-

BASIC listing of the Ping-Pong ball problem.

Pascal listing of the Ping-Pong ball problem.

Pascal's data structures are declared with const, type, and var statements. Strong typing features.

Looping accomplished with for...do statements.

Note that selection control is implemented without the use of IF statements.

Comments can be anywhere in the program and are enclosed by (•····•).

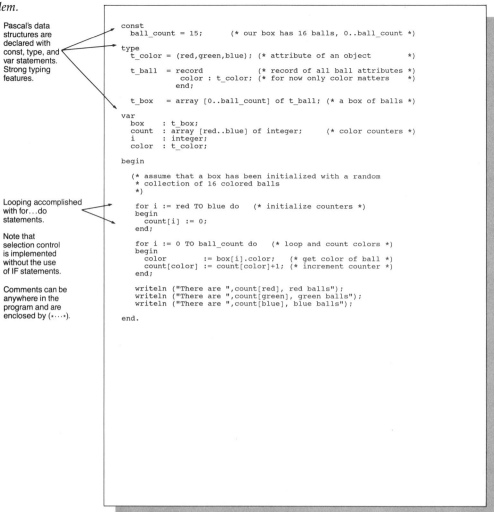

```
const
  ball_count = 15;        (* our box has 16 balls, 0..ball_count *)

type
  t_color = (red,green,blue); (* attribute of an object        *)

  t_ball  = record          (* record of all ball attributes *)
              color : t_color; (* for now only color matters  *)
            end;

  t_box   = array [0..ball_count] of t_ball; (* a box of balls *)
var
  box    : t_box;
  count  : array [red..blue] of integer;      (* color counters *)
  i      : integer;
  color  : t_color;

begin

  (* assume that a box has been initialized with a random
   * collection of 16 colored balls
   *)

  for i := red TO blue do    (* initialize counters *)
  begin
    count[i] := 0;
  end;

  for i := 0 TO ball_count do    (* loop and count colors *)
  begin
    color        := box[i].color;    (* get color of ball *)
    count[color] := count[color]+1; (* increment counter *)
  end;

  writeln ("There are ",count[red], red balls");
  writeln ("There are ",count[green], green balls");
  writeln ("There are ",count[blue], blue balls");

end.
```

plished by blocks of code called procedures, functions, or units. The procedures and functions are given names and are called from other parts of the program. This facilitates the implementation of well-structured code.

Pascal was one of the first languages to support the concept of strongly typed data. The analogy of adding apples and oranges is a good example of typed data. In language that does not support typing—such as BASIC, COBOL, or FORTRAN—data could be classified as apples and oranges, but it would be the programmer's responsibility to see that they did not get added. In Pascal, the programmer can specify type apple and type orange. Then, a programming statement that tried to add the two together could be "spotted" by the compiler and flagged as a type mismatch error. In addition to common data types such as integers and characters, Pascal supports the following data structures: sets (as in mathematical sets), arrays, records, files, pointers, enumerations, and programmer-defined data types.

C

C was originally developed in England under the name of BCPL. It was adapted at Bell Laboratories in the United States by Brian Kernighan and Dennis Ritchie and transformed into a language called B, which was then improved and modified in 1974 into what is now known as C. It was used to write the Unix operating system and subsequently became a popular language for programmers.

Like Pascal, C is a structured language and encourages the modular approaches to programming. A C program consists of a main module and a number of smaller units called functions, which are equivalent to Pascal's functions. Although it does contain some English-like statements, C has a less demanding syntax, so programs written in C can look like assembler

C listing of the Ping-Pong ball problem.

```c
#include "stdio.h"

typedef enum
{
  red,
  green,
  blue

} COLOR;

#define cntBalls  16      /* our box will have 16 balls, 0..cntBalls-1 */
#define cntColors (blue+1) /* we will be counting 3 colors            */

typedef struct    /* structure of all ball attributes */
{
  COLOR color;    /* for now only color matters       */

} BALL;

void CountColors(void)
{
  BALL    box[cntBalls];          /* a box of balls  */
  int     count[cntColors];       /* color counters  */
  int     i;                      /* loop counter    */

  /* assume that box has been initialized with a random */
  /* collecton of 16 colored balls */

  for (i = 0; i < cntColors; i++)  /* initialize counters */
     count[i] = 0;
  for (i = 0; i < cntBalls; i++)   /* loop through box counting colors */
     count[box[i].color]++;

  printf("There are %d red balls\n",  count[red]   );
  printf("There are %d green balls\n",count[green]);
  printf("There are %d blue balls\n", count[blue]  );

} /* CountColors */
```

a structures
lemented through
ne statements.
ing is supported

ping implemented
a for loop.

nments can be
where in the
gram, surrounded
/ */*

programs. C implements its control structures through the use of IF ELSE statements and FOR, WHILE, and DO WHILE loops.

ADA

Ada is a general-purpose programming language developed in 1979 for the U.S. Department of Defense by an international team of computer scientists led by Jean Ichbiah. It was named after Augusta Ada Byron, Countess of Lovelace, who is considered the first programmer because of her work with Charles Babbage. The Pentagon has declared that software for military systems should be written in Ada. By virtue of that mandate alone, it is guaranteed a position in the software development community.

Ada is considered by many programming experts to be the most advanced programming language ever designed. It combines and refines many features of previous languages into a completely structured language.

Ada implements its control structures in much the same way as Pascal with its FOR loops and IF THEN ELSE control looping. A package can be written, compiled, and tested separately, a feature that helps to promote modularity. Ada has stronger typing features than Pascal and, most significantly, allows the construction of programs that consist of several tasks that execute in parallel.

REVIEW

Software development is a discipline that is constantly evolving. As the push for more and better software continues, new tools and techniques are created for use in solving problems. The prominent ideas are

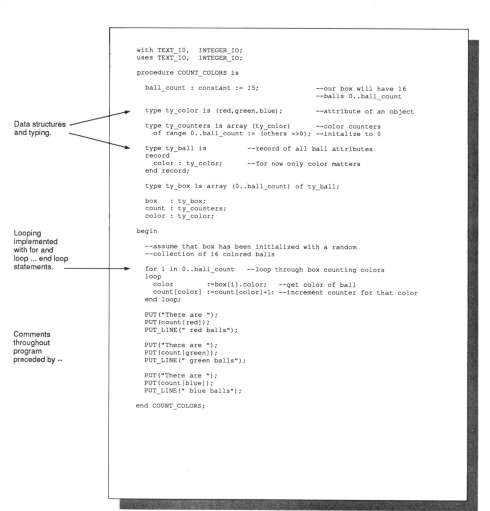

```
with TEXT_IO,  INTEGER_IO;
uses TEXT_IO,  INTEGER_IO;

procedure COUNT_COLORS is

   ball_count : constant := 15;            --our box will have 16
                                           --balls 0..ball_count

   type ty_color is (red,green,blue);      --attribute of an object

   type ty_counters is array (ty_color)    --color counters
     of range 0..ball_count := (others =>0); --initalize to 0

   type ty_ball is          --record of all ball attributes
   record
      color : ty_color;     --for now only color matters
   end record;

   type ty_box is array (0..ball_count) of ty_ball;

   box   : ty_box;
   count : ty_counters;
   color : ty_color;

begin

   --assume that box has been initialized with a random
   --collection of 16 colored balls

   for i in 0..ball_count   --loop through box counting colors
   loop
      color      :=box[i].color;  --get color of ball
      count[color] :=count[color]+1: --increment counter for that color
   end loop;
   PUT("There are ");
   PUT(count[red]);
   PUT_LINE(" red balls");

   PUT("There are ");
   PUT(count[green]);
   PUT_LINE(" green balls");

   PUT("There are ");
   PUT(count[blue]);
   PUT_LINE(" blue balls");

end COUNT_COLORS;
```

Data structures and typing.

Looping implemented with for and loop ... end loop statements.

Comments throughout program preceded by --

Ada listing of the Ping-Pong ball problem.

modularization and structured design, both of which can be effectively used before a program is coded. Once the program is ready to be developed, following accepted and standardized methods helps the programmer to create better and more correct software. A disciplined approach to program design, coding, translating, linking, testing, and documentation further increases the chances of software being correctly developed and on schedule. Even though structured programming is the most commonly accepted way of developing software, newer methods such as object-oriented programming are becoming quite popular. COBOL, FORTRAN, BASIC, Pascal, C, and Ada were compared in terms of their abilities to be used as structured tools for creating software.

REFERENCES

1. Harel, David. *Algorithmics: The Spirit of Computing.* Reading, Mass.: Addison-Wesley, 1987, p. 152. This book is an excellent introduction to algorithms, but the reading gets very dense rather quickly as it assumes some background in programming.

2. Ibid., p. 124.

3. Love, Tom. "Message Object Programming: A New Approach to System Building." Sandy Hook, Conn.: Productivity Products International, Inc., November 1984, pp. 8-11.

RESOURCES

BOOKS

Brooks, Frederick. *The Mythical Manmonth.* Reading, Mass.: Addison-Wesley, 1975. Frederick Brooks was the "father of the IBM System/360" and served as project manager for its development and manager of the Operating System/360 software project. This book is a set of essays on the management of computer programming and is a highly readable classic in the field.

Freeman, Peter. *Software Perspectives: The System Is the Message.* Reading, Mass.: Addison-Wesley, 1987. This book is a somewhat nontechnical discussion of the software development life cycle. It also contains some interesting arguments about the nature and quality of software.

Hu, David. *Object-Oriented Environment in C++.* Portland, Ore.: Management Information Source, 1990. An introductory book with plenty of programming examples that explains concepts, the Smalltalk language, user-interface design, and C++.

Lammers, Susan, ed. *Programmers at Work.* Redmond, Wash.: Microsoft Press, 1986. A fascinating look at 19 programmers and the way they approached the development of programs such as 1-2-3, Microsoft Word, dBase II, and Framework.

MAGAZINES

Computer Language. San Francisco, Cal.: CL Publications. A monthly magazine that focuses on the changing issues and trends in computer programming.

STUDY GUIDE

Match the following key terms to the appropriate definition:

A.

1. ____ Software development
2. ____ Software engineering
3. ____ Top-down design
4. ____ Bottom-up design

5. ____ Structure chart
6. ____ Module
7. ____ Algorithm
8. ____ Structured programming

9. ____ Control structure
10. ____ Flowchart
11. ____ Pseudocode

a. A step-by-step set of instructions for solving a specific problem.

b. A written description of a program using English statements.

c. The process of analyzing the requirements of a system, then designing, writing, and testing the software.

d. Starting with the parts and trying to build a whole.

e. The application of top-down design methods to programming.

f. The application of scientific and mathematical principles to the design and development of producing software.

g. Statements in a program that control the order in which the instructions are executed.

h. A set of instructions that can be tested and verified independently of its use in a larger program.

i. Going from general terms to finer and finer details.

j. A diagram that serves as a model for modularizing a structured program.

k. A graphic way of representing the thinking that goes into solving a problem.

B.

12. ____ Coding
13. ____ Structured programming language
14. ____ Source program
15. ____ Object program

16. ____ Interpreter
17. ____ Compiler
18. ____ Debugging
19. ____ Linker
20. ____ Loader

21. ____ Program testing
22. ____ Program documentation
23. ____ Object-oriented programming

a. A program that brings programs stored in a program library into memory for execution.

b. Writing a program in a specific programming language.

c. A program that has been translated into machine language.

d. A technique in which the programmer works with predefined objects.

e. Written information necessary to support the software.

f. A program that translates interactively each programming statement into an immediately usable machine language instruction.

g. A program that translates correct high-level programming statements into machine language instructions all at one time.

h. A language specifically designed for breaking a program into smaller units or modules.

i. A program written in a programming language such as BASIC or Pascal.

j. The process of uncovering errors in a program.

k. The process of verifying a program for its ability to perform its intended functions and to not do anything unexpected.

l. A program that combines separate modules into one executable program.

True/False:

24. ____ The first programmers used Ada as their programming language.

25. ____ The initial applications for computers in the early 1960s were in areas that already had standardized manual procedures.

26. ____ In the early days of programming, software was usually unique to the problem being solved.

27. ____ The process of programming is very effective when one person is responsible for all aspects of completing a specific program.

28. ____ The process of changing an existing program is known as program maintenance.

29. ____ A module cannot be coded, debugged, and tested without writing an entire program.

30. ____ Algorithms are an excellent source of problem-solving information.

31. ____ A basic premise of structured programming is that all programs can be written using one basic control structure.

32. ____ In the program design phase, a problem can be understood by engineering a solution.

33. ____ An advantage of pseudocode is the ability to write statements that are flexible enough to be coded in different programming languages.

34. ____ The finished results of testing are input to a compiler or an interpreter.

35. ____ Bugs are another name for errors.

36. ____ Interpreting each program statement considerably speeds up the execution speed of a program.

37. ____ When a program has been debugged, it can be assumed that it will work properly.

38. ____ A software engineer will often write a user's manual at the same time he or she prepares the requirements list.

Multiple Choice:

39. Software development has evolved over the last 20 years because of
    a. A rise in computer prices.
    b. The constant development of new programming languages.
    c. Large-scale efforts to test and validate new programming methods.
    d. Growth in the demand for software.

40. Which of the following statements is not an advantage to top-down design?
    a. A hierarchy chart is a useful visual model.
    b. Top-down design specifies how to combine smaller modules into a whole program.
    c. The programmer does not have to be concerned with specific details.
    d. The programmer can start with the whole and work toward the parts.

41. Independent modules can work as parts of a larger program because
    a. They can be tested and verified separately.
    b. They are well-defined processing tasks.
    c. They are conceptual tools.
    d. They can communicate by passing data.

42. The purpose of structured design is to
    a. Provide the means for teams of programmers to communicate.
    b. Modularize the problem.
    c. Start with the whole and work toward the parts.
    d. Allow modules to communicate with one another.

43. The design task of breaking a problem into modules is finished when
    a. The modules are tested and verified.
    b. A hierarchy chart is completely drawn.
    c. There is no misunderstanding about what the modules do.
    d. All the lower-level functions are known.

44. Which of the following does a flowchart use as symbols for processing operations?
    a. Ovals.
    b. Diamonds.
    c. Parallelograms.
    d. Rectangles.

45. The task of coding a program is easiest to accomplish with which of the following tools?
    a. Preprinted coding sheets.
    b. An automatic flowchart generator.
    c. An interactive terminal or personal computer.
    d. Programming languages with line numbers.

46. A compiler can do many kinds of error checking because
    a. The rules for writing programs are so rigid.
    b. Programmers do not make many errors.
    c. Spelling and grammar errors are easy to catch.
    d. It can transform instructions into a low-level language.

47. Testing a program is finished when
    a. A programmer finds all errors in the code with a compiler.
    b. All the expected things that can go wrong with a program are found.
    c. All possible conditions that can occur in a program have been explored.
    d. The documentation is complete.

48. Program documentation is concerned with

   a. User or instruction manuals.
   b. Drawing diagrams of program modules.
   c. Maintaining the software throughout its life cycle.
   d. Preprinted coding sheets.

49. Which of the following concepts does not characterize object-oriented programming?

   a. Class.
   b. Inheritance.
   c. Messages.
   d. Order.

Thought Questions:

50. What is the difference between a compiler and an interpreter? What are the advantages and disadvantages of each?

51. Why was software easier to write in the early 1960s than it is now?

Projects:

52. Visit an organization that employs programmers. Interview one of the programmers to find out what languages and techniques are used for software development. Report your findings to the class.

53. Research books and magazines to find articles that compare programming languages. Write a brief paper comparing two programming languages. Include the history of the languages.

SOFTWARE EXERCISES

As you have learned, software development consists of a sequence of activities necessary to design, code, test, and document the software. The time one programmer spends developing a program is divided among those four activities in the following manner: 35 percent in designing, 25 percent in coding, 35 percent in testing, and 5 percent in documenting. (These percentages are based on American Management Association figures.)

Assume that you are given 12 weeks to complete the task of developing the Ping-Pong application. Use your word processor to create a project schedule similar to the one shown here. Allocate the time for each of the four activities according to the percentages given. Use next Monday's date as the start date for your schedule.

```
Software Development Project Schedule
            June             July          August
       1  8 15 22 29   6 13 20 27   3 10 17
Design    <------->
Code               <-------->
Test                        <-------->
Document                             <--->
```

ANSWERS

1. c, **2.** f, **3.** i, **4.** d, **5.** j, **6.** h, **7.** a, **8.** e, **9.** g, **10.** k, **11.** b, **12.** b, **13.** h, **14.** i, **15.** c, **16.** f, **17.** g, **18.** j, **19.** l, **20.** a, **21.** k, **22.** e, **23.** d, **24.** F, **25.** T, **26.** T, **27.** T, **28.** T, **29.** F, **30.** T, **31.** F, **32.** F, **33.** T, **34.** F, **35.** T, **36.** F, **37.** F, **38.** T, **39.** d, **40.** b, **41.** d, **42.** b, **43.** c, **44.** c, **45.** c, **46.** a, **47.** c, **48.** c, **49.** d.

STEVE FREEDMAN

Profession: President, Vesalius, Inc., a multimedia publishing corporation, Berkeley, California.

Profile: After obtaining his M.D. from Stanford's Medical School, Dr. Freedman began researching the field of electronic books and multimedia communication systems. His latest production, the Electric Cadaver, is a multimedia anatomical reference encyclopedia that incorporates motion video, computer graphics, text, and sound.

Quote: "In the long term, computers will be seen primarily as a communications medium."

CHAPTER 15

END-USER DEVELOPMENT

PREVIEW

When personal computers first emerged in the late 1970s, they were considered a novelty and ignored by established MIS organizations. However, two trends have emerged. First, over the last decade, personal computers have become more powerful, less expensive, and easier to use. Second, the skills needed to implement major computer applications have shifted away from narrow technical specialties to a more balanced mix of strategic business skills coupled with a broad, general understanding of computer based technologies. Taken together, these two trends have resulted in personal computers being used by end users to develop applications of strategic importance to their organizations. As a result the entire application development process, as well as the set of people that participate in that process, has changed.

This chapter explores the continuum between traditional programming and many new application development alternatives and shows why particular choices between the alternatives are made. It discusses the diversity of tools and explains some of the newer trends and tools in application design. You should review the material on graphical user interfaces in Chapter 2 before reading the latter parts of this chapter.

In this chapter, you'll learn

- The need for end-user development.

- Alternatives to traditional programming.

- The types of end-user development tools.

- The differences among macro languages, program generators, database programming languages, interface builders, hybrid approaches, authoring systems, and object environments.

- End-user development trade-offs.

THE NEED FOR END-USER DEVELOPMENT

In the past, centralized MIS departments were expected to satisfy all the application development needs of an entire organization. However, the proliferation of departmental, work group, and individual computer systems has placed an emphasis on developing applications by non-computer specialists at the end-user level. The reasons for this emphasis are that:

• MIS departments cannot satisfy the large number of requests for application development. It is not unusual to find MIS departments with a two- to four-year backlog.

• Historically, MIS departments have often focused on technical aspects and overlooked the strategic business aspects of problems that needed to be solved. Applications developed solely by MIS departments have often failed to solve adequately the problems for which they were intended.

• Programming can be very difficult because it requires a very high level of technical knowledge and specialized training. Few end users have the time or motivation to master the necessary skills.

Keep in mind that this emphasis does not mean an end to traditional programming or large-scale MIS development. Programming is the appropriate approach for large-scale software development. When end users develop their own applications, the information center role of MIS takes on additional importance. MIS departments can help users find corporate data to process and provide additional levels of technical support. End-user development simply adds additional choices along a continuum of development options that ranges from traditional programming to off-the-shelf application software.

ALTERNATIVES TO TRADITIONAL PROGRAMMING

As you learned in Chapter 13, developing an application to meet a set of requirements requires answers to several planning and design questions. Does software that will solve the problem already exist? How have others solved similar problems? Are the requirements so unique that a new application must be developed from scratch? The answers to these questions involve defining (1) the scale of the application (e.g., are there tens of thousands of records involved or only a few?), (2) the scope of the application (i.e., Is the application general purpose or targeted to a very specialized need? Will the application be used outside the company or by just a few individuals within the company?), and (3) the type of data involved in the application (e.g., Raw data from the corporate database, spreadsheet cells, images, or a combination of all of these data types?).

Even after needs have been identified and an application defined, there is a wide range of development tools from which to choose.

• *Traditional programming languages*, such as C, COBOL, and BASIC. This approach, which was discussed in Chapter 14, generally costs the most and takes the longest amount of time to learn.

• *Macro languages* that can be found as a component of word processing, spreadsheet, and database programs.

• *Program generators* or nonprocedural application generators. These offer a nonprogramming alternative for custom development. Depending on the circumstances, these packages can often be used as is, with little customization.

• *Database programming languages*. While similar to traditional programming languages, they are generally easier to learn.

• *Interface builders*, such as Hypercard for the Macintosh and Toolbook for MS-DOS computers. This approach combines (1) the ability to assemble user interfaces from graphic objects with (2) a simple programming language.

• *Hybrid approaches*, which involve the use of a combination of tools such as Hypercard or Toolbook, databases, and traditional programming languages.

- *Authoring systems*, which are specialized application generators that can be used to create interactive learning or training programs. They often involve the use of tools such as Hypercard, Guide, or Macromind Director.

- *Object environments* in which it is possible to create applications using object-oriented techniques similar to those that were discussed in Chapter 14.

Keep in mind that there is no best way to develop an application. However, there are ways that have proven to be better in specific situations. The conceptual and logical approaches to solving an application development problem are the same regardless of the tools used. A spectrum of technology alternatives simply makes it easier to implement some kinds of applications. When developing an application, part of the planning and design problem involves picking and choosing among the best of the available tools.

PROTOTYPING

Success at end-user development is enhanced by obtaining feedback from the people who are affected by the application. Instead of following a rigid development plan, an end-user developer is more likely to succeed through **iterative prototyping**—the process of building working models of the application, trying them out, and modifying them in response to new ideas.

With a prototype of the application, users can gain hands on working experience with the model and more quickly evaluate the ability of the application to meet their needs. Typically, as people begin to work with an application, they change their ideas about what they want.

Building a model also helps to decide which tools to use in the long term. A prototype may be used as a simple demonstration and then discarded, or it may be possible to continue refining the prototype until it becomes the actual application. It is always possible to move on to more sophisticated tools such as having the application redone in a traditional programming language. On the other hand, it is usually more desirable to

stay within a single method or tool. For example, don't start with Hypercard to prototype a database application. Start with a specific database application generator and continue to build with that tool.

THE LIFE CYCLE APPROACH

Adhering to the **life-cycle approach**, which consists of determining the user's requirements, designing the application, writing the application, testing it, and maintaining it as the inevitable bugs appear and as user requirements change, is considered de rigueur by all application developers, regardless of the methods and tools used.

For example, a team of engineers designing a new generation of automobiles doesn't begin by making a full-scale metal mockup of the proposed design. That would be too time consuming and expensive. Instead, they start with rough sketches and refine them, after which they take clay and make several models, before settling on a full-scale mockup for tooling. It's usually better to make several models and discard the unusable ones.

MACRO LANGUAGES

A **macro** is a single command that executes a sequence of other commands. Virtually all spreadsheet programs

Macro languages. Shown here is a sample macro language with built-in commands.

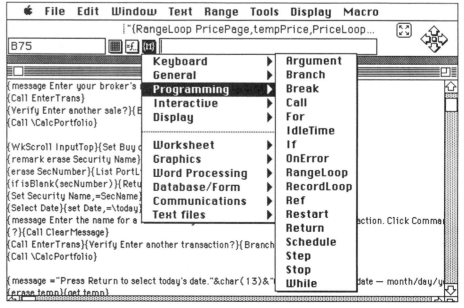

and most database and word processing programs implement a macro language facility.

Macros can be used to automate repetitive or complex time-consuming tasks. You can record a series of actions, then play them back by pressing a key you define. Or you can create a custom macro in a manner similar to writing a program. A *macro language* is a special-purpose programming language embedded inside an application. They are usually easier to use than a traditional programming language because they are limited to handling a few kinds of data that are part of the application and with which the user is already familiar. For example, you could:

• Record a macro to automatically create a letterhead.

• Record a macro that consolidates a series of five regional spreadsheets into one sales report.

• Create a custom set of menu bars, menus, and dialog boxes for a special-purpose application.

Macro languages do not eliminate the tasks of analyzing requirements, defining the problem, and planning and developing the solution. Their advantage lies in the rapidity with which applications can be developed by nonprogrammers. Their disadvantage is that they often fail to meet the criteria for good structured programming languages. The applications developed with macro languages are usually unstructured and undocumented. For example, suppose a manager informally developed a spreadsheet macro upon which an entire department became dependent, then re-

signed from the company. The new manager likes the macro, but wants to expand its functionality. If the macro was not properly documented, problems can occur if it needs to be changed or maintained.

COMMAND FILES

Closely related to the idea of macro is a *command file*, a series of operating system commands that is played back when the command file is executed. Like macros, command files can be used to automate repetitive or complex time-consuming tasks. You can enter a series of commands into a file, name the file, and then play the commands back by executing the file. In the MS-DOS operating system, command files are called *batch files*.

For example, suppose you had a word processing application in which you needed to back up 10 files at the end of each day's writing. In MS-DOS, this would involve typing 10 COPY commands each time you needed to perform the back up. You can put the ten COPY commands into a batch file and assign the file a name. Then to do the back up, you simply type the name of the batch file. Your commands in the batch file are processed as if they were entered from the keyboard.

A common example of an MS-DOS batch file is called AUTOEXEC.BAT. When the computer is turned on, the batch file, if it exists, is executed automatically when the system starts up. An AUTOEXEC.BAT file might perform tasks such as setting up a RAM disk, checking a hard disk, and invoking a specific application program.

Command files. A sample MS-DOS batch file for copying a specific file from drive a: to drive b:.

```
echo off
rem This is a batch file for backing up
rem chap1.doc from drive a: to drive b:
echo Place the original data disk in A:
echo And the backup disk in B:
pause
if exist a:chap1.doc goto backup
echo File in Drive A: does not exist
goto end
:backup
echo backing up...
copy a:chap1.doc b:
goto end
:end
```

PROGRAM GENERATORS

Program generators, sometimes called *application generators* or *fourth-generation languages*, offer a way to generate a program based on writing specifications about the problem to be solved. Program generators can be found in personal computer database packages and as stand-alone packages for larger systems. For example, a *report generator* is a special type of program generator that can generate only one type of program—a report from a database. If you want to have a weekly sales report produced from an existing file, you could use a report generator to specify the report's title, column headings, and fields from the existing file to be printed. The specifications would then be used to generate a program to print the report.

When building a database application with a program generator for example, start by specifying what data are to be stored in the database and how that data should be processed. If a data dictionary for existing databases is available, consult it for specifications. After defining the needed databases, you can define a description, data type, field width, and validation rules for each database field. An hourly pay field, for example, would be defined as a monetary amount and might include a range validation check to make sure the value does not exceed a specific amount.

After the database design is complete, you can create the layouts for menus, data-entry screens, help screens, query screens, and reports. Once all the pieces of the application are specified, the program generator creates the programs for the application. The program generator should also provide the means to create documentation for the application such as the database, the structure of the application, the programs, and screen and report definitions.

Program generators are called *nonprocedural languages* because you define problems in terms of the results desired instead of in procedural programming terms. Program generators enable you to avoid the programming steps that must be specified in a language such as COBOL or C; however, a program must still be designed, generated, tested, and documented. A person using a program generator must still understand the problem and engineer a solution. Only the tools he or she uses have changed.

An example of an application generator on a larger scale is a product called Application Development Facility (ADF) by IBM. ADF allows a person with minimal programming training to write specifications in the

characteristics of the desired programming language, which are used to generate a program automatically. Using ADF, a programmer with a minimum of skills could quickly and easily generate a complete application, which would help to speed up the software development cycle.

Although program generators may work well when it comes to noncritical applications, they are usually not considered for critical production applications such as order processing or payroll. Such applications, which involve long life spans and many end users, are usually considered as candidates for development with a traditional programming language from the MIS department.

DATABASE PROGRAMMING LANGUAGES

Database programming languages are similar to traditional programming languages, but they are generally easier to learn because they, like macro languages, limit the types of problems they are used to solve to those devoted to inputting, storing, retrieving, sorting, and reporting of data. Developing applications with database languages can be fast, flexible, and inexpensive because they are problem oriented. They can solve a smaller set of problems better than a general-purpose programming language.

DATABASE PROGRAMMING ISSUES

Despite the potential time and money savings of using a database in lieu of a programming language, there are several issues to consider. First, consider the style and boundaries of the database programs in question. As discussed in Chapter 11, for example, a single flat file may not be an appropriate tool for developing a complete application. A relational database may be needed. An application written in a database language may run relatively slowly because it is *interpreted*; that is, the database commands are translated and executed one at a time. For higher

```
┌─ PROGRAM.PRG ──────────────────────────────────┐
│Msum   = 0                                       │
│                                                 │
│do while Mloop < 100                             │
│    ? "Name: "+TRIM(Fname)+" "+TRIM(Lname)+" State: "+State│
│    if Mloop > 50                                │
│       Mpage = 2                                 │
│    endif                                        │
│    Msum = Msum + 1                              │
│    Mcount = Mcount + Mloop/Msum                 │
│    Mloop = Mloop + 1                            │
│enddo                                            │
└─────────────────────────────────────────────────┘
┌─ DISPLAY ─────────────────┐ ┌─ BREAKPOINTS ──────┐
│Mloop         :        10  │ │1: Mloop = 10        │
│Mcount        :       209  │ │2: Mloop = 20        │
│DATE() + 14   : 02/11/88   │ │3: Mloop + Msum > 1000│
│Msum          :         9  │ │4:                   │
└───────────────────────────┘ └─────────────────────┘
┌─ DEBUGGER ─────────────────────────────────────────────────┐
│Work Area: 1    Database file: CUSTOMER.DBF   Program file: PROGRAM.DBO│
│Record:    1    Master Index:                 Procedure:    PROGRAM│
│ACTION:    _                                  Current line: 19   │
└────────────────────────────────────────────────────────────┘
Stopped for step.
```

Database programming. dBase IV contains a programming language and debugging facility for custom application development.

defining and documenting the system.

From an end-user point of view, just because an application works doesn't mean that below the surface it's structured and designed well, and capable of being maintained. Database development environments make it easy to be negligent. Of course, that can happen in any environment, but professional programmers learn the discipline along the way. An end user can get a functional application developed very quickly without a lot of discipline. But proper design, development, and implementation are important if the application will be used for a long period of time or is of strategic importance to the organization. Whether databases or programming languages are used, the time must be taken to understand, comment on, and document the structure of the program.

performance, execution speed can be increased by using a database compiler. Like the programming language compilers discussed in Chapter 14, a *database compiler* translates all the programming statements into a machine language program that is executed at once. For example, a program called Clipper can translate dBase programming statements into a machine language program that can be executed without the line-by-line translation steps.

Second, because there are many different database packages available, invest the time to learn about the strengths and weaknesses of the various products. Learn about the various database tools and their capabilities, as well as the existing development done in those environments. The time spent in obtaining such information will pay off in the long run.

The time it takes to become proficient in using a database language is often underestimated, even though vendors claim that databases are easy to use. Learning how to use a complex database product is not a trivial task.

Databases offer reasonable alternatives to the challenge of programmer productivity, but writing the program represents only a fraction of the of the cost and time of the total application development life cycle. The rest is in

INTERFACE BUILDERS

An *interface builder* allows you to assemble a user interface, also called a front end, from a library of predefined graphic objects such as windows, buttons, and scroll bars. With the addition of programming in a simple language, entire applications can be developed.

Hypercard for the Macintosh and Toolbook for MS-DOS-based computers with Microsoft Windows are good examples of interface builders. Both provide a customizable graphical user interface and the means to create programs called scripts. Hypercard calls its programming or scripting language Hypertalk, whereas Toolbook uses the term "Openscript." Hypercard uses the term "stack" as the metaphor upon which applications are based; Toolbook uses the term "book." Hypercard stacks are made up of cards, Toolbook books of pages. Both cards and pages can contain text, input fields, and graphics. Both can contain buttons to allow the user to start a process, select an option, or branch or jump from one card or page to another.

Taken together, these tools add up to a framework for developing a wide range of applications that can include text, graphics, video, sound, and animation. Custom front ends for existing applications, interactive tutorials, reference works, and desktop presentations are natural candidates for interface builders.

How do you build an application with an interface builder? Let's take the case of a simple address book as an example. (Refer to the discussion of creating the People File in Chapter 8.) Your application is based on a familiar metaphor, the physical address book. For simplicity sake, it will contain one page per person. You need not worry about how many pages to create; you can add them as you go along. Next, you would define the objects that are to appear on each page. For example, you need to create some text fields so that you can enter the person's name, title, company, address, and so on. You could also add a background color or pattern to your pages for aesthetics or added emphasis. If you had access to a scanner, you could add a graphics field to your pages. Then by scanning photographs of people, you could copy the scanned image to the graphics field in the appropriate page.

Finally, you need a means to navigate through the pages in your application. For that you create buttons. (Recall that when using a graphical user interface you press a button on the screen by positioning the cursor with a mouse, then pressing a button on the mouse.) To navigate sequentially through your address book, you would create two buttons with the graphic symbols [<] to go to the previous page and [>] to go to the next page. When you create the [<] button, for example, you would also create a simple script that tells the application to go to the previous page. How would you find a particular individual's name in your address book? A built-in search command allows you to navigate to a particular page in the application in which a specific field of text appears.

Of course, buttons can do more than simply move among pages. For example, if you want to print a mailing list when you press a button, you can attach a script to the button to tell the application to print the mailing list. A button can also trigger a search through an external database. Thus

quite complex applications can be created. For example, an accounting firm had an auditing application in which auditors used manual searches to find specific answers to specific questions from a 12-foot shelf of reference manuals. These thousands of pages of text cover everything from company policies to the Securities and Exchange Commission regulations to the latest tax codes. Part of the solution involved shrinking the multivolume reference set onto a CD ROM disk. But storing a large amount of data is one thing; retrieving it is another. After reviewing the technology tools available, the accounting firm chose Hypercard to replace manual searches with a Macintosh-based retrieval system. The application began as a prototype, by simply mocking up a user interface. Through reiteration based on user feedback, the product evolved into a functional retrieval application.

With an interface builder's buttons and scripting language, you can create *multimedia applications* that combine multiple information types such as text, graphics, video, music, voice, and animation. For example, one developer produced an electronic sales brochure designed to help dealers sell

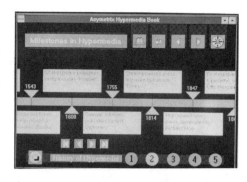

Interface Builder. *Toolbook's navigation capabilities allow users to create books.*

Buttons. *Behind a button is a script that tells the button what to do.*

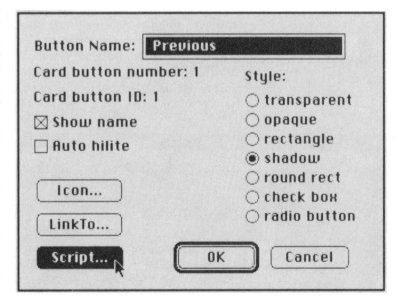

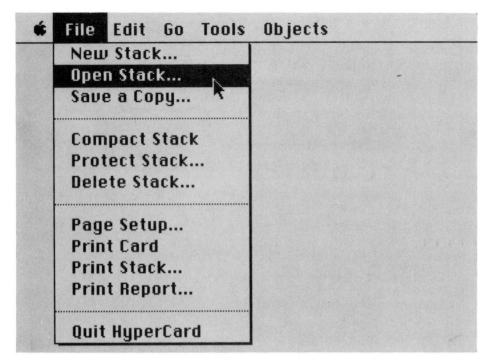

Interface builder. Hypercard uses the term "stack" as a metaphor for custom applications.

Hybrid approach. Shown here is a frame from The Electric Cadaver, a multimedia anatomical reference encyclopedia.

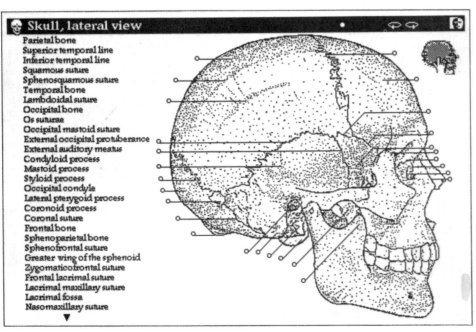

desktop-publishing systems. A potential customer fills out an on-screen qualification form in which he or she makes choices that determine how a subsequent interactive desktop presentation featuring scanned images, voice, and music, will proceed. At the end of the presentation, the salesperson can print an order form to help close the sale.

Another example: an "electronic employee handbook," in which new employees can browse through the benefits section, fill out a card to select the desired type of benefit package, and have the card automatically sent to the personnel department via a local-area network.

HYBRID APPROACHES

Hybrid approaches enable you to assemble systems out of existing tools to develop an application to meet a specific need. For example, in a bank, rather than having MIS develop a new application for loan processing, an experienced loan analyst might opt to access a customer database, write a macro to link fields in the selected database record to a spreadsheet for financial analysis, and produce a finished loan report for management. Thus two application programs are used at the end-user level to create a single small-scale information system.

Through buttons that trigger special commands, interface builders can link to a variety of external devices, systems, or other applications. For example, at a steel plant, a group of process-control minicomputers monitors the steel-making operation. Engineers and metallurgists access data on Macintoshes running Hypercard, which is networked to the process-control computers; they select various sets of data, and then transfer those data to spreadsheets and other applications for analysis. In effect, Hypercard serves as the user interface for the minicomputers.

Based on experience gained in this project, the company plans to use the same techniques to link shop-floor Macintoshes to a manufacturing resource planning (MRP) system to provide management with data about the steel-making operation.

By combining tools, it is often possible to create an expressive environment that combines several multimedia possibilities. For example, to explore the nature of dynamic documentation, Stanford's Steve Freedman developed the Electric Cadaver, a multimedia anatomical reference encyclopedia. Not for the squeamish viewer, the application uses a videodisk on which the whole human anatomy is precisely cataloged, with images ranging from detailed autopsy photographs to video clips of surgical procedures. With Hypercard acting as directory and videodisk controller, the user can navigate through each muscle, organ, and bone in the body.

AUTHORING SYSTEMS

An *authoring system* is a specialized application generator that combines hardware and software tools for designing interactive programs. Any program that can control events through time is an authoring system. A good example of this is lighting a stage play. The task involves coordinating the timing of lights with the timing of actors and actions on the stage (e.g., fade to dark at the end of Act 1, flash background strobe lights to create the illusion of a sudden storm). The task can be quite formidable if done manually, but a computer-controlled lighting board, which is a special-purpose authoring system, allows the technical director to preprogram the sequence, duration, intensity, and color of the lights for an entire play. (The system also includes a manual override in case the actor's timing is off or something unexpected happens during the course of the play.) In a personal computer system, the stage is the display screen, and the authoring system is programmed to control the sequence, duration, and timing of the audio and visual elements of a presentation.

A common application for authoring systems is the production of *courseware,* programs for which the main purpose is teaching. In the past, courseware, also known as computer-assisted instruction, consisted of simple drill-and-practice tutorials or fill-in-the-blanks tests. Today's authoring systems enable teachers to create interactive simulations that integrate pictures, animation, and sound to appeal to a student's emotional and intellectual reasons for learning. They can be used to augment lectures, as laboratory tutorials, and as library reference material.

As with any specialized technology, authoring systems extract trade-offs from their developers. One of the biggest problems is the tremendous versatility of such systems. Users accus-

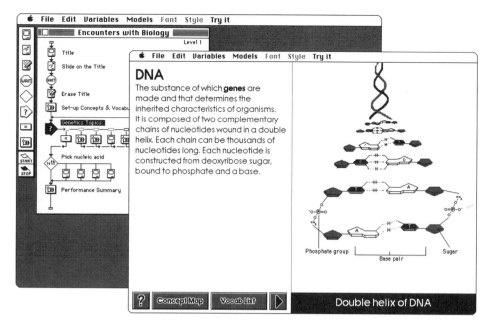

Authoring systems. *Building custom courseware that includes text and graphics.*

tomed to developing text-based applications may have trouble with the transition to an authoring system's visual and graphic orientation.

Using an authoring system is more like making a movie than it is like traditional application development. As a consequence, developers use *storyboards*—sequencing techniques borrowed from the movie industry. With a storyboard, an end user can visually map out a sequence of actions and coordinate events, such as synchronizing soundtracks, actions, and dialog. Large-scale projects developed with authoring systems are complicated enough to require a team ap-

Authoring systems. *Animation is made possible by manipulating the score shown in the lower left corner.*

proach, often consisting of a project manager, graphic designers, production artists, illustrators, instructional designers, copywriters, and editors.

An example of an authoring system that uses animation is a product called Director from Macromind, Inc. To create the illusion of motion in animation, a series of single frames is projected in a sequence. Director uses a score to enable users to create pictures and sound one frame at a time. As in music, the score reads from left to right and the columns contain activities such as pictures, text, sound or music, narration, and buttons during each frame. The user can view single frames or compress time so that a sequence spanning a number of frames can be viewed.

For example, to show customers how calls are routed through switches over a telephone network, switching equipment manufacturer Northern Telecomm uses animated multimedia presentations to help customers understand the switching process. Flashes of color coupled with multiple colors and color changes are used to represent call traffic. In between the routing animation, the presentation features graphs and text describing the process.[1]

OBJECT ENVIRONMENTS

Object environments. New Wave represents objects with icons on the display screen.

Object-oriented application environments are derivatives of the object-oriented programming paradigm that was discussed in Chapter 14. *Object environments* exploit the availability of prefabricated software components called objects. In these environments predesigned objects can be easily combined and modified, in many different ways, to produce a new application. Examples include Hewlett-Packard's NewWave, IBM's OfficeVision, and Metaphor Computer System's Data Interpretation System (DIS).

Object environments use three generic kinds of objects:[2]

- *Application objects* are data and their instructions combined into a single module of software.

- *Container objects* are similar to file folders. They can hold other objects so they can be easily stored, filed, or sent through electronic mail.

- *Resource objects* are devices or services such as a printer or a file-server object.

Object environments are used with graphical user interfaces such as Microsoft Windows. Once things are defined as objects, they can be represented as *icons* on a display screen. For example, an application object's icon might look like a document; a container object's icon might look like a file folder. Taken together, these generic objects form a system of software building blocks with which you can develop applications.

For example, the Metaphor Data Interpretation System uses object-oriented concepts in a specialized application to simplify the gathering and analysis of data in brand management applications. Brand managers are people in the food industry in charge of a specific product line. If a brand manager has to analyze the results of a sales promotion and create a report for upper management, he or she builds an application object called a *capsule*— a group of objects represented by icons that are linked together—to record the set of actions necessary to gather the sales data and analyze them. The capsule might contain a database query object, a spreadsheet object, a charting object, and a printer object. The brand manager builds a flow diagram in the capsule that links the objects together. The end result is a custom application

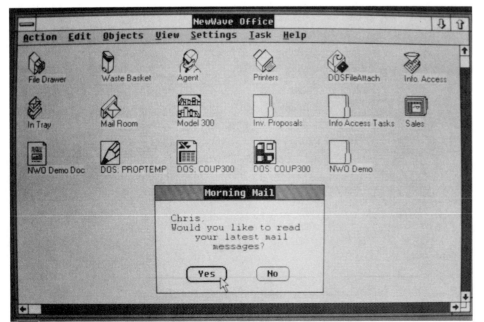

tailored to the brand manager's needs.

The Hewlett-Packard Company is using an object environment in a product called NewWave. NewWave uses object-oriented concepts combined with the Windows graphical user interface to permit you to create applications by manipulating icons. In NewWave, an application object, represented by an icon, is simply the appropriate data files linked to an application program. An object management facility keep track of all links between data files. Suppose, for example, a spreadsheet and a chart in a document have been defined in an application object. If data in the spreadsheet change, the chart is updated automatically. More complex tasks that require multiple steps can be automated via the use of another type of object called an *agent*.

You would create an agent object in much the same way that you would create a macro—by recording a series of actions which the agent translates into commands. To create an employee review application for example, you would record the following tasks. (1) Querying the corporate personnel database over the local-area network to determine which employees are eligible for review. (2) Moving the data into a spreadsheet for analysis. (3) Creating a report that combines salary data with a performance review. Once recorded, the application can be played back, and even scheduled to run automatically on certain dates, such as once every quarter.

Like object-oriented programming, object environments are still in their infancy. There are not very many object libraries from which end users can draw, and object environments sold by different vendors are not compatible.

END-USER DEVELOPMENT TRADE-OFFS

Developing applications with end-user tools can be fast, flexible, and inexpensive, and such savings in time and money are the hard numbers with which application developers justify their use. End-user development is problem oriented. In many cases, it is

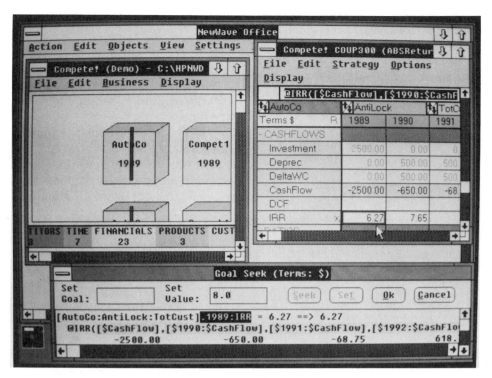

Object environments. New Wave users can integrate information from several different applications.

more powerful than a programming language because it sacrifices generality for specificity in a narrow range of problems.

However, end-user tools are not an end-all development environment. There are cases in which traditional programming languages are better suited for developing applications—accounting, such as general ledger and

SPOTLIGHT ON...

Hypercard Applications

Apple's bundling of Hypercard with every new Macintosh is alluring to people who have no programming experience. Hypercard promises help for people who want to develop applications but who do not want to learn how to program.

But Hypercard is not an end-all tool. There are cases in which traditional programming languages or database programs will be better suited for developing applications than Hypercard. What does Hypercard offer the programmer that the traditional tools don't?

• *Style.* Applications can be created that combine text, graphics, video, music, voice, and animation.

• *Creativity.* Hypercard can provide a rich, interactive, graphic environment using pictures and graphics instead of words.

• *Flexibility.* Hypercard exploits the potential of prototyping (discussed in Chapter 12) by making it easy to create an initial working model, then easily modify it.

As with any new technology, Hypercard requires trade-offs. Arguably, the biggest drawback is Hypercard's own tremendous versatility. Programmers accustomed to developing text-based applications may have trouble with the transition to its visual and graphic orientation. And Hypercard is, in many ways, more like making a movie than it is like programming.

To learn more, read Danny Goodman's Hypercard Developer's Guide. *Illustrated paperback, 644 pp. New York: Bantam Books, 1988.*

accounts payable, and corporate databases are among them.

There are several factors that can adversely affect an organization's ability to use alternative tools to develop new applications. Among the most important of these is resistance to change. People often spend a great deal of time learning how to use a particular program. They develop a level of comfort and expertise with the program and do not want to abandon those levels to take the risk involved in learning a new program. Despite this, an end user should always ask: Would I be better off learning a new tool? Will the investment in learning pay off?

In the long term, developing a new application is more likely to succeed by changing some basic attitudes and behavior. For example, a new application should be developed so that it's easy for people to accomplish new ways to do work. As mentioned in Chapter 10, it's not the technology that will decide the success of the application; human factors such as social structures and work and communication patterns and habits will determine whether the application will be used.

REVIEW

End-user development has emerged because of the widespread growth of departmental, work group, and individual computer systems. It adds additional choices along a continuum of development options. The type, scale, and scope of the application determine which methods and tools to use for development. The choices of tools include traditional programming, macro languages, program generators, database programming languages, interface builders, hybrid approaches, authoring systems, and object environments.

Although there is no best way to develop an application, certain choices have proven to be better in specific situations. In the long term, however, it's not the technology, but how well people can use technology that determines the choice of development tools. Also, adhering to the life-cycle approach, in which requirements are determined and the application is designed, written, and maintained, is required regardless of the tool chosen.

As with any specialized technology or tool, alternatives to traditional programming extract trade-offs from their users. Alternative tools can be more powerful because they are problem oriented and thus sacrifice generality for specificity in a narrow range of problems. And end-user tools are not an end-all development environment. The user must pick and choose from among the best of the available tools.

REFERENCES

1. Lockwood, Russ. "Multimedia in Business: The New Presentations." *Personal Computing*. Totowa, N.J.:, June 29, 1990, p. 126.

2. Rymer, John. *Object Orientation: Concepts and Implementations*. Boston, Mass.: Patricia Seybold's Office Computing Group, 1990, p. 129.

RESOURCES

BOOKS

Ambron, Sueann, and Kristina Hooper, eds. *Interactive Multimedia*. Redmond, Wash.: Microsoft Press, 1988. A collection of articles from different authors based on a 1986 conference on multimedia in education. Each author provides his or her perspective on building multimedia presentations.

Pierce, Joseph. *ToolBook Companion*. Redmond, Wash.: Microsoft Press, 1990. This book is an excellent tutorial and reference guide to the Toolbook interface builder program.

STUDY GUIDE

Match the following key terms to the appropriate definition:

A.

1. ____ Iterative prototyping
2. ____ Life-cycle approach
3. ____ Macro
4. ____ Macro language
5. ____ Program generators
6. ____ Report generator
7. ____ Nonprocedural languages
8. ____ Interface builder

a. A special type of program generator that can only generate one type of program: a report from a database.

b. A single command that executes a sequence of other commands.

c. The process of building working models of the application, trying them out, and modifying them in response to new ideas.

d. A way to generate a program based on writing specifications about the problem to be solved.

e. A language in which the user defines problems in terms of the results desired instead of in procedural programming terms.

f. Determining the user's requirements, designing the application, writing the application, testing it, and maintaining it.

g. A special-purpose programming language embedded inside an application.

h. A tool that allows an end user to assemble a user interface from a library of predefined graphic objects such as windows, buttons, and scroll bars.

B.

9. ____ Multimedia applications
10. ____ Hybrid approaches
11. ____ Authoring system
12. ____ Courseware
13. ____ Object environments
14. ____ Application objects
15. ____ Container objects
16. ____ Resource objects

a. Approaches that enable a user to assemble systems out of existing tools to develop an application to meet a specific need.

b. A specialized application generator that combines hardware and software tools for designing interactive programs.

c. Devices or services such as a printer or a file-server object.

d. Objects that can hold other objects so they can be easily stored, filed, or sent through electronic mail.

e. Applications that combine multiple information types such as text, graphics, video, music, voice, and animation.

f. Data and their instructions combined into a single module of software.

g. The use of prefabricated software components called objects that can be easily combined and modified in many different ways, to produce a new application.

h. Programs for which the main purpose is teaching.

True/False:

17. ____ The skills needed to implement major computer applications must combine technical specialties with strategic business skills.

18. ____ Programming can be very easy and most end users can master the necessary skills.

19. ____ End-user development means an end to large-scale MIS development and traditional programming.

20. ____ There is no best way to develop an application.

21. ____ Typically, as people begin to work with an application, they change their ideas about what they want.

22. ____ Macro languages eliminate the tasks of analyzing requirements, defining the problem, and planning and developing the solution.

23. ____ Program generators are nonprocedural because the user defines problems in terms of the results desired instead of in programming terms.

24. ____ Database programming languages are generally easier to learn than programming lan-

guages because they limit the types of problems they are used to solve.

25. ____ Often, end-user applications began as a prototype, by simply mocking up a user interface.

26. ____ Interface builders make it easy to navigate through massive amounts of information without getting lost.

27. ____ Any language or program that can control events through time is an authoring system.

28. ____ Using an authoring system is more like making a movie than it is like traditional application development.

29. ____ Object environments do not work well with graphical user interfaces.

30. ____ An application object can be thought of as the appropriate data files linked to a program.

31. ____ Today, extensive object libraries exist from which end users can draw upon.

Multiple Choice:

32. Which of the following has contributed least to end-user application development?
    a. Departmental computer systems.
    b. Workgroup computer systems.
    c. Individual computer systems.
    d. Centralized management information systems.

33. Why is it useful to build a working model of a potential application?
    a. Users will not change their ideas about what it is they want.
    b. The model will not change.
    c. Users can decide which tool to use in the long term.
    d. The model can be thrown away.

34. Which of the following is true about macro languages?
    a. They eliminate the tasks of analyzing requirements.
    b. They facilitate rapid application development.
    c. They are harder to use than traditional programming languages.
    d. Macro applications are usually structured and documented.

35. When building a database application with a program generator, the user should start by

a. Defining a description, data type, field width, and validation rules for each database field.
    b. Creating the layouts for menus and data-entry screens.
    c. Creating help screens, query screens, and reports.
    d. Specifying what data are to be stored in the database.

36. Databases offer reasonable alternatives to the challenge of programmer productivity because
    a. Database languages are procedure oriented.
    b. They can solve a smaller set of problems better than a general-purpose programming language.
    c. The learning curve to become proficient in using a database language is short.
    d. Writing the program represents only a fraction of the cost and time of the total application development life cycle.

37. Which of the following would not be considered an application area for an interface builder?
    a. Reference works.
    b. Interactive tutorials.
    c. Electronic sales brochures.
    d. Order entry.

38. Which of the following is not a

likely application for courseware?
    a. Fill-in-the-blanks tests.
    b. Augmenting lectures.
    c. Laboratory tutorials.
    d. Library reference materials.

39. What is one of the biggest problems the user of an authoring system faces?
    a. Developing text-based applications.
    b. The tremendous versatility of such systems.
    c. Using a storyboard.
    d. Developing a reference work.

40. Which of the following is false about object environments?
    a. Generic objects form a system of software building blocks.
    b. Object environments and graphical user interfaces are unlikely partners.
    c. Once things are defined as objects, it is ideal to represent them as icons on a display screen.
    d. Predesigned objects can be easily combined and modified, in many different ways, to produce a new application.

41. In an object environment, which of the following is not considered to be a generic type of object?
    a. Data.
    b. Application.
    c. Container.
    d. Resource.

Thought Questions:

42. In this chapter, we introduced macro languages, program generators, database programming languages, interface builders, hybrid approaches, authoring systems, and object environments. Which did you find the easiest to understand? Why? Which was the most difficult or obscure? Why?

43. How are object environments similar to the other tools mentioned in this chapter? How are they different?

Projects:

44. Choose one of the categories of end-user development tools mentioned in this chapter, then visit a computer store and find a program that fits the category you choose. Prepare a report describing the program.

45. Contact an organization that has an MIS department. Prepare a brief report that addresses the following questions: Has decentralization affected the way that the organization does business? Are applications developed at the end-user level in the organization? If they are, how does the MIS department support end-user development? Present your findings to the class.

SOFTWARE EXERCISES

For this exercise, you are going to use your word processor to write an MS-DOS batch file that copies a file from one disk to another, and then displays the directory of the disk on which the file has been copied. You will need to consult your school computer lab's MS-DOS Reference Manual to do this assignment, but keep in mind the following: (1) After you have typed the commands with your word processor, make sure to save your file as an ASCII text file. (2) The file name for the batch file must include .BAT as the extension.

ANSWERS

1. c, 2. f, 3. b, 4. g, 5. d, 6. a, 7. e, 8. h, 9. e, 10. a, 11. b, 12. h, 13. g, 14. f, 15. d, 16. c, 17. T, 18. F, 19. F, 20. T, 21. T, 22. F, 23. T, 24. T, 25. T, 26. F, 27. T, 28. T, 29. F, 30. T, 31. F, 32. d, 33. c, 34. b, 35. d, 36. b, 37. d, 38. a, 39. b, 40. b, 41. a.

APPENDIXES

PREVIEW

A. THE HISTORY OF COMPUTERS

A comprehensive timeline of computer and information technology "firsts" that starts in the 1600s. It presents an overview of the major inventions and developments in the history of computers.

B. SHOPPING GUIDE

The personal computer industry currently has a wide variety of hardware and software from which to choose. This appendix outlines a process that you can use to choose among this wide variety. It contains useful, up-to-date information about software and hardware choices so that you can match a personal computer system to your own needs.

C. NUMBER SYSTEMS, DATA REPRESENTATION, AND CODES

Appendic C contains an explanation of different number systems, how they are used in computer systems, and how data are represented in computers. This appendix also contains a useful reference table of both the EBCDIC and ASCII codes.

D. GLOSSARY

This appendix contains a comprehensive, up-to-date reference to computer and communication terminology. It includes definitions of all the key terms used in the text as well as hundreds of additional important terms.

The abacus was the first implementation of the notion that machines could be used to perform intellectual work.

APPENDIX A
THE HISTORY OF COMPUTERS

PREVIEW

Wilhelm Schickard didn't know he was making history in 1623. He was simply trying to build a calculator for the famous mathematician Johannes Kepler. Nor did Vannevar Bush, who in 1931 was trying to figure out ways to solve differential equations and thus developed the first analog computer. Neither did Grace Hopper, who in 1960 was trying to figure out how to make a program written for one computer run on another computer and consequently wrote the first practical compiler program. They were too intensely involved in their day-to-day problems to think about historical consequences.

Nor were the great technical achievements always awarded the approval of the marketplace. Blaise Pascal could never sell his automatic calculator. Charles Babbage could only complete a small part of his difference engine. And Richard Greenblatt's first chess-playing programs were no match for humans.

But today, we look back in awe at what they and many other scientists, inventors, and mathematicians accomplished. As we trace the long history of computers, keep in mind that the limitations are no longer technical, but economic, legal, and political. Today, we have reached an era in which anything we might want to do with computers is possible.

1617   1621   1623

JOHN NAPIER'S "BONES." The Scottish mathematician John Napier (1550-1617) is best known for the invention of logarithms—numbers that enable multiplication and division to be reduced to addition and subtraction. Toward the end of his life, he invented sets of calculating rods made of sticks of bone or ivory, hence the name "Napier's bones." These sticks made multiplication and division easier by being, in essence, movable multiplication tables. They influenced the invention of the slide rule and some of the calculating machines that followed.

THE SLIDE RULE. William Oughtred (1575–1660), an English mathematician, invented a circular slide rule that translated Napier's logarithms onto a set of rotating scales. The device is considered to be one of the earliest analog computing devices.

FIRST MECHANICAL CALCULATOR. Wilhelm Schickard (1592-1635), in Germany, designed the Calculating Clock, a calculating machine that incorporated "Napier's bones" onto cylinders that could be rotated to perform calculations. It accomplished multiplication and division by converting numbers to logarithms, adding or subtracting them, and converting back. Schickard commissioned one of his machines to be built for the famous mathematician Johannes Kepler but, when half-built, the machine was destroyed by fire. Before it could be rebuilt, Schickard died in the plagues that accompanied the Thirty Years War.

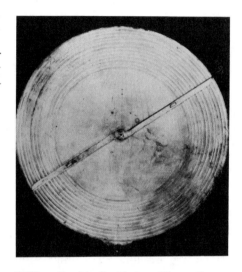

William Oughtred's Circles of Proportion was the first slide rule.

Schickard's calculator used a variation of Napier's bones on rotating cylinders. Shown is a model that was reconstructed in the 1960s.

Napier's bones, engraved in ivory, were movable multiplication tables, the first modern step in the mechanization of calculating.

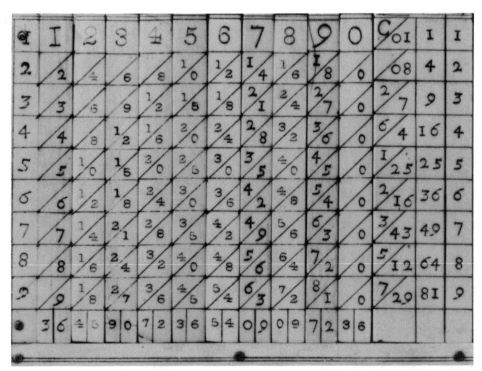

1642   1666   1673

FIRST AUTOMATIC MECHANICAL CALCULATOR. Blaise Pascal (1623-1662) invented the Pascaline, which is considered to be the first automatic calculating device. The machine, which could only add and subtract, was the first to be based on extremely precise interconnected gears, a principle that persisted for hundreds of years in mechanical calculators. Pascal thought his machine would be a commercial success, but even the simple operation of subtraction required interpreting results on the machine instead of actually reading the results. That plus resistance to change severely limited widespread adoption of the machine.

FIRST MULTIPLYING MACHINE. Sir Samuel Morland (1625-1695)—former secretary to Oliver Cromwell and, at the time of his invention, master of mechanics to King Charles II of England—invented a machine that incorporated a steel pin that moved a series of dial plates and small indexes that allowed addition, subtraction, multiplication, and division to take place. The device was clumsy and not always reliable and did not include automatic carryover like Pascal's calculator.

FIRST GENERAL-PURPOSE CALCULATING MACHINE. Gottfried von Leibniz (1646-1716) tried to attach a multiplication and division mechanism to Pascal's machine but could not make it work so he decided to design his own machine. The result was the cylinder with stepped teeth now known as the Leibniz wheel. It was the first general-purpose calculating device able to meet the needs of mathematicians, but it still suffered from reliability problems.

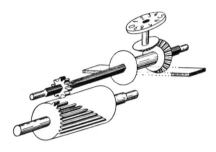

The stepped cylinder principle invented by Leibniz.

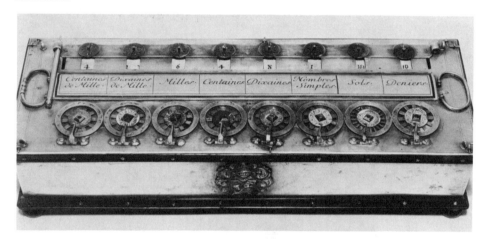

An eight-digit version of the Pascaline, a device originally invented to mechanize the tedious calculations of Blaise Pascal's father, who was a tax collector.

Leibniz's calculating machine departed from Pascal's gear design and incorporated a cylinder with stepped teeth.

The operator of Moreland's multiplying machine used a steel pin to move a series of dials.

1777

FIRST LOGIC MACHINE. Charles Mahon (1753-1816) invented a "logic demonstrator." It was a simple, pocket-sized instrument and could solve traditional syllogisms, numerical problems in logical form, and also elementary questions of probability. The device is thought to be the forerunner of the decision-making and logic capabilities of computers.

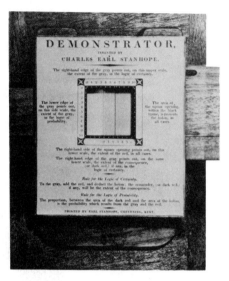

Charles Mahon's (the Earl of Stanhope) pocket-sized logic demonstrator.

1804

FIRST PUNCHED-CARD MACHINE. Joseph-Marie Jacquard (1752-1834) was inspired by a punched-paper barrel organ and invented the punched-card loom attachment that revolutionized the French silk-weaving industry. This was important because the truly automatic calculator could not be made until a mechanical method could be found to input information and control its operations. The principle of the Jacquard loom would later be applied to many computing devices.

Jacquard's loom, although not a computer, strongly influenced the development of punched card input and output.

Joseph-Marie Jacquard.

1820

FIRST MASS-PRODUCED CALCULATING MACHINE. Charles Thomas de Colmar (1785-1870) began selling his "arithmometer" to Parisian insurance houses. Thomas's machine used a simplified and refined version of Leibniz's stepped wheel, in which a drum containing nine teeth, each a different length, turned a small, slidable wheel that operated the counters. It became a popular calculating machine and won a medal at the International Exhibition in London in 1862. Over the next 30 years, approximately 1500 arithmometers were manufactured.

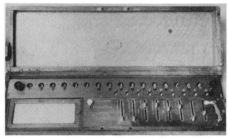

Thomas's commercially successful calculating machine.

1822   1833   1854

THE DIFFERENCE ENGINE. Charles Babbage (1791-1871) was intrigued by the problem of errors in the hand calculation of complex mathematical tables. He was inspired by Charles Mahon's logic machine, which he used as a starting point, and a working difference engine was completed in 1822 and was used to calculate simple tables. In 1833 Babbage abandoned the project and began work on his real dream, the "analytical engine," a general-purpose machine that would be capable of performing any type of digital calculation. Although his analytical engine was never built, Babbage did succeed in mapping out all the principles and procedures from which all modern digital computers have followed. As a result, he is considered to be the source of the automatic computer.

FIRST IDEA OF PROGRAMMING. Augusta Ada (1815-1853), Countess of Lovelace and daughter of the poet Lord Byron, was an amateur mathematician and close friend of Charles Babbage. She worked closely with Babbage and proposed the idea that it would be possible to program the analytical engine with a single set of cards for recurring sets of instructions, two concepts that today are known as the conditional loop and the subroutine.

PUBLISHING OF BOOLEAN ALGEBRA. George S. Boole (1815-1864), an English logician, published what was to become the foundation for the design of all logic circuits in computers. His theory of logic, based on the three operators *and*, *or*, and *not*, reduced logic to a simple form of algebra so that many arguments could be handled as simply as mathematical formulas.

George Boole is considered by many as the father of information theory as a result of his publishing of Boolean algebra.

Augusta Ada, the Countess of Lovelace, is considered to be the first programmer. The programming language Ada is named after her.

A reconstructed model of Babbage's Difference Engine, which was used to calculate simple tables.

Charles Babbage.

1869   1874   1879

INVENTION OF A LOGIC MACHINE. William S. Jevons (1835-1882) considered Boole's algebraic logic as the greatest advance in logic since Aristotle. His machine, which used a logical alphabet of four terms, was built to perform operations on Boolean principles. It was the first to have the power to solve complicated problems faster than the unaided logician.

FIRST PINWHEEL ADDING MACHINE. W. T. Odhner (1845-1905), a Swedish engineer, patented a "pinwheel" method for adding any digit from 1 to 9, now known as the Odhner wheel. Calculators based on the pinwheel were widely used until the introduction of the electronic calculator in about 1960.

THE ANALOG TIDE PREDICTOR. William Thomson, Lord Kelvin (1824-1907), a nineteenth-century scientist who is best known for the Kelvin temperature scale, built the "tide predictor." It was a mechanical system of drums, cables, and dials and showed that differential equations, which deal with relationships among variables, could be solved by machine. It was applied to the calculation of tide tables, which were necessary for coastal navigation, and could predict the times of tides and the height of water around the coast of Great Britain for any number of years ahead.

Odhner's pinwheel adding machine influenced the design of many calculators.

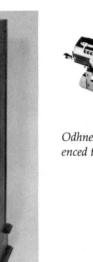

William Jevon's logic machine.

Kelvin's Analog Tide Predictor.

1885   1886   1890

FIRST SUCCESSFUL KEY-DRIVEN CALCULATOR. Dorr Eugene Felt (1862-1930) designed a calculating machine that was the forerunner of today's key-driven calculators. His initial machine was called Felt's "macaroni box" because he could not afford metal parts and had to settle for a grocer's wooden macaroni crate for the casing. Felt finished his model of the first operative multiple-order, key-driven calculating machine in 1885. By 1887 Felt had produced eight of his "comptometers," which he sold to the U.S. Treasury and the New York State Weather Bureau.

FIRST ELECTROMECHANICAL PUNCHED-CARD SYSTEM. Dr. Herman Hollerith (1860-1929), a statistician with the U.S. Census Bureau, knew of Jacquard's method and applied it to a tabulating machine. Its first practical application was tabulating the 1890 census. After completing the census, Hollerith started the Tabulating Machines Company. Through acquisitions and mergers, the Tabulating Machines Company grew to become International Business Machines (IBM).

FIRST ADDING AND LISTING MACHINE. William S. Burroughs (1857-1898), a young bank accountant, had begun work in 1882 to build an adding machine. Burroughs was inspired by Felt and ultimately obtained financing for his machine, and in 1886 the predecessor to the Burroughs Company, the American Arithmometer Company, was formed and began successful production in 1890 of the Burroughs adding and listing machine.

Felt's Comptometer, the first successful key-driven calculator.

Burroughs's early device for listing as well as calculating.

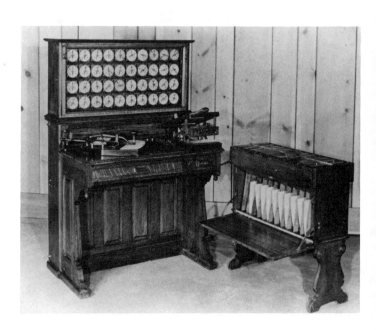

Hollerith's counting machine (left) and sorting machine (right) were the first use of punched cards for tabulating.

1893   1906   1919

FIRST SUCCESSFUL DIRECT-MULTIPLICATION MACHINE. Otto Steiger (1858-1923), of Zurich, developed a machine in 1893 that was, in effect, an automated version of Leibniz's machine. Between 1894 and 1935, 4655 calculators were sold under the name "Millionaire." For many years, it was also one of the most important devices used for scientific calculation.

FIRST VACUUM TUBE. Lee De Forest (1873-1961), an American, invented the audion, the first three-element vacuum tube, which is capable of detecting and amplifying radio signals from an antenna. In the late 1930s, the vacuum tube would play an important role in the development of computers.

INVENTION OF THE FLIP-FLOP. W. H. Eccles and F. W. Jordan, both Americans, invented the flip-flop, a binary circuit capable of assuming one of two stable states at any given time. The flip-flop is an essential building block that permits the storage of one bit of information—it is an invention that would have enormous influence on the design of computer memory.

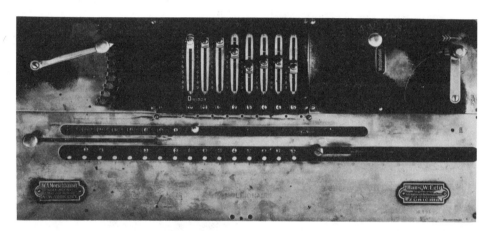

Steiger's Millionaire.

Lee De Forest.

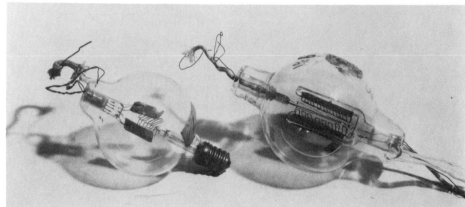

On the left is a 1912 version of De Forest's audion. On the right is a 1913 telephone vacuum tube.

1920   1931   1933

FIRST AUTOMATIC CALCULATING MACHINE. Leonardo Torres y Quevedo (1852-1936), a Spanish inventor, combined electromechanical calculating techniques with his theory of automata and constructed an automatic calculating machine. Arithmetic problems were typed in on a typewriter, and the arithmometer caused the typewriter to type out the answers. At about the same time, Torres also built what is considered to be the first decision-making automatic machine —a chess-playing machine.

FIRST ANALOG COMPUTER FOR DIFFERENTIAL EQUATIONS. At MIT, Dr. Vannevar Bush (1890-1974) constructed the first analog computer to solve differential equations. Called the Differential Analyzer, it was mechanical, apart from electric motors, and used differential gears whose angular rotation indicated quantities. The quantities being computed were represented by the number of degrees through which certain gears had rotated; this meant that the accuracy of the computations was limited by the precision with which the angles could be measured.

FIRST MECHANICAL PROGRAM. Wallace J. Eckert (1902-1971) linked together the IBM 601 multiplying punch, the credit balance accounting machine, and the summary punch. To run these machines as a unit, Eckert made a mechanical program that controlled the devices through a plug-cable relay box. His unique arrangement of machines was the forerunner of scientific computing at Columbia University.

An early photo of Wallace J. Eckert, inventor of the first mechanical program.

Leonardo Torres y Quevedo.

The Differential Analyzer built by Dr. Vannevar Bush at MIT, with integrating units in foreground.

Torres's automatic calculating machine used an automatic typewriter for input and output.

1936 1937 1938

FIRST GENERAL MODEL OF LOGIC MACHINES. Alan M. Turing (1912-1954) wrote the classic paper "On Computable Numbers," which was published in 1937 in the *Proceedings of the London Mathematical Society.* In this paper he described a hypothetical machine—an abstract general model now known as the Turing machine—that used ideas that would influence the structure, feasibility, and limitations of future digital computers.

FIRST APPLICATION OF BOOLEAN ALGEBRA TO SWITCHING FUNCTIONS. Claude E. Shannon (b. 1916) published his master's thesis at MIT in which he described a technique that demonstrated the parallel between algebraic logic and switching circuits. He continued his research at Bell Laboratories and greatly influenced the design of logic circuits for telephone equipment and computers. In 1948 Shannon formalized "information theory," which permits precise measurement of the amount of information delivered in a communication system and the efficiency with which the devices handle it.

FIRST ELECTROMECHANICAL CALCULATOR. George R. Stibitz (b. 1904) used electromechanical circuits for telephone relays at Bell Laboratories to construct the "Complex Calculator I." This machine was controlled manually via keyboard and was used for engineering calculations. In 1940 the machine was demonstrated by Teletype, probably the first example of linking a computing device to a remote terminal.

Alan M. Turing, an influential computer pioneer who developed the first general model for logic machines and the first test for machine intelligence called the Turing test.

A 1949 photo of Claude Shannon with his maze-solving mouse, a device built to study telephone switching systems. (Like the mouse, a telephone call must make its way to its destination by the shortest possible path.)

Stibitz's Complex Calculator used electromechanical relays.

A 1981 photo of George Stibitz.

1939   1941   1943

FIRST ELECTRONIC DIGITAL COMPUTER. Dr. John V. Atanasoff (b. 1904), a mathematics professor at Iowa State College, with his assistant Clifford Berry (1918-1963), designed and built the ABC (Atanasoff Berry Computer), an operating prototype of the first electronic digital computer. It was the first machine to use vacuum tubes for the logic circuits.

FIRST GENERAL-PURPOSE PROGRAM-CONTROLLED COMPUTER. Konrad Zuse (b. 1910), along with Helmut Schreyer, built the Z3 electromechanical relay computer in 1941. Its program was entered on punched film. Zuse escaped from the Nazis in Berlin in March 1945 with a dismantled scientific computer, the Z4. After the war, Zuse's relay computers were combined with a punched-card device and were marketed in Switzerland by Remington Rand.

FIRST ENGLISH ELECTRONIC CALCULATING MACHINE. In early 1940, Britain lived under the threat of possible invasion. It recruited a team of experts, Alan Turing among them, to develop a machine called the Colossus for cryptoanalysis to break the code of the German code machine, the Enigma. Although it was, in theory, a powerful general-purpose computer, the Colossus was dedicated solely to code breaking and was classified until well after the war.

John V. Atanasoff's prototype of the first electronic digital computer.

A 1981 photo of Konrad Zuse.

The Colossus at Betchley Park, England.

1944   1945   1946

FIRST AMERICAN PROGRAM-CONTROLLED COMPUTER. Howard Aiken (1900-1973) began work on the Automatic Sequence-Controlled Calculator (ASCC) Mark I in 1939. The Mark I was patterned after Babbage's analytical engine. Numbers were stored on "registers" containing sets of wheels, and each wheel rotated according to its number and was controlled by a telephone relay. Punched paper tape carried the instructions, and because each step was specified separately, programming was tedious. It was presented to Harvard, where it was used for 15 years.

THE FIRST BUG. While development was proceeding on the Mark I's successor, the Mark II, a relay failed. Inside the failed relay, the researchers found a moth that had been beaten to death. The development team carefully removed the moth and taped it into their log book. From that time on, when the computer was not working, the development team members said they were debugging the computer, which is thought to be the origin of the terms "bug" and "debugging."

FIRST LARGE-SCALE ELECTRONIC DIGITAL COMPUTER. The Electronic Numerical Integrator and Calculator (ENIAC) became operational in 1946. It was programmed by externally set plugs and switches, and therefore was not considered a true stored-program computer. ENIAC was widely used for scientific calculation until the early 1950s.

Harvard's Mark I Automatic Sequence-Controlled Calculator was the first American program-controlled computer.

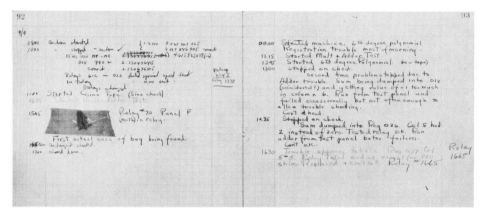

The first bug was a moth that was beaten to death by one of the Mark II's electromechanical relay switches.

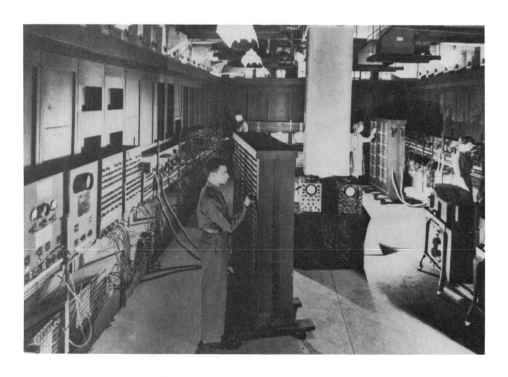

ENIAC—the first large-scale electronic digital computer—contained 18,000 vacuum tubes.

1946 1947 1949

PUBLISHING OF THE STORED-PROGRAM COMPUTER CONCEPT. Before ENIAC was completed, its designers, aided by mathematician John von Neumann (1903-1957), began work on its stored-program successor, the Electronic Discrete Variable Automatic Computer (EDVAC). The idea of a stored-program computer was publicized by the 1945 write-up of the EDVAC team's discussions and by a 1946 lecture series at the University of Pennsylvania's Moore School. It was an electronic serial vacuum tube machine with mercury delay lines and magnetic wire secondary memory, but it was not completed until 1952.

The EDVAC team who first proposed the design of a stored-program computer.

A 1954 photo of John von Neumann, who is often credited with the development of the stored program concept. He contributed to many early computer designs, including ENIAC and EDVAC.

FIRST TRANSISTOR. John Bardeen (b. 1908), Walter H. Brattain (b. 1902), and William Shockley (1910-1989) invented the transistor at Bell Laboratories. It provided a smaller, faster, and more efficient switch. The three shared a Nobel Prize in 1956 for that invention.

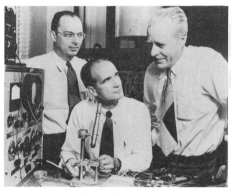

A 1956 photo showing the winners of the Nobel physics prize. Seated is Dr. William Shockley. Standing are Dr. John Bardeen (left) and Dr. Walter Brattain (right). The transistor is a tiny device that replaced the vacuum tube and ushered in the ear of microelectronics.

FIRST WORKING FULL-SCALE STORED-PROGRAM COMPUTER. Maurice V. Wilkes (b. 1913), who attended the 1946 Moore School EDVAC lectures, led the development of Cambridge University's Electronic Delay Storage Automatic Calculator (EDSAC). This electronic computer used mercury delay lines, punched paper tape input, and teleprinter output. It was the first full-scale stored-program computer to operate, although a small-scale stored-program computer called Manchester Mark I (1946-1948), built by F. C. Williams and T. Kilburn to test the CRT memory tube that Williams invented, was operated at Manchester University in 1948, a year before EDSAC was completed.

EDSAC—England's version of the full-scale stored program computer—was the first to operate.

FIRST CORE MEMORY. In 1949 Jay Forrester (b. 1918) was trying to solve the problem of a more reliable memory for computers. In those days, tubes were a serious shortcoming in computer design because they were unreliable and burned out. Forrester's idea was to interconnect doughnut-shaped magnetic rings or cores on wire. Four years later, a working core memory was to be installed on the "Whirlwind" computer.

FIRST INTERACTIVE REAL-TIME COMPUTER. Jay Forrester began work on the "Whirlwind" in 1944. The interactivity came from the idea to link the computer to a CRT and to a light gun (the forerunner of the light pen) that could interact in real time with the CRT. In 1953 it also became the first computer to use core memory. The Whirlwind was the prototype, for a network of computers and radar stations called SAGE (Semi-Automatic Ground Environment), which was from 1958 to 1983 an important part of the U. S. air defense system.

FIRST ENGLISH LARGE-SCALE ELECTRONIC DIGITAL COMPUTER. Alan M. Turing specified the design of a computer called the Automatic Computing Engine (ACE) for the National Physical Laboratory in 1945. Edward Newman and James Wilkinson had the electronic Pilot ACE operational by 1950. It first used mercury delay lines for memory and later added a drum for storage.

Looking through a magnifying glass at an early magnetic core memory. Magnetic core memory planes were the predominant form of memory in the 1950s and early 1960s.

The Whirlwind Computer, designed at MIT.

1951   1951   1954

FIRST COMMERCIALLY AVAILABLE COMPUTER. In 1947 J. Presper Eckert (b. 1919) and John W. Mauchly (1907-1979) formed the Eckert Mauchly Computer Corporation, built a small binary computer for Northrop, and then began the UNIVersal Automatic Computer (UNIVAC) for the Bureau of the Census. It was delivered on June 14, 1951. Until that time, computers were one-of-a-kind laboratory instruments. The financial backer of Eckert Mauchly was killed in an airplane accident, and the two designers sold their company to Remington Rand, which later became Sperry Rand.

FIRST DESCRIPTION OF MICRO-PROGRAMMING. Maurice V. Wilkes, who developed the EDSAC, first proposed the concept of microprogramming, which was to have a profound effect on later mainframe, minicomputer, and microcomputer design. By the early 1960s, microprogramming was an established way of designing and building computer systems.

FIRST TRANSISTORIZED GENERAL-PURPOSE COMPUTER. TRADIC (TRansistorized Airborne DIgital Computer) was built in 1954 by Bell Laboratories (where the transistor was invented). It contained 800 transistors. This signaled a new generation of computers, in which transistors replaced vacuum tubes as the basis for the internal circuitry of computer systems. TRADIC was also the first computer to be operated successfully in aircraft, an environment that had proved hostile to earlier types of computers.

A recent photo of Maurice Wilkes.

A 1952 photo of developers Eckert and Mauchly with UNIVAC I.

The TRADIC was the first completely transistorized general-purpose computer.

1956   1957   1958

FIRST RANDOM-ACCESS STOR-AGE SYSTEM. The RAMAC 305 (Random-Access Method for Accounting and Control) was the first system to permit files to be stored in a randomly accessible form. RAMAC used 50 magnetic disks that could store 5 million characters with an access time to any record of less than a second. The next major innovation in mass storage was the replaceable disk pack concept in 1962.

FIRST HIGH-LEVEL PROGRAM-MING LANGUAGE. FORTRAN (FORmula TRANslator) was introduced to improve automatic programming. A small group of IBM employees headed by John Backus began work in 1954 to develop a high-level programming language for use by scientists, mathematicians, and engineers.

FIRST ARTIFICIAL INTELLI-GENCE PROGRAMMING LAN-GUAGE. John McCarthy invented the LISP (LISt Processor) programming language that was suitable for symbol and list manipulating required for artificial intelligence research.

John McCarthy.

The RAMAC 305 was the forerunner of modern disk-based systems.

An early photo of the FORTRAN development team. John Backus is second from the right.

1958   1960   1960

FIRST INTEGRATED CIRCUIT.
Jack S. Kilby (b. 1928) of Texas Instruments came up with the idea of manufacturing all circuit components in one operation with one material. In August 1958, he assembled a unit of discrete silicon elements, and on September 12, he demonstrated the first working integrated circuit. This development paved the way for a cost-effective method for placing an ever-increasing number of components on a single silicon chip.

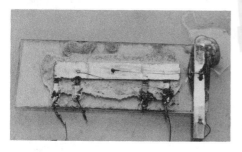

The original integrated circuit built by Jack Kilbey of Texas Instruments.

FIRST TRANSPORTABLE HIGH-LEVEL PROGRAMMING LANGUAGE. In 1959 a user group met at the University of Pennsylvania to explore solutions to the problem of program transportability (i.e., programs written for one computer could not be executed on a different model or make of computer). The result was the Department of Defense-sponsored CO-BOL (COmmon Business Oriented Language). One of the most influential people on the committee was Grace Hopper (1906-1989), who also wrote the first practical compiler program and was a pioneer in the field of computer languages.

A 1982 photo of computer pioneer Grace Hopper.

FIRST LASER. Theodore H. Maiman, working at Hughes Research Laboratories in Malibu, California, announced the operation of a laser (*l*ight *a*mplification by the *s*timulated *e*mission of *r*adiation) based on a crystal of synthetic ruby.

An early experimental ruby maser amplifier used for radio astronomical work.

A COBOL program.

```
001010 IDENTIFICATION DIVISION.
001020 PROGRAM-ID. PINGPONG.
001030
001040 REMARKS.  THIS PROGRAM COUNTS THE NUMBER OF RED,
001050           GREEN, AND BLUE PING-PONG BALLS IN A BUCKET
001060           OF 16 BALLS.
001070
001080 ENVIRONMENT DIVISION.
001090 CONFIGURATION SECTION.
001100 SPECIAL-NAMES. CONSOLE IS SCREEN.
001110
001120 DATA DIVISION.
001130 WORKING-STORAGE SECTION.
001140 01  BUCKET.
001150     05  BALL  OCCURS 16 TIMES  PIC 99.
001160
001170 01  SUB                       PIC 99.
001180 01  RED-COUNT                  PIC 99 VALUE 0.
001190 01  BLUE-COUNT                 PIC 99 VALUE 0.
001200 01  GREEN-COUNT                PIC 99 VALUE 0.
001210
002000 PROCEDURE DIVISION.
```

1961   1961   1962

FIRST VIRTUAL MEMORY. In 1961 a group of people in Manchester, England, proposed a method for overlaying portions of stored programs in memory without the programmer knowing it was happening. It was used on a number of computers associated with research projects in computer systems design. By the early 1970s, virtual memory had become available on most computers.

FIRST SIMULATION LANGUAGE. GPSS (General-Purpose Systems Simulator) was the first language capable of simulating natural systems, making simulation a practical tool for people to use.

FIRST INTERACTIVE REAL-TIME GRAPHICS. Ivan Sutherland (b. 1938) developed a computer program called Sketchpad that allowed a user to draw interactively on a CRT screen. At the same time, other workers at MIT, Itek, and Bolt Beranek and Newman were actively engaged in similar research.

A 1962 photo of Ivan Sutherland using Sketchpad on a TX-2 computer at the MIT Lincoln Laboratory.

1963   1964   1964

FIRST MINICOMPUTER. A number of smaller companies in the computer field began to introduce small computers. The most successful among these was the Digital Equipment Corporation (DEC), which inaugurated the market for minicomputers. One of the founders, Ken Olsen, first worked on the Whirlwind and TX-0 computers at MIT. He, Stan Olsen (his brother), and Harlan Anderson joined in 1957 to begin DEC, which manufactured basic circuit board logic modules. In 1959 the firm demonstrated its first computer, the PDP-1. In 1963 DEC shipped its PDP-8, the first commercially successful minicomputer.

IBM SYSTEM/360 INTRODUCED. On April 7, 1964, IBM announced a new family of computers called System/360, which launched an era of computing in which integrated circuit technology, called solid logic technology (SLT), replaced transistors. (Volume manufacturing of integrated circuits had not yet been accomplished.) The System/360, which represented a major reorientation in computer design, had a tremendous impact on the computer industry. Thirty-three thousand units were sold, making all prior commercial computers obsolete.

FIRST BASIC PROGRAM IS RUN. In May 1964, the inventors of BASIC, Thomas Kurtz and John Kemeny, ran the first BASIC program at Dartmouth College, Hanover, New Hampshire. The Dartmouth College BASIC System was an influential prototype of time-sharing computer systems.

A recent photo of Thomas Kurtz (left) and John Kemeny with their latest implementation of BASIC—True BASIC.

An IBM System-360 computer, which launched a new generation of computing.

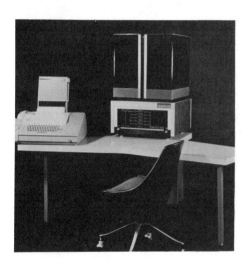

The DEC PDP-8 was the first successful commercial version of the minicomputer.

A BASIC program.

```
100 REM  Ping-Pong ball problem
110 REM
120 REM The variable A is an array of
130 REM 16 Ping-Pong balls
140 REM Subroutine 500 initializes the array
150 DIM A(15)
160 X = 0
170 Y = 0
180 Z = 0
190 GOSUB 500
200 GOSUB 600
210 GOSUB 700
220 END
230 REM
240 REM Intialize a bucket with a random collection
250 REM of balls with the following colors:
260 REM Red = 0, Green = 1, Blue = 2
270 FOR I = 0 TO 15
280     B = INT(RND * 10)
290        IF B > 2 GOTO 540
300 NEXT I
310 REM
```

1964

1967

1968

FIRST COMMERCIALLY AVAILABLE SUPERCOMPUTER. Control Data Corporation delivered the first CDC 6600, which was to be the fastest and most powerful computer available for several years. Although the first computers to which the term supercomputer was applied were the IBM Stretch and the Univac LARC (both developed in the late 1950s), each of these computers was an experimental prototype. (Eventually eight IBM Stretch computers were produced.)

FIRST PROGRAM TO PLAY CHESS SUCCESSFULLY AGAINST PEOPLE. In 1949 Claude E. Shannon published a paper in which he discussed the problems of a computer playing chess. This paper laid the groundwork for chess-playing programs. In 1956 the Maniac I computer was programmed to play chess on a simplified 6 x 6 board that paved the way for play against people. In 1967 MacHack, a program written at MIT by Richard Greenblatt, played well enough to enter a tournament and win at the novice level. Research into game-playing programs would have a great influence on the emerging field of artificial intelligence.

FIRST STRUCTURED PROGRAMMING CONCEPTS. Edsger Dijkstra published the paper "Go To Statement Considered Harmful," which, in essence, stated that the number of programming errors could be greatly reduced by elimination of the GO TO statement. Since then, virtually all programming textbooks have adopted the structured techniques.

Edsger Dykstra.

The Control Data CDC 6600.

1969   1970   1970

FIRST 16-BIT MINICOMPUTER SHIPPED. In 1968 a newly formed company, Data General Corporation, began development of a 16-bit minicomputer called the Nova. (The previously mentioned PDP-1 and PDP-8 were 12-bit minicomputers.) The first Nova was shipped in 1969.

FIRST COMMERCIALLY PRODUCED FIBER-OPTIC CABLE. Corning Glass Works, Inc., developed a process to produce strands of glass that act as light pipes, called fiber-optic cable. Optical circuits have a speed and capacity advantage over conventional metal wire or cable.

FIRST SEMICONDUCTOR LASER. Bell Laboratories announced a solid-state laser. Until that time, lasers were bulky, gas-filled tubes, usually confined to research laboratories or large-scale instrumentation. Semiconductor lasers offered the promise of cost-effective use in conjunction with fiber-optic cables for computer and communication systems.

The first 16-bit minicomputer, the Data General Nova.

A modern semiconductor laser shown positioned in the head of a pin.

A modern fiber-optic cable.

1970　　　1971　　　1971

FIRST RELATIONAL DATABASE MODEL. E. F. Codd (b. 1923), who at the time was working at the IBM Research Laboratory in San Jose, California, published a classic paper titled "A Relational Model of Data for Large Shared Data Banks." That paper is now credited as the origin of the entire field of relational database technology.

E. F. Codd

FIRST MICROPROCESSOR CHIP. Intel Corporation introduced the first microprocessor chip, called the 4004, that, when combined with the 4001 ROM chip and the 4002 RAM chip, made up a microcomputing system. Intel called the 4004 its "Microprogrammable Computer on a Chip." The term microprocessor was not used until 1972. It caused the computer industry and its suppliers to rethink the future role of the computer. The 4-bit 4004 had 2250 transistors on a 1/6-inch-long by 1/8-inch-wide chip; it almost matched ENIAC's 1946 total computational power.

FIRST PROGRAM TO UNDERSTAND NATURAL LANGUAGE. Terry Winograd (b. 1945) completed his master's thesis at MIT; it included a program called SHRDLU. Although earlier programs could converse with humans, SHRDLU was the first to combine parsing (analyzing) English statements, putting events into context, problem solving, and natural language response. It could analyze a conversation about a toy world containing blocks of various sizes, shapes, and colors.

Terry Winograd.

> Pick up a big red block.
>
> *OK.*
>
> Grasp the pyramid.
>
> *I don't understand which pyramid you mean.*
>
> Find a block that is taller than the one you are holding and put it in the box.
>
> *By "it" I assume you mean the block that is taller than the one I am holding.*
>
> What does the box contain?
>
> *The blue pyramid and the blue block.*

A SHRDLU conversation.

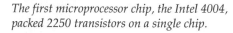

The first microprocessor chip, the Intel 4004, packed 2250 transistors on a single chip.

1971   1971   1977

FIRST EXPERT SYSTEM COMPLETED. DENDRAL, which was started in the mid-1960s at the artificial intelligence lab of Stanford Research Institute, mimics the behavior of an expert chemist who is determining the structure of molecular compounds.

Recent photo of Edward Feigenbaum, who, with Bruce Buchanan and Joshua Lederberg, began work on the first expert system, Dendral, in 1965.

FIRST PERSONAL COMPUTER. The personal computer revolution began when *Scientific American* ran an ad for the Kenbak—the first personal computer—in its September 1971 issue. John Blankenbaker (b. 1930), the designer and builder of the Kenbak, intended to sell his computer to educators, but only 40 of the $750 Kenbak computers were sold. The Kenbak bore little resemblance to today's personal computers. Instead of using a keyboard, the computer was programmed by setting switches on the computer's front panel. Blinking lights represented output in lieu of a display screen. The processor consisted of a set of small-scale integration (SSI) chips, and total memory capacity was 256 bytes.

FIRST COMMERCIAL LOCAL-AREA NETWORK (LAN). Datapoint Corporation announced ARCNET, the first commercially available local area network. ARCNET transmits data at 3 million bits per second over a coaxial cable.

The Kenbak-1, the first personal computer, was akward to use by today's standards. All input was via eight data buttons and seven command buttons on the front panel. Output was provided by eight lights.

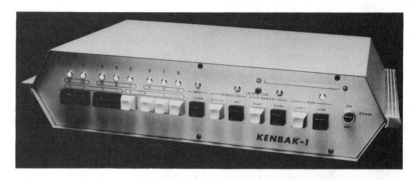

Datapoint's ARCnet local-area network.

1977   1979   1980

FIRST COMPLETELY ASSEMBLED PERSONAL COMPUTERS. In 1977 Apple Computer, Radio Shack, and Commodore announced or made available completely assembled personal computers.

VISICALC INTRODUCED. On May 11, 1979, at the West Coast Computer Faire, the first commercial program designed for an inexperienced user on a personal computer was introduced. VisiCalc was the forerunner of personal computer application software.

FIRST RISC PROCESSOR PROTOTYPE. John Cocke (b. 1925) and a group of collaborators at IBM completed the 801 minicomputer, the first Reduced Instruction Set Computer (RISC). RISC computers use simple machine language instructions, the great majority of which can be executed in a single machine cycle. In January 1986, IBM introduced the RT PC, the first commercial RISC computer from a major computer vendor. Today, RISC computers are offered by Hewlett-Packard, Sun, Motorola, Apollo, Intergraph, and others.

Apple II computer—a sample of one of the first completely assembled personal computers.

John Cocke with the IBM 801 minicomputer, the first RISC computer.

A VisiCalc screen.

1980   1981   1981

FIRST 32-BIT MICROPROCESSOR CHIP. Bell Laboratories invented and developed the Bellmac-32, the first true single-chip microprocessor with 32-bit internal architecture and a 32-bit data bus.

IBM PERSONAL COMPUTER INTRODUCED. IBM introduced its first personal computer, an event that would legitimize the idea of the personal computer in the business world.

FIRST COMMERCIAL PARALLEL COMPUTER. BBN Advanced Computers, Inc., began shipping the Butterfly, a parallel computer that can combine up to 256 microprocessors to achieve single-program parallel processing. Computer scientists believe that parallel processing will eventually prove more suitable than serial processing for most computing applications. For example, a flight simulator program might have independent modules that control different parts of a simulation. Each part or module could then be assigned to its own processor.

An early model of the Bellmac-32, the first 32-bit microprocessor.

BBN Advanced Computer's Butterfly, the first commercial parallel processing computer.

The IBM Personal Computer.

1983   1987   1989

FIRST EXPERIMENTAL VERSION OF AN OPTICAL TRANSISTOR. The optically based "transphaser" is, in theory, capable of switching 1000 times faster than is an electronic switch. By using the properties of certain crystals and laser technology, an optical computer could be built to process information in much the same way as an electronic computer, but much faster.

HYPERCARD INTRODUCED. On August 11, 1987, Apple Computer, Inc. introduced Hypercard, an inteface builder and software development environment for the Macintosh conceived by a team of developers headed by Bill Atkinson.

FIRST MILLION-TRANSISTOR MICROPROCESSOR. Intel Corporation introduced the i860, a 64-bit RISC microprocessor, the first time over 1 million transistors had been placed on a single chip. The highly integrated chip includes built-in three-dimensional graphics and floating-point processors and has a speed of 33 MIPS at 40 MHz.

An early optical transistor.

Bill Atkinson.

The Intel i860 RISC microprocessor.

1989 1990

FIRST OPTICAL NEUROCHIP.
Kazuo Kyuma, working at Mitsubishi Electric in Osaka, Japan, developed a prototype optical neural network chip. The chip is an optoelectronic device (it contains both electronic and optical components). It contains 32 neurons that send and receive signals through LEDs and photodiodes. The chip is capable of recognizing the 26 letters of the Roman alphabet and paves the way for optically based computer systems that can recognize images and patterns and understand speech.

FIRST OPTICAL COMPUTER. A team headed by Alan Huang at AT&T Bell Laboratories built a processor that uses light rather than electricity to process information. Called a digital optical processor, the invention uses lasers to carry information and optical devices to store and process it. The optical devices are known as S-SEEDs (Symmetric Self-Electro-optic Effect Devices). Light can change the transparency of these devices, which makes it possible to use them as switches.

The first optical processor. This AT&T prototype is the forerunner of optical processors that are expected to operate 1000 times faster than their electronic counterparts.

REFERENCES

Augarten, Stan. *Bit by Bit: An Illustrated History of Computers*. New York: Ticknor & Fields, 1984.

The Charles Babbage Institute for the History of Information Processing, 104 Walter Library, University of Minnesota, Minneapolis, Minn. 55455.

The Computer Museum, 300 Congress Street, Boston, Mass. 02210.

Eames, Charles. *A Computer Perspective*. Cambridge, Mass.: Harvard University Press, 1973.

Evans, Christopher. *The Making of the Micro*. New York: Van Nostrand Reinhold, 1981.

Goldstine, Herman. *The Computer from Pascal to Von Neumann*. Princeton, N.J.: Princeton University Press, 1972.

Lubalin, Irwin. "History of Computers." In *Avnet 1982 Annual Report*. New York: Avnet, Inc., 1982.

Ralston, Anthony, ed., and Edwin D. Reilley, Jr., assoc. ed. *Encyclopedia of Computer Science and Engineering*. New York: Van Nostrand Reinhold, 1983.

Rheingold, Howard. *Tools for Thought*. New York: Simon & Schuster, 1985.

Trask, Maurice. *The Story of Cybernetics*. London: Studio Vista Ltd., 1971.

Computer stores carry a wide variety of personal computer systems and application software.

APPENDIX B
SHOPPING GUIDE

PREVIEW

In Chapter 2, we discussed some uses for personal computer systems. In Chapter 13, we discussed how to buy a personal computer system. Other chapters in the book have pointed out the various options for input, output, and mass storage.

In this appendix, we present a minicatalog of personal computer software and hardware products. Our minicatalog is divided into several major categories. Each category begins with a discussion of the overall purposes and benefits of products in that category. Following the introductory material are descriptions of individual products. Each product description includes a discussion of how the product is best used, its strengths and weaknesses, its suggested price (which may vary considerably from our listed figures), and where to obtain more information. In the software categories,

hardware requirements are also listed.

To select products to address your needs, start by determining the software category that most closely describes your needs and then read the individual product descriptions. After that, read the hardware section. Check the hardware requirements and operating systems when matching software to hardware.

Much of the information that appears in this appendix is provided by the manufacturer and does not constitute an endorsement or review of the product mentioned. Also keep in mind that there are many more products in each category than we have listed. With over 15,000 software packages and hundreds of computer systems on the market, we are only trying to present an overview of the kinds of hardware and software that are available.

APPLICATION SOFTWARE

Personal computer software comes in many different varieties, and the applications number in the thousands, so it is useful to know how individual programs are categorized. The broadest classifications of software are system software and application software.

System software includes

- *Operating systems.*
- *Programming languages.*

Application software includes

- *Special-purpose programs.* Dedicated to performing single-use tasks, such as payroll, accounting, bookkeeping, education, entertainment, or statistical analysis, in which the program contains built-in problem-solving features specially designed for those particular tasks.

- *General-purpose programs.* Adaptable to a wide variety of tasks, such as word processing, spreadsheet calculating, record keeping, graphics, or communications, in which the user defines the problem and the procedure and uses the software to assist in preparing a solution.

GENERAL-PURPOSE PROGRAMS

General-purpose software packages have been developed in response to the general problem-solving needs of people whose work includes such common tasks as planning, writing, record keeping, calculating, and communicating. Part of general-purpose software's usefulness derives from the fact that it is not dedicated to any specific use but can be adapted to a wide variety of tasks. The categories of general-purpose application software are the following:

- *Writing.* One of the most common general applications for personal computers is writing. This category includes word processors, which allow you to write anything from a simple note to a book about computers; outline processors, which allow you to enter ideas in any order; desktop publishing, which allows you to prepare and print typeset or near-typeset-quality documents; and spelling checker, mail merge, and indexing programs that work in conjunction with word processors.

- *Spreadsheets.* Another common general application is the spreadsheet, which allows you to build and analyze financial models, balance sheets, budgets, and other types of financial projections.

- *Database.* Database programs, also called data management programs, let you create, index, and access files, such as personal notes, customer lists, or inventories. You can also create and print complex reports based on those files.

- *Integrated.* These are multifunction general-purpose programs that combine at least two functions with the ability to share data among the functions. For example, integrated application programs might combine word processing, spreadsheet, and database functions. They can also include graphics and communication capabilities.

- *Graphics.* This category includes drawing, analytical graphics, and presentation graphics programs.

- *Communications.* Communications software allows you to link your personal computer into a larger network, such as The Source or CompuServe, or it provides you with the option to communicate directly with other personal computer owners.

Some categories of special-purpose application software are the following:

- *Managing.* Includes personal information managers, project management, decision modeling, and statistical analysis programs.

- *Accounting and bookkeeping.* Ranges from simple personal budgeting systems and income tax programs to complex integrated accounts payable, accounts receivable, and general ledger systems.

- *Vertical business applications.* These are specialized programs that meet the specific business needs of professions such as lawyers, dentists, doctors, real estate agents, contractors, and distributors. Note: The vertical market segment is too diverse to cover in this appendix. No product descriptions exist in this category.

- *Entertainment.* Consists primarily of computer games.

- *Education.* Education can easily overlap with entertainment in the form of simulations and games, but education also includes tutorials.

- *Scientific and engineering.* This category contains a wide variety of statistical, analytical, design, and testing programs.

- *Utilities.* This category includes disk and file management, data protection and recovery, and desktop utilities such as calendars, calculators, and notepads.

Writing

WordStar 6.0

Wordstar features a keyboard command structure supplemented by pull-down menus and function keys. Features include a telecommunications program, an outliner, spelling checker, thesaurus, extensive support for laser printers, and page preview.

WordStar runs on MS-DOS–based computers with 512K RAM and two disk drives. The program is not copy protected. Suggested price is $495.

WordStar International Corporation, 201 Alameda del Prado Avenue, Novato, Calif. 94949; (415) 382-8000.

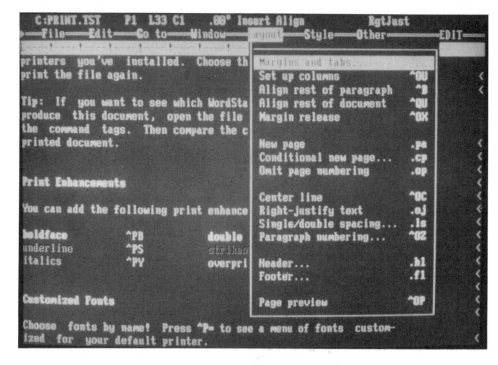

Writing

ForComment

ForComment is an editing program designed for situations in which word processing documents must be reviewed and edited by several people. Up to 15 reviewers can make comments and suggest revisions to a document. The program records and collates all the comments, providing an audit trail of who made which comments. The completed file is then reviewed by the author before making revisions. Files can be as large as 32,000 lines of text plus 32,000 lines of comments.

ForComment runs on MS-DOS–based computers with 320K RAM and two disk drives. The program is not copy protected. Suggested price is $295.

Broderbund Software, Inc., 17 Paul Drive, San Rafael, Calif. 94903; (415) 492-3200.

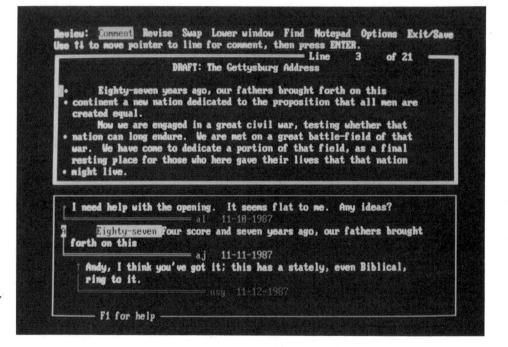

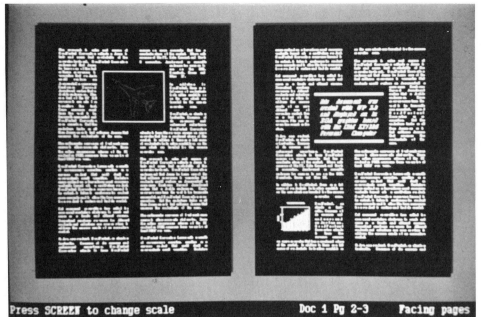

Press SCREEN to change scale   Doc 1 Pg 2-3   Facing pages

Writing

WordPerfect

WordPerfect is a highly functional word processor best suited for power users where typing speed is critical. It is considered to be difficult to learn, although good written tutorials accompany the software. WordPerfect supports an on-line thesaurus and a 115,000-word spelling checker; two windows open concurrently (split-screen editing); the ability to sort lines, paragraphs, pages, and merged records; integration of text and graphics; the ability to calculate averages and totals; extensive support for laser printers; and page preview.

WordPerfect runs on MS-DOS–based computers with 384K RAM and two disk drives. Versions are also available for the Macintosh, Atari ST, and UNIX-based computers. The program is not copy protected. Suggested price for the MS-DOS version is $495.

WordPerfect Corporation, 288 West Center Street, Orem, Utah 84057; (801) 225-5000.

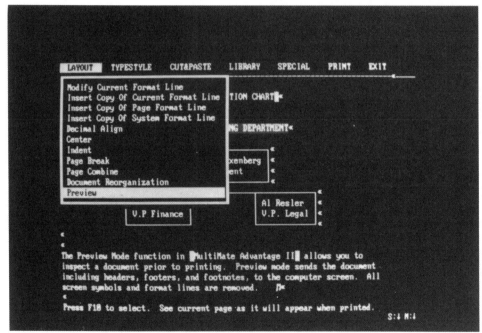

Writing

MultiMate Advantage

MultiMate Advantage emulates the Wang dedicated word processor, a popular office machine. The program, designed primarily for secretarial use, is highly functional and easy to use. It combines a command-driven interface with an optional pull-down, menu-driven interface. Features include a built-in spelling corrector, dBase mail merge, math capabilities, disk indexing through document summary screens, built-in cardfile database, automatic footnotes, line and box drawing, section numbering, and automatic table of contents.

MultiMate Advantage runs on MS-DOS–based computers with 384K RAM and two disk drives. The program is not copy protected. Suggested price is $565.

Ashton-Tate, 20101 Hamilton Avenue, Torrance, Calif. 90502; (213) 329-8000.

Writing

Professional Write

Professional Write is a menu-driven word processing program that features a menu bar with pull-down menus, a spelling checker with a built-in 77,000-word dictionary, and a thesaurus with 20,000 words. The program also features mail-merge capabilities, an "address book" database, and the ability to draw lines in the document.

The program runs on MS-DOS–based computers with 256K RAM and two disk drives. The program is not copy protected. Suggested price is $249.

Software Publishing Corporation, 1901 Landings Drive, Mountain View, Calif. 94043; (415) 962-8910.

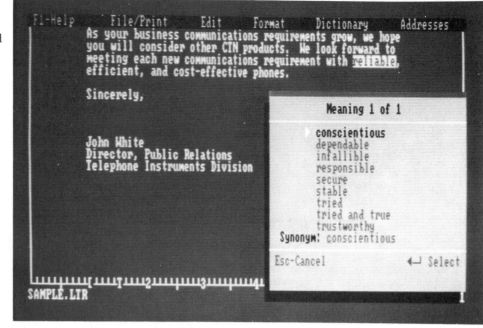

Writing

Microsoft Word

Word is a menu-driven, almost what-you-see-is-what-you-get word processor. It supports up to eight different windows with an easy way to cut and paste between windows. Its screen display lets you see true underlining, boldface, italic, and overstrike. (A Macintosh version also allows you to see different fonts and type sizes.) The program includes extensive support for laser printers and page preview. The program is designed to work with a mouse, but you can do everything with the keyboard if you prefer.

Word runs on MS-DOS–based computers with 512K RAM, and the Apple Macintosh with 512K RAM. Both versions require two disk drives. The program is not copy protected. Suggested MS-DOS version price is $450. The Macintosh version's suggested price is $395.

Microsoft Corporation, 16011 NE 36th Way, Redmond, Wash. 98073; (206) 882-8080.

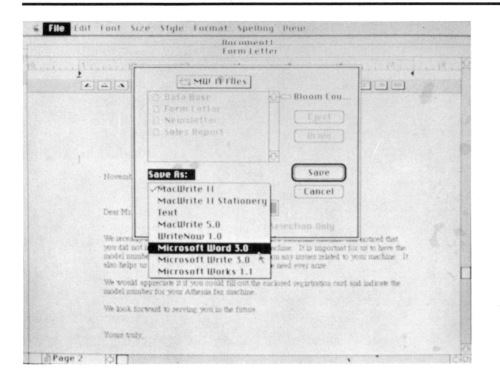

MacWrite II

MacWrite II is a very inviting what-you-see-is-what-you-get word processor that enables you to mix and match type fonts and sizes within a document and has the ability to paste in drawings from a MacPaint file. The program rates very high in the ease-of-learning-and-use category.

MacWrite II runs on the Macintosh computer with 1-MB RAM and two disk drives. The program is not copy protected. Suggested price is $249.

Claris Corporation, 5201 Patrick Henry Drive, Santa Clara, Calif. 95052; (408) 987-7000.

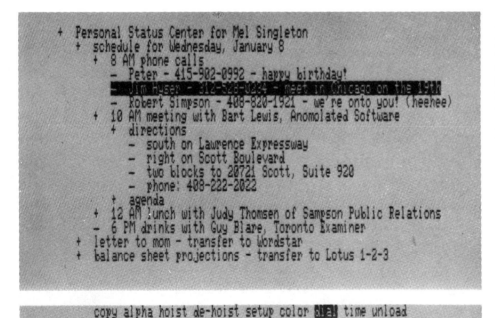

Ready

Ready is an outline processor that is always ready, because it is memory resident. It allows you to enter ideas or notes as single sentences in an outline, then expand on them by opening multiple sublevels in the outline and rearrange them in any order. To turn your outline into a finished document, Ready is compatible with most word processors and other programs, such as 1-2-3 and dBase III.

The program runs on MS-DOS–based computers. The program is memory resident and requires 128K RAM to run, so you must add the 128K to the memory requirements of any program you want Ready to run with. At least 256K RAM is suggested. The program is not copy protected. Suggested price is $99.95.

Symantec, Living Videotext Division, 117 Easy Street, Mountain View, Calif. 94043; (415) 964-6300.

Writing

Turbo Lightning

Turbo Lightning is a memory-resident, interactive look-up system that gives you access to the 83,000 word *Random House Concise Dictionary and Thesaurus* while using another application program. It functions as an interactive proofreader and informs you as soon as it detects a misspelled word, and has an on-line synonym finder. Turbo Lightning can be used in conjunction with other programs, such as WordStar, Word, PFS:Write, MultiMate, 1-2-3, and the dBase series.

Turbo Lightning runs on MS-DOS–based computers. The program is memory resident and requires 54K RAM to run, so you must add the 54K to the memory requirements of any program you want Turbo Lightning to run with. At least 128K RAM is suggested. The program is not copy protected. Suggested price is $99.95.

Borland International, 4585 Scotts Valley Drive, Scotts Valley, Calif. 95066; (408) 438-8400.

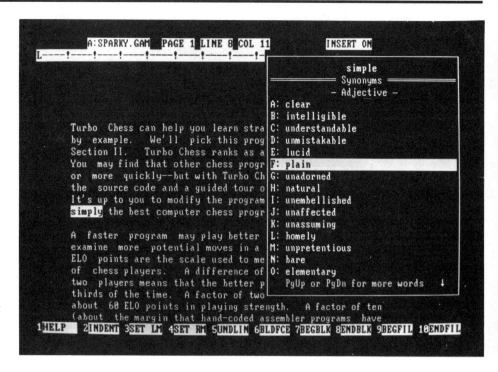

Writing

Microsoft Bookshelf

Bookshelf is a memory-resident, interactive, general-purpose reference work database on a CD ROM disk. You access Bookshelf within a word processor while editing a document. You can look up information from 10 references, including *The American Heritage Dictionary*, *Roget's II: Electronic Thesarus*, and *The Chicago Manual of Style*.

Bookshelf runs on MS-DOS–based computers with 640K RAM. It requires two disk drives, but you must also purchase a CD ROM disk drive, which adds an extra $1000 to the price of the software. The program is not copy protected. Suggested price is $295.

Microsoft Corporation, 16011 NE 36th Way, Redmond, Wash. 98073; (206) 882-8080.

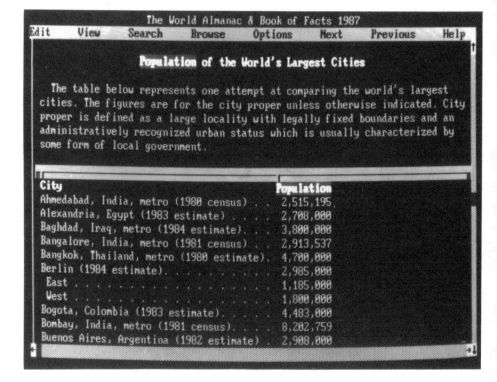

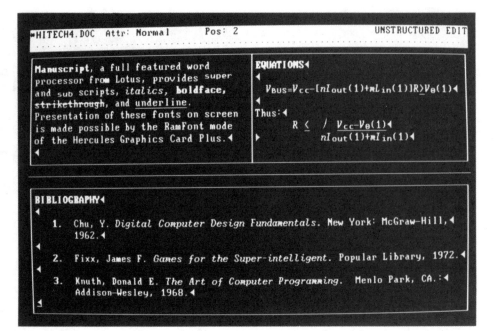

Lotus Manuscript

Manuscript is a word and document processor for technical and scientific writing. It has an outliner, a print formatter that allows you to mix text (including multiple fonts) and graphics, a spelling checker, and a document comparison feature that automatically highlights changes between revisions of documents.

The program runs on MS-DOS–based computers with 512K RAM and requires a hard disk. The program is not copy protected. Suggested price is $495.

Lotus Development Corporation, 55 Cambridge Parkway, Cambridge, Mass. 02142; (617) 577-8500.

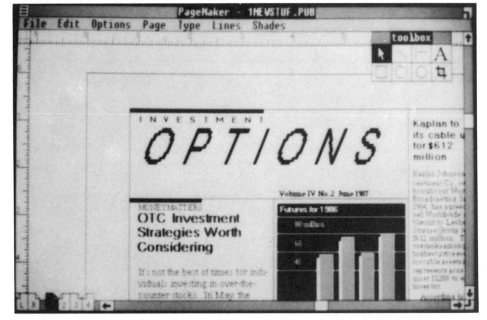

PageMaker

PageMaker is a desktop-publishing program. The program sets up the display screen as an electronic paste-up board and gives the user a toolbox of design aids for electronic page composition. The program permits integration of text and graphics, has a built-in text editor, and will import data from various word processors and graphics programs. Although the program is easy to use and powerful, a mouse and a high-resolution large-screen display are needed.

PageMaker runs on MS-DOS–based computers with 640K RAM, and the Apple Macintosh with 1-MB RAM. Both versions require a hard disk. The MS-DOS version of the program is not copy protected. Suggested price is $695.

Aldus Corporation, 411 First Avenue South, Suite 200, Seattle, Wash. 98104; (206) 628-2352.

Spreadsheet

1-2-3 Release 3

1-2-3 is perhaps the most popular application program available for personal computers and has thus become a de facto standard. Its features include three-dimensional worksheets, access to external databases, relational data management capabilities, macro capabilities, string functions, string arithmetic, efficient memory management, and programming capabilities. An interactive hands-on tutorial is included. Graphics capabilities include the ability to create presentation-quality pie, line, or bar charts from spreadsheet data. The program is menu driven but complex. Spreadsheet size is 256 worksheets by 8192 rows by 256 columns.

The program runs on 80286- and 80386-based computers with 1-MB RAM (3-MB under OS/2) and a hard disk. The program is not copy protected. Suggested price is $595. MS-DOS–based users should investigate 1-2-3 Release 2.2 priced at $495.

Lotus Development Corporation, 55 Cambridge Parkway, Cambridge, Mass. 02142; (617) 577-8500.

Spreadsheet

Quattro

Quattro's spreadsheet has built-in presentation graphics with 10 customizable graph types. The program's user interface features pull-down menus as well as control-key operation to bypass the menus. Also included is a programmable application development environment for building dedicated applications.

The program runs on MS-DOS–based computers with 384K RAM. Two disk drives are required. The program is not copy protected. Suggested price is $247.50.

Borland International, 4585 Scotts Valley Drive, Scotts Valley, Calif. 95066; (408) 438-8400.

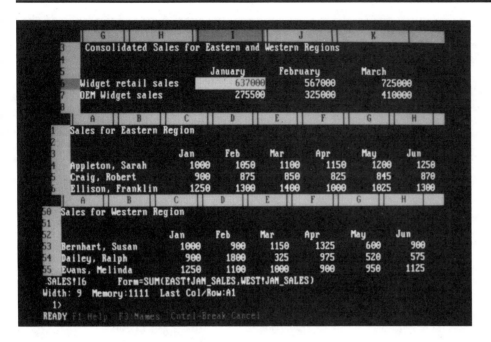

Spreadsheet

SuperCalc5

SuperCalc5 integrates support for multiple and linked spreadsheets. Up to 255 pages or spreadsheets can be linked. A built-in auditing module helps users debug their spreadsheets. Presentation-quality charting and graphics capabilities along with a report function enhance the quality of displayed and printed output.

SuperCalc5 runs on MS-DOS–based computers (DOS 3.0 or higher) with 512K RAM and two disk drives. The program is not copy protected. Suggested price is $495.

Computer Associates, 1240 McKay Drive, San Jose, Calif. 95131; (408) 432-1727.

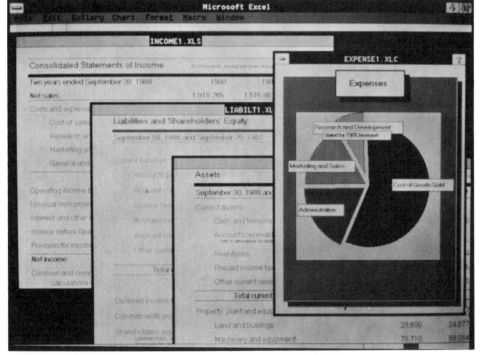

Spreadsheet

Microsoft Excel

Excel is a powerful and sophisticated spreadsheet program that also combines graphics, data management, and a macro language facility for automating repetitive functions. Excel offers the ability to format cells with underlines or outlines and the ability to display boldface and italic type of different styles and sizes. You can display multiple spreadsheets and associated graphs concurrently. Because of the Macintosh interface, Excel is easy to learn to use yet contains some of the most sophisticated features that are possible in a spreadsheet program. Spreadsheet size is 16,384 rows by 256 columns.

Excel runs on the Apple Macintosh computer with 512K RAM and two disk drives, and on MS-DOS–based computers with Microsoft Windows. The program is not copy protected. Suggested Macintosh price is $395; MS-DOS price, $495.

Microsoft Corporation, 16011 NE 36th Way, Redmond, Wash. 98073; (206) 882-8080.

Spreadsheet

Professional Plan

Software Publishing Corporation studied the spreadsheet market and came up with an easy-to-use program with features that include typing in the spreadsheet model instead of an editing line, using the row and column headings in formulas instead of cell numbers, and the ability to perform keyword calculations. Spreadsheet size is a maximum of 32,000 rows by 32,000 columns. Analytical graphics include bar, line, pie, and scatter charts.

Professional Plan runs on MS-DOS–based computers with 384K RAM and two disk drives. The program is not copy protected. Suggested price is $249.

Software Publishing Corporation, 1901 Landings Drive, Mountain View, Calif. 94043; (415) 962-8910.

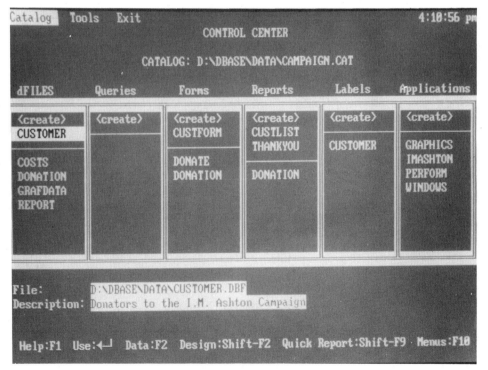

Database

dBase IV

dBase IV is a multifile relational database program that features support for SQL, a forms manager, a query-by-example interface, and a report writer. The user interface features a control center—six on-screen graphic panels—that provides menu access to the program, as well as an optional command-driven interface. The package also includes the dBase programming language and an applications generator for developing more complex applications.

dBase IV runs on MS-DOS–based computers with 640K RAM and two disk drives. A hard disk is recommended. The program is not copy protected. Suggested price is $795.

Ashton-Tate, 20101 Hamilton Avenue, Torrance, Calif. 90502; (213) 329-8000.

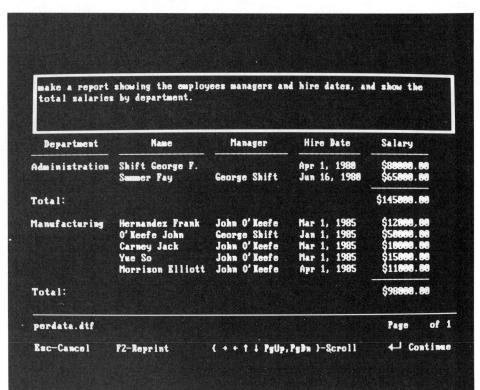

Database

Q&A

Q&A is a menu-driven single-file database program integrated with a word processor. The program contains a built-in natural language interface called the Intelligent Assistant. With it, you can query the database, create reports, and create, change, or delete forms from a database. Although the natural language interface makes the program very easy to use, it also slows down queries. The word processor uses memory-based files so it can store only limited amounts of information.

Q&A runs on MS-DOS–based computers with 512K RAM and two disk drives. The program is not copy protected. Suggested price is $349.

Symantec Corporation, 10201 Torre Avenue, Cupertino, Calif. 95014; (408) 253-9600.

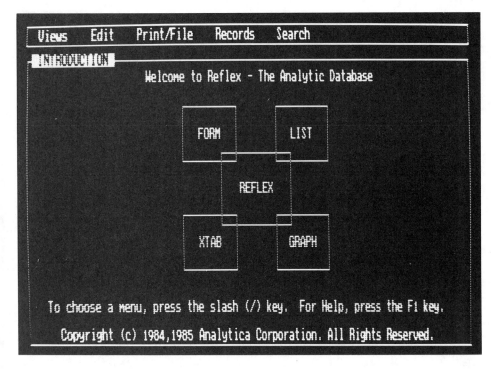

Database

Reflex

Reflex is a single-file database program that supports five views of a file. Users can display their data in a form view, a list view, a graph view, a cross-tab view, and a report view. The program's menu bar, pull-down menus, windows, and graphics make it very easy to use. The report view feature also allows users to import and export files to and from 1-2-3, dBase, and PFS files. Support for a mouse is also included.

Reflex runs on MS-DOS–based computers with 348K RAM and two disk drives. The program is not copy protected. Suggested price is $149. A version called Reflex Plus is available for the Macintosh.

Borland International, 4585 Scotts Valley Drive, Scotts Valley, Calif. 95066; (408) 438-8400.

Database

Professional File

Professional File is a single-file database program. You can use the program for file creation, maintenance, and query through the form generator. You can also produce a wide variety of reports including mailing labels and cross-tabulated reports. The program is compatible with its companion programs Professional Write and Professional Plan.

Professional File runs on MS-DOS–based computers with 256K RAM and two disk drives. The program is not copy protected. Suggested price is $249.

Software Publishing Corporation, 1901 Landings Drive, Mountain View, Calif. 94043; (415) 962-8910.

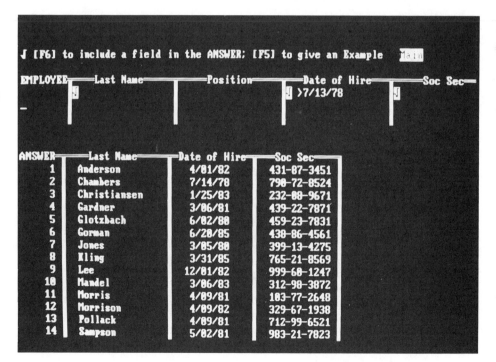

Database

Paradox

Paradox is a multifile relational database program that uses a visual interface that resembles a 1-2-3 spreadsheetlike grid of rows and columns. This interface makes it quite easy to create, modify, and combine databases while hiding a powerful internal structure. The package also includes the Paradox Application Language (PAL), a programming language for developing applications.

Paradox runs on MS-DOS–based computers with 512K RAM and two disk drives. A hard disk is recommended. The program is not copy protected. Suggested price is $695.

Borland International, 4585 Scotts Valley Drive, Scotts Valley, Calif. 95066; (408) 438-8400.

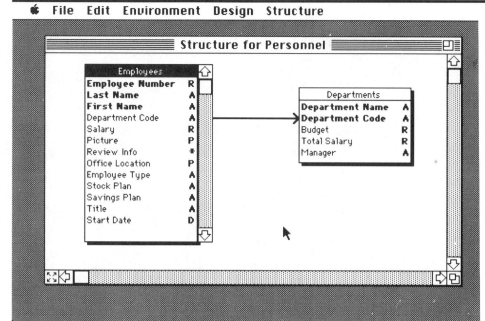

Database

4th Dimension

4th Dimension is a multifile relational database program. With it you can design your own layouts, store pictures, create presentation-quality graphics, and create custom applications with the built-in programming environment. The program rates very high in the ease-of-learning-and-use category.

4th Dimension runs on the Macintosh computer with 1-MB RAM and two disk drives. A hard disk is recommended. The program is not copy protected. Suggested price is $695.

ACIUS, Inc., 10351 Bubb Road, Cupertino, Calif. 95014; (408) 252-4444.

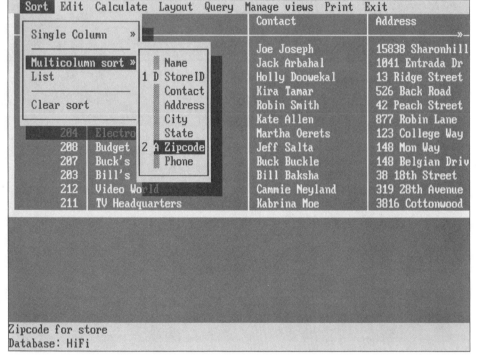

Database

R:Base 3.0

R:Base 3.0 is a multifile relational database program. It includes a set of menu-driven Express facilities for creating forms and reports and for generating applications without programming. The prompt-by-example mode is an easy way to perform a complete range of query operations. For those who prefer programming, a high-level procedural language is also built into R:Base 3.0.

The program runs on MS-DOS–based computers with 640K RAM and two disk drives. A hard disk is recommended. The program is not copy protected. Suggested price is $725.

Microrim, Inc., 3925 159th Avenue N.E., Redmond, Wash. 98052; (206) 885-2000.

Integrated

AppleWorks

AppleWorks is an integrated program that combines a word processor, a database, and a spreadsheet. The programs share a common user interface, and you can cut or copy data from the spreadsheet or database and paste them into documents created by the word processor.

AppleWorks runs on the Apple II family of computers with 128K RAM and two disk drives. Suggested price is $295.

Claris Corporation, 5201 Patrick Henry Drive, Santa Clara, Calif. 95052; (408) 987-7000.

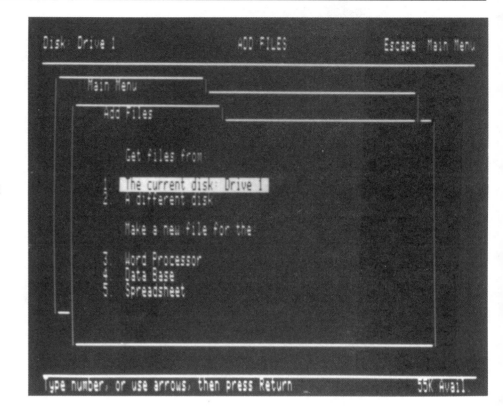

Integrated

Microsoft Works

Microsoft Works is an integrated program that combines a word processor with spelling checker, a spreadsheet with charting, a database with reporting, and communications. You can easily switch among the modules and also cut and paste data among them.

The program runs on MS-DOS–based computers with 512K RAM, and the Apple Macintosh with 128K RAM and one floppy disk drive. The program is not copy protected. Suggested price is $295 for the Macintosh version, $149 for the MS-DOS Version.

Microsoft Corporation, 16011 NE 36th Way, Redmond, Wash. 98073; (206) 882-8080.

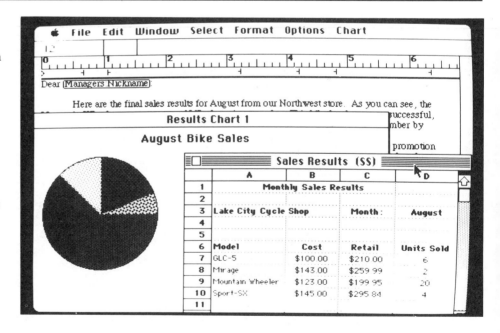

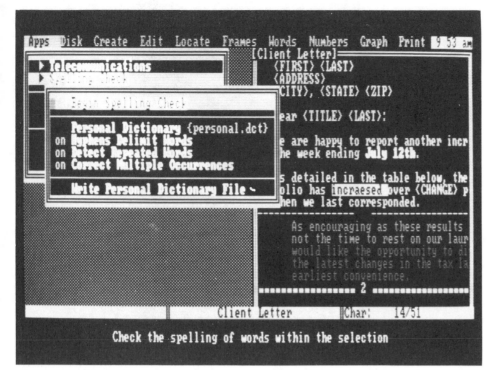

Framework

Integrated

The functions of Framework include word processing, spreadsheet, database with forms processing, business graphics, and an outline processor. Its unique feature, as the name suggests, is the use of an outlining structure for storing information and organizing it into frames. Frames can be linked together and organized by the outline processor, which allows you to create and modify a large integrated file.

Framework runs on MS-DOS–based computers with 384K RAM and two disk drives. The program is not copy protected. Suggested price is $695.

Ashton-Tate, 20101 Hamilton Avenue, Torrance, Calif. 90502; (213) 329-8000.

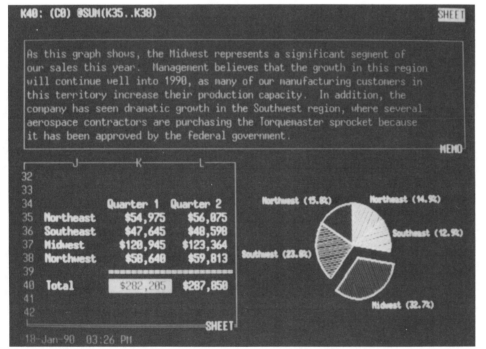

Symphony

Integrated

Symphony is an integrated program that supports spreadsheets, word processing, forms-oriented database, graphics, and communications. The program uses the spreadsheet metaphor to store all its data. You can build windows for each type of application, and the program is upwardly compatible with 1-2-3. The spreadsheet size is 8192 rows by 255 columns.

Symphony runs on MS-DOS–based computers with 384K RAM and two disk drives. The program is copy protected. Suggested price is $695.

Lotus Development Corporation, 55 Cambridge Parkway, Cambridge, Mass. 02142; (617) 577-8500.

Graphics

MacPaint

MacPaint is a freehand drawing program for producing black-and-white pictures. You can add type fonts, sizes, and styles to your drawings and paste them into MacWrite documents. The program is imaginative and extremely easy to use.

MacPaint runs on the Apple Macintosh with 512K RAM and one disk drive. The program is not copy protected. Suggested price is $125.

Claris Corporation, 5201 Patrick Henry Drive, Santa Clara, Calif. 95052; (408) 987-7000.

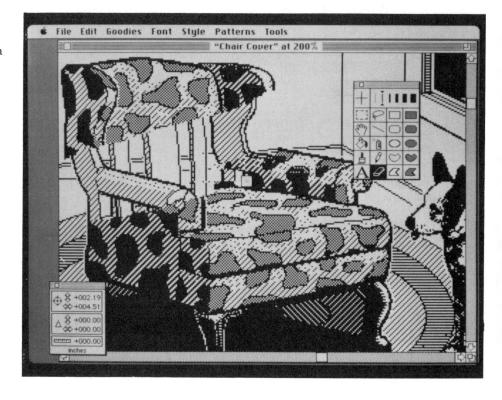

Graphics

Harvard Graphics

Harvard Graphics is a business graphics program that produces graphs and charts. Graph types include pie and pie-bar combinations, horizontal and vertical bar, clustered, overlapped and stacked bar, area, line, curve, trendline, scatter graph, and high-low-close charts. Text chart types include title charts, lists, bullet points, and two- and three-column charts. You can enter data from the keyboard or read data from Lotus files, ASCII files, or other Software Publishing programs.

The program runs on MS-DOS–based computers with 512K RAM and a hard disk drive. The program is not copy protected. Suggested price is $495.

Software Publishing Corporation, 1901 Landings Drive, Mountain View, Calif. 94043; (415) 962-8910.

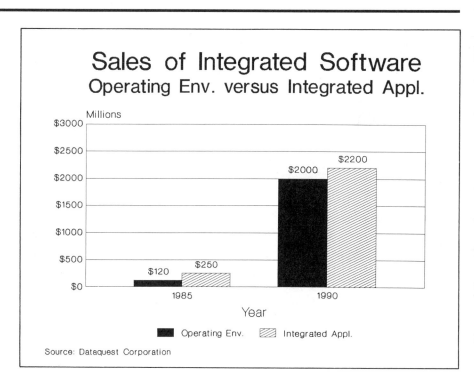

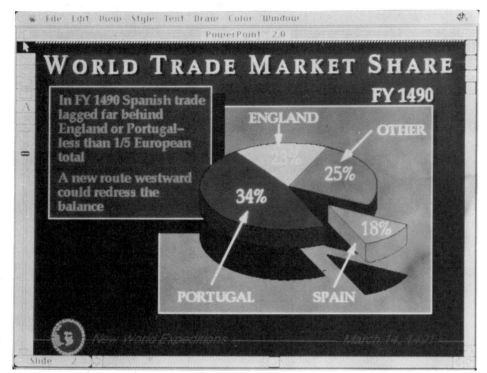

Graphics

PowerPoint

PowerPoint is a desktop presentation program that can produce a variety of charts, diagrams, and graphs. The user types text onto blank "slides" on the Macintosh screen, selects the appropriate background and text colors, inserts graphics, and arranges the slides in order. Output can be black-and-white overheads, color overheads, transparencies, or 35-mm slides. You can also display the slides in sequence on the Macintosh screen.

The program runs on the Apple Macintosh with 1-MB RAM and two disk drives. The MS-DOS version of the program is not copy protected. Suggested price is $395.

Microsoft Corporation, 16011 NE 36th Way, Redmond, Wash. 98073; (206) 882-8080.

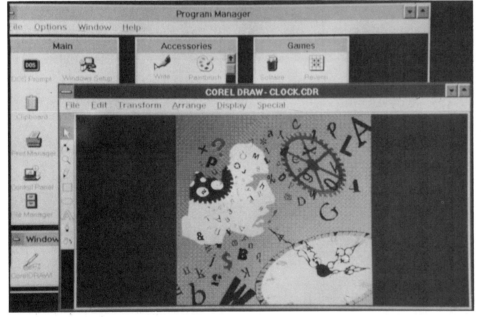

Graphics

CorelDraw

CorelDraw is a freehand color drawing program with which high-quality graphics can be created. You can import your drawings into most word processing and desktop-publishing programs. Features include a tracing program, built-in typefaces, and a clip art library. Full color images can be output to inkjet, thermal, or dot-matrix printers and slidemakers or plotters. The program can also produce spot color overlays or color separations for color offset printing.

The program runs on the MS-DOS–based computers with 640K RAM and a hard disk. The program requires Microsoft Windows. Suggested price is $595.

Corel Systems Corp., 1600 Carling Avenue, Ottawa, Ontario, Canada K1Z8R7; (613) 728-8200.

Graphics

35mm Express

35mm Express is targeted toward slide production. The program offers drawing tools; has a built-in communications module; and plots data in 3-D, area, word, bar, line, and pie charts. The program is menu driven and requires familiarity with business graphs to master the program thoroughly.

35mm Express runs on MS-DOS–based computers with 256K RAM and two disk drives. The program is not copy protected. Suggested price is $495.

Business and Professional Software, Inc., 143 Binney Street, Cambridge, Mass. 02142; (617) 491-3377.

Communications

Crosstalk

Crosstalk is a personal computer telecommunications program that provides the following features: smart terminal operation, including automatic log-on; automatic telephone dialing; the ability to capture data onto a disk; and the ability to send disk files to other computer systems.

Crosstalk runs on MS-DOS–based computers with 64K RAM and one floppy disk drive. The program is not copy protected. Suggested price is $195. The program can also be found bundled with selected modems.

Crosstalk Communications, Inc., 1000 Holcomb Woods Parkway, Suite 440, Roswell, Ga. 30076; (404) 952-0267.

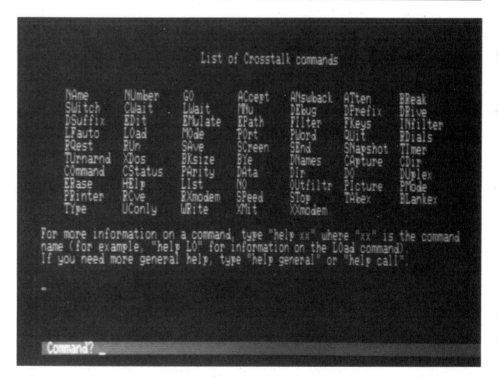

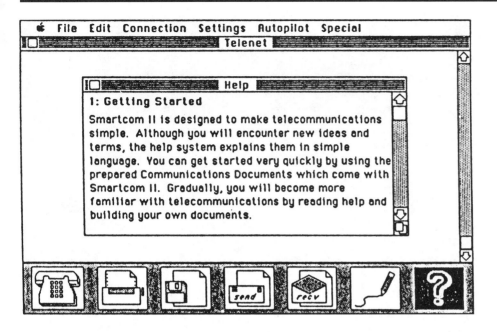

Hayes Smartcom

Hayes Smartcom is a personal computer telecommunications program that supports macro commands for dialing up to 25 information services, unattended remote operation, and the ability to send and capture ASCII or binary files to and from other computer systems. It features XMODEM and Hayes Verification protocols for error-free data transfer and terminal emulation. The program is easy to learn and use.

Hayes Smartcom runs on MS-DOS–based computers, and the Apple Macintosh with 128K RAM and one floppy disk drive. The program is not copy protected. Suggested price is $149. The program is also bundled with Hayes Smartmodem 1200B.

Hayes Microcomputer Products, Inc., 5923 Peachtree Industrial Boulevard, Norcross, Ga. 30092; (404) 449-8791.

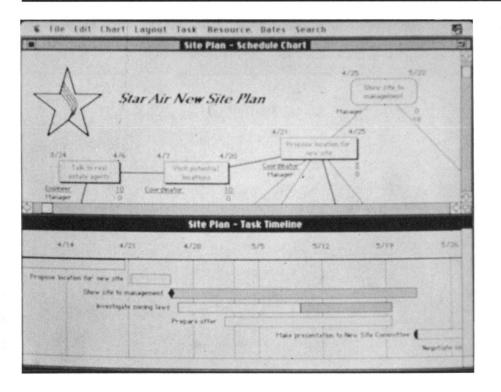

Managing

MacProject II

MacProject II produces start-to-completion project schedules in either text or bar chart form. You can also produce status or budget reports, and a calendar program is included. The critical path is automatically calculated and *what-if* questions can be used to schedule changes.

The program runs on the Apple Macintosh with 512K RAM and one floppy disk drive. The program is not copy protected. Suggested price is $495.

Claris Corporation, 5201 Patrick Henry Drive, Santa Clara, Calif. 95052; (408) 987-7000.

Managing

Agenda

Agenda is a personal information manager. It differs from database programs in that no structure for the data need be set up before entering data. The user enters data in units called items. Items may have notes attached to them and can be assigned to categories. The user can query the information to obtain a view. Views are user defined and may link several categories.

Agenda runs on MS-DOS–based computers with 640K RAM and two disk drives. A hard disk is recommended. The program is not copy protected. Suggested price is $395.

Lotus Development Corporation, 55 Cambridge Parkway, Cambridge, Mass. 02142; (617) 577-8500.

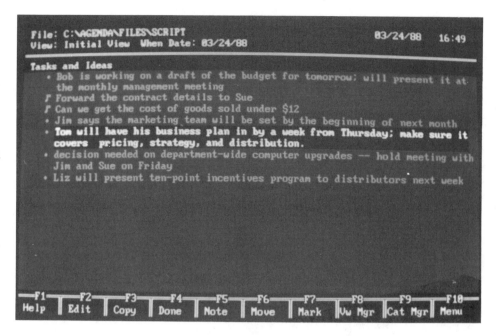

Accounting and Bookkeeping

One-Write Plus

One-Write Plus is a checkbook-writing and cash-journal system designed for small business accounting or personal finances. The program can handle debits and credits, prepare simple financial reports, and write checks. It is an extremely easy-to-use program, especially for people with no accounting background. However, since this is not a double-entry bookkeeping system, data-entry errors are harder to catch and must be checked manually.

One-Write Plus runs on MS-DOS–based computers with 256K RAM and two disk drives. The program is copy protected. Suggested price is $250.

Great American Software, Inc., P.O. Box 910, Amherst, N.H. 03031; (603) 889-5400.

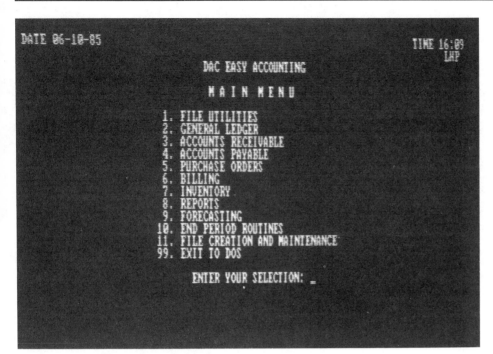

Accounting and Bookkeeping

DAC-Easy Accounting

DAC-Easy Accounting is a simple yet powerful menu-driven integrated accounting package that provides general ledger, accounts receivable, accounts payable, inventory, purchase order, billing, and forecasting functions. It provides good standard accounting for small- and medium-sized businesses and an exceptionally good value for the price.

DAC-Easy Accounting runs on MS-DOS–based computers with 128K RAM and one floppy disk drive. The program is copy protected. Suggested price is $99.95.

DAC Software, Inc., 4801 Spring Valley Road, Dallas, Texas 75244; (214) 458-0038.

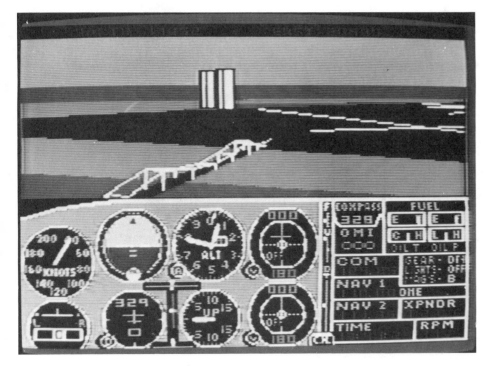

Entertainment

Flight Simulator

Flight Simulator is one of the most popular games for the IBM PC; the program simulates flying a Cessna 182 single-engine airplane, and you control the plane by manipulating an instrument panel via the keyboard as you view a simulated display out the cockpit window.

Flight Simulator runs on MS-DOS–based computers with 64K RAM and one floppy disk drive. The program is not copy protected. Suggested price is $50.

Microsoft Corporation, 16011 NE 36th Way, Redmond, Wash. 98073; (206) 882-8080.

Entertainment

Pinball Construction Set

Not only can you play electronic pinball, but with Pinball Construction Set you can construct your own pinball game. You can change the location of bumpers and flippers; add decorations, sounds, and shapes; and then play the game you have created. A fascinating and educational simulation.

Pinball Construction Set runs on the Apple II family, certain Atari computers, the Commodore family, and MS-DOS–based computers with 64K RAM and one floppy disk drive. The program is copy protected. Suggested price is $40.

Electronic Arts, 2755 Campus Drive, San Mateo, Calif. 94403; (415) 571-7171.

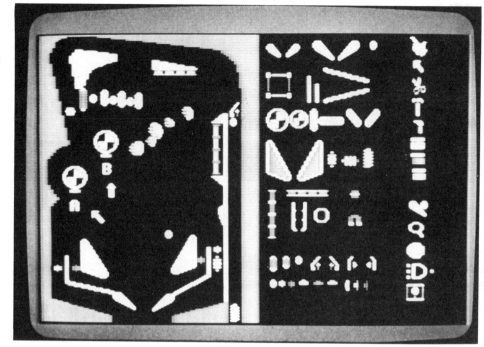

Education

Discovering Microsoft Works

The educational version of Works is a limited-capacity educational version of the Works integrated software package. It combines word processing, spreadsheet with graphics, database with reporting, and communications. The program ranks high on performance, versatility, and ease of use. The software is accompanied by a textbook.

The educational version of Works runs on MS-DOS–based computers with 384K RAM and two disk drives. The program is not copy protected. Suggested price is $20.

John Wiley & Sons, Inc., College Division, 605 Third Avenue, New York, N.Y. 10158; (212) 850-6000.

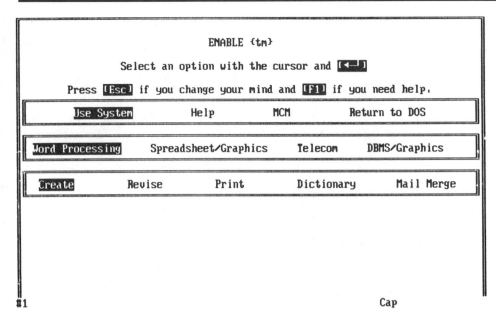

Enable 2.14

The educational version of Enable is a limited-capacity educational version of the Enable integrated software package. It combines word processing, spreadsheet, database, graphics, and communications. The program ranks high on performance and versatility. The software is accompanied by two student manuals.

The educational version of Enable runs on MS-DOS–based computers with 256K RAM and two disk drives. The program is not copy protected. Suggested price is $35.

John Wiley & Sons, Inc., College Division, 605 Third Avenue, New York, N.Y. 10158; (212) 850-6000.

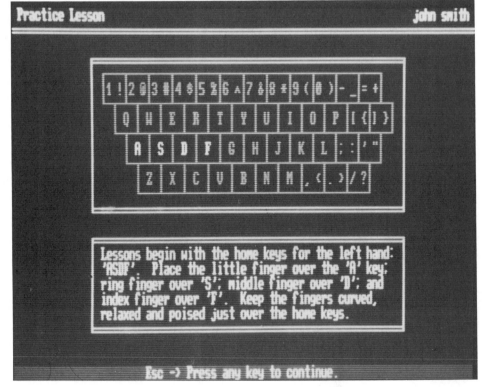

Typing Tutor

If you can't type, or still use the hunt-and-peck method of typing, learning how to use a computer may seem to be a formidable barrier. This program teaches fundamental typing skills. It can adjust itself to your skill level and create custom-designed lessons. It also graphs your progress after each lesson, showing your speed, accuracy, and strengths and weaknesses.

Typing Tutor runs on MS-DOS–based computers, the Apple II family, and the Macintosh 128K RAM and one floppy disk drive. The program is not copy protected. Suggested price is for the MS-DOS version is $49.95.

Simon & Schuster Software, 1 Gulf + Western Plaza, New York, N.Y. 10023; (212) 373-8500.

Scientific and Engineering

AutoCAD

AutoCAD is a multipurpose computer-aided drawing program with two-dimensional drafting and three-dimensional visualization capabilities. The program is menu driven and supports a mouse, light pen, or digitizing tablet. Although the program is easy to use and powerful, a number of additional hardware features are recommended. A digitizing tablet is best for drawing. A hard disk is recommended, and a math coprocessor, such as the 80287, speeds up the program considerably.

AutoCAD runs on MS-DOS–based computers with 512K RAM and two disk drives. The program is not copy protected. Suggested prices vary from $300 for the basic drafting package to $2500 for a full-scale, three-dimensional design tool.

Autodesk, Inc., 2320 Marinship Way, Sausalito, Calif. 94965; (415) 332-2344.

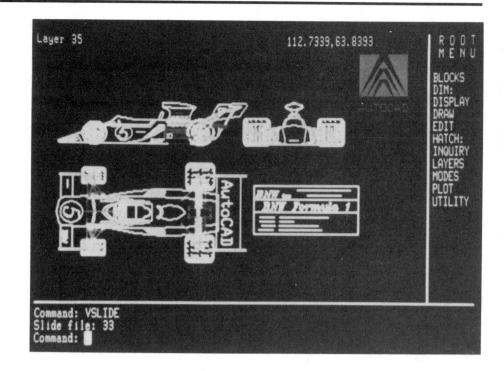

Scientific and Engineering

Mathematica

Mathematica is a comprehensive software system for mathematical computations. The program can solve equations, perform numeric calculations and symbolic manipulations, and draw two- and three-dimensional graphs with animation. It also includes a high-level interactive programming language.

Mathematica can run on a wide variety of computers from personal computers to workstations to supercomputers, but requires several megabytes of memory. The Macintosh version, for example, requires 2.5-MB RAM. Suggested price for the standard Macintosh version is $495.

Wolfram Research, Inc., P.O. Box 6059, Champaign, Ill. 61821; (217) 398-0700.

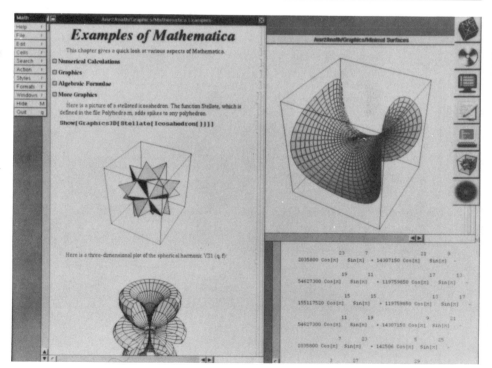

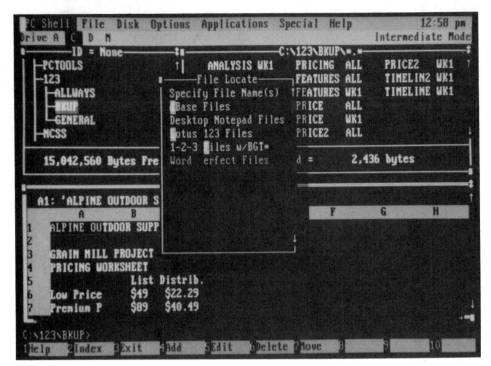

Utilities

PC Tools Version 6

PC Tools Version 6 is a collection of disk and file management, data protection and recovery, and desktop management tools. The program is easy to learn and use.

PC Tools runs on MS-DOS–based computers with 512K RAM and one floppy disk drive. The program is not copy protected. Suggested price is $149.

Central Point Software, Inc., 15220 N.W. Greenbrier Parkway, Suite 200, Beaverton, Ore. 97006; (503) 690-8090.

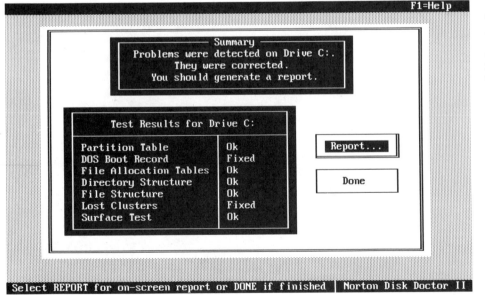

Utilities

The Norton Utilities

The Norton Utilities is a collection of disk and file management, data protection and recovery, and desktop management tools. The program is easy to learn and use.

PC Tools runs on MS-DOS–based computers with 512K RAM and one floppy disk drive. The program is not copy protected. Suggested price is $149.

Peter Norton Computing, Inc., 100 Wilshire Blvd., 9th Floor, Santa Monica, Calif. 90401;(213) 319-2000.

HARDWARE

To sort out the wide variety of personal computer systems, we classify them into the following categories:

- *Notebooks.* The notebook-sized personal computer derives its name from its $8\frac{1}{2}$-inch by 11-inch by under 2-inch measurements. Notebook-size personal computers fit into a briefcase, weigh less than 8 pounds, and are battery powered in their normal mode of operation. Prices vary widely. They sometimes offer operating system and application software in ROM.

- *Laptops.* Laptops are portable computers. They are battery powered in their normal operation, weigh less than 20 pounds, contain a flat-panel display screen, typically come with one or two disk drives and a built-in modem, and have ports for peripheral devices, such as printers, mice, or external disk drives.

- *Desktops.* The desktop category is the most popular configuration of all personal computers. Desktop computers typically contain a medium-sized system unit that can accommodate several expansion slots and have a separate keyboard and monitor. With options, prices can exceed $10,000, but $3000 is closer to an average price.

- *Workstations.* The workstation category resembles the desktop category in appearance, but workstations are associated with high-performance specialized applications such as computer-aided design and publishing, modeling, and visualization. Most employ multiple 32-bit processors; some are based on 64-bit RISC processors. Because they use the Unix operating system, most of the software listed in this appendix is not applicable. With options, prices can exceed $50,000, but $10,000 is closer to an average base price.

The following is a representative sampling of computer systems. It is not meant to be complete, but it will give you an idea of the variety of computer systems that are available. As with software, actual prices may vary considerably from the suggested prices listed in this appendix.

Notebook

Atari Portfolio

Portfolio is a hand-held IBM PC-compatible computer. ROM-based applications include a word processor, a spreadsheet, a personal calendar, and a phone directory. A port is included for file exchange with other personal computers.

Standard features include an Intel 80C88 microprocessor, 128K RAM, 32K or 128K RAM cards that replace disk drives, and an 8-line by 40-character LCD display. The computer is powered by three standard AA batteries. Weight is 1 pound. Suggested price is $399.

Atari Corporation, 1265 Borregas Avenue, Sunnyvale, Calif. 94806; (408) 745-2000.

Notebook

GridPad

The most interesting feature of the GridPad is the fact that it has no keyboard. You can enter hand-printed characters with a stylus and software recognizes those characters and turns them into typed text. You can also use the stylus to point to commands on the screen and use the GridPad as an MS-DOS–based computer. An optional 3-pound expansion unit adds a 40-MB hard disk and a $3\frac{1}{2}$-inch floppy disk drive.

Standard features include a 10-MHz 80C86 microprocessor, 1-MB RAM, and a 10-inch LCD display with 640- by 400-pixel resolution. Weight is 4.5 pounds. Suggested price is $2370.

Grid Systems Corporation, 47211 Lakeview Boulevard, Fremont, Calif. 94537; (415) 656-4700.

Notebook

Sharp PC-6220

The PC-6220 is an $8\frac{1}{2}$-inch by 11-inch by 1.4-inch notebook computer. Options include an external $3\frac{1}{2}$-inch floppy disk drive, an internal modem, two internal expansion slots, and an add-on battery that increases the battery life to five hours.

Hardware features include a 12-MHz 80C286 microprocessor, 1-MB RAM, a 20-MB hard disk, and a backlighted 10-inch black-and-white VGA (640- by 480-pixel resolution) LCD display. Weight is 4 pounds. Suggested price is $3995.

Sharp Electronics Corporation, Sharp Plaza, Mahwah, N.J. 07430; (201) 529-8965.

Notebook

Toshiba T1200XE

The T1200XE is a 12-inch by 11-inch by 2-inch notebook computer. Options include a built-in modem, expandable memory, color monitor, and an external disk drive.

Hardware features include an 12-MHz 80C286 microprocessor, 1-MB RAM, a 20-MB hard disk, a $3\frac{1}{2}$-inch floppy disk drive, and a sidelight LCD display with 640- by 400-pixel resolution. Weight is 8 pounds. Suggested price is $3995.

Toshiba America, Inc., Information Systems Division, 9740 Irvine Boulevard, Irvine, Calif. 92718; (714) 583-3000.

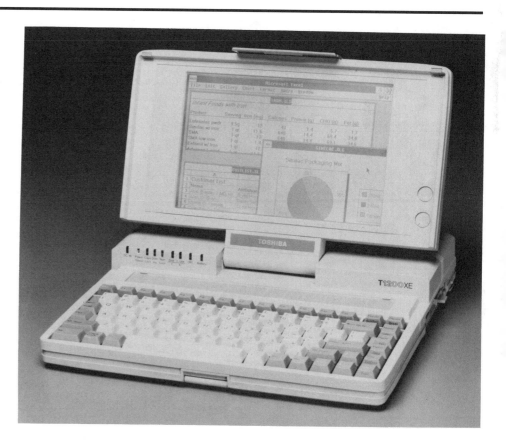

Notebook

Compaq LTE/286

Compaq LTE series of computers measures in at $8\frac{1}{2}$-inches by 11-inches by 2-inches.

Standard features include a 12-MHz Intel 80C286 microprocessor, 640K RAM, one $3\frac{1}{2}$-inch 1.44-MB floppy disk drive, a 20-MB or 40-MB hard disk, and a supertwist LCD display with 640- by 350-pixel resolution. Weight is 6.2 pounds. Suggested price is $4499 with a 20-MB hard disk; $4999 with a 40-MB hard disk.

Compaq Computer Corporation, 12330 Perry Road, Houston, Texas 77070; (713) 370-7040.

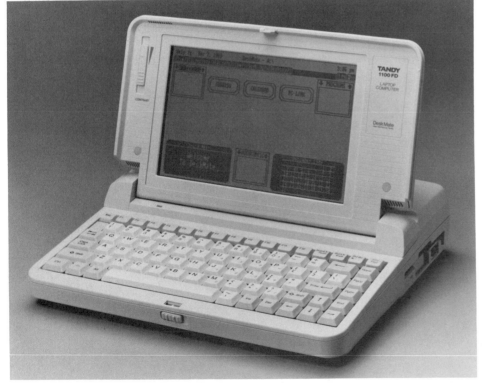

Laptop

Tandy 1100 FD

The Tandy 1100 FD is a small-sized MS-DOS–based laptop computer. The Tandy 1100 FD features a back-lighted supertwist LCD display with 640- by 200-pixel resolution plus eight shades of gray for graphics. Also included is Tandy's own DeskMate graphical user interface in ROM.

Standard features include an NEC V-20 microprocessor, 640K RAM, one $3\frac{1}{2}$-inch floppy disk drive, and a removable rechargeable battery pack with ac adapter. A 2400-baud internal modem is optional. Weight is 6.5 pounds without battery. Suggested price is $999.

Tandy Corporation, 1800 One Tandy Center, Fort Worth, Texas 76102; (817) 390-3011.

Laptop

Toshiba T1600

The Toshiba T1600 is an MS-DOS portable computer. It has a backlighted supertwist LCD screen with 640- by 400-pixel resolution, or an optional reflective LCD screen to conserve battery power. Standard features include an Intel 80C286 microprocessor, 1-MB RAM, one built-in $3\frac{1}{2}$-inch floppy disk drive, and a 20-MB hard disk. A 40-MB hard disk and a modem are optional.

A removable battery can be recharged in the computer, or in an optional external battery charger. The computer has space for two batteries. Weight is 11.6 pounds. Suggested price is $4699.

Toshiba America, Inc., Information Systems Division, 9740 Irvine Boulevard, Irvine, Calif. 92718; (714) 583-3000.

Laptop

TurboSport 386

This 80386-based system features a high-contrast "Page White" display to provide darker and sharper images in a CRT-quality display. This feature helps readability in all lighting conditions.

Standard features include a 12-MHz 80386 microprocessor, 2-MB RAM, one $3\frac{1}{2}$-inch floppy disk drive, a 40-MB hard disk drive, an 80-character by 25-line fluorescent backlighted LCD display with 640- by 400-pixel graphics resolution, and built-in chargeable battery pack with ac adapter. Weight is 15 pounds. Suggested price is $7999.

Zenith Data Systems, 1000 Milwaukee Avenue, Glenview, Ill., 60025; (312) 699-4839.

Laptop

Compaq SLT/286

The SLT stands for Super Lap Top, and this smaller version of Compaq's transportable computers features a high-contrast graphics display to provide darker and sharper gray-scale images with CRT quality. An intelligent power management system allows the SLT/286 to conserve power, permitting up to three hours of operation before recharging the batteries. An optional desktop expansion base accommodates two expansion slots.

Standard features include a 12-MHz 80C286 microprocessor, 640K RAM, one $3\frac{1}{2}$-inch floppy disk drive, a 20-MB hard disk drive, a paper white backlighted fluorescent LCD display with up to 640-by 480-pixel graphics resolution, detachable keyboard, and built-in chargeable battery pack. Weight is 14 pounds. Suggested price is $5399.

Compaq Computer Corporation, 12330 Perry Road, Houston, Texas 77070; (713) 370-7040.

Laptop

Toshiba T5200

The Toshiba T5200 is a high-powered top-of-the-line portable personal computer that Toshiba claims has all the power of a desktop 386-based computer. The clamshell design has VGA graphics capability.

Standard features include a 20-MHz 80386 processor, 2-MB RAM, a $3\frac{1}{2}$-inch floppy disk drive, a 40-MB hard disk drive, and an 80-character by 25-line gas plasma display with VGA graphics resolution. Options include an internal modem, an expansion chassis, and a 2-MB memory expansion board. Weight is 15 pounds. Suggested price is $9499.

Toshiba America, Inc., Information Systems Division, 9740 Irvine Boulevard, Irvine, Calif. 92718; (714) 583-3000.

Laptop

Macintosh Portable

The Macintosh Portable incorporates all traditional Macintosh features into a laptop computer. The LCD screen size features 640- by-400 pixels and uses active-matrix technology to achieve high contrast. The computer uses rechargeable lead acid batteries that can last six hours.

Standard features include a 16-MHz CMOS Motorola 68000 microprocessor, 1-MB RAM, a built-in LCD screen, one $3\frac{1}{2}$-inch 1.4-MB floppy disk drive, and a trackball. Weight is 15.7 pounds. Suggested price is $5799. With a 40-MB hard disk, the price is $6499.

Apple Computer, Inc., 20525 Mariani Avenue, Cupertino, Calif. 95014; (408) 996-1010.

Laptop

Grid 1450SX

The Grid is a MS-DOS–based portable computer housed in a sleek black magnesium case. Because Grid Systems research determined that most users would want to use this computer with ac power, the battery packs, which slide under the system unit, are optional.

Standard features include a 16-MHz 803886SX microprocessor, 1-MB RAM, one $3\frac{1}{2}$-inch floppy disk drive, a 20-MB hard disk, and a high-contrast LCD display screen with electroluminescent lighting. Weight is 11.8 pounds. Suggested price is $4995.

Grid Systems Corporation, 47211 Lakeview Boulevard, Fremont, Calif. 94537; (415) 656-4700.

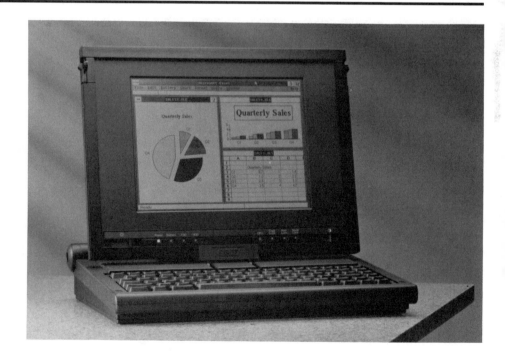

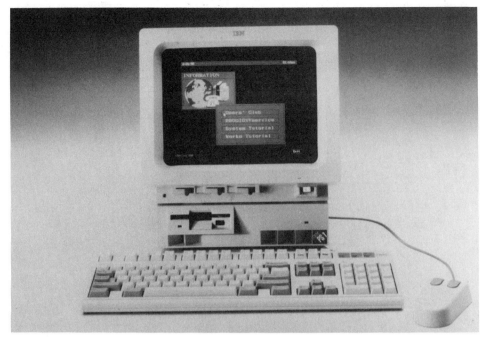

Desktop

IBM PS/1

IBM is targeting the entry-level market by calling its PS/1 personal computer a home computing system. You can take the PS/1 out of its shipping box, plug in a few cords, turn it on, and begin to use it, thanks to MS-DOS in ROM.

Standard features include a 10-MHz 80286 processor, a $3\frac{1}{2}$-inch floppy disk drive, a built-in modem, a mouse, and Microsoft Works and Prodigy. Options include a monochrome or color monitor and a 30-MB hard disk. Suggested price starts at $999 for a monochrome monitor, $1649 for the addition of a hard disk, and $1999 for a hard disk and color monitor.

IBM Entry Systems Division, P.O. Box 1328, Boca Raton, Fla. 33432; (407) 443-2000.

Desktop

Commodore Amiga 500

The Commodore Amiga 500 is a scaled-down version of the Amiga 1000. It is a sophisticated home computer that includes graphics, video, four-channel sound, and built in speech synthesis. It is not a toy however, but is a good beginning computer. You can obtain a wide variety of educational, game, and business software; for programming in BASIC, the Commodore Amiga 500 offers very good color and sound.

Standard features include a Motorola 68000 microprocessor, 512K RAM, and a $3\frac{1}{2}$-inch floppy disk drive. Options include a monochrome or color monitor. Suggested price is $699.

Commodore International, Computer Systems Division, 1200 Wilson Drive, West Chester, Penn. 19380; (215) 431-9100.

Desktop

Commodore Amiga 2000

Commodore's Amiga 2000 features a built-in operating environment (GEM) that was inspired by the Macintosh interface. IBM compatibility is an option that is achieved by adding the A2088 Bridge Board.

Standard features include a Motorola 68000 microprocessor with custom chips for sound, graphics, and animation; 1-MB RAM; one $3\frac{1}{2}$-inch floppy disk drive; and a mouse. An optional color monitor must be purchased separately. Suggested price is $1995.

Commodore International, Computer Systems Division, 1200 Wilson Drive, West Chester, Penn. 19380; (215) 431-9100.

Desktop

Atari 520ST

The Atari 520ST is a powerful, low-cost computer system with a built-in GEM desktop operating environment. For the programmer who wants a computer with a lot of potential, the 520ST is very advanced. The novice or businessperson interested in ready-made application software should adopt a wait-and-see attitude.

Standard features include a Motorola 68000 microprocessor, 512K RAM, 192K ROM, and a mouse. Optional equipment includes a $3\frac{1}{2}$-inch floppy disk drive and a monochrome or color monitor. An enhanced Atari 1040 features 1-MB of RAM. Suggested price is $799.

Atari Corporation, 1265 Borregas Avenue, Sunnyvale, Calif. 94806; (408) 745-2000.

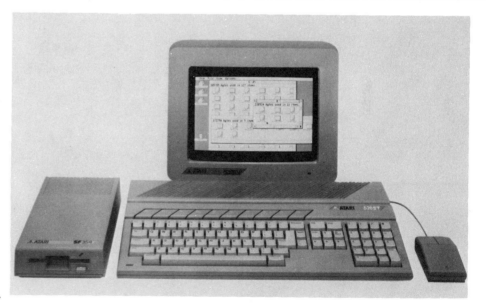

Desktop

Macintosh LC

The Macintosh LC is an entry-level color Macintosh computer. Its enhancements over earlier models include high-resolution color, high-performance sound capabilities with its built-in microphone and audio digitizer, and built-in mouse.

Standard features include a 16-MHz Motorola 68020 microprocessor, 2-MB RAM, one $3\frac{1}{2}$-inch 1.4-MB floppy disk drive, and a keyboard. Options include monochrome or color displays, and a 40-MB hard disk. Suggested price starts at $2499. A plug-in board that allows the Macintosh LC to function as an Apple IIe is available for $199.

Apple Computer, Inc., 20525 Mariani Avenue, Cupertino, Calif. 95014; (408) 996-1010.

Desktop

IBM Personal System/2 Model 30

The IBM Personal System/2 Model 30 is a low-end desktop system designed to replace IBM's earlier PC XT model. The Model 30 incorporates many built-in features, including serial, parallel, and pointing device ports; a processor support chip that provides clock generator, bus controller, and video clock functions; and a graphics controller that provides several levels of resolution.

Standard features include an Intel 8086 microprocessor, 640K RAM, three expansion slots, and two $3\frac{1}{2}$-inch 720K floppy disk drives. Suggested price is $1695. With a 20-MB hard disk, the price is $2295.

People who are more budget minded might look at the more compact IBM Personal System/2 Model 25, which is priced at $1350 with a built-in monochrome display or $1695 with a built-in color display. The Model 25, however, has no provision for a hard disk.

IBM Entry Systems Division, P.O. Box 1328, Boca Raton, Fla. 33432; (407) 443-2000.

Desktop

Tandy 1000 TX

The Tandy 1000 TX is a low-priced entry in the MS-DOS–compatible arena. Its features and options parallel those of the IBM PC XT, and it runs all the software that runs on the IBM computer. Also included is Personal Deskmate 2, an integrated program that includes word processing, spreadsheet, filing, calendar, and telecommunication modules along with a menu-driven user interface.

Standard features include an Intel 80286 microprocessor, 640K RAM, five expansion slots, and one $3\frac{1}{2}$-inch floppy disk drive. Options include a monochrome or color monitor. Suggested price is $1199.

Tandy Corporation, 1800 One Tandy Center, Fort Worth, Texas 76102; (817) 390-3011.

Desktop

IBM Personal System/2 Model 55SX

The Model 55SX is a desktop system that implements IBM's video graphics array (VGA) display standard and a 16-bit Micro Channel bus. The system unit contains three general-purpose expansion slots.

Standard features include an Intel 80386SX microprocessor, 2-MB RAM, one $3\frac{1}{2}$-inch, 1.44-MB floppy disk drive, and a 30-MB or 60-MB hard disk. Suggested price with a 30-MB hard disk is $3895; with a 60-MB hard disk, $4295.

IBM Entry Systems Division, P.O. Box 1328, Boca Raton, Fla. 33432; (407) 443-2000.

Macintosh Classic

The Macintosh Classic is an updated version of the traditional all-in-one Macintosh. The Classic includes a built-in AppleTalk networking interface, Small Computer Systems Interface (SCSI), and sound output. A good first computer for the novice user.

Standard features include an 8-MHz Motorola 68000 microprocessor, 1-MB RAM, a built-in 9-inch monochrome monitor, a $3\frac{1}{2}$-inch 1.4-MB floppy disk drive, and a mouse. Suggested price starts at $999. The Macintosh Classic 2/40 with 2-MB RAM and a 40-MB hard disk is priced at $1499.

Apple Computer, Inc., 20525 Mariani Avenue, Cupertino, Calif. 95014; (408) 996-1010.

Macintosh IIsi

The Macintosh IIsi is the entry-level computer in Apple's Macintosh II family. It includes one internal expansion slot, built-in microphone and audio digitizer for sound functionality, a built-in video port that supports 640- by 480-pixel resolution, and support for 256 simultaneous colors when combined with an optional 12-inch RGB color monitor.

Standard features include a 20-MHz Motorola 68030 microprocessor, 2-MB RAM, one $3\frac{1}{2}$-inch 1.4-MB floppy disk, a 40-MB hard disk, and a mouse. Suggested price is $3769 without a monitor or keyboard. A color monitor is $599, a keyboard is $129.

Apple Computer, Inc., 20525 Mariani Avenue, Cupertino, Calif. 95014; (408) 996-1010.

Desktop

IBM Personal System/2 Model 70 386

The PS/2 Model 70 386 is IBM's high-end desktop personal computer. There are three models in the family and each is capable of running MS-DOS, OS/2, or AIX, IBM's version of Unix.

Standard features include a 16-MHz Intel 80386 microprocessor, 1-MB RAM, a $3\frac{1}{2}$-inch floppy disk drive, a 60-MB hard disk, three expansion slots, and VGA graphics capability. Suggested price starts at $5795.

IBM Entry Systems Division, P.O. Box 1328, Boca Raton, Fla. 33432; (407) 443-2000.

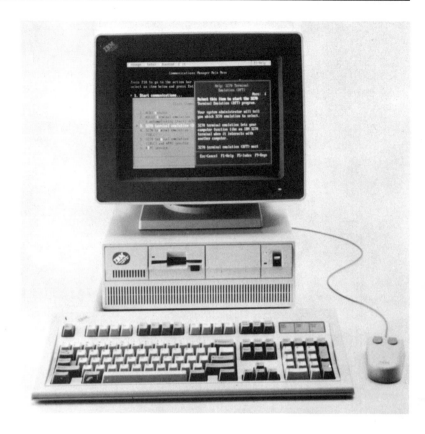

Desktop

Hewlett-Packard Vectra QS/16S

The Vectra QS/16S is Hewlett-Packard's entry-level 80386-based personal computer. The 80386SX processor, unlike its larger brother the 80386, contains a 16-bit data bus. You can also purchase HP Touch, the optional touchscreen accessory for the Vectra.

Standard features include an Intel 16-MHz 80386SX microprocessor, 1-MB RAM, and one $3\frac{1}{2}$-inch or $5\frac{1}{4}$-inch floppy disk drive. A variety of hard disks and display options are available. Suggested price with a 40-MB hard disk is $4395.

Hewlett-Packard, 1020 N.E. Circle Boulevard, Corvallis, Ore. 97330; (503) 757-2000.

Desktop

Compaq Deskpro 486/25

The Compaq Deskpro 486/25 is designed for compute-intensive and specialized applications such as a local-area network server.

Standard features include a 25-MHz Intel 80486 microprocessor, 4-MB RAM, a $5\frac{1}{4}$-inch floppy disk drive, and a 120-MB hard disk drive. Suggested price starts at $12,999.

Compaq Computer Corporation, 12330 Perry Road, Houston, Texas 77070; (713) 370-7040.

Desktop

HP Vectra 486 PC

The HP Vectra 486 PC is optimized for applications, such as computer-aided design, departmental multiuser computing, and local-area network server functions. Eight 32-bit expansion slots are available.

Standard features include a 25-MHz Intel 80486 microprocessor, 2-MB RAM, a $5\frac{1}{4}$-inch floppy disk drive, and a 152-MB hard disk drive. Suggested price starts at $13,999.

Hewlett-Packard, 1020 N.E. Circle Boulevard, Corvallis, Ore. 97330; (503) 757-2000.

Workstation

Sun SPARCstation SLC

The SPARCstation SLC incorporates the computer's processor and memory inside the monitor cabinet to optimize desktop space. The computer uses Sun's own proprietary SPARC RISC processor.

Standard features include a 20-MHz SPARC microprocessor, 8-MB RAM, and a 17-inch monochrome monitor. An optional hard disk drive is available. Suggested price is $4995.

Sun Microsystems, Inc., 2550 Garcia Avenue, Mountain View, Calif. 94043; (415) 969-9131.

Workstation

NextStation

The NextStation is a more powerful down-sized version of the original Next Computer System. It's hardware components include a math coprocessor, a digital signal processor, and an integrated channel processor. Perhaps the computer's most distinguishing characteristic is NextStep, the object-oriented graphical user interface, programming language, and interface building tools that are bundled with the computer. An optional 400-dot-per-inch laser printer is $2000.

Standard features include a 25-MHz 68040 microprocessor, 8-MB RAM, one 2.88-MB floppy disk drive, a 105-MB hard disk, a 17-inch high-resolution monochrome monitor, a mouse, and the Mach operating system (compatible with the UNIX 4.3BSD operating system). Suggested price is $4995. A Postscript color version of the NextStation is available for $7995.

Next, Inc., 3475 Deer Creek Road, Palo Alto, Calif. 94304; (415) 424-0200.

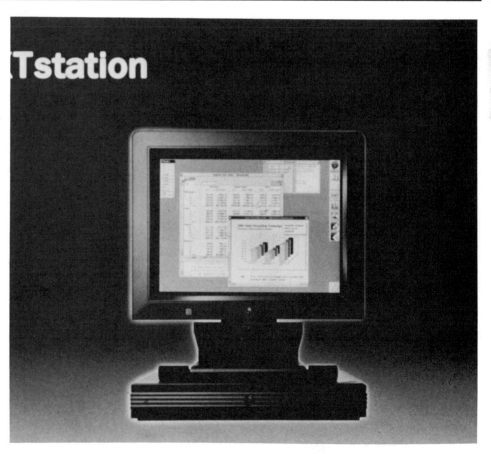

Workstation

HP Apollo 9000 Model 425t

The HP Apollo 9000 Model 425t is the midrange desktop workstation in the Series 400 product family. With its HP Vue graphical user interface, the Model 425t is designed for computer-aided software engineering and electrical and mechanical engineering applications.

Standard features of the diskless unit include a 25-MHz 68040 microprocessor, 8-MB RAM, a 19-inch high-resolution (1280- by 1024-pixel) monochrome monitor, and the Domain/OS and HP-UX Unix-based operating systems. Suggested price is $8990.

Hewlett-Packard Company, 3000 Hanover Street, Palo Alto, Calif. 94304; (800) 752-0900.

Workstation

IBM System/6000 POWERstation 320

The POWERstation 320 is the desktop entry in IBM's family of RISC-based workstations called the System/6000. (POWER is an acronym for Performance Optimization With Enhanced RISC.) The workstations are designed for scientific, technical, and multiuser commercial applications.

Standard features include a 20-MHz RISC microprocessor, 8-MB RAM, a 120-MB disk drive, a 19-inch high-resolution (1280- by 1024-pixel) monochrome monitor, a mouse, and the AIX operating system (IBM's version of the Unix operating system). Suggested price starts at $12,995.

IBM Corporation, 1133 Westchester Avenue, White Plains, N.Y. 10604; (203) 352-7611.

Workstation

Digital DECstation 5000 Model 200

The DECstation 5000 Model 200 is at the high end of Digital's family of workstations. It is designed for graphics applications such as electronic and mechanical design, molecular modeling, and 3-D modeling and animation.

Standard features of the diskless unit include a 25-MHz R3000 RISC microprocessor, 8-MB RAM, a 19-inch high-resolution (1280- by 864-pixel) monochrome monitor, and Ultrix, Digital's Unix-based operating systems. Suggested price starts at $14,995.

Digital Equipment Corporation, 3000 Hanover Street, Palo Alto, Calif. 94304; (800) 752-0900.

NUMBER SYSTEMS, DATA REPRESENTATION, AND CODES

PREVIEW

Computer and communication systems represent information and data in a coded form that is directly related to the binary number system. Therefore, understanding number systems in general and the binary number system specifically is helpful in understanding how data are represented.

Today, we take for granted the decimal number system, where 10 symbols—0, 1, 2, 3, 4, 5, 6, 7, 8, and 9—are combined in various ways for counting and calculating. Two major concepts are important for understanding any number system: (1) the base of the number system and (2) positional notation.

The odometer in most cars is made from an interconnected set of wheels that rotate in relation to the number of miles traveled. If the odometer were binary instead of decimal, each wheel would only have the digits 0 and 1 instead of the familiar digits 0 through 9.

The odometer is initially set to 0's.

As the car moves, the odometer rotates and the number 1 comes up first.

As the zero comes up, the digit to the left is triggered and rotates to 1.

As the 1 comes up, no action is triggered until…

the next 0 comes up, triggering both the adjacent left digit and the one adjacent to it.

See if you can fill in the next three rotations of the odometer.

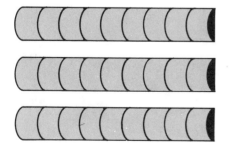

THE BASE OF A NUMBER SYSTEM

The base of a number system refers to how many symbols are used. The decimal system we use for counting and calculating uses a base of 10 and, therefore, has 10 symbols (0 through 9). The choice of base 10 may simply have been the result of the number of fingers on our hands.

The binary system, which is used in computers and communications (from the Latin word *binarius*, meaning "two at a time"), employs a base of 2 and, therefore, has two symbols (0 and 1). The choice of binary stems from an early decision to use bistable devices (those with only two stable states) as the major component in computer hardware. For example, the most commonly used bistable device for primary storage or memory is called RAM (random-access memory). RAMs contain an array of memory "cells" that store digital bits (0's and 1's) as the presence or absence of an electrical charge. Technically speaking, a RAM memory cell is made of one transistor and one capacitor. The transistor is used to charge the capacitor; that is, the transistor reads and writes the memory cell. The two different symbols, 0 and 1, can easily be matched to the two different states of a bistable device that can be either on (the presence of a charge) or off (the absence of a charge).

A simple table for a few binary numbers and their decimal equivalents follows:

Binary	Decimal	Binary	Decimal
0	0	1000	8
1	1	1001	9
10	2	1010	10
11	3	1011	11
100	4	1100	12
101	5	1101	13
110	6	1110	14
111	7	1111	15

POSITIONAL NOTATION

Positional notation refers to the fact that each of the symbols represents a different value depending on the position it occupies in the number. For example (using * for the multiplication sign), the decimal number 2222 means $2 * 1000 + 2 * 100 + 2 * 10 + 2 * 1$. It is the position in which each 2 stands that indicates whether it means thousands, hundreds, tens, or ones. Another example of positional notation is the difference between the number 287 and the number 872. Both use the same set of digits, but again the position of each digit signifies the value that the digit assumes.

Consider the decimal number 345.23. Using positional notation, this number can be represented as the addition of the five numbers

$$300 + 40 + 5 + .2 + .03$$

Breaking the number down further we arrive at

$$3 * 100 + 4 * 10 + 5 * 1 + 2 * .1 + 3 * .01$$

And in what mathematicians call conventional form, we have

$$3 * 10^2 + 4 * 10^1 + 5 * 10^0 + 2 * 10^{-1} + 3 * 10^{-2}$$

Conventional form uses the shorthand symbol *power* or *exponent* to express positional notation. In the case of 10^2, the number 2 indicates the power and is a shorthand way of expressing $10 * 10$, or 100. Similarly, the negative powers signify the decimal fractions: 10^{-2} means $1/10^2$ or $1/100$, or .01. The meaning of 10^0 is defined as being equal to 1, because it lies between 10^1 and 10^{-1}, or between 10 and $1/10$. Except for zero itself, any number raised to the zero power is also defined as being equal to 1.

Mathematicians have derived a general formula for base 10 numbers that looks like this:

$$N_{10} = x_n * 10^n + ... + x_2 * 10^2 + x_1 * 10^1 + x_0 * 10^0 + x_{-1} * 10^{-1} + ...$$

where the letter *N* represents the complete number, the subscript 10 means that the number is written with base 10 symbols, the letter *x* refers to the position of the number in the sequence, and the ellipses (...) mean that the series can extend as far as you want it to.

There is nothing fundamental or special about the base 10 number system. It is simply the one we use and are accustomed to. The symmetry of using powers extends to any number system, and the powers of any other number system will fulfill all the mathematical requirements, as demonstrated by substituting the letter B to represent the base in the following conventional form:

$$N_B = x_n * B^n + ... + x_2 * B^2 + x_1 * B^1 + x_0 * B^0 + x_{-1} * B^{-1} + ...$$

version may not necessarily be possible. The following conversion of 101.101_2 to its decimal equivalent shows some of the complexity involved with a decimal point.

$$N_2 = 1 * 2^2 + 0 * 2^1 + 1 * 2^0 + 1 * 2^{-1} + 0 * 2^{-2} + 1 * 2^{-3}$$

By converting the base 2 number into decimal form, we obtain

$$N_{10} = 1 * 4 + 0 * 2 + 1 * 1 + 1/2 + 0/4 + 1/8$$

$$N_{10} = 4 + 0 + 1 + .5 + .0 + .125$$

$$N_{10} = 5.625$$

CONVERTING A GIVEN BASE NUMBER TO A DECIMAL NUMBER

When converting a number from its base to a decimal number (base 10), the following steps can be taken. First, write the number in conventional form, where B is the base of the number. For example, the binary number 11011_2 would be

$$N_2 = 1 * 2^4 + 1 * 2^3 + 0 * 2^2 + 1 * 2^1 + 1 * 2^0$$

Now convert the conventional binary form into conventional decimal form by using decimal arithmetic:

$$N_{10} = 1 * 16 + 1 * 8 + 0 * 4 + 1 * 2 + 1 * 1$$

$$N_{10} = 16 + 8 + 0 + 2 + 1$$

$$11011_2 = 27_{10}$$

Converting 1111_2 to its decimal equivalent yields the following results when converting into conventional decimal form:

$$N_2 = 1 * 2^3 + 1 * 2^2 + 1 * 2^1 + 1 * 2^0$$

$$N_{10} = 1 * 8 + 1 * 4 + 1 * 2 + 1 * 1$$

$$N_{10} = 8 + 4 + 2 + 1$$

$$1111_2 = 15_{10}$$

Although this general formula does not work in reverse, it is possible to convert numbers of any base to numbers of any other base; however, it should be noted that when working with fractional numbers, an exact con-

CONVERTING DECIMAL NUMBERS TO BINARY NUMBERS

A convenient way to convert decimal numbers to binary numbers is called the *remainder method*. It consists of dividing the decimal number and all successive answers by 2 until the process is finished. The binary value is then read from the remainders, with the most significant digit being the final remainder. For example, to convert 341_{10} to a binary number

341 divided by 2 is 170
   with a remainder of 1
170 divided by 2 is 85
   with a remainder of 0
85 divided by 2 is 42
   with a remainder of 1
42 divided by 2 is 21
   with a remainder of 0
21 divided by 2 is 10
   with a remainder of 1
10 divided by 2 is 5
   with a remainder of 0
5 divided by 2 is 2
   with a remainder of 1
2 divided by 2 is 1
   with a remainder of 0
1 divided by 2 is 0
   with a remainder of 1
$341_{10} = 101010101_2$

Another example is the conversion of 156_{10} to its binary equivalent:

156 divided by 2 is 78

  with a remainder of 0

78 divided by 2 is 39

  with a remainder of 0

39 divided by 2 is 19

  with a remainder of 1

19 divided by 2 is 9

  with a remainder of 1

9 divided by 2 is 4

  with a remainder of 1

4 divided by 2 is 2

  with a remainder of 0

2 divided by 2 is 1

  with a remainder of 0

1 divided by 2 is 0

  with a remainder of 1

$156_{10} = 10011100_2$

In fact, to convert decimal numbers to any other number system, we can use the remainder method by simply using the base of the desired number system as a divisor. For example, to convert 1326_{10} to an 8-based number system (octal),

1326 divided by 8 is 165

  with a remainder of 6

165 divided by 8 is 20

  with a remainder of 5

20 divided by 8 is 2

  with a remainder of 4

2 divided by 8 is 0

  with a remainder of 2

1326_{10} equals 2456_8

OTHER NUMBER SYSTEMS

One major rationale for developing a number system was the ease with which arithmetic could be accomplished. For over half the course of civilization, people used a base 60 numbering system worked out by the Mesopotamians. Although 60 is an extremely large number to use as a base, it can be evenly divided by 1, 2, 3, 4, 5, 6, 10, 12, 15, 20, 30, and 60, which means that arithmetic problems came out with even answers more frequently than with a base-10 system. The base 60 system remains in use today. We divide our hour into 60 minutes, a minute into 60 seconds, and a circle into 60 * 60 degrees. If someone says it is 4:57:03 A.M., we know it means 4 hours, 57 minutes, and 3 seconds after midnight. The equivalent of the Mesopotamian 60-based number 4,57,3 in decimal form is

$$4 * 60^2 + 57 * 60^1 + 3 * 60^0$$

$$4 * 3,600 + 57 * 60 + 3 * 1 \text{ or } 17,823$$

which, by the way, is exactly what 4:57:03 A.M. means: 17,823 seconds after midnight.

Another number system that is commonly used because of simpler arithmetic is a base 12 system. Since 10 is only evenly divisible by 1, 2, 5, and 10, whereas 12 is evenly divisible by 1, 2, 3, 4, 6, and 12, a base 12 system was commonly used for commercial transactions (dozens and grosses) and especially fractional portions of those transactions. (It is also used for measurements in cooking.)

You will find that when working with computers, the most common bases are 2 and 16. As a matter of practical convenience, the 10 symbols of the decimal number system are used in all systems. In addition, when a system requires more than 10 symbols, such as in the base 16 system, letters of the alphabet have been adopted for use as symbols. A base 16 number system is represented by the symbols 0, 1, 2, 3, 4, 5, 6, 7, 8, 9, A, B, C, D, E, and F. This system, known as the hexadecimal system, is primarily used as a shorthand system for writing binary numbers, which we will discuss later.

BINARY ARITHMETIC

The binary system makes some of the operations of arithmetic very simple. For example, the binary arithmetic table looks like this:

0 plus 0 equals 0

0 plus 1 equals 1

1 plus 0 equals 1

1 plus 1 equals 10

The last one may, at first, look confusing, but remember that there is no symbol beyond 1 in a binary system, and since we already know about positional notation (and carrying from our decimal arithmetic days), we put down the 0 and carry the 1. Addition can be very simple. For example, adding from right to left

```
  11011101        1101101
+  100010         + 1111
  11111111        1111100
```

Note that in the second example 1 + 1 = 10 and 10 + 1 = 11, so you put down the 1 and carry the 1 just as you would in decimal arithmetic. It does get more confusing when you have to add more than two numbers, such as

```
  11      1 + 1 + 1 = 11
 101      Put down the 1 and
  11      carry the 1 to the
+101      left.
1101
          1 + 0 + 1 + 0 = 10
          Put down the 0 and
          carry the 1 to the
          left.

          1 + 1 + 1 = 11
```

```
  10      1 + 1 + 1 + 1 = 100
  10      Put down the 0 and
  11      carry the 10 to the
  11      left.
  11
 +11      0 + 1 + 1 + 1 + 1 =
1100      100
          Put down the 0 and
          carry the 10 to the
          left.
```

You have a 1 and a 1 left over in two different columns, so put them down.

Multiplication is even simpler in binary:

0 times 1 equals 0

1 times 0 equals 0

1 times 1 equals 1

```
    1001          1101
  *  101        * 1010
    1001          0000
    0000          1101
    1001          0000
  101101          1101
              10000010
```

The arithmetic operations of subtraction and division prove somewhat more difficult, because it is more difficult to "think" binary when performing them. However, like any arithmetic, knowing the tables and practicing can make binary arithmetic as easy as decimal arithmetic.

DATA REPRESENTATION AND CODES

The bit (binary digit) is the smallest unit of data or information in a computer or communication system. Because it is only capable of representing two values, 0 or 1, bits must be combined with other bits to form a code that is capable of representing such things as letters (both uppercase and lowercase), numbers, and special characters. By definition:

1 bit can equal 2 different combinations (0 or 1)

2 bits can equal 4 different combinations (00, 01, 10, 11)

4 bits can equal 16 different combinations (0000, 0001, 0010,

0011, 0100, 0101, 0110, 0111, 1000, 1001, 1010, 1011, 1100, 1101, 1110, 1111)

8 bits can equal 256 different combinations as shown in the chart (2 to the eighth power)

Designers of computers have gravitated toward an 8-bit code. It is closely related to both a 2-based system and a 16-based system and provides enough combinations for (1) all the letters, including both uppercase and lowercase, (2) the numbers and special punctuation characters; and (3) special 1-byte control codes that are used by programmers and have enough room left over for expansion. In computer jargon, 8 bits grouped together are called a byte. Generally speaking, a byte is the equivalent of one character of data.

HOW TO USE THE TABLE

Two character sets and their equivalent binary codes are presented in the table. ASCII-8 (American Standard Code for Information Interchange) is most commonly used in personal computers and communication systems. EBCDIC (Extended Binary Coded Decimal Interchange Code) is important because it was developed by IBM and is found on many IBM computers. Neither is superior to the other, but, as you can see in the table, there are differences.

When data are input to a computer or communication system, they must be encoded into a form suitable for information processing or transmission. A simple example of encoding is when you press keys on a computer or terminal keyboard. Each time you

press a key, the device translates the keystroke into the equivalent binary code. (In Chapter 4 terminology, the keystroke is encoded.) For example, pressing the space bar translates into a binary code of "01000000" in both ASCII and EBCDIC. By pressing the letter *H*, we can see from the table that the ASCII binary code is "10101000," whereas the EBCDIC code is "11001000." The binary code is what the internal circuits of the computer store and process. It is also how data are transmitted in a communication system and how data are stored on auxiliary storage, such as a disk.

Also shown is the hexadecimal (base 16) equivalent of the binary code. The binary translation into hexadecimal follows:

Binary	Hex	Binary	Hex
0000	0	1000	8
0001	1	1001	9
0010	2	1010	A
0011	3	1011	B
0100	4	1100	C
0101	4	1101	D
0110	6	1110	E
0111	7	1111	F

The hexadecimal code requires only two digits to represent the eight binary digits; it is used as a shorthand method for writing binary codes. By grouping the 8-bit binary code into two groups of four each, and using the conversion table, it is fairly easy to convert an 8-bit binary code into hexadecimal.

It is also easy to convert any binary number into hexadecimal by using the grouping method, as the following example shows. Breaking the binary number 101010111001 into groups of four each (working from right to left) yields the following: 1010 1011 1001. Look up the equivalent hexadecimal number in the binary/hex table and you will get 1010 = A, 1011 = B, 1001 = 9, so $AB9_{16}$ = 101010111001_2. If the number has an odd number of places, the method will still work. For example, the binary number 1110011 translated into groups of 4 yields 0111 0011, where 0111 = 7 and 0011 = 3, or 73 in hexadecimal.

A byte of data can be conceptually represented as eight consecutive on or off switches where on switches represent 1s and off switches represent 0s. The topmost figure represents the binary code 01000000 or a space character (what you get when you press the space bar on the keyboard). The next figure represents 10101000 or the letter "H." What do the next figures represent?

Binary Code	Decimal Equivalent	Hexadecimal Equivalent	ASCII-8 Character	EBCDIC Character
00000000	0	00	NUL	NUL
00000001	1	01	SOH	SOH
00000010	2	02	STX	STX
00000011	3	03	ETX	ETX
00000100	4	04	EOT	PF
00000101	5	05	ENQ	HT
00000110	6	06	ACK	LC
00000111	7	07	BEL	DEL
00001000	8	08	BS	
00001001	9	09	HT	
00001010	10	0A	LF	SMM
00001011	11	0B	VT	VT
00001100	12	0C	FF	FF
00001101	13	0D	CR	CR
00001110	14	0E	SO	SO
00001111	15	0F	SI	SI
00010000	16	10	DLE	DLE
00010001	17	11	DC1	DC1
00010010	18	12	DC2	DC2
00010011	19	13	DC3	TM
00010100	20	14	DC4	RES
00010101	21	15	NAK	NL
00010110	22	16	SYN	BS
00010111	23	17	ETB	IL
00011000	24	18	CAN	CAN
00011001	25	19	EM	EM
00011010	26	1A	SUB	CC
00011011	27	1B	ESC	CU1
00011100	28	1C	FS	IFS
00011101	29	1D	GS	IGS
00011110	30	1E	RS	IRS
00011111	31	1F	US	IUS
00100000	32	20		DS
00100001	33	21		SOS
00100010	34	22		FS
00100011	35	23		
00100100	36	24		BYP
00100101	37	25		LF
00100110	38	26		ETB
00100111	39	27		ESC
00101000	40	28		
00101001	41	29		
00101010	42	2A		SM
00101011	43	2B		CU2
00101100	44	2C		
00101101	45	2D		ENQ
00101110	46	2E		ACK
00101111	47	2F		BEL
00110000	48	30		
00110001	49	31		
00110010	50	32		SYN
00110011	51	33		
00110100	52	34		PN
00110101	53	35		RS
00110110	54	36		UC
00110111	55	37		EOT
00111000	56	38		
00111001	57	39		
00111010	58	3A		
00111011	59	3B		CU3
00111100	60	3C		DC4
00111101	61	3D		NAK
00111110	62	3E		
00111111	63	3F		SUB
01000000	64	40	SP	SP
01000001	65	41	1!	
01000010	66	42	"	
01000011	67	43	#	
01000100	68	44	$	
01000101	69	45	%	
01000110	70	46	&	
01000111	71	47	'	
01001000	72	48	(	
01001001	73	49	)	
01001010	74	4A	*	¢
01001011	75	4B	+	
01001100	76	4C	,	<
01001101	77	4D	-	(
01001110	78	4E	.	+
01001111	79	4F	/	'
01010000	80	50	0	&
01010001	81	51	1	
01010010	82	52	2	
01010011	83	53	3	
01010100	84	54	4	
01010101	85	55	5	
01010110	86	56	6	
01010111	87	57	7	
01011000	88	58	8	
01011001	89	59	9	
01011010	90	5A	:	!
01011011	91	5B	;	$
01011100	92	5C	<	*
01011101	93	5D	=	)
01011110	94	5E	>	;
01011111	95	5F	?	-
01100000	96	60		_
01100001	97	61		/
01100010	98	62		
01100011	99	63		
01100100	100	64		
01100101	101	65		

Binary Code	Decimal Equivalent	Hexadecimal Equivalent	ASCII-8 Character	EBCDIC Character	Binary Code	Decimal Equivalent	Hexadecimal Equivalent	ASCII-8 Character	EBCDIC Character
01100110	102	66			10011001	153	99		r
01100111	103	67			10011010	154	9A		
01101000	104	68			10011011	155	9B		
01101001	105	69			10011100	156	9C		
01101010	106	6A			10011101	157	9D		
01101011	107	6B		'	10011110	158	9E		
01101100	108	6C		%	10011111	159	9F		
01101101	109	6D		-	10100000	160	A0	@	
01101110	110	6E		>	10100001	161	A1	A	
01101111	111	6F		?	10100010	162	A2	B	s
01110000	112	70			10100011	163	A3	C	t
01110001	113	71			10100100	164	A4	D	u
01110010	114	72			10100101	165	A5	E	v
01110011	115	73			10100110	166	A6	F	w
01110100	116	74			10100111	167	A7	G	x
01110101	117	75			10101000	168	A8	H	y
01110110	118	76			10101001	169	A9	I	z
01110111	119	77			10101010	170	AA	J	
01111000	120	78			10101011	171	AB	K	
01111001	121	79			10101100	172	AC	L	
01111010	122	7A		:	10101101	173	AD	M	
01111011	123	7B		#	10101110	174	AE	N	
01111100	124	7C		@	10101111	175	AF	O	
01111101	125	7D		'	10110000	176	B0	P	
01111110	126	7E		=	10110001	177	B1	Q	
01111111	127	7F		"	10110010	178	B2	R	
10000000	128	80			10110011	179	B3	S	
10000001	129	81		a	10110100	180	B4	T	
10000010	130	82		b	10110101	181	B5	U	
10000011	131	83		c	10110110	182	B6	V	
10000100	132	84		d	10110111	183	B7	W	
10000101	133	85		e	10111000	184	B8	X	
10000110	134	86		f	10111001	185	B9	Y	
10000111	135	87		g	10111010	186	BA	Z	
10001000	136	88		h	10111011	187	BB	[	
10001001	137	89		i	10111100	188	BC	\	
10001010	138	8A			10111101	189	BD	]	
10001011	139	8B			10111110	190	BE	^	
10001100	140	8C			10111111	191	BF	_	
10001101	141	8D			11000000	192	C0		
10001110	142	8E			11000001	193	C1		A
10001111	143	8F			11000010	194	C2		B
10010000	144	90			11000011	195	C3		C
10010001	145	91		j	11000100	196	C4		D
10010010	146	92		k	11000101	197	C5		E
10010011	147	93		l	11000110	198	C6		F
10010100	148	94		m	11000111	199	C7		G
10010101	149	95		n	11001000	200	C8		H
10010110	150	96		o	11001001	201	C9		I
10010111	151	97		p	11001010	202	CA		
10011000	152	98		q	11001011	203	CB		

Binary Code	Decimal Equivalent	Hexadecimal Equivalent	ASCII-8 Character	EBCDIC Character	Binary Code	Decimal Equivalent	Hexadecimal Equivalent	ASCII-8 Character	EBCDIC Character
11001100	204	CC			11100110	230	E6	f	W
11001101	205	CD			11100111	231	E7	g	X
11001110	206	CE			11101000	232	E8	h	Y
11001111	207	CF			11101001	233	E9	i	Z
11010000	208	D0			11101010	234	EA	j	
11010001	209	D1		J	11101011	235	EB	k	
11010010	210	D2		K	11101100	236	EC	l	
11010011	211	D3		L	11101101	237	ED	m	
11010100	212	D4		M	11101110	238	EE	n	
11010101	213	D5		N	11101111	239	EF	o	
11010110	214	D6		O	11110000	240	F0	p	0
11010111	215	D7		P	11110001	241	F1	q	1
11011000	216	D8		Q	11110010	242	F2	r	2
11011001	217	D9		R	11110011	243	F3	s	3
11011010	218	DA			11110100	244	F4	t	4
11011011	219	DB			11110101	245	F5	u	5
11011100	220	DC			11110110	246	F6	v	6
11011101	221	DD			11110111	247	F7	w	7
11011110	222	DE			11111000	248	F8	x	8
11011111	223	DF			11111001	249	F9	y	9
11100000	224	E0			11111010	250	FA	z	
11100001	225	E1	a		11111011	251	FB	{	
11100010	226	E2	b	S	11111100	252	FC			
11100011	227	E3	c	T	11111101	253	FD	}	
11100100	228	E4	d	U	11111110	254	FE	~	
11100101	229	E5	e	V	11111111	255	FF	DEL	

Control Character Representations

ACK	Acknowledge	ENQ	Enquiry	PF	Punch off
BEL	Bell	EOT	End of Transmission	PN	Punch on
BS	Backspace	ESC	Escape	RES	Restore
BYP	Bypass	ETB	End of Transmission Block	RS	Reader Stop
CAN	Cancel	ETX	End of Test	SI	Shift In
CC	Cursor Control	FF	Form Feed	SM	Set Mode
CR	Carriage Return	FS	Field Separator	SMM	Start of Manual Message
CU1	Customer Use 1	HT	Horizontal Tab	SO	Shift out
CU2	Customer Use 2	IFS	Interchange File Separator	SOH	Start of Heading
CU3	Customer Use 3	IGS	Interchange Group Separator	SOS	Start of Significance
DC1	Device Control 1	IL	Idle	SP	Space
DC2	Device Control 2	IRS	Interchange Record Separator	STX	Start of Text
DC3	Device Control 3	IUS	Interchange Until Separator	SUB	Substitute
DC4	Device Control 4	LC	Lowercase	SYN	Synchronous Idle
DEL	Delete	LF	Line Feed	TM	Tape Mark
DLE	Data Link Escape	NAK	Negative Acknowledge	UC	Upper Case
DS	Digit Select	NL	New Line	VT	Vertical Tab
EM	End of Medium	NUL	Null		

STUDY GUIDE

Convert the following numbers from their specified base into decimal-based numbers:

1. 1001_2
2. 120_3
3. 132_4
4. 4221_5
5. 125_8
6. 236_8
7. 463_8

Convert the following decimal numbers to binary:

8. 38_{10}
9. 67_{10}
10. 131_{10}
11. 250_{10}

Perform the following binary additions:

12. $1101 + 1010$
13. $11101 + 00111$
14. $1001101 + 11001$
15. $111 + 101 + 110$
16. $10 + 110 + 1011 + 11$

Perform the following binary multiplications:

17. $101 * 1101$
18. $1111 * 11$
19. $1010 * 1010$
20. $11001 * 111$

Find the binary code for the following ASCII characters:

21. ACK (Control character)
22. A
23. =

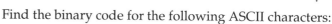

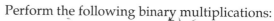

ANSWERS

1. 9, **2.** 15, **3.** 30, **4.** 561, **5.** 85, **6.** 158, **7.** 307, **8.** 100110, **9.** 1000011, **10.** 10000011, **11.** 11111010, **12.** 10111, **13.** 100100, **14.** 1100110, **15.** 10010, **16.** 11010, **17.** 1000001, **18.** 101101, **19.** 1100100, **20.** 10101111, **21.** 00000110, **22.** 10100001, **23.** 01011101.

APPENDIX D
GLOSSARY

A

Access time. The amount of time it takes for information to be read from or written to a disk. The sum of search time plus seek time.

Accumulator. A register used to temporarily store data being manipulated by the CPU. (See *Register*.)

Acoustic modem. A modem using a coupler into which the telephone handset is plugged. Also called an acoustic coupler. (See *Modem*.)

Acronym. A word formed by taking the first letters or sounds of each word in a phrase and capitalizing them. For example, RAM (pronounced as a word) is an acronym for random-access memory.

Ada. A U.S. Defense Department-sponsored high-level programming language named after Augusta Ada (Countess of Lovelace), the world's first programmer and Charles Babbage's associate.

Adder. The circuitry that performs addition on data received by the CPU.

Address. (1) A location in memory where data are stored and can be retrieved. (2) The part of an instruction that identifies the specific location of the data to be operated on by that instruction.

Address bus. An electrical pathway that carries the addresses of data from memory to the processor. (See *Bus*.)

Address register. A register containing the storage location of the next data item to be retrieved from memory.

Algorithm. A predetermined set of instructions for solving a problem in a finite number of steps. (See *Heuristic*.)

Alphanumeric. Data represented in both alphabetic (the letters A–Z) and numeric (the numbers 0–9) form.

ALU. An acronym for arithmetic/logic unit. The component of the CPU that is responsible for performing arithmetic and logic operations.

Analog. Pertaining to the representation of numerical quantities, such as the measurement of speed by an analog speedometer.

Analog computer. An early type of computer that was designed to process data obtained directly from measurable quantities, such as voltages, resistances, or rotations. (See *Analog-to-digital converter*.)

Analog-to-digital converter. A device that converts analog quantities, such as voltages, resistances, rotations, light, pressure, or temperature, into digital numbers for processing by a computer.

Analytical graphics. Graphics that are intended to help the user of a computer analyze data from spreadsheets and databases. Usually includes simple bar, line, and pie charts.

Antenna. A device for sending and receiving electromagnetic waves.

APL. An acronym for A Programming Language. An interactive scientific programming language designed for on-line use.

Application. What is done with a computer system.

Application generator. A program that writes other programs based on the user's input. (See *Fourth-generation language*.)

Units of Measure Used in Computers and Information Systems			
Time and speed	Second	1/1	one
	Millisecond	1/1000	one-thousandth
	Microsecond	1/1,000,000	one-millionth
	Nanosecond	1/1,000,000,000	one-billionth
	Picosecond	1/1,000,000,000,000	one-trillionth
Memory and storage capacity	Byte	1	2^0
	Kilobyte (KB)	1,024	2^{10}
	Megabyte (MB)	1,048,576	2^{20}
	Gigabyte (GB)	1,073,741,824	2^{30}
	Terabyte (TB)	1,099,511,627,776	2^{40}

Units of measure used in computers and information systems.

Application object. Data and their instructions combined into a single module of software. (See *Object environment*.)

Application programmer. A person who writes computer programs, such as spreadsheets, word processors, database programs, and specific application programs (e.g., accounting or inventory programs). There are two categories: business application programmers and scientific or engineering application programmers.

Application software. A computer program or set of programs intended to perform a specific function, such as accounting, payroll, word processing, spreadsheet calculating, or database management.

Application-specific integrated circuit (ASIC). An integrated circuit designed to fill the specific requirements of an application.

Architecture. A term used by computer designers to designate the structure of complex information processing systems. It includes the kinds of instructions and data used, the memory organization and addressing, and the methods by which the system is implemented.

Arithmetic expression. An expression consisting of only numbers and operators, for example, 7 + 6. (See *Arithmetic operator*.)

Arithmetic/logic unit. See *ALU*.

Arithmetic operator. A symbol that tells the computer to perform an arithmetic operation. The operators are (+) for addition, (-) for subtraction, (*) for multiplication, (/) for division, and (**) for exponentiation.

Arithmetic unit. The functional unit of a central processing unit that performs adding, subtracting, multiplying, dividing, and shifting of numbers. (See *ALU*.)

Array. A type of data structure that consists of two or more related data elements identified by a single name. (See *Data structure*.)

Artificial intelligence (AI). The branch of computer science that attempts to understand the nature of intelligence and produce new classes of intelligent machines. Areas of study include robotics, speech recognition, image recognition, natural language processing, and expert systems.

Artificial language. A language whose syntax, grammar, and rules were developed prior to its use. Programming languages are examples of artificial languages. (See *Natural language, Programming language*.)

Ascending order. Sequential arrangement from lowest to highest. A telephone book, for example, lists names in ascending order. (See *Descending order*.)

ASCII. An acronym for American Standard Code for Information Interchange. A code that specifies a unique set of binary digits that represent a character set.

Assembler. A program that translates an assembly-level language into machine language.

Assembly-level language. A low-level computer language consisting of symbolic instructions and addresses that translate into machine codes on a one-to-one basis.

Asynchronous transmission. A mode of communication in which individual data characters are sent at random time intervals. (See *Synchronous transmission*.)

Attribute. A column in a two-dimensional database. (See *Relation, Tupple*.)

Audio digitizer board. A board that plugs into a computer's expansion slot and turns analog sound waves into digital files for playback.

Automatic teller machine (ATM). A special-purpose computer that allows bank customers to perform routine banking transactions themselves, rather than having to wait for a bank employee.

Authoring system. A specialized application generator that combines hardware and software tools for designing interactive programs.

Automation. Short for **automa**tic oper**ation**. The process of mechanizing or computerizing functions so they perform without human intervention.

B

B-tree. A file in which the records are structured into an inverted tree based on a series of midpoints. For example, the root of the tree is the midpoint of a file, at the second level are more midpoints, and so on.

Background study. The analysis of an existing system for the purpose of performing a requirements analysis.

Backing up. Copying program or data files in case the original is lost or destroyed.

Backup file. A copy of a file made for safekeeping in case the original is lost or damaged.

Band/belt/train printer. An impact printer that uses one striking mechanism for each character position across a line. Sometimes called a line printer.

Bandwidth. The term used as a measure of the capacity of a communication channel, expressed in bits per second.

Bank switching. A technique used to increase a computer's memory. For example, the Lotus/Intel/Microsoft Expanded Memory Specification can expand the 1-MB memory limitation of the 8088/8086 microprocessor by adding additional banks of memory and bank switching among them.

Bar code. A series of thick and thin stripes used to represent numbers and characters.

BASIC. An acronym for Beginners All-purpose Symbolic Instruction Code. A high-level programming language originally intended for time-sharing systems, but now used primarily in conjunction with microcomputers.

Batch processing. A method by which a computer performs one job at a time, with no human interaction occurring during the job.

Baud. A unit of information transfer that is synonymous with one bit per second.

Bidirectional printing. Printing lines of output in alternate directions. For example, if the first line is printed left to right, the next line will be printed right to left.

Binary digit. The smallest unit of information capable of being represented in a computer or communication system. (See *Bit*.)

Binary numbers. A number system that uses only the symbols 0 and 1 to represent digits (from the Latin *binarius*, meaning "two at a time").

Binary search. A search method in which a list of items is successively halved until the sought item is located.

Binary signal. A computer circuit that is represented by two different levels (high and low) of voltage.

Biometric device. An instrument that performs mathematical analysis of biological characteristics. Examples include analyzing speech, handwriting, fingerprints, or eye retina features.

BIOS. An acronym for basic input/output system. The part of an operating system that links the specific hardware devices to the software.

Bistable. A hardware device, such as a switch, that can only assume two stable states, such as on or off.

Bit. Short for **bi**nary dig**it**. (See *Binary digit*.)

Bit map. A technique for dividing a display screen into a very fine grid of pixels that uses a video memory, in which bits represent pixels on a display screen. With bit mapping, a grid of pixels on a display screen is represented by a light or dark point on the surface of the display screen. (See *Pixel*.)

Bits per second. The number of bits of information that pass a given point in one second. A measure of the carrying capacity of a channel. Sometimes called baud rate.

Boolean algebra. An algebra that is used to manipulate symbols according to the operators *and*, *or*, and *not*. It allows logic to be handled as simply as mathematical formulas. Developed by George Boole in 1847.

Bootstrap loader. An initialization program that sets up and readies the computer when it is turned on.

Bottom-up design. In software development, a technique that starts with the parts or most basic functional components and proceeds to build a whole or completed program.

Branch. A type of program instruction that performs a test on a register or flag and, depending on the results, continues on with the next instruction in sequence or branches (or jumps) to another instruction in the program.

Buffer. A device (usually a memory) that temporarily stores data while it is being routed to a destination, such as a printer, mass storage, or a communication channel.

Bug. A computer term for an error. A software bug is a programming error; a hardware bug is a malfunction or design error in the computer or one of its components.

Bundled. A computer system sold as a complete system. A typical bundled system would include all the necessary hardware components along with a variety of software programs for various applications. Often called a turnkey system.

Bus. The electrical pathway used to transfer information from one point in a computer to another.

Bus network. A system in which all computers or terminals communicate via a common distribution channel or bus.

Business systems analyst. A systems analyst who is in an organizational department other than the data processing department.

Buzzwords. Popular cliches used by a group of people.

Byte. A sequence of eight consecutive bits used in coding systems to represent one character of data or information.

C

C. A high-level programming language that is very popular with system programmers because of its transportability between computer systems.

Cache. A high-speed buffer memory filled from lower-speed mass storage. Frequently used instructions and data can be fed to and from the CPU much faster when located in a cache. Pronounced as "cash."

Cathode ray tube. See *CRT*.

CD ROM. An acronym for compact disk read-only memory. An optical disk on which data are encoded for retrieval by a laser. (See *Optical disk*.)

Cell. In a spreadsheet, the space representing the intersection of a row and column.

Cellular mobile radio. A technique for dividing a geographical area into hexagonal-shaped cells. A local antenna within each cell is used to transmit via noninterfering frequencies. As mobile radio users move from cell to cell, telephone calls continue uninterrupted while a central computer adjusts transmit and receive frequencies. Cellular mobile radio service is an alternative to the more limited single-antenna mobile telephone services.

Central electronic complex. The processor and memory of a computer system along with some pathways for information to travel between the two. (See *Memory, Processor*.)

Central processing unit. See *CPU*.

CGA. Short for color graphics adapter, an IBM video board that plugs into an expansion slot and provides 320- by 200-pixel resolution and a 16-color palette on the display screen. (See *EGA, VGA*.)

Channel. A pathway for the transmission of data or information to and from a computer or communication system.

Character map. A technique for dividing the display screen into a grid that is 25 rows high by 80 columns wide. Each location on the grid can correspond to a character, such as a letter, number, or punctuation mark. A ROM stores each character as a pattern of dots.

Chip. A small piece of silicon or other semiconducting material containing an integrated circuit.

Circuit. (1) In a computer, an interconnected set of components that performs an electronic function. (2) In communications, an electrical connection between two nodes.

Circuit switching. A physical (electrical) connection between two nodes in a communication network that dedicates the entire bandwidth of that circuit until the connection is dropped. (See *Packet switching*.)

Client. An end user or computer program that requests resources across a network. (See *Server*.)

Client/server model. A combination of clients and servers that provides the framework for distributing files and databases across a network. (See *Client, Server*.)

Clock. A computer circuit that uses

regular electrical pulses to trigger, time, and synchronize various events within a computer.

CMOS. An acronym for complementary metal oxide semiconductor. A technique for producing integrated circuits that have lower power consumption than do regular integrated circuits. CMOS circuits are widely used in portable battery-powered computers.

Coaxial cable. A channel medium consisting of wire surrounded by a flexible metallic shielding.

COBOL. An acronym for COmmon Business Oriented Language. A high-level programming language that is used primarily for business-oriented applications.

Code. (1) A set of symbols, such as the dots and dashes of the Morse code, that represents another set of symbols, such as the letters of the alphabet. (2) The set of rules that defines the way in which bits can be arranged to represent numbers and letters. Example: ASCII. (3) To write a computer program in a specific programming language.

Collision. In a communications network, when two messages are transmitted at the same time, they will collide, resulting in a garbled transmission with neither message arriving intact at its destination.

Collision detection. A task performed in a network system to prevent two computers from transmitting at the same time and having the messages collide.

Command. An instruction that tells a computer to perform an operation.

Command-driven software. Software that takes action as a result of the user typing single letter, word, or line of commands.

Command processor. A program that examines what you type in when interacting with an operating system.

Communication. (1) A process by which information is exchanged between individuals through the use of a commonly agreed-on set of symbols. (2) From an engineering standpoint, the movement of electronic traffic from one point to another.

Communication processor. A device that interfaces a central computer to a number of terminals.

Communication server. A device that connects local-area networks to wide-area or telecommunication networks.

Communication system. A system that consists of senders (transmitters), physical channels, and receivers.

Compatibility. (1) The ability to connect different computer systems or devices so they can work together. (2) The capability of different computer systems to process the same applications.

Compiler. A computer program (software) that reads a high-level program to (1) check it for spelling and grammar errors and (2) translate it into lower-level language instructions.

Component. In the computer industry, an elementary part, such as an integrated circuit, memory chip, or microprocessor, that can be connected to other parts to form larger systems.

Computer. A system consisting of at least one CPU, input, output, memory, and software that can follow instructions (programs) to manipulate symbols (information).

Computer-aided design (CAD). The use of a computer system to aid the process of design.

Computer-aided engineering (CAE). The use of a computer system to produce, analyze, test, and design systems and components.

Computer-aided manufacturing (CAM). The use of a computer system to assist in a manufacturing process.

Computer-assisted instruction (CAI). The use of a computer system to provides instruction and drill-and-practice in basic computation and language skills.

Computer graphics. A broad term that refers to the methods and techniques used to draw pictures or images on display screens or on special graphic printers and plotters.

Computer-integrated manufacturing (CIM). Computer-based systems in different company departments that integrate independent design, manufacturing, and administrative functions. For example, drafting accomplished on a CAD system might be directly linked to a numerically controlled CAM factory machine tool.

Computer literacy. The knowledge and skills required to use a computer as a problem-solving tool.

Computer science. The science of problem-solving techniques using computers.

Computer systems analyst. A systems analyst who is in the data processing department and is concerned with the technical aspects of system design.

Computer-telephone. A device that combines a computer, a modem, and a telephone into one unit.

Computerization. The reshaping of society by the widespread adoption and use of computers.

Computerized information services. On-line databases to which subscribers can gain access via telephone lines. (See *Database, On-line processing*.)

Computerphobia. The fear of computers.

Concentrator. A device that combines data from several sources into a smaller number of channels for retransmission.

Conceptual tool. A tool for working with ideas instead of things.

Concurrent program execution. The execution of two or more programs at the same time. They actually take turns using the computer so rapidly that they give the illusion of operating concurrently.

Configuration. A set of computer equipment programmed and/or physically linked together to operate as a system.

Container object. An object that holds other objects so they can be easily stored, filed, or sent through electronic mail. (See *Object environment*.)

Control bus. An electrical pathway used to signal various parts of a computer when to transfer information and when the transfer is complete. (See *Bus*.)

Control key. A key that when pressed in combination with other keys generates control characters for use by a program. For example, pressing a control key in conjunction with the *D* key might mean delete a character in a word processing program.

Control structures. Statements in the program that control the order in which the instructions are executed. Examples include sequence, selection, looping, and case.

Control unit. The functional unit of the CPU that is responsible for retrieving instructions from memory, determining their type, and breaking each instruction into a series of simple, small steps or actions.

Coprocessor. A processor that adds additional functions to the central processor. Examples include math and graphics coprocessors.

Copy protect. A technique used by software developers to make a disk difficult, if not impossible, to copy.

Courseware. Programs for which the main purpose is teaching. (See *Computer-assisted instruction*.)

CP/M. An acronym for Control Program for Microcomputers. A trademark of Digital Research, Inc., CP/M was a common operating system on early 8-bit microcomputers.

CPU. An acronym for central processing unit. The part of the computer system that interprets and executes instructions, performs arithmetic and logic operations, and directs the input, storage, and output operations. Also called a processor.

CRT. An acronym for cathode ray tube. A type of screen found in television sets and computer displays in which an electron beam scans a phosphor-coated surface, leaving light or dark points of light (pixels) on the inside face of the screen. (See *Pixel*.)

Cursor. A visual aid on a display screen, usually in the form of an arrow, blinking block, or blinking underline, that indicates where the next symbol will appear.

Cursor-movement keys. Keys that move the cursor in a particular direction when pressed.

Cybernetics. The science of communication and control in living organisms and machines. Includes the study of messages as a means of controlling machinery and society, the development of automation, and the study of psychology and the nervous system.

Cycle. A set of operations that is repeated regularly in the same sequence.

Cylinder. The imaginary surface composed of all the tracks that lie directly above and below one another on a multiple-platter disk pack.

D

Daisy wheel. A printer type element that contains a series of spokes attached to a central hub. Each spoke contains a fully formed character at its tip.

Data. A general term meaning the facts, numbers, letters, and symbols processed by a computer or communication system to produce information. (See *Information*.)

Data bus. An electrical pathway over which data and instructions travel to and from the processor. (See *Bus*.)

Data communications. The transfer of data or information between computer-related devices.

Data dictionary. (1) In system design, a listing of all the data elements and data structures within a system. (2) In a database system, a file that contains descriptions of and relationships among a collection of data.

Data-flow diagram. In systems analysis, a series of blocks that represents processes or procedures that are connected by flow lines.

Data integrity. Techniques for protecting a database against invalid alteration or destruction.

Data processing. A general term that stands for all the logical, arithmetic, and input/output operations that can be performed on data by a computer.

Data processing analyst. A systems analyst who is in the data processing department of an organization and is concerned with the technical aspects of system design. Also called computer systems analyst.

Data processing (DP) department. The combination of the information system and the people who support it. The DP department combines computer and communication hardware and software with manual procedures and models for analysis, planning, control, and decision making.

Data security. Techniques for protecting a database against access or modification without authorization.

Data structure. A term that refers to the techniques used to structure or organize data so that they can be stored, retrieved, and manipulated by a program.

Database. (1) A collection of different types of data organized according to a structure that minimizes redundancies and facilitates the manipulation of the data. (2) A collection of one or more files treated as a whole unit.

Database management system (DBMS). Software that organizes, manipulates, and retrieves data stored in a database.

Database manager. A database program that manages two or more files at the same time. (See *File manager*.)

Database model. A model that identifies the major parts (e.g., files, records, and fields) of a database and illustrates how these parts fit together.

Database server. Software that services requests to a database across a network.

Database system. An information system that integrates a collection of data and makes it available to a wide variety of people in an organization.

Database transaction. A group of database modifications treated as a single unit.

Debug. The process of going through a program (software) or component (hardware) to remove errors.

Decimal number. Referring to the base 10 number system we normally use for arithmetic. Some early computers used decimal numbers instead of binary numbers. (See *Binary number*.)

Decision-support software. Knowledge-based software that builds decision-making models.

Decision-support system. Applications within MIS that directly support specific decision making. (See *Management information system*.)

Decode. To modify information from a computer-readable form into a form that people can read or use. (See *Encode*.)

Decryption. The decoding of a cryptic electronic transmission. (See *Encryption*.)

Dedicated. Something designed for a specific use, such as a leased line for data transmission or a computer intended only for word processing.

Default. An action or value that a computer automatically assumes unless a different action or value is specified.

Descending order. Arrangement of information in sequence from highest to lowest. (See *Ascending order*.)

Desktop publishing. The use of personal computers to prepare and print a wide variety of typeset- or near-typeset-quality documents. The process involves composing the text, manipulating graphics, making up or composing the document, and publishing the finished product on a laser printer or typesetter.

Detail documentation. Documentation that provides a programmer with sufficient information to write the program.

Device driver. Programs that interface with the operating system to control the operation of the hardware components of a personal computer system. The device driver is responsible for translating instructions from the application into commands the hardware understands.

Dial-up line. The normal switched telephone line that is used as a transmission medium for communications.

Digital. Relating to the technology of communications and computers by which information is stored and transmitted in binary ones and zeros.

Digital computer. A type of computer capable of representing binary digits by producing and sensing discrete on or off states represented by binary ones and zeros.

Digitizing. The process of translating analog data into digital data.

Digitizing camera. A camera coupled with a processor used for encoding highly detailed images, such as pictures or three-dimensional objects, into digital data.

Direct file. A type of file organization scheme designed for processing records in an order other than sequential. Also called a random access file.

Direct-source input. Data that are captured directly from their source without the requirement of a separate transcribing step. (See *Transcribed input*.)

Disk. A circular platter on which a magnetic or reflective coating is ap-

plied. Used for long-term storage of data.

Disk array. The combination and synchronization of multiple disk drives into one self-contained unit. A disk array features faster data access and higher data throughput than an equivalent-sized single disk drive.

Disk cartridge. Removable disks that are sealed in a container similar to a videotape cartridge.

Disk drive. A device that houses the motor to spin the disk and the read/write head for accessing and storing information on the disk.

Disk pack. A removable stack of hard disks joined together by a common spindle.

Display. A method or device for representing information that is output from a computer system. Usually found in the form of a cathode ray tube (CRT) or flat-panel display. (See *CRT, Flat-panel display*.)

Distributed computing. A type of processing that utilizes a number of small computers distributed throughout an organization.

Distributed database. A capability in which different parts of a database reside on physically separate computers. The goal is to access information without regard to where the data might be stored.

DMA. An acronym for direct-memory access. A technique by which the CPU is placed in a wait state while another device transfers data to or from memory at a high rate.

Document. Any text or collection of characters (letters, numbers, spaces, punctuation marks, and other symbols). Usually associated with word processing and desktop-publishing applications.

Documentation. (1) The books, manuals, or tutorials that accompany a computer-related product. (2) Written specifications that are a part of the process of developing software.

DOS. An acronym for disk operating system. (See *Operating system*.)

Dot-matrix printer. A printer that uses a selected pattern of dots transferred by impact to produce images on paper.

Download. A method of sending a copy of data, such as a file, from a central location to a remote location and storing it there for future use.

DRAM. An acronym for dynamic random-access memory, a memory that is constantly refreshed with electrical pulses. Pronounced "dee-ram."

Draw program. A graphics program that provides commands to create lines, circles, rectangles, and other shapes, as well as do freehand sketching, while allowing the objects created to be resized, or moved around without affecting other objects. Examples include MacDraw for the Macintosh and Windows Draw for MS-DOS computers. (See *Paint program*.)

Duplex. A data communications term that indicates in how many directions data can flow at one time. In half-duplex, data move in one direction at a time; in full-duplex, data move in two directions at a time.

E

EBCDIC. An acronym for Extended Binary Coded Decimal Interchange Code. An 8-bit code designed by IBM that assigns binary digits to specific symbols. Used primarily by IBM computers.

Edit. To make changes in data, a program, or a document.

EGA. Short for enhanced graphics adapter, an IBM video board that plugs into an expansion slot and provides 640- by 350-pixel resolution and a 16-color palette on the display screen. (See *CGA, VGA*.)

Electroluminescent display (ELD). A display device that produces light through the application of electric current on a sensitive surface.

Electromechanical relay. A mechanical switch that is opened and closed by an electromagnet.

Electronic conference. A meeting that is conducted over an electronic network using terminals or personal computers.

Electronic data interchange (EDI). The computer-to-computer electronic transmission of standard documents such as invoices and purchase orders. EDI makes possible the translation of paper-based documents into and out of a generic form so that they can be transferred electronically among different computers.

Electronic mail. An electronic technology that handles the sending and receiving of messages.

Electronic mailbox. A file stored on disk in which each record represents a message and serves as an interface for electronic mail.

Electronic marketplace. The buying and selling of information through information services and videotex services. Examples of services that can be subscribed to include Prodigy, The Source, CompuServe, Dialog, and Nexis.

Electronic printer. A printer that uses a laser to record an image on an electrically charged drum or belt that is then transferred onto paper. (See *Laser printer*.)

Electronic transaction. The electronic transfer of funds in lieu of conventional paper transactions, such as checks.

Electrostatic printer. A printer that uses electricity to transfer images onto specially coated paper.

Emulation. The imitation of one computer system or part of a computer system by another. For example, a newer IBM 3031 computer can be made to emulate an older IBM System/370 computer for purposes of running the older computer's software without changing it.

Encode. To modify information into a desired pattern for transmission or processing. (See *Decode*.)

Encryption. The coding of an electronic transmission for purposes of security or privacy. (See *Decryption*.)

End user. A person who uses a product, as opposed to persons who develop or market the product.

End-user development. The use of tools, such as macros, program generators, inteface builders, by noncomputer specialists to develop applications that those individuals will use.

Ergonomics. The science of the study of how people use tools to perform work and how they physically relate to their environment.

Error checking. In communications, software routines that identify and often correct erroneous data.

Execute. To run a computer program or part of a program.

Expansion slot. A series of sockets into which additional circuit boards can be plugged. Many personal computers and minicomputers use an "open architecture" by which additional hardware devices can easily be added to the system via expansion slots. (See *Architecture*.)

Expert system. A computer program that solves specialized problems at the level of a human expert.

Expert-system shell. A development environment that uses rules or examples as its input, but eliminates the need for programming.

F

Facsimile. A method for electronically copying and transmitting an image.

Fault. A condition that causes a functional component to fail to operate in the required manner.

Fault-tolerant computer. A computer that uses redundant hardware or software components to prevent failure from disrupting the operation of the system. The system can continue processing while the faulty component is replaced or repaired.

Fiber optics. Transmitting information by using infrared or visible light frequencies through glass fibers.

Field. The smallest unit of named data that has meaning in a record. A field usually describes an attribute of the record, such as a name or address.

File. A collection of organized data stored as one complete unit for processing.

File manager. A database program that manages entering, modifying, retrieving, and printing information from one file at a time. (See *Database manager*.)

File server. A device that interfaces files or databases to a local-area network.

Firmware. Software that has been copied on integrated circuits, usually ROM (read-only memory).

First generation. Referring to computers of the period 1951–1958 that used vacuum tubes.

Fixed-length operations. The type of operations performed by a word-addressable computer.

Flat file. A single file consisting of rows (records) and columns (fields) of data that resemble a two-dimensional spreadsheet.

Flat-panel display. A display characterized by a thin panel consisting of rows and columns of pixels. Digital circuits feed signals to each row and column. For example, sending a low voltage down a row while sending higher voltages across selected columns causes the pixels at the intersections to light up. (See *LCD, LED, Pixel*.)

Floppy disk. A flexible plastic disk coated with a magnetic recording material.

Flowchart. A graphic representation used in the design phase of programming to represent the logic of a program or module. (See *System flowchart*.)

Format. (1) The process of preparing a magnetic storage medium, such as a floppy disk, to store data in specified places (i.e., tracks and sectors). (2) The way information is physically organized on a display screen, printed page, or disk.

FORTRAN. Short for FORmula TRANslator. A high-level computer programming language used primarily for scientific and engineering applications.

Fourth generation. Referring to computers of the period 1975 to the present that use various forms of microprocessor and other VLSI chips. (See *Microprocessor, VLSI*.)

Fourth-generation language. A term that encompasses (1) presentation languages, such as query languages and report generators; (2) specialty languages, such as spreadsheets and database languages; (3) application generators that define, input, modify or update, and report data to build applications; and (4) very-high-level languages that are used to generate application code. Often abbreviated as 4 GL.

Frame. (1) A basic unit of information (equivalent to one full screen) in a videotex system. (2) The vertical section of magnetic tape that corresponds to one byte of data.

Frame buffer. In graphics, a special area of random-access memory that holds the contents of a screen display. The processor can perform manipulations on information in a frame buffer before it is displayed. Sometimes used interchangeably with the term "bit map."

Frequency. The rate at which a signal pattern is repeated.

Frequency-division multiplexing. The communication process of assigning a channel to several users on the basis of splitting the frequency of the channel into narrower bands.

Front-end processor. A computer that handles communications between terminals and a central computer.

Full-duplex. A mode that allows two computers to send and receive data at the same time. (See *Half-duplex*.)

Full-text retrieval software. Software that allows text to be indexed, edited, annotated, linked, and searched for in an electronic document. (See *Text database*.)

Function key. A key, usually labeled [F1] through [F10] or [F12], that tells a program to perform a specific action. Pressing the [F1] key, for example, might invoke a help system.

Functional specification. A precise description of the functional requirements of a computer system.

G

Garbage in–garbage out. A term referring to information processing that has been distorted by invalid input.

Gas plasma display. A display device in which a gas, usually a mixture of neon and argon, is trapped between flat glass plates. A grid of electrodes permits the turning on and off of pixels.

Gate array. A standardized design for an integrated circuit consisting of a fixed number of logic gates that can be interconnected according to customer specifications.

General-purpose computer. A type of computer that can be programmed for a wide variety of tasks or applications.

General-purpose programs. Programs that are adaptable to a wide variety of tasks, for example, word processing, spreadsheet, database management, graphics, and communications. Also called general-purpose application software.

Gigabyte (GB). A unit of measure that is the equivalent of 2^{30}, or 1,073,741,824, bytes.

Geographical information system (GIS). A system that digitizes maps and images of distributions of statistical data and displays them as graphics.

Graphical user interface. An interface that uses pictures and graphic symbols to represent commands, choices, or actions.

Graphics. The term encompassing several elements, including color, motion, and resolution, that together result in the ability of a computer to show line drawings, pictures, or animation on a display screen or printer.

Guided-vehicle system. Robots that can find their way around a factory either by sensing guide wires embedded in the floor or through a vision system.

H

Hacker. A term for a person who gains access to computer systems without authorization.

Half-duplex. A mode that allows two computers to send and receive data, but only in one direction at a time. For example, if one computer is receiving data, it must wait until transmission is complete before sending data. (See *Full-duplex*.)

Handshaking. A procedure or protocol used to establish if two computers or a computer and a peripheral are ready to exchange information.

Hard automation. Dedicated equipment that can only perform a single operation under carefully controlled circumstances, for example, a factory assembly line that can automatically weld certain types of car parts.

Hard copy. Output from a computer system that is in the form of images recorded on paper or film.

Hard disk. A disk made of a rigid base, such as aluminum, and coated with a magnetic oxide layer. (See *Disk*, *Floppy disk*.)

Hardware. The physical components associated with a computer or other system. (See *Software*.)

Hashing. A mathematical technique for assigning a unique number to each record in a file.

Heuristic. Exploratory methods for problem solving in which an evaluation is made of the progress toward the goal using a series of approximate results. Sometimes associated with trial-and-error methods or rules of thumb. (See *Algorithm*.)

Hexadecimal number. A number system that uses a base of 16. Its symbols consist of 0, 1, 2, 3, 4, 5, 6, 7, 8, 9, A, B, C, D, E, and F. It is often used as a shorthand method for writing binary numbers. (See *Binary number*, *Decimal number*.)

Hierarchical model. A method for storing data in a database that structures data into an inverted tree in which records contain (1) a single root or master key field that identifies the type, location, or ordering of the records, and (2) a variable number of subordinate fields that define the rest of the data within a record.

Hierarchical network. A central controller coupled to a series of nodes, or subcontrollers, that are connected to several terminals or personal computers.

Hierarchy chart. A diagram for showing the interrelationships among program modules. Also called a structure chart.

High-level language. A programming language that allows a programmer to specify instructions in English-like statements that are closer to the problem being solved than the computer language in which they are written. Examples are COBOL, FORTRAN, BASIC, Pascal, Ada, C, PL/1, and Modula-2. (See *Low-level language*.)

Human factors. Those elements that pertain to the design of the software interface between people and computers. For example, the design of icons and windows is a human factors concern.

Hybrid approach. An approach that enables the assembly of systems from two or more existing tools.

Hybrid computer. A type of computer designed for highly specialized tasks and one that combines the features of both digital and analog computers.

Hypermedia. An extension of hypertext that includes graphics, video, sound, and music.

Hypertext. Electronic books in which a author can link information and create nonlinear paths through related material.

I

IBG. An acronym for interblock gap. The empty space on a magnetic device between physical records.

Icon. A picture on a display screen that represents a physical object, such as a file folder, memo, letter, in-basket, or wastebasket. (See *Graphical user interface.*)

Image scanner. A device that converts optically focused images, such as photographs or drawings, into digital images that can then be processed like any other digital data. A photoreceptor device is required to convert reflected light into digital images.

Immediate addressing. An addressing technique in which the contents of an address portion of an instruction contain an operand instead of an address. (See *Operand.*)

Impact printer. A printer that operates on the principle of a striking mechanism transferring an image through a ribbon onto paper.

Index. A list containing an entry for each record in a file organized in a certain way.

Index file. In a database, a file that keeps track of the addresses where records can be found.

Index sequential. A file organization method that provides both sequential and direct access capability.

Industrial work. Work involving the production of goods and services. Often associated with blue-collar factory workers. (See *Information work.*)

Inference engine. The part of an expert system that performs the reasoning. (See *Expert system.*)

Information. (1) Data that have a context. (2) Data used in decision making.

Information processing. The work that information systems perform, consisting of responding to input, processing that input according to instructions, and providing output.

Information revolution. (1) A term used to indicate the point at which modern society shifted from being an industrial society to being an information society. No agreed-on date. (2) The reshaping of economic, social, political, and technical structures as a result of people and computers teaming up.

Information society. A society structured around the principles of information as a commodity and as a strategic resource.

Information system. A system that takes input, processes it, and produces information as output.

Information technology. A collective term for computer and communication hardware and system and application software.

Information theory. The branch of computer science that studies the properties of information and how it is measured.

Information work. Work involving professionals, managers, clerks, and administrators who produce information. (See *Industrial work.*)

Inkjet printer. A printer that uses a selected pattern of dots to form images that are transferred by spraying droplets of ink.

Input. (1) The use of a device to encode data. (2) The process of transferring data into a computer system.

Instruction. A basic unit of a program that specifies what action is to be performed on what data.

Instruction counter. A register used to store the address (location) of the next instruction to be executed by the CPU. (See *Register.*)

Instruction set. The unique set of software operations that comes with every processor and helps to define the

architecture of the processor. (See *Architecture.*)

Integrated application software. Software that combines several applications under one consistent user interface.

Integrated circuit. A system of interrelated circuits packaged together on a single silicon chip.

Integrated link software. Software partially residing in a personal computer and partially in a mainframe or minicomputer that bridges the incompatibility between the two.

Interactive. A computer system that provides response to all inquiries by the user.

Interface. The hardware and/or software necessary to interconnect components of a computer system or to connect one computer system to another.

Interface builder. A program that allows you to assemble a user interface, also called a front end, from a library of predefined graphic objects such as windows, buttons, and scroll bars. Examples include Hypercard for the Macintosh and Toolbook for MS-DOS–based computers..

Interpreter. A computer program that translates an instruction into machine language, executes it, and then repeats the process for each instruction in a program until the program is finished.

Interrupt. A signal that causes a processor to suspend the instruction that it is currently executing and transfer control to a special interrupt-handler program. Interrupts may occur because of an exception, such as an arithmetic overflow or data transfer error.

I/O port. An abbreviation for input/output port. A device connected to a computer that allows the input or output of data and instructions. (See *Port.*)

Iterative prototyping. The process of building working models of the application, trying them out, and modifying them in response to new ideas. (See *Prototyping.*)

J

Jargon. The vocabulary peculiar to a

profession or group.

Joystick. A lever, pivoted to move in any direction, that controls the movement of a cursor on a display screen. Similar to a mouse, but used mostly in game programs. (See *Cursor.*)

K

K. An abbreviation for 1024 bytes.

Key. A field in a file used to identify records for purposes of retrieval or sorting.

Key-to-disk or key-to-tape device. A device in which data are entered on a keyboard and directly recorded on a disk or tape.

Keyboard. Keyswitch technology coupled with electronic circuitry that is used to encode input data.

Keypunch machine. An early type of input device in which data are entered on a keyboard and transcribed by punching combinations of holes into specially designed cards.

Kilobyte (KB). A unit of measure equal to 2^{10} or 1024 bytes. (See *K.*)

Knowledge base. The collection of facts, data, beliefs, assumptions, and heuristic methods about a problem area.

Knowledge engineer. A systems designer who designs expert systems.

Knowledge representation. The formal method for representing facts and rules about the area under consideration in an expert system.

Knowledge work. A term used for occupations in which the primary activities involve receiving, processing, and transmitting information. Often called information work.

L

Laptop computer. A term used to indicate a portable computer that can be operated while on a person's lap. Laptop computers are battery powered in their normal operation.

Laser disk. See *Optical disk.*

Laser printer. A printer that uses a laser to record an impression on a drum or belt, which is then transferred to paper.

LCD. An acronym for liquid crystal display. A liquid-filled display surface that, when electrically charged, creates images using ambient light. Typically used in watches, calculators, and portable computers.

LED. An acronym for light-emitting diode. A semiconductor device used as a display in watches, calculators, and instruments.

Letter-quality printer. A printer that uses a cylinder, typeball, daisy wheel, or thimble to transfer formed characters by impact through a ribbon onto paper.

Life-cycle approach. An approach used in system design and software development that proceeds from definition to design and development to implementation.

Light-emitting diode. See *LED.*

Light pen. A hand-held light-sensitive device that allows a user to point to or write information on a display screen.

Line printer. A printer that prints character by character or dot by dot, but the process happens so fast that it seems to be printing one line at a time. (See *Band/belt/train printer.*)

Linear density. The number of bits per inch on a disk track. (See *Track, Track density.*)

Linker. A program that combines separate modules into one executable program.

Liquid-crystal display. See *LCD.*

LISP. Short for LISt Processor. A language used primarily by artificial intelligence programmers for general symbol manipulation and list processing.

Loader. A program that brings programs stored in a program library into memory for execution.

Local-area network (LAN). A communication channel along with interface circuitry that connects devices, such as computers or peripherals, within a limited geographical distance.

Logical record. A record that is defined according to its content or function. (See *Physical record.*)

Loop. A series of program instructions that are performed repeatedly until a specified condition is satisfied.

Low-level language. A programming language that uses symbolic codes that closely resemble the machine language into which they are translated. Example: assembler language. (See *High-level language.*)

LSI. An acronym for large-scale integration, a process that packs thousands of transistors on a single chip.

M

Machine cycle. The length of time required to perform one specific machine (computer) operation.

Machine language. A computer-specific set of primitive or elementary instructions that allows people to communicate with a particular computer.

Macro. (1) A single command that executes a sequence of other commands. For example, displaying your name, address, and phone number by typing [Ctrl] A. (2) When used as a shortened version of macroinstruction, a single instruction that represents a given sequence of instructions in a program.

Macro language. A special-purpose programming language embedded inside an application. Usually found in word processor, spreadsheet, and database programs.

Magnetic ink character recognition. See *MICR.*

Magnetic printer. A printer that projects a selected pattern of charged particles onto a drum that is then transferred onto paper. Also called an ion printer.

Magnetic tape. A tape, similar to audiotape, that is coated with a film on which data can be magnetically recorded.

Mainframe computer. A class of computer providing large storage capacity, high-speed processing, and complex data-handling capabilities.

Management information system (MIS). A system that gathers, condenses, and filters data until it becomes information, then makes it available on time, and in a useful form, for use in decision making at various levels of management within an organization.

Mapping. A term that programmers use to describe the correspondence between the logical and the physical structure of a file. For example, if a physical record and a logical record happen to be equal in size, there is said to be one-to-one mapping.

Mask. In integrated circuit design, a glass photographic plate that contains the circuit patterns used in fabricating a chip.

Mass storage. The storage of mass data. Commonly used to replace the term auxiliary storage; includes storing data on disks, tapes, and drums.

Master file. A type of file that can be thought of as a relatively permanent collection of records.

Megabyte (MB). A unit of measure that is the equivalent of 2^{20}, or 1,048,576, bytes.

Megahertz (MHz). A term used in computers and communication as a unit of frequency. It means million cycles per second. One megahertz (MHz) =1,000,000 hertz.

Memory. The component of a computer system that stores programs and data while waiting to be processed by the CPU. Also called primary storage.

Memory mapped. A technique for accessing input or output devices as if they were memory locations.

Menu. A list of options from which a user must make a choice so that processing can continue.

Menu-driven software. A technique for getting the user to make choices between several different options.

Metaphor. In software development, the use of words or pictures to suggest a resemblance. For example, the Apple Macintosh uses a desktop metaphor with its icons for paper, folders, files, wastebaskets, and so on.

MICR. An acronym for magnetic ink character recognition. Devices that are capable of recognizing patterns written or printed in magnetic ink. Used primarily by the banking industry on checks.

Micro Channel. A hardware bus with a 32-bit data path used in some IBM Personal System/2 computers. It is a trademark of IBM. (See *Bus*.)

Microcomputer. A computer system based on a microprocessor as the central processing unit. (See

Personal computer.)

Microelectronics. The electronic logic represented as microscopic circuits on a chip.

Microfiche. A 4- by 6-inch sheet of photo film used to store miniature images of documents as frames.

Microfilm. A roll of photo film used to store images of documents in miniature.

Micron. A unit of measure equivalent to one-millionth (1/1,000,000) of a meter.

Microprocessor. The central processing unit (CPU) implemented on an integrated circuit chip or set of chips.

Microprogram. The lowest level of software instructions that operates directly on the hardware circuitry of a computer.

Microsecond. A measure of time equivalent to one-millionth (1/1,000,000) of a second.

Millisecond. A measure of time equivalent to one-thousandth (1/1000) of a second.

Minicomputer. A type of medium-sized computer introduced in the 1960s that provides lower-cost processing and storage capacities than the larger mainframe computers.

MIPS. An acronym for million instructions per second. Most often used as a unit of measure for comparing the processing speed of different computers.

Modeling. A partial simulation of real or possible situations or conditions.

Modem. Short for **Mo**dulator **dem**odulator. A device that changes digital computer signals into analog computer signals for transmission over telephone lines and, in reverse, transforms analog signals into digital signals.

Modulation. Controlling a communication signal so that it contains information in the necessary format for transmission.

Module. A set of programming instructions that can be tested and verified independently of its use in a larger program.

Monitor. A television receiver or CRT used for computer output display.

MOS. An acronym for metal oxide semiconductor. The traditional material used in fabricating integrated circuits. (See *CMOS*.)

Mother board. A fiberglass circuit board that contains sockets into which chips can be plugged and a set of tracks (printed on the circuit board) that connects the various chips.

Mouse. A device used to position the cursor on a display screen in lieu of cursor control keys. A mouse also has buttons for selecting options.

MS-DOS. An acronym for Microsoft Disk Operating System. It is a trademark of Microsoft Corporation and is a widely used operating system for personal computers.

MS-DOS–based computer. A personal computer that runs the Microsoft MS-DOS operating system.

Multimedia applications. Applications that combine multiple information types such as text, graphics, video, music, voice, and animation. (See *Hypermedia*.)

Multiplexer. A device that allows several communication signals to share the same channel concurrently.

Multiprocessing. A computer system that uses two or more processors that share memory and input and output devices.

Multiprogramming. A computer system in which two or more programs are executed concurrently by one computer. In effect, the programs take turns running, usually giving the user the illusion that he or she is the only user of the system.

Multitasking. A technique for concurrently executing tasks, or basic units of work performed by a program, on the same computer system. It is similar to multiprogramming, except the processor may be working on several portions of a program instead of several programs.

Multiuser. Systems that allow several users to share a computer's processor, memory, and mass storage simultaneously. Often characterized by systems with several terminals connected to a single central processor.

Musical instrument digital interface (MIDI). A technology that interconnects electronic music instruments and computers.

N

Nanosecond. A measure of time equivalent to one-billionth (1/1,000,000,000) of a second.

Natural language. Languages, such as English, used by humans that develop over time through usage. (See *Artificial language.*)

Natural language interface. An interface that allows the user to input simple English or other natural language phrases in lieu of complex computer commands.

Network. Two or more communicating devices that are connected to form a system.

Network computing. Computer and communication technology that combines geographically dispersed office workers, computing resources, and information into a single integrated environment.

Network model. A technique used in database systems to store data by combining records with a linked list of pointers.

Neural network. An experimental computer that has a memory that is modeled on the human brain. The memory consists of thousands of interconnected "neurons" that receive input from their neighboring neurons. They can perform very simple processing based on patterns of input, and then produce results by sending their output back to neighboring neurons.

Node. The term for a device, such as a terminal, computer, or disk drive, connected to a communication network. (See *Topology.*)

Noise. In communications, an unwanted signal that was not part of the original transmission.

Nonimpact printer. A printer that prints without a striking mechanism impacting a ribbon. Examples include thermal, thermal transfer, electrostatic, inkjet, and laser printers.

Nonvolatile storage. Memory devices, such as ROMs, magnetic tape, and magnetic disk, that can retain data when electric power is shut off. (See *Volatile storage.*)

O

Object. A data element that includes data plus the allowable operations that can be performed on that data. In software engineering, an object is an instance of a class or a logical grouping of objects.

Object code. Output from a compiler or assembler that is linked with other code to produce executable machine language code.

Object environment. A development environment that exploits the availability of prefabricated software components called objects. In these environments predesigned objects can be easily combined and modified, in many different ways, to produce a new application.

Object-oriented model. In database systems, a model that groups data into collections that represent some kind of object or thing and allows records to inherit information from ancestor records.

Object program. See *Object code.*

Object-oriented programming. A programming technique in which the programmer builds a program by combining predefined objects. An example: Smalltalk. (See *Object.*)

OCR. An acronym for optical character recognition. A process that scans a printed image, reads the symbols, and translates them into computer-readable codes.

Office. A place where information is acquired and processed and more information is produced as output.

Office automation. The application of computer and communication technologies to enhance office functions and procedures.

Office of the future. A metaphor applied to the way in which most office workers will handle their daily tasks. It consists of a set of electronic tools and techniques for handling work.

On-line processing. Processing where data enter the system directly from the point of origin and the input and output devices are under direct control of the CPU. (See *Batch processing.*)

Operand. Something that is to be operated on or manipulated, such as the part of an instruction that contains the addresses of data to be manipulated by the instruction. (See *Operation.*)

Operating environment. Programs that combine independent programs into a single environment and allow them to be integrated and their user interfaces simplified. An example: DeskView.

Operating system. A set of programs that manages the overall operation of the computer system. Software that manages routine procedures within a computer system, such as input, output, scheduling, job management, file management, and task management. Examples are MS-DOS, OS/2, Unix, VM, and VMS.

Operation. The part of an instruction that specifies the function that is to be performed. (See *Operand.*)

Optical character recognition. See *OCR.*

Optical disk. Disks that record and retrieve data using laser beams of light instead of magnetic methods. There are three types of optical disks: read only, also called CD ROM; write once, which can be recorded on once by the end user; and erasable, which combines optical and magnetic techniques to record on the surface of the disk.

OS/2. An acronym for Operating System/2, a personal computer operating system jointly developed by Microsoft and IBM.

Output. (1) The use of a device to decode symbols into a form people can use. (2) The results of computer processing.

Overlay. To divide a program into sections that are stored on a mass-storage device and then are brought into main memory as needed. Used when a program is too large to fit into main memory.

P

Packaged application software. Programs that are already written and tested and that may be purchased off the shelf in retail computer stores or through mail-order outlets.

Packet switching. A method for breaking messages into smaller units that can be transmitted separately over communication networks and reassembled into the original message at the destination.

Paging. A memory-management technique for mapping virtual addresses on disk to real addresses in memory. (See *Segmentation.*)

Paint program. A graphics program that provides commands to create lines, circles, rectangles, and other shapes, as well as do freehand sketching. Examples are MacPaint for the Macintosh and Windows Paintbrush for MS-DOS computers. (See *Draw program.*)

Parallel. The transmission, processing, or storage of data such that all parts of a byte are handled simultaneously. (See *Serial.*)

Parallel computer. A computer in which multiple computing nodes that are self-contained microcomputers join together to speed the execution of a single program. A parallel computer may combine from tens to thousands of microcomputers to increase the speed and improve the performance of a complex program.

Parallel processing. The combination of multiple processors and software techniques to facilitate executing parallel instructions.

Parity. A bit that is part of a binary code that indicates the number of 1's in the code and that is used for error checking.

Parsing. Taking a sentence or command and breaking it down into its components to determine what action to take.

Pascal. A high-level programming language developed to teach the concepts of structured programming. It is used as both a teaching tool and for general-purpose software development; named after the seventeenth-century French mathematician Blaise Pascal.

Password. A unique, usually secret, code used to identify users and allow them to access a system that can be accessed by multiple users.

Peripheral. A device that operates in conjunction with, but is not a part of, a computer, such as a printer, disk drive, or graphics tablet.

Personal computer. A microcomputer usually targeted to the information processing needs of an individual. Often called a microcomputer. (See *Microcomputer.*)

Photolithographic process. The procedure used to print the mask pattern of integrated circuits on a silicon wafer.

Physical file. The way in which the actual data in a database system are stored and accessed on a medium such as a disk.

Physical record. A record that is composed of one or more logical records. (See *Logical record.*)

Picosecond. A measure of time equivalent to one-trillionth (1/1,000,000,000,000) of a second.

Pipelining. The overlapping of fetch and execute cycles within a processor. For example, while one instruction is being executed, the processor will begin fetching the next instruction to be executed.

Pixel. Short for picture element, which is a light or dark point on the surface of a display screen.

Plotter. A device that produces an image by controlling the motion of a pen carriage.

Pointer. An address that specifies a storage location where data can be found.

Pointing device. A device for moving the cursor and interacting with a display screen.

Point-of-sale system. A computer input device located at the point at which goods and services are paid for.

Polling. A communications control method in which a master computer "asks" remote terminals whether or not they have any information to transmit.

Port. The location through which the computer exchanges information with an external device. A port has a physical connector and an address so that programs know where to send information.

Power supply. A device consisting of a transformer and related components that transforms household current into the direct voltages used by a computer.

Presentation graphics. Graphics that are intended to communicate information to other people. Example: graphics used at a sales presentation.

Print buffer. A hardware device that attaches to a printer, stores characters, and controls printing.

Print server. A device that connects printers to a local-area network.

Printer. A device that produces hard copy output from a computer system by transferring an image onto paper.

Procedure. A detailed set of instructions that identifies what is to be done, who will do it, when it will be done, how it will be done, and why it will be done.

Procedure-oriented language. A programming language that describes the steps necessary to solve a problem. Most high-level languages, such as COBOL, BASIC, or FORTRAN, are procedure oriented.

Process. A systematic series of actions directed toward a goal.

Processor. A functional unit that interprets and carries out instructions. (See *CPU.*)

Productivity crisis. A term used to describe a lack of productivity increase in proportion to the amount of technology applied to office work.

Program. (1) A set of instructions that tells a computer what to do. (2) The activity involved in creating a program.

Program design language. See *Pseudocode.*

Program documentation. Written or printed information necessary to support the ongoing existence of the software.

Program generator. Automatic generation of a program as a result of writing specifications about the problem to be solved.

Program testing. The process of verifying a program for its ability to perform its intended function and not to perform anything unexpected.

Programmable industrial automation. Flexible, easy-to-learn-and-use, intelligent automation applied to factory systems. Includes robotics, vision systems, and information systems.

Programmer. A person who creates computer programs.

Programmer analyst. A job classification that combines the functions of a programmer and a systems analyst.

Programming language. A formally constructed artificial language in which the syntax and grammar are stated so precisely that a computer can analyze, interpret, and understand the meaning of that language. Examples are Ada, Assembly language, C, COBOL, FORTRAN, and Pascal.

Protocol. A formal set of rules for specifying the format and relationships when exchanging information between communicating devices.

Protocol converter. Hardware or software that translates the codes of one computer or terminal into the code of another computer or terminal. It enables incompatible computers or terminals to communicate with one another.

Prototyping. The process of building working models of a system's inputs, outputs, and files.

Pseudocode. A method for writing English-language statements that are equivalent to programming-language statements in their sequence. Often used as an alternative to flowcharting. Sometimes called program design language.

Pull-down menu. A menu that is hidden from view until needed.

Q

Query. A question or request for information.

Query by example (QBE). A fill-in-the-blanks approach to questioning a database. The user searches for information by filling out a query form on the display screen.

Query language. The capability to question a database or file of information without any knowledge of how or where the information is stored.

Qwerty. An abbreviation used to designate a standard typewriter keyboard layout, indicated by the first six letters in the first row of alphabetic characters.

R

RAM. An acronym for random-access memory. A temporary memory that is empty until the microprocessor needs to use it, that is, load programs and data into it. RAM is often called read/write memory, meaning that the microprocessor can read its contents and write programs or data into it. Its name comes from the method used to access information from the memory, that is, random access. This means that it takes the same amount of time to access any one piece of information as it does another.

Random access device. A device that can read and write information at any location on the device in the same amount of time, regardless of its physical location.

Random-access memory. See *RAM*.

Random-access method. A method of accessing a file that allows a program to read or write any record in the file in the same amount of time without regard to its physical location.

Read. A program instruction that acquires a copy of a block of data from a storage medium, such as disk or tape.

Read-only memory. See *ROM*.

Read-only optical disks. Optical disks that cannot be written on and so have the functional equivalency of read-only memory (ROM).

Real-time processing. A processing method in which the immediate response requirements limit the running time of the program. For example, a program monitoring a critically ill patient needs to give immediate responses and cannot spend an excessive amount of time processing the input data.

Record. A collection of related data treated as a unit. For example, the payroll information about one person.

Reentrant routine. A module of programming code that is executed simultaneously by more than one software module.

Refresh. The reactivation of electronic components, such as dynamic random-access memory (DRAM) and phosphor-coated display screens, to maintain information that would otherwise leak or fade away.

Register. A small amount of memory, usually one or two bytes, reserved to function as a temporary storage area during program execution.

Relation. A two-dimensional table in the formal terminology of relational databases. (See *Attribute, Tupple*.)

Relational model. A technique used in database systems in which one or more flat files or tables create relationships among the tables on the basis of a common field in each of the tables. (See *Flat file*.)

Requirements list. Formally written statements that specify what the software must do or how it must be structured.

Resource object. A device or service such as a printer or a file-server object. (*See Object environment*.)

Ribbon cable. A group of attached parallel wires commonly used to connect a printer or disk drive to a computer.

Ring network. An approach for linking terminals or personal computers by using a closed-loop communication channel.

RISC. An acronym for reduced instruction set computer. RISC is a combination of hardware and software that reduces the number of instructions in a computer's instruction set and attempts to execute each instruction as quickly as possible.

Robot. A programmable general-purpose motion machine.

ROM. An acronym for read-only memory. A permanent memory that the microprocessor can read information from, but whose contents can neither be erased nor written over-thus the name, read-only memory. ROM stores the instructions that start up the computer when the power is turned on, and stores some additional programs.

RS-232C. A term designating the industry standard for a 25-pin physical interface that connects computers with peripheral equipment, such as printers or modems.

Rule. A statement about the relationships of various facts or data.

S

Save. To store information in a file.

Scanner. A device that examines a

pattern and converts it into a digital representation suitable for computer processing. Patterns can then be manipulated into a form suitable for the application.

Scrolling. Using directional keys (cursor control keys) to move the contents of a display screen up, down, left, or right.

Search time. The time required to rotate the needed record under the read/write head of a magnetic disk.

Second generation. Refers to computers in the time period 1958-1964 that used transistors to replace vacuum tubes.

Secondary storage. The component of a computer system in which programs and data are stored while not in use. (See *Mass storage*.)

Sector. The smallest block of physical data that can be written to or read from a disk device.

Seek time. The time required to position the read/write head over the proper track on a magnetic disk.

Segmentation. A memory management technique for allocating and addressing memory. (See *Paging*.)

Semiconductor. A material (usually silicon) with properties between those of a conductor and insulator. Its resistance can be changed by electricity.

Sensor. An instrument capable of directly encoding a physical event. Used as an input device for computer systems.

Sequencer. Software that can capture, edit, and play back music.

Sequential. A file organization method that involves storing records in a predetermined sequence based on one or more key fields.

Serial. The transmission, processing, or storage of data one bit at a time. (See *Parallel*.)

Server. A computer running software that fulfills requests from clients across a network. (*See Client*.)

Silicon. A nonmetallic element that is commonly used in the fabrication of integrated circuit chips.

Silicon compiler. A program used in the development of integrated circuits that translates high-level block diagrams into detailed transistor circuits.

Simulation. A computerized representation of a process or set of activities.

Smart sensor. Devices that combine a computer and a sensor on a single silicon chip. (See *Sensor*.)

Soft copy. The recording of an image (computer output) on a surface such as a display screen.

Software. Programs that control the functions of a computer system. (See *Hardware*.)

Software development. The process of analyzing the requirements of a system, then designing, writing, and testing the software.

Software engineering. The application of scientific and mathematical principles to the design and development of producing software.

Software maintenance. The job of modifying existing programs to fix bugs or make requested changes.

Software piracy. The term used to describe the illegal or unauthorized copying of software.

Sort. To arrange records in a file into a preidentified sequence, such as alphabetically or numerically from lowest to highest.

Source code. The set of statements that make up a computer program.

Source document. A tangible piece of paper or form from which data are entered as input to a computer system.

Source program. See *Source code*.

Special-purpose computer. A computer that is dedicated to a single purpose. (See *General-purpose computer*.)

Special-purpose program. Programs that are dedicated to performing single-use tasks, for example, medical billing, patient tracking, or contract writing. Also called special-purpose application software.

Speech coding. A technique for voice output from a computer that uses prerecorded human speech as the source of the output.

Speech recognizer. A device for voice input that is capable of recognizing an individual person's voice.

Speech synthesis. A technique for voice output that uses phonemes or basic speech sounds to imitate the human voice.

Spelling checker. A program that checks documents for spelling errors. Also called a spelling corrector.

Spool. An acronym for Simultaneous Peripheral Operations On-Line. A program that allows printing to occur simultaneously with other computer operations.

Spreadsheet program. A program that models the way in which financial people solve problems, such as budgeting and estimating.

SQL. Short for Structured Query Language. A query language for manipulating data in a relational databases.

Standard cell. A technique for designing integrated circuits by which predefined functions, such as processing elements and memories, are obtained from libraries and used in the design process.

Star network. A central controller with a separate communication channel attached to each device connected to it.

Statistical multiplexing. A technique for allocating a communication channel among several users on the basis of idle time on the channel. A statistical multiplexer fills the idle time gaps between transmissions with parts of other transmissions.

Stored-program concept. The storage of data and instructions using the same memory so that the computer can become a general-purpose system. Used in lieu of hand wiring the computer each time a specific task is to be performed.

Strategy. A plan of action designed to cope with change, competition, and uncertainty.

Streaming tape. A form of magnetic tape that is specifically designed to store backup copies of disk files. Also called cartridge tape.

Structure. In database programs, the manner in which the fields of a record are organized or interrelated. Also called record structure.

Structure chart. A diagram that serves as a model for modularizing a structured program. (See *Hierarchy chart*.)

Structured analysis. The examination of a complex problem by dividing it into simple functions.

Structured design. The process of designing the components of a computer program and their interrelationships in the best possible way.

Structured programming. The application of top-down design methods to programming.

Structured programming language. A programming language that facilitates the idea of breaking the program into smaller units or modules to allow clearer expressions of the problem and simpler organization. Examples are Pascal, C, Modula-2, and Ada.

Structured walkthrough. A peer review designed to evaluate and challenge specifications. The proposed specifications are presented to other analysts, programmers, or system developers for feedback, comments, and criticism.

Style checker. A program that hyphenates words, checks for punctuation errors, and flags awkward usage.

Subroutine. A part of a program that can be executed repeatedly by a single statement.

Supercomputers. The fastest computers made.

Supervisor. The operating system control program responsible for deciding which application program will have use of the CPU.

Switch. A device capable of making or breaking one or more connections in a circuit. Also called a gate.

Synchronous transmission. Data communications in which a synchronizing clock signal is used to transmit large blocks of data between sending and receiving devices.

Synthesizer. A device that electronically generates sound instead of picking it up with a microphone.

System. (1) In general systems theory, a set or arrangement of parts acting together to perform a function. (2) In systems analysis, a network of interrelated procedures performed by people with the aid of tools or machines.

System flowchart. A graphic representation of the components, flow, and relationships among elements of a system.

System software. Programs or commands used to control the operation of the computer system.

Systems analyst. A person in an organization who performs the interfacing between users and programmers.

T

Talkwriter. A word processor that transforms speech into text. (See *Speech recognizer*.)

Tape drive. A device that stores data recorded on magnetic tape. A form of mass storage.

Technology. (1) The practical application of knowledge. (2) Activities that are directed toward the satisfaction of human needs that produce alterations in the material world.

Telecommunications. Communications over a long distance.

Telecommuting. The electronic transportation of information instead of the physical transportation of people.

Template. In a spreadsheet, a partially completed worksheet designed to assist the user in entering data.

Terabyte. A unit of measure equivalent to 2^{40}, or 1,099,511,627,776 bytes. Used to measure capacities of optical disk mass-storage devices.

Terminal. A device that is used in communication systems to enter or receive data.

Text database. A collection of words such as articles in *The Wall Street Journal* or a series of legal abstracts. Text databases are either stored on-line or on CD ROM optical disks and include the means to search through massive amounts of data to answer specific questions.

Thermal printer. A printer that uses a selected pattern of dots to form images that are transferred by heat onto specially coated paper.

Thermal-transfer printer. A printer that uses heat to melt wax particles that contain ink, which are then transferred to paper.

Thin-film disk. A disk that contains a metallic layer as opposed to a magnetic oxide layer on its surface. This permits higher recording density because the read/write head can travel closer to the disk's surface owing to more precise tolerances.

Thin-film head. A disk read/write head made from the same photolithographic process as integrated circuits. It permits individual data bits to be stored closer to each other on the surface of the disk.

Third generation. Referring to computers in the time period 1964-1977 that used integrated circuits to replace transistors.

Throughput. The total volume of work performed by a system in a given period of time.

Time-division multiplexing. Assigning a communication channel to several different users on the basis of fixed time intervals.

Time-sharing. A method that allows multiple users of a computer system to share the computer, giving the illusion of having simultaneous access.

Token. In local-area networks, the electronic equivalent of an envelope. A token contains a fixed amount of information and a destination address.

Token-ring network. A type of local-area network in which a single token passes from computer to computer and carries messages around the network.

Top-down approach. A technique used by systems analysts and software developers that refers to starting with the whole problem and developing more and more detail as the solution develops.

Top-down structured design. An approach for program design that involves proceeding from general terms to finer and finer details until no more detail is necessary.

Topology. In a computer network, the interconnection of devices and communication channels into a network configuration.

Total systems concept. An MIS concept popular in the late 1960s in which a single centralized repository of information would represent all the organization's activities.

Touch screen. A plastic membrane or set of infrared sensors placed over a display screen to enable the user to select actions or commands by touching the screen.

Track. Refers to concentric circles where data are stored on a disk.

Track density. The number of tracks per inch on a disk. (See *Linear density*.)

Transaction. An event about which data are recorded and processed. For example, a request for a seat on an airline flight.

Transaction file. A type of file in which records created during the input process are stored until needed for further processing.

Transaction-oriented processing. A type of processing in which transactions activate processing. For example, an airline reservation system.

Transcribed input. Data that are captured by transcribing them from source documents onto another medium that is capable of being input to a computer system. (See *Direct-source input, Source document*.)

Transistor. A tiny, solid-state device that performs the switching functions of a vacuum tube.

Transparent. A term used by computer designers to indicate a function that the user is not directly aware of. In effect, the user "sees right through it" and does not notice that it is around.

Tupple. A row in a two-dimensional database. (See *Attribute, Relation*.)

Turnkey. A computer system that includes all the necessary hardware and software and that is built, tested, and installed by the vendor.

Tutorial. A set of instructions designed for self-taught learning about computers.

U

UART. An acronym for *u*niversal *a*synchronous *r*eceiver *t*ransmitter. An integrated circuit that performs the function of translating parallel data into serial data, and vice versa.

ULSI. An acronym for *u*ltra*l*arge-*s*cale *i*ntegration. ULSI etches 100 million to 1 billion transistors and other circuit elements on a single chip.

Unix. A trademark of Bell Laboratories. An operating system designed for minicomputers and microcomputers.

UPC. An acronym for Universal Product Code, a bar code consisting of thick and thin stripes that can be read by an optical reader. Used primarily to identify supermarket items.

Update. A term for the modification of records in a master file by replacing older information with more current information.

Upward compatible. A term used when a new piece of equipment or computer system can produce identical results as the equipment or system it replaces.

User analyst. A systems analyst who is in an organizational department other than the data processing department.

User friendly. A term describing how easy a system or program is to learn and use and how gently it tolerates errors or mistakes on the part of the user.

User group. An informal organization of people who use the same type of computers or software and have regular meetings to swap information and programs.

User interface. That portion of a program that handles the human interaction with the program.

Utilities. (1) In system programming, programs that perform functions that are required by many of the programs using the system. (2) In database systems, programs that allow a user to maintain a database.

V

Variable-length operations. The type of operations performed by character (byte)-addressable computers.

Vertical recording. A recording technique that stands the magnetic particles on the surface of a disk on end so that the north-south poles point up and down or vertically toward the surface of the disk. This effectively increases the density of the disks because more magnetic fields can be packed into a given area on the disk.

VGA. Short for video graphics array, an IBM video chip on the PS/2 mother board that provides 640- by 480-pixel resolution and a 256-color palette on the display screen. (See *CGA, EGA*.)

Video capture board. A board that plugs into an expansion slot and turns full-motion video signals into digitized files.

Video conference. A conference held by means of one- or two-way interactive television.

Videotex. A form of electronic publishing.

View. In a database, a group of data associated with a specific user.

Virtual circuit. A logical connection between nodes in a communication network that can be accomplished with many different physical circuits during the transmission of messages.

Virtual memory. A technique for storing programs or data on mass-storage devices and creating the illusion that data are in memory by swapping pages or segments in and out of memory when needed.

Virtual-memory operating system. A type of operating system that automatically manages program overlays, bringing them in and out of memory as needed.

Vision system. A robotic system that uses a television camera coupled with image processing software to allow a robot to see.

Visualization. A term that applies to representing complex mathematical phenomenon or simulations with images. The more visual the representation of data, the easier it is to completely and more accurately understand the data.

VLSI. An acronym for very-large-scale integrated circuit. VLSI etches 100,000 to 100 million transistors and other circuit elements on a single chip.

Voice recognizer. See *Speech recognizer*.

Voice training. The process of recording an individual's voice patterns when speaking specific commands. The voice patterns are stored for future matching when the device is actually in use.

Volatile file. A file in which a high percentage of records accessed are changed or records are added or deleted.

Volatile storage. Memory devices, such as dynamic random-access memory (DRAM), that lose all data when electric power is cut off. (See *Nonvolatile storage*.)

von Neumann computer. The traditional form of computer architecture named after John von Neumann (1903-1957), in which the computer has one central processor and one memory connected via a single channel. Also used to indicate a computer in which programs and data share the same memory.

W

Wafer. A thin disk of pure silicon on which multiple copies of integrated circuits are fabricated.

What-if analysis. Use of a spreadsheet to compare alternatives.

Wide-area network. A geographically dispersed communication network linking computers for the purpose of communicating with one another. A nationwide network of airline reservation terminals is an example of a wide-area network.

Winchester disk. A high-speed, medium- to large-capacity, sealed magnetic storage medium for computer systems.

Window. A variable-sized rectangular area on a display screen.

Word processing. An application program designed to compose, revise, print, and file written documents.

Word recognizer. A device for voice input that is capable of responding to individually spoken words or commands.

Word size. The term used to describe the size of operand registers and buses in computer systems. Also called word length.

Word wrap. A feature of many computer programs that allows you to continue typing beyond the end of a line without having to press the return key.

Workgroup computing. Computer and communication technology that facilitates the process of people working together in groups that are electronically connected.

Workstation. A type of small computer targeted to the needs of high-performance specialized applications such as computer-aided design and publishing, modeling, and visualization.

Write. A programming statement that causes a permanent copy of a block of data to be recorded on a storage medium, such as a disk or tape.

Write-once optical disks. Blank disks that are recorded on by the user. To write data, a powerful beam of laser light burns tiny spots or pits into the coating that covers the surface of these disks. Once burned in, the spots are not erasable. Also called write-once, read-mostly, or WORM.

Write-protect ring. A plastic ring that prevents writing on the tape when removed from the back of a tape reel.

WYSIWYG. An acronym for what-you-see-is-what-you-get. The display of information in a form that resembles very closely what will eventually be printed. The term is used often in word processing, desktop publishing, and typesetting.

PHOTO CREDITS

Chapter 1 Opener: Courtesy Spectrum Holobyte. Page 5 (top): Courtesy IBM. Page 5 (bottom): Courtesy Apple Computer, Inc. Page 6: Courtesy Samna Corp. Page 7 (top): Courtesy Apple Computer, Inc. Page 7 (bottom) Courtesy Microsoft Corp. Page 8: Courtesy Microsoft Corp. Page 9: Courtesy Digital Equipment Corp. Page 13: Courtesy Cadam, Inc. Page 15 : Courtesy AT&T Bell Labs. Page 16 (top): Courtesy IBM. Page 16 (bottom): Courtesy Aldus Corp. Page 17: Courtesy Princeton Graphics Systems. Page 18: Courtesy IBM. Page 19 (top): Courtesy Kodak. Page 19 (bottom): Courtesy Apple Computer, Inc.

Chapter 2 Opener: Courtesy Alan Kay. Page 29 (top): Courtesy Microrim. Page 29 (bottom): Courtesy Ashton-Tate, Inc. Page 30 (top): © 1989 Next, Inc. Reprinted by permission. Page 30 (bottom): Courtesy Microrim. Page 31: Courtesy Quarterdeck. Page 32: Courtesy Microsoft Corp. Page 33: Courtesy Sun Microsystems, Inc. Page 34: Courtesy Microsoft Corp. Page 36 (top): Courtesy Lotus Development Corp. Page 36 (bottom): Courtesy Microsoft Corp. Page 37 (top): Courtesy Reference Software. Page 37 (bottom): Courtesy Microsoft Corp. Page 38: Courtesy Aldus Corp. Page 39: Courtesy Hewlett-Packard. Page 41 (top): courtesy Microsoft Corp. Page 41 (bottom): Courtesy Computer Associates. Pages 43 and 44: Courtesy Borland International. Pages 45 and 46 (top): Courtesy Lotus Development Corp. Page 46 (bottom): Courtesy Microsoft Corp.

Page 47 (top) Courtesy Polaroid. Pages 47 (bottom) and 48 (top): Courtesy Apple Computer, Inc.

Chapter 3 Opener: Courtesy Clifford Stoll. Page 57: Courtesy Data General. Page 58: Courtesy Chrysler Corp. Page 59 (top): Mark Pokemper/Black Star. Page 59 (bottom): Courtesy Lotus Development Corp. Page 60: Courtesy Prodigy Information Services. Page 61: Joel Gordon. Page 63 (top): Courtesy Buick Motor Division. Page 63 (bottom): John Zoiner/International Stock Photo. Page 65: Courtesy CompuServe. Page 68 (top): Courtesy Interface Group. Page 68 (bottom): Terry Parke. Page 69: John Foraste/Brown University. Page 70: Stuart Bratesman/Apple Computer, Inc.

Chapter 4 Opener: Courtesy EDventure Holdings. Page 82: Courtesy Hewlett-Packard. Pages 84 (top): Courtesy IBM. Page 84 (bottom): Courtesy General Electric. Page 86 (top): Courtesy Robotic Research, University of Rhode Island. Page 86 (bottom): Courtesy Ford Ford Motor Co. Page 87: Courtesy Recognition Equipment, Inc. Page 88: Courtesy Grid Systems. Page 91: Courtesy IBM. Page 92: Courtesy Digital Research. Page 93 (bottom): Courtesy Grid Systems. Page 94: Courtesy Evans & Sutherland Computer Corp. Page 95: Courtesy IBM. Page 96: Courtesy Owl International.

Chapter 5 Opener: Courtesy IBM. Pages 112 and 114 (top): Courtesy

IBM. Page 114 (bottom): Courtesy Mouse Systems, Inc. Pages 115 (bottom) and 116: Courtesy Unisys. Page 117 (top): Courtesy Lockheed, California. Page 117 (bottom): Courtesy Datacopy Corp. Page 118: Courtesy IBM. Page 119 (top): Courtesy Koala Technologies. Page 119 (center): Courtesy UPC. Page 120 (top): Courtesy Hewlett-Packard. Page 120 (bottom): Courtesy Scan Optics. Page 121 (top): Courtesy IBM. Page 121 (bottom): Courtesy Xerox Imaging Systems/Kurzweil. Page 122: Courtesy Image-In, Inc. Page 123: WAK Pictures/Ameritech.

Chapter 6 Opener: Courtesy Watzman & Keys. Page 133: Courtesy Department of the Treasury. Page 134 (top): Courtesy Toshiba America, Inc. Page 134 (bottom): Courtesy Kodak. Pages 135 and 136: Courtesy IBM. Page 137 (top): Courtesy Epson. Page 137 (bottom): Courtesy Okidata Corp. Page 138: Courtesy Xerox. Page 139 (top): Courtesy IBM. Page 139 (bottom): Courtesy Okidata Corp. Page 140: Courtesy Apple Computer, Inc. Page 141: Courtesy Epson. Page 142: Courtesy Toshiba America, Inc. Page 144 (top): Courtesy Kodak. Page 144 (bottom): Courtesy Xerox. Page 145 (top): Courtesy Hewlett-Packard. Page 145 (bottom): Courtesy Digital Equipment Corp.

Chapter 7 Opener: Courtesy Next, Inc. Page 154: Courtesy Intel. Pages 158 and 162: Courtesy IBM. Page 164 (top): Courtesy Control Data Corp. Page 164 (bottom): Courtesy Amdahl.

Page 165: Courtesy Unisys. Page 166: Courtesy IBM. Page 167: Courtesy NCR. Page 168 (top): Courtesy IBM. Page 168 (bottom): Courtesy Digital Equipment Corp. Page 169 (top): Courtesy IBM. Page 169 (bottom): Courtesy Tandem Computers. Page 170: Courtesy Visual, USA. Page 171: Hank Morgan. Page 172: Courtesy IBM.

Chapter 8 Opener: Courtesy T/Maker Corp. Page 180: Courtesy IBM. Page 181: Courtesy Maynard Electronics. Page 182: Courtesy Apple Computer, Inc. Page 184 (top): Courtesy Storage Technology Corp. Page 184 (bottom): Courtesy Hewlett-Packard. Page 185: Courtesy Unisys. Page 186 (top) Courtesy Plus Development Corp. Page 186 (bottom): Courtesy Iomega Corp. Pages 187 and 189: Courtesy IBM. Page 190: Courtesy Tab Products Co.

Chapter 9 Opener: Courtesy The Travelers Companies. Page 198: Charles Harbutt/Archive Pictures. Page 199 (top): Courtesy NASA. Page 199 (bottom): UPI/Bettmann Newsphotos. Page 200 (top): Courtesy AT&T. Page 200 (bottom): Courtesy IBM. Pages 202 and 203: Courtesy AT&T. Page 204 (top): Courtesy Epson. Page 204 (bottom): Courtesy Digital Equipment Corp. Page 205: Courtesy IBM. Page 206: Courtesy Apple Computer, Inc. Page 207 (top): Courtesy Murata. Page 207 (bottom): Courtesy Ricoh. Page 210: Courtesy AT&T. Page 211: Courtesy Motorola, Inc.

Chapter 10 Opener: Courtesy Cincinnati Milacron. Page 229: Courtesy IBM. Page 230 (top): Courtesy Metaphor Computer Systems. Page 230 (bottom): Courtesy Datapoint Corp. Page 231: Courtesy Xerox. Page 234 (top): Courtesy Aetna Life Insurance Co. Page 234 (bottom): Courtesy Digital Equipment Corp. Page 236: Courtesy Symantec Corp., Living Videotext Division.

Chapter 11 Opener: Courtesy GO Corp. Page 244: Courtesy Odesta Corp. Page 249: Courtesy Ashton-Tate. Page 250: Courtesy Oracle. Page 251 (top): Courtesy Borland International. Page 251 (bottom): Courtesy Microrim. Page 252 (top): Courtesy Cosmos. Pages 252 (bottom), 254, and 257: Courtesy Ashton-Tate. Page 258: Courtesy Microrim.

Chapter 12 Opener: Courtesy Nicholas Negroponte. Page 267 and 268: Courtesy Advanced Information and Decision Systems. Page 269: The New York Times. Page 272 (top): Courtesy General Electric. Page 272 (bottom): Courtesy Owl International. Page 273 (top): Courtesy Gold Hill Computers. Page 273 (bottom): Courtesy Texas Instruments.

Chapter 13 Opener: Courtesy ASK Computer Systems. Page 282 (top): Elyse Rieder. Page 282 (bottom): Rick Browne/Picture Group. Page 283: Joe Munroe/Photo Researchers. Page 290: Courtesy Excelerator. Page 292: Courtesy Borland International. Page 293: Courtesy Lotus Development Corp. Page 294: Robin Meyer/Black Star.

Chapter 14 Opener: Courtesy Microsoft Corp. Page 302 (top): Courtesy Unisys. Page 303: Bruce Flynn/Picture Group. Page 304: Courtesy Caseworks, Inc.

Chapter 15 Opener: Courtesy Stanford University. Page 329: Courtesy Lotus Development Corp. Page 332: Courtesy Ashton-Tate. Page 333: Courtesy Asymetrix Corp. Page 334: Courtesy Apple Computer, Inc. Page 335 (top): Courtesy Authorware, Inc. Page 335 (bottom): Courtesy Macromind, Inc. Page 336: Courtesy IBM. Page 337(top): Courtesy Hewlett-Packard. Page 338: Courtesy Apple Computer, Inc.

Appendix A Pages 345, 346, and 347: Courtesy IBM Archives. Page 348 (top left) and 348 (top center): Courtesy IBM. Page 348 (bottom): Courtesy New York Public Library Picture Collection. Pages 348 (right) and 349 (left): Courtesy The Computer Museum. Page 349 (bottom center): Courtesy New York Public Library Picture Collection. Pages 349 (top center) and 349 (right): Culver Pictures. Page 350 (cen-

ter): The Bettmann Archive. Page 351 (left): Courtesy The Computer Museum. Page 351 (center): Courtesy IBM Archives. Page 351 (right): The Bettmann Archive. Page 352 (top): Courtesy The Computer Museum. Page 352 (bottom right): Courtesy AT&T. Page 352 (bottom left): Courtesy The Institute of Electrical Engineers. Page 353 (top right): UPI/Bettmann Newsphotos. Page 354 (top left): Courtesy The Computer Museum. Page 354 (top center, top right, & bottom): Courtesy AT&T Bell Labs. Page 355 (top): Courtesy The Computer Museum. Page 355 (bottom left): *COMPUTERWORLD* photo by A. Dooley. Page 355 (bottom right): Courtesy National Archives, Kensington, England. Page 356 (top left): Courtesy Harvard Archives. Page 356 (top right): Courtesy Naval Surface Weapons Centers. Page 356 (bottom): Courtesy Unisys. Page 357 (top left): Courtesy Moore School of Electrical Engineering, University of Pennsylvania. Page 357 (bottom left) and 357 (top center): UPI/Bettmann Newsphotos. Page 357 (right): Courtesy University of Cambridge Computer Lab. Page 358 (top): Courtesy MIT Archives. Page 358 (bottom): Courtesy Mitre Corp. Archives. Page 359 (left): Courtesy Unisys. Page 359 (center): Courtesy The Computer Museum. Page 359 (right): Courtesy AT&T Bell Labs. Page 360 (top left): Courtesy IBM Archives. Page 360 (bottom): Courtesy Dan Leeson. Page 361 (top left): Courtesy Texas Instruments. Page 361 (top center): UPI/Bettmann Newsphotos. Page 361 (top right): Courtesy AT&T. Page 362: Courtesy MIT Museum. Page 363 (top left): Courtesy Digital Equipment Corp. Page 363 (top center): Courtesy IBM. Page 363 (top right): Courtesy Dartmouth College. Page 364 (left): Courtesy Control Data Corp. Page 364 (right): Courtesy The University of Texas. Page 365 (left): Courtesy Data General. Page 365 (bottom) and 365 (right): Courtesy AT&T. Page 366 (top): Courtesy The Relational Institute. Page 366 (bottom left): Courtesy Intel Corp. Page 366 (right): Courtesy Stanford University. Page 367 (top left): Courtesy E. Feigenbaum/Photo by Marek Majewski. Page 367 (top right): Courtesy Martha Everson/The Computer Museum. Page 367 (bottom): Courtesy Datapoint Corp. Page 368 (top) and 368 (bottom): Courtesy Apple Computer, Inc. Page 368 (right): Courtesy IBM. Page 369 (left): Courtesy AT&T Bell Labs. Page 369 (bottom): Courtesy IBM. Page 369 (right): Courtesy BBN, Inc. Page 370 (left): Courtesy AT&T Bell Labs. Page 370 (right): Courtesy Apple Computer, Inc. Page 370 (bottom): Courtesy Intel. Page 371: Courtesy AT&T Bell Labs.

Appendix B Page 374: Michael Kagan/Monkmeyer Press Photo. Page 377 (top): Courtesy Wordstar International. Page 377 (bottom): Courtesy Broderbund Software, Inc. Page 378 (top): Courtesy WordPerfect Corp. Page 378 (bottom): Courtesy Ashton-Tate. Page 379 (top): Courtesy Software Publishing Corp. Page 379 (bottom): Courtesy Microsoft Corp. Page 380 (top): Courtesy Claris Corp. Page 380 (bottom): Courtesy Symantec, Living Videotext Division. Page 381 (top): Courtesy Borland International. Page 381 (bottom): Courtesy Microsoft Corp. Page 382 (top): Courtesy Lotus Development Corp. Page 382 (bottom): Courtesy Aldus Corp. Page 383 (top): Courtesy Lotus Development Corp. Page 383 (bottom): Courtesy Borland International. Page 384 (top): Courtesy Computer Associates. Page 384 (bottom): Courtesy Microsoft Corp. Page 385 (top): Courtesy Software Publishing Corp. Page 385 (bottom): Courtesy Ashton-

Tate. Page 386 (top): Courtesy Symantec Corp. Page 386 (bottom): Courtesy Borland International Page 387 (top): Courtesy Software Publishing Corp. Page 387 (bottom): Courtesy Borland International. Page 388 (top): Courtesy ACIUS, Inc. Page 388 (bottom): Courtesy Microrim, Inc. Page 389 (top): Courtesy Claris Corp. Page 389 (bottom): Courtesy Microsoft Corp. Page 390 (top): Courtesy Ashton-Tate. Page 390 (bottom): Courtesy Lotus Development Corp. Page 391 (top): Courtesy Claris Corp. Page 391 (bottom): Courtesy Software Publishing Corp. Page 392 (top): Courtesy Microsoft Corp. Page 392 (bottom): Courtesy Corel Systems, Inc. Page 393 (top): Courtesy Business and Professional Software, Inc. Page 393 (bottom): Courtesy Crosstalk Communications. Page 394 (top): Courtesy Hayes Microcomputer Products, Inc. Page 394 (bottom): Courtesy Claris Corp. Page 395 (top): Courtesy Lotus Development Corp. Page 395 (bottom): Courtesy Great American Software, Inc. Page 396 (top): Courtesy DAC Software, Inc. page 396 (bottom): Courtesy Microsoft Corp. Page 397 (top): Courtesy Electronic Arts. Pages 397 (bottom) and 398 (top): Courtesy John Wiley & Sons, Inc. Page 398 (bottom): Courtesy Simon & Schuster Software. Page 399 (top): Courtesy Autodesk, Inc. Page 399 (bottom): Courtesy Wolfram Research, Inc. Page 400 (top): Courtesy Central Point Software, Inc. Page 400 (bottom): Courtesy Peter Norton Computing.

Pa[...]
tems[...]
Sharp [...]
(bottom): [...]
Inc. Page 404 [...]
Computer. Pag[...]
tesy Tandy Corp[...]
Courtesy Toshiba Am[...]
405 (bottom): Courtesy [...]
Systems. Page 406 (top):[...]
Compaq Computer. Page 4[...]
tom): Courtesy Toshiba America[...]
Page 407 (top): Courtesy Apple Co[...]
puter, Inc. Page 407 (bottom): Courtesy Grid Systems Corp. Page 408 (top): Courtesy IBM Entry Systems Division. Pages 408 (bottom) and 409 (top): Courtesy Commodore International. Page 409 (bottom): Courtesy Atari Corp. Page 410 (top): Courtesy Apple Computer, Inc. Page 410 (bottom): Courtesy IBM Entry Systems Division. Page 411 (top): Courtesy Tandy Corp. Page 411 (bottom): Courtesy IBM Entry Systems Division. Page 412 : Courtesy Apple Computer, Inc. Page 413 (top): Courtesy IBM Entry Systems Division. Page 413 (bottom): Courtesy Hewlett-Packard. Page 414 (top): Courtesy Compaq Computer. Page 414 (bottom): Courtesy Hewlett-Packard. Page 415 (top): Courtesy Sun Microsystems, Inc. Page 415 (bottom): Courtesy Next, Inc. Page 416 (top): Courtesy Hewlett-Packard. Page 416 (bottom): Courtesy IBM Corp. Page 417: Courtesy Digital Equipment Corp. Page 418: George Malave/Stock Boston.

Page 402 (top): Courtesy Atari Corp. Page 402 (bottom): Courtesy Grid Systems Corp. Page 403 (top): Courtesy Electronics Corp. Page 403 Courtesy Toshiba America, (top): Courtesy Compaq 404 (bottom): Cour- erica, Inc. Page Page 405 (top): Zenith Data Page Courtesy Inc. 06 (bot-

INDEX

Abacus, 344
Access time, definition, 431
Accounting and bookkeeping, 376
    information as strategic resource,
        60–62
Accounting and bookkeeping
        software, 35, 376
    DAC-Easy Accounting, 396
    One-Write Plus, 395
Accumulator, definition, 431
Acoustic modem, 206, 431
Acronym, definition, 431
Ada, 349, 431
Ada, Augusta (Countess of
        Lovelace), 349, 431
Adaptation, need for, 65
Adder, definition, 431
Address, 157
    definition, 431
Address bus, 158, 159
    definition, 431
Address register, definition, 431
Administration, 99
Agenda, 395
Agent object, 337
AI, *see* Artificial intelligence
Aiken, Howard, 356
Airlines:
    reservations, DBMS application
        example, 247–248
    information as strategic resource,
        60–62, 88
Algorithm, 307–308
    definition, 431
All-computer technocracy, 66–67
Alphanumeric, definition, 431
[Alt] key, 113
ALU, 156
    definition, 431
American Arithmometer Company,
    351
American Standard Code for
    Information Interchange,
    413–416
    key layout, 112
Amiga 2000, 409
Analog, definition, 431
Analog computer, 346, 353
    definition, 431
Analog tide predictor, 350
Analog-to-digital converter,
    definition, 431
Analytical engine, 349
Analytical graphics, 46–47, 431
Anderson, Harlan, 363
Anderson, John, 270

Antenna, definition, 431
APL, definition, 431
Apple II computer, 368
AppleWorks, 389
Applications, 14–15, 332–333
    definition, 431
    developing, 281
Application-development tools,
    254
Application Development Facility
    (ADF), 331
Application generator, 254,
    330–331
    definition, 431
Application object, 336
    definitions, 432
Application programmer, 97
    definition, 432
Applications development group,
    227
Application software, 34–35, 48,
    376
    definition, 432
Application-specific integrated
    circuit (ASIC), 157, 432
Architecture, definition, 432
ARCNET, 367
Arguments, 29
Arithmetic expression, definition,
    432
Arithmetic/logic unit, **see** ALU
Arithmetic operations, 156
Arithmetic operator, definition,
    432
Arithmetic unit, definition, 432
Arithmometer, 351
Array, definition, 432
Art, computer assisted, 90
Artificial intelligence (AI),
        267–277
    computer-integrated
        manufacturing, 86
    definition, 432
    factory automation, 84–86
    natural language processing,
        270–272
    neural network, 275–277
    occupational demand, 97
    programming language, 361
    thinking about thinking, 269
    from thinking to intelligent
        behavior, 269–270
    Turing test, 268–269
Artificial language, definition, 432
Ascending order, definition, 432
ASCII, 424–427

definition, 432
    key layout, 112
Assembler, definition, 432
Assembly, factory automation, 248
Assembly-level language,
    definition, 432
Asynchronous transmission,
    definition, 432
Asynchronous mode, 217
Atanasoff, John V., 355
Atari 520St, 409
Atari Portfolio, 402
Atkinson, Bill, 370
ATM, *see* Automatic teller machine
Attribute, definition, 432
Audit trail, 256
Authoring system, 334–336
AUTOEXEC.BAT, 330
AutoCAD, 399
Automatic Computing Engine
    (ACE), 358
Automatic teller machine (ATM),
    61, 115
    definition, 432
Automation, 87, 272
    definition, 432
Automobiles, computerized,
    62–64, 82–83

Babbage, Charles, 349
Background study:
    definition, 432
    systems analysis, 286
Backing up, definition, 432
Backup file, 184, 330, 432
Backus, John, 317, 360
Balanced tree, 259
Band printer, 135–136, 432
Bandwidth:
    communication channels,
        203–204
    definition, 432
Banking:
    electronic, types, 61
    information as strategic resource,
        60–62
Bank switching, definition, 432
Baran, Paul, 215
    definition, 432
Bar codes, 119
Bardeen, John, 357
Base of number system, 410
BASIC, 318–319, 363
    definition, 432
Batch files, 330
Batch processing, definition, 432

Batch-processing system, 110
Baud:
    definition, 432
    rate, 203
BBN Advanced Computer
    Butterfly, 369
Beginner's All-purpose Symbolic
    Instruction Code, *see* BASIC
Bell, Alexander Graham, 201
Belle, 269
Bellmac-32, microprocessor, 369
Belt printers, 135–136
    definition, 432
Bernoulli Box, 187
Berry, Clifford, 355
Bidirectional printing, definition,
    432
Binary arithmetic, 422–423
Binary code, 423–428
Binary digit (BIT), definition, 12,
    432
Binary number, 419–422
    conversion of decimal number,
        421–422
    definition, 432
Binary search, 258, 433
Binary signal, 433
Binary system, 11, 420
Bin-picking robot, 85
Biometric device, definition, 433
BIOS, definition, 433
Bistable, definition, 433
Bit, 11, 432
8-Bit code, 423
Bit map, 140, 433
Bits per second, 203, 433
Blankenbaker, John, 367
Boolean algebra, 349
    application to switching
        functions, 354
    definition, 433
Boole, George S., 349
Bootstrap loader, definition, 433
Bottom-up design:
    definition, 433
    software, 306
Branch, definition, 433
Brattain, Walter H., 357
Bridge, 236
Broadband channel, 204
B-tree:
    database management systems,
        259
    definition, 432
Buchanan, Bruce, 367
Buffer, definition, 433

453

Bug, 313, 356
  definition, 433
Bundled, definition, 433
Burnes, Mary Jo, 224
Burroughs, William S., 351
Bus, 158, 160, 433
Bush, Vannevar, 353
Business application, COBOL, 317
Business plan, spreadsheet use, 41
Business systems analysts, 284
  definition, 433
Bus networks, 211–212
  definition, 433
Butterfly, 172, 369
Buttons, 333
Buzzwords, definition, 433
Byte, 157, 433

C, 300, 320–321, 422
Cache, definition, 433
Cache memory, 162
CAD, 46, 82–83, 92
CADUCEUS, 89
CAE, 83
CAI, see Computer-assisted
  Instruction
Calculator:
  digital, 157
  electromechanical, 354
  electronic, 355
  mechanical, 346, 347, 348–352
CAM, 82–83
Camera, electronic, 121
Camera-output systems, 145
Capsules, 336
Cards, 332
Carr, Robert, 244
Cartridge tape, 183–184
CASE, 291–292
Cassette tape, 183
Cathode ray tube (CRT), 16, 141
  definition, 433
CCITT Group, 211
CDC 6600, 364
CD ROM, 94, 192, 433
Cell, 433
Cellular mobile radio, definition,
  433
Cellular radio, 211
Central electronic complex,
  154–163, 172
  buses, 158, 160
  clock speeds, 162
  definition, 433
  increase in word size, 161
  memory, 157–158
  memory management, 162
  processor, 155–156
  random-access memory, 157
  read-only memory, 158
  RISC, see Reduced Instruction
    Set Computers
Central processing unit, see CPU
CGA, definition, 433
Channel, 165, 433
Character map, 140, 433
Chess computer programs,
  268–270
Chip, 11, 12, 163
  32-bit microprocessor, 369
  definition, 433
  design, 163
  making, 163
  microprocessor, 366
  small-scale integration, 367
Church–Turing thesis, 268
Circles of Proportion, 346
Circuit, 11
  definition, 433

Circuit switching, 215
  definition, 433
CISC processor, 163
Class, 315
Clerical worker productivity,
  229–230
Client, definition, 433
Client/server model distributed
  database, 256–257
  definition, 433
Clock, 155
  definition, 433–434
  speed, 162
CMOS components, 170, 434
Coaxial cable, 202, 434
COBOL, 316–317, 361
  definition, 434
Cocke, John, 368
Codd, E. F., 249, 366
Code, 11, 423
  definition, 434
Coding program, 312
Colab, 235
Colby, Dr. Kenneth, 68
Collaborative work, 235
Collision, definition, 434
Collision detection, definition, 434
Color CRTs, 141
Color displays, 141
Colossus, 355
COM (computer output to
  microfilm or microfiche), 145
Command, definition, 434
Command-drive interfaces, 28–29
Command-driven software,
  definition, 434
Command file, 330
Command processor, definition,
  434
Commodore Amiga 500, 408
Commodore Amiga 2000, 409
Common Business Oriented
  Language, see COBOL
Common carrier, communications,
  213–214
Communication, definition, 434
Communication channels,
  202–205
  bandwidth, 203–204
  fiber-optic systems, 205
  LAN, 210
  media, 202–203
  microwave systems, 204
  satellite systems, 204–205
Communication processor,
  definition, 434
Communications, 13, 35, 199
  common carriers, 213–214
  computers and, 200–201
  computer-to-computer, 47
  Crosstalk, 393
  FAX machines, 209–210
  forms of, 233
  Hayes Smartcom, 394
  historical perspectives, 201–202
  modems, 206
  multiplexers, 216–217
  protocols, 217
  satellites, 202, 204–205
  scope of, 200–201
  switching concepts, 215–216
  terminal emulation, 207–208
  terminals, 206–207
  transmission modes and types,
    217
Communications industry,
  213–215
Communications processor,
  208–209

Communication server, 236, 434
Communication skills, 99
Communication software, 47–48,
  376
Communication systems, 12–13,
  434
Compact disk read-only memories,
  192
Compaq Deskpro 486 Model 25,
  414
Compaq LTE/286, 404
Compaq SLT/286, 406
Comparable worth, 99
Compatibility, 166
  definition, 434
  software evaluation, 296
Compiler, 313
  definition, 434
  silicon, 163
Complementary metal oxide
  semiconductor, see CMOS
Complex calculator, 354
Complex instruction set
  computers, 163
Component, definition, 434
Composing, word processing, 36
Composite color CRTs, 141
Comptometer, 351
Computer, definition, 434
Computer-aided design (CAD),
  46, 82–83, 92
  definition, 434
  integrated circuits, 163
Computer-aided engineering
  (CAE), 83
  definition, 434
  integrated circuits, 163
Computer-aided manufacturing
  (CAM), 82–83
  definition, 434
  integrated circuits, 163
Computer-aided publishing, 145
Computer-aided software
  engineering (CASE), systems
  analysis, 288–289, 291–292
Computer-assisted instruction
  (CAI), 95
Computer crime, 70–71
Computer designers, 98–99
Computer graphics, definition, 434
Computer hardware engineers, 98
Computer III Report and Order,
  214
Computer-integrated manufacturing
  (CIM), 86–87, 434
Computerization, definition, 434
Computerization of society, 56–75
  banking, 61–62
  coping with effects, 66–71
  education, 69–70
  effect on smokestack industries,
    64
  ethics and, 70–74
  telecommuting, 68–69
Computerized information
  services, 57–61, 434
Computerless society, 67
Computer literacy, 6–9, 19
  definition, 434
  experience with computers, 7
  levels of, 6
  programming, 8–9
  read about computers, 6–7
  tutorial, 8
Computer monitoring, productivity,
  66–67
Computer networking, see
  Networking
Computer programs, see Program;

Software
Computer operators, 97
Computerphobia, definition, 434
Computers:
  arts and design, 89–92
  careers, 97–100
  communication and, 200
  crime and, 70–73
  definition, 4, 434
  education and, 70–71, 95–97
  ethics, 70–73
  experience with, 7–8
  future, 99–100
  game playing, 376
  general purpose, 5
  government, 93
  hypothetical, 160–161
  law, 94–95
  medicine and healthcare, 88–89
  military, 93–94
  movies and television, 90
  operators, 97
  perceptions, 66
  privacy, 73–74, 215
  professional compensation, 360
  retailing, 87–88
  sales and marketing, 98
  service and repair, 97
  shopping for, 375
  society and, 56, 63
  sound, 90
  special purpose, 4
  support personnel, 98
  as systems, 9–10, 153
  thinking and, 268–269
  training, 99–100
  types of, 4–6
  uses, 4–5
  virus, 71–72
Computer science, definition, 434
Computer systems, evolutionary
  trends, 163–170
  channels, 165
  compatibility, 166–167
  mainframes, 164–165
  microcomputers, 169–170
  microprogramming, 167
  minicomputers, 167–169
  time-sharing, 165–166
Computer systems analyst, 284
  definition, 434
Computer technicians,
  occupational demand, 97
Computer-telephone, definition,
  434
Computer-trained people, supply
  and demand, 97
Concentrator, 216, 434
Conceptual tool, definition, 434
Concurrent program execution,
  definition, 434
Configuration, definition, 434
Connection Machine, 172
Container object, 336
  definition, 434
Control bus, 160, 434
Control character representations,
  428
Control key [Ctrl], 91, 434
Control program for
  microcomputers, see CP/M,
  definition
Control structures:
  definition, 434
  software, 308–309
Control unit, 156, 435
Conversion, to new system, 293
Coprocessor, 143
  definition, 435

COPY, 29
Copy protection, 74, 435
CorelDraw, 392
Core memory, invention, 358
Corning Glass Works, Inc., 365
Cost:
  integrated circuit design, 164
  software evaluation, 296
  systems analysis, cost-benefit
    estimate, 289
Courseware, 335
  definition, 435
CP/M, definition, 435
CPU, 17, 155
  definition, 435
  selection, 297
Crash, 169
Crawford, Curtis, 108
Cray-2, 171
Cray-3, 171
Cray Y-MP series, 171
Crime, computers and, 70–74
Crosstalk, 393
CRT, 16, 141
  definition, 435
Cryptoanalysis, 355
Cursor, 36
  definition, 435
  movement keys, 413, 435
Cybernetics, definition, 435
CYBER Series, 171
Cycle, definition, 435
Cylinder, 185–186, 435

DAC-Easy Accounting, 396
Daisy wheel, definition, 435
DAT, 184
Data, 10–11, 184–185
  definition, 10, 435
  independence, 255
  integrity, 255
  security, 256
Database, 35, 42–45
  applications, 43
  definition, 42, 435
  file manager, 43
  on-line, 58–60
  personal information managers,
    45
Database compiler, 332
Database management system
    (DBMS), 245–260. See also
  Management information
    system
  application example, 247–248
  B-trees, 259
  characteristics, 248
  data dictionary, 259–260
  data manipulation, 251–252
    application-development
      tools, 254
    basic operations, 251
    data independence, 255
    data integrity, 255–256
    data security, 256
    on-screen form, 252
    query languages, 252–254
    report generation, 44–45, 254
    sorting, 252
  definition, 435
  distributed, 256
  hashing, 259
  indexing, 258
  need for, 246–247
  physical files, 258
  utilities, 260
Database manager, 43
Database models, 248–251
  definition, 435

differences among, 251
flat file, 248–249
hierarchical, 249–250
network, 250
object-oriented, 250–251
relational, 249
Database programming languages,
  316, 331–334
Database programs, 376
  dBase IV, 385
  4th Dimension, 388
  Lexis, 94
  Paradox, 387
  Professional File, 387
  Q&A, 386
  R:Base 3.0, 388
  Reflex, 386
  Westlaw, 94
Database server, 257, 435
Database specialists, 98
Database system, definition, 435
Database transaction, 255–256, 435
Data communications, 200, 435
Data bus, 158, 435
Data dictionary, 259–260, 288, 291
  definition, 435
Data Discman, 96
Data diddling, 71
Data-entry clerks, 97
Data-flow diagram, 288, 435
Data General Nova, 365
Database system, definition, 435
Data integrity, definition, 435
Data processing (DP), definition,
  435
Data processing analyst, definition,
  435
Data representation, 423–424
Data security, definition, 435
Data structure, definition, 435
dBase IV, 385
DBMS, see Database management
  system
Debug, 435
Debugging, 313
Decimal number:
  conversion to binary number,
    421–422
  converting number from its
    base, 421
  definition, 435
Decision-support software,
  definition, 435
Decision support systems, 226,
  435
Decode, definition, 435
DEC PDP-8, 363
Decryption, 73
  definition, 435
Dedicated, definition, 435
Dedicated file server, 257
Deep thought, 270
Default, definition, 435
Defining a file, 181
DeForest, Lee, 352
Delete [Del] key, 113
DENDRAL, 273–274, 367
Descending order, definition, 435
Design automation, integrated
    circuits, 91–92
  integrated circuits, 163
Design process, new system, 290
Design review, 291
Desktop computers, 401, 408–414
Desktop presentation, 47
Desktop publishing, 34–35, 39, 376
  applications, 39
  definition, 436
  software, 39

Detail documentation, 291, 436
Device driver, definition, 436
Dial-up line, definition, 436
Difference engine, 349
Differential Analyzer, 353
Digital, definition, 436
Digital audio tape, 184
Digital calculator, 157
Digital computer:
  definition, 436
  first, 355
Digital DECstation 5000 Model
  200, 417
Digital optical processors, 371
Digital signal processors, 157
Digitizer tablets, 116
Digitizing, 116, 436
Dijkstra, Edsger, 364
Direct conversion method, 293
Direct files, 182, 436
Direct memory access, see DMA,
  definition
Director, 335
Directory, 32
Direct-source input, 110, 111, 436
Disabled persons, enabling
    computer applications, 68
Discovering Microsoft Works, 397
Disk, 18, 436
Disk array, defined, 436
Disk cartridges, 187, 436
Disk drive, 436
Disk operating system, see DOS
Disk pack, 186–187, 436
Display:
  definition, 436
  selection, 297
Distributed computing, 167–168,
  436
Distributed database, 256–257, 436
Distributed file servers, 257
Distributed filing, 34
DMA, definition, 436
Document, see also Word
    processing
  definition, 436
Documentation, 7. See also Tutorial
  definition, 7, 436
  detail, 291
  high-level, 291
  program, 292–293
  software evaluation, 295
  style of, 295
  support personnel, 359
  system, 290–292
  system flowchart symbols, 291
  technical, 292
  user, 292–293
DOS, definition, 436
Dot-matrix printers, 19, 134–135
  definition, 436
Download, 207, 436
DRAM (Dynamic random access
    memory), testing for, 436
Draw program, 46, 436
DSS, 226
Dumb terminal, 206
Duplex, definition, 436
Dynabook, 142
Dynamic binding, 315
Dynamic RAM, 157
Dyson, Esther, 80

EBCDIC (Extended Binary-Coded
    Decimal Interchange Code),
    424–427, 436
Eccles, W. H., 352
Eckert, J. Presper, 359
Eckert, Wallace J., 353

Economics, of information, 58–62,
  75
EDI, see Electronic data
    interchange
Edit, definition, 436
EDSAC, 357
Education, 99–100
  future and, 70
Educational software, 376
  Discovering Microsoft Works,
    397
  Enable 2.14, 398
  Typing Tutor, 398
EDVAC, 357
EGA, definition, 436
ELD panels, 142
Electroluminescent display (ELD),
  142, 436
Electromechanical relay, definition,
  436
Electronic banking, 61–62
Electronic books, 95–96
Electronic calendar, 238
Electronic camera, 121
Electronic conferencing, 235, 436
Electronic data interchange (EDI),
  61, 436
Electronic Delay Storage Automatic
    Computer, 357
Electronic Discrete Variable
    Automatic Computer, 357
Electronic drawing, 116
Electronic funds transfer, 61
Electronic mail, 235, 437
Electronic mailbox, 235, 437
Electronic marketplace, definition,
  437
Electronic Numerical Integrator
    and Calculator, see ENIAC
Electronic photography, 121–122
Electronic printer, definition, 437
Electronic sweatshop, 66–67
Electronic transactions, 61, 437
Electrostatic printers, 137–138, 437
Embezzlers, using computers, 70,
  71
Emulation, definition, 437
Enable 2.14, 398
Encode, definition, 437
Encryption, 73, 437
End user, definition, 437
End user development, 337–338,
  437
Engelbart, Doug, 114
Engineering software, see Scientific
    and engineering software
ENIAC (Electronic Numerical
    Integrator and Calculator),
    356, 357
Enter key, 113
Entertainment software, 34, 376
EPCOT Center, touch screens,
    115–116
Erasable optical disk, 193
Erasable programmable read-only
    memory (EPROM), 190
Ergonomics, definition, 437
Errors, 313–314
  checking, 437
Escape key [Esc], 113
Ethics, and computer, 70–74
  crime, 70–71
  privacy, 73–74
  security, 72–73
  software piracy, 74
Execute, definition, 437
Expansion slots, 18, 437
Expert systems, 89, 267, 272–275,
  367

Expert systems (*Continued*)
from databases to knowledge bases, 272
definition, 437
drawbacks, 274
how they work, 273–274
inference engine, 273
prospects, 274
shells, 274–275, 437
Exponent, 420
Export utility, 260
Extended Binary Coded Decimal Interchange Code, 424–427, 436

Facsimile, definitioln, 437
Facsimile machines, 209–210
Factory automation, 84–87
inspection and quality control, 85
materials handling, 84–85
packaging and shipping, 86
production and assembly, 85
Fair Credit Reporting Act of 1971, 73
Fault, 169, 437
Fault-tolerant computers, 169–170, 437
FAX machines, 209–210
FCC, see Federal Communiciations Commission
Feature analysis, 120
Federal Communications Commission (FCC), 214
Feigenbaum, Edward, 367
Felt, Door Eugene, 351
Fiber-optic cable, 202, 205, 365
Fiber optics, definition, 437
Fiber-optic systems, communication channels, 205
Field engineers, 97
Fields, 43, 437
File manager, 43, 437
Files, 31, 437
defining, 181
index sequential, 182
logic structure, 180
mass storage, 180–181
physical structure, 180
random access, 182
requirements, systems analysis, 288
sequential, 181–182
File servers, 257, 437
Filing, 38
Firmware, 190, 437
First generation, definition, 437
Fixed-length operations, definition, 437
Flat-bed plotters, 145
Flat file, 248–249, 437
Flat-panel display, 16, 142–143
definition, 437
Flight Simulator, 94, 396
Flip-flop, 352
Floor standing personal computer, *see* Workstations
Floppy disks, 18, 184–185
definition, 437
Flowchart, 311
definition, 437
symbols, 311
ForComment, 377
Form, 252
Format, definition, 437
Forrester, Jay, 358
FORTRAN, 317–318, 343, 360
definition, 437

4th Dimension, 388
Fourth generation, definition, 437
Fourth-generation language, 294
definition, 437
Frame, definition, 437
Frame buffer, definition, 438
Framework, 390
Freedman, Steve, 326
Frequency, definition, 438
Frequency-division multiplexing, 216, 438
Front-end processors, 208, 438
Full-duplex, 217, 438
Full-text retrieval software, 94, 438
Functional specification, 285
definition, 438
systems analysis, 289
Function keys, 112–113, 438
Fuzzy sets, 277

Games, *see also* Entertainment software
artificial intelligence, 269
Flight Simulator, 396
Pinball Construction Set, 397
Garbage in-garbage out, definition, 438
Gas plasma display, 142
definition, 438
Gate arrays, 438
Gates, William, 302
Gateway, 236
General-purpose computers, 5
definition, 438
history, 355
General-purpose programs, 34, 35, 48, 376
as alternative to programming, 290
definition, 438
Geographical information system (GIS), definition, 438
Gigabyte (GB), definition, 438
Gigaflop, 171
GO TO Statement, 364
GPSS, 362
Graphical user interface (GUI), 29–30, 332, 336
definition, 438
Graphic design, 89–90
Graphics, 35, 45–48, 143–144, 367
analytical, 46–47
CorelDraw, 392
definition, 45, 438
draw program, 46
Harvard Graphics, 391
high-resolution, 144
interactive real-time, 362
low-resolution, 144
MacPaint, 391
near-photographic quality, 144
paint program, 46
PowerPoint, 392
presentation, 46–47
software, 143
35mm Express, 393
Graphics adapter board, 47
Greenblatt, Richard, 364
Grid1450SX, 407
GridPad, 402
GTE Telenet, 216
Guided vehicle systems, 85, 438

Hacker, 71, 438
Half-duplex, 217, 438
Hand-held personal computer, 402
Handshaking, 217, 438
Handwriting recognition, 272

Hard automation, 84, 438
Hard copy, 133, 438
Hard disk, 185–186, 438
capacity, 185
cylinder, 185
disk cartridges, 187
disk packs, 186–187
Winchester drives, 187
Hardware, 14. *See also* Integrated circuit; *specific devices*
changing role, 161–172
CRTs, 139–140
definition, 438
digitizer tablets, 116
keyboards, 111–113
light pen, 116
magnetic ink character recognizer, 118–119
matching, to software, 297
mouse, 114
printers, *see* Printers
raster displays, 144
selecting, 296–297
sensors, 122–123
from software to firmware, 190
touch technology, 114–115
Hardware engineering, 154–157
Hardware selection, 296–298
display capability, 297
keyboard, 297
mass storage, 297–298
memory capacity, 297
places to shop, 298
processor, 297
Harvard Graphics, 391
Hashing, 259, 438
Hayes Smartcom II, 394
Health Care, computer applications, 88–89
Heuristic, definition, 438
Heuristic methods, 272
Hewlett Packard HP Apollo 9000 Model 425t, 416
Hewlett-Packard HP Vectra 486 PC, 414
Hewlett-Packard Vectra QS/16S, 413
Hexadecimal number, definition, 438
Hexadecimal number system, 422, 424–427
Hierarachical database, 249–250
Hierarchical model, definition, 438
Hierarchical networks, 211, 438
Hierarchy chart, 306, 438
High-level documentation, 291
High-level language, definition, 438
High-resolution graphics, 144
High-tech/high-touch 68, 70
education, 69–70
telecommuting, 68–69
Hitachi S-810/20 supercomputer, 171
Hoff, Ted, 169
Hofstadter, Douglas, 268
Hollerith, Herman, 351
Home personal computer, *see* Personal computer systems
Hopper, Grace, 316, 361
Human factors, definition, 438
Hybrid approach, definition, 439
Hybrid computer, definition, 334, 439
Hypercard, 332, 370, 376
applications, 334
Hypermedia, 96

Hypertalk, 332, 439
Hypertext, 96, 439

IBG, definition, 439
IBM 3090 mainframe, 172
IBM Personal Computer, 369
MS-DOS, 32, 33
OS/2, 33–34
IBM Personal System/1, 408
IBM Personal System/2:
Model 30, 410
Model 70, 386, 413
Model 55 SX, 411
IBM RP3, 172
IBM Stretch, 364
IBM System/360, 363
IBM System/370 series, 166–167
IBM System/6000 POWERstation 320, 416
Icon, 336, 439
Image processing, 121–122
Image scanner, 117–121, 439
Immediate addressing, definition, 439
Impact printer, 133–135
band, belt, and print train, 135–136
definition, 439
dot-matrix, 134–135
letter-quality, 133–134
Implementation phase, systems analysis, 292
Import utility, 260
Index, definitiion, 439
Index file, 258, 439
Indexing, database management systems, 258
Index sequential, definition, 439
Index sequential file, 182
Industrial work, 57, 439
Inference engine, definition, 439
Information, 10–11
codes, 11
as commodity, 58–59
data, 10
definition, 10, 439
economics of, 58–59, 75
as political resource, 58
as strategic resource, 59–62
Information center, 227
Information explosion, 229
Information networks, 200
Information processing, 10, 439
Information Revolution, 56, 439
Informatioin society, 56–57, 439
Informatioin system, 12–13, 109, 225
Information technology, 227, 238–239, 439
Information theory, 354, 439
Information work, 56–57, 439
Information worker, obsolescence and, 65
Inheritance, 315
Inkjet printer, 136, 439
Input, 110–111
definition, 110, 439
devices, 16
direct source, 88–89, 110, 111
keyboards, 111–113
pointing devices, 113–116
requirements, systems analysis, 287–288
scanners, 117–122
sensors, 122–123
transcribed, 110–111
voice, 123–124
Input/output port, *see* I/O port,

definition
Inspection, factory automation, 85
Installation, ease of, 295
Instruction, definition, 439
Instruction counter, definition, 439
Instruction set, 155, 166, 439
Insurance, information as strategic
    resource, 60
Integrated application software,
    389–390
    definition, 439
Interface builder, 328, 332–334
    applications, 333
    definition, 439
Integrated circuit, 11, 157,
    163–166, 361
    chips, 11, 12, 16–17, 163
    definition, 439
    quest for smallness, 163
    VLSI, 163–164
Integrated link software, definition,
    439
Integrated programs, 35
Integrated Services Digital
    Network, 213
Integrated software, 48, 376
    AppleWorks, 389
    Framework, 390
    Microsoft Works, 389
    Symphony, 390
Intel i860 RISC microprocessor,
    370
Intel 8086, 161
Intellect, 271
Intelligence, definition, 268
Intelligent terminal, 206
INTELSAT series, 202
Interactive, definition, 439
Interactive videodisk programs,
    193–194
Interblock gap, see IBG, definition
Interface, definition, 439
Interface builder, 328, 332–334
    applications, 333
    definition, 439
Interpreter, 313, 439
Interrupt, definition, 439
I/O port, definition, 439
Ion printers, 138
Iterative prototyping, 329, 439. See
    also Prototyping

Jacquard, Joseph-Marie, 348
Jargon, 9, 439–440
Jevons, William S., 350
Jobs, supply and demand, 97
Jobs, Steven P., 152
Jordan, F. W., 352
Joystick, definition, 440
Just-in-time inventory approach,
    85

K, definition, 440
Kay, Alan, 26
Kemeny, John G., 318, 363
Kenbak-1, 367
Kernel, operating system, 31
Kernighan, Brian, 320
Key, definition, 440
Keyboard, 16, 111–113
    construction, 111–113
    cursor movement keys, 113
    definition, 440
    function keys, 112–113
    personal computer, 112–113
    selection, 297
    special control keys, 113
    typewriter layout, 112

uses, 111–112
Key field, 182, 248–249
Key-driven calculator, 351
Keypunch machine, 110, 440
Key-to-disk system, 110, 440
Key-to-tape system, 110, 440
Kilburn, T., 357
Kilby, Jack S., 361
Kilobyte (KB), definition, 440
Knowledge base, 272–273, 440
Knowledge engineer, 273, 440
Knowledge representation, 273,
    440
Knowledge work, 56, 440
Kurtz, Thomas E., 318, 363
Kurtzig, Sandra, 281
Kurzweil, Raymond, 120
Kurzweil reading machine,
    120–121
Kyuma, Kazuo, 371

LAN, 210, 367, 440
Laptop computer, 170, 401,
    404–407
    definition, 440
    display capability, 297
Large-scale integration (LSI), 163,
    440
Laser, 205
    invention, 361
    semiconductor, 365
Laser-based optical transmitters,
    203
Laser disk, see Optical disk
Laser printers, 138–139, 440
LCD, 17, 440
LED, definition, 440
Lederberg, Joshua, 367
LED printers, 139
Lehigh virus, 72
Leibniz, Gottfried von, 347
Leibniz wheel, 347
Letter-quality printers, 19, 133–134
    definition, 440
Life-cycle approach, 284, 329, 440
Light-emitting diode, definition,
    440
Light-emitting diode printers, 139
Light pen, 116, 440
Lightwaves, 205
Linear density, 184, 440
Line printer, 135, 440
Linker, 314, 440
Liquid crystal display, see LCD
LISP (LIST Processor), 360
Loader, 314, 440
Local-area network (LAN), 210,
    440
    definition, 440
    history, 367
Logarithms, 326
Logical error, 313–314
Logical record, 180, 440
Logic demonstrator, 348
Logic machine, 350
    general model, 354
Logic operations, 156
Logic structure file, 180–181
Logic systems, 277
Loop, definition, 440
Looping control structure, 309
Lotus Manuscript, 382
Low-level language, definition, 440
Low-resolution graphics, 143
LSI, definition, 440

Machine cycle, definition, 440
Machine language, 155, 440

Machine readable data, 132
Macintosh, operating system, 33,
    190
Macintosh IIsi, 412
Macintosh Classic, 412
Macintosh LC, 410
Macintosh Portable, 407
MacPaint, 391
MacProject II, 394
Macro, definition, 440
Macro languages, 329–330, 440
Macromind, Inc., 335
MacWrite II, 380
Magnetic disk, 18, 184–189
    floppy, 184–185
    hard, 185–189
    linear density, 184–185
    physical record storage,
        188–189
    sectors, 185
    thin-film, 189
    thin-film read/write heads, 189
    track density, 184
Magnetic ink character recognition,
    see MICR
Magnetic printer, 138, 440
Magnetic storage media, 190–191.
    See also Magnetic disk
Magnetic tape, 183–184, 440
Magneto-optical disks, 193
Mahon, Charles, 348, 349
Mailing list, 11–12
Maiman, Theodore, 361
Mainframe-centric model, 256
Mainframe computer, 5, 164–167
    channels, 165
    compatibility, 166–167
    definition, 440
    microprogramming, 167
    time-sharing, 165–166
Management, 99
Management information system
    (MIS), 225, 239
    components, 227
    definitioin, 226, 440
    effects on people, 238–239
    foundations, 226–227
    information explosion, 229
    information technology tools,
        231
    network computing, 236–238
    operational level, 228
    organizational perspectives,
        228–231
    personal computing, 231–233
    productivity, 229
    retailing, 87
    strategic level, 228
    strategic management, 226
    structure, 227–228
    tactical levle, 228
    workgroup computing, 233–236
Managerial productivity, 230
Managing software, 376
    Agenda, 395
    MacProject II, 394
Manchester Mark I, 357
Mapping, 180, 440
Marconi, Guglielmo, 201
Marketing support people, 98
Mark I, 356
Mask, 441
Mass storage, 179–194
    cartridges, 191
    definition, 441
    files, 181–182
    hardware selection, 296–298
Master file, definition, 441

Material Requirements Planning
    (MRP), 83
Materials handling, factory
    automation, 84–85
Math game, structure diagram, 311
Mathematica, 399
Matrix matching, 120
Mauchly, John W., 359
McCarthy, John, 361
Mechanical mouse, 114
Medical applications, computer,
    88–89
    diagnostic systems, 89
    medical imaging, 89
    patient monitoring, 88
Medium-bandwidth channels, 204
Megabyte (MB), 161, 441
Megahertz (MHz), 156, 441
Memory, 17, 157–159
    amount addressed, 160
    cache, 162
    capacity, 157, 297
    definition, 441
    hierarchy, 162
    management, 162
    paging, 162
    random-access, 17–18, 157–158
    read-only, 17, 158
    segmentation, 162
    virtual, 32, 162, 362
Memory mapped, definition, 441
Menu, 441
Menu-driven software, definition,
    441
Mesopotamian base-60 system,
    422
Message, 233–234, 315
Metal oxide semiconductor, see
    MOS, definition
Metaphor, definition, 441
Metaphor Data Interpretation
    System, 336
MICR, 118, 119, 441
Micro Channel, definition, 441
Microcomputers, 169–170
    economic feasibilities, 169
    definition, 441
    fault-tolerant computers,
        169–170
    smart cards, 170
    very small computers, 170
    virtual machines, 170
Microelectronics, 62, 441
Microfiche, 145, 441
Microfilm, 145, 441
Micron, definition, 441
Microprocessor, 17
    chip, 366
    definition, 441
    million-transistor, 370
Microprogram, definition, 441
Microprogramming, 167, 359
Microsecond, definition, 441
Microsoft Bookshelf, 381
Microsoft Disk Operating System,
    see MS-DOS
Microsoft Excel, 384
Microsoft Word, 379
Microsoft Works, 389
Microwave systems,
    communication channels, 204
Microwave transmitters, 203
MIDI, 441
Midrange computers, see
    Minicomputers
Million instructions per second
    (MIPS), 161, 441
Millisecond, definition, 441

Miniaturization, electronic circuits, 163–164
Minicomputers, 5, 167–169
  16-bit, 365
  definition, 441
  invention, 363
MIPS, 161
  definition, 441
MIS, *see* Management information system
MIS department, 284–285
  organization, 226–227
Model, 329
Modeling, definition, 441
Modem, 47, 48, 206, 441
Modular conversion method, 293
Modularization, software, 306–307
Modulation, definition, 441
Module, 306–307, 401
Monitor:
  definition, 441
  selection, 297
Monochrome CRT displays, 141
Morland, Samuel, 347
Morse code, 11, 201
Morse, Samuel F. B. 11, 201
MOS, definition, 441
Mother board, 18, 441
Motorola 68030, 161
Mouse, 16, 114, 441
MRP, 83
MS-DOS, 32–33, 441
MS-DOS-based computer, definition, 441
MultiMate Advantage, 378
Multimedia application, 333–334
Multiplexer, 216–217, 441
Multiplying machine, 347
Multiprocessing, 171–172, 441.
  See also Hypermedia
Multiprogramming, definition, 441
Multitasking system, 32
Multiuser system, 32, 168, 441
Musical instrument digital
  interface (MIDI), 91, 441–442
MYCIN, 89

Naisbitt, John, 56
Nanosecond, definition, 442
Napier, John, 346
Napier's bones, 346
National Crime Information
  Center, 73
Natural language:
  definition, 442
  interface, 30, 253, 429, 442
  processing, 270–272, 277
  understanding, 270–272, 366
Near-photographic quality
  graphics, 144
Negroponte, Nicholas, 266
Network, 13–14, 210–215, 218
  bus, 211–212
  configurations, 210–211
  definition, 442
  hierarchical, 211
  local-area, 210, 235–236
  private branch exchanges, 212
  ring, 211
  star, 210
  wireless, 211–212
Network computing, 236–238, 442
Network model, 250, 442
Neural-net computer, 276
Neural network, 275–277, 371
  applications, 276
  definition, 242
Newman, Edward, 358

NewWave, 336
NextStation, 415
Node, definition, 442
Noise, definition, 442
Nonimpact printer, 136–139, 442
  electrostatic, 137–138
  inkjet, 136–137
  lasers, 138–139
  magnetic, 138
  thermal, 137–138
  thermal transfer, 138
Nonprocedural languages, 331
Nonvolatile read only memory, 158
Nonvolatile storage, definition, 442
Norton Utilities, 400
Notebooks, 401, 402–404
  Atari Portfolio, 402
  Compaq LTE/286, 404
  GridPad, 402
Number systems:
  base, 420
  base, 2, 422
  base-60, 422
  base-16, 422
  base-12, 422
Numeric keypad, 16

Object, 315, 442
Object code, definition, 442
Object environments, 336–337
  definition, 442
Object-oriented database, 250
Object-oriented model, 442
Object-oriented programming, 315–316, 442
Object program, 313, 442. *See also* Object code, definition
Obsolescence, computer and, 64–65
OCR, 120–121, 442
Odhner, W. T., 350
Office, definition, 442
Office automation, definition, 442
Office of the future, definition, 442
Olsen, Ken, 363
Olsen, Stan, 363
1-2-3 Release 3, 383
ONCOCIN, 89
One-Write Plus, 395
On-line databases, 58–59
On-line processing, definition, 442
On-line transaction processing, 111
Operand, 155, 442
Operating environment, definition, 442
Operating system, 49
  definition, 30, 442
  functions, 31
  kernel, 31
  Macintosh, 33
  MS-DOS, 32–33
  multitasking, 32
  multiuser, 32
  OS/2, 33–34
  Unix, 33
  software evaluation, 296
  virtual memory, 32
Operating system/2, 33–34
Operation, 155, 442
Operations group, 227
Optical character recognition
  (OCR), 120–121, 442
Optical computer, 371
Optical disk, 18, 191–194
  definition, 442

erasable, 193
multimedia applications, 193–194
  read-only, 192–193
  write-once, 193
Optical mouse, 114
Optical neural network chip, 371
Optical transistor, 370
Optical transmitters, 203
Organizational structure changes, 230
OS/2, 33, 442
Oughtred, William, 346
Outline processors, 35
Output, 131–133
  camera-output systems, 145
  computer-aided publishing, 145
  definition, 442
  devices, 133
  plotters, 145
  types, 132
  voice, 145–146
Output requirements, systems
  analysis, 287
Overlay, definition, 442

Packaged application software,
  definition, 442
Packaging, factory automation, 87
Packet switching, 215–216, 442
Page composition software, 39
PageMaker, 382
Page printers, 139
Paging, memory, 162, 443
Paint program, 46, 443
Pajitnov, Alexey, 2
Papert, Seymour, 269
Paradigm shift, 269, 315
Paradox, 387
Parallel, definition, 443
Parallel computer, 369, 443
Parallel conversion method, 293
Parallel processing, 172, 443
Parity, definition, 443
Parry program, 268
Parsing, 271, 443
Pascal, 319–320, 443
Pascal, Blaise, 347
Pascaline, 347
Password:
  definition, 443
  protection, 72
Patient monitoring, 88
PBX, 210
PC cards, 190
PC DOS, 32
PC Tools Version 6, 400
People Express, 247–248
Performance evluation:
  software, 295
  systems analysis, 293
Peripherals, 154, 443
Personal computer systems, 5,
  15–19, 401, 402–414
  definition, 443
  desktop, 401, 408–414
  disks and disk drives, 18
  display, 16–17
  hand-held, 402
  history, 367, 368
  keyboard, 16
  laptops, 401, 404–407
  new applications, 232–233
  notebooks, 401, 402–404
  operating system, 30–34
  printers, 19
  software, 28
  software selection, 294–296

system unit, 16–18
terminal emulation, 207–208
transportable, *see* Personal
  computer systems, laptops;
  Personal computer systems,
  notebooks
  user interfaces, 28–30
  workstations, 401, 415–416
Personal computing, management
  information systems, 231–232
Pflager, Helmut, 268–269
Photography, electronic, 121–122
Photolithographic process, 443
Photonics, 205
Photonic switches, 205
Physical files, database
  management systems, 258,
  443
Physical records:
  definition, 443
  storage or disk, 188–189
Physical structure, 180–181
Picosecond, definition, 443
Picture element, *see* Pixel
Pilot test conversion method, 293
PIN, 61
Pinball Construction Set, 397
Pin Wheel Adding Machine, 350
Pipelining, definition, 443
Pixel, 140, 143
Plotters, 145, 443
Pointers, 250, 443
Pointing devices, 113–116, 443
Point of sale system, 87
  definition, 443
Political resources, information as,
  58
Polling, definition, 443
Port, 19, 443
Portable computer, 170, 190. *See
  also* Laptop computer;
  Notebooks
Portfolio, 402
Positional notation, 420–421
Postimplementation study, 293
Postscript, 143
Power, 420
PowerPoint, 392
Power supply:
  definition, 443
  in system unit, 17
Pragmatics, 271
Presentation graphics, 46–47, 443
Pressure transducer, 111
Print buffer, definition, 443
Printers, 19, 133–139
  band, belt, and print train,
    135–136
  definition, 443
  dot-matrix, 134–135
  electrostatic, 137–138
  inkjet, 136
  laser, 138–139
  letter-quality, 133–134
  magnetic, 138
  nonimpact, 136–139
  thermal, 137–138
  thermal transfer, 138
Print server, definition, 443
Printing, 38
Print train printers, 135
Privacy, 73–74
Privacy Act of 1974, 73
Private branch exchanges (PBX),
  210
Private identification number
  (PIN), 61
Problem definition, 289

Procedure, definition, 443
Procedure-oriented language, 443
Process, definition, 443
Processing requirements, systems
 analysis, 288–289
Processor, 17, 155–156
 arithmetic/logic unit, 156
 control unit, 156
 definition, 443
 functional components, 156
 hardware selection, 297
 register, 156
 RISC, 162–163
Production, factory automation, 87
Productivity, 229–231, 289
 computer monitoring, 66–67
Productivity crisis, definition, 443
Professional File, 387
Professional Plan, 385
Professional productivity, 230
Professional Write, 379
Program, *see also* Software
 definition, 443
 design language, *see* Pseudocode
 documentation, *see*
  Documentation
 maintenance, 305
 testing, 313–314, 443
Program counter, 160
Program generator, 330–331, 443
Programmable industrial
 automation, definition, 443
Programmer, 443
 in professional environment,
  305
Programmer analyst, 97–98, 284,
 444
Programming, 8–9, 304. *See also*
 Software development
 alternatives to, 328–329
 history, 304
 object-oriented, 315–316
 structured, 306–307
Programming environment, 305
Programming language, 8–9, 343
 Ada, 349
 artificial intelligence, 360
 BASIC, 318–319
 C, 320–321
 COBOL, 316–317
 comparison, 316
 compilers *vs.* interpreters, 313
 database, 331–334
 definition, 444
 FORTRAN, 317–318
 Pascal, 319–320
 structured, 312
 syntax and logical errors,
  313–314
 translation, 313
Protocols, 217, 444
Protocol converter, definition,
 444
Prototyping, 290, 329, 444
Pseudocode, 312, 444
Public Utility Commission, 214
Publishing, computer-aided, 145
PUCs, 214
Pull-down menu, 29, 444
Punched-card machine, 348
Punched-card system,
 electromechanical, 351
Pyramid organization, 230

Q&A, 386
Quattro, 383
QBE, 252–253
Query, definition, 444

Query by example (QBE),
 252–253, 444
Query language, 252–254, 444
Qwerty, definition, 444
Quevedo y, Leonard Torres, *see*
 Torres y Quevedo, Leonardo

RAM, 17–18, 157–158, 420, 444
RAMAC 305, 360
RAM disk, 162
Random access device, definition,
 444
Random access files, 182
Random-access memory (RAM),
 17–18, 157–158, 420, 444
Random access mehtod, definition,
 444
Random Access Method for
 Accounting and Control, 360
Raster display, 144
R:Base 3.0, 388
Read, definition, 444
Read-only memory, *see* ROM
Read-only optical disk, 192–193,
 444
Read/write head, 183
 thin-film, 163
Ready, 380
Real-time processing, definition,
 444
Record, 43, 444
 locking, 255, 257
Reduced instruction set computers
 (RISC), 162–163, 368, 370
Reel-to-reel tape, 183
Reentrant routine, definition, 444
Reflex, 44, 386
Reformatting, 37
Refresh, definition, 444
Register-oriented processor, 156,
 444
Relation, 249, 444
Relational database, 249, 366
Relational model, definition, 444
Remainder method, 421
Remote job entry terminals (RJE),
 207
Report generation, 254
Report generator, 45, 330–331
Requirements, definition, 444
Requirements analysis, 285–287
 constraints, 288–289
Requirements list, 310, 444
Requirements planning, 287–289
Resolution:
 CRT, 141
 graphics, 141, 144
Resource object, 336, 444
Retailing, 60–61
Return key, 113
Revising, word processing, 36–37
RGB (red, green, blue) CRT, 141
Ribbon cable, definition, 444
Ring network, 211, 444
RISC, 37, 368, 370, 444
Ritchie, Dennis, 320
Robot, 190, 444
Robotics, 83–87. *See also* Factory
 automation
 guided vehicle systems, 85
Roizen, Heidi, 178
ROM, 17, 158
 definition, 444
 firmware, 190
Root directory, 33
Rotating drum plotter, 145
RS-232C, definition, 444
Rule, definition, 444

SABRE, 60, 201, 247
SAGE, 358
Salami slicing, 71
Sales representative, 98
Satellites, communications, 202
Satellite systems, communication
 channels, 204–205
Save, definition, 444
SBDS, 272
Scanner, 87, 117–122
 applications, 117–121
 bar codes, 119–120
 definition, 444–445
 image processing, 121–122
 magnetic ink character
  recognition, 118–119
 optical character recognition,
  120–121
Schickard, Wilhelm, 346
Schreyer, Helmut, 355
Scientific and engineering
 applications, FORTRAN, 318
Scientific and engineering
 software, 34, 376
 AutoCAD, 399
 Mathematica, 399
Scrolling, 37, 445
SDI, *see* Strategic Defense
 Initiative
Searching, database, 44–45
Search time, definition, 445
Secondary storage, definition, 445
Second generation, definition, 445
Sectors, 159, 445
Security:
 communications industry, 215
 ethics, 72–73
SEED, *see* Self Electro-optical
 Effect Device (SEED)
Seek time, definition, 444
Segmentation, memory, 162, 445
Selection control structure,
 308–309
Selectric key layout, 112
Self Electro-optical Effect Device
 (SEED), 205
Semantics, 271
Semi-Automatic Ground
 Environment (SAGE), 358
Semiconductor, 163, 445
Semiconductor laser, 365
Sensors, 122–123, 445
Sequence control structure, 308
Sequencer, definition, 445
Sequential, definition, 445
Sequential access, magnetic tape,
 183
Sequential files, 181–182
Serial, definition, 445
Server, definition, 445
Service Bay Diagnostic System, 86
Service Employees International
 Union (SEIU), telecommuting
 and, 68
Service-oriented jobs, effect on of
 computer technology, 65
Service technicians, 97
Shannon, Claude E., 270, 354, 364
Shareware, 74
Sharp PC-6220, 403
Shipping, factory automation, 86
Shockley, William, 309, 357
SHRDLU, 271, 366
Silicon, definition, 444
Silicon chip, 163, 164
Silicon compiler, 315, 445
Simulation, 444
Simulation language, 362

Site licensing, 74
16-bit processor, 161
Slide rule, 346
SLT, 363
Small-scale integration chips, 367
Smart cards, 170
Smart sensors, 123, 445
Soft copy, 133, 445
Software, 14
 application, 34, 376
 definition, 14, 445
 evaluation, 293
 firmware, 190
 graphics, 143
 maintenance, definition, 445
 matching to hardware, 297
 personal computer, 28
 piracy, 74, 445
 productivity tools, 305–306
 system, 34, 366
 transportability, 361
 user interface, 28–30
 for writing, *see* Word processing
Software development, 303–304,
 321–322
 algorithms, 307–308
 alternatives to writing programs,
  328–329
 bottom-up design, 306
 coding, 312
 control structures, 308–309
 database programming
  languages, 331–334
 definition, 444
 documentaiton assembly, 314
 evolution of, 304–306
 flowcharting, 311
 hybrid approaches, 334
 Hypercard, 332
 language translation, 313–315
 linking program, 314
 macro languages, 329–330
 modularization, 306–307
 new tools and techniques,
  305–306
 phases, 309–315
 problem definition, 310
 program generators, 330–332
 prototyping, 290
 pseudocode, 312
 solution planning, 310–312
 structure chart, 306
 testing, 314
 top-down design, 306
Software engineering, 291–292
 beginnings, 304–305
 definition, 444
 occupational demand, 97
Software engineers, 98–99
Software selection, 294–296
 compatibility, 296
 documentation, 295–296
 ease of installation, 295
 evaluation checklist, 294–296
 operating system, 296
 performance, 295
 price, 296
 support, 296
 user interface, 294–295
Solid logic technology, 363
Sorting, 252
 database, 44
 definition, 445
The Source, 216
Source code, definition, 445
Source document, 110, 445
Source program, 313
Speaker verification, 123

Special effects, for television and movies, 144
Special-purpose application software, as alternative to programming, 290
Special-purpose computers, 4, 445
Special-purpose programs, 34–35, 376, 445
Spectrograms, 124
Speech coding, 146, 445
Speech recognizer, definition, 445
Speech recognition, 124, 272
Speech synthesis, 146, 445
Spelling checker, 38, 445
Spool, definition, 445
Spreadsheet, 8, 35, 40–42, 376
    definition, 40, 445
    Microsoft Excel, 384
    model, 40
        building, 41
        comparing, 41–42
    1-2-3 Release 3, 383
    Professional Plan, 385
    Quattro, 383
    SuperCalc5, 384
Sputnik 1, 202
SQL, 226, 445
S-SEED, 371
SSI, see Small-scale integration chips
Stacks, 332
Stackware, 332
Standard cell, 445
Star networks, 211–212, 445
Static RAM, 157
Statistical multiplexer, 216–217
Statistical multiplexing, 445
Steiger, Otto, 352
Stibitz, George R., 355
Stoll, Cliff, 54
Storage, requirements, systems analysis, 288
Stored-program concept, definition, 445
Storyboards, 335
Strategic Defense Initiative (SDI), 93
Strategic management, 226–227
Strategic resources, information as, 59–62, 74–75
    accounting, 61
    airlines, 60
    banking, 61–62
    insurance, 60
Strategy, definition, 445
Streaming tape, 183, 445
Structure, definition, 445
Structure chart, 306, 445. See also Hierarchy chart
Structured analysis, definition, 446
Structured design, 446
Structure diagram, math game, 311
Structured program design, 306–309
Structured programming, 308, 364
    Ada, 321, 349
    C, 320
    definition, 446
    Pascal, 319–320, 348–349
Structured programming language, 312, 446
Structured query langbuages (SQL), 252, 445
Structured walk-through, 289, 446
Style checker, definition, 446
Stylus, 142
Subdirectories, 33

Subroutine, definition, 446
Sun SPARCstation SLC, 415
SuperCalc5, 384
Supercomputers, 170–171, 446
    commercially available, 364
Supertwist crystals, 142
Supervisor, definition, 446
Support, software evaluation, 296
Sutherland, Ivan, 362
Switch, 11, 12, 446
Switching concepts, 215–216
Symmetric Self-Electro-optic Effect Devices (S-SEED), 371
Symphony, 390
Synchronous mode, 217
Synchronous transmission, definition, 446
Syncom II, 202
Syntax, 271
    error, 313–314
Synthesizer, 91, 440
System, 9–10
System flowchart:
    definition, 446
    symbols, 291
System/360, see IBM System/360
System/370, see IBM System/370 series
Systems analysis, 283
    alternatives to programming, 290
    background study, 286–287
    case study, 293–298
    computer-aided software engineering, 291–292
    constraints, 288–289
    conversion, 293
    cost-benefit estimate, 289
    data dictionary, 288
    data-flow diagram, 288
    definition phase, 285–289
    design and development phase, 290–292
    design review, 291
    detail documentation, 291
    documentation techniques, 292–293
    evaluating performance, 293
    evaluation, 289
    file and storage requirements, 288
    functional specifications, 285, 289
    high-level documentation, 291
    implementation phase, 292–293
    input requirements, 287–288
    installation, 292
    life-cycle approach, 284
    output requirements, 287
    process, 284
    processing requirements, 288–289
    requirements analysis, 285–287
    requirements planning, 287–289
    role, 284
    structured walk-through, 289
    testing, 292
    top-down approach, 284
    user documentation and training, 292–293
Systems analyst, 97–98
    definition, 446
    role, 284
Systems group, 227
Systems life cycle, 284–285
System software, 48, 446
Systems programmers, 98
System unit, 17–18

Tabulating Machines Company, 351
Talkwriter, 124, 446
Tandy 1100 FD, 404
Tandy 1000 TX, 411
Tape, 182–184
Tape drive, definition, 446
T1 channels, 204
Technical documentation, 292–293
Technical writers, 359
Technology, 62–65, 75
    computer-aided engineering, design, and manufacturing, 62–63
    definition, 62, 446
    effects on society, 63–64
    need to adapt, 65
    obsolescence and computer, 64–65
Technology planning group, 227
Telecommunications, 200, 446
Telecommuting, 68–69, 446
Telegraph, 11, 201
Telenet, 216
Telephone, 201
Telstar, 202
Template, definition, 446
Terabyte, 190, 446
Teraflop, 171
Terminals:
    communications, 206–208
    definition, 446
    emulation, 207–208
Testing:
    program, 314, 444
    systems analysis, 292
Text, 132, 133
Text database, 246–247
Thermal printers, 137–138, 446
Thermal transfer printers, 138, 446
Thesaurus programs, 38
Thin-film disks, 189, 446
Thin-film read/write heads, 189, 446
Thinking, 268–270
    about thinking, 269
    intelligent behavior, 269–270
Third generation, definition, 446
35mm Express, 393
32-bit processor, 161, 369
Thomas (de Colmar) Charles, 348
Thomson, William (Lord Kelvin), 350
Throughput, definition, 446
Time-division multiplexing, 216, 446
Time-sharing, 165–166, 168, 446
Time-slicing, 166
Toffler, Alvin, 56
Token, 211, 446
Token-ring network, 211, 446
Toolbook, 332
Top-down approach, 284, 446
Top-down design, 306
    structured, 446
Topology, definition, 446
Torres y Quevedo, Leonardo, 353
Toshiba T1200XE, 403
Toshiba T1600, 405
Toshiba T5200, 406
Total system concept, 226, 446
Touch pad, 116
Touch-panel, integrated with flat-panel displays, 142–143
Touch screen, 114–115, 446
Touch technology, 114–116
Towers of Hanoi puzzle, 308
Track, 184, 189, 447

Track density, 184, 187, 447
TRADIC, 359
Training, 99–100
    sources of, 99
    user, 292–293
Train printer, 136
Transaction, definition, 447
Transaction file, definition, 447
Transaction-oriented processing, 231, 232, 447
Transaction terminals, 207
Transcribed input, 110, 447
Transducers, 122–123
Transistors, 163–164
    definition, 447
    invention, 357
    optical, 370
Transistorized Airborne Digital Computer, 359
Translation, programming language, 313–314
Transmission modes and types, 217
Transparent, definition, 447
Transphaser, 370
Transportable personal computers, see Laptop computer; Notebooks
Trojan horse, 71
Tupple, 447
Turbo Lightning, 381
TurboSport, 405
Turing, Alan M., 268, 354, 355, 358
Turing test, 268–269
Turnkey, definition, 447
Tutorial, 8, 447
Twisted pair wires, 202
Typesetting, computer-aided, 145
Typewriterlike terminals, 207
Typing Tutor, 398

UART, definition, 447
Ultralarge-scale integration (ULSI), 164, 447
UNIVAC, 359
Universal asynchronous receiver transmitter, see UART, definition
Universal Product Code (UPC), 119, 447
Unix, 33, 447
Update, definition, 447
Upward compatible, definition, 447
User analyst, 284, 447
User diagnostics, 292
User documentation, 292–293
User friendly, 30, 447
User group, definition, 447
User interfaces, 28–30, 48
    command-driven, 28–29
    definition, 447
    graphics-oriented, 29–30
    menu-driven, 29
    natural language, 30
    software evaluation, 294–295
Utilities, 376, 400
    database management systems, 260
    definition, 447

Vacuum tube, history, 352
Value-added network (VAN), 213
Variable-length operations, definition, 447
Vertical market applications, 34, 376
Vertical recording, 189, 447

Very small computers, 170
Very-large-scale integration
    (VLSI), 163–164, 171
    definition, 447
VGA, definition, 447
Video capture board, definition,
    447
Video conferencing, 236, 447
Videodisk programs, interactive,
    193–194
Videodisks, see Optical disks
Video-display technology,
    139–143
Video graphers array, see VGA,
    definitioni
Video memory, 140
Videotex, 236, 447
View:
    database management systems,
    260
    definition, 447
Virtual circuit, definition, 447
Virtual machines, 170
Virtual memory, 32, 162, 362, 447
Virtual-memory operating system,
    definition, 447
Virus program, 71–72
VisiCalc, 368
Vision system:
    definition, 447
    robots, 85

Visualization, definition, 477
VLSI, see Very-large-scale
    integration (VLSI)
Vocabulary, 9
Voiceband channels, 203
Voice input, 111, 123–124
Voice mail, 234–235
Voice output, 145–146
Voice recognizer, see Speech
    recognizer, definition
Voice training, definition, 447
Volatile RAM, 157
Volatile file, definition, 447
Volatile storage, definition, 447
von Neumann approach, 172
von Neumann computer, 165, 448
von Neumann, John, 357
Voyager space mission, image
    processing, 121
VP-100 super computer, 171

Wafer, definition, 448
Waltrip, T. Travers, 198
Waltzman, Susanne, 130
What-if analysis, 41–42, 448
Whirlwind Computer, 358
White collar work, 56
Wide-area networks, 236–238, 448
Wilkes, Maurice V., 167, 357, 359
Wilkinson, James, 358
Williamson, F. C., 357

Winchester disk, definition, 448
Winchester drives, 18, 187
Windows, 30, 448
Winograd, Terry, 271, 366
Wireless computer networks,
    212–213
Wirth, Niklaus, 319
Women, proportion of workforce,
    99
Word length, see Word size
WordPerfect, 378
Word processing, 35–38, 376
    composing, 36
    definition, 35, 448
    filing, 38
    ForComment, 377
    impacts on offices, 229–230
    Lotus Manuscript, 382
    MacWrite II, 380
    Microsoft Bookshelf, 381
    Microsoft Word, 379
    Microsoft Word, 379
    MultiMate Advantage, 378
    PageMaker, 382
    printing, 38
    Professional Write, 379
    Ready, 380
    revising, 36–37
    spelling checker, 38
    Turbo Lightning, 381
    WordPerfect, 378

Word Star 6.0, 377
Word processors, 34, 38
Word recognition, 123
Word recognizer, definition, 448
Word size, 156, 161, 448
WordStar 6.0, 377
Word wrap, 36, 448
Workgroup computing, 233–236
    collaborative work, 235–236
    definition, 445
    electronic conferencing, 235
    electronic mail, 234–235
    voice mail, 234–235
Workstations, 401, 415–417
    definition, 448
WORM, see Write-once optical
    disk (WORM)
Write, definition, 448
Write-once optical disk (WORM),
    193, 448
Write-protect ring, definition,
    448
Writing, software, see Word
    processing
WYSIWYG, definition, 448

Xerox Corporation, collaborative
    work, 235

Zue, Victor, 124
Zuse, Konrad, 355